The Selected Letters of Jane Welsh Carlyle

Seaforth –
Sunday
10 Augt 1845 before post time

["Monsieur le President! I begin to be weary of the treatments I experience here"! – Always my "bits of letters" and "bits of letters" as if I were some nice little Child writing in half-text on ruled paper to its Godpapa! – Since Jeffrey was pleased to compliment me on my "bits of conditions", I have not had my "rights of Woman" so trifled with! He payed the penalty of his assurance in losing from that time forward my valuable correspondence; with you I cannot so easily cease to correspond, "for reasons which it may be interesting not to state": but a woman of my invention can always find legitimate means of revenging herself on those who do not "treat her with the respect due to Genius" – who put her off with a pat on the head or a chuck under the chin, when she

Jane Welsh Carlyle to Thomas Carlyle, 10 August 1845, National Library of Scotland; MS 603.187

The Selected Letters of Jane Welsh Carlyle

A Victorian and a Contemporary

Drawn from the Duke-Edinburgh Edition (1970–2024)

Edited by Richard Lansdown

EDINBURGH
University Press

Edinburgh University Press is one of the leading university presses in the UK. We publish academic books and journals in our selected subject areas across the humanities and social sciences, combining cutting-edge scholarship with high editorial and production values to produce academic works of lasting importance. For more information visit our website: edinburghuniversitypress.com

Edinburgh University Press Ltd
13 Infirmary Street, Edinburgh, EH1 1LT

Typeset in 11/12.5 Baskerville by
IDSUK (DataConnection) Ltd

A CIP record for this book is available from the British Library

ISBN 978 1 3995 2346 2 (hardback)
ISBN 978 1 3995 5720 7 (paperback)
ISBN 978 1 3995 2347 9 (webready PDF)
ISBN 978 1 3995 2348 6 (epub)

Contents

Illustrations

Preface and Acknowledgements

In 'A Brief History of the Duke-Edinburgh Edition of the Carlyle Letters' (*Studies in Scottish Literature*, 17 (1982)) Charles Richard Sanders tells the origin story of this book. Guided by personal enthusiasm, Sanders visited Britain from the United States in 1952 in search of the papers that Thomas Carlyle had left to his literary executor James Anthony Froude (1818–1894) on the condition that they be handed on to Thomas's niece, Mary Aitken, once Froude had made use of them in writing his four-volume biography of the author, completed in 1884. Sanders found most of these documents at the National Library of Scotland in Edinburgh; others, he learned, were at New York Public Library and Yale University. This collection amounts to about half the Carlyle letters that we know of—though as Sanders points out, many letters must have been lost or destroyed over the years, as is always the case. He went on to throw out numerous lines of enquiry concerning Carlyle, steadily discovering library holdings, transcripts and facsimiles: the 'fugitive letters', as he called them, outside the Froude-Aitken archive. His purpose back in 1952, he recalled thirty years later, was a modest one: to collect and collate what he called the 'pen portraits' with which Carlyle's correspondence abounded, and (perhaps) to catalogue the letters as a whole. To prepare a complete edition of the letters would be a 'gigantic task' and he had other fish to fry.

By 1955 Sanders realised that Jane Welsh Carlyle's letters must join her husband's, even in the 'pen portrait' line. (Her letters were 'essentially and vitally complementary to his', as he wrote in the Introduction to the first volume of *The Collected Letters of Thomas and Jane Welsh Carlyle*—referred to throughout as *CL*—in 1970, just as his are complementary to hers, of course.) Then in 1959 Gordon Ray (an authority on the Victorian novelist William Makepeace Thackeray) visited Sanders' English Department at Duke University, North Carolina, and urged him to go for broke, with some Guggenheim Foundation funding Ray might direct his way. Still modest, Sanders volunteered to edit the letters up to 1834, when the Carlyles established their famous home on Cheyne Row, Chelsea. This target Sanders achieved as general editor in seven volumes, by 1977, but he remained on post until 1980, two years before his article, when the story had reached 1837, and he was succeeded as general editor by Clyde Ryals at Duke.

In this initial undertaking Sanders was joined by fellow academics at the University of Edinburgh, in particular by Kenneth Fielding. The National Library of Scotland remained central to the project, and at Duke Sanders was joined by John Clubbe, expert on both Carlyle and Lord Byron. By the time Sanders reported in 1982 8,000 letters by Thomas had been collected and 4,000 by Jane, and he anticipated that the collection would be completed in ten or fifteen years: by 1995, perhaps.

In 2024, this extraordinary endeavour is finally complete, in what will be over fifty volumes, taking us beyond Jane's death in 1866 to Thomas's in 1881. A transatlantic enterprise that has its origins in the year Queen Elizabeth II ascended the British throne has outlived even her; and so it is that this selection from one third of the Carlyle correspondence—the female third, Jane's third—forms a monument to a monument, as one might say, or a chapel to a cathedral. Sanders' comments on the value of what he and his many collaborators have done over all these years are worth quoting, echoing strangely as they do at the time I add them. 'Certainly the Carlyle letters will not help us to get rid of inflation,' he wrote; 'reduce unemployment, taxes, or money spent for welfare, or cure the ills being suffered by the automobile business in the United States':

> They will not help us solve the energy problem. But neither would Vergil's poetry or Shakespeare's plays. We must think of the values inherent in the Carlyle letters in terms not directly related to the problems which cause us great concern today. Our problems are in the main concerned with technology, with discovering the means by which ends may be achieved. The Carlyles were chiefly concerned with the ends themselves, with the values that make life worth living [. . .] Like one of Carlyle's heroes, Dr Samuel Johnson, they led lives and made statements that were commentaries on the art of living. Though they did not perfect this art, they experienced many hours of a very rare quality as recorded in the letters; and fortified and illumined by extensive reading, they observed the lives of those around them and evaluated their own experiences from day to day while at the same time they were writing letters which recorded their conclusions. Hence it is possible for us to read the letters not merely for the pleasure that they bring to us but also for what they may teach us about the most difficult and the greatest of the arts.

That—the study of the centrality, complexity and perplexity of 'the values that make life worth living', and 'the most difficult and the greatest of the arts': how to *live*—is perhaps the central credo of literary study as it has traditionally been understood. And the Carlyles' letters give us raw materials for analysis by the cubic metre.

Many people have been involved with the Duke-Edinburgh project in an editorial role since 1952. I list the main figures, current and retired, in alphabetical order: Bill Bell, John Butt, Ian Campbell, Aileen Christianson, John Clubbe, Kenneth Fielding, Katherine Inglis, Brent Kinser, Stacy Lavin, Sheila McIntosh, Clyde Ryals, Charles Sanders, Hilary Smith, David Sorensen, David Southern, Liz Sutherland, Janetta Taylor and Jonathan Wild; there must be dozens of other contributors in libraries and private collections all around the world, who made the edition possible, not to mention the publishing and academic teams at the two universities. At the permissions department at Duke University Press Diane Grosse and Kerin Ogg kindly granted me the freedom to quote from the Carlyle text; I am profoundly grateful for the Press's support, without which this book could not have eventuated. On the other side of the Atlantic Emily Sharp, Elizabeth Fraser, Fiona Conn, and their colleagues at Edinburgh University Press have been wonderful. The book was meticulously copy-edited by Cathy Falconer, who saved me from errors by the score. Closer to home, my families, English and Australian, continue to put up with this sort of activity, much as Jane put up with Thomas, 'in the valley of the shadow of Frederick'. Thanks, too, to Gene Montgomery for the wonderful cover illustration, and to Rosemary Ashton for all her support.

To members of Karl Miller's English Department at University College London, 1979–1989,
who saw more potential in me than I did.

Introduction

In the nineteenth century the English woman writer came into her own, professionally speaking, chiefly via the novel. Works like *Jane Eyre* and *Adam Bede* earned their authors serious popularity, and it came as no surprise, then, that Charlotte Brontë's friend Elizabeth Gaskell published her biography in 1857, or that George Eliot's husband John Walter Cross published hers in 1885. (In 1869 the novelist's nephew James Edward Austen Leigh issued his *Memoir of Jane Austen* in a more circumscribed and guarded spirit.) The appearance in 1883 of the *Letters and Memorials of Jane Welsh Carlyle*, edited by her husband Thomas and his friend and literary executor James Anthony Froude, was unexpected by comparison. Jane Welsh Carlyle—and she insisted on the retention of her maiden name, just as the poet Elizabeth Barrett Browning did; the practice among married women (especially in Scotland) is not a modern invention—had published not a word in her lifetime (1801–1866) and was known to the Victorian reading public, if at all, only as the wife of the fuliginous intellectual and gadfly Thomas Carlyle (1795–1881): author of *Sartor Resartus*, *The French Revolution*, *Past and Present* and other works of historical biography and social critique.[1] Nor were Jane's letters the reasonably anodyne ones written by Austen and Eliot. They were vivid by the standards of conventional Victorian femininity, and they painted an often lonely picture of her existence and her relationship with her husband. Mrs Alexander Ireland followed the *Letters and Memorials* with a candid, indeed plainspoken, *Life of Jane Welsh Carlyle* in 1891, and spoke of her subject's 'deep, isolated nature, her shining gifts, her unique charm', but also of 'her life of pain'. The *Letters and Memorials*, she said, 'gave us a revelation': 'a Rembrandt-like portrait of a woman, touched with strongest lights and deepest tragic shades—a faithful and unerring portrait, self-depicted.'[2]

1. Carlyle's standing in his own lifetime was immense; nowadays he is an object of neglect verging on dismissal. To take one area: the attitudes he expressed on matters of race are comparable with those of T. S. Eliot, though the poet's views are psychologically more murky and are communicated more equivocally ('the Jew is underneath the lot', and so forth). But Eliot's life and works continue to merit countless column inches in the broadsheet papers and the reviews, whereas Carlyle is mostly regarded as an irrelevant and nasty antique.
2. Mrs Alexander Ireland, *Life of Jane Welsh Carlyle* (London, 1891), v, 2. The *Letters and Memorials* included Thomas's annotations, but no general preface or introduction.

Jane died in 1866, Thomas in 1881. He had all the time in the world, therefore, and perhaps every good reason, to destroy—or at least bowdlerize and repress—the record of unhappiness his wife left in her letters.[3] That he never did so but reverentially collected, prepared and annotated them for publication, and also left a searingly grief-stricken and guilt-ridden memoir of her that he allowed Froude to publish in his *Reminiscences* directly after his death, must redound greatly to his credit. He did not go so far as to accuse himself of being the source of her desolation but did acknowledge his own 'black electricities and consuming fires' as an intellectual, wondered 'how miserable my Books must have been to her', and remembered 'a noble fight at my side; a valiant strangling of serpents day after day—done gaily by *her* (for the most part), as I had to do it angrily and gloomily; thus we went on together [. . .]'.[4] Mrs Ireland identified the paradox of a 'strange blindness' in this posthumous remorse on Thomas's part. 'Those clear eyes which saw through the eternities', she wrote, 'had limited vision in the little spot of earth on which he moved, and ears which were open to the great inarticulate cry of humanity, were unaccountably deaf, at times, to the distinct voice of pain in the utterance of the heart nearest his own.' Rosemary Ashton, too, speaks of his 'curiously frank yet unself-knowing' attitude to what Jane left him with.[5] Yet he was loyal to his late wife's abilities, almost to a fault:

> As to 'talent,' epistolary and other, these *Letters*, I perceive, equal and surpass whatever of best I know to exist in that kind; for 'talent,' 'genius,' or whatever we may call it, what an evidence, if my little woman need that to me! Not all the [George] *Sands* and [George] *Eliots* and babbling *cohue* [throng] of 'celebrated scribbling women' that have strutted over the world, in my time, could, it seems to me, if all boiled down and distilled to essence, make one such woman.[6]

3. The destruction of such documents was by no means unusual in the nineteenth century. Byron's memoirs were famously burnt in his publisher's office soon after his death in 1824, Cassandra Austen destroyed the majority of Jane's letters to her shortly before her death in 1843, and Dickens made bonfires of his correspondence in 1860 and 1869. Where Jane is concerned we have only eight letters—five very small—to her close friend the novelist Geraldine Jewsbury (who destroyed her correspondence), and no letters from her to either her mother or her devoted supporter Erasmus Darwin. Those she wrote to Thomas immediately after her mother's death in 1844 are also gone.
4. Thomas Carlyle, *Reminiscences*, ed. Kenneth J. Fielding and Ian Campbell (Oxford, 1997), 149, 147, 145.
5. Ireland, *Life*, 79; Rosemary Ashton, *Thomas and Jane Carlyle: Portrait of a Marriage* (London, 2002), 95. 'After her death, Carlyle cursed himself for his blindness to Jane's unhappiness, yet he channelled all his guilt into confessing his insensitivity to her *physical* ill health, never really allowing himself to see that she had been for long periods unhappy and unfulfilled' (ibid.).
6. Carlyle, *Reminiscences*, 138.

Thomas—who had wanted the edition to be of six volumes rather than the eventual three—prepared the *Letters and Memorials*, therefore, out of love, regret, respect and regard, but also out of something husband and wife shared, again almost to a fault. 'His writings, every one of them,' Froude observed, 'were to the same purpose and on the same text—that truth must be spoken and justice must be done; on any other conditions no real commonwealth, no common welfare, is permitted or possible.' To which we can perhaps only observe that what is philosophically necessary for a commonwealth might not be good for a marriage. Jane, too, Froude said, 'had a terrible habit of speaking out the exact truth, cut as clear as with a graving tool, on occasions, too, when without harm it might have been left unspoken'. No wonder he concluded that 'Two diamonds do not easily form cup and socket'.[7]

But sometimes Froude's instinct to state and drive home inconvenient truths itself led to distortions. 'The victory was won', he said of Carlyle's career, 'but, as of old in Aulis, not without a victim.'[8] But Thomas was no Agamemnon, leading his ships to Troy, and Jane was no Iphigenia, an innocent girl caught up in the trammels of fate and divine retribution. 'Throughout the later nineteenth century and all of the twentieth, one of the most tenacious stereotypes clinging to Jane Welsh Carlyle', Kathy Chamberlain suggests, 'was that of victimized wife, miserably, helplessly put upon by an insensitive literary man.'[9] As this selection may help to demonstrate, the situation was more complicated than one of victim and oppressor. Two of my editorial predecessors, Alan and Mary McQueen Simpson, entitled their 1977 selection of Jane's letters *I Too Am Here*, which is an excellent choice, drawn from an important letter of June 1835 to John Sterling. 'You did kindly to send the little separate note,' Jane told Sterling:

> the least bit 'all to myself,' (as the children say) was sure to give me a livelier pleasure, than any number of sheets in which I had but a secondary interest. For in spite of the honestest efforts to annihilate my *I-ity*, or merge it in what the world doubtless considers my better half; I still find myself a self-subsisting and alas! selfseeking *Me*. Little Felix, in the Wanderjahre, when, in the midst of an animated scene between Whilelm and Theresa, he pulls Theresa's gown, and calls out, '*Mama Theresa I too am here!*'

7. John Clubbe (ed.), *Froude's Life of Carlyle* (London, 1979), 413, 403, 146.
8. Ibid. 201. It is important to remember that Froude was a latter-day friend of Carlyle's: he only met the couple in 1849, and came really to know Jane between 1861 and her death in 1866, when she was often very ill.
9. Kathy Chamberlain, *Jane Welsh Carlyle and her Victorian World: A Story of Love, Work, Friendship, and Marriage* (London, 2017), 289–90.

> only speaks out with the charming trustfulness of a child, what I am perpetually feeling, tho too sophisticated to pull peoples skirts, or exclaim in so many words; Mr Sterling '*I* too am here.'[10]

It is a good title, but whether Jane's self-infantilisation in this passage or her assertion that she experienced this child-like marginalisation 'perpetually' is truly just remains an open question. In any event, few people who knew the couple needed reminding that Jane was there. Two other editorial predecessors, Kenneth Fielding and David Sorensen, remembering Froude's Euripidean metaphor, speak of the need to produce a 'domestic account' of Jane's existence rather than 'mount a Greek tragedy'.[11] In the context of Thomas's reverential editorship we should also recollect the huge value he placed on letters and personal documents throughout his writing life, but in his Oliver Cromwell and Frederick the Great projects of the 1840s and 1860s in particular. 'The letter hangs there in the dark abysses of the Past,' he wrote in the introductory 'Of Oliver's Letters and Speeches':

> if like a star almost extinct, yet like a real star; fixed; about which there is no caviling possible. That autograph Letter, it was once all luminous as a burning beacon, every word of it a live coal, in its time; it was once a piece of the general fire and light of Human Life, that Letter! [. . .] well read, there is still in it light enough to exhibit its own self; nay to diffuse a faint authentic twilight some distance round it.[12]

Thomas was to Jane, then, more Mentor than Agamemnon, encouraging her by direct appreciation from their earliest days in the exercise of an epistolary talent he valued as highly as any other historian or critic in the language.[13]

10. *CL* 8: 138. Goethe's *Wilhelm Meister's Journeyman Years* (1821 and 1829) was the sequel to *Wilhelm Meister's Apprenticeship* (1796); together they form one vast *Bildungsroman* about a bourgeois hero in search of himself in the theatre and society. Thomas's translation of the first part of the novel was published in 1824.
11. Kenneth J. Fielding and David R. Sorensen (eds.), *Jane Carlyle: Newly Selected Letters* (Aldershot, 2004), xiv.
12. Thomas Carlyle, *The Letters and Speeches of Oliver Cromwell*, 3 vols. (London, 1926), i. 61.
13. Thomas's tutelary role established itself even in their courting days. 'He was teaching the most apt student of the art of writing letters produced by the nineteenth century, and he very early discovered the fact' (*CL* 1: xvi).

Given the marital ideology of the day, it was difficult for any Victorian wife to be seen outside of her relationship with her husband; and nothing much is to be gained by attempting to peel Jane Welsh Carlyle away from hers retrospectively, biographically speaking. Accusations of neglect verging on cruelty have been made, certainly.[14] But if Virginia Surtees described the famous Carlyle house on Cheyne Row (No. 24 now, No. 5 then) as a 'house of desolation', and their marriage as 'a monument to unremitting egotism and perverseness almost unique in nineteenth-century literary circles', the leading modern historian of their relationship uses more balanced language, telling a story of 'psychological and emotional tension', but also of 'astonishing literary, intellectual, and social success'.[15] Thomas 'was no John Stuart Mill', Rosemary Ashton concludes, 'no progressive advocate of sexual equality', but then 'Nor, really, was Jane, though she resented her subjection'. Her reward for that subjection 'was to share the years of success—phenomenal success—when all the world, British, American, European, made for their shabby-genteel corner of Chelsea'[16]—hardly a house of desolation therefore.

And come the world did, to encounter him, to encounter her, or to encounter them both. It is not true to suggest that 'the big names were those who sought out Carlyle, while she seemed only to attract the exiles

14. The most alarming piece of evidence dates from 26 June 1856, when Jane recorded 'blue marks on my wrists' in her journal; marks that she apparently told Geraldine Jewsbury the next day had been caused by Thomas during an argument (*CL* 30: 259). Bruises on both wrists would be hard to explain otherwise.
15. Virginia Surtees, *Jane Welsh Carlyle* (Salisbury, 1986), 1; Ashton, *Portrait of a Marriage*, 7. There were a fair number of unhappy literary marriages in the nineteenth century, from Byron to Hardy and Dickens to Tolstoy.
16. Ashton, *Portrait of a Marriage*, 448. In a manner familiar to unhappy couples the world over, camps established themselves in the wake of the *Reminiscences*, the *Letters and Memorials*, and Froude's four-volume biography of Thomas (1882–1884). The Froude side wanted the ('tragic', Euripidean) truth to be told and justice to be done to Jane, whereas the Carlyle family—particularly Thomas's nephew Alexander—defended their relative from charges of selfishness and even sexual impotence. Thus Alexander published his own selection of Jane's letters in 1903, seeking to save Thomas's reputation (perhaps to whitewash it: Ashton, *Portrait of a Marriage*, x), and his own selection of Thomas's letters the following year, using every opportunity to paint his uncle as the long-suffering husband of a drug-dependent neurotic. Froude's children responded by publishing their father's *My Relations with Carlyle* in 1903, and Alexander (backed up by the eminent psychiatrist James Crichton-Browne) replied the same year with *The Nemesis of Froude*. (Froude had published a scandalous novel, *The Nemesis of Faith*, in 1849.) A year before his death in 1931 Alexander was still infuriated, and published *The Carlyle Myth Refuted*, thirty-six years after Froude had died.

and the strays'.[17] Emerson, Mill, Robert Browning, Edward Fitzgerald and Froude mostly came to see Thomas; and Geraldine Jewsbury, Erasmus Darwin and Mazzini mostly to see Jane. But Francis Jeffrey, Leigh Hunt, Dickens, his friend and biographer John Forster, Harriet Martineau, John Sterling, Thackeray, Ruskin and Tennyson came to see both or either, and varying records emerged as a result. When Samuel Butler suggested in 1884 that it was 'very good of God to let Carlyle and Mrs Carlyle marry one another, and so make two people miserable instead of four',[18] he was writing from no personal knowledge. Neither was Frederic Harrison, reviewing Froude's biography of Carlyle, when he said of the couple's correspondence, 'Husband and wife rail at each other like giants and giantesses in a fairy tale; when they have a tiff, it stuns us like the Tower of Babel.'[19] But the first-hand testimony is conflicting, even if we put aside the well-known capacity of married couples to put on a front. Harriet Martineau testified that 'No kind of evening was more delightful to me than those which were spent with the Carlyles', before mentioning 'the marvellous talk of both husband and wife'.[20] Perhaps not the most astute judge of character, Ralph Waldo Emerson recorded in 1847 that 'Carlyle and his wife live on beautiful terms: Nothing can be more engaging than their ways [. . .]'.[21] David Masson, the future literature professor and historian, met the couple as a young man down from Scotland in 1843, and remembered 'the demeanour of this famous couple to each other in their domestic privacy' as 'uniformly exemplary and loving in all essential respects, with a kind of stately gallantry on Carlyle's part when he turned to his Jane, or she interposed one of her remarks; and, on her part, the most admiring affection for him in all that he said or did'.[22] Masson described 'this remarkable lady' with care, noting 'a delicately cut and

17. Surtees, *Jane Welsh Carlyle*, 186. As readers will see in the course of her correspondence Jane certainly was sympathetic to foreigners such as Amely Bölte, Godefroi Cavaignac, Stavros Dilberoglue, Spiridione Gambardella, Giuseppe Mazzini, Count Carlo Pepoli and Richard Plattnauer—as was Thomas, to some extent. Bölte and Plattnauer were particularly needy, but to call them 'strays' is going too far. One stray she certainly did adopt was the much-treasured Maltese-cross Nero, sent to her from Manchester by Dilberoglue in 1850, who survived numerous scrapes before dying in 1860; he figures largely below.
18. Geoffrey Keynes and Brian Hill (eds.), *Letters between Samuel Butler and Miss E. M. A. Savage, 1871–1885* (London, 1935), 349–50.
19. Frederic Harrison, *The Choice of Books and Other Literary Pieces* (London, 1886), 179.
20. Harriet Martineau, *Autobiography*, 2 vols. (London, 1877), i. 377–8.
21. Ralph L. Rusk and Eleanor M. Tilton (eds.), *The Letters of Ralph Waldo Emerson*, 10 vols. (New York, 1939–1995), iii. 424.
22. David Masson, *Memories of London in the 'Forties*, ed. Flora Masson (Edinburgh, 1908), 53.

rather pained face of dun-pale hue, very dark hair, smoothed on both sides of an unusually broad forehead, and large, soft, and lustrous eyes of a gypsy black'.[23] Ten years later, the Irish nationalist and parliamentarian Charles Gavan Duffy described a similar woman: 'Her face was colourless but most expressive, answering promptly to every emotion; her eyes were frank and pleasant, and her smile, which was gracious, passed easily into banter or mockery.'[24] The same physical impression was made on Froude, in 1849: 'Her features were not regular, but I thought I had never seen a more interesting-looking woman. Her hair was raven black, her eyes dark, soft, sad, with dangerous light in them.'[25] The Carlyles' friend, the preacher Edward Irving (early in their marriage, it is true), could speak in somewhat nauseating terms of her being like an Eve and making a little Paradise wherever she was, and Froude could chime in as regards her 'genius for small evening entertainments',[26] but perhaps it was that 'dangerous light' that produced mixed feelings in others. On receipt of a particularly self-pitying letter from Jane, Harriet Martineau asked a mutual friend, '*What* is it? and what *is* she?'[27] 'She is so coquettish,' Martineau wrote to a friend as early as 1838: 'so different when she & I are alone, & when others are by; & she breaks in with little jokes & wanting notice when we are talking.'[28] Hardly an Iphigenia, then. The poet Arthur Hugh Clough's fiancée found her 'very flighty sharp; nothing whatever gentle and female about her [. . .] like a spoiled child'. Robert Browning called her a 'hard, unlovable woman', and Charles Darwin (brother of Erasmus) admitted that 'It is high treason, but I cannot think that Jennie is either quite natural or lady-like. She certainly is very far from natural; or to use the expression Hensleigh [Wedgwood, Darwin's cousin] so often quotes, she is not an unconscious person.'[29] Eliza Forster, wife of John, had no time for accounts of Jane's marital oppression at Thomas's hands. 'Don't you believe all that!' she apparently told the neurologist James Crichton-Browne. 'She was rather an actress, and liked to pose

23. Ibid. 36.
24. Quoted in Lawrence Hanson and Elisabeth Hanson, *Necessary Evil: The Life of Jane Welsh Carlyle* (London, 1952), 433. Duffy later became an Australian politician, serving as the eighth premier of Victoria in the early 1870s. In 1856, while working at the Lands Department, he proposed and planned a new township in the county of Bogong, on the New South Wales border, to be named 'Carlyle', main streets 'Thomas' and 'Jane'. It was never built, though a parish in the region retains the name.
25. Clubbe, *Froude's Life*, 477.
26. Hanson and Hanson, *Necessary Evil*, 183; Clubbe, *Froude's Life*, 204.
27. Surtees, *Jane Welsh Carlyle*, 214.
28. E. S. Arbuckle (ed.), *Harriet Martineau's Letters to Fanny Wedgwood* (Stanford, 1983), 11.
29. See Ashton, *Portrait of a Marriage*, 336, 369; Hanson and Hanson, *Necessary Evil*, 238.

as a martyr, talking of her sufferings and getting sympathy. I assure you he was the great sufferer.'[30]

These varying impressions and perspectives are remote from the point but also prove it: these witnesses may not have known the whole truth, but their incommensurable accounts clearly suggest that something was up. 'The only certain thing', Rosemary Ashton concludes, 'is that the relationship between Carlyle and Jane was not entirely happy.'[31] On the one side Thomas: 'a man driven by physical and spiritual demons that were impervious to her influence'; 'fevered, hag-ridden, fiercely self-involved'; 'brusque and self-centred'; who 'found it easier to express affection for her on paper than face to face'; apparently with 'little time for pity, and none for comprehension of Jane's feelings' yet also in fact the possessor of 'the softer heart' of the two.[32] On the other side Jane: 'a sounding-board for Carlyle's frustrations, miseries, and the other manifestations of his selfishness, which depressed her to the point of madness'; 'her own worst enemy'; 'clever and facile' ('too intelligent to be completely contented with the life she was most fitted for, and insufficiently thoughtful or deeply-feeling to find the serious work she believed herself called to do [. . .] and so led always to depression and a sense of futility'); carrying with her always a 'longing for notice and approbation and appreciation which underlay all her daring and spirited ways'; and her 'need to be constantly winning small battles' going along with an inability 'to let go of any strong emotion, however wasteful of energy or destructive of peace and progress it might be'.[33] 'A push and pull existed in Jane,' Kathy Chamberlain remarks, 'sometimes unconscious, sometimes not, between the allure of the shadows—passivity, privacy, invalidism—and the desire to stand up for herself and assume a role on the social stage.'[34] 'She wanted to be needed, and she needed to be adored', yet on the other hand she was the victim of an 'ingrained habit [. . .] to view life ironically, a defensive mechanism which afforded her some intellectual satisfaction but no happiness'.[35] An ironist seeking adoration; an introvert repressing extrovert impulses; an insufficiently thoughtful intellectual; a victim of selfishness who was her own worst

30. Quoted in Simon Heffer, *Moral Desperado: A Life of Thomas Carlyle* (London, 1995), 349.
31. Ashton, *Portrait of a Marriage*, 11.
32. Ibid. 35; Ireland, *Life*, 130; Heffer, *Moral Desperado*, 57, 315; Hanson and Hanson, *Necessary Evil*, 485; Surtees, *Jane Welsh Carlyle*, 128.
33. Heffer, *Moral Desperado*, 414; Surtees, *Jane Welsh Carlyle*, 198; Hanson and Hanson, *Necessary Evil*, 228; Ireland, *Life*, 149; Ashton, *Portrait of a Marriage*, 173, 100.
34. Chamberlain, *Jane Welsh Carlyle and her Victorian World*, 135.
35. Ashton, *Portrait of a Marriage*, 252, 270.

enemy: perhaps only a George Eliot—or a Flaubert—could have encompassed Jane's moral nature.

Of course, alongside these forces pulling the couple apart there were interests they shared: theirs was, when all is said and done, a remarkable partnership. I have already mentioned their arguably over-zealous commitment to telling the truth, no matter the personal cost. Both, too, were basically philistines, with no interest in the arts to speak of (visual, musical or architectural; though Jane did appreciate Chopin when he visited London in 1848), and only a limited tolerance for imaginative literature, though Jane consumed bales of cheap novels and did genuinely admire both Charlotte Brontë and George Eliot. (Her dismissive comments on Austen, Keats, Browning and even Dickens are dismaying, and Thomas had no time for poetry whatsoever. They failed to appreciate Ruskin's feverish aestheticism, too.) Their attitudes to religion—his yearnful, given his hatred of Victorian materialism, hers utterly sceptical—also converged in essence. On the other hand, after their arrival in London in 1834 eight years after their marriage, they never shared a bed. 'You might indicate', Froude wrote to Mrs Ireland as she worked on her biography, 'that there was only companionship',[36] and a marriage not based on a sexual relationship loses an immense source of tenderness and trust. But Kathy Chamberlain astutely suggests that the couple's manic and lifelong hypochondria, reported in exhaustive detail in letters to each other, was itself a 'displacement' or sublimation of that need: 'a way of continuing to care for each other's bodies' in an asexual way.[37] Illness was a never-ending resource for the pair of them, and what Jane calls the 'bad habit of constantly talking with exaggerative Carlyleian eloquence of all his ailments great and small' (*CL* 35: 248) was by no means confined to her husband. Rosemary Ashton relates Thomas's 'dyspepsia' (for want of a better word; probably chronic constipation, or ulcers of some description) to Charles Darwin's similar sufferings, involving 'physical weakness and mental depression, and, most alarmingly for both these meticulous men, self-disgust proceeding from the embarrassment of wind and the irregularity and sometimes torture of passing bowel movements'.[38] In later years Jane, too, self-medicated on 'eternal dosing with laxatives'. Modern medicine regards such conditions as mostly brought on by bad diet, and certainly Jane regarded fruit, for example, as a thing 'for no use but to give people a cholic'.[39] She and Thomas

36. Clubbe, *Froude's Life*, 55.
37. Chamberlain, *Jane Welsh Carlyle and her Victorian World*, 148.
38. Ashton, *Portrait of a Marriage*, 36.
39. Surtees, *Jane Welsh Carlyle*, 252, 160.

comment on food in their correspondence frequently enough; neither so much as mentions a green vegetable. Lamb chops and porridge are the most commonly mentioned foodstuffs, and anything with feathers on it produced only consternation. Other Victorian complaints they reported to one another in hypertrophic detail remain opaque to us in a similar way, occupying as they do the borderland between the somatic and the psychological: 'neuralgia', 'lumbago', 'rheumatism', '*nerves*' and so forth. Even before they became man and wife in 1826 they shared 'letters of similar hypochondriacal self-indulgence, each feeding off the other, setting a tone for their marriage'.[40] Still, it was by no means all hypochondria; Jane clearly did suffer from appalling migraines, whatever their source. 'Such headaches I never witnessed in my life,' Thomas recorded:

> agony of retching (never anything but phlegm) and of spasmodic writhing that would last from twenty-four to sixty hours, never the smallest help affordable. Oh, what of pain, *pain*, my poor Jeannie had to bear in this thorny pilgrimage of life; the unwitnessed Heroine, or witnessed only by me,—who never till now *see* it *wholly*![41]

It seems that she also perhaps suffered from premenstrual dysphoric disorder as well as more or less annual influenzas that kept her indoors for weeks in the winter; her insomnia was almost constant, as was her husband's. And she suffered a woeful injury in the street in 1863, with various obscure side effects. Such afflictions brought the couple together if only as topics for conversation.

Other things they had in common included the apparently endless strings of protégés and protégées—many foreign—the couple picked up, and about whom they compared notes regarding their foibles, characteristics and eccentric English idiom, which generated a good deal of what Thomas called the couple's '*coterie sprache*'.[42] Then there was their role as tenants in one of the most famous houses in English literary history, on Cheyne Row, which Thomas found and chose in 1834, which

40. Heffer, *Moral Desperado*, 72.
41. Carlyle, *Reminiscences*, 67.
42. Tantalisingly, the Russian radical and autobiographer without equal Alexander Herzen (1812–1870) was one of these visitors, much taken by Carlyle's seriousness on social ideas, despite their very different attitudes to them. He visited Cheyne Row in September 1852 while Thomas was in Germany, and they did meet in December of that year, but not much more came of it. 'He is a brave energetic looking man Herzen', Jane reported to Thomas's brother John, 'but with a basis of *barbarian*. His tawny eyes have a hungry animal look that made me feel as if he might easily spring at me and eat me' (*CL* 27: 289).

they never owned yet never left, and in which they lived sometimes in a sort of nomadic state as Thomas shifted his study from room to room and floor to floor, including eventually an ambitious but unsuccessful soundproofed box in the roof, designed to protect his morbid sensitivities from neighbouring roosters, street-vendors and piano-players. The house contained and still contains furniture from Jane's childhood home, yet intermittently in Thomas's absence she conducted almost military campaigns of cleaning and redecorating that exhausted and infuriated her, but were also welcome bouts of physical activity. (Her attitude to builders and related tradesmen is withering but also exhilaratingly comic.) Then there were the servants the house necessarily relied upon (though one at a time was all they could afford or countenance for many years), thirty-three of whom came and went during their tenancy, providing endless opportunities for hilarity and exasperation. (The most remarkable of them, 'Kirkcaldy Helen' Mitchell, worked for them from 1837 to 1846 before descending into total alcoholism and an attempted suicide, but her reign gave Thomas and Jane a copious supply of anecdotes and recitals to share, and injected 'something akin to liveliness into the discordant climate in that unhappy house'.[43]) Then, everywhere around them, there was London itself, the largest and most stupendous city in the world, to which both gravitated like iron filings to a magnet, but about which both of them complained incessantly as regards its beggars, noise, smells and fogs, not to mention its dreadful *milk*. 'Though [. . .] Jane could make a comic anecdote out of a broom handle even in the lonely wilds of Craigenputtoch,' Rosemary Ashton points out, 'her joy at having so much to observe, to describe, and to criticise in London shines out of her letters'[44]—and it is in the capital that her correspondence really comes alive, accordingly. The horrors of the Great Wen inspired Thomas with numerous resolutions to return to the rural Scotland of his childhood, but Jane's memories of their exile in Dumfries during their early married years ensured that those ideas remained theoretical. Still, as the years went by, the couple insisted on taking annual holidays—mostly separately, sometimes disastrously together—to friends and relations in lowland Scotland, England's north and its south coast to get away from it all, from which locations they sent protracted letters of complaint to each other before dashing back to Chelsea to grumble about the city once more: a double bind of the centrifugal and the centripetal worthy of Geoff Dyer and *Out of Sheer Rage*. 'The fact was', Virginia Surtees

43. Surtees, *Jane Welsh Carlyle*, 138.
44. Ashton, *Portrait of a Marriage*, 159.

rightly concludes, 'that Jane was never satisfied anywhere but in her own house giving her own orders.'[45]

'To whom can we complain', Thomas wrote therefore, 'if not to one another, after all?'[46] First and foremost there was the *posture* they brought to all these issues and topics: a frenzied hyper-sensitivity they ramped up in each other in happiness and misery alike—misery that was a source of happiness, indeed. We have already noted Frederic Harrison on the couple railing at one another like giants and giantesses from a fairy tale. Rosemary Ashton pictures them as 'like two Othellos bellowing about life and death over the dropping of a handkerchief', and Froude, too, spoke of Thomas's 'Titanesque power of making mountains out of molehills'.[47] Yet this hyper-sensitive and co-dependent irritability went in different directions, or found different outlets. 'As a writer and conversationalist', Kathy Chamberlain remarks, 'Jane Carlyle was in essence a comedian, not a tragedian' as her husband was. Yet, 'Comedian and tragedian may see the world from sharply different angles but they see the same sort of world—as Samuel Johnson put it, a world that is too often "bursting with sin and sorrow."'[48]

'Bursting' is a perfect word for the pair of them, in their letters and their company alike: bursting with hilarity and outrage, to be sure, but also with frustration and disgust. (Western culture is well stocked with cultural pessimists, from Jean-Jacques Rousseau to F. R. Leavis, but like Ruskin Thomas Carlyle brings a new and catastrophist meaning to the term.) We have seen Jane discussing her all-important '*I-ity*' and David Masson commenting on Thomas's 'stately gallantry' in the Cheyne Row parlour as Jane 'interposed one of her remarks'. Occasionally, Masson recorded, Thomas would resort to 'playful teasing' and 'rhetorical mastery even against *her*':

> Far more frequent [. . .] were her little witticisms at his expense. She was fond of entertaining her friends with sprightly stories of any recent misbehaviours of his; and on such occasions he would listen most benignantly and approvingly, with the pleased look of a lion whose own lioness was having her turn in the performance.[49]

45. Surtees, *Jane Welsh Carlyle*, 208. 'With the Carlyles', Rosemary Ashton notes (*Portrait of a Marriage*, 176), 'absence always made the heart grow fonder, apart from sulks and tiffs over missed posts and continuations of arguments begun before they parted.'
46. Quoted in Hanson and Hanson, *Necessary Evil*, 399.
47. Ashton, *Portrait of a Marriage*, 447; Clubbe, *Froude's Life*, 350. 'He saw his ailments through the lens of his imagination, so magnified by the metaphors in which he described them as to seem to him to be something supernatural [. . .]' (ibid. 148).
48. Chamberlain, *Jane Welsh Carlyle and her Victorian World*, 211. 'He was misanthropic, she was gregarious' (Surtees, *Jane Welsh Carlyle*, 138).
49. Masson, *Memories of London*, 53–4.

It is a revealing reminiscence. Jane's witticisms are 'little' and her stories are 'sprightly', as befits the Victorian wife she manifestly was not. She entertains only *her* friends with them, never his. The lion looks on benignly and approvingly all the while, as his glamorous assistant takes her turn in the ring. Given the forces at play, it is not altogether surprising that this fireside ritual and its epistolary equivalent grew more bitter as the years went by—and particularly after Thomas fell under the mysterious spell of the mannish Lady Harriet Baring in the 1840s, provoking understandable grief and jealousy in his wife. The 'battles of wit' that had begun in the couple's courting days gradually became something more like a performance, genius for small entertainments notwithstanding. 'Many acquaintances commented on her self-appointed role, apparently complacently tolerated by Carlyle, of mockingbird and put-upon wife of genius presiding over the tea table.' 'However complacent Carlyle may have been on these occasions,' Rosemary Ashton goes on,

> he was not always disposed to be amused at Jane's sharpness, and she was not always able to channel her frustration into biting humour, but sometimes wept or sulked instead. Increasingly this became the Carlyles' *modus vivendi*; Jane was licensed to criticise Carlyle in front of others, Carlyle's concession being to tolerate the criticism [. . .] and so a kind of serio-comic double act grew up alongside Carlyle's solo performances.[50]

Here was another cycle of rivalry and co-dependency, like the trips north and south, the house, the projected escapes to the country, the servant 'problem' and Thomas's embarrassing prostration before Lady Harriet. In time it became embittered: 'Hitherto', Lawrence and Elisabeth Hanson remark regarding the mid-1850s, 'she had confined herself to satirical stories about him at which he laughed along with the rest. Now she interrupted him, talked across him at table, seized every opportunity to assert herself.'[51] 'I too am here', with a vengeance.

In sum, 'He thought of a wife as a companion to himself who would make life easier and brighter to him'—and by no means the intellectual companion Jane hoped that she might become. (Tellingly, she 'never wavered in her pride in Carlyle, and yet there is scarcely a comment in her letters about the quality of his individual works'.[52]) 'He observed

50. Ashton, *Portrait of a Marriage*, 173, 193, 220.
51. Hanson and Hanson, *Necessary Evil*, 436–7.
52. Ashton, *Portrait of a Marriage*, 254. On his books she wrote to John Forster on 14 December 1845 (*CL* 20: 76): 'I am always so thankful to have them *done* and out of the house, that the praise or blame they meet with afterwards is of the utmost insignificance to me.'

nothing [. . .] about her which called his attention from his work and from what was round him.'[53] He 'loved his wife dearly to the end but' paradoxically 'was incapable of telling her so except in letters', regarding Jane basically 'more like a live-in sibling' than a wife: 'a family member one quarreled with, was annoyed by, counted on, intermittently felt a strong affection for, and could not do without.'[54]

❧

I said that we cannot peel Jane off from Thomas, biographically speaking, as his wife. But as a writer the case is different. 'Had she been placed in a congenial relationship, with a man many degrees less intellectual than Thomas Carlyle—a man with whom the deeper sympathies of a woman's heart had met full response—we cannot doubt that the world would have known Jane Welsh Carlyle as a writer.'[55] Mrs Ireland's is a noble sentiment, but I am not sure that it is true. George Eliot was fortunate in having the unwavering support of her partner, George Henry Lewes; Jane Austen's family recognised her talent; and Charlotte Brontë had her like-minded sisters, in league with her as she with them. But intellectual support alone does not make a novelist (and I assume it is Jane as a novelist that Mrs Ireland had in mind). To be one of them, one must be a poet and a social analyst, too—as those three nineteenth-century cases show.[56] We have some evidence to the effect that Jane entertained authorial ambitions. As a teenager she wrote a novel and a Romantic tragedy, 'The Rival Brothers'—as did many another early nineteenth-century adolescent. She wrote poetry for some years and as a young woman was greatly taken by Lord Byron—ditto. She had a literary bonfire of some kind in January 1825, involving 'the beginnings of *five* novels in various stages of progress' (*CL* 3: 239). 'She had written at one time something of her own early life; but she gave

53. Clubbe, *Froude's Life*, 171, 282.
54. Surtees, *Jane Welsh Carlyle*, 3; Chamberlain, *Jane Welsh Carlyle and her Victorian World*, 301.
55. Ireland, *Life*, 307.
56. Jane wrote to Thomas on 18 January 1823 about their early creative plans for her: 'If you have one spark of humanity within your breast send me an outline of some tale to work on; else I shall never get on; for no sooner has my brain got up something like a plot, than I perceive it to be the veriest imbecility, and cast it away for some other, that is, in its turn, discarded with no less contempt' (*CL* 2: 271). We could never imagine the young Henry James, say, being caught short of a *donnée* like this.

up, and burnt it,' Thomas recollected. 'She wrote at various times in Note-books; refusing all sight of them even to me: but she has destroyed nearly every vestige of them.'[57] In the winter of 1833 he also recorded 'that Jane was writing—"*what* she will not tell me"', and in 1836, while he was slaving on *The French Revolution*, she was apparently working on some French translations.[58] In 1837 she wrote a jejune 'Dialogue' called 'The Bird and the Watch' about the timepiece she inherited from her mother. In November 1852, without warning, she wrote a 'semi-autobiographical, semi-fictional tale',[59] '*The Simple Story* of my own First Love', luxuriating in nostalgia for her childhood self. There is the 'Much Ado about Nothing' journal, reproduced below, serio-comically describing a return visit to her home town of Haddington in 1848, and some other fragmentary diaries: precious little more.[60] Even keeping a journal was something she only very intermittently committed to: 'one may keep a journal very minutely and regularly', after all (she wrote when starting one in October 1855), 'and still be a great fool!—all the greater perhaps for this very labour of selfconsciousness which is so apt to degenerate into a dishonest striving "to make a silk purse out of a sows ear"—for posthumous admiration or sympathy—from one's Executors; or even for present self-complacent mistification of *oneself*!' (*CL* 30: 199). Her art was that of a letter-writer, and the presence of an interlocutor, virtual but known, was essential to release her from that 'selfconsciousness' every serious writer, in whatever medium, ultimately needs to escape. Thus in an important sense the imperfect relationship she had with her husband, lacking in response to the 'deeper sympathies of a woman's heart' as it evidently was, was a matrix as well as a restraint.

But if Jane did not necessarily have the poetic and sociological instincts of a novelist she remains a supreme storyteller, as several of the letters reproduced below demonstrate. To take a case almost at random: in July 1836, only a few years after the couple's arrival in Chelsea, Jane visited her mother at home in Templand, Dumfriesshire, where Grace Welsh had moved after Thomas and Jane married. The visit was not an entirely successful one, and in future years Jane came to realise that she and her mother could not be under the same roof for any serious length of time. By the end of August she turned for home on a series of coach connections: exactly the set of experiences that her epistolary

57. Carlyle, *Reminiscences*, 55.
58. Ashton, *Portrait of a Marriage*, 137, 174.
59. Ibid. 326.
60. Jane's notebook of 1845–1852, '*The Simple Story*', and her journal of October 1855–July 1856 are reproduced in *CL* 30.

talent thrived upon. 'Now that I am fairly settled at home again, and can look back over my late travels with the coolness of a spectator,' she wrote to her aunt Mary Welsh on 4 September, 'it seems to me that I must have tired out all men, women, and children that have had to do with me by the road':

> I got into that mail the other night, with as much repugnance and trepidation as if it had been a Phalaris's brazen bull, instead of a christian vehicle, invented for purposes of mercy not of cruelty: There were three besides myself when we started, but two dropt off at the end of the first stage, and the rest of the way I had as usual half the coach to myself. My fellow passenger had that highest of all terrestrial qualities which, for me, a fellow passenger can possess, *he was silent*.— I think his name was Roscoe, and he read sundry long papers to himself with the pondering air of a lawyer. We breakfasted at Litchfield [Lichfield, Staffordshire], at five in the morning, on muddy coffee and scorched toast, which made me once more lyrically recognise in my heart (not without a sigh of regret) the very different coffee and toast with which you helped me out of my headach.

Absolutely nothing, the modern reader notes to him- or herself, has changed about travel and its discontents with the passage of nearly 200 years—though which of us would have the wit, the imagination and the knowledge to compare the airliner, train carriage or coach we submit ourselves to with the hollow bronze bull in which an ancient Sicilian tyrant liked to roast his victims in order to compare their screams with the animal's bellowings? And which of us could produce out of nowhere the 'pondering air' that infallibly indicates a member of the legal fraternity?

But there is more to come:

> At *two*, there was another stop of ten minutes, that might be employed in lunching or otherwise— [F]eeling myself more fevered than hungry, I determined on spending the time in combing my hair and washing my face and hands *with vinegar*,—in the midst of this solacing operation I heard what seemed to be the mail resuming its rapid course, and quick as lightening it flashed on me 'there it goes!—and my luggage is on the top of it!—and *my purse* is in the pocket of it!—and here am I stranded on an unknown beech, without so much as a sixpence in my pocket to pay for the vinegar I have already consumed!' Without my bonnet, my hair hanging down my back, my face half dried, and

> the towel with which I was drying it firm grasped in my hand, I dashed out,—along,—down,—opening wrong doors,—stumbling over steps,—cursing the day I was born,—still more the day on which I took a notion to travel,—and arrived finally, at the bar of the inn in a state of excitement bordering on lunacy. The bar-maids looked at me 'with weender and amazement'— 'Is the coach gone?' I gasped out.— 'The coach? Yes!' 'O! and you have let it away without *me*! O! stop it,—cannot you, stop it?' and out I rushed into the street with streaming hair and streaming towel, and almost brained myself against—*the Mail*! which was standing there in all stillness without so much as horses in it!— [W]hat I had heard was a heavy coach!— And now having descended like a maniac, I ascended again like a fool, and dried the other half of my face, and put on my bonnet, and came back 'a sadder and a wiser' woman—

The irrational but utter panic that travel via public provision provokes in us as 'quick as lightening'—the overwhelming desire for privacy and cleanliness the gratification of which seems itself like an invitation to fate; the dread-cum-realisation that all our effects, documents and currency must have been carried away in one fell swoop by forces beyond our control, leaving us worse than naked, unidentifiable and actually penniless; the paranoid belief that trusted auxiliaries in the process (cabin crew, coach drivers, hotel staff, 'security') have no comprehension of either the gravity of the situation or our state of mind with respect to it; and the humiliating absurdity of finding that every one of those feelings was totally and as it were *visibly* groundless—all those twentieth-century experiences Jane has magically anticipated, even as she inserts herself retrospectively into (of all English classics) 'The Rime of the Ancient Mariner': 'A sadder and a wiser man / He rose the morrow morn.'

But she and her audience are not home yet. Thomas, it goes without saying, is not at the London inn to meet the coach:

> I did not find my Husband at the *Swan with two necks*; for we were *in*, a quarter of an hour before the appointed time. [S]o I had my luggage put on the backs of two porters and walked on to Cheapside, where I presently found a Chelsea Omnibus. By and by however, the omnibus stopt, and amid cries of '*no room Sir*'—'*Cant get in*'— Carlyle's face beautifully set off by a broad-brimmed white hat gazed in at the door,—like the Peri who '*at the gate-of heaven stood disconsolate*'— [I]n hurrying along the Strand pretty sure of being too late,—amidst all the imaginable and

> unimaginable phenomena which that immense thorough fare of a street presents; his eye (heaven bless the mark) had lighted on *my trunk* perched on the top of the omnibus and had recognised it! This seems to me one of the most indubitable proofs of *genius* which he ever manifested— [H]appily a passenger went out a little further on, and then he got in— (*CL* 9: 47–8)

Here is the other aspect of the Janus-faced god of long-distance travel: the paranoiac nightmare of being left behind suddenly resolves into the dream of being reclaimed, inevitably by one's hopelessly unreliable spouse, his face 'beautifully set off' by the traveller's fatigue and over-stretched expectation, the battered suitcase a metonym for its exhausted owner. Jane is absolutely at the centre of this delectable narrative—'*my purse*', 'without *me*', '*my trunk*'—but the extent of her artistic control is in fact a guarantee against egoism. It is her journey but it is also the journey of every passenger, whether from Edinburgh to London in Victoria's time or Sydney to Dubai in our own age.

So the Hansons are not wrong to say that 'Nothing, short of death, could for long keep down the zest for life which again and again lifted her above prostration, sickness, headache, sleeplessness'[61]—not to mention the other personal difficulties and dissatisfactions that dogged her. In fact those difficulties and dissatisfactions were at the centre of her genius as they were at the centre of her unhappiness. Jane, Froude suggested (with regard to their Craigenputtoch period, but with general application), 'took refuge in a kind of stoicism, which was but a thin disguise for disappointment and at times for misery'.[62] Once, 'a kind of stoicism' suggested itself to me as the title for this selection as 'I too am here' suggested itself to the McQueen Simpsons. But again it will not do. Jane's personality—her 'zest for life' as revealed in her letters—was too dynamic for a concept like stoicism usefully to characterise it. As early as December 1830 she wrote to her friend Eliza Stodart from Craigenputtoch, aged twenty-nine, that she had learned 'to produce letters as the silk-worm spins, all out of my own inside' (*CL* 5: 207), and certainly when she arrived in London three years later she (belatedly) blossomed as a writer. The invention of the penny post in 1840 (a campaign that Thomas had thrown his weight behind from the beginning) seems to have released her in that respect, as it did so many other Victorians. 'The writing and receiving of personal letters had become woven into the fabric of daily life' during Jane's lifetime, as Kathy Chamberlain

61. Hanson and Hanson, *Necessary Evil*, 348.
62. Clubbe, *Froude's Life*, 277.

remarks: 'vital to human connectedness, intimacy, and entertainment. Increasingly in the Victorian era, letters were expressions of individuality, for men and women alike.'[63] For middle-class women like her—literate, mostly denied the opportunity to work, and trapped in domestic servitude (in Jane's case, childless as she was, of a fairly light variety)—the postal reform must have been as revolutionary as social media are for us today. Her talent alchemically transformed a 'strongly accentuated emphasis on ordinary matters'[64] into authentic if unpremeditated and unpondered reflections of and on the human spirit. For these reasons, not to mention the intimations we can make out in her epic journey from Templand to Chelsea in 1836 and countless other instances besides, 'A Victorian and a Contemporary' seems a better title when all is said and done, though an expression she used in '*The Simple Story* of my own First Love'—'in advance of the Century'—captures something of the same issue. I stress this not because Carlyle was the possessor of 'advanced views' or suchlike,[65] but because her response to life is so uncannily like our own. Like us she maintains marital relations and deals with relations on both sides of the partnership; she runs a household, with its multiple petty frustrations; she suffers from house guests and high-maintenance friends; she copes with shopping at one end of the moral spectrum, and with illness and bereavement at the other; she must even contend with pandemics like typhus (which killed her father) and cholera. Thus it is that much in Victorian life is still with us, even as Jane and Thomas were among the first generation of individuals frequently to use railway transport and the postage stamp. Some of that life is still with us as regards married existence, too. But Jane Welsh Carlyle has the ability to look into the depths of these things with a vision not altogether of her time, like some tutelary spirit dead in 1866 but still alive today. Let us return to the issue of health and medicine, for example. It is easy to smile at blue pills and green vitriol, morphine, pepsine, quinine and iodine (thirty drops, *before* breakfast), senna pods and castor oil, camphor, henbane, Quassia and 'Indian hemp',

63. Chamberlain, *Jane Welsh Carlyle and her Victorian World*, 82.
64. Ireland, *Life*, 69.
65. Jane was dismayed by the drafts of Geraldine Jewsbury's sexually explicit novel *Zoe: The History of Two Lives* (1845), which she edited. In August 1849 she wrote to her friend Martha Lamont about her newly published *The Fortunes of Woman: Memoirs* to say, 'Good luck to you and it. I hope it wont be to write up what they call "The rights of Women" at all rates— I am so weary of hearing about these *rights* of ours—and always to the tune of "don't you wish you may get them"?' (*CL* 24: 157). Yet she also joined George Eliot and 2,000 other women to sign the 1856 petition for a married women's property act (reproduced in *CL* 31: 29–36), legislated the following year.

hydrotherapy, phrenology and the rest. Phrenology we have abandoned, even if we have hung on to homoeopathy, which Jane scouts utterly in her letter to John Forster of 28 August 1841, below. When we look at these things, Victorians like her appear safely in the remote past of medical and scientific absurdity. But then if we are honest we recall our own paramedical and sub-medical addictions: float tanks, aromatherapy, reflexology, colonic irrigation, dermabrasion, ear-candling, *reiki*, *feng shui*, crystals, 'mindfulness', colouring-in books for grown-ups, probiotics, and all the vitamins and supplements we dose ourselves with and which have so little verifiable effect between the oesophagus and the urethra. When we look at ourselves in the light of things like that the Victorians appear to be breathing down our necks—only we have the advantage of a century and more of scientific progress and education.

Jane made no claims on her own behalf as regards being in advance of her century. 'For *me*', she wrote to her niece Helen Welsh in October 1848, 'I am incorrigible as to "the welfare of others"—at least in the matter of letter writing the idea of *giving pleasure* cannot prevail with me to write and I write always from one of two motives, from a *need* to *receive* a letter, only to be extracted by giving one, or from gratitude for what is vouchsafed me "on the voluntary principle["]' (*CL* 23: 141). But the pleasure of writing a letter must be bound up with the pleasure it affords its recipient. 'If Carlyle's letters complement his writings', as Rosemary Ashton remarks, 'Jane's form a body of literature in themselves', allowing her, as Kathy Chamberlain sees it, 'to control the narrative of her life, to shape the way her actions were interpreted, to indicate to her audience how she wished to be seen. She could attempt, at least, to edit her life through her letters, and make of living something like art',[66] as every great English letter-writer (from Byron to Virginia Woolf, and Henry James to D. H. Lawrence) essentially does. She herself described 'writing so many letters as I write' as '*strenuous idleness*' (*CL* 18: 252): a paradoxical condition not altogether remote from imaginative literature in the conventional sense. Epistolary art is about *presence*, and her letters convey this elusive quality perhaps even more directly than Byron's own. (As we have seen, she conveys her effects mostly by means of narrative; he, ever the poet, could depend on a Shakespearean mastery of prose rhythm.) And her husband was by no means alone in the value he placed on her achievement. 'They are wholly apart from all other letters,' Harriet Martineau believed, and John Sterling told a

66. Ashton, *Portrait of a Marriage*, 9; Chamberlain, *Jane Welsh Carlyle and her Victorian World*, 117.

friend that she was 'the most brilliant letter-writer' that he knew.[67] 'Few people, indeed,' Virginia Woolf suggested in 1905, 'have been able to cast so brilliant an image of themselves upon paper', and seventy years later Elizabeth Hardwick agreed, finding Jane's letters 'more brilliant, lively, and enduring than all except the best novels of the period'.[68]

But even feminists like Woolf and Hardwick have been capable of constructive belittlement when it comes to seeing Jane's achievement in its true light, beyond her husband's shadow.[69] 'Her genius, in her letters and in her character,' Hardwick suggested (and, being the ex-wife of Robert Lowell, Hardwick wrote from personal experience of male 'gigantism'),

> was to turn his gigantism into a sort of domestic comedy, made out of bedbugs, carpets, soundproof rooms, and drunken serving girls. Just as the form and style of Carlyle's works set no limit upon themselves, so she sets limits upon everything. His grandiosities were accomplished in the midst of her minute particulars.[70]

'While her husband sat upstairs in the sound-proof room deciphering the motives and characters of the actors in some long-forgotten drama, Mrs Carlyle', Woolf wrote, 'was practising the same art over her tea-cups.'[71] The tendency to miniaturisation is very marked: 'Imagining Mrs Carlyle as a novelist is a natural extension of her letters', Hardwick goes on, 'with their little portraits of ordinary people, their gift with anecdote, their fluent delight in the common events of the day.' 'Mrs Carlyle,' Woolf chimes in, 'like the true humorist she was, has eyes for all sides of the little dramas that enact themselves in her drawing-room and never loses her sense of proportion.'[72] 'Little portraits', 'ordinary people', 'anecdote', 'delight', 'common events' (even 'gift' and 'fluent': like Milton looking down his nose at Shakespeare, warbling his native

67. Chamberlain, *Jane Welsh Carlyle and her Victorian World*, 14; Ashton, *Portrait of a Marriage*, 214.
68. Andrew McNeillie (ed.), *The Essays of Virginia Woolf, Vol. 1: 1904–1912* (London, 1986), 54; Elizabeth Hardwick, *Seduction and Betrayal: Women and Literature* (New York, 1975), 166.
69. A readable survey of the ways in which Jane has been identified with Thomas as a writer as well as a wife, even by feminist critics, is Anne Skabarnicki, 'Seeing Jane Plain: Recovering the Art of Welsh Carlyle', *Modern Language Studies*, 27:3/4 (Autumn–Winter 1997). See also Aileen Christianson, 'Jane Welsh Carlyle's Private Writing Career', in Douglas Gifford and Dorothy Macmillan (eds.), *A History of Scottish Women's Writing* (Edinburgh, 1997).
70. Hardwick, *Seduction and Betrayal*, 165.
71. Woolf, *Essays, Vol. 1*, 55.
72. Hardwick, *Seduction and Betrayal*, 166; Woolf, *Essays, Vol. 1*, 56.

wood-notes wild); the 'little dramas' of the drawing-room: the attitude betrays itself—in its condescending attitude to fiction, never mind Jane Carlyle.[73] It is easy to understand this tendency to see Thomas contemplating kings at his desk while Jane dealt with cabbages at the tea-table. (Thomas himself, having praised his wife to the skies in comparison to George Eliot and George Sand, still referred to her as 'my *little* woman', as we have seen.) But on the other hand where is it written that Frederick the Great is automatically more interesting than, say, Elizabeth Bennet; or Oliver Cromwell automatically more interesting than Maggie Tulliver? The world has long since put those questions to rest and decided that Austen's 'three or four families in a country village' reproduced on her 'little bit of ivory' reflect at least as much of human nature as the behemoths Thomas spent long and bitter years biographising. Jane Welsh Carlyle's letters may not have the geographical and experiential scope of Byron's, or the aesthetic intensity of John Keats's. Very well; she was neither of those individuals. As Thomas decided in his *Reminiscences*, '*human* was what she looked at, and what she was'.[74] Her husband's literary contribution in his sphere was magnificent—indeed nowadays woefully underrated—but her contribution in her sphere was just as important and original. A world bursting with sin and sorrow—and other things besides—can be seen through a multiplicity of lenses, so long as they are bright and clear.

The principles of the selection are threefold and simple. First (hopefully), a revelation of Jane Carlyle's epistolary art, alongside the other

73. '"*Monsieur le President!* I begin to be weary of the treatments I experience here"!', Jane wrote to Thomas on 10 August 1845. '—Always my "bits of letters" and "bits of letters" as if I were some nice little Child writing in half-text on ruled paper to its Godpapa!— Since [Francis] Jeffrey was pleased to compliment me on my "bits of convictions"; I have not had my "rights of Woman" so trifled with! *He* payed the penalty of his assurance in losing from that time forward my valuable correspondence; with *you* I cannot so easily cease to *correspond* [. . .]: but a woman of my invention can always find legitimate means of revenging herself on those who do not "treat her with the respect due to Genius"—who put her off with a pat on the head or a chuck under the chin, when she addresses them in all the full-grown gravity of five feet-five-inches-and-three-quarters—without her shoes! So let us hear no more of my *bits of letters*, unless you are prepared to front a nameless retribution!' (frontispiece, and *CL* 19: 137–8).

74. Carlyle, *Reminiscences*, 105. An important element in Jane's epistolary success was that she wrote to a wide array of individuals, as did Byron. Vincent van Gogh's letters are important, no doubt; but as so many of them are addressed to his brother Theo, his correspondence feels limited by comparison.

great letter-writers in English literature and beyond: her force of expression, her narrative gift, her humour and her pathos. Second, the letters taken in chronological sequence must amount to something of an informal autobiography—a 'faithful and unerring portrait'—even if letters (like diaries) generally are a form that militates against both prolepsis and retrospection, unlike the memoir.[75] Third, Carlyle is a superb reflector of her own time, even as she anticipates ours: a time when the stagecoach gave way to the steam train; when universal postage was introduced; when poetry gave way to the novel and the Romantic and Regency worlds disappeared in the flood tide of bourgeois 'Victorian' morality; when French thought gave place to German ideas, and English science reached its apogee; when nationalism abroad and Chartism at home pressed their claims most urgently; when typhus and cholera stalked the land, and public health and hygiene roused itself in response, even on the Chelsea embankment; when food standards, prison conditions and mental disability became subjects of genuine if haphazard concern; when taxation gradually became efficient and ubiquitous; when political, social and economic reform began to gather pace; when change in the lives of women began (albeit very slowly) to move in positive directions, at least in the domestic and marital spheres for the middle class; and when people looked in every direction—as we do now—for guidance in a rapidly evolving and unpredictable world.

75. For a little more on these particular 'theoretical' issues the reader might like to consult my 'Crucible or Centrifuge? Bronislaw Malinowski's *Diary in the Strict Sense of the Term*', *Configurations*, 22 (2014), 29–55, and 'Berlioz' Memoirs and Delacroix's Journal: Context, Personality, Ethos', *Romanticism*, 23:1 (2017), 1–14.

Chronology

(Please note: Jane Welsh Carlyle's life does not lend itself to standard chronologies, and will emerge via her letters and the chapter introductions below. This list attempts to contextualise her life rather than to summarise it.)

1758	Birth of James Carlyle, TC's father
1771	Birth of Margaret Aitken, TC's mother
1775 or 1776	Birth of John Welsh, JWC's father
1782	Birth of Grace Welsh, JWC's mother
1795	James and Margaret marry; birth of TC (4 December), Ecclefechan, Dumfriesshire; birth of John Keats
1796	Death of Robert Burns
1797–1813	Birth of TC's six siblings (Alexander, John, Margaret, James, Mary, Janet)
1801	Birth of Jane Baillie Welsh (14 July)
1803	Birth of Ralph Waldo Emerson
1806	TC sent to Annan Academy, and learns Greek, French and Latin; birth of John Stuart Mill and Elizabeth Barrett (later Browning)
1809	TC enrols at Edinburgh University, supported by his family, studying Greek, mathematics and logic; birth of Charles Darwin
1810	Birth of Elizabeth Gaskell
1811	Birth of William Makepeace Thackeray
1812	Birth of Charles Dickens, Robert Browning and Geraldine Jewsbury
1814	TC leaves university to teach at his detested old school, Annan Academy; preparing for a church career
1815	JWC, 'The Rival Brothers', a drama (*CL* 3)
1816	TC meets Edward Irving while teaching at Kirkcaldy; birth of Charlotte Brontë
1817	TC abandons plans for entering the ministry; loss of faith; reads Madame de Staël's *De l'Allemagne*, Hume and Gibbon; first efforts in journalism and poetry; his mother has an obscure but dangerous collapse, which he can-

not help but associate with her disappointment in him as regards a religious vocation

1818 TC leaves Kirkcaldy and returns to university to study natural history; he never took a degree

1819 TC teaches himself German, discovers Goethe; meets the editor of the *Edinburgh Encyclopaedia* and writes articles; death of JWC's father and her loss of faith; birth of Queen Victoria, George Eliot and John Ruskin; Peterloo Massacre

1820 Death of George III and ascent of George IV

1821 TC resolves to become an author, and meets JWC at Haddington with Irving; first article in the *New Edinburgh Review*

1822 TC takes up a tutorship with the Buller family; birth of Matthew Arnold

1823 TC starts a biography of Schiller and a translation of Goethe's *Wilhelm Meister's Apprenticeship*

1824 TC's relations with JWC become serious; his first and revelatory visit to London; also visits John Badams in Birmingham for two months and sees British industrialism; visits Paris (October); gives up tutoring; sends *Wilhelm Meister* to Goethe; death of Byron

1825 *Schiller*; TC lives and works at the family farm in Hoddam Hill, Dumfriesshire, and rids himself of the 'Mud-gods of my Epoch' (atheistical and religious); JWC visits the family successfully; first English railway opens; first horse-drawn omnibuses in London, now the world's largest city

1826 TC and JWC marry (17 October) and live at 21 Comely Bank, Edinburgh

1827 TC's translation plans fail; meets Francis Jeffrey; applies unsuccessfully for professorial positions at St Andrews and University College London

1828 TC and JWC move to Craigenputtoch, Dumfriesshire (May; till May 1834); Burke and Hare murder trials in Edinburgh

1829 'Signs of the Times' in the *Edinburgh Review*; Catholic emancipation; Metropolitan Police established

1830 Death of TC's sister, Margaret; death of George IV and ascent of William IV; Liverpool and Manchester railway; Charles Lyell, *Principles of Geology*

1831 *Sartor Resartus* completed; TC visits London (August) to seek publication, where JWC joins him (October), and where Irving has become a celebrity preacher; cholera pandemic and multiple railway extensions in Scotland

1832 Death of TC's father and of Goethe; return to Craigenputtoch (March); death of Walter Scott and Jeremy Bentham; cholera pandemic in London; passage of the Great Reform Bill and Scottish Reform Act

1833 *Sartor Resartus* serialised; residence in Edinburgh (January–May); Ralph Waldo Emerson visits at Craigenputtoch; Alfred Tennyson, *Poems*; Slavery Abolition Act; Factory Act restricts child employment

1834 TC and JWC set up home in Cheyne Row, Chelsea (June); TC starts work on *The French Revolution* and applies unsuccessfully for an astronomy professorship at Edinburgh Observatory; death of Coleridge and of Irving; New Poor Law enforces the workhouse; Houses of Parliament consumed by fire

1835 First part of *The French Revolution* burned by accident by John Stuart Mill's servant; friendship with John Sterling, Erasmus Darwin; JWC learns Italian; Darwin at Galapagos; Cruelty to Animals Act; last capital punishment for buggery

1836 *Sartor Resartus* published in Boston with Emerson's help; University of London founded

1837 TC's breakthrough: *The French Revolution* completed, and first set of lectures, on German literature; Dickens, *The Pickwick Papers*; death of William IV and ascent of Victoria; opening of London's first mainline station (Euston)

1838 TC's second lecture series, on the history of literature; he joins campaign for penny post; *Sartor Resartus* published in London; *Critical and Miscellaneous Essays* published in Boston; Dickens, *Oliver Twist*; Chartist campaigns for male suffrage in Scotland and England; National Gallery opens

1839 TC starts reading on Cromwell and joins campaign for the London Library; first meeting with Lady Harriet Baring (later Ashburton); his third series of lectures, on European revolutions (Reformation, English and French); joins the 'Condition of England' question with *Chartism*; Dickens, *Nicholas Nickleby*; first telegraph line; Custody of Infants Act increases maternal access

1840 Penny post introduced; TC's fourth (and last) lecture series, on heroes and hero-worship; declines chair in history at Edinburgh

1841 *On Heroes, Hero-Worship and the Heroic in History*; Emerson, *Essays: First Series*; London Library founded

1842 JWC's mother dies; Alfred Tennyson, *Poems*; Browning, *Dramatic Lyrics*; Copyright Act; Income Tax Act; Edwin Chadwick's report on sanitary conditions; Victoria tours Scotland

1843 *Past and Present*; TC becomes closer to Lady Harriet Ashburton; Dickens, *A Christmas Carol*; Hood, 'The Song of the Shirt'; Ruskin, *Modern Painters*, vol 1; completion of Nelson's Column, Trafalgar Square

1844 Death of John Sterling; JWC refurbishes No. 5; TC declines professorship at St Andrews; Emerson, *Essays: Second Series*; Disraeli, *Coningsby*; Factory Act; stock exchanges open in Glasgow and Edinburgh

1845 JWC, intermittent Notebook (April 1845–November 1852: *CL* 30); *Oliver Cromwell's Letters and Speeches, with Elucidations*; Disraeli, *Sybil, or The Two Nations*; Geraldine Jewsbury, *Zoe: The History of Two Lives*; railway mania at its peak; Great Famine in Ireland

1846 TC tours Ireland; JWC concerned about her sanity and insomnia; relations with TC at a low level regarding Lady Harriet; Dickens, *Dombey and Son*; repeal of the Corn Laws; Highland potato famine

1847 Thackeray, *Vanity Fair*; Charlotte Brontë, *Jane Eyre*; Emily Brontë, *Wuthering Heights*; second Factory Act

1848 TC, articles on the Irish question; Emerson lectures in London; Chopin visits the capital; cholera pandemic; Thackeray, *Pendennis*; John Stuart Mill, *Principles of Political Economy*; Caledonian Railway establishes connections between England and Scotland; cholera in Edinburgh; Chartism reaches a climax; Public Health Act; birth of the Pre-Raphaelite Brotherhood

1849 TC tours Ireland, while JWC returns to Scotland; her 'Much Ado about Nothing' journal (August: *CL* 24); JWC is given a dog, Nero; Dickens, *David Copperfield*; Charlotte Brontë, *Shirley*; Charles Kingsley, *Alton Locke*

1850 *Latter-Day Pamphlets* and 'Occasional Discourse on the Negro Question'; redecorating at No. 5, JWC strains her chest and shoulder; Tennyson, *In Memoriam*; Elizabeth Barrett Browning, *Poems*; death of Wordsworth; the 'Great Stink' of untreated sewage in the Thames

1851 *Life of John Sterling*; TC's interest in Frederick the Great awakens; Great Exhibition in Hyde Park

1852 Large-scale changes at No. 5 after a thirty-one-year lease is signed; JWC, '*The Simple Story* of my own First Love' (*CL* 30); TC tours Germany; Dickens, *Bleak House*; Public Libraries Act

1853 House rebuilding continues for most of the year; death of TC's mother

1854 TC commits to *Frederick*; his upstairs study a failure and is rebuilt; his infatuation with Lady Harriet Ashburton at its height; Dickens, *Hard Times* (dedicated to TC); Coventry Patmore, *The Angel in the House*; Britain joins Crimean War

1855 TC meets Ruskin; JWC explodes over household finances; house-painters once more; JWC Journal, October 1855–April 1856 (*CL* 30); her friend Ellen Twisleton records JWC's experiences at Craigenputtoch (November: *CL* 30); Tennyson, *Maud*; first pillar boxes installed in London

1856 Work on *Frederick* continues; JWC in poor health in autumn; in February alongside 2,000 others she signs the petition 'To the Laws of Property as they Affect Women'; Elizabeth Barrett Browning, *Aurora Leigh*; National Portrait Gallery established; end of Crimean War

1857 JWC's health improves in spring; death of Lady Ashburton; JWC revisits Haddington; Tait works on his painting *A Chelsea Interior*; Matrimonial Causes Act makes divorce a civic procedure; Victorian and Albert Museum founded

1858 JWC receives George Eliot's *Scenes of Clerical Life*; *History of Friedrich II of Prussia, Called Frederick the Great*, vols. 1 and 2; TC's second tour of Germany; Lord Ashburton remarries; *English Woman's Journal* established; divorce courts start to function; the 'Great Stink' returns

1859 JWC receives George Eliot's *Adam Bede*; her health poor; Dickens, *A Tale of Two Cities* (substantially influenced by *The French Revolution*); Charles Darwin, *On the Origin of Species*; John Stuart Mill, *On Liberty*; Tennyson, *Idylls of the King*; 'Big Ben' first sounds at the Houses of Parliament

1860 Death of Nero (February); JWC falls and breaks a rib; two servants at No. 5 henceforth; Ruskin, *Unto This Last*; George Eliot, *The Mill on the Floss*; Dickens, *Great Expectations*; the Oxford evolution debate; Food and Drink Act makes adulteration illegal; first regulated nursing school

1861 JWC's health continues to come and go; death of Elizabeth Barrett Browning; Criminal Law Consolidation Acts

1862 JWC makes an intense acquaintanceship with Charlotte Cushman; *Frederick*, vol. 3; London to Edinburgh express train; Joseph Bazalgette begins construction of London embankments

1863 JWC visits St Leonards-on-Sea for her health (June); injured on the street in Cheapside (September); death of Thackeray; John Stuart Mill, *Utilitarianism*; first section of London Underground

1864 JWC remains seriously ill, and returns to St Leonards in spring; Lord Ashburton dies; JWC travels to Scotland, begins to recover; returns to No. 5 (October); TC buys her a carriage for exercise; *Frederick*, vol. 4; Browning, *Dramatis Personae*; Tennyson, *Enoch Arden*

1865 JWC has another health collapse (February); her intimacy with the second Lady Ashburton grows; *Frederick*, vols. 5 and 6; JWC reduced to writing with her left hand; TC elected Lord Rector of Edinburgh University and chairs a committee in defence of Governor Eyre of Jamaica, removed for cruelty; death of Elizabeth Gaskell; modern sewerage begins in London; New Poor Law Act reforms workhouses; fourth cholera pandemic

1866 A new dog, Tiny, enters No. 5; TC gives his rectorial address at the University of Edinburgh (2 April); delayed in Scotland by a sprained ankle; JWC dies while on her daily drive (21 April); funeral in Haddington (26 April); George Eliot, *Felix Holt*; London Fire Brigade founded; last London cholera outbreak

1867 TC starts writing *Reminiscences*; 'Shooting Niagara: And After?' in opposition to the Second Reform Bill

1868 Mary Aitken Carlyle moves in to No. 5 to assist editing JWC's letters

1876 Important letter from Geraldine Jewsbury to James Anthony Froude, TC's biographer, on their marriage (22 November: *CL* 30)

1881	Death of TC (5 February); *Reminiscences*
1883	*Letters and Memorials of Jane Welsh Carlyle*
1895	No. 5 Cheyne Row, now No. 24, is purchased by public subscription, and handed over to the Carlyle's House Memorial Trust; thence to the National Trust in 1936

Editorial Note

With the publisher's permission the entire text of the letters is drawn from *The Collected Letters of Thomas and Jane Welsh Carlyle* (Durham, NC: Duke University Press, 1970–2024), cited as *CL*; and *The Carlyle Letters Online* (https://carlyleletters.dukeupress.edu).

'Jane's letters, in particular,' the editors noted, 'are in a very unconventional form' (*CL* 1: xxvii); she did not date her letters, capitalised irregularly, and punctuated with dashes, as so many nineteenth-century letter-writers did. In so far as typography can reproduce orthography, the Duke edition assiduously respects Jane Carlyle's text as received in print or manuscript. But the purpose of this selection is not identical to the parent edition. It is aimed at the general reader as well as the scholarly one, and certain editorial changes have been introduced accordingly for ease of readership, in the knowledge that the Duke original remains in print and online for readers of all kinds to refer to. In particular, Jane used the dash as we all do, to offset subordinate clauses and phrases within sentences and at their end; but she also ubiquitously uses it instead of a full stop. Nor does she always capitalise the first letter of a new sentence thereafter. Perhaps the most important editorial intervention I have made—on a case-by-case basis rather than dogmatically—is to open up a space after a 'dash full stop' and insert a capital letter for the new sentence. This seemed less necessary, from the reader's point of view, after either an exclamation mark or a question mark, so I have left the first letter of the new sentence after these marks in lower case. Jane—like many writers of English—was also irregular in her use of the semi-colon, mostly treating it as a comma; I have left her usage alone, and inserted commas and full stops only when clarity and prose-rhythm seemed to require them. She occasionally misspells, as all letter-writers do. I have left alone that which seems characteristic ('headach' for 'headache', for example, or 'doze' for 'dose') but silently corrected simple oversights ('the' for 'they', or 'sich' for 'six', for example). I have kept [*sic*] to the bare minimum.

Otherwise, I have transferred quotation marks from American usage to British: 'singles', with "doubles" within singles. I have removed the full stop and the superscript from constructions like 'D^{r}.', 'M^{r}.' and 'M^{rs}.', or '1st' and '2nd'. I have converted words in capitals to small capitals to avoid 'screaming' emphasis—though perhaps sometimes that is exactly what Jane intended! Following the guidance of the Duke edition I have also taken full control of Jane's address line and date, given in italics before each letter. I have used the editorial ellipsis [. . .] on comparatively few occasions: mostly when Jane either added a superfluous postscript or introduced a paragraph of personal detail that would have required inordinate annotation.

Annotation is all my own, but I have depended hugely on my Duke predecessors, and sometimes simply quoted a note that could not be improved upon in my view, or borrowed one of Thomas's from the 1883 *Letters and Memorials* quoted in the collected edition. Jane's letters are chock-full of references, allusive and elusive, not all of which can be traced and many of which fall into the category of what she and Thomas called '*coterie sprache*' ('coterie speech'), developed between them with contributions from friends, family and servants alike. (The exiled Italian nationalist Giuseppe Mazzini was a particularly prodigious contributor to this private argot, as he translated literally from his native tongue to English in conversation: *quà giu* as 'here down' and so on. Another key source was the maidservant 'Kirkcaldy Helen' Mitchell.) Where the reference could not be traced, or the coterie idiom holds sway, I have not troubled the reader with a note; on the other hand I hope I have not too often (to use Thomas's expression from his review of Boswell's *Johnson*) 'punctually explained what is already sun-clear'. The correspondence between Jane and Thomas, in particular, must be one of the most substantial such marital relations in history: the same names recur again and again across the years. Rather than repeat myself in the notes ad nauseum I have appended a list of 'Characters and Correspondents' at the end of the book, to which readers can refer.

Further Reading

Allingham, H. and D. Allingham (eds.), *William Allingham's Diary* (London, 1907).

Ashton, Rosemary, *Thomas and Jane Carlyle: Portrait of a Marriage* (London, 2002).

Blunt, Reginald, *The Carlyles' Chelsea Home* (London, 1895).

Campbell, Ian, 'Carlyle House', *Carlyle Annual*, 11 (1991).

Carlyle, Thomas, *Reminiscences*, ed. Kenneth J. Fielding and Ian Campbell (Oxford, 1997).

Chamberlain, Kathy, *Jane Welsh Carlyle and her Victorian World: A Story of Love, Work, Friendship, and Marriage* (London, 2017).

Christianson, Aileen, 'Constructing Reality: Jane Welsh Carlyle's Epistolary Narratives', *Carlyle Studies Annual*, 16 (1996).

——, 'Jane Welsh Carlyle's Private Writing Career', in Douglas Gifford and Dorothy Macmillan (eds.), *A History of Scottish Women's Writing* (Edinburgh, 1997).

Christie, William (ed.), *Letters of Francis Jeffrey to Thomas and Jane Welsh Carlyle* (Abingdon, 2008).

Clarke, Norma, 'Jane Welsh Carlyle: The Letters, the Self, and the Literary', *Carlyle Studies Annual*, 16 (1996).

Clubbe John (ed.), *Froude's Life of Carlyle* (London, 1979).

Codr, Ariana, 'Rethinking the Marriage Plot: Self-Consciousness in the Letters of Jane Welsh Carlyle and Thomas Carlyle', *Modern Philology*, 115 (2018).

Cumming, Mark (ed.), *The Carlyle Encyclopedia* (Madison, NJ, 2004).

Drew, Elizabeth, *Jane Welsh and Jane Carlyle* (London, 1928).

Espinasse, Francis, *Literary Recollections and Sketches* (London, 1893).

Fielding, Kenneth J., 'Robert Scott Tait: His Portraits and Photographs of the Carlyles in their "Chelsea Interior"', *Review of Scottish Culture*, 13 (2000).

—— and David R. Sorensen (eds.), *Jane Carlyle: Newly Selected Letters* (Aldershot, 2004).

Gray, Beryl, '"Nero, c'est moi": Jane Welsh Carlyle and her Little Dog', *Carlyle Studies Annual*, 22 (2006).

Hanson, Lawrence and Elisabeth Hanson, *Necessary Evil: The Life of Jane Welsh Carlyle* (London, 1952).

Heffer, Simon, *Moral Desperado: A Life of Thomas Carlyle* (London, 1995).

Holme, Thea, *The Carlyles at Home* (London, 1965).

Ireland, Mrs Alexander [Annie], *Life of Jane Welsh Carlyle* (London, 1891).

Jones, Sarah Olwen, 'Staging the Interior: The Public and Private Intimacies of Thomas and Jane Welsh Carlyle's Domestic Lives', *Journal of Victorian Culture*, 18 (2013).

Kaplan, Fred, *Thomas Carlyle: A Biography* (Cambridge, 1983).

Larkin, Henry, 'Carlyle and Mrs Carlyle: A Ten Years' Reminiscence', *British Quarterly Review*, 74 (1881).

Masson, David, *Memories of London in the 'Forties*, ed. Flora Masson (Edinburgh, 1908).

Morrison, N. Bryson, *True Minds: The Marriage of Thomas and Jane Carlyle* (London, 1974).

Rose, Phyllis, *Parallel Lives: Five Victorian Marriages* (London, 1984).

Skabarnicki, Anne, 'Seeing Jane Plain: Recovering the Art of Welsh Carlyle', *Modern Language Studies*, 27:3/4 (Autumn–Winter 1997).

Sorensen, David and Rodger Tarr (eds.), *The Carlyles at Home and Abroad* (London, 2004).

Surtees, Virginia, *Jane Welsh Carlyle* (Salisbury, 1986).

Tarr, Rodger and Fleming McClelland (eds.), *The Collected Poems of Thomas and Jane Carlyle* (Greenwood, FL, 1986).

Wasko, Jean, 'The Angel in the Envelope: The Letters of Jane Welsh Carlyle', *Modern Language Studies*, 27 (1997).

Figure 1: Kenneth Macleay, *Jane Baillie Welsh, Mrs Thomas Carlyle, 1801–1866. Wife of the Historian, Thomas Carlyle* (1826), National Galleries of Scotland; presented by Alexander Carlyle 1930

Prelude: Youth, Courtship, Marriage, 1801–1828

In an essay comparing Jane Welsh Carlyle to her friend the novelist Geraldine Jewsbury, Virginia Woolf suggested of the former that 'something of the narrowness and something of the prudery of a Scottish country doctor's daughter clung to her'.[1] (Woolf's friend T. S. Eliot would make similarly snobbish and ignorant comments about the nonconformist culture into which D. H. Lawrence was born.) Jane Baillie Welsh was born on 14 July 1801, the only child of the leading general practitioner in Haddington, the ancient, neat and prosperous county town of East Lothian, seventeen miles east of Edinburgh: a family and an environment almost devoid of narrowness and prudery. John and Grace (both named Welsh, but unrelated) originated in Dumfriesshire in Scotland's lowland west, as did Thomas Carlyle's family, but their social standing was very different, Thomas being the son of a stonemason.

Both parents doted on Jane, as parents of single children often do; but each had a different expectation, nonetheless. In terms we might borrow from *Pride and Prejudice*, the mother thought she had been blessed with a Jane Bennet, the father was sure he had a Lizzy. Grace anticipated a conventionally marriageable young lady of the kind she herself had been; John recognised an intellectual talent like his own and fed it, sending Jane to school like the local boys to learn mathematics and Latin. In due course he would take the still more unusual step of hiring a tutor, Edward Irving (theology student at Edinburgh University, aged eighteen), for his precocious nine-year-old. In due course Grace exerted her authority and had her way: the teenaged girl was sent to a couple of boarding schools (the first in Haddington, the second in Edinburgh) designed to furnish and finish the attributes of the standard young lady. Jane clearly idolised

1. Stuart N. Clarke (ed.), *The Essays of Virginia Woolf, Vol. 5: 1929–1932* (London, 2009), 19. In the last chapter of his autobiography, *Praeterita* (1885–1889), John Ruskin says of 'the rural towns of South Scotland' of the mid-nineteenth century that they possessed 'greater refinement in them, and more honourable pride, than probably [. . .] any other district of Europe'.

her father, taken from her tragically by typhus in September 1819 when she was only eighteen, he only forty-four: 'the being that I loved more than all the world besides,' she told her friend Eliza Stodart a week after the event, 'although he is no longer conscious of my affection' (*CL* 1: 199).[2] His death undermined her religious belief, and like many father-directed daughters she went on to have a difficult relationship with her mother. Whether she subliminally sought to replace John Welsh via her choice of husband is another possibility altogether.

Irving left Haddington in the summer of 1812 and returned to university, where he met Thomas Carlyle, three years younger than him but of a similar background, chalk and cheese though they were in other respects. In 1819 Jane would come up to Edinburgh and be as Rousseauistically smitten by her ancient tutor as he was by her—only he had promised himself to another woman. He tried to extricate himself from that commitment but could not, and married in 1823. During this difficult period—reminiscent once more of Jane Bennet's sufferings over Mr Bingley—Irving continued to visit Haddington, with Grace's fulsome approval. He brought his young friend, too, in June 1821, with Dr Welsh fewer than eight months in the grave, to meet mother and daughter—the latter transformed from local tomboy to the cynosure of every eye in Haddington. Appropriately enough, Jane was now knee-deep in Romantic literature, and this new young man—as rough a diamond as Irving was a polished one—volunteered to guide her reading. He sent her Madame de Staël's *De l'Allemagne* (1817) and followed that up with the originals, Schiller and Goethe, steering her powerfully in a new and deeper intellectual direction, as her father once had done. On 11 November 1822 she wrote Thomas a letter from which, in a sense, there could be no turning back—not that she didn't try:

> My dear friend
>
> If ever I succeed in distinguishing myself above the common herd of little Misses, thine will be the honour of my success. Repeatedly

2. Jane wrote to her cousin Helen on 6 December 1850: 'I wonder after all how I come to be grown such a coward, for I was certainly one of the bravest little children alive—used to bear pain like an Indian—take hissing *Ganders* by the neck—and show myself up to every emergence—I suppose my bravery active and passive must have been like most of my other good qualities "for the occasion got up"—*assumed* to gain my Fathers approbation, to be *praised* by him, and kissed, and "loved very much indeed"—' (*CL* 25: 304). An open-and-shut case, one would have to say. Jane wore mourning clothes until the day she married Thomas, who was as fixated on his mother as Jane was on her father, with a parallel set of implications not so much for his choice of a wife as for his idea of marriage. In due course Thomas would be buried alongside his mother at Ecclefechan, Jane alongside her father at Haddington.

> have your salutary counsels, and little well-timed flatteries roused me from inactivity when my own reason was of no avail. Our meeting forms a memorable epoch in my history; for my acquaintance with you has from its very commencement powerfully influenced my character & life. When you saw me for the first time, I was wretched beyond description—grief at the loss of the only being I ever loved with my whole soul had weakened my body and mind—distraction of various kinds had relaxed my habits of industry—I had no counsellor that could direct me—no friend that understood me—the pole-star of my life was lost, and the world looked a dreary blank— Without plan, hope, or aim I had lived two years when my good angel sent you hither— I had never heard the language of talent and genius but from my Father's lips— I had thought that I should never hear it more—you spoke like him—your eloquence awoke in my soul the slumbering admirations and ambitions that *His* first kindled there— I wept to think, the mind he had cultivated with such anxious, unremitting pains was running to desolation; and I returned with renewed strength and ardour to the life that he had destined me to lead— But in my studies I have neither the same pleasures, or the same motives as formerly— I am *alone*, and no one loves me better for my industry—this solitude together with distrust of my own talents, despair of ennobling my character, and the discouragement I meet with in devoting myself to a literary life would, I believe, have, oftener than once, thrown me into a state of helpless despondency; had not your friendship restored me to myself, by supplying (in as much as they can ever be supplied) the counsels and incitements I have lost— You see I am not insensible to the value of your friendship, or likely to through [throw] it away; tho' you have sometimes charged me with inconstancy and caprice— (*CL* 2: 196–7)

There was a lot of coming and going in a protracted courtship, which Grace evidently regarded with disfavour: she tried to forbid a correspondence with Thomas while encouraging one with Irving. 'From the summer of 1821 until they finally married in October 1826,' as Rosemary Ashton reminds us, 'Thomas and Jane met in person only two or three times a year, sometimes less, and then either in snatched half-hours at Mr Bradfute's house in Edinburgh or under the generally baleful eye of Mrs Welsh in Haddington.'[3] In August 1823 (addressed from '*Hell*'), Jane told Thomas, 'I owe you much! feelings

3. Rosemary Ashton, *Thomas and Jane Carlyle: Portrait of a Marriage* (London, 2002), 34. Bradfute was the uncle of Jane's friend Eliza Stodart.

and sentiments that ennoble my character, that give dignity interest and enjoyment to my life—in return, I can only love you, and *that* I do, from the bottom of my heart' (*CL* 2: 416). In September she stepped back into the idiom of romantic fiction: 'Oh no! Your Friend I will be, your truest and most devoted friend, while I breathe the breath of life; but your wife! Never never!' (*CL* 2: 427). Yet he could see what she could see sometimes, too, but sought to deny, having more than a pinch of her mother's native snobbishness: 'No my dearest friend, you are not happy,' he wrote near Christmas 1823: 'indeed how could you be so? What communion has light with darkness; or you with the inane people your lot is cast among? You are encircled with driveling and folly; nothing that your mind can relish or care for; companionless, tho' your heart is full of warm affections' (*CL* 2: 492). The doctor's daughter from bourgeois Haddington was dying to launch yet dreading to commit; she exhibited her smitten and woebegone suitors, she subtly channelled her mother's disparagement about the impossibility of it all, and she wriggled on the hook most piteously; but she had met her Waterloo. By May 1824 the couple had reached 'an understanding', and by January 1825 marriage with Thomas was 'the most *probable* destiny for me' (*CL* 3: 266). By May she was able to say 'I love you with all my soul' (*CL* 3: 322), and by July she had taken the important step of clearing the decks by confessing her infatuation with Irving: 'I told you that I did not care for Edward Irving, took pains to make you believe this— It was false; I loved him—must I say it—*once* passionately loved him— [. . .] Write I beseech you instantly, and let me know my fate [. . .] Say if you *can* that I may come to you—that you will take me to your heart after all as your own, your trusted Jane and I will arrange it as soon as ever I am able—' (*CL* 3: 356–7). By 8 December she had visited Thomas's family successfully and the die was cast, with a quote from Byron to drive it home:

> for strange as you may think it, young Man, I have an affection for thee which it is not in the power of language to express; and I wot not what evil or accumulation of evils could prevail to make me entirely wretched; while thou art within reach to comfort me with sweet words of hope and love, and while it is written, as with a sunbeam, on my soul 'He loves me! He is mine!'— Yes, 'mine, with life to keep, and scarce with life resign.' Is it not so? (*CL* 3: 425)

Her mother accepted the inevitable, sold the family home to her dead husband's partner (one of Jane's suitors, in point of fact), went to live with her father and sister at Templand (a farm near Thornhill, back home in Dumfriesshire), and rented a pleasant little house in Comely Bank, suburban Edinburgh, for the newlyweds to live in once the ceremony took place, finally, on 17 October 1826, more than five years after they had clapped eyes on each other. Jane Baillie Welsh had passed away, and Jane Welsh Carlyle was born, for better or for worse.

Figure 2: William Young, *Thomas Carlyle, 1795–1881. Historian and Essayist. (View of Carlyle's House at Craigenputtoch)* (1883), National Galleries of Scotland; purchased 1919

1

'The Dreariest Spot in all the British Dominions': 1828–1834

After so long a courtship—and a year's separation before the event—the Carlyles' marriage was likely to be anticlimactic, and so it proved. Once the 'odious ceremony' had been performed (CL 4: 136), the patterns that it was intended to resolve began to assert themselves. 'Yes, you will marry,' Thomas told Jane in November 1823 (CL 2: 472): 'but do something far more glorious than "make puddings": you shall make immortal food for the souls of generous men in lands and ages that you have never seen and never can see.' Six months before the wedding day his roots were showing (CL 4: 69): 'The Man should bear rule in the house and not the Woman.'

But there was another contradiction running alongside that between romantic idealism and patriarchal reality. 'All your faults', Jane had told Thomas in November 1824, with a wisdom beyond her years (CL 3: 191), 'are the effects of your isolated way of life: if you seclude yourself altogether from your fellows, as sure as fate, you will sink in a year or two, into the most surly, misanthropic, self-opinionative, dreadfully disagreeable person alive.' Yet on the other hand both of them, from the beginning of their relationship, fantasised about 'Quietness and fresh air—quietness deep as of the grave, and breezes free as they blow over the summit of Cairngorm' (Thomas), and playing the role of 'Hermitess in some wild highland glen' (Jane) (CL 2: 259, 263). In 1827 she was still playing the same tune—this time to Anna Montagu, who had played an essential role in their coming together—regarding a plan 'to settle down in the wildest place of all Dumfriesshire, leaving the world to run its own race and bear away its prizes; content might we but walk *thro' life with unfettered limbs' (CL 4: 221).*

Given this pattern, settlement in a newlyweds' dream home at No. 21 Comely Bank, suburban Edinburgh—a city which Thomas had known for fifteen years without making any substantial inroads into its intellectual core—was unlikely to be successful, being the product of Grace Welsh's bourgeois vision of her daughter and her uncouth husband. They took up residence at this still pleasant-looking terraced house in October 1826 and left in April 1828, and though Jane referred to it as a 'pepper box' in retrospect there is hardly anything from her in situ. Thomas met Francis Jeffrey, began to publish in the great man's Edinburgh Review, and the couple held Wednesday-evening 'at homes' where men like Jeffrey might gather. But clearly there was something missing, for Thomas at least. With a high hand he had the current tenants evicted in April 1827 from a substantial farm in Dumfriesshire—the only property left to Jane by her father, but settled by her on her mother at marriage—and prepared his wife for moving there in May 1828. All this on the grounds of his health, it was made clear—which did not prevent him applying (unsuccessfully) for professorships of various kinds at the all-new University of London.

Craigenputtoch ('the Hill of the Hawk') would be their home, off and on, for the following six years. In fact, Jane had mentioned the place to Thomas back in 1824, in jest, before saying, 'I would just as soon think of building myself a nest on the Bass-rock [a volcanic gannet rookery in the Firth of Forth].' 'Depend upon it,' she went on, 'you could not exist there a twelvemonth. For my part I would not spend a month on it with an angel' (CL 3: 249). But the 'Hermitess' role was now thrust upon her, willy-nilly. At Craigenputtoch Thomas wrote 'Signs of the Times', 'Characteristics', and above all and in particular his brilliant fantasy, Sartor Resartus, *which he took to London to find a publisher in August 1831. Jane joined him in October, and they returned, defeated in that respect, but with a new sense of London as a destination, in March of the following year. (They had another break in Edinburgh, January–May 1833.) At Craigenputtoch, too, they were visited by guests from the future like Jeffrey and Ralph Waldo Emerson; but there, too, they suffered that 'isolated way of life' Jane had warned about four years before their arrival.*

Twenty years after she left the farm and escaped to Chelsea Jane's friend Ellen Twisleton transcribed her recollection of her existence there (CL 30: 267–74). 'Living at Craigenputtoch, it wasn't as if I saw anything of Carlyle':

> he went to his own room directly after breakfast, & worked there till 2 hours before dinner, & always rode those two hours. And he rode *alone*, because he only galloped or walked, and it fretted him to have my horse cantering along by the of his side [*sic*], so he rode alone & I rode alone, then he came to dinner very much *worked-up*, as bilious people always are by a ride, & he was 'dangerous,' you know, & there was no freedom of communication during dinner; then he went to walk for an hour, which wasn't very wholesome, I always tho't, right after eating, & to his room till tea; & afterward to his room, until about ten o'clock, & then he'd come in, quite tired out with his work, & say, 'Jane, will ye play me a few of those Scotch tunes'—& so I would sit down & play Scotch tunes till he went to bed,—oftenest with the tears running down my face the while I played.—

'I used to go out & sit down in the middle of the moor, on a stone,' Jane recalled, '& wonder *if this were I, & how the same person could live such a life, that had lived the one I'd been used to before,—so petted generally, (though I got whipping enough, to be sure, at times;) but, being an only child, even if I was* punished, *I always felt*

myself an object of importance, at any rate.' The account is warped by long pent-up dissatisfaction (in it, for example, Comely Bank is transformed from a 'pepper box' to a 'little jewel of a house'). It was also surely embittered by Thomas's infatuation with the London socialite Lady Harriet Ashburton; and we have letters from Jane from Craigenputtoch of a different note and nature, below. But her life there must have been a hard one, nonetheless.

The question of whether the Carlyles ever had a sexual relationship has been debated since Froude's biography of Thomas. Aside from the tenderness of some of the letters here, there is one in particular that sheds light on their Craigenputtoch life, from Jane to her bed-bug bedevilled 'Dearest Love', alone in London with the Sartor manuscript in September 1831:

> You were not 'happy'— And I not with you! No Goody to kiss you into good humour, or if that were found impossible to bear you company in ill humour. I thought of you and dreamt of you all night in your solitary 'manger,' and shall have no peace till we are reunited— I will make you up a bed on the drawing-room floor, and sleep on it beside you (better than I have done of late in our own fine red one) if there be no other way of escaping vermin. (*CL* 5: 422)[1]

Such tender interludes notwithstanding—and the Carlyles could be wonderfully loving to each other via their preferred go-between, the Post Office—it was certainly true that she was unhappy and neglected at Craigenputtoch, and forced to confront a form of life she had known nothing of before, as the princess of Haddington and the apple of her father's eye. (See 11 January 1857, below.) In the end, it was essential for the wellbeing of them both that they escaped the breezes off the Cairngorms, the 'wild Highland glen' and the 'isolated way of life'—where making puddings turned out to be all too serious a responsibility—and began a new home in London.

To Johann Wolfgang von Goethe, Craigenputtoch, 10 June 1828

Respected Sir
The Bearer of this is Mr May, a Merchant of Glasgow, and my esteemed acquaintance; who in passing thro' Weimar wishes, as he says himself, to see with his own eyes 'the first man of the age,' I embrace the

1. 'It is just possible', Rosemary Ashton remarks, 'that Jane thought herself pregnant at this time.' She mentioned fainting fits, and Thomas asked her to be careful travelling to London: 'there is more than thy own that thou carriest with thee' (*Thomas and Jane Carlyle: Portrait of a Marriage* (London, 2002), 121). But unambiguous evidence is not available.

opportunity of sending you by him, in my own and my Husband's name, the continued assurance of our affection and grateful regard; and am ever, with the truest sentiments,

Your Scholar and Admirer,
Jane W. Carlyle.

❧

To Eliza Stodart, Craigenputtoch, 28 July 1828

'My dear dear Angel Bessy'!!!

What a world of trouble is in these words announced to you! In fact my tea is done, and my coffee is done, and my sugar white and brown; and without a fresh supply of these articles my Husband would soon be done also: it might be got at Dumfries—but bad; and so I have bethought myself of your kind offer to do my commissions as of old, and find it come more natural for me to employ *you* in this way than another.

To proceed then, at once, to business; that so I may afterwards proceed with freedom to more grateful topics: will you order for me at Polland's in North Hanover Street[2] (nearly opposite Miss Grey's) two stones of brown sugar at 8d and one stone—*very* brown at 6d½; as also a small loaf of white at 12d—with five pounds of ground rice.[3] Then Angel Bess you must not go home by the Mound but rather along the Bridges that you may step into the new tea establishment in Waterloo place and get me four pounds of tea at five and four pence per pound—two pounds at seven shillings—and two pounds of ground coffee at two shillings— [T]his the Cockneys must be instructed to wrap up in strong paper and carry to Pollands addressed to Mrs Carlyle Craigen &c &c[.] And you will have the goodness to tell Polland before hand, that such a parcel will be sent to him to forward along with his sugar—and that he must pack the whole nicely up in a box and send it to the first Dumfries carrier addressed to me to the care of Mr [James] Aitken Academy Street Dumfries. Now one thing more thou Archangel Bessy

2. North Hanover Street, Waterloo Place and The Mound are all streets in central Edinburgh. A set of bridges still cross the dip in the terrain in the New Town, occupied by Waverley station and the Princes Street Gardens.
3. The stone as a measurement of human weight in the United Kingdom is fourteen pounds, but the measurement has varied greatly both historically and in terms of the substance to be measured. The 'stone' for sugar was normally around eight pounds in the nineteenth century. Refined sugar was sold in the sugarloaf form produced by the moulds in which it was processed; the weights of such loaves also varied.

you will pay these things (somewhere about 4 pounds as I calculate) in the trembling hope of being repaid by the earliest opportunity— And unless it goes hard with me I will take good care that you are not dissappointed— The truth is I have no five pound note to send you and four small ones would make rather a bulky letter— And here you may draw your breath as I do mine; for I have nothing farther to trouble you with except on recollection half a pound of Dickson's mustard; not even a long-winded apology for the trouble already given.

By this writing you will know that I have survived my astonishing change—and the talk about tea &c will show you that I even look hopefully into life. Indeed Craigenputtoch is no such frightful place as the people call it: till lately indeed our existence here has been made black with smoke; and confusion unspeakable was nearly turning our heads. But we are begining to get a settlement made at last; and see a distinct prospect of being more than tolerably comfortable[.] The solitude is not so irksome as one might think. [I]f we are cut off from good society, we are also delivered from bad; the roads are less pleasant to walk on than the pavement of Princes Street but we have horses to ride; and i[nstead] of shopping and making calls I have bread to bake and chickens to hatch— I read, and work & talk with my Husband and never weary.

I ride over to Templand occasionally; and my Mother and Agnes Ferguson were here last week[.] They seemed content with the aspect of things[,] but my Mother is so confined at home now! she cannot be absent one night, and *that* home, I fear is no peaceful place for *her*[.] I am sadly vexed about her she is looking so ill and so unhappy.

You will write and tell me how all is going on at 22 and in Edinr generally. [D]ear Edinr I was very happy there; and shall always love it and hope to see it again often and often before I die— Will you give my kind regards to Mr Simpson when you see him and tell him I was well pleased to hear of his success. Remember us also to Mr Aitken and most affectionately to your Uncle. Do you know of any good Habit maker in Edinr (not very expensive)? I have got fine cloth for a habit and am almost afraid to risk the making of it in Dumfries. Perhaps you could make enquiry for me and let me know the charge. and whether a habit could be made from a pattern gown or peliss.[4] Grace Macdonald is turning out a most excellent servant and seems the carefullest honestest creature living. She broke her arm soon after we came hither but it is now almost quite stron[g ag]ain. I never miss a drop of '*broth*.' [And?] my linens are all entire

4. In masculine couture a pelisse is a short over-jacket worn slung on the shoulder by cavalrymen; for women, a long, buttoned coat or dress, with or without sub-military frogging.

My best wishes for Maggy and her new child and '*I hope Mr Dudgeon is quite well.*'[5] Letters from Germany and all parts of the earth reach us here just as before. It is so strange to see Craigenputtoch written in Goethe's hand!— But my paper is done Ever Truly [Your] friend,

JW Carlyle

❧

To Eliza Stodart, Craigenputtoch, 5 February 1830

Dearest Eliza

This has been the unluckiest new-year to me! Every day some Job's-post[6] or other tempts me to curse my stars! It began with the death of my pig—my sweet, wise, little pig, who was the apple of my eye—he got a surfeit one evening, and next morning I was pigless! and just when my long cherished hopes of him were approaching their fulfilment, and a few weeks more would have plumped him out into such delicate bacon! So the glory of this world passeth away![7] On the back of this severe family-affliction followed a disaster occasioned by a quite opposite cause, being the consequence not of overfeeding but pure starvation: a stranger cat under the pangs of famine rushed wildly into our larder one day, making straight in the direction of a beefsteak—and, before you could bless yourself, snack went the steak, and smash went a *corner dish*; which you know was as bad as if the whole four corner dishes had been broken or at least a pair of them. And alas! this was only a beginning—this smash, it seemed, was but a signal for the breakage of all the crockery glass and china about the house— For now Nancy became as it were suddenly possessed with a demon of destruction which shivered everything she laid hands on—nay—the supper-tray with all its complement of bowls, plates &c &c she '*soopit ower wi her tails*' [swept over with the tail of her dress]! one fell *soop*!— But already I must have filled your eyes with tears—and will not tax your sympathy with a detail of *all* my grievances—indeed one sheet would not hold them. Only attend to the last, which you must help me to remedy, being in truth the main cause of my writing again so soon— Last week we were despatching a boxfull of books to

5. Eliza's sister Margaret was married to a Mr John Dudgeon; her uncle was Edinburgh publisher, John Bradfute, with whom Thomas had dealings (see next letter).
6. A message or messenger of disaster; from the story of much-afflicted Job in the Old Testament, which Jane had been reading of late.
7. 'Sic transit gloria mundi': a warning about the impermanence of worldly things, issued to the pope at his coronation; now proverbial.

Sam[8] to be transmitted to their various owners in Edinr— None of our own people being 'at *the* town' that Wednesday it was entrusted to the Carrier, who naturally was charged *to pay it*—but our ill luck pursuing us even in this small matter, the carrier either misunderstood or proved oblivious; and so the package was despatched with all its charges to be defrayed at Bank-street!— Now, tho' intrinsically considered the damage done by this mistake be trifling, yet you will understand how one should find it abundantly vexatious—and I beseech you to explain to Mr Aitken how the omission which must have appeared to him so singularly inconsiderate occured—and to charge him (by his Lady's love or whatever he values most) to place this with every expence which these book commissions cost him, to Carlyle's account. If he does not we shall not be able to apply to him with any freedom, and I doubt if in all Edinr we could find another as helpful.

And now contrary to my usual practice 'I must plant a remark' or two on the weather— It is well we have meat and fire '*within ourselves*' (as Mrs Roughhead used to say) otherwise we should live in hourly apprehesion of being snowed up, and consequently starved to death without even the mournful alternative of '*eating our own children*.' Oh for a sight of the green fields again or even the black peat-moss—anything rather than this wide waste of blinding snow! The only time when I can endure to look out (*going* out is not [to] be dreamt of) is by moonlight, when the enclosure before the house is literally filled with hares—and then the scene is really very picturesque—the little dark forms skipping and bounding over the white ground so witch-like! A still more novel spectacle exhibited itself the other day at broad noon—seven black-cocks [grouse] '*as fine*' (or perhaps finer) '*as ever stepped the streets of Greenock*' came running down the wood to within a few yards of the door— Such are the pleasing varieties of life here!— You will allow they are extremely innocent—

Carlyle inquired if I had sent his love the last time—and charges me to remember it now—we speak of your uncle and you over our evening fire both often and kindly—my kindest regards are with you both—my Grandfather continues much the same— God bless you—always affectionately yours

Jane W Carlyle

8. Samuel Aitken, Thomas's contact at publisher and bookseller Bell and Bradfute, Bank Street, Edinburgh; Eliza Stodart became Mrs Aitken in 1829, but her husband was a churchman, the Rev. David Aitken.

To Eliza Stodart, Craigenputtoch, 20 April 1831

My dearest Eliza

My first determination after reading your letter and tasting your barleysugar was to write the very next week along with a Manuscript[9] for Cochrane— But the manuscript for Cochran did *not* go the next week; nor the next again. nor is it gone at this hour: but rather doubts are rising in mens minds whether it is ever to go at all. In which circumstances, 'necessity Mother of invention' has put me on the discovery, that there is *no* indissoluble connection between the said manuscript and the said letter: and this fact being once clearly demonstrated to my understanding I lose not another moment in courteously saluting you— as in duty and affection bound. 'Get ye good morning Audrey'!—[10] And a fine sunshiny spring morning it is[.] Our woods have put on their green again—and black birds are sweetly singing; and hens profitably cackling; and the Bubbly[11] goggeling neither sweetly nor profitably; and in short even here one feels oneself still in the land of the living in the place of hope.

My Cousin! did you ever watch a goose hatching—or a turkey—or any hatching thing? If not you can form no adequate conception of the hopes and fears which at present agitate my breast. I have a goose sitting on five eggs—a rather flighty sort of character—quite *a goose of the world* in fact who from time to time drives me to the brink of despair by following her pleasures whole hours with the other geese to the manifest danger of cooling her eggs. I hover about the nest during these long absences with a solicitude quite indescribable and it will end I believe in my sitting down on the eggs myself— My Turkey again sits like a very vegetable (indeed she could not well do otherwise being secured under an inverted crate) but she is a born idiot; and I dread that the offspring will be all creatures of weak intellect also—nay, more—that one by one they will be overlaid or otherwise 'die from neglect' like Roberts little daughter— 'The troubles that afflict the just &c &c'![12] '*Now this comes of having the world*'! as Carlyle's Grandmother said, when by some miracle she found herself in possession of an entire gold guinea; and was at her wits end where on all the earth to secure it from thieves— When I had no stock I was comparatively tranquil.

9. Thomas had written an article, 'German Literature of the Fourteenth and Fifteenth Centuries', accepted by J. G. Cochrane, editor of the London-based *Foreign Quarterly Review*; it would be published in October.
10. Shakespeare, *As You Like It*, V. i. 13–15: the quotation is inexact.
11. 'Bubbly-jock': Scots for turkey-cock.
12. Psalms 34: 19.

'Angels and ministers of grace defend us'! 'Art thou a Spirit of health or goblin damned'?[13] O Eliza Eliza! We were sitting at breakfast yesterday morning suspecting nor evil nor good—sipping a highly nutritive beverage of tea and whipt egg—and talking pleasantly enough on some transcendental subject—when suddenly—an unusual sound of carriage wheels, louder and louder, nearer and nearer, interrupted the whole operation[.] I thought it could be no one else but Miss Anderson of Stroquhan; and ran to receive her 'in my choicest mood': but Lord have mercy! what was I come out for to see? seated in an open gig—muffled curiosly in Indian shawls, my astonished eyes rested on the large musculal figure of—Miss Scot! yes Mary Scot of Haddington—'*Hee hee hee—Mrs Caarlile—hee hee hee*'[.] But it was no heeheeing to me! the intensity of my astonishment quite paralized me—and it was minutes before I could express the joy which I really always feel at recognising a Haddington face—belong to whom it may. She was obliged to be off the same evening— But we made the best use of our time. I took nothing in hand the whole day but *milking* news from her (a rather rural metaphor) which she with unabating copiousness supplied. [A]nd could I tell you but a tenth of the facts wherewith I in this way stored my mind you would wonder equally at the capacity of the Instructor and the Learner. Nothing I think in her whole budget [contents of a bag] amused me so much as a *Tale of a nettle*—a still more serious nettle-feud than the '*Jenny Nettles*' of Ancient times.[14] Mary Davidson one day stuck a fine fresh little nettle in the back part of Dr Fyffe's hat—while he was paying a professional visit— The Dr claped on the hat without noticing the emblem— Walked thro the whole town with it and finally mounted and rode off thro' the County— But he detected it at last—the hateful ridiculous too appropriate nettle—and then what were his feelings—his boiling rage! 'Indignation' (they say)[15] 'makes verses'— Accordingly the Dr indited 'one of the most impertinent' and I will be bound to say unintelligible poems ever penned, against the fair offender whom he styled '*a flirting fool*,' and sent it to the house instead of his further medical attendance— Here is a Doctor for you of a right independent spirit!

Do you know any thing of our Mother?— She is gone out of sight for two weeks at least out of my sight and if I do not hear tell of her soon, I must be *after* advertising her.

13. Shakespeare, *Hamlet*, I. iv. 18–19.
14. A Fifeshire maiden of folklore and song deserted by her soldier lover, who hangs herself in grief.
15. Juvenal, *Satires*, i. 79.

Carlyle was for writing a letter to your Uncle [Bradfute] *on his own bottom*—but I advised him to add a postcript here by way of saving postage. And now 'from thee Eliza I must go'—being constrained by what is called the iron law of necessity to take steps (as many as are between here and the next farm town) towards getting the above written sent off [. . .]

Aye! will you not come! and eat home grown strawberries on my Birth day? I know not when I shall see you unless you come hither—My kind regards and C's to Sam [Aitken]— The Barleysugar was a precious goody—I had not tasted a morsel for three years—

God bless you—Ever affectionately yours
Jane Baillie Pen[16]
Welsh Carlyle

To Thomas Carlyle, Craigenputtoch, 6–9 August 1831

Best & Dearest

So you are really gone! and I—ich bin allein [I am alone]! [E]very instant I feel this; yet I am not so miserable as might be supposed—at least not more miserable *here* than I should be in any other place where you were not. It would be infinitely worse to be obliged to make the agreeable among people whom I was all the while wishing annihilated—as I should be constrained (notwithstanding my true tho' perhaps feeble attachment to my species) to wish, with hardly any exception all creatures of the human kind that 'obtruded' themselves on me in my present humour. As it is, Heaven be thanked I have ample room and verge enough to ray forth darkness; and to meditate on 'the mill of death' or 'the monstrous twelve yards long puddings in our insides' or any other earthly or unearthly topics that seems good to me, without the smallest interruption.[17]

I went to bed when the sound of your wheels could no longer be heard; and cried myself into a troubled sleep. The first thing that met my eyes on waking was your night cap lying on my pillow; whereupon I fell a-crying anew, and actually kissed it I believe, tho' you know I

16. A childhood nickname of Jane's, from Penfillan, the home of her paternal grandfather, as there were Janes and Jeannies in her mother's side of the family.
17. A trio of allusions in this sentence: to Thomas Gray's 'The Bard' (l. 52), to German Romantic poet and mystic Novalis, and to lecturer John Waugh's dissection of a porpoise's stomach, witnessed by Thomas at university in 1818.

hate *red* nightcaps. New trials awaited me when I got out of bed and found some article of your dress in all parts of the room: but the worst of all was when I sat down to breakfast, and noticed the *one* cup and *one* everything, and thought how long *this* must last. My heart was nearly failing me altogether; my *head did* fail me—and the whole of that day and part of the following, I had to keep my bed. Fate seemed minded to spare me the trouble of seeking myself employment in your absence. To day I am in my usual middle state—and have been going about 'siding things' as they say in Liverpool—in East lothian dialect, 'redding up' [thoroughly cleaning] or in your 'brief and energetic' dialect 'making an earthquake.' And now my house is all in order (*'swept and garnished'*) and tea has been made *for some hours* for Jemmy who is late (it is near eleven)[.] I may mention further that Harry has got his sides tarred; and that old Mary has found a nest of twelve turkey eggs—which I could have broken, in spite that they were not put in the canister.[18] Nothing of more importance has 'transpired'— Good sleep to you my Darling and good dreams.

Monday [8 August]—Jemmy did not appear on Saturday— I sat up for him till twelve. Yesterday was my worst day since you went. A *betterish* dinner having been prepared for Jemmy I thoughtlessly—*madly* I should say—invited Alick and Jenny. Alick indeed took off (aus ins Freie [out into the open]) so soon as the repasts were ended: but she sat *on*—*on* the unspeakable eye-sorrow, toning forth an occasional 'ee-a' and 'doost,' till I was within a hairsbreadth of telling her that if I was going to keep *any*body about the house in these times it would *not* be she. Jemmy's arrival at nine was a real deliverance— He left them all well at Scotsbrig— He brought me an affectionate little letter from Mary excusing her shyness at our last meeting and accompanied with 'a riband for my wearing cap'—both which made me very wae [sad]. We sat looking at the randzeichnungen[19] till Midnight (Jemmy & I)—for I am as wakeful as if I had a Teufelsdreck in petto [in mind]. 'When I lie down I say when shall I arise and the night be gone'[20]—and I am on foot again the first in the house—to do—what? to dream—

This morning we were two at Breakfast, and *I rang twice*; then started and exclaimed almost in tears 'O Mercy, what am I doing'—and frightened Jemmy into whiteness of face. The people are gathering

18. Jemmy: Thomas's brother James; Harry: the farm horse; Mary: a servant brought from Templand. For 'swept and garnished', see Matthew 12: 44. Alick is Thomas's brother Alexander, Jenny his sister.
19. Goethe had sent Thomas a copy of Eugen Napoleon Neureuther's vignettes on his ballads and romances, published in 1830.
20. Job 7: 4.

for the roup;[21] several have landed themselves in the complete inclosure before the house, and dashed off over the wall as if we had been discharging cannon from the windows. One man with a pot belly hung on the top till I thought he was going to become a fixture; for the war[ning] of other travellers in this remote part of King Williams dominions. The cruelest midge that ever was born has alighted in the very centre of the little *disease* on my face and inflicted a most severe bite and my head is not well— Poor Goody! sorely flamed on from the Hell beneath!— The roup is concluded and has turned out surprisingly—considering the handful of people—The corn brought considerably more than Alick calculated[;] the hay rather less, the potatoes found no purchaser except a small lot which was sold to a drunk man (the most diverting drunk man he seems to have been for he clapped a *second* saddle on Samuel Macadam's horse and insisted on riding it off as his own). A Hundred and forty five pounds was the price of the corn and Hay exclusively of what Alick kept for his own use[.] And Macadam proposes to take all the potatoes at the Candlemas price— This is rather what Mr De Quincey[22] would think a too *Theresa*like paragraph— I have sent Betty home for two days to see her Babe—and old Mary is officiating as housemaid. The only *visible* work I have done since you left me has been creating her a bonnet out of an old petticoat which has made her the happiest of old women. But I have also read some little in the Chaos[23] and the book of Job—Jemmy said when he found me today sitting amidst a litter of books papers needlework &c 'You are not without a *sort* o wark here I think, but you never seem to get *fettled* [settled down] to'— So it is—my head achs & achs, and I dream dream[.] And now to bed where I shall not sleep— Good night—and Heaven keep you—

Tuesday [9 August]— Well I too have 'a Most excellent passivity'[.] Behold me I toil not neither do I spin,[24] yet somehow the day always slips over if not without wishing yet without weariness— O the magic of the imagination! For what would one exchange the power to fancy? I shall hear on Saturday— This I expect will reach you before then—

21. Auction of farm produce and equipment.
22. Autobiographer and critic Thomas De Quincey (1785–1859) had reviewed Thomas's translation of *Wilhelm Meister* and commented on Goethe's heroine's habit of mixing financial reflections up with romantic ones.
23. The poet's daughter-in-law Ottilie von Goethe had started a literary journal with this title in 1829.
24. Matthew 6: 28.

I have your profil[e] stuck up on the mantelpiece— Rembrances to John— How I long for your letter— Bless you Bless you my dear good Husband. I am ever thine

Jane W Carlyle

The whole parcel of arsenic disappeared in Alicks house—it seemed not improbable we should every soul of us be poisoned. It was found after a time

To Thomas Carlyle, Craigenputtoch, 1–3 September 1831

Beloved Good—'Balm best and holiest'[25]

Blessings on thee for thy precious letters! truly they are my life in death! O had you seen me last night—seen the almost insupportable impatience of thy Goody; and then her transports—you would hardly have known whether to laugh or weep. Betty returned with a long story about Macknight having been late. 'For gods sake give me the letters!' 'He left the town too at the usual hour Mam but—' 'For the love of God will you produce the letters!' So seeing that I would positively not hear *her* out first, she at last handed me *the little bag* I had sent, in case of one being lost by the way—for the various imaginations I fall on to torment myself with are altogether wonderful—

And now I was happy, happy—indeed *too* happy[,] for the intensity of the feeling was sickening— My fire burned clear—my candle was lit—all in readiness—and I seated myself at my little table (for one) and spread out both the letters before me, and tried to read them *both at once*—and finding that impossible even to love—finally began with the beginning and read on to the end—at which point I felt a strong disposition to rush out into infinite space, and tell the dead craigs and running brooks, that my Husband was well and took up with no other women! God help me I am a great fool— 'Now you will put yourself off your sleep Mam' said Betty when she came in with porridge and found me walking at quick time about the room—and she never said a truer thing—for not *one* wink of sleep have I got this night— About one I rose, put on my dressing gown, lit my candle, looked vacantly on the Dumfries Courier for two hours, and—smoked half an inch of a cigar— Not I declare to thee for the love of the cigar, but because I had

25. Bernard Barton, 'The Field of Waterloo', from *Napoleon and Other Poems* (1822).

a pleasure in mimicing thee. Then I returned to bed again but sleep was out of the question— My heart now beat audibly—the wind too was making strange noises—for the first time I felt a little nervous about our unprotected state, and regretted that I had not yet learned, as I was meaning, to fire the Gun! And so between vague apprehensions and anxious listening, on the one hand, and thoughts of thy love and goodness on the other—of my probable journey to London—my meeting with my own—Johns good fortune—Mrs Montagu's desertion to the Dragons—Badams's misfortunes and all the interesting things you tell me—I tumbled on till seven, when I had tea in bed, and after one other unavailing attempt at sleep I put on my clothes—and here am I—not a bit weary—without headach or other ailment only *very much detached.*[26] But tomorrow will come when I shall be 'more stilly laid,' as the song says,[27] so it is best to write while I may: besides it will help to compose my mind.

I should have liked better certainly if John had got an appointment of a more permanent sort, altho' less showy—but let us be thankful and hope the best—it is infinitely better than none nay it is a fair and even splendid carreer laid open to him in which he has only to avoid kicking over apple-baskets and he will get along bravely— Offer him my sincere congratulations— I will send on the note for Alick by the earliest opportunity, I had a note from *Him* this morng (by Macadam!) written before he got my letter— Which letter was one long shriek of apprehension and entreaty—but no matter—it came from the heart and therefore it would go to the heart. He will mind my words for he loves me, I rather take it, far better than I thought—and thus will good come out of evil. I *discovered* much that night in Dumfries which I will tell you of hereafter. At present let me turn to what is naturally upermost in my thoughts—My coming to you[.] Say but this—that you do not for the purpose of *procuring me a pleasure* make any sacrifice of your own wishes or convictions; and without an instants hesitation I am decided to come—so soon too as I can get things arranged for leaving— 'The town is empty'[:] O Mercy—it will be full enough any day of the year for one who has been so long used to a desert— Every way of it were pleasant for me[.] I should like to go to Cornwall—like to go to Enfield like to stay with *you*, so that on that ground there need be no delay, and

26. Thomas's London friend Anna Montagu sought to advance both his career and his brother John's. She had also introduced Thomas to John Badams, a Birmingham medical graduate she was sure could cure his dyspepsia. But Thomas reported her mistreating him, and Badams would later dissolve into alcoholism and indebtedness.
27. Walter Scott's 'The Heath this Night' from *The Lady of the Lake* (1810).

neither on any other ground that I can see were it judicious. I should not add to your expenses living *with* you in London (so far as I see into it) more than if I were keeping a *separate* establishment here— And there seems every chance of *your* being detained in London some time yet— At all rates (if it be decided that we winter in London, which indeed appears to me almost as a *necessity*) the saving (if any) of returning hither for a few weeks were not worth the fatigue and disconvenience; and while the expense of *my* journey up is the same whether incurred now or a month or two later—

Now consider what a time elapses before one can get an answer to a letter here— And also how very slowly one gets on even with the most trivial arrangements if these depend not wholly on oneself—and so tell me in the *very next* letter (if I be really to come) all that you would have me to do— First as to Betty—shall I dismiss her or let her stay on and take care of the house till the term— I have been thinking the last way were perhaps the best for the house, and the cheapest. She would have potatoes butter bacon without cost—a little tea and sugar would complete her outfitting— I shall be sorry to lose her but the keeping of *pets* is too expensive a taste for people in our way— The same remark applies to Harry; but some means may perhaps be fallen upon of keeping *him* on without expense— Here he canna be for obvious reasons connected with his own personal comfort poor little beast. They keep beehsts in beehsts place—and would break the heart of a beesht that has had the life of an entire gentleman— Perhaps my Mother will take him in the mean time and send her shelty [pony] here— This is the only outlook that I have for him as yet— However if you would wish him sold and out of the road—tell me— The cow is sure of a welcome go where she will— You would like her sent to Scotsbrig I suppose? And the Turkeys with *your* compliments— The chickens I am resolved to eat as many of as I can—

Next as to what I am to bring with me or send— Am I to bring anything except my wearing apparel[?] Is there any need of sheets or tablecloths &c[?] Do you want any books or clothes? would it be worth while to carry meal—butter bacon so far? The eatables might be packed together in one barrel—the other things (if wanted) in your large trunk and shipped in the steam-boat with me— My Uncle[28] would be able to point out the safest and cheapest way of getting them transported afterwards— But, you must explain to me at least give me *some idea* of the sort of things that you feel in want of—

28. Liverpool John Welsh, one of Jane's most significant relations in later life.

I can take an inventory of all the articles in the house, and *where* they are—and leave it with the keys in charge to my Mother so that at any future time should anything be required it may be come at and sent—

And now having written myself almost out of breath I shall rest a little—and recommence if possible with a better pen—

Next Saturday the devil and his angel, the Monnihive [Moniaive] Carrier shall *not* prevail against me— I have been out examining Harrys sides—I think they may bear the saddle—will try him at least for a mile or two this very night—and if so I will ride for the letter *myself*, and save three days of impatience indignation and despair—

I feel strong enough when I see any *enterprise* before me—but indeed my health is improved— I was persuaded to take portwine at Templand and since my return, I have drunk one of our *two* bottles—a glass every forenoon[—]and have been distinctly very much the better for it. The disease on my face too is fading into invisibility— When I was at Templand my Mother said 'I will tell you Jeanie what you should do for that spot on *your* face—bathe it every morng and evening with springwater &c &c'[.] 'But I was flattering myself that the spot on my face was nearly gone'— '*By the by* I think it is' (with a look of disappointment)— Robert Barker seemed to think it no blemish; he is as much or more in love with me I verily believe than ever he was—I observed one night to the ladies that he was surely getting into strange conditions— 'He is madly in love with another man's Wife' says my Mother 'that's all'—'And a good deal too much I think, could you not either of you advise him to bestow his valuable affections more to the purpose?'

And Jeffrey admired the sleeping city—[29] Thank him for nothing— He would have been the dullest of mortals if he had not— My beloved Dreck! my jewel of great price! The builders despise thee; but thou wilt yet be *brought out with shouting* and I shall live to see thee in thy place— All these discouragements do but increase my confidence—as a candle burns brighter for being snuffed—for Dreck is imperishable, indestructible as the substance of the four elements—and all Booksellerdom all Devildom cannot prevail against him! But I must leave the next half sheet to be filled up at Dumfries— God bless thee Darling

Friday night [2 September].

29. In *Sartor Resartus*, i. 3: Jane's 'beloved Dreck', from *Teufels-dreck*, an early title for the novel, meaning devil's-dust, to be 'brought out with shouting' as in 2 Samuel 6: 15 and Psalms 118: 22.

Little sleep last night either—and today one of my worst heads— Had any traveller landed here this forenoon and explored his way thro' the deserted *toon* to my apartment, he might have fancied himself in a scene of enchantment. There, on my bed, lay collected all the *life* remaining in the place, and that apparently extinct or spell-bound: I had been fainting, and Betty leaning over me, holding salts to my nose, in which position we both finally fell asleep! Now I am up and better, and still resolutely bent on the post office to-morrow— Indeed Mr C[ar]l[y]le a's maist ashamed to say it, but a's far too impetuous—my speculative ardor I feel will shorten my life— But I must not fill up my paper till tomorrow— Goodnight my Beloved—

Dumfries, Saturday [3 September].

Well dearest here am I! have ridden down in safety after a gentle nights sleep of *fifteen minutes*, and without having broken my fast! *Gleg* [sharp] as a hawk—more fluent more ready for adventure than ever I was in my life—only feeling 'a strong inclination to bark'[30] or rather to rush out *as a sign*, and tell the 'machine of society' '*for gods sake to get on*' God help me! I wish I were safe in your arms; for this sort of life is too agitating—would soon kill me outright— I am the veriest fool— I never knew I was such a fool before— I try all I can to be quiet patient reasonable—but the struggle only makes the fever of my mind the greater[.] Well it will not last long— I will direct this almost frightful activity to accomplish all that is to be accomplished with the speed of light—and then! then shall I fly away and be at rest! I have your precious letter—burst it open in the street—read it in the Apothecary's hall where I am now writing— Fear not but I shall get all managed and soon. Already are my arrangements put on a train and next letter perhaps I shall be able to say *when*

Here is a letter from Goethe which alas I cannot read!— But you will read it to me ere long— I have written a note to the noble Lady. Oh how sadly you have defaced her fair image in my soul; but I must still *try* to love her—there are so few women in the world to be loved—! This Mrs Austin indeed![31] Take care! God bless you— I have no quiet

30. From an old Punjabi tale, 'The Four Associates', involving a crow, a jackal, a camel and a hyena; the jackal's urge to bark reveals the presence of his friends in a field of melons.

31. See Thomas's letter to Jane of 31 August, in which he describes a visit to the wife of a law professor 'in the despised and despicable London University' in strikingly ambivalent terms. On 29 August he had described a visit to Anna Montagu, nicknamed 'the noble lady' by Edward Irving, though she was in fact the daughter of a Yorkshire wine merchant. Mrs Montagu had, Thomas reported, '"written you a Letter calling for a speedy answer" and was anxious &c'. See next letter.

or calmness to think of anything practical here— Fail not to write for next Saturday— I will make sure of the let[ter.]

Thy own

Jane

To Margaret Carlyle, London, 6 October 1831

My dear Mother

The newspaper would give you assurance that I was arrived in London,[32] and in a condition to write your name; but further particulars concerning myself and the barrel, you are still anxiously waiting for, and now that I find myself at liberty to write, it were inhuman to keep you longer in suspense.

To begin with the beginning— After leaving you all with a sad enough heart, and comitting myself to the mercy of the waves, my case was none of the pleasantest— Alick recommended me to go down to the cabin till the vessel got underway—and I *saw* no more of the sea till I stepped on shore at Liverpool. It was very stormy, and I was mortally sick the whole twenty four hours. Happily there was no cabin-passenger besides myself. So I had 'ample room and verge enough'[33] to make what demonstrations I pleased. My cousin Alick was waiting for me on the dock with a hackney coach which in a few minutes landed me with my trunks &c at my Uncles—one of his men took the barrel in a cart to the office from which it was to be forwarded by the canal. They were all very glad to see me at Maryland Street—and feeling entirely exhausted with my sea-sickness I stupidly let myself be persuaded not to proceed till the Wednesday. And by Wednesday I was in worse *fettle* for travelling than when I arrived for I had almost no sleep the whole time of my stay owing to a Lady in the same room snoring like ten steam engines.

32. Before the introduction of the uniform penny post in 1840 letters were paid for by the addressee, depending on weight and origin; but newspapers could be sent at standard lower rates before that date, so they could be used as Jane uses one here: to tell the addressee where you were or to send simple messages on the wrapper: see her comment on John Carlyle's travels, below. The very last communication in this volume, from John in the aftermath of Jane's death, shows that newspaper postage continued to be used in this way in the 1860s.

33. Thomas Gray, 'The Bard', II. 1. Thomas's brother Alick saw her off from Dumfries; Uncle John Welsh's son Alick met her at Liverpool, where the family resided at Maryland Street, in what is now known as the 'Knowledge Quarter'.

My seat was taken in a coach that came straight thro' so that I had no shifting of luggage to embarass me. My travelling companions were two irish Ladies—who neither *picked my pocket of my purse nor watch.* [A]nd twenty four hours after I started, I had the satisfaction of jumping out into Carlyles arms who with John was waiting for me at a certain Angel Inn [Islington, north London]—you may imagine the sight of their faces among so many hundreds of strange ones was a joyful sight. They were both looking well—John thinish but clear and healthy looking. They had a nice little dinner of chops and rice pudding in readiness— Edward Irving came up in the evening and all was well— But I was not to escape so easily— The next day and the next my head was so ill I had to be in bed— On Sunday I got out a little—and saw the Montagus— On Monday we were hunting after new lodgings—George Irving's being intolerably noisy and still infested with bugs which few houses here are without. We succeeded in realizing a much better up-putting for the same money—in the house of a Mrs Miles and Mrs Page— english people—where I now write— The barrel had arrived the end of the week and been unpacked—so that our flitting was no such light matter[,] and occupied all Tuesday— Yesterday I had a headach again and to day is the first that I can call my own.

I hope we shall be very comfortable here—the people are of a prepossessing appearance—and the house is the only clean one I have seen since I left Scotland[.][34] We have a Drawingroom about the size of our own at Craigenputtoch—more elegantly fitted up—with a small but comfortable bedroom opening from it with large folding doors. [I]t is in an airy and remarkably quiet street—and the people assure us they *very seldom see* a bug. I have no notion of London house keeping yet but am lying back till with 'weender and amazement.'[35] I have reviewed the ground—one fact I may mention as a sample potatoes are a penny a pound—so that we pay three half pence for barely as many as we need—the milk too is ridiculously dear and such stuff after Nooly's— Thank Heaven we have good butter without running to the shops— And Carlyle has fastened a lid with a padlock on the can— But what place unites all the advantages of both town and country?

I have seen few people yet—not even Jeffrey who is very ill— confined to bed— I was to have gone to him yesterday but could not for my head— Carlyle and I are thinking to walk over tonight when his Ladies are at the House of Lords—which will suit me best.

34. Their lodgings were at 4 Ampton Street, off Gray's Inn Road, a short distance south of the present King's Cross mainline station.

35. A frequently reiterated piece of coterie speech. 'Nooly' was the cow at Craigenputtoch.

John set off on Tuesday Morning to join his Countess[36] at Dover— [A] newspaper has since intimated his safe arrival so far— He was in good spirits for the enterprise and we hope it will be the beginning of much good for him—

Carlyle is reading today with a view to writing an article—to keep Mall—in shaft—[37] They are not going to print the book after all— Murray has lost heart lest it do not take with the public and so like a stupid ass as he is has sent back the manuscript[.] The *deevil* may care[;] it *shall* be printed in spite of Murray some time and in the meanwhile it is not losing any of its worth by lying—Jane W Carlyle

To Mary Welsh, London, 27 December 1831

My dear Aunt

When I returned from Enfield, where I had been for a week; I found the box containing the memorials of my heedlessness,[38] along with the welcome letter, awaiting me on the top of a cistern outside our staircase window; and our Landlady assures me with the utmost selfcomplacency that she had done all she could for it, in the way of keeping it perfectly cool! She looked rather blank when after duly commending her care, I informed her it was probably a cloak and shawl which she might now bring in out of the rain with all dispatch. Only to the intellect of a Cokney would a deal box have suggested the *exclusive* idea of game.

The cloak I got died a more sober colour, and lined and furred so as effectually to exclude the cold;—no slight conquest of art over Nature in these days— Some people here have the impudence or ignorance to congratulate me on the agreeable change of climate I have made: but truly if my contentment depended mainly on weather I should wish myself back to our own hilltop without delay. Regarded as a place merely, this 'Noble City' is simply the most detestable I ever lived in. One day a ferocious frost; the next a fog, so thick you might put it in your pocket; a dead sea of greencoloured filth under foot; and above an atmosphere like one—of my Uncle's sugar-boilers. But as the French

36. John had been employed by a certain Lady Clare, who spent much of her time in Italy: details are scant.
37. The mall is the head of a hammer or similar steel tool, through which the wooden handle is fastened.
38. Clothes she had left behind in Liverpool.

say *il faut se ranger* [you have to settle in]! and so day after day I rush forth with desperate resignation; and even find a sort of sublimity in the infinite horror thro' which I must make my way, or—die of indigestion. If I am inclined to reflect on the *place*, however (perhaps not without a touch of national prejudice) it is certainly my bounden duty to speak well of the people— Nowhere have I found more worth, more talent or more kindness; and I must doubly regret the ill health I have been suffering under, since it has so curtailed my enjoyment of all this— Nevertheless tho I dare seldom accept an invitation out, I have the pleasantest evenings at home. Scarce a night passes that some acquaintance new or old does not drop in at tea, and then follow such bouts at talking! not of one 'Book' (as my Uncle named Carlyle) but several *Books*— I have seen most of the Literary people here, and, as Edward Irving said after his first interview with Wordsworth, 'I think not of them so highly as I was wont.' These people who have made themselves *snug little reputations*, and on the strength of such hold up their heads as 'one and somewhat' are by no means the most disting[ui]shed th[at] I meet with either for talent or cultivation[.] Some of them indeed (Charles Lamb[39] for instance) would not be tolerated in any society out of England—

But I must abruptly conclude while I am yet but beginning—the young man who is to be the bearer of this and whom I have requested to deliver it in person being just ready to start[.] [. . .] My kindest love to my Uncle and all the weans [children]— My mother writes that he had *written* her a letter—which I was truly happy to hear. God bless you all Your affectionte

Jane W Carlyle

To Eliza Stodart, Craigenputtoch, 10 October 1832

My dearest Eliza

'It is surprising to see all how they *ack* [act, behave] i' the various places,' as Mrs Jeffrey's Maid, who now poor creature, acts no longer on this planet, used to preface her travel's history on the dicky [outside seat] of her Master's chaise—an Ominous beginning, which like our

39. Lamb (1775–1834), essayist and *littérateur*, co-author with his sister Mary of the *Tales from Shakespeare*, best known for his *Essays of Elia* (1823). Jane and Thomas had met him with John Badams in Enfield, east London, when he was drunk on gin and water.

Mother's 'O I must tell you about Aberdeen!' had always the effect of instantaneously scattering her fellowservants to the four winds as if a bombshell had been thrown into the midst of them. It is really surprising how they ack! not knowing but the next hour may be their last—certain that a *last* must come *soon*—yet leaving the most palpable duties undone as if there were all eternity to do them in. You may guess I am incited to this highly novel and striking reflection, by the consideration that my last letter to you has been left unanswered for one year and half—that from anything I hear you are not even *remotely* purposing to answer it—have not a single compunctious visiting[40] about the matter. Yet how many years and half think you, even at the longest allowance shall we remain sojourners together on the same earth? and how will the surviver like to remember periods of silence like this when the possibility of friendly intercourse then for the first time, like all things *past*, not only rightly estimated, but overestimated, will exist no more for ever? Nor in censuring you do I pretend alltogether to clear myself—I should have written again and again[.] Not only Scripture[41] which bids you turn the other cheek when one is smitten—but my own experience of how naturally one may fall into a fault from which it is extremely difficult to get out, as well as kindness which is continually reminding me that you are my earliest friend[;] all counselled this—but pride and indolence carried the day. In prolonged bad health and worse spirits I judged there could be small call upon [me] to be sending letters out as it were, into infinite space—no sound of them ever more heard—still vainer seemed it to apply for simpathy to one who was apparently nowise concerning herself whether I remained behind in a nice flower-potted London churchyard, or returned in a state of total wreck to my own country. A few days before I left London a certain Dr Allan said to Carlyle in a complimentary tone as I left the room—'Mrs Carlyle has the remains of a fine woman!' [T]hink of that now! at thirty to pass for a remains! judge if I must not have suffered somewhat! and if loss of health and loss of looks were not a decent sort of excuse at least, for not enacting the amiable part of turning the second cheek, or in other words writing the second letter— The short and the long of the matter is we are both in fault—let us mutually forgive—Kiss and be friends and draw this practical inference that indolence as the copy line says is truly the root of all evil—[42]

The special object of my breaking silence this day is to give you a commission which I think will gratify you—not, of the petty needle

40. Shakespeare, *Macbeth*, I. v. 45.
41. Matthew 5: 39.
42. 1 Timothy 6: 10.

and staylace sort—but what think you? to look about in your walks between this and the beginning of winter for a little furnished house to contain my husband self and a maid for as many months as we see good to exchange our country life for your town one— The grim prospect of another winter in this solitude is too frightful for my husband, who finds, that it is absolutely essential for carrying on not only his craft, but his existence to hear from time to time a little human speech[;] accordingly we are to neighbour you this wint[er] and let us see to make better of it than on [the] former occasion— As to the manner of hou[se] I may begin by restricting your quest by three limitations—first it must be free of bugs, secondly of *extraordinary* noises—and lastly of a high rent. [S]uch a place as that my Mother tenanted of Miss Sheriff would answer well enough— [P]erhaps Miss Dora if it were modestly suggested to her might make another migration into the country—she never seemed to stay at home on any account but because she had a house on [her] hands. Henry Inglis[43] represented Comely Bank as being inhabited now by strange haggard ruffian-looking people whose calling was questionable— [I]n that case it were no longer pleasant but otherwise I should still prefer it to any part of the new town— [A] floor in the heart of the town were my last recource—any *suburban* situation especially if self contained were preferable—the nearer yourself the better [. . .]. With respect to house room—there would be required at least a sitting room and bedroom with some sort of adjunct that might be slept in 'at a time'—a kitchen and six feet for the Maid[;] a small patch of outdoors accomodation were extremely desirable where my husband might smoke— It was most piteous to see him reduced to perform that process in London on the top of a cistern! looking as he stood perched aloft 'on that bad eminence'[44] with the long pipe in his mouth, for all the world like the emblem over a Tobacconist's door. Now look round you and see what is to be had and on what terms—and report progress—and as the time draws on and my knowledge increases—I will give you more definite instructions.

Does your Uncle ever make the *smallest* mention of me? ever inquire if the mischievous creature who broke his folder[45] is still working devilry on this planet[?] Alas no! She is sober enough now—a long succession of bad days and sleepless nights have efectually tamed her— O Bess, for

43. Edinburgh lawyer, businessman and sometime poet (1806–1886); still in touch with the Carlyles in London in the mid-1850s.

44. Milton, *Paradise Lost*, ii. 6.

45. It seems Mr Bradfute, in his profession of publisher and bookseller, always used a folding paper knife, which perhaps young Jane had managed to damage.

one good laugh with you, for the sake of old times! I do not remember the time when I laughed. C[rying is] now the order of the day.

Colera is raging in Dumfries—and the whole town and County in a state of distraction—as if death were now presented to them for [the] first time because it is presented in a new shape!— As if God had not appointed to all Men once to die![46]

A kiss to your Uncle—kind regards to Sam— What is Mr Simpson doing? Your Cousins? every body? For god sake write to me soon— My Mother is bilious and terrified— My Grandfather as usual[.] I am going over tomorrow to rouse her.

God bless you
I am always your affectionate friend /
Jane W Carlyle

To Eliza Stodart, Craigenputtoch, 24 May 1833

My dear Eliza

You have been thinking doubtless (for the heart of woman is prone to evil thoughts) that I did not display alacrity enough in writing to you. But judge not without knowledge: first hear the dolorous tale I have to tell; and you will find that my friendship has in this case been without reproach.

You have first to learn that we were in Edinr *two days* after you and all our acquaintance supposed us gone! actually *secreted* in Mrs Blackey's house, with feelings which I should suppose akin to a Gohsts—for, O tell it not in Gath![47] Eliza! we had—missed the coach! the *old* horror had been transacted anew! And well might we keep ourselves secret! well might we hide our diminished heads,[48] and shun the cheerful face of a friend! You know *my* way of being always too early—perhaps you do *not* know, that my Husband always puts off till the last moment— [T]his, almost the only, discrepancy in our habits has produced many little argumentations betwixt us which on that illfated morning I for the *first time* determined to evade. Accordingly

46. Cholera came to Dumfries from September to November 1832; around 1,100 people were infected in the area, half of whom died of the disease.
47. 2 Samuel 1: 20.
48. A much-favoured quote, initially from *Paradise Lost*, iv. 34–5, then in Alexander Pope, 'Epistle to Bathurst', 281–2.

tho' up in good time (indeed I did not close my eyes the whole night) dressed and breakfasted in good time, we somehow trifled away *five minutes* over and above what there was to work on, and on reaching the starting place, bag and baggage, saw our '*Convenience*' (as Mrs Rennie[49] used modestly to call her carriage) vanishing at the far end of Princes Street! Let us drop a veil over the disgraceful home-march! Enough to say that I was forthwith deposited in bed with the dreadfulest headach, and remained there, most of the time we had to wait; glad my existence was unknown, that so I might be left in quiet. It was now too apparent to me that I had got Influenza; I only hoped that I might brave it out, and keep up till I was landed at *home*. But I could get no further than Templand, after suffering by the way such misery as I shall not soon forget. There I had to keep my bed for a week— My Mother too was laid up with it for three days, so I had the additional vexation of being looked on as a pestilence. On Monday I took the road again—reached the goal of all my wishes, for the time being—again had a bad turn that confined me in bed— And only yesterday felt myself like living and today eat half of a salt herring to breakfast on the strength of which I write— So confess that I have lost no time—but on the contrary am displaying a most satisfactory ardour in the matter.

We found the house—not merely standing but in the best order— The Woman who had charge of it thro' the winter had kept the damp out—and Nancy had sorted it to a wonder without my superintendence. My Cow is at the point of calving— My little horse is in high mettle—my hens are fat and laying—and all have returned from their diverse winter-quarters—making together with ourselves a '*reunion*' of the most Idyllic discription! So far we have cause to be thankful. But as there is always some confounded drag on the contentment that is of this world—so a spectacle presented itself on our return enough to have made a passionate person *explode*[,] but me who am an example of patience and submission it only moved to tears. One of the woods (just think of it) the one on your left as you approach the house was burnt to cinders! a melancholy mass of blackened stumps, while all around was shining in new verdure. The Tenant had been burning heather—the trees had caught fire—and he simply retired into his house and left it to burn! O Eliza—I could cry yet to think of this—to think of my Father taking such a world of pains to plant these woods—to think they have had rain and sunshine vouchsafed them

49. Mother of George Rennie, an erstwhile admirer of Jane's, who would return in later life.

for more than twenty years, to be finally consumed in one night thro' the carelessness of a lout like Macadam.[50] But he pays his rent, and that is everything—the appearance of Craigenputtoch is of consequence only to *us*. Well be it so! we shall not stay to see it reduced to its original desolation. I wish its improvement had not been my Fathers work, and then I should not care tho it were let on a nineteen years lease to the Devil himself.

One thing however I shall insist on—namely that I should hereafter have the melancholy privelege of being *informed* when my property is burnt or otherwise destroyed—instead of having the fact concealed from me till it could be concealed no longer—even my own servant commanded by my Mother not to tell me of it— You see I am angry—more so perhaps than becomes a pretender to some Philosophy— But I am giving vent to my feelings on the occasion *here* for the first time—as a way of getting in some measure rid of them— To turn to a more agreeable topic— Will you give our affectionate regards to your Uncle; of whose kindness to us during our stay in town—from the first day to the last (a sort of kindness so much after our own hearts—) my Husband and I have many times gratefully commemorated— Do you too my dear Eliza accept our kind remembrance of your kindness— Write to me soon—and love me always— Your affectionate

Jane W Carlyle [. . .]

❧

To Henry Inglis, Craigenputtoch, 23 November 1833

My dear Sir

I beseech you, do not estimate my gratitude for your letter, by the alacrity I have displayed in answering it. It was delightful to laugh with you again at anything, even a fellow creature's indigestions; and still more delightful to find I was remembered by you, while modestly supposing myself forgotten of the whole earth: I thanked you, then, from the very bottom of my heart; and would have told you so on the instant but for an inveterate habit of procrastination I have somehow acquired. Whatever is to be done, tho' it were but to stich a button on my Husband's shirt; I must put off till 'a more convenient season': and it is inconceivable what woes are thus originated,—just in that single matter

50. The neighbour mentioned on 6–9 August and 1–3 September 1831, above.

of shirt-buttons, to go no further. 'Females' that are fulfilling the end of their being, videlicet, 'bringing up children,' should be attentive to whip at the very first symptom of this tendency.

Why did you not come in Autumn, and make amends to us for the loss of Hunt? '*Craigen-poo-toch*' looked so well this year, and I felt so well, and could have enjoyed your company after a quite other fashion than thro' the last winter; *when 'my memory was a long train of indigestions,—my prospects more of the same*.'[51] John Mill had to go to France; so we were disappointed of him also: and were thankful to Providence for the windfall of a stray American, 'come out for to see whatsoever things were wise and of good report,[']—from one end of Europe to the other.[52] With such accuracy of investigation did he prosecute this object, that he arrived, by paths unknown, at the door of Craigenpootoch, which was, of course, opened to him with all the pleasure in life. To find the Christian charities inside, and even the Graces[53] seemed to occasion him the most agreeable surprise. Carlyle had been represented to his transatlantic imagination, quite *Teufelsdreckish*,—a man severe—living in complete isolation, and partial barbarism: the Individual before his bodily eyes was shaven and shorn, overflowing with the milk of human kindness,[54] *und mit Weib im Hause* [and with a wife in the home]; a blessing which the amiable American estimated highly—himself having *lost it* after an *exceedingly brief* trial.[55] He went 'on-on'—and we saw him no more. Our next inmate was a broken-down Barrister who some years ago enjoyed the threefold reputation of a Scholar, Genius, and Gig Man;[56] but who is now literally lying among the pots,—having made his last stand against the world, on a not too solid basis of whisky and water— He with a pretty pettish wife of the fine Lady sort, but also taking into whisky exhibited to us for one mortal week a specimen of that sort of company which is worse than none; which at Craigenputtoch of all places one is tempted to deny the possibility of. But they also passed on, and again all was silent and

51. In all likelihood quoting something Thomas has said.
52. The stray American is Ralph Waldo Emerson; the quote is from Philippians 4: 8. 'John Mill' is the liberal philosopher John Stuart Mill.
53. In Christianity, faith, hope and love; in Greek myth the *Charites*, Aglaea ('shining'), Euphrosyne ('joy') and Thalia ('blooming').
54. Shakespeare, *Macbeth* I. v. 17.
55. Emerson's wife, Ellen Louisa Tucker, had died of tuberculosis in 1831, aged twenty; the couple had married only in 1829.
56. A vital early coinage of Thomas's, from 1830 or so, to mean a person who measured their success purely in terms of material achievements like the ownership of a gig (small carriage): an 'aspirational' Philistine.

continues silent to this hour.[57] Yet here in the midst of this almost fearful silence we are fixed for the winter—resolute to assert the superiority of mind over matter, by neither going out of our wits nor attempting our lives thro' the dismalities of the ensuing season. Would *you* but come at Christmas it were an act of Mercy never to be forgotten! But alas! you are 'an *ornament to Society in every direction*' and society will not part with you, and you will not part with society to console suffering virtue in its Patmos—[58] Yet it is better to be loved than admired—better to have one *friend* than one thousand *acquaintances*—I doubt if there be one individual alive, out of your own family, that loves [you] more truly than Carlyle does; or even than I do, which however is less to the purpose—yet who of your whole acquaintance sees less of you than we? This is not as it should be— I put it to your conscience, whether the '*infinitismal system*' be a whit more rational in the practice of Friendship, than in the practice of Medicine? One meeting in the course of half a dozen years seems to me as great an absurdity as an ounce of salt put into the Pacific Ocean—and the Friend must [su]ffer equally with the Patient under such a treatment. Will you come then? O do! I want to ask you about the amiable '*In-deeed*',—about that fearful *Epergne* [table centrepiece]; and fifty things that you only understand the true essence of, and can satisfactorily describe to me.[59] Come! and I will show you a caricature that you will never forget—and more—will *give* you a beauty of a teapot! I know it would do you good to revive your impressions of the contrast between *this* life and *your* life—to try how locusts and wild honey[60] taste after the luxuries of civilized cookery[.] But if it caused '*an indigestion*'? no fear! the only things a truly catholic '*disguster*' (such as yours is) '*likes as ill as a piece iron*' (borrowed from an Annandale lady who thus expressed her decided disapprobation of yew-cheese) are *stupidity falsity*, and *gigmanity*. From these you cannot pray the good Lord to deliver you more heartily than we do. But I was to leave space

57. In a letter to John Carlyle of 1 October Thomas comments mordantly on the sad case of William Gray and his wife: 'No visit that we ever had here was so intolerable to both of us: at last, after five mortal days they went out, without being thrown out. I think they will not trouble us again. For poor Gray, a man not without force, quickness, light-gleams in all kinds [. . .] I feel much pity: but how can you help a man that will not help himself; that in all straits finds a present aid in the whisky-bottle? One night I lectured him earnestly; he was in tears albeit unused to that mood; but, next day, must again demand "a little whisky to mix with it, if you'll allow me."'
58. The Aegean island on which the exiled St John the Divine was granted the visions that formed the biblical book of Revelation.
59. The last few sentences are clearly in response to a letter from Inglis.
60. Matthew 3: 4: the sustenance of St John the Baptist, Christ's precursor, 'crying in the wilderness'.

for some story about books—and I am almost at the end of my sheet— Will you give my kindest regards to your sweet gentle wife—and a kiss for me to that poor babe who is likely to be mismanaged as his Mother, I take it, has not studied either Anatmony or Phrenology. [. . .]

If my letter is worth nothing to you; at least it shall cost you nothing— I enclose it to the Advocate.[61]

[no signature]

To Eliza Miles, Craigenputtoch, late January? 1834[62]

As my parting counsel (which being a fellow-sufferer I may be permitted to offer) beware of *Doctors*! swallow anything (poison excepted) rather than a *prescription*— 'They are all Physicians of no value'—their prescriptions are slow death— Put your trust in diet, exercise, a[nd the Hand] of Providence— A new order of M[edicine may] arise; cant and quackery and pu[blic fraud?] be swept overboard with the his[tory of medicine?] before Doctors regain their old usef[ulness,] their old honour among mankind— Let you and I and all saneminded Dispep[tics] minister to ourselves—

And now God bless you— Remember me to all the household— to Mrs Page in particular who was oftenest in collision with me, and always kindly— I assure you we thought ourselves very fortunate in having fallen among such worthy and friendly people—and we often talk of you as *friends* now that our other relation no longer exists— Again God bless you my dear Eliza— Think of me ever as your affectionate friend and wellwisher

Jane W Carlyle [. . .]

61. Again, Jane is getting around the postage charge by sending her letter via Francis Jeffrey, who was appointed Lord Advocate under the Crown in Scotland—and who accordingly did not have to pay for his mail.
62. Eliza Miles was the daughter of the house where Jane and Thomas lodged at Ampton Street, much taken with Jane on brief acquaintance; Jane Page co-managed the establishment.

Figure 3: Robert Scott Tait, '5 Cheyne Row' (1857), Thomas Carlyle Papers, Rare Book & Manuscript Library, Columbia University in the City of New York

2

Arrival in Chelsea: 1834–1837

For Jane, Rosemary Ashton suggests, 'Craigenputtoch was a battle lost, whereas for Carlyle, it was, eventually, a battle won.'[1] *Thomas had written his version of Wordsworth's Prelude, Sartor Resartus, setting the growth of his mind in order. He had completed his understanding of both German Romanticism on the one hand and the Enlightenment on the other. Out of those twin understandings he hoped to steer a course between the Scylla of rationalist atheism and the Charybdis of religious revival—between the utilitarian Mill-ites and the evangelist or High Church Millenarians, as he put it. But Jane had lost a dream: that of being the intellectual helpmeet and associate in that process. Her 1824 vision of Thomas had been of 'one warmhearted, highminded* dearest *Friend, whose sublime Genius would shed an ennobling influence on all around him; whose graceful and splendid qualities would inspire a love that should be the heart and soul of my life!' (CL 3: 176).*[2] *Her Craigenputtoch experience showed her a man who was intellectually and emotionally an utter loner, the reverse of the refulgent benignity of which she had dreamed. It was a painful lesson, indeed.*

But the exile played into Thomas's hands in another sense, too—in coming to which it is worth remembering that he was born in the same year as John Keats, but whereas the latter has gone down in history as the eternally flickering Romantic ephebe, the former has been consolidated as the quintessentially whiskery and earthbound Victorian, simply by virtue of living longer. In the couple's London foray of 1831–1832, Thomas began to encounter (if not always at first hand) the rump of the English Romantic revolution: William Godwin, Charles Lamb, Leigh Hunt, William Hazlitt, Thomas De Quincey and—worst of all in terms of disappointment—Coleridge, the 'Sage of Highgate', wandering, as Thomas put it, 'like a man sailing among many currents, whithersoever his lazy mind directs him'.

1. Rosemary Ashton, *Thomas and Jane Carlyle: Portrait of a Marriage* (London, 2002), 105.
2. Thomas idealised from the other direction in June 1826, almost on the eve of the wedding: 'O my little *Weibchen*! The next Book I write, *another* shall help me to correct and arrange! And my fairest recompense will be the glad look of two kind black eyes, thro' which a soul is looking that belongs to my soul for ever and ever! Let us not despond in the life of honourable toil which lies before us' (*CL* 4: 103).

(He would complete the circle of disaffection by meeting Wordsworth in 1835, a year after Coleridge's death, and Jane would share his estimation of literary London in that period.) The great second-generation Romantic poets were dead, and something else was waiting to be born; the stage was shifting, but no actors were available to fill it. Indeed, when Thomas took Sartor to town he discovered that publishers weren't interested in imaginative speech at all, and that the uncertain progress of the Great Reform Bill through Parliament—like 'Brexit' and 'Covid' in that respect—had drained every iota of interest from the literary sphere. A disappointment where that particular book was concerned, this would be a revelation for its author's career. (After Sartor, his next important work would be called, simply, 'Signs of the Times'.)[3] *When we look at the brilliant circle the Carlyles would establish about themselves in Chelsea, most of it foregathers from this time on, and quite quickly: literary people, certainly (Emerson, Dickens, Thackeray, Macready, John Sterling, John Forster and Geraldine Jewsbury), but also intellectuals (John Stuart Mill, Harriet Martineau and the Wedgwood-Darwin circle), journalists (Edward Sterling), English politicians (Richard Monckton Milnes) and exiled Continental nationalists and/or revolutionaries (Cavaignac and Mazzini). This new era and new amalgam, carried onward and upward by the 'Condition-of-England' arguments of the 1840s, was the perfect context not only for Thomas's career, navigating those quintessentially Victorian currents between rationalism and belief, but for his and Jane's social success and pleasure, too. The cultural tradition being what it was, it was not possible for a Victorian woman to be a salonnière in the French style (though perhaps Lady Harriet Ashburton had an eye on the role). Jane's was far too informal and personal a set of connections for that to be the right word. But her modest house in Chelsea—hers in every sense, knowing every inch of shelving and every carpet nail in it as she did—would be neither a Cairngorm fantasy nor a Bass Rock hermitage but a substantial and authentic institution, standing as she left it to this day.*

Thus No. 5 Cheyne Row is nothing less than the third pillar in our triad. Thomas found it on 19 May 1834 but wisely awaited his wife's arrival, inspection and approval. He wrote on 21 May, having visited another possibility in Brompton, too, for comparison—and already his extraordinary powers of descriptive retention, as like to Dickens as gold is like to gold, are in evidence:

> The street is flag-pathed, sunk-storied, iron-railed, all old-fashioned and tightly done up; looks out on a rank of sturdy

3. Jane and Thomas alike normally took a baleful view of poetry in this post-Romantic world. In August 1844 Elizabeth Barrett Browning sent Thomas her *Poems*, and he wrote kindly in response, but suggested she 'use "speech" rather than "song" in these days of crisis' (Philip Kelley et al. (eds.), *The Brownings' Correspondence* (Winfield, KS, 1984–), ix. 122).

old *pollarded* (that is *beheaded*) Lime-trees, standing there like giants in *tawtie* [shaggy] wigs (for the new boughs are still young) beyond this a high brick-wall, on the inside of which, from our upper stories, appear a garden surrounded with rather dim houses and questionable miscellanea, among other things, clothes drying. Backwards, a Garden (the size of our back one at Comely Bank) with trees &c, in bad culture; beyond this green hayfields and tree-avenues (once a Bishop's pleasure-grounds) an unpicturesque, yet rather cheerful outlook. The House itself is eminent, antique; wainscotted to the very ceiling, and has been all new-painted and repaired; broadish stair, with massive balustrade (in the old style) corniced and as thick as one's thigh; floors firm as a rock, wood of them here and there worm-eaten, yet capable of cleanness, and still with thrice the strength of a modern floor. And then as to room, Goody! [. . .] Three stories besides the sunk story [basement]; in every one of them *three* apartments in depth (something like 40 feet in all; for it was 13 of my steps!): Thus there is a front dining room (marble chimney-piece &c); then a back dining-room (or breakfast-room) a little narrower (by reason of the kitchen stair); then out from this, and narrower still (to allow a back-window, you consider), a china-room, or pantry, or I know not what, all shelved, and fit to hold crockery for the whole street. Such is the ground-area, which of course continues to the top, and furnishes every Bedroom with a dressing room, or even with a *second* bedroom. [. . .] Neither this nor the Brompton house have a kitchen-*range* [. . .], but only a grate with moveable niggards [firebricks or plates] &c. In Chelsea is, or lies ready for being, a kitchen-jack [mechanical spit]; from the boiler-house the boiler ('*Coppa*') is taken out, but 'would be replaced.' No back-door (communicating with the street); bells in disorder but would be rectified; new locks, some of which threatened to act *à la Puttoch*, but seemed very oilless. On the whole a most massive, roomy, sufficient old house; with places, for example, to hang say three dozen hats or cloaks on; and as many crevices, and queer old presses, and shelved closets (all tight and new painted in their way) as would gratify the most covetous Goody. Rent £35! (*CL* 7: 172–3)

The stage was set, Comely Bank be damned. By 1837 Jane would acknowledge 'almost a cat-like attachment to my own home' (CL 9: 168), and earlier yet, three months after getting the keys, she wrote proudly to Mrs Carlyle: 'I must tell you what Car will not tell of himself—that he is rapidly mending of his Craigenputtoch gloom and acerbity— He is really at times a tolerably social character and seems to be regarded with a feeling of mingled terror and love in all companies' (CL 7: 288). The gloom and acerbity would return in spades, but Jane had a victory now.[4]

❧

To Eliza Stodart, Chelsea, circa August 1834

Our well-beloved Friend and Cousin

Mrs Montagu who has made '*the fine arts*' her peculiar study has a pretty and original way of knitting up a ravelled correspondence—[5] Instead of outraging the already outraged with a lengthened apology, she commences with a lively attack[:] 'is astonished that you have not written to inquire the reason of her silence'—'thinks it strange that you should adopt with her the formal letter for letter system'[—]'Is hurt,' 'is angry' is every thing but what you expected namely ashamed of herself—and you find yourself suddenly much to your surprise transformed into the offending party and thankful for the kind forgiveness with which she ends— This beats out and out our old simple fashion of making confessions of indolence &c &c or telling lies about excessive occupation and so forth. But having let you into the secret I need not play it off upon you this time, only I let you see what I might do if I liked—and I give you instead of a useless apology a useful hint which you may find your account in against enraged correspondents—

Well! is it not very strange that I am here? sitting in my own hired house by the side of the Thames as if nothing had happened; with fragments of Haddington, of Comely Bank, of Craigenputtoch interweaved

4. The story of the Carlyles and No. 5 is told from the inside (as the author was resident in the house at the time of writing) by Thea Holme, in *The Carlyles at Home* (London, 1965; reprinted by Persephone in 2002). Holme includes an invaluable appendix, 'The Servants at Cheyne Row during Mrs Carlyle's Lifetime', but also reminds us how difficult servant-life was in a house dating from Queen Anne's time: 'To cook a meal by the light of the fire and one candle [. . .]; to wash up without being able to see which was a stain and which the pattern on the plate; to pack away food in deep-set cupboards where it was difficult to make out what stood at the back of the shelf; to keep every corner swept clean of the stone-flagged floor, where stray crumbs attracted armies of black-beetles and mice housed in the wainscot; all this must have presented problems to the conscientious servant. To clean and be clean, in perpetual twilight, by means of pump-water and kettles, required a high degree of patience, hardihood and industry' (10). Her chapter 10, on the garden, is particularly noteworthy.
5. Shakespeare, *Macbeth*, II. ii. 36.

with *cokneycalities*[6] into a very habitable whole? Is it not strange that I should have an everlasting sound in my ears, of men, women, children, omnibuses, carriages glass coaches, streetcoaches, waggons, carts, dog-carts, steeple bells, doorbells, Gentlemen-raps, twopenny-post-raps, footmen-showers-of raps, of the whole devil to pay, as if plague pestilence, famine, battle, murder sudden death[7] and wee Eppie Daidle were broken loose to make me diversion.— And where is the stillness, the eternal sameness, of the last six years—? Echo[8] answers[,] at Craigenputtoch! There let them 'dwell with Melancholy' and old Nanny Macqueen[,] for this stirring life is more to my mind, and has besides a beneficial effect on my bowels. Seriously I have almost entirely discontinued drugs, and look twenty percent better, every one says, and 'what every one says must be true.' This being the case, You may infer that I am tolerably content in my new position; indeed I am more and more persuaded that there is no complete misery in the world that does not emanate from the bowels.

We have got an excellent lodgement; of most antique physiognomy, quite to our humour; all wainscoated carved and queer-looking; roomy substantial, commodious, with closets to satisfy any Bluebeard, a chinacloset in particular that would hold our whole worldly substance converted into china! Two weeks ago there was a row of ancient trees in front, but some crazy-headed Cokneys have uprooted them— [B]ehind we have a garden (so called in the language of flattery) in the [wo]rst order, but boasting of two vines which produced two bunches of grapes, in the season, which 'might be eaten'; and a walnut-tree from which I have gathered almost sixpence worth of walnuts. 'This large and comfortable tenement' we have, *without bugs*, for some two or three pounds more rent than we paid for the pepper box at Comelybank. This comes of our noble contempt for fashion—Chelsea being highly unfashionable.[9] The only practical disadvantage in this circumstance

6. 'Cockneycalities': qualities associated with the speakers of cockney English from London's East End, and by extension to the capital as a whole. Jane frequently drops the second 'c' in the word, the origins of which are obscure.
7. See 'The Litany' in the English *Book of Common Prayer*; Eppie Daidle wags school 'as bairns will do', according to his grandmother, to see an execution in Walter Scott's *Heart of Midlothian* (1818), 'as was natural for a wean'.
8. From the Narcissus tale in Ovid's *Metamorphoses*: the lover of the self-obsessed hero, who can only repeat the last words she hears. 'Dwell with Melancholy': Milton, 'Il Penseroso', 175–6.
9. Hard to believe in this day and age, when Chelsea is one of London's most affluent suburbs, but true at the time, when London was far smaller and even central areas like Camden Town were beyond the pale. If Chelsea had a reputation it was as a raffish and bohemian district, home to artists and the like.

is that we are far from most of our acquaintance; a disadvantage which I endeavour to obviate by learning to walk; my success is already considerable[:] I have several times walked ten miles without being laid up. Besides we are not wholly isolated. Leigh Hunt lives a few doors off. The Celebrated Mrs Somerville is at Chelsea Hospital within five minutes walk, and Mrs Austin is coming to introduce me to her tomorrow—and within a mile I have a *circle* of acquaintances—[10] [O]ne of these who lives in prodigious *shine* with wife and family, you may happen to recollect something about— A grave handsome man who has been here repeatedly, and treats me with infinite respect, and takes immensely to my Husband—a sort of person with whom one talks about 'the condit[i]on of art' in this cou[n]try—and such like topics of general interest and studies to support the reputation of a rather intellectual and excessively reasonable woman— Can you divine who I mean? impossible—George Rennie! How has it happened? quite simply. I am one of the most amiable women living; tho like your Uncle 'My virtues are unknown'— I am incaplable of cherishing resentment even against a faithless lover[.] I heard he was there, I wondered what he was like; I sent him my address. He came instantaneously with his Sister Margaret—'Bess did I feel awkward?[']' to be sure I did, and looked awkward for I was within an ace of fainting and he looked like one of his own marbles— But neither of us I believe entertained a particle of tenderness for the other nevertheless—it was mere queaziness from the intense sensation of the flight of time which such a meeting occasioned one—fifteen years! only think! He is much improved by age, in appearance, manner, and also I think in character—but he lives in the wretchedest atmosphere of '*gigmanity*'—his wife is a perfect fool—the whole kin of them are fools— And poor George must either go in with their folly to a certain extent, or break his heart, or blow up his whole household sky-high— Moreover he is still self-willed and vain enough to show me as often as I see him that I made an escape— I go often to Margaret's, who lives in style also, but seems to feel rather out of her element here. Lady Kinloch[11] is close by the Rennies— [S]he was amazed to see me, and is very kind— I am glad she is not '*dead*'

For the rest our society with a few additions and [subtractions is] mu[ch] the same that we had when here formerly—only I find it much pleasanter now being in better ease for enjoying it— John Mill, Leigh Hunt and Mrs Austin remain my favourites. I know some Elliots

10. Mrs Austin was mentioned by Jane in her letter of 1–3 September 1831, above. Mary Somerville (1780–1872) was a scientist and mathematician, after whom an Oxford college for women students came to be named in 1879.

11. Lady Isabella Kinloch (1773–1861), widow of the baronet of Gilmerton, near Haddington.

acquaintances of David Aitken[12] who are very agreeable people.— By the by did Mr Aitken tell you what a franticly affectionate reception I gave him at Craigenputtoch— [H]e looked rather fearful for the consequences to his cloth— I shall never learn to give up these outbreakings of the old woman in me from time to time— [T]he other morning when Mr Terrot came in (who is to carry this) I sprang into his arms and I believe almost stifled him with the ardour of my embrace— He returned it however with more sympathy than was to have been anticipated.[13] I have wondered at my audacity ever since[,] for the thought of such an attempt in a cool moment would have made me quake[.] For God sake write and tell me what everybody in Edinr is doing—especially my own relations whom methinks I ought to know something about— I so seldom hear out [of] Scotland— My Mother is most scrupelous about putting me to the expence of postage— I shall be down perhaps next year—and then it will be hard if I do not see you— But will you never come here? I declare to Heaven there is nobody except my Mother I should welcome with such delight— After all you are the only right female friend I ever had in the world—the only one I can to all lengths and without the least misgiving talk nonsense to—and that I consider a pretty good test of friendship— Here I must be always so *sensible* it is really quite frightful— Carlyle wrote to your Uncle and sent a book—did he get either letter or parcel? He now sends his constant regards— God bless you my dear Eliza— I am always in spite of neglect in the article of writing

your truly attached Friend—

Jane W Carlyle—

You will remark again 'Jane once wrote a beautiful hand'— Well it cannot be helped—the pen is bad—and I am in haste [. . .]

To John Sterling, Chelsea, 4 June 1835

My dear Sir

You did kindly to send the little separate note: the least bit 'all to myself,' (as the children say) was sure to give me a livelier pleasure,

12. Rev. David Aitken (1796–1875), known to Thomas in early 1827, when he wrote the reverend a reference in support of his application for the chair of church history at the University of Edinburgh. Aitken later used it in 1829 to become the minister at Minto, Roxburghshire, Scotland, and in 1836 he would marry the recipient of this letter, Eliza Stodart.
13. Rev. Charles Hughes Terrot (1790–1872) would in due course become Bishop of Edinburgh.

than any number of sheets in which I had but a secondary interest. For in spite of the honestest efforts to annihilate my *I-ity*, or merge it in what the world doubtless considers my better half; I still find myself a self-subsisting and alas! selfseeking *Me*. Little Felix, in the Wanderjahre,[14] when, in the midst of an animated scene between Whilelm and Theresa, he pulls Theresa's gown, and calls out, '*Mama Theresa I too am here*!' only speaks out with the charming trustfulness of a child, what I am perpetually feeling, tho too sophisticated to pull peoples skirts, or exclaim in so many words; Mr Sterling '*I* too am here.'

But I must tell you, I find a grave fault in that note about the last fault I should have dreamt of finding in any utterance of yours: it is not believing but faithless! In the first place the parenthesis '(if ever)' seems to me a wilful questioning of the goodness of Providence. Then you say; if in some weeks I can bring myself to think of you with patience perhaps &c—now both the 'if' and '*perhaps*' displease me. Only the most inveterate Sceptic could, with your fineness of observation, have known me for two weeks, without certifying himself that my patience is infinite, inexhaustible! that in fact I, as well as yourself combine 'the wisdom of Solomon with the patience of Job.'[15]

Far from being offended by your desertation on the Sartor I think it the best that has been said or sung of him. [E]ven where your criticism does not quite fall in with my humble views, I still love the spirit of the critic. For instance, I am loth to believe that I have married a Pagan,—but I approve entirely of the warmth with which you warn your Friend against the delusion of burning pastils before a statue of Jupiter and such like extravagancies. I suppose it is excessively heterodox and in a catholic country I should be burnt for it, but to you I may safely confess that I care almost nothing about *what* a man believes, in comparison with *how* he believes.[16] If his belief be correct, it is so much the better for himself; but its intensity, its efficacy is the ground on which I love and trust him. Thus you see I am capable of appreciating your fervour

14. The little scene plays out in Thomas's translation of Goethe's *Wilhelm Meister's Apprenticeship* (1824), ii. 123.
15. 1 Kings 10: 4 and James 5: 11.
16. A view of belief that has been itself described as quintessentially Romantic: see, for example, the first chapter of Isaiah Berlin's *The Roots of Romanticism* (2013). It was a principle that the Carlyles followed, by and large, not only in terms of the people whom they welcomed under their roof, but in Thomas's writings, too: his book on hero-worship gives as much credit to the prophet Muhammad as the presbyterian John Knox. The 'Thirty-nine Articles' (1571) constitute the founding doctrines of the Church of England, found in the *Book of Common Prayer*; Sterling had been ordained a deacon of the church in 1834.

in behalf of the thirtynine articles, without being afflicted because my Husband is accused of contumacy against them.

But what do you mean by speaking of 'a few weeks'! When you went, you said, with an *appearance* at least of good faith, that you would be back in London—in three weeks: And one week and half of another is already gone.

I hope you will keep your time for several reasons; chiefly for this one, that our continuance in London has of late days become more uncertain, the America speculation having suddenly received a more practical form; and if we depart for Scotland without seeing you any more, and afterwards our good or evil star actually shoots over the Atlantic; surely to some of us at least it will [be] a matter of regret rather than of self congratulation that our acquaintance should have begun.

I have seen your Mother twice, she is very good to me. I have moreover been reviving one of my young-lady-accomplishments for her sake, painting flowers on a portfolio, to keep those verses in which she was so troubled about losing

Your Father has been here since I began writing, to ask us to dinner on Saturday— We played a *drawn* game at chess, and Carlyle and he debated more loudly than logically on the subject of Napoleon's morality. He is just gone to inquire about the house in Cheyne Walk, in which good work I was meaning to have forestalled him and communicated the result in my letter.[17] If a Fairy would gran[t] me three wishes this evening; my first would be that we might remain where we are, my second that you might be settled in Cheyne Walk, and the third like a thrifty Scotch woman I would beg leave to lay by in reserve for future need.

And now I must go and array myself with all possible splendour for a rout [party] at Mrs Bullers, where O'Conell is to be and all the earth that is to say all the radical earth. Wish me good speed— May I offer my good wishes and prospective regards to your wife?

Affectionately yours /

Jane W Carlyle

17. Sterling was looking for a London home, and his strong-minded father, Edward (who will feature largely in Jane's life and correspondence), was acting for him; Cheyne Walk runs along the Thames, at right angles to Cheyne Row.

To Jean Carlyle Aitken, Chelsea, mid-August 1835

My dear Jane

Even the doubt, expressed in your last letter, about the durability of my affection was more agreeable to me than the brief notice which you usually put me off with, 'remember us to Mrs Carlyle—,' or still worse—'remember us to *your Lady*.' I have told you often, that it afflicts me to be always, in the matter of correspondence with you, obliged like the Annandale man to thank God 'for the blessings made to pass *over my head*.' It *ought* not perhaps to make any particular difference whether your letters be addressed to *him* or me but it *does*— You never in your life *answered* a letter of *mine* (and I have written you several) except little business notes from Dumfries, which could not be considered any *voluntary* expression of kind remembrance.— Had you even expressed a wish to hear from me since I came here; I would nevertheless have written, being of a disposition to receive thankfully the smallest mercies, when greater are denied—but as I said you have always put me off with a bare recognition of my existence which was small '*encooragement*.' The fact is we are both of us I believe too proud: we go upon the notion of '*keeping up our dignity Mr Arnot*.'[18] *You* have it by inheritance from your Mother who (as I have often told herself) with a great profession of humility is swallowed up in this sin; and I have possibly been seduced into it, by her example which I was simple enough to consider a safe one to imitate in all respects.

For my part however, I am quite willing to enter into a compact with you henceforth to resist the Devil—*in so far* as he interferes with our mutual good understanding; for few things were more pleasant for me than to '*tell you sundry news of every kind no rather every thought which enters in within this shallow mind*:[’] had I but the least scrap of assurance of your contentment therewith.

Now that my Mother is actually coming, I am more reconciled to my disappointment about Scotland. Next year God willing I shall see you all again

Meanwhile I am wonderfully well hefted here—the People are extravagantly kind to me—and in most respects my situation is out of sight more suitable than it was at Craigenputtoch. Of late weeks Carlyle has also been getting on better with his writing which has been uphill work since the burning of the first manuscript.[19]

18. Thomas annotated here, about 'a little Laird, come almost to starvation, by drinking &c.—a poor creditor', whose wife whispered this remark to him on some occasion (*CL*).

19. One of the most famous accidents in English literary history. In February Thomas had leant the MS of the first volume of *The French Revolution* to John Stuart Mill, whose housemaid took it for waste paper and fed it to the fire in early March. There was no alternative: Thomas sat down to rewrite the whole thing.

I do not think that the second version is on the whole inferior to the first— [I]t is a little less vivacious perhaps but better *thought* and put together— One chapter more brings him to the end of his *second first* volume and then we shall sing a *te deum* and get drunk— For which by the way we have unusual facilities at present; a Friend (Mr Wilson) having yesterday sent us a present of a hamper (some six or seven pounds worth) of the finest old Madiera wine.

These Wilsons are about the best people we know here—the Lady verging on *old maidism* is distinctly the *cleverest* woman I know— Then there are Sterlings—who from the Master of the house down to the footman are devoted to me body and soul—it is between us as between 'Beauty and the Beast.'

Speak your wishes speak your will
Swift obedience meets you still!

I have only to say 'I should like to see such a thing,' or 'to be at such a place' and next day a carriage is at the door or a boat is on the River to take me if I please to the ends of the Earth—thro them we have plumped into as pretty an Irish connexion as one would wish. Among the rest is a Mr Dunn an Irish Clergyman—who would be the delight of your Mothers heart—a perfect personification of the spirit of Christianity— You may take this fact to judge him by that he has refused *two* Bishopricks in the course of his life for conscience sake. We have also some Italian acquaintances—an Italian Countess Clementina Degli Antoni is the woman to make my Husband faithless if such a one exist—so beautiful so graceful so melodious so witty so every thing that is fascinating for the heart of man— I am learning from her to speak Italian—and she finds she says that I have a divine talent ('*divino talento*')[.][20] She is coming to tea this evening and another Italian Exile Count de Pepoli and a Danish young Lady '*Singeress* to the King of Denmark' and Mr Sterling and my old lover George Rennie. '*The victualling*' of so many people is *here* a trifle or rather a mere affair of the imagination—tea is put down and tiny biscuits—they sip a few drops of the tea and one or two sugar biscuits victuals a dozen ordinary eaters—so that the thing goes off with small damage to even a long necked purse— The expenditure is not

20. Clementina Betti degli Antoni (1802–1862), Faenza-born singer; in due course Count Pepoli would write the epitaph for her grave at the Sala del Colombario at the Bologna Charterhouse. She was teaching Jane Italian. Thomas wrote to his brother John on 15 June 1835: 'a Bologna liberal and banished: a beautiful Lombard woman, with the finest Lombard grey eyes: she had no English [. . .] and we talked in French jargon and dumb shew. The poor Countess, once rich, is obliged to teach music here, and sing!'

of one's money, but of one's wits and spirits—and that is sometimes so considerable as to leave one too exhausted for sleeping after.

I have been fidgeted with another change of servants— The woman recommended to me by Mrs Austin—turned out the best servant I had ever had, tho a rather unamiable person in temper. We got on however quite harmoniously and the affairs of the house were conducted to my entire satisfaction.— When suddenly she was sent for home to attend a sick Mother, and after three weeks absence during which time I had to find a chair-woman [charwoman] to supply her place she sent me word the other day that in the state of uncertainty she was kept in she could not expect her place to remain longer vacant for her. The next day I lighted on an active tidy looking Irish Roman catholic—in a way so singular that I could not help considering her as intended for me by Providence—and boding well of our connexion— She is not come yet but will be here on Wednesday—and in the mean while my chair-woman, who has her family in the work house, does quite tolerably.

The comfort is, that I have not to puddle about myself here as I used to have with the '*soot Drops*'[21] at Craigenputtoch—the people actually do their own work better or worse— We have no bugs yet to the best of my knowledge, and I do not know of one other house among all acquaintance that so much can be said for. For all which and much more we have reason to be thankful.

I must not finish without begging your sympathy in a disaster befallen me since I commenced this letter—the Cat has eaten one of my Canaries! not [C]hicco poor dear but a young one which I hatched myself—[22] I have sent the abominable monster out of my sight for ever—transfered her to Mrs Hunt. With kindest regards to every one of you[,] prattlers included yours

affectionately Jane Carlyle

To Thomas Carlyle, Chelsea, 12 October 1835

Dearest

A newspaper is very pleasant when one is expecting nothing at all, but when it comes in place of a letter it is a positive insult to ones

21. 'Soot' has meant 'sweet' as well as 'smoky residue': perhaps Jane implies that her Scots servants were softies compared to her London ones.
22. Brought down from Scotland, Chico the canary, Thomas notes (*CL*), 'was a very bad husband & father'; no wonder Jane had to hatch his offspring.

feelings. Accordingly your first newspaper was received by me in choicest mood, and the second would have been pitched in the fire had there been one at hand, when after having tumbled myself from the top story at the risk of my neck, I found myself deluded with '*wun penny im*.'[23] However I flatter myself you would experience something of a similar disappointment on receiving mine, and so we are quits and I need not scold you—

All is going as well with me, as I am thankful to find it is with you. I have not been a day in bed since you went have indeed been almost quite free of headach and all other aches, and every body says Mrs Carlyle begins to look better and what every body says must be true. With this improved health every thing becomes tolerable, even to the peesweep Sereetha (for we are still without other Help)[.][24] Now that I do not see *you* driven desperate with the chaos; I can take a quiet view of it, and even reduce it to some degree of order. Mother and I have fallen naturally into a fair division of labour and we keep a very tidy house. Sereetha has attained the unhoped for perfection of getting up at half after six of *her own accord* lighting the parlour fire, and actually placing the breakfast things (nil desperandum me duce [never despair with me as leader]!) I get up at half after seven and prepare the coffee and bacon-ham (which is the life of me making me always the hungrier the more I eat of it)[.] Mother in the interim makes her bed and sorts her room— After breakfast Mother descends to the inferno, where she jingles and scours and from time to time scolds Sereetha; till all is right and tight there— I, above stairs, sweep the parlour, blacken the grate—make the room cleaner than it has been since the days of Grace Macdonald—then mount aloft to make my own bed (for I was resolved to enjoy the privilege of having a bed of my own) then *clean myself* (as the servants say) and sit down to my Italian lesson. A bit of meat roasted at the oven supplies two days cold and does not plague us with cookery— Sereetha can fetch up tea things—and the porridge is easily made on the parlour fire—the kitchen one being allowed to go

23. 'One penny, him', the cockney postman says, that being the price for accepting a newspaper by mail.
24. Again, Thomas's note (*CL*) is irresistible: '"Sereetha"; in the interval of Servants (rebellious Irish [one] packed off, and Ann Cook not yet come with me), I rem[em] ber this poor little Chelsea Specimen, picked out as stop-gap from some of the neighb[ourin]g huts here. A very feeble, tho' willing little girl, introduced by the too romantic-looking name "Sereetha,"—wh[ic]h, on quest[ionin]g her little Self I discovered to be Sarah Heather (Sar' 'Eather, Sir!); much to our amuse[men]t for the moment! "Peesweep" is *Peewit*, Lapwing; with wh[ic]h swift but ineffectual bird, Sereetha seemed to have similarity.' Grace Macdonald, below, was an Edinburgh servant they took to Craigenputtoch.

out (for economy) when the peesweep retires to bed at eight o'clock— That we are not neglected by the public you may infer from the fact that this very night Peesweep fetched up *four* teacups in the tray, and when I asked the meaning of the two additional, she inquired with surprise '*were there to be no gentlemen*'? In fact the kindness of these people! 'beats the WORLD'[.] I had some private misgiving that your men would not mind me when you were not here, and I should have been mortified in that case, tho' I could not have blamed them—but it is quite the reverse— Little Grant has been twice to know if he could '*do any thing for me*'—Garnier has been twice!![25] the first time by engagement to you the second time to meet Pepoli whom he knew in Paris and wished to reknow and who proved *perfido* [unfaithful] on the occasion— Pepoli has been twice and is gliding into a flirtation, with—mia madre [my mother]! who presented him in a manner molto graziosa [extremely graceful] with her tartan scarf. From John Mill I have been priviledged with two notes and one visit— He tried evidently to yawn as little as possible and stayed till the usual hour lest, I suppose, he should seem to have missed your conversation—John Sterling and the Stimabile[26] of course—the latter was at tea last night to meet Mr Gibson—one of my fatal attempts at producing a *reunion*—for they coincided in nothing but years. The Stimabile was at Brighton for several days and goes again next week so that he has not been deadly. Our visiting has been confined to one dinner and *two teas* at the Sterlings and a tea at Hunts!! You must know Susan Hunter[27] came the day after you went and stayed two days— [A]s she desired above all things to see Hunt I wrote him a note asking if I might bring her up to call— He replied he was just setting off to town but would look in at eight oclock— I supposed this as usual a mere off put but he actually came—found Pepoli as well as Miss Hunter[,] was amazingly lively, and very lasting; for he sta[yed] till near twelve— Between ourselves it gave me a poorish opinion of him to see how uplifted to the third Heaven he seemed by Susans compliments and sympathizing talk. He asked us all with enthusiasm to tea the following Monday[.] Susan came from town on purpose and

25. The first, Thomas tells us, was an official at the East India Company and a friend of John Stuart Mill; for Garnier, see Characters and Correspondents.
26. Italian, 'Estimable', by which the Carlyles referred to Edward Sterling forever after, because of his ample self-conceit. Degli Antoni had set Jane as an Italian project a pretend letter to Sterling, beginning '*Stimabile Signor*', and it stuck. For William Gibson, see Characters and Correspondents; Jane calls him 'the Silverheaded' below.
27. An acquaintance from St Andrews, Thomas tells us, who became 'a sturdy admirer & benefactor' of Leigh Hunt. Her brother became professor of logic and rhetoric at St Andrews.

slept here— Mrs Hunt behaved smoothly and looked devilish and was drunkish. He sang, talked like a pengun,[28] ever to Susan, who drank it all in like nectar; while my Mother looked cross enough—and I had to listen to the whispered confidences of Mrs Hunt— But for me, who was declared to be grown '*quite prim and elderly*' I believe they would have communicated their mutual experiences in a retired window seat till morn[in]g— '*God bless you Miss Hunter*' was repeated by Hunt three several times in tones of ever increasing pathos and tenderness as he handed her down stairs behind me— Susan for once in her life seemed past speech. At the bottom of the stairs a demur took place— I saw nothing but I heard with my wonted glegness [keenness]—what think you?—a couple of handsome *smacks* [kisses]! and then an almost inaudibly soft God bless you Miss Hunter! Now just remember what sort of looking woman is Susan Hunter and figure this transaction! If he had kissed me it would have been intelligible but Susan Hunter of all people!— By the way Mr Craik is immensely delighted with you and grateful to Susan for having brought you together— Mrs Cole came the other day and sat an hour waiting for me while I was out and finally had to go—leaving an obliging note offering me every assistance in procuring a servant— Mrs John Sterling takes to me wonderfully—but John I perceive will spoil all with his innocence— He told her the other day when she was declaring her wish that he would write on theology rather than make verses that she 'might fight out that matter with Mrs Carlyle who he knew was always on the side of the poetical'—tho he accompanied his words with a sort of *hug* I saw by the colour that came to her face that he had done me an ill turn. He (Sterling) has written a positively splendid poem of half an hour length—an Allegorical shadowing of the union of the Ideal and actual— It is far the best thing he ever did—far beyond any thing I could have supposed him capable of— He said when he was writing it he thought sometimes 'Carlyle will be pleased with that'

To descend to the practical or I should rather say ascend, for I have filled my whole paper with mere gossip. I think you seem so far as human calculations avail, to have made a good hit for to the servant—character is not worth a straw but you say she looks intelligent and good humoured is young and willing[—] [F]etch her then in Gods name—and I will make the best I can of her— After all we fret ourselves tomuch about little things[;] much that might be laughed

28. Not a *penguin*, as we might guess, but a Scottish phrase, 'to crack like a pen-gun' (a kind of popgun made from a quill pen, according to *OED*): to be voluble.

off, if one were well and cheerful as one ought to be, becomes a grave affliction from being too gravely looked at— Remember also [*sic*] Saturday night

[*sic*] meal and o for goodness sake procure a *dozen* of bacon-hams! There is no bottom to my appetite for them. Sell poor Harry [the horse] by all means or shoot him—we are too poor to indulge our *fine feelings* with keeping such large pets (especially at other peoples expence)— What a pity no frank is to be got!— I have told you nothing yet— No word ever came from Basil Montague— I have translated some songs into Italian written a long excessively spirituosa [spirited] letter to 'mia adorabile [my adorable] Clementina,' and many graziosa cartuccia [elegant notes] besides. In truth I have a divino ingegno [divine spirit].

You will come back strong and cheerfuler will you not? I wish you were come any how. Dont take much castor—eat plenty of chicken broth rather—dispense my love largely

Mother returns your kiss with interest— We go on tolerably enough but she has vowed to hate all my people except Pepoli so that there is ever a '*dark-brown shad*[*e*]' in all my little reunions. She has given me a glorious black velvet gown realizing my beau Ideal of puzz [*putz*: finery]. I shall keep the beverage[29] for you darling.

Did you take away my folder pen knife? We are knifeless here—

We were to have been to Richmond today with the Silverheaded but to my great relief it turned out that the steam boat is not running.

God keep you my own dear Husband and bring you safe back to me. The house looks very empty without you and my mind feels empty—
Your Jane

To Eliza Stodart, Chelsea, circa 29 February 1836

Dear Dear Eliza

It has several times occurred to me of late, with a painful force of apprehension, that I am what is called *bewitched*. I sit here week after week, month after month, looking at things which I have the most evident call to do, and with apparently no more power to bestir myself than the Lady in Comus![30] For instance with respect to yourself; I have

29. A dialect term now, according to *OED*, meaning a drink or other gratuity (a kiss, say) offered by someone wearing a new suit of clothes.

30. Milton's masque on the theme of chastity (1634), in which 'the Lady', deserted by her two brothers, heroically resists the temptations offered her by the eponymous magician.

wished to tell you, have meant to tell you, and by all laws of good loving ought to have told you, ages ago; that I am still alive, and true to you as in the days of my '*wee existence*'! And yet for no visible reason, I have gone on telling you nothing of the sort—nothing of *any* sort—but leaving you to suppose me a heartless renegade, unless indeed your faith be greater than that of woman. Well! believe it or no, as you like and can; I love you still with all the *ardour of my young enthusiasm*—much more heartily and trustfully than I am apt to love nowadays with my middleaged discretion. Yet I have set myself very seriously to the business of loving since I came here—conscious that my long sojourn in the wilderness had developed certain misanthrophical tendencies in me that were leading me rather devilward,—into the region of hatred and all uncharitablness! With a good deal of effort I have got up a sentiment for several men and women which has a good right to go by the name of friendship in these days. I have even executed two or three *innocent flirtations* with good effect, and on the whole live in great amity with my fellow creatures. They call me '*sweet*,' and '*gentle*'; and some of the men go the length of calling me 'ENDEARING' and I laugh in my sleeve and think oh Lord! if you but knew what a brimstone of a creature I am behind all this beautiful amiability! But my *sentiment* for *you* dearest, is not '*got up*,' but grown up with me out of my sunny childhood, and wears always a sunny healthful look that these half-literary half-sentimental intimacies contracted after thirty can never match. The fault however is not in the *people* but in the *time*. 'You great fool' said my Uncle Robert, once to me, when I was flying into somebody's arms on the North Bridge,[31] 'you will surely learn sometime or other that every body is not in such ecstacies to see you as you are in to see everybody'!! My judicious Uncle! you were there and then a true Prophet! I have long ago learnt to distrust the ecstacies produced at sight of me in others, and consequently cease to give way to any sort of ecstacy in myself. When I fly into any ones arms *now* and '*swear everlasting friendship*' it is always with a secret misgiving, and a secret and almost risibile conscious of a certain *theatricality* in the transaction. The words '*forever*' '*eternal*' '*constant*' '*faithful*' and such like applied to the friendships and loves that one *begins* at the years of discretion never fall on my ears except accompanied by something like the distant laugh of malicious friends. Melancholy effects of age!! 'O the days when I was young'! and confident and foolish! Do *you* like to be wise Bess? I dont at all!—but one is obliged to put a good face on the matter. And so I sit here in no 5 Cheyne Row and make grave

31. A road bridge above Waverley station linking the Old and New Towns of Edinburgh, originally built in the second half of the eighteenth century and replaced in 1897.

pantomime, and grave speech in acknowledgement of all the wisdom I hear uttered by the celebrated men and women of the age; thinking my own thought all the while which is often this or something like this— 'Was not sitting under a hay-stack in a summers day with Bess and George Rennie—or even weeping childlike purely affectionate tears at the sound of the *Castle bugles*; when in reply to my demand to be allowed to marry, they[32] sent me two halfcrowns and some barley-sugar; worth a whole eternity of this idle speculation and barren logic'? But the people here are good people, and with many noble gifts in them, and to me they have been quite incomprehensibly kind so that I ought not to feel discontent with THEM because the magic of the *imagination* in me has got impaired by years, and no spectacles that *reason* can invent does any thing at making the world so green and glorious for me as it once was. My chief intimates are a family of Sterlings— The Father known by the na[me] of '*the Thunderer of the Times*'—a clever, tumultuous, vapid sort of a half-Irishman,—the Mother a kind sincere wellenough cultivated most motherly half Scotchwoman—the Son! [John]—An angel of Heaven! *ostensibly* a Clergyman of the church of England, and author of Arthur Coningsby a highly original Novel; He has also a wife, very fat, and good natured and fine ladyish in the *best* sense of the term. These people, as the elder Sterling told Susan Hunter when she was here, '*all adore me*'! Certainly they load me with kindnesses and treat me as if I were a sort of necessary to their existence: The very footman and Ladysmaid 'have been quite anxious' if I have staid away half a week[;] Mrs Sterlings portrait in oil hangs over my Mantle-piece— and the whole thing is in the most flourishing condition—if it do but last[;] then I have an Italian Conte, one of the first poets of Italy, the handsomest and bestmannered of men, who comes twice a week or so and makes my thoughts melodious for the rest of the day. He was my Mothers chief indeed I think *only* favorite here among all our people; which was curious as they had no medium of communication but their eyes! For my part I speak Italian now like a nightingale, and *will* I am told soon write it '*better* than any native Signora'! Like the man and the fiddle nobody knows what he can do till he try. Did you hear tell of my Darling Degli Antoni?—your recent distress prevented me introducing

32. Presumably blown by domestic militia in the 'French Wars' up until 1814. The Edinburgh lawyer and politician Henry Cockburn was in charge of a troop of the Midlothian Volunteers alongside Walter Scott at the time, and remembered 'The parades, the reviews, the four or six yearly inspections at Dalmahoy, the billettings for a fortnight or three weeks when on "permanent duty" at Leith or Haddington—what scenes they were!' (*Memorials of his Time*, ed. Karl Miller (Chicago, 1974), 181).

her to you among the rest of my Edinr friends. She is another of my special friends: it is so delightful to be called '*carissima amica*' [dearest friend] &c that it is worth while to keep up an Italian friendship or two for the purpose. But oh my dear Eliza would you but come and *see* all that I have—in the way of friends, in the way of house room in the way of hearts room! what glorious days we might still have together after all that is come and gone! Your Uncle, I rejoice to hear is better again, can you not come then? The journey is a mere trifle. [T]he [we]lcome would be a great reality! To me y[ou w]ould indeed be welcome as flowers in May—or rather were it not better to say as flowers in December; and to my Husband you would be welcome—as a cigar in a land destitute of tobacco!!— Oh Bess will you will you come? Kisses to your uncle— My Husband is pretty well—almost thro the second volume of his illfated book—thinks of your Uncle and you with grateful affection—is on the whole the cleverest man I meet with still and the truest. I have never yet thanked you with my own hand for your beautiful stockings but I never wear them without thanking you silently. Godbless you Dearest write to me soon tho I do not deserve it—and love me always—your own Jane Welsh

To Mary Welsh, Chelsea, 4 September 1836

My dear Aunt

Now that I am fairly settled at home again, and can look back over my late travels with the coolness of a spectator; it seems to me that I must have tired out all men, women, and children that have had to do with me by the road. The proverb says '*there is much ado when cadgers ride*.' I do not know precisely what '*cadger*' means;[33] but I imagine it to be a character like *me*; liable to headachs, to seasickness, to all the infirmities 'that flesh is heir to,'[34] and a few *others* besides: the friends and relations of *cadgers* should therefore use all soft persuasions to induce them to remain at home. I got into that mail the other night, with as much repugnance and trepidation as if it had been a Phalaris's brazen bull,[35]

33. *OED*: 'a species of itinerant dealer who travels with a horse and cart' taking produce from rural areas to the town and vice versa.
34. Shakespeare, *Hamlet*, III. i. 62.
35. An ancient Sicilian tyrant king, given to roasting people to death inside a bronze replica bull.

instead of a christian vehicle, invented for purposes of mercy not of cruelty: There were three besides myself when we started, but two dropt off at the end of the first stage, and the rest of the way I had as usual half the coach to myself. My fellow passenger had that highest of all terrestrial qualities which, for me, a fellow passenger can possess, *he was silent.*— I think his name was Roscoe, and he read sundry long papers to himself with the pondering air of a lawyer. We breakfasted at Litchfield, at five in the morning, on muddy coffee and scorched toast, which made me once more lyrically recognise in my heart (not without a sigh of regret) the very different coffee and toast with which you helped me out of my headach. At *two*, there was another stop of ten minutes, that might be employed in lunching or otherwise— [F]eeling myself more fevered than hungry, I determined on spending the time in combing my hair and washing my face and hands *with vinegar*,—in the midst of this solacing operation I heard what seemed to be the mail resuming its rapid course, and quick as lightening it flashed on me 'there it goes!—and my luggage is on the top of it!—and *my purse* is in the pocket of it!—and here am I stranded on an unknown beech, without so much as a sixpence in my pocket to pay for the vinegar I have already consumed!' Without my bonnet, my hair hanging down my back, my face half dried, and the towel with which I was drying it firm grasped in my hand, I dashed out,—along,—down,—opening wrong doors,—stumbling over steps,—cursing the day I was born,—still more the day on which I took a notion to travel,—and arrived finally, at the bar of the inn in a state of excitement bordering on lunacy. The bar-maids looked at me 'with weender and amazement'— 'Is the coach gone?' I gasped out.— 'The coach? Yes!' 'O! and you have let it away without me! O! stop it,—cannot you, stop it?' and out I rushed into the street with streaming hair and streaming towel, and almost brained myself against—*the Mail*! which was standing there in all stillness without so much as horses in it!— [W]hat I had heard was a heavy coach!— And now having descended like a maniac, I ascended again like a fool, and dried the other half of my face, and put on my bonnet, and came back 'a sadder and a wiser' woman—[36]

I did not find my Husband at the *Swan with two necks*; for we were *in*, a quarter of an hour before the appointed time. [S]o I had my luggage put on the backs of two porters and walked on to Cheapside, where I presently found a Chelsea Omnibus. By and by however, the omnibus stopt, and amid cries of '*no room Sir*'—'*Cant get in*'— Carlyle's face beautifully set off by a broad-brimmed white hat gazed in at the door,—

36. The penultimate line of Coleridge's 'Rime of the Ancient Mariner' (1798).

like the Peri who '*at the gate-of heaven stood disconsolate*'[37]— [I]n hurrying along the Strand pretty sure of being too late,—amidst all the imaginable and unimaginable phenomena which that immense thorough fare of a street presents; his eye (heaven bless the mark) had lighted on *my trunk* perched on the top of the omnibus and had recognised it! This seems to me one of the most indubitable proofs of *genius* which he ever manifested— [H]appily a passenger went out a little further on, and then he got in— My Brother-in-law had gone two days before, so my arrival was most well-timed. I found all at home right and tight, my maid seems to have conducted herself quite handsomely in my absence—my *best* room looked really *inviting*. A bust of Shelly (a present from Leigh Hunt) and a fine print of Albert Durer's handsomely framed (also a present) had *still further ornamented* it during my absence— I also found (for I wish to tell you all my satisfaction) every grate in the house furnished with a supply of coloured clippings!—and the holes in the stair-carpet all darned so that it looks like new— They gave me tea and fried bacon and staved off my headach as well as might be. They were very kind to me, but on my life, every body is kind to me! and to a degree that fills me with admiration—I feel so strong a wish to make you all convinced how very deeply I feel your kindness!—and just the more I would say; the less I am able to say anything.

Please tell my Uncle that Carlyle has been about the stocking—and the people engaged to have it ready and sent to Mr Fowns in Tavistock Square[38] (according to their orders) on Tuesday night. If it do not come shortly tell us and we will leave them no peace till they send it.

I expect in a day or two to be quite recovered from the fatigue of my wanderings and then that I shall begin to reap the good effects— Now, I do not expect dear Aunt that *you* should write to me, when you have so much else to do but certainly the rest might be well employed (could they but think so) in sending me news from time to time. God bless you all. Love to all, from the head of the house down to Johnny—

your [affec]tionate

Jane W Carlyle

I left a pair of stockings behind. Pray have the kindness to give them to Margaret (of course I mean Margaret the maid)

37. Thomas Moore, 'Paradise and the Peri', from *Lalla Rookh* (1817), ii. 1–2.
38. *CL* suggests Fownes Brothers, 'Leather-dressers and glove manufacturers, 4 Tavistock St.' Clearly a medical requisite for Uncle John.

To Thomas Carlyle, Foley Arms, Great Malvern, Worcestershire, 11 August 1837

Husband of me—I hope you duly received the large packet I sent enclosed to Henry Taylor; otherwise you must be thinking me a rather degenerate Goody.[39] Honourable members are such *rari aves* [rare birds] here as yet, that even Mr Gibson could not get me a common frank;[40] so I was constrained to address myself to *the Government*. On the faith that it is all right I shall take up the thread of narration where I broke off at Chelsea; under no very comfortable circumstances, for my head was so bad that I had to go to bed three times while writing that letter, tho' I would not tell you so *then* for fear of making you anxious. By the way it is a great *sottise* [stupidity] that of the *two strokes* on the newspaper—the less one is *all well* the more careful one is that no want of strokes shall let the truth be suspected; it is when one is well enough to be taking no thought of wellness or illness that the strokes are apt to be forgotten.

Allons donc [let's go on then]! my run-away husband— On Monday (being the 7th of August 1837) I arose and put on clean raiment, and having for the hundredth time recommended to Ellen my roses and silver spoons, and myself to the Great disposer of all, I seated myself beside Mr and Mrs Sterling in their new carriage, with much the same sensations as I might have felt beside Mr and Mrs Graham in their new balloon;[41] to drive wheresoever the wind listed, and be landed where it should please the pigs: so great was the horror of doubt and fluctuation which involved our whole expedition to my thinking! The same day however, about eight in the evening, we actually gained Oxford as proposed; and descended '*da carroza*' [from the carriage] less fatigued and more pleased with our day's-work than '*I as one solitary individual*' had anticipated.— On my life, there is '*a fund of vitality*' in that man, which covereth a multitude of sins. What a taste he still has for '*innocent pleasures*'! I, who at half his age have already exhausted all that, can do nothing but stare at his preternatural effervescences and raptures.— *The Angel Inn*, where we staid at Oxford, gave me a rather unpleasant impression of the *tone* of that place (for travellers always get very decided and of course infallible impressions of places from the Inns where they

39. Henry Taylor (1800–1886), dramatist and important acquaintance of the Lake poets Wordsworth and Southey, introduced to Thomas by John Stuart Mill in 1831.
40. Like sending a newspaper, another means of coming by cheap postal communication. Members of Parliament had the privilege of appending their signatures ('franks') to mail for free delivery. When sending a newspaper a correspondent might use a system of marks ('*two strokes*', below) to send a simple message to the recipient.
41. Margaret and George Graham were pioneering balloonists of the period. In 1824 Margaret made the first female ascent, and her three daughters all followed in her footsteps. She died in poverty in 1864.

eat or sleep)—not that the bread butter et cetera was not first rate, and the silver forks in 'good' style: what disgusted me was to observe in every bed room, *laid before the looking glass, a bible* and *book of prayers* with a small hassock underneath (and this preparation I was told was universal thro' all the Inns at Oxford)[;] *my* particular hassock (of green cloth) had a drawing printed on it, which I was at pains to examine—it represented a sportsman (for consistency's sake let us hope *a parson*) in the midst of a stubble field taking aim at three birds which he could not fail to hit, the tips of their wings being touching the muzzle of his gun! Moreover the Waiters, all large elderly men, had a sort of 'mazed abstractedness and sad gravity of look which gave one a notion they must have some time or other been unsuccessful graduates: while the maids *my-ladied* at us at such a rate, and made their reverences so profoundly that the free Breton-blood[42] rushed to my face in very shame for them— From all which I inferred that Oxford was a place much under the domination of Cant—Cant in its two most killing shapes, of *Religion* that *keeps its hassock* and *Respectability* that *keeps its gig.*

The Colleges however, which we saw the best part of during Tuesday forenoon under the guidance of Jacobson, interested me beyond measure—not only as being a splendid memorial of past ages but as shaping for me into actual stone and mortar, and painted glass, and illuminated manuscripts and square-capp'd blackgowned figures et cetera, the vague notions I had gathered in my girlhood, out of novels and histories, of a Great English University.— But nothing of all that I saw gave me so lively an emotion of pleasure as—a very small thing indeed—neither more nor less than *Guy Fox's Lantern* preserved under a glass case![43] and what gave Mr Sterling the liveliest emotion of *dis*pleasure, was a question I addressed, with no ill intention but in pure unsophisticated curiosity, to the gentleman who showed us the Bodleian Picture Gallery, viz: 'how came it that I saw no picture of Oliver Cromwell there, seeing that they had raked together so many insignificant persons of his time?'[44] A broad stare was all the answer I

42. The Bretons, inhabitants of Brittany in north-west France (anciently Armorica) and originally from Celtic Britain, are a notoriously independent ethnic group; whether Jane was of Celtic descent would be hard to prove in the absence of DNA.

43. Guy Fawkes, famous coadjutor in the 'Gunpowder Plot' of 1605 to blow up the Houses of Parliament; his lantern was on him when he was arrested, and was displayed at the Bodleian Library before being moved to the Ashmolean Museum in Oxford in 1887, where it remains on display.

44. Sterling's displeasure and the guide's discombobulation are understandable; Oxford had been a major centre of royalist loyalism during Cromwell's Civil War of 1642–1651. It would be a year or two before Thomas's Cromwellian studies would become all-consuming, but he had doubtless admired the Protector long since.

received to this natural enquiry, from which the gentleman's features did not relax so long as I remained in his company. I hope he is now more at ease. There were also many gloriously illuminated manuscripts shown me, which I could have spent much more time in looking at than Mr Sterling would allow—especially a Plato and Tacitus—and a greek testament bound in solid silver having a carved ivory Monk in relief on one side and on the other a Greek inscription purporting the 'that Maker thereof particularly wished God would bless himself and his family.'— And there was Queen Elizabeth's Latin exercise-book (putting me very much in mind of my own) along side of Tippo Saib's gold-lettered *Koran*![45] But I should need more sheets than one to enumerate all the curiosities and niceties I saw.

With all its magnificence it seems to me that the Bodleian Library must be a most perverse place to study in; for this reason above all, that the numerous private libraries left to it in donation, of which it is chiefly composed, are and *must be* kept *apart* and *entire*; so that instead of *one* great Library arranged under general heads, you have as it were a great many little libraries arranged under one general roof. They told me the inconvenience of this was obviated by the perfection of the *catalogues* to which I can only say the perfection of the catalogues must be much beyond the perfection of the *Librarians*. One of whom, grown grey in the service, I made as red as a lobster with asking him simple questions which he could nowise answer.

On the Afternoon of the same day we visited Blenheim where amidst much that was note-worthy I remarked most note-worthy of all, and a sort of epitome of the whole, two pictures hung on the same wall,—the one, Old Sarah in her loneliness and her pride,—the other Miss Glover in—her blue satin![46] (Miss Glover, for to be sure you do not know it, being a trashy actress's daughter, at present officiating as Mistress to his grace of Marlborough, a man of Seventy with a wife living in London) I could not but wish that a picture might have spoken for once, and the beautiful termagant might have there and then opened her tinkler-jaw

45. Tipu Sultan, 'the Tiger of Mysore' (1751–1799), who defied the British East India Company in the four Anglo-Mysore Wars of the late eighteenth century. He was killed at Seringapatam (Mandya) in 1799, and his Islamic holy book was taken from his library in the aftermath.

46. Sarah Churchill (1660–1744) was the first Duchess of Marlborough and wife of the triumphant British general, John Churchill, whose great house (the only non-royal, non-episcopal palace in Britain) was Blenheim, near Woodstock, Oxfordshire. The actress Julia Glover was by no means trashy but, be that as it may, her daughter Matilda (1802–1876) was mistress of the fifth Duke, George Spencer Churchill (1766–1840), and had several children by him.

on that trumpery damsel, and asked her in the Devil's name what *she* was doing in *her* Blenheim as '*one of the family*' (to use our Cicerone's delicate phraseology)?— [B]ut so is it ever, pride before destruction—the haughty spirit before a fall!— We slept that night at a country Inn near Burford some sixteen miles on the other side of Blenheim, and proceeded hither, next day, by Cheltenham and Tewksbury (not without poking into every crevice of the old church at the latter place)—across the Severn (a marvellously clear flowing river for England) and so thro' a country as full as it could cram of apple-orchards growing on the greenest sward,—patches of the yellowest corn,—thatched homesteads up to the knees in hollyhocks,—and all soft, sweet, picturesque objects, which Nature in her profusion could be suffered to have flung together. For Malvern itself, it only half pleases me—the situation is magnificent, it stands a little way up on a hill or hills, from the top of which you see over *ten* counties, and the window of our sitting-room commands the richest, most extensive prospect I ever saw with my eyes—but as a village it is preposterous—at a little distance it looks as if it had been built with a pack of cards—all so white and twostoried and formal! at hand you find it consists of a great many smart, roman-cemented cockney-built *Villas* with a sprinkling of '*gin pallace*'-looking Hotels, grouped stupidly, or in strait lines at regular distances—all which seems so out of character on the slope of a romantic hill and alongside of a fine old Monastery and some two or three *old* houses in the gothic style!— But it will do well enough for all I am likely to *want* with it— Pray heaven you may not find me fallen into that arch-sin—a taste for description of natural scenery— For the present then you are to figure your *povera piccola* [poor little one] settled in one of these gin-pallace Hotels (*of course* the most aristocratic—when my Lord this and My Lady that breathe the same atmosphere that we breath—) tolerably well off as to things temporal, but for the spiritual part looking forward to better times; we have private rooms like the rest of the *great* people, and are served with excellent food, and Mrs S sews at her worsted work, and I work at your purse and the [Stimabile] exclaims '*By Jove Hester this tranquillity is—delicious*,' but from the fierce tone he begins in, tho' sinking into dieaway softness at the close, I am always expecting the '*delicious*' will come out a '*damnable*'—and when there is no more to be done 'we go about worship' and so to bed where I for one, tho' quiet enough, sleep no better than at Chelsea—that is to say badly as can be. For all this we pay some guinea a-day *each*!—the more's the pity for him that pays it all. By the way there is certainly a good deal of practical kindness in supporting *me* here at any such rate— However they both seem to think themselves obliged by having my company—and show me all the attention possible—so that I go by the name of '*the young Lady*' in the house—and in short tout va bien [all goes well]—so far. How long it will go so well is another question— He talks of being absent a month. But I guess that either he will return sooner, or I will separate myself from the Great Balloon and alight in a parachute, before that time. I have stood the travelling better than I expected hitherto—going at ones own time in ones own carriage, with an officious Stephen to look after ones odds and ends, and officious Landlords to serve up tender roast chickens and 'exquisite sherry' is a very different sort of thing from dashing over the country in disarray, in doubt and destitution at the blast of a mail coach horn— But I *must* stop. God bless you my beloved. Write instantly on receipt of this—to my present Address—and tell me if you think of coming back—I do not want to hurry you—but—it is so long that we have not seen each other—at least to me it seems long— Love to all— Again God bless my—Genius—Jane Carlyle.

Pray say something pretty to the Sterlings—they send you their kindest regards.

You had better enclose this letter to my Mother— It will give me more time to swallow the *fresh* air on the hills if I make it stand for two.

To Thomas Carlyle, Clifton, 29 August 1837

Dearest Love

I have been too long waiting for certainties—*hithering and thithering* being a condition under which I find it almost impossible to write or indeed to do any thing except fret myself to fiddlestrings. What I generally do in such cases is to shape out a decision with all despatch for *myself*, and leave the others to welter on after their own fashion; accordingly when I found on our arrival at Clifton, that it was all in the wind whether we should stay there one week or two or three, and whether we should return straight to London, or by Brighton, or by the Isle of Wight, or first making '*a run over to Dublin*,' I immediately announced my intention of descending by *parachute*, and was only prevented from carrying it into effect by humane consideration for the Parties in the Balloon, where there was evidently going to be an alarming explosion in case of my departure. Mrs Sterling having set her heart on a visit of some length to the Bartons, and his Whirlwindship finding the whole Barton generation '*creatures without stimulus*' whom he was desirous to cut and run from by '*feeling it his duty to see poor Mr[s] Carlyle* OME!' His secret purpose was evidently to take himself and me back in the carriage and leave Mrs S to follow as she could—and this I felt would have been a very ungracious proceeding towards that good soul who treats me with such kindness and consideration. I now perceive the use my company is of to them both, better than I did when we set out— I furnish, as it were, the sugar and ginger which makes the alkali of the one and the tartaric acid of the other effervesce into a somewhat more agreeable draught for 'the *effervescing* of these people'!— To say the least '*it is very absurd*'! But I shall keep all my stock of *biographic* NOTICES to enliven our winter evenings. Meanwhile you are to know that we left Malvern for Clifton a week ago, all of us with very dry eyes. Mr S on finding that certain Lords who smiled decietful at the Carlton Club,[47] were absolutely inaccessible at the Foley Arms, suddenly discovered that '*your beautiful scenery was a great humbug, as you had only to strip the soil a foot deep and it would be a vile black mass.*' Mrs Sterling in her querulous qualifying about it and about it way—doubted whether it was 'wholesome to overlook such a flat' 'not but what it was very well to have seen it *for once*—or if there was *any necessity* for living here—of course one would not object &c &c—['] and for me—poverina [poor little thing]—from the first moment I set my eyes on the place, I foresaw that it would prove a failure—that it would neither make me a convert to *nature*, nor find me in a new nervous system— [E]very day of our stay there I arose with a headach—and my nights were unspeakable; every day I felt more emphatically that *nature* was an intolerable bore— Do not misconstrue me—genuine unsophisticated nature I grant you is all very amiable and harmless—but beautiful nature which Man has *exploited* as a Reviewer does a work of genius—making it a peg to hang his own conceits upon, to enact his *Triomphe der Empfindsamkeit* in[48]—beautiful nature which you look out upon from pea-green arbours—which you dawdle about in on the backs of donkies—and where you are haunted with an everlasting smell of roast meat—all that I do declare to be the greatest of bores—and I would rather spend my days amidst downright acknowledged brick houses and paved streets than any such fool's paradises. So entirely *unheimlich* [dismal] I felt myself that the day I got your letter I cried over it for two or three hours. In other more favourable circumstances I should have recognised the tone of sadness that ran all

47. One of London's great members' clubs, founded as an organ of the Conservative Party in 1832 in the aftermath of the Great Reform Bill; it still operates in St James's Street, Westminster, and is highly exclusive.

48. 'The Triumph of Sensitivity' (1777): a romantic and idealistic drama of Goethe's, accompanied by music, much concerned with nature and humanity.

thro' it, as the simple effect of a tiresome Journey and a doze of physic at the end, but read at Malvern with headach and sleeplessness and ennui for interpreters!— Alas what could I do but fling myself on my bed and cry myself sick. I said to myself you were no better than when you left me and all this absence was gone for nothing. I wanted to kiss you into something like cheerfulness and the length of a kingdom was betwixt us—and if it had not—the probabilities are that *with the best intentions* I should have quarrelled with you rather. Poor men and women! what a time they have in this world—by destiny and their own deserving— But as Mr Bradfute used to say 'tell us something we do not know.' Well then it is an absolute fact that his Whirlwindship and I road to the top of Malvern hill, each on a live donky! Just figure it! with a Welch lad whipping us up from behind; for they were the slowest of donkies tho' named in defiance of all probability *Fly* and *Lively*. 'The Devil confound your donkies,' exclaimed my vivacious companion (who might really I think '*but for the honour of the thing*,' and perhaps some small diminution of the danger of bursting his lungs, have as well walked) 'they are so stupidly stubborn that you might as well beat on a stick'! 'And isn't it a good thing they be stubborn Sir' said the lad 'as being, ye see, that they have no sense, if they warnt "stubborn" they might be for taking down the steep and we wants no accidents Sir.' 'Now' said I, 'for the first time in my life I perceive why Conservatives are so stupidly stubborn[;] *stubborness*, it seems, is a succedaneum [substitute] for *sense*.' A flash of indignation—then in a soft tone 'Do you know Mrs Carlyle you would be a vast deal more amiable if you were not so *damnably* clever'! This is a fair specimen of our talk at Malvern from dewy morn to balmy eve.[49]

My procedure at Worcester (where we passed two days and whence I sent a newspaper) was unexpected and *disappointing* in the extreme. I walked into the house of the illustrious Archdeacon, along a lengthy passage, down two steps into an antique looking drawing room or suit of drawingrooms; without giving proof of being anything out of the common—I cast my nota-bene eyes over the man—a large portly figure belonging to the rotund school—the very beau ideal of an old Abbot—with a countenance full of twinkling intelligence and gregarious good humour, having a high metallic tone of voice, and a whisking suddeness of movement accompanied by a peculiar fling of the coat-skirts which reminded me forcibly of the *Archivarius Lindhurst*—[50] I also

49. John Henry Newman, 'Snapdragon: A Riddle for a Flower Book' (1827), derived from Milton, *Paradise Lost*, i. 742–3.
50. Archivarius Lindhorst, a sinister and awesomely prepotent character in E. T. A. Hoffman's fantastic novella, 'The Golden Pot' (1814): the 'father of a green serpent', below.

flung a cursory glance on a table where a massive lunch was spread out, such as realized one's sublimest conceptions of a Convent refectory, and then—without more said or done I pitched myself into a *fluffy* snowwhite bed which was shown me as mine where I lay twenty four hours—not out of sheer contradiction but because I really could no longer hold myself erect. In vain the prim archdeaconian *Perpetua* came at stated intervals to know 'if I wanted any thing' receiving always for answer 'to be let alone'—and in vain the Whirlwind himself came at intervals not stated, to ask in a tone of deep tho' loud pathos (for it was from outside the door) '*if I believed that he was exceedingly sorry*,' receiving also one unvarying answer '*Yes Yes*'[.] My headach refused to listen to the voice of either charmer till it had run its course. It was indeed a strange preternatural night the first I passed in that prebendary establishment, right under the stroke (it seemed to me) of the great Cathedral clock, which strikes even the quarters, haunted by the images of the large Archdeaconus and large pigeon pie I had seen below, and taken together had to my overexcited imagination a cast of magic! especially in the dead of night, with a rushlight dimly lighting the chamber and my head quite mistified between this Worcester Archdeacon and the german Archivarius—and could by no possibility *decide* whether Archdeacon Singleton was not also the father of a green serpent and could make his face into a bronze knocker[!] Worthy man when he welcomed me anew next day with the broadest smiles he little suspected what strange thoughts I had had of him.— But I have quite miscalculated my distance—and have left no room for my travels history since. The loss will not be material— Suffice it to say we came from Malvern to Cheapstow all in one day besides '*doing*' Eastnor Castle, Goodrich Castle, Tintern Abbey and Cheapstow Castle—and the next on to Clifton—thoroughly tired body and soul.[51] We are in lodgings here—I have a quiet room—and sleep better— [E]very day we dine with the Bartons—the kindest people to dine with that one could wish, but as he says—there is a lack of *stimulus*. The brother that is returned from India [Anthony] is the most wonderful compound in appearance of Cavaignac and—Mr Bradfute[:] Ecco la combinazione [Behold the combination]!—And now here is surprising news for you—John Sterling is to be back in London with his wife and her little ones about the twe[lf]th—[h]e himself having turned towards Madeira—in consequence of the

51. A worthy tour, of castles near Ledbury and Monmouth, the abbey immortalised in Wordsworth's poem, and Chepstow, all in the counties of Hereford and Monmouth, either side of the English-Welsh border, before the travellers resort to the Bristol suburb of Clifton.

Colera abroad, and the family to remain at Knight[s]bridge—which I do not think his Father half likes—poor John is really a little flighty—'*after all*'. I fondly hope to quit Clifton the end of this present week and to go home by the base of the isoceles triangle which the Isle of Whight makes with Clifton and London instead of along the two sides— I long for home—and to be putting in order for your coming— I shall send you a newspaper immediately on my landing—and then you will write to say *when*— O my darling we will surely be better both of us *there* again—effervescing even. Dont you think so?— I made no mark—wrote nothing on any newspaper—it must have been some editorial mark of Mr S's which I had not noticed— I have sent you papers from every large town where I have been.

I have left no room for kind messages—say for me all that you know I would wish to say— I saw the Crawfords at Monmouth— Mr C. is most emphatic for another course of lectures—the *Characters* he thought a most glorious project—[52] I have no doubt but you will find an audience prepared to be enchanted with you whenever you want one

The Book seems to be much more *popular* than I ever expected—Archdeacon Singleton finds 'nothing radical in it'!!

If you could fall in with a copy of the Scotch Worthies I want it to give away.[53]

[no signature]

52. On 12 December 1837 Thomas would write to his brother John about his 'dream of a Series of Literary characters, Homer, Virgil, Dante, Shakspeare Cervantes, Voltaire &c.' in essay form.

53. John Howie, *Biographia Scoticana* (1775), detailing the lives of dozens of Scottish religious figures.

Figure 4: Elizabeth Paulet, *Notre Dame de Chelsea* (1844), Thomas Carlyle Papers, Rare Book & Manuscript Library, Columbia University in the City of New York

3

'The Lion's Wife': 1838–1842

By no means did Thomas awake and 'find himself famous' after the publication of The French Revolution in May 1837, as Byron had after the publication of Childe Harold's Pilgrimage in 1812. But as that year went on he became established in the literary landscape—in Britain but also in the United States (aged forty-three, though; not Byron's twenty-four). Sartor Resartus would finally be published in book form in London in July 1838, Critical and Miscellaneous Essays would follow a year later, and though the money took time to catch up it eventually did in 1839 and released the Carlyles from financial anxiety, especially when added to the income from his four annual lecture series of 1837–1840.

Never one to rest on his laurels—or anything else, come to that—Thomas threw his energies into any number of campaigns, each (one might say) concerned with taxation on knowledge: the penny post, the founding of the London Library, and author's copyright. In the end, they would all be successful: in 1840, 1841 and 1842, respectively. He also (on the one hand) started serious preparatory work for something on Oliver Cromwell and (on the other) deepened his interest in contemporary working-class unrest among the Chartists, seeking electoral reform. In March 1839 he first met a prodigious socialite and lion-hunter, Lady Harriet Baring, of whom we shall hear more in Chapter 5.

That Jane was gratified by this success can be in no doubt. But as it was won in some ways at her expense, her response became ambivalent and accordingly ironic: in a letter of 26 August 1838 Thomas refers to her as 'thou sharptempered Goody' (CL 10: 154), which is significant. Recovering from the wintry new year of 1838 she supported her husband at his second set of lectures in May (at first, she wrote, 'as white as a pocket handkerchief—but he made no gasping and spluttering as I found him doing last year at the fourth lecture'), and then saw the back of him in summer as he went to Scotland from August to October. The following year—Mrs Welsh having visited Chelsea in February and March, and Thomas having lectured once more, on European Revolutions—the couple took the unusual step of holidaying in Scotland together from July to September, though Jane spent time with her mother by the sea at Ayr, too. In May 1840 the last series of lectures would take place, on heroes and hero-worship, and Jane would take shelter from a hot summer in her narrow, tall, cool house near the Thames. The following winter was a harsh one, and Jane remained confined, but in April she took advantage of Thomas's absence for one of her Herculean spring-cleans before joining him in Scotland in July for an unsuccessful and expensive holiday at Newbie, on the Solway Firth.

Amidst this rhythm of Thomas's social endeavours and his lecturing, the couple and the house were extending their influence steadily. In early 1840, for example, Thackeray and Dickens joined the circle, as did Tennyson by the autumn. But they were also visited the following year by Geraldine Jewsbury, the strong-minded daughter of a Midlands cotton manufacturer, who had contacted Thomas for literary advice after her father's death in 1840 and who would become a demanding and possessive friend of Jane's thereafter. Frances Wedgwood, Erasmus Darwin, John Forster and Catherine Macready also attached themselves to Jane in this period, as did, most preciously of all, the exiled Italian nationalist Giuseppe Mazzini. Mazzini's importance for her is hard to over-estimate but also hard to quantify, as her letters to him do not survive. He told his mother that Jane was 'the only woman here who knows and understands me', and it is clear that she shared confidences with him about her relations with both her mother and her husband, the extent of which we can only guess at. Another vital import at No. 5 was the most colourful of all the servants, straight out of the novels of Tobias Smollett: 'Kirkcaldy Helen' Mitchell, who plays a kind of working-class Scottish alter ego alongside Jane, expressing on her behalf reactions she could not voice herself. But these life-affirming novelties notwithstanding, some old rhythms were locked into the fabric of the building, too: not least Thomas's futile and misguided sense that he should leave it and disappear to Dumfries once more, in search of a peace he might have known he could never find. 'My one hope and thought for the most part', he recorded in his journal at Christmas 1840,

> is that very shortly it will be over, my very sore existence ended in the bosom of the Giver of it—at rest somehow. Things might be written here which it is considerably better not to write. As I live, and have long lived, death and Hades differ little to me from the earth and life.[1]

The best he could offer Jane in this vein, it seemed, was 'mutual misery' (CL 13: 82). Not, then, an easy person to do business with; and certainly not one to appreciate and to share social and intellectual success, even with his wife. But we can take pleasure in one development, at least: it is during this period that letters from Jane become significantly more frequent. Earlier in their married life there are many gaps, but by 1841 the Collected Letters editors were able to say that 'Jane's part now increases [. . .] from this point her own brilliant contributions will be seen increasingly balancing Carlyle's' (CL 13: x).

1. Rosemary Ashton, *Thomas and Jane Carlyle: Portrait of a Marriage* (London, 2002), 217.

To Leigh Hunt, Chelsea, early 1838?

My dear Sir—

My Husband is just gone out leaving orders with me to write you a note inviting you to come to tea— I said it was of no use; you were predetermined *not* to come, especially if *I* asked you— He answered I could try at least, and tell you he had finished his days work, and was really very desirous you would come. So behold I try! and what can I do more? I cannot annihilate your laziness, or dislike, or pet, or caprice or whatever it is that makes you so obstinately stay away— I cannot make you as happy to come to us, as we are to have you come. I can but (as Edward Irving recommends in all such emergencies) '*pray to the Lord*'! and assure you, that in *your* solitary instance at least, I break thro my established prenciple of liking, in throwing away a very large quantity of affection on you which you seem totally insensible of and of course ungrateful for— Mrs Hunt also takes but a Motherless charge of me— Bless you all nevertheless

Yours sincerely /
Jane W Carlyle

To Frances Wedgwood, Chelsea, 7 March 1838

My dear Mrs Wedgwood

My Husband is gone to dine with your Husband, and 'Erasmus,' at Mr Erskine's. Thence they proceed together to a '*flare up*' at Miss Martineaus; (which I wish success to with all my heart—at lowest, that it may consume its own smoke!) And now while these our so-called Lords and Masters are following their pleasing without us; a pretty idea is come to me, that I all alone *here* will have a little quiet talk with you all alone *there*. For I feel a sympathetic assurance that you are alone at this moment even as I am—your feet on the fender as mine are—looking into the fire as I was doing until I began to write. And if any one says you are idly employed or that I was idly employed I declare the fault-finder to be entirely ignorant of what *looking into the* fire means. For my part I find it the very hardest work I ever apply myself to: my eyes are no sooner fairly rivetted on the red embers, than I seem to be changed into the Dove of the Ark sent forth 'ere yet the waters were abated,' to fly and flutter in all directions, finding no rest for the sole of its foot.[2] For

2. Genesis 8: 8–9.

you, indeed, with your better and happier nature, the world can never, I should think, become as a watery waste—there must always be some dry land—some green sunshiney spot where you see little children playing among the flowers! but even you I am sure often feel fatigued, as with a long journey, after a long look into the fire: and the Baby's-cap which you might have made in the interim, or the volume of *Western Travel*[3] you might have read would not have proved such full occupation. Dear Mrs Wedgwood when shall I see you again? I hope and pray that for once the battle may be for the strong, and the Secretaryship for the man that deserves it! And that we shall know you again in the place whence you can be so ill spared. A woman who, as my Husband might say is no *Chimera*, no *Incarnated formula*, but a *Reality*—a *genuine woman* is so great a rarity with us in this *dishumanizing* City: that such a one, when known of, should be sought after, and brought back, in spite of all obstacles; like the *Twelfth Statue for the vacant pedestal*, in the Arabian Tale. If you were to be recovered, as the Statue was by slaughter of giants and wildbeasts, I should entertain high hopes at present: for *Cavaignac* were the very man for such an exploit! and Mr Wedgwood has engaged him to visit you. They met here one evening and liked each other. The only happy combination that took place! The rest of the people were the most incompatible that I even, who am remarkable for making the worst assorted parties in Nature, could have brought together. Mr Darwin has often helped me at such a Deadlift, but that evening he seemed to have privately made up his mind, that he would not speak a word or move a muscle, except according to his own sweet will, tho' it were to save us all from perdition! Indeed, it strikes me that he and the whole of us are '*demoralizing*' since you went—there are wars and rumours of wars, tempests in teapots, *flare-ups*, rather of the tar-barrel sort.[4] 'The thing which is to day is (not) the same that was yesterday, nor will be tomorrow.' We want *reality*, stability, composure of soul—above all it seems to me, we all of us want a sound sleep!

3. Harriet Martineau, *Retrospect of Western Travel* (1838), based on her 1834 travels in the United States. Hensleigh Wedgwood was a police magistrate: indeed he presided over the first stages of a trial that eventually resulted in the last execution for sodomy in Britain (1835), and petitioned the Home Secretary for a commutation of the sentence. But he also had ethical objections to the administration of oaths, so he resigned his post and left London in poverty with his wife. Later this year he was appointed Registrar of Metropolitan Public Carriage: perhaps that is the 'Secretaryship' Jane alludes to.
4. It is not easy to establish what Jane had in mind: there was an 'Opium War' in the Far East, an incipient Afghan War in the Middle East, and the less alarming Mormon-Missouri and 'Pastry' wars in the Americas. The nineteenth-century press was like our own in its appetite for conflict.

My Husband is to give new Lectures in May, on the subject of National Literature. This time he positively set his face against *'fire-eating'* in Willis's Rooms, amidst Harp-players and Dancing Masters and such like; whereupon Mr Darwin after much rumaging has found him a less *fashionable* quarter (near Portman Square) where he expects to feel less like a Mountebank.[5] Meanwhile his frequent prayer is 'O for a little impudence and good health'! but as for the first *non omnia possunt omnes* [everyone cannot do everything]! He can do much, but he cannot be *impudent* for the life of him: and a vehement longing for *good health* is apt to defeat its object.

Mr Scott lectures in Exeter Rooms and Darwin goes to hear him!! Such changes doth fleeting time procure! Time and Mrs Rich.[6]

I have been interrupted so often in writing this letter that I have lost all heart in making it longer. I am plainly writing with adverse Fates, and if I insist on going on shall probably spill *all* the ink (as I have already done part) over my paper, or in some other way render it quite useless— So good night and God bless you! Yours affectionately

Jane Carlyle

To Thomas Carlyle, Chelsea, 18 September 1838

My *sweet* Love

Thank you deeply for your kind letter—which (to rise a degree beyond your Mother) made me as *light* as swan-down. I send you our Doctor [John Carlyle] very grey, very thin, but healthy, and locomotive as ever— I wish I could send him with one *certainty* in his pocket—in which case he would be a help more meet for you—but the man is born to IFS as the sparks fly upwards,[7] lives and has his being in a *grand*

5. Willis's Rooms, better known as Almack's, were on King Street, St James's, in London's exclusive West End, and were frequently used for lectures and readings. Portman Square is a mile to the north-west, in less fashionable Marylebone.
6. Perhaps Alexander John Scott (1805–1866), theologian and eventually professor of English at University College London, who published *Lectures, Expository and Practical, on the Epistle to the Romans* in 1838. I assume they were given at the long-since demolished Exeter Hall, on the Strand, which frequently hosted religious addresses. (The Hall replaced the Exeter Exchange, a menagerie where Byron saw a pair of tigers in 1813.) Mary Rich was the wife of British traveller and Assyriologist Claudius Rich, who died young in Persia in 1821, after which she returned to London and took up residence in Woolwich.
7. An oft-used expression: Job 5: 7.

peutêtre[8]—and the only thing one can do alongside of him is to be oneself as *positive* as twenty mules— Do *you* then my precious good indulge in no *iffing* that can be avoided; but say in all cases *I* WILL or I *will not*—for instance 'I *will* go back to my wife that is waiting for me in Chelsea within a *fixed* time' (as short as you like—say a fortnight—a week) and '*I* will *not* go to Italy for one—to be "dadded a abreed" [led abroad] and have my bits of glimpses into "*a glancing future*" all obscured again under a mist of purposelessness and idle dreams.['] Rome may be the best place for him—but for you it were great nonsense to quit the pool you have waited by so long, just at the instant when the Angel is beginning to trouble the waters—[9] You think, infatuated man that you are, it is the greatest of hardships to have a house and wife tied about your neck, so that you cannot follow every fly-away impulse, but I declare, looking at the matter in pure abstraction, I consider it to have been a real blessing for you, that you have been hindered in this way from bolting out into infinite space[10]—where you may rely on it you would not have the faculty of always '*bobbing up*' again like Ulysses— And I also regard it as a blessing for you that you have had to *work* on the impulse of *hunger*—If you had been born to the fortune of Byron[11] I question if you would have done any good in the world, or if I should have been able to exist beside you for above six months at longest— As to John I should not like to have any hand in deciding him one way or other—this only is clear to me; better to be a peripatetic Doctor than no Dr at all—and it is to be strongly doubted that he will never screw himself up to practicing his profession with the necessary energy and endurance in London.

—The Elliots returned last Thursday so I am again carriageless, returned to an earth not worthy of me— I have still however the occasional disposal of the great Sterlingian Apparatus and the Darwingian Cab—the former a thing to stand amazed before as in presence of the infinite—such '*Bays*'—! such a coachmanized Tiger! and footmen!

8. The 'great perhaps': famous deathbed remark made by French writer Rabelais (1490?–1553) about life after death.
9. John 5: 3–4, on a miraculous healing pool for the halt, the lame and the sick: 'For an angel went down at a certain season into the pool, and troubled the water: whosoever then first after the troubling of the water stepped in was made whole of whatsoever disease he had.' Thomas's career was at a breakthrough moment after *The French Revolution* and the final publication of *Sartor Resartus*; to go abroad with John would be to lose an opportunity.
10. Shakespeare, *Hamlet*, II. ii. 255; Homer's hero of *The Odyssey* was the survivor of many marine adventures.
11. In point of fact, Byron was born into conditions of some penury, his father having run through most of the poet's mother's inheritance; but he did have fortune in the sense of luck.

both of them with new buttons and gold banded hats &c &c— But I have a sort of idea that it will all be destroyed one day by spontaneous combustion— I have got the medallion of John—not like I think, but it gives the liveliest contentment to any body else—so I am sure I need not be discontented— And I have something more to the purpose—dear Good—Lawrence's last sketch of *you*![12] Where on earth were our eyes when we did not perceive it to be one of the most spirited likenesses? He is to do me a large one in oil on his return from Italy, and in the mean time this is very satisfactory indeed.— It was hanging on the wall at my back the day after it came and I had forgotten it for the moment—when I saw it, all of a heap, in the mirror of my work-box, looking over my shoulder as it were—whereupon I gave a loud scream—(screamichen!)[13] [I]t is a strange deffective yet superior thing! gives the idea the old Ass says of 'a man whose chronic state is *moroseness* and his occasional impulses ferocity'!— Helen says 'its his livin sell when he's in his best clais'!— I forgot to tell you a bit of comfort last time—the *Tin-man* is to move at Christmas— He is building!—a fine house with a pond for gold fish and another for silver—and a third for Waterfowl! all this being in Beaufort Street!!— [B]ut at any rate the dogs are all sunk dumb long ago— In fact nothing can be quieter than we are here at present—

Since writing the above I have had 'a breath of beloved Hampstead'! I happened to say on my last drive with the Sterlings that I had never been there yet—whereupon the Tempest exclaimed 'by Jove! Mrs Carlyle! why DID you not mention that when we started'? [B]ecause I said having lived four years without seeing Hampstead I hoped (knowing his business that day lay else where) that I might still hang together four and twenty hours without seeing it— But an expedition to Hampstead must be appointed on the spot, and today it took effect. So you are to suppose me returned with such an accession of ideas as was to be gained by driving all thro' that Cokney paradise and gaping a few minutes over what they call a 'heath'![14] Indeed that sort of ideas are the only

12. English portrait-painter Samuel Laurence (1812–1884) did a pigeon-pair of chalk sketches of Thomas and Jane: two of the most winning images we have of their younger selves. They remain at the Carlyle House on Cheyne Row.
13. One of Thomas's pet names for Jane. The 'old Ass' is Edward Sterling, the 'Stimabile'. It is the inimitable housemaid 'Kirkcaldy Helen' Mitchell who comments that the portrait is 'his living self, when he's in his best vein (or groove, or mood)'.
14. Hampstead Heath is set on a high ridge to the north of central London, running between Hampstead and Highgate. The campaign to save it for public access began in the late 1820s and continued to the 1870s. It remains unashamedly a cockney paradise, though hardly a heath in the scientific sense.

new ones I am getting in your absence—to tell the truth nothing can exceed my *dolce far niente* [sweet idleness]— The upstairs bed is all rehabilitated—and looks 'particular neat' and I have had the feathers out of both beds a-airing in the garden—and this is all that I have to say for myself in the way of household-industry— [A]s for study; I have read ONE book *The letters of Ortis*—a wersh [insipid] kind of Werter—by Ugo Fosculo[15]—and I have now commenced the *Souvenirs du Duc de Vicence*[:] promising enough— But then I flatter myself that I am laying in a little stock of strength and spirits for the winter; and in the meantime I am keeping myself very quiet and cheerful—which if not the chief end of man is surely the chief end of woman.— A woman in a state either of 'excitement' or '*melanconia*' is a sort of woman 'one does *not* like to see'—

I had a very surprising *treat* the other evening— Leigh Hunt wrote me a gracious little note inviting me to come and hear his play read[16]—and '*stand by him with some new friends*'— The said new friends turning out to be of the Taylor set[,] Margaret Gillies and her Sister &c &c—[17] One man was introduced to me very particularly—but Baron Alsdorf[18] being blethering [chattering] about his letter to you at the moment I missed the name— The introduction seemed going to turn out much like Cavaignac's and Mrs Grote's till towards the close of the business that the man and I suddenly found ourselves in the middle of the room together, apparently selected by destiny to represent the two extremes of human opinion on the question of whether *Conventionality* was or was not the strongest thing in this world— I spoke with that faith in human nature and in the force of truth which thank God I have never lost and which my observations in the *Lecture time* gave new vigour to—and the man spoke it seemed to me with a poor rascally disbelief in all that, made rabid by the fact that himself had never been believed in by any man or body of men— It was one of the curiousest *shines* [parties] that

15. Ugo Foscolo (1778–1827), Ionian-born Italian author and revolutionary, whose melodramatic and depressive novel *The Last Letters of Jacopo Ortis* (1798) certainly owes a debt to Goethe's sensational (and suicidal) *The Sorrows of Young Werther* (1774). The Napoleonic memoirs of Armand-Augustin-Louis de Caulaincourt, Duke of Vicenza (1773–1827), were published in Paris in 1837.
16. *A Legend of Florence: A Play in Five Acts*, duly published in 1840.
17. Harriet and John Taylor, Unitarians; Margaret and Mary Gillies, artist and children's author, respectively, also associated with that movement. Thomas wrote to Jane amusingly on 24 July 1836 about an abortive introduction of Cavaignac to Harriet Grote, conversationalist and biographer. Dr Southwood Smith, below, was another Unitarian, and significant authority on that key Victorian matter, health and sanitation.
18. Can this be the Charles Ernest, Baron von Alzdorf (b. 1815), who travelled to Wellington, New Zealand, in 1840 to take charge of the Commercial Hotel there, and who was killed in an earthquake in 1855?

I ever played a part in—and I cannot imagine yet where I got the courage to stand and debate there long and loud among so many people, with an elderly gentleman in breeches and evidently (in his own estimation and Miss Margaret Gillies at least) a man of mark— 'Dr'—said somebody— [']Dr what['] I asked little Lawrence who stood by me— '[D]ont you know him? Dr Southwood Smith'[.] My dear never do you get acquainted with Dr Southwood Smith if you can help it—he is a bad man or I am no physiognomist— As for the play it is plain as a pike staff why Macready would not play it—it is something far worse than '*immoral*'—'*anticonventional*'—it is mortal dull—a beautiful insipidity reigns thro'out—and for the regenerating truths it is calculated to teach the conventional heart—they would need to be *shot at it* (as we do our truths) from the mouth of a cannon, not timourosly *pleadingly tendered* to it before it were fair to expect that they should take the least effect—

But here is John come in, and I must give over this splashing as if I had all eternity and time to boot for writing in—

I will not go to Ramsgate now—the days are too short and the weather too cold for sailing and a Land journey of such extent were too fatiguing—as well as too expensive. It is probably just as well—house-robberies having been very rife in our neighbourhood—

I heard of two reviews of your poor beast[19] one of which I send—but you must bring it back as I only *borrowed* it from Saunders & Otley— The other is to the same flaming tune—in the Monthly— There *have* also been various newspaper criticisms[,] say what you will—

And so god bless you Dear and put home-tendencies into your head and feet— My love to all—even the most minute child— Write as soon as possible

Your povera piccola [poor little one]
Jane W Carlyle

To Grace Welsh, Chelsea, 7 April 1839

Dearest Mother— It is a week past on Thursday since you went away, and really that one week looks longer than all the time you were here. Parting is one of the few hardships in this world which one does *not*

19. *Sartor Resartus*, published by Saunders and Otley and reviewed in the *Metropolitan Magazine* and the *Monthly Review* in September. The *Globe* newspaper also reviewed it that month.

'use to'; indeed the last time seems always the worst. It was quite heart-breaking leaving you in that tremendous apparatus, given up as it were to an irresistible destiny; to be shot away from one like an arrow into space![20] I cried all the way home; and then sat down so *dowie* [sad] by the fire, indisposed to speak to any son or daughter of Adam. But Helen was determined I should not despond for lack of a little of her Job's comfort;[21] so she broke the silence by an announcement that we were 'out of baith dips and moulds.' 'There,' said I, giving her money, and returned to look into the fire. But she lingered as she went, and at the door she made a stand and gave a great sigh, and then broke forth, 'I declare it's no like the same hoose, sae dull and dismal-like, it's just as if a *corp* [corpse in a coffin] had gaen oot! She was so attached!' What could one do in such a case but either jump up and fell her, or burst into new weeping? Having little spirit remaining, I chose the latter alternative. Then as if on purpose to keep alive my regrets, ever so many things have turned up, since you went, that I should have liked you to have been present at. The very next evening came the French Catholic Rio,[22] that Carlyle had described to us as such a striking man. He pleased me much, tho' resembling the description in no one particular except the duskiness of his complexion. I had fancied him a stern, bigoted enthusiast, whereas he is a sort of French John Sterling; if possible even more voluble and transparent; and his Catholicism sits on him just about as lightly as John's Church-of-Englandism sits on him. I happened to ask him if he knew Cavaignac: 'Ah, who does *not* know Cavaignac by name? But *I*, you know, am a victim of *his* party, as *he* is a victim of Louis Philippe. Does Cavaignac come here?' 'Yes, we have known him long.' 'Good gracious! How strange it would be for us to meet in the same room! How I should like it!' 'Well,' I said, 'he is to dine here on Monday.' 'I will come; good gracious, it will be so strange': and he seemed amazingly charmed with his prospect. Not so Carlyle, who began, before he was well out at the door, 'Mercy Jane, are you distracted?' 'What *can* you do with these two men?' etc., etc. I assured him it would go off without bloodshed, and began to think of my *dinner.*

20. Jane frequently referred to train travel in these melodramatic terms; trains in the 1830s ran at about thirty miles per hour.
21. Job 2: 11. As *CL* tells us, 'Candles were made by dipping a wick into melted tallow or pouring wax in moulds.'
22. Alexis-François Rio (1797–1874), French art historian specialising in the medieval age, and thus of interest to both Carlyle and (in due course) Ruskin. Politically opposed to a republican like Cavaignac, who was marginalised by the conservative King Louis Philippe, crowned in 1830. In his journal (*CL*) Rio noted that Cavaignac 'was much less interesting to me than my hosts by whom I was more and more enchanted. I do not know any other man in London with conversation as inspired as Carlyle's. I wish I could recall his fine words on Goethe and the painter Hogarth whom he regards as a genius.'

In addition to the boiled leg of mutton already projected for the sake of the capers, I decided on a beefsteak pie; and, that care off my mind, I trusted in Providence that the men would not come to an explosion.

The dinner, however, could hardly be called a 'successful one.' Rio appeared on the scene at half-past three, as if he could not have enough of it. Latrade[23] came as the clock struck four. But Cavaignac— Alas! Two of his friends were on terms about blowing each other's brains out, and Cavaignac was gone to bring them to reason; and not till they were brought to reason would he arrive to eat his dinner. Now, whether the men would be brought to reason before the dinner was quite spoiled, was a delicate question that Latrade himself could not answer. So, one half hour being gone, and still no appearance of him, I was on the point of suggesting that we should wait no longer, when a carriage drove up and deposited Mrs Macready and Macready's Sister. Was ever beeksteak pie in such a cruel predicament! There was no help, however, but to do the amiable, which was not ill to do even in these trying circumstances, the visitors were such attractive sort of people. Mrs Macready asked me how I liked Harriet's Book.[24] I answered 'how do *you* like it?' She made wide eyes at me and drew her little mouth together into a button. We both burst out a-laughing, and that is the way to get fast friends. An hour and half after the dinner had been all ready we proceeded to eat it,—Rio, Latrade and we. And when it was just going off the table cold, Cavaignac came, his hands full of papers and his head full of the Devil knows what; but not one reasonable word would he speak the whole night. Rio said nothing to his dispraise, but I am sure he thought in his own mind. 'Good Gracious! I had better never be in the same room with him again!'

But there has been another Frenchman here that I would have given a gold guinea that you had seen: To-day gone a week the sound of a whirlwind rushed thro' the street, and there stopt with a prancing of steeds and footman thunder at this door, an equipage, all resplendent with skye-blue and silver, discoverable thro' the blinds, like a piece of the Coronation Procession, from whence emanated Count d'Orsay![25]

23. Louis Chassaignac de Latrade (1811–1883), another French republican in exile.

24. Harriet Martineau's first novel, *Deerbrook* (1839), concerning two young sisters' descent on an English village and their associated romantic entanglements.

25. Alfred Guillaume Gabriel Grimod d'Orsay, Comte d'Orsay (1801–1852), dandy and socialite; erstwhile travelling companion of the flashy Earl and Countess of Blessington and via them acquaintance of Lord Byron; habitué at Marguerite Blessington's London home after the Earl's death in 1829; and future close friend of the young Benjamin Disraeli. Accompanied on this occasion by Henry Fothergill Chorley (1808–1872), journalist and critic. Jane's comment about d'Orsay's looks, 'of no sex', is interesting: he has been thought to have been sexually involved with both the Earl and the Countess; he certainly married the Earl's daughter (by a previous marriage) when she was only fifteen—though the marriage did not last.

ushered in by the small Chorley. Chorley looked 'so much alarmed that he was quite alarming'; his face was all the colours of the rainbow, the under-jaw of him went zig-zag; indeed, from head to foot he was all over one universal quaver, partly, I suppose, from the soul-bewildering honour of having been borne hither in that chariot of the sun; partly from apprehension of the effect which his man of Genius and his man of Fashion were about to produce on one another. Happily it was not one of my nervous days, so that I could contemplate the whole thing from my *prie-Dieu* ['pray god': armless, straight-backed kneeling stool designed for prayer] without being infected by his agitation, and a sight it was to make one think the millenium actually at hand, when the lion and the lamb, and all incompatible things should consort together. Carlyle in his grey plaid suit, and his tub-chair, looking blandly at the Prince of Dandies; and the Prince of Dandies on an opposite chair, all resplendent as a diamond-beetle, looking blandly at *him*. D'Orsay is a really handsome man, after one has heard him speak and found that he has both wit and sense; but at first sight his beauty is of that rather disgusting sort which seems to be like genius, 'of no sex.' And this impression is greatly helped by the fantastical finery of his dress: sky-blue satin cravat, yards of gold chain, white French gloves, light drab great-coat lined with velvet of the same colour, invisible inexpressibles, skin-coloured and fitting like a glove, etc., etc.[26] All this, as John says, is '*very* absurd'; but his manners are manly and unaffected and he convinces one, shortly, that in the face of all probability he is a devilish clever fellow. Looking at Shelley's bust, he said 'I dislike it very much; there is a sort of faces *who* seem to wish to swallow their chins and this is one of them.' He went to Macready after the first performance of *Richelieu*,[27] and Macready asked him, 'What would you suggest?' 'A little more fulness in your petticoat!' answered d'Orsay. Could contempt for the piece have been more politely expressed? He was no sooner gone than Helen burst into the room to condole with me that Mrs Welsh had not seen him—such a '*most* beautiful man and most beautiful carriage! The Queen's was no show i' the worl' compared wi' that! Everything was so grand and so preceese! But it will be something for next time.'

26. 'Inexpressibles': the never-to-be-adverted-to flesh-coloured leggings always associated with the Regency dandy; by 1839 long since replaced by looser, thicker trousers properly so called.
27. *Richelieu: or, The Conspiracy* (1839), a drama about the sixteenth-century French cardinal and statesman by Edward Bulwer-Lytton (1803–1873), voluminous scribbler in a variety of formats. The play is noteworthy only for contributing the saying 'the pen is mightier than the sword' to the English language.

I have heard from Elizabeth (not Countess Pepoli yet). She says of him merely: 'one of the pleasantest things that has happened to me since I came' (the place it seems is horribly dull) 'has been a most cheerful Letter from Pepoli on leaving the Quadrant. He says he does not mean to see you till he has completed his arrangements.' [. . .]

The Coolidges called yesterday to take leave and beg an autograph.[28] I am giving away the whole of the manuscript of the *French Revolution*, in pages. She (Mrs Coolidge) asked most politely after you, and was sure I must 'miss you sadly.' Creek[29] has been but once since you went away: Carlyle was in the midst of *Deerbrook* when he came in, and gave such a smack with his teeth as could hardly escape notice, and has produced this amelioration of our lot. Rio has taken up *his* mantle, has been three times last week and comes again to-night; but he returns into Monmouthshire to-morrow and is making the best of his time.

. . . I hope my Uncle continues improving. My kindest regards to him and the rest.— Carlyle sends his kind love. He has been saying up to last night, 'One misses her much.' God bless you.

Your affectionate /
Jane Carlyle

To Margaret Carlyle, Chelsea, 5 May 1839

My dear Mother

Our second lecture '*transpired*' yesterday,[30] and with surprising success—literally surprising—for he was imputing the profound attention with which the audience listened, to an awful sympathizing expectation on their part of his momentary, complete break-down, when all at once they broke into loud plaudits, and he thought they must all have gone clean out of their wits!— But as does not happen always, the majority were in this instance in the right, and it was *he* that was out of *his* wits to fancy himself making a stupid lecture, when the fact is, he really *cannot* be stupid if it were to save his life— The short and the long of it was, he had neglected to take a pill the day

28. Joseph and Ellen Coolidge: he an international businessman from Massachusetts, she Thomas Jefferson's granddaughter.
29. For George Lillie *Craik* see Characters and Correspondents.
30. On 'Protestantism, Faith in the Bible, Luther, Knox, and Gustavus Adolphus', which eventually formed a chapter in *On Heroes, Hero-Worship and the Heroic in History* (1841).

before, had neglected to get himself a ride, and was out of spirits at the beginning— [E]ven I who consider myself a perfectly unprejudiced judge, did not think he was talking his best or anything like his best, but the '*splendids*' '*devilish-fines*,' '*most trues*' and all that which I heard heartily ejaculated on all sides, showed that it was a sort of mercy in him to come with bowels in a state of derangement, since if his faculties had had full play, the people must have been all sent home in a state of excitment bordering on phrenzy— The most practical good feature in the business, was a considerable increase of hearers—even since last day—the audience seems to me much larger than last year, and even more distinguished— The whole street was blocked up with 'fine yellow (and all other imaginable coloured) deliveries'[31]—and this is more than merely a dangerous flattery to one's vanity—the fashionable people here being (unlike our scotch *gigmen* and *gigwomen*) the most open to light (above all to *his* light) of any sorts of people one has to do with— Even John Knox, tho' they must have been very angry at him for demolishing so much beautiful architecture, which is quite a passion with the English, they were quite willing to let good be said of, so that it was indisputably true—nay it was in reference to Knox that they first applauded yesterday— Perhaps his being a Countryman of their favorite Lecturer's might have something to do with it!— [B]ut we will hope better things tho we thus speak—

You will find nothing about *us* in the Examiner of this week— Leigh Hunt who writes the notices there did not arrive at the first Lecture in time to make any report of it—having come in an Omnibus which took it in its head to run a race with another Omnibus after a rather novel fashion, that is to say, each trying which should be *hindmost*. *We* go to Lecture this year very commodiously in what is called a *Fly* (a little chaise with one horse) furnished us from a Livery stable hard by at a very moderate rate— Yesterday the Woman who keeps these stables sent us a *flunky* more than bargain, in consideration that I was 'such a very nice Lady'—showing therein a spirit above slavery and even above *Livery*— Indeed as a foolish old woman at Dumfries used to say 'every body is kind to *me*' and I take their kindness and am grateful for it without inquiring too closely into their motives— Perhaps I am a genius too as well as my Husband—indeed I really begin to think so—especially since yesterday that I *wrote down* a parrot! which was driving us quite desperate with its screaching. Some new neighbours that came a month or two ago brought with them an accumulation

31. The remark of a female domestic, many years before, on seeing fashionably painted carriages in the street: stored up by the Carlyles in typical 'coterie speech' fashion.

of all the things to be guarded against in a London neighbourhood— viz a pianoforte, a lap-dog and a Parrot—the two first can be born with as they carry on the glory within doors but the Parrot since the fine weather has been holding forth in the Garden under our open windows— Yesterday it was more than usually obstreperous—so that Carlyle at last fairly sprang to his feet declaring he could 'neither think nor live'— Now it was absolutely necessary that he should do both—so, forthwith, on the inspiration of conjugal sympathy I wrote a note to the Parrot's mistress (name unknown) and in five minutes after Pretty Polly was carried within and is now screaching from some subterrane[an] depth whence she is hardly audible— Now if you will please to recollect, that at Comely Bank I also *wrote down* an Old Maid's house-dog and an only son's pet-bantamcock you will admit I think that my writings have not been in vain.

My Mother is still in Liverpool, having been detained there by an operation which has to be performed on one of my Uncle's eyes— but as he is doing very well I suppose she will now be thinking of Templand—she was very happy here last time—and very sensible to Carlyle's kind treatment of her— He had been 'every thing' she said 'that heart could desire'— When I wonder will *you* be justified in saying as much of *me*? We have blessed weather now which makes me feel as strong again— I hope it will have the same effect on Isabella—. We have been very comfortable in our household this long while— My little fifeshire Maid grows always the longer the better—and never seems to have a thought of leaving us any more than we have of parting with her— My kindest love to all the 'great Nation'[32] into which you are grown. affectionately yours

Jane Carlyle

To Thomas Carlyle, Ayr, 18 August 1839

Dearest

It is *fifty six* miles to Ayr, the way we came, and we were as long about it, as would have taken me from Liverpool to London—to say nothing of the superior jumbling— Add to this that the fatigues of the day had to be borne on one bad sandwich, and without any particle of

32. Genesis 12: 22. Isabella was James Carlyle's wife; she gave birth to a son, Thomas, in November 1838, now five months. Margaret's clan was increasing in size.

that contentment which gives a charm to even the dinner of herbs,[33] and you will think it no shame that I arrived here in a state of wera [very] desperation. Poor old Gibson however served as a sort of spiritual feather-bed, on which the wearied ~~Cresoot~~ (I cant spell it.) (soot essence)[34] might at length fling itself down and taste of brief repose— He had tea and *fried whitings*, all prepared for us at the Lodgings—had sent in coal and candle, tea sugar and extras and shown himself as usual 'the kindest of men'— Even I could pardon his prosing, for the sake of his good-humour—a thing which I have been so little used to of late—and up to this hour my patience with him is still holding out— He had got us excellent Lodgings a dining-room about the size and shape of Mrs Colquhouns at Stock Bridge—but more plenished looking—and two very excellent bedrooms—mine, which is an attic, has curious dark nooks in it where in a revolutionary period one might secret two or perhaps even three Aristocrats—its window looks away over a *beautiful* prospect of—house-tops—and I feel in it quite a Mrs Teufelsdröck[.] The Landlady is a writers widow and looks quite satisfactory— The greatest drawbacks to the comfort of the location are its vicinity to the townclock which chimes every quarter, and rings for a long time at six in the morning with a sort of passionate solemnity which I should think must drive sleep far from every eye in Ayr— This is one great nuisance and the 'brattling and branging' of the servant maids is another— 'There never was any thing in the least like it'! late and early—dump dump, clash brash and towards breakfast time, a universal quoit-playing with all the crokery! Of course I get little sleep, but I was sleeping so wretchedly ill at Templand where there was perfect quietness that I am less irritated by the noise than I should otherwise have been— For the place itself, I can fancy it might be very pleasant to live in under conceivable circumstances— The next time we come to Scotland I think we must try 'a bit *hadin* [a little house] o'oor ain' *here*, at a proper distance from the town clock. The town and surrounding country have a look of cheerful sufficiency which is quite refreshing after the gigmanic stagnation of Dumfrieshire— There are the prettiest little villas all about, where one can fancy people living without being tempted to commit suicide—the country people look lively and intelligent and the town people actually rather cultivated—

33. Proverbs 15: 17.
34. 'Spirit of Soot' was a pet name Thomas had for Jane, 'in laughing acceptance of some particularly clever & well-deserved bit of satire she had been reporting to me' (*CL*); the chemical creosote is a distillate of tar. For William Gibson see Characters and Correspondents. *Sartor Resartus* has a wonderful passage on the rooftop vistas of its fictional town, Weissnichtwo ('don't-know-where').

and then there are capital good shops and markets, and even a circulating Library— And for people that like seabathing, better cannot be found—so good that (only think) I bathed the day before yesterday— It was an awful enterprise truly— I thought the wind would have cut me in pieces while I was stripping off my clothes—and when I ran madly into the waves to be at the end of it; it was like cramp the whole way up as the water deepened— But at last I bobbed down the head of me twice and when I ran out thereupon tho' my *wet* flannel gown was clinging all round me I felt quite warm— My Mother poured a gulp of brandy down my throat—and I ran home (only some three or four minutes walk) with little regard to appearances— I felt better for it all afternoon and meant to repeat the thing next day, but I had such a nervous horrid night and next day felt so like taking a great cold that I durst not— However the sun has shone out now for the first time and if it be as bright a day tomorrow, I have a mind to try another time—no sea can be clearer, and smoother at bottom, and the shore is all solitary as if nobody bathed at all— (I have a horrid pen and no knife so do not loose temper with this writing) Yesterday we dined with Mr Gibson at his farm, a nice house bui[lt] for the father of Lord Alloa— He hired a Phelanthon to convey us, and showed us Burns Monument birthplace &c &c[35] and Thom's Tam o Shanter and Johnny for which a pretty establishment has been built beside the monument—and having crammed us with victuals brought us back at night— 'The kindness of that man'— It was very pleasant to see all these Burns memorabilia—but as 'there is always a something' it rained on us the whole way— He is to get me the loan of a mule however and I will ride back to the place again— If it were only to get a little more speech with the ploughman who shows the monument.— who is a great philosoph[er] and deals in figurative language—

Poor Gibson has pleasure-drives enough laid out for us to occupy the next month and consume his whole stock of spare cash—but I suppose we shall be returning about the end of the week— If my mother wants to stay a few days longer however I shall not object—for I am *not* afraid of my life here— I know a very intelligent shoemaker—and several other people of that sort, and the time does not stifle me as it did at Templand— There is even in this very house a fat scullion whom

35. Scottish judge Lord Alloway had an estate outside that Scottish village, south of Ayr, with a roofless 'Auld Kirk' that features in Burns' 'Tam o' Shanter', next to which are monuments to the poet, as well as his cottage. 'Phelanthon' does not figure in *OED*; perhaps Jane meant a phaeton: a four-wheeled open carriage, ideal for touring—unless it rains.

it is cheering to talk to, she looks so struck by what one says to her, and sometimes falls into a great clash of laughter—that puts one in mind that there is such a thing as mirth in the world— I cannot write here the house feels always so *open* but I am not thro Nickelby yet[36] and I am netting at times— My Mother continues the worst-natured of women—but I let her be doing and 'keep never minding'— Once a day—generally after breakfast she tries a fall with me—and in three words I give her to understand that I will not be snubbed—privately resolving to be sore *up* in the world indeed, before I subject myself to such unreasonable usage again— I will send a newspaper on arriving at Templand—and you will then come I trust and take me away—Answer this immediately—address Post office

Kind regards to all—

[no signature]

To Margaret Carlyle, Chelsea, 27 October 1840

Dear Mother

I make no excuse for being so long in complying with your often repeated hint that I should write to you—it is for the like of '*Tom*' to '*take the hint*'—but for me, your highly original daughter-in-law, I am far beyond hints, or even direct commands, in the matter of letter-writing— I have now in fact no character to lose and make myself quite comfortable in the reflection that far from feeling any indignant surprise at my silence, my friends will henceforth receive any communication I may vouchsafe them in the course of years as an unexpected favour for which they cannot be too thankful—

What do I do with my time you wonder? with such '*a right easy seat of it*' one might fancy I should be glad to write a letter now and then just to keep the devil from my elbow— But Alicks Jenny and all of you were never more mistaken than when you imagine a woman needs half a dozen squeeling children to keep her uneasy—she can manage to keep herself uneasy in a hundred ways without *that*. For my part I am always as busy as possible—on that side at least I hold out no encouragement to the Devil—and yet, suppose you were to look thro' a microscope—

36. Dickens' third novel, *Nicholas Nickleby*, was being serialised: the penultimate instalment appeared in August 1839. Netting is surely a disappeared homecraft now: the making of fabric meshwork for hair nets, purses and so forth.

you might be puzzled to discover a trace of what I do—nevertheless depend upon [it] my doings are not lost—but invisible to human eyes they 'sail down the stream of time into the ocean of eternity' and who knows but I may find them after many days.[37]

At present I have got a rather heavy burden on my shoulders[:] the guarding of a human being from the perdition of strong liquors. My poor little Helen [Mitchell] has been gradually geting more and more into the habit of tippling—until some fortnight ago she rushed down into a fit of the most decided drunkeness that I ever happened to witness— Figure the *Head of the Mystic School* and a delicate female like myself up till after three in the morning, trying to get the maddened creature to bed, not daring to leave her at large for fear she should set fire to the house or cut her own throat— Finally we got her *bolted* into the back kitchen in a corner of which she had established herself all coiled up and *fuffing* like a young tiger about to make a spring—or like the *Bride of Lammermuir*[38] (if you ever read that profane book)— [N]ext day she looked black with shame and despair and the day following, overcome by her tears, and promises, and self-upbraidings I forgave her again very much to my own surprise— About *half an hour* after this forgiveness had been accorded I called to her to make me some batter—it was long of coming—and I rung the bell—no answer. I went down to the kitchen to see the meaning of all this delay—and the meaning was very clear, my penitent was lying on the floor dead drunk—spread out like the three legs of Man[39]—with a chair upset beside her and in the midst of a perfect chaos of dirty dishes and fragments of broken crockery—the whole scene was a lively epitome of a place that shall be nameless— And this happened at ten in the morning!— All that day she remained lying on the floor insensible—or occasionally sitting up like a little bundle of dirt—executing a sort of *whinner* [feeble whine]— We could not imagine how she came to be so long of sobering—but it turned out she had a whole bottle of whiskey hidden within reach, to which she crawled *till it was finished* thro'out the day— After this, of course I was *determined* that she should leave— My friends here set to work with all zeal to find me a servant—and a very promising young woman came to stay with me until a permanent character should turn up— This last scene '*transpired*' on the Wednesday[;] on the Monday she was to sail for Kirkaldy— All the intervening days—I held out

37. Ecclesiastes 11: 1.
38. Walter Scott, *The Bride of Lammermoor* (1819), iv.
39. The triskelion, symbol of the Isle of Man, is presumably related to its motto, 'Wherever you throw it, it shall stand', but is of mysterious origin—perhaps in Sicily.

against her pale face, her tears, her despair—but I suffered terribly for I am really much attached to the poor wretch who has no fault under heaven but this one— [O]n the Sunday night I called her up to pay her her wages and to inquire into her future prospects—her future prospects! it was enough to break any body's heart to hear how she talked of them— It was all over for her on this earth, plainly, if I drove her away from me who alone have any influence with her— Beside me she would struggle—away from me she saw no possibility of resisting what she had come to regard as her Fate— You may guess the sequel— I forgave her a third time—and a last time— I *could* not deny her this *one* more chance—the creature is so good otherwise— Since then she has abstained from drink, I believe, in *every* shape—finding abstinence, like old Samuel Johnson,[40] easier than temperance—but how long she may be strong enough to persevere in this rigid course, in which lies her only hope—God knows. I am not very sanguine—meanwhile I feel as if I had adopted a child— I find it necessary to take such an incessant charge of her—bodily and mentally—and my own body and soul generally keep me in work enough without any such additional responsibility.

Carlyle is reading voraciously great folios preparatory to writing a new book[41]—for the rest he growls away much in the old style—but one gets to feel a certain indifference to his growling—if one did not, it would be the worse for one— I think he committed a great error in sending away his horse—it distinctly did him good—and would have done him much more good if he could have 'damned the expence'— Even in an economical point of view he would have gained more in the long run by increased ability to work than he spent in making himself healthier—but a willful man will have his way— My kind love to Isabella—and all of them— I hope she is stronger now—it was all she seemed to want to be a first rate wife— I never forget her kindness to me last year—tho I do not write to her any more than to others

affectionately yours /
Jane W Carlyle

40. 'Abstinence is as easy to me, as temperance would be difficult': a remark of the inimitable essayist and critic, recorded in the memoirs of Hannah More.
41. The project that would after many domestic sufferings become *Oliver Cromwell's Letters and Speeches, with Elucidations* (1845); Carlyle's later biography of the similarly heroic figure, Frederick the Great of Prussia, would be even more draining and time-consuming.

To Susan Stirling, Chelsea, 8 January 1841

My dear Susan

I always thought you a woman of admirable good sense; and I rejoice to see that marriage has not spoiled you. This speaks well for your Husband too; for I defy any woman unless she be no better than a stone, to hinder herself from taking something of the colour of the man she lives beside all days of the year. We women are naturally so impressible, so immitative! the more shame to men if we have all the failings they charge us with! Our very self-will, I believe[,] which they make such a fuss about, is after all only a reflex of their own!

I find in your letter no less than three several proofs of this 'admirable good sense'—first you love *me* the same as ever—*that* is highly sensible in you—secondly you improve in admiration of my Husbands writings; *that* also is highly sensible—thirdly you understand that my silence means nothing but—that I am silent; and *that* (to use my Mothers favourite phrase) is sensible 'to a degree.' Indeed if my silence is indicative of any thing at all dear Susan, it indicates more trust in *your* steady sentiments of kindness towards me, than I have in the generality of people who profess to love me best—if I thought that you imagined me forgetful when I am only not making periodical affirmations of my remembrance of you, and that you were to cast me out of your remembrance in consequence, I would write certainly, would conquer my growing repugnance to letter-writing, rather than risk the loss of your affection—but I should not feel so grateful to you as now, with the assurance I have that I may give way to my indolence and keep your affection nevertheless.

In fact in my character of *Lion's* wife here I have writing enough to *do*, by constraint, for disgusting even a Duchess of Orleans[.] Applications from young Ladies for autographs, *passionate* invitations to dine, announcements of inexpressible longings to drink tea with me—all that sort of thing which as a provincial girl I should have regarded perhaps as high promotion, but which at this time of day I regard as very silly and tiresome work, fritters away my time in fractionary writing, against the grain, and leaves me neither sense nor spirit for writing the letters which would suggest themselves in course of nature. Dear Susan I am sorry to say this world looks always the more absurd to me the longer I live in it! Human beings always the more like sheep! But thank heaven I am not the shepherd set over them: so let them go their way, while we who are a little higher than the sheep go ours! Now dont be fancying that I am growing into a '*proud Pharisee*,'[42] which were even a degree

42. Luke 18: 11.

worse than a sheep! Not at all! I have a bad nervous system keeping me in a state of greater or less physical suffering all days of my life, and *that* is the most infallible specific against the sin of spiritual pride that I happen to know of.

I am better this winter however than I have been for the last *four* winters—only the confinement—for I never get across the threshold in frost—is rather irksome, and increases my liability to headach—but it is a great improvement to have no cough and to be able to keep in the perpendicular.

For my Husband he is as usual, never healthy, never absolutely ill—protesting against 'things in general' with the old emphasis—with an increased vehemence just at present, being in the agonies of getting underway with another book. He has had it in his head for a good while to write a life of Cromwell and has been sitting for months back in a mess of great dingy folios, the very look of which is like to give me lock-jaw. [. . .]

What a likeable man, by the way, your Brother in Edinr is. So intelligent and so unpretentious—a combination not often to be found in Edinr, so *quietly* clever and *quietly* kind. I love *quiet* things, and *quiet* good things still carry me to enthusiasm. Tho' for the rest, my quality of enthusiasm is pretty well got under— God bless you dear— Kind regards to your husband and sister— Carlyle joins me in all good wishes your affectionate J Carlyle

Need I tell you that I am always very happy to have a letter from you

To John Sterling, Chelsea, circa 9 March 1841

My dear John—'after all'![43]

In God's name *be* 'a hurdygurdy,' or whatever else you like![44] You are a good man anyhow, and there needs not your '*dying*' to make me know this at the bottom of my heart, and love you accordingly. No—my excellent Sir, you are a blessing which one knows the value of even *before* one has lost it: and it is just because I love you better than most

43. More coterie speech. Thomas explains (*CL*): '"Poor fellow, after all!" was very often the *finish* of my Brother [John] in summing up his censures of men;—so often that we had grown to expect it, and banter it.'
44. Sterling forsook the church for poetry; the hurdy-gurdy is a cranked, droning, solo folk string instrument: a self-deprecating metaphor for self-expression as mere noise.

people that I persecute you as I do—that I *flare up* when you touch a hair of my head (I mean my *moral* head)—so now we are friends again, are we not? If indeed thro' all our mutual impertinences we have ever been anything else!

You see I am very lamb-like today—indeed I could neither '*quiz*' nor be 'polite' to you today for the whole world—the fact is, I also have had a fit of illness which has softened my mood, even as yours has been softened by the same cause. These fits of illness are not without their good uses for us people of *too poetic* temperaments—for my part I find them what the touching of their Mother Earth was for the giants of Old[45]—I arise from them with new heart in me for the battle of existence—and you know, or ought to know what a *woman* means by new heart—not new brute force as you men understand by it—but new power of loving and enduring—

We have been really in a rather deplorable plight here for a good while back—ever since a certain trial about a patent! So strangely are things linked together in this remarkable world!— My poor Man of Genius had to sit on a Jury two days—to the ruin of his whole being physical, moral, and intellectual—and ever since he has been *reacting* against the administration of British Justice to a degree that has finally mounted into Influenza[46]—while I poverina [poor thing] have been reacting against his reaction—till that malady called by the Cocknies 'mental worry' fairly *took me by the throat*—and threw me on my bed for a good many days—and now I am but recovering—as *white* as the paper I write upon, and carrying my head as one who had been making a failed attempt at suicide—for in the ardour of my medical practice I flayed the whole neck of me with a blister— So you see it is a good proof of affection that I here give you, in writing thus speedily, and so long a note— God bless you dear John, and all that belongs to you

With all my imperfections believe me ever, faithfully and affectionately yours Jane Carlyle

No Lectures to be this Spring or ever more— God willing

45. The story of Antaeus, in Greek myth, who recovered himself in conflict as Jane describes.
46. It would be hard to imagine anyone less well suited to jury service than Thomas, especially on a case regarding theft of patent in a cotton-carding machine in Manchester: 'Maddest thing I ever saw,' he recorded; 'clear to myself in the first half hour [. . .] Intolerable suffering, rage, almost despair (and resolute[io]n to quit London) on my part' (*CL*).

To John Sterling, Chelsea, 29 April 1841

My dear John

I do not know whether for you as for old Burton 'a woman in tears be as indifferent a spectacle as *a goose going barefoot*'?[47] If so; I make you my compliments, and you need not read any further! But if you have still enough of human feeling (or as my Husband would call it '*Minerva-press-tendency*')[48] about you, to feel yourself more or less *comoved* by such phenomena; it may interest you to know, that on opening your letter the other day, and beholding the little 'feminine contrivance' inside, I suddenly and unaccountably fell a-crying as if I had gained a loss! I do not know what of tender and sad and '*unspeakable*' there lay for my imagination in that lace article folded up—unskillfully enough—by man's fingers—*your* fingers—and wrapped round with kind written words! but so it was. I wept—and if this was not receiving your remembrance in the *proper* way—I beg of you to read me no *lecture* on the subject—for your lectures are hateful to me beyond expression, and their only practical result is to strengthen me in my own course—

My Husband is not returned yet—is now at his Mothers in Scotland— He will come I suppose the beginning of next week— These three weeks of solitude have passed very strangely with me— I had been worn out with what the Cocknies call 'mental worry'— His Jurytrial, his Influenza, &c all things had been against me! For the first time in my life I could sympathize with Byrons Giaour[49]—and, so soon as I had the house all to myself, I flung myself on the sofa with the feeling

'I would not, if I might be blest;
I want no paradise but *rest*.'

And accordingly the scope of my being ever since has been to approximate as nearly as possible to nonentity And I flatter myself that my efforts have been tolerably successful— Day after day has found me stretched out on my sofa with a circulating Library book in my hand—which I have read, if at all, in [George] Darley's fashion 'with one eye shut, and the other not open'—evening after evening[.] I have dreamt away in looking into the fire, and wondering to see myself here in this great big absurdity of a world! In short my existence since I was

47. Proverb employed by Robert Burton in his miscellany, *The Anatomy of Melancholy* (first edition 1621 and ultimately reprinted in 1800). A favourite with Thomas.

48. A late eighteenth- and early nineteenth-century London-based publishing house, famed for its addictive Gothic and sensational novels.

49. The enigmatic hero of Byron's sensationally successful follow-up to *Childe Harold's Pilgrimage*: first of his 'Turkish Tales' set in the Aegean (1813). Jane quotes lines 1,269–70.

left alone, has been *an Apathy tempered by emanations of the Minerva-press*! Promising— Well I shall have to return to my post again presently— one has to *die* at one's post has one not?— The wonderful thing for me is always the prodigiously long while one takes to *die*. But 'That is the mystery of this

wonderfully history
And you wish that you could tell'![50]

There is a copy of Emerson's Essays come for you here—I wish you good of them!— I find him getting affected, stilted, mystical, and in short 'a considerable of a bore'[.] A bad immitation of Carlyle's most Carlylish *translations* of Goethes most Goetheish passages!

You have to thank me for making them send you an Examiner—
God bless you—
Ever your affectionate
Jane Carlyle

To John Forster, Chelsea, 10 July 1841

dear Mr Forster

You are dreaming perhaps that I am gone away without sending the address—but no fear of that, or perhaps I should rather say, no *hope* of it! The fact is I am still here, feeling more like a Gohst that cannot get itself *laid*[51] than anything else in prose or verse! I begin to be ashamed of showing my face even to the unknown persons who pass me by in the streets— I fancy them all saying to themselves 'Chirst Almighty! what is that woman still doing above ground?' What indeed but waiting for the crowing of the cock![52]—and no cock will crow! 'Did you ever know anything in the least like it?' (as my good Mother says).— He went according to the programme, and since his arrival has written me three letters, each promising that the next should contain 'some thing definite,' and the whole three proceeding in a rapidly increasing ratio towards 'confusion worse confounded'— Today's beats the world! If you only read it you would not know whether to laugh or cry over

50. Romantic poet Robert Southey, 'A True Ballad of St Antidius, the Pope, and the Devil' (1802), 84–5.
51. Shakespeare, *Cymbeline*, IV. ii. 278.
52. Shakespeare, *Hamlet*, I. i. 157.

it!—five pages of infinitismal details about houses issuing like one of our friend Oliver's parliamentary speeches in simple zero! 'And now,' he says, 'comes the practical question what are YOU to do?' God knows! unless I set about getting a divorce, and marry again, some man with *common sense* instead of *Genius*!

Perhaps—indeed positively—if he do not forbid—I will cut the matter short at once, by putting myself and my maid on the Railway next week and going straight to the Mother that bore me—some thirty miles *beyond* that *Annan* of his—having placed *her* in safe keeping, for she cannot be trusted on her own—*you remember*!— I could then join this much-agitated *Calebs in search of a house*[53] and *make* him find one, or else resign himself with a good grace to live in the open air!— Will not this be my best course think you? 'He that considers everything will never decide on anything' and *this* man considers *everything* and some things more—

Meanwhile it is a pity you are so far off, or you might come and give me your ideas 'on things in general'—for seeing you always does me *real* good—there is something *sunshiny* about you, that cheers my gloom,—for little as you may suspect it I am in a state of almost continual blue-devils— I do not mean that your head wears a halo—like holy family—saint—or martyr-heads but you have a *sunny* manner of being that makes itself felt. [. . .]

It will be the end of next week I imagine before I can get away now

Ever affectionately yours /

Jane Carlyle

To John Forster, Chelsea, 28 August 1841

My dear Mr Forster

Mrs Macready writes to me today words which make me shudder—Voila!— 'Mr Forster consults Dr Quin[54] and is getting thin and industrious'!— [T]he 'industrious' I do not object to—'the Devil' I have heard [']is always at the elbow of an idle man'—and far be it from me, your friend, and the wellwisher of humanity to prefer that you should have so *uncanny* a neighbour— [B]ut against Dr Quin and the *thinning*

53. An oft-employed reference to *Coelebs in Search of a Wife* (1809), an earnest novel about virtuous marriage by evangelist writer Hannah More (1745–1833).

54. Frederic Hervey Foster Quin (1799–1864), founder of the Homeopathic Society in London in 1844.

I feel myself called upon to protest, seriously, loudly, with all the emphasis that is in me, which, let me tell you, is considerable!— Is this all that my little Gods have done for you?—worthless Deities that they are, fit only to be broken and cast under the grate! I will bring you a new little God from Scotland who will look better to your interests; if you will but in the meanwhile abjure Dr Quin and keep the flesh on your bones!— Do dear Mr Forster consider my words; Dr Quin is an emissary of Beelzebub! homeopathy an invention of the father of lies!— I have *tried* it, and found it wanting, I would swallow their whole doll's-medicine-chest for sixpence and be sure of finding myself neither better nor worse for it. But then they cut off ones coffee, and wine, and tea— ones cigars too, if I am not mistaken— [T]hey strip existence of all its best realities,—till at last just when one is 'almost trained to live on air,' like the Annandale man's horse, one *dies*[.] Now will you give up this nonsense which can come to nothing but harm?— It not only grieves but irritates me to think of a man with your eyes to see and heart to understand, *letting* himself be mistified with spoonfuls of cold water!— No one knows better than myself that there is a sort of reaction against medical science, as one sees it in the present day, which predisposes [one] to take up with any sort of bold quackery in preference but your life and health are precious—and so for Godsake leave Dr Quin to administer his infinitesimal dozes to fine Ladies and the like whom the world can better spare! We shall be home presently— We have quitted Newby[55] and hope never to look upon its like again— Oh such a place! Now that I am fairly done with it I look back upon it all as a bad dream! never shall I forget its blood-red, moaning sea—its cracked looking-glasses its 'industrious fleas,' its desolation and hugger-mugger [disorder] such as hath not entered into the heart of man to conceive!— This Templand looks a paradise in comparison—never before did I know how to appreciate material comforts! My heart dilates over the *white* sheets, the soft carpets, the silver spoons in which one can see oneself, and above all over one's own *clean* nice looking lady-Mothers, 'studious of household good'—[56] My Husband however with an infatuation which there is no accounting for, is off again to his barbarous Annandale— He talked of making an excursion into Cumberland and visiting the Speddings who live there [Keswick, Cumbria]— I who have not the strength of a robinredbreast left in me, would no wise undertake to accompany him. And so I wait here till he have 'come to a

55. Village and harbour on the Solway Firth, on Scotland's south-west border with England.
56. A favourite quotation, from Milton, *Paradise Lost*, ix. 233.

decision' on the grand question of what he is next to make of himself.— Most probably he will be content with a very few days of Speddingdom and then go straight to Chelsea— I shall in that case go off to Harriet Martineau in the first instance and then home by railroad— You know we never travel *together*—he does not like the *fash* [bother] of a woman with band-boxes—

If you like to send me one line to say how you are, it will find me here for a week yet at all events Templand—Thornhill—Dumfries [. . .]

God bless you— My Mother desires to be kindly remembered to you—

Ever affectionately yours /
Jane Carlyle

To Thomas Chalmers, Chelsea, 22 October? 1841

My dear Sir

That letter from you 'all to myself,' as the children say, made me both proud and glad. My romantic journey with you thro' beautiful dream-like places, seen then for the first time, and the last, with poor Edward Irving following desperately in our track, your and your wife's kindness to the audacious stranger-girl,—all *that* was not likely ever to die out of my recollection: but in reading, here, at Chelsea, kind words to me under your own hand; it seemed as if I were still hearing your voice in *the improvised cart*, amidst lochs and hills, or in the steam-boat on the Clyde! I have *seen* you, however, more recently than you think—both seen and heard you, while I was the last person you were dreaming of— Some years ago, when you preached in the Swallow-Street-Chapel[57] I was sitting there looking wistfully in your face, and feeling, at the *rousing* you were giving the people, almost as if I had a hand in it! It was the Preacher of *my* country, the Apostle of *my* youth, whom they were there listening to in breathless attention; and I felt as if I had a part and lot in you which *they* had not— I took such a long look at you in coming away that I think you must have felt some emotion *at your heart* without knowing what could be the cause of it! But I was no longer the head-long young Lady that used to start away at a tangent and catch people by the skirts in the open street; 'actually believing' as

57. A Presbyterian church off Piccadilly in London's West End, demolished in 1915.

my sarcastic uncle used to tell me 'that every body was as pleased to see me, as I to see every body'! I could still have found in *my heart* to run after you, and catch you by the skirt, and take my chance! but my *head* protested against a procedure so startling, so affronting to all the *conv-enances* [propriety] of this world. I feared to importune you—to make a fool of myself—and so—let you go—with a sigh!— Next time that you come to London, you will perhaps be kind enough to tell me how you may be arrived at in a way more suitable to my years, and grave manners; or perhaps you will find your road to Chelsea, if it were only to give yourself the benevolent pleasure of seeing how improved I am—*in common decency*—whether or no in anything else; I never feel perfectly sure! Meanwhile I will read your Mrs Marshalls books—very thankful to have them recommended to me by *you*, just at a crisis in my history when I was feeling 'rather exquisitely' that the generality of books do not 'touch upon *my* crime,' as the strangler Burke neatly phrased it.[58] I do not disclaim the opportunities of making them more known which you attribute to my position, as my position is not of *my* making—and in all modesty I may own to its *publicity*.

My dear Mother, thank God is still spared to me, and enjoying tolerable health. I spent a month in Dumfriesshire with her this summer—after a separation of two years. I often think, because perhaps, having no children of my own, I am interested in finding reasons for not regretting it—how little good poor Mothers get of their married daughters, whom they have had such a world of plague in bearing, and nursing up, and training, and teaching, until they could shift for themselves! She will be heartily gratified by your remembrance of her, which I forwarded in my last letter.

My husband is upstairs with his inkstand and books—*au secret* [in solitary confinement]—in so very strict a sense that even *I* dare not intrude upon him to tell him that I am writing to you—otherwise doubtless he would send some answer to your message, which I can answer for it he *looked* gratified in receiving—

Be kind enough to remember me *affectionately* to Mrs Chalmers, on my own account, and also on poor Edward Irving's who always talked of her to me with grateful affection. Alas! what traces of himself has that noble spirit left on this earth!—a few shrieking bewildered men collecting the rabble—and the police—at street corners! But surely *that* cannot be all! '[T]hrow thy bread on the waters and thou shalt find

58. Margaret Hermiston Marshall, of Manchester, was the author of numerous Christian tracts; William Burke was a partner in the notorious 'Burke and Hare' murders and pathological redistributions in Edinburgh, 1828.

it after many days.'[59] He threw his bread on the waters and—his life-blood after it—shall it not be made good to him even here?—

ever cordially and respectfully yours
Jane Carlyle

To Isabella Carlyle, Chelsea, 10? November 1841

My dear Isabella

The packages arrived last night all safe and satisfactory— So that we have only been out of meal *one night*!— This will seem to you hardly credible; but so it is, whether by natural or miralculous means, the little bag of meal we brought along with us—not only became quite excellent after the journey but has held out till Monday last. I was almost glad when Helen said, 'you have the last of it now'; for I was beginning to think there was something *uncanny* in the business— What a glorious prospect of food for many days! such as we starved wretches in towns hardly ever see the like of, buying as we do, I know not why, every thing in pennyworths— I can say nothing as to the taste yet of any one article for Carlyle would not leave his work last night to break up the lids—but I never saw any thing that was not *good* come out of your hands and so in my next I expect to tell you that butter cheese meal and bacon is all what the ravenous heart of man could wish it to be— I was rather provoked to have to go to bed without seeing my plaid—but now I have had it about me for the last two hours[,] and like it very much indeed— C trys to persuade me that I cannot wear such a thing here, in the idea I plainly perceive that he will *get it to himself* to go out at nights in—but I not only *can* but *will* wear it!— [I]ndeed if he kept his eyes open where women are concerned he would perceive that there are hundreds of women going about this winter in plaids of every colour and quality under the sun—so that I shall be able to get the good of my comfortable wrappage without exciting the slightest consternation to the fashionable world— I have often however regretted that I said anything about it, and so gave you all the plague of getting it made for me—you have worries enough at home; delicate as you are, without my willfully adding to them— And now I wish I could send the shawl *by post*—as I shall no longer require it—but it must wait I suppose till some

59. Ecclesiastes 11: 1.

old clothes be going—as it is not worth carriage by itself— If the plaid is not warm enough there will be nothing for me but to *wear one* of *Mrs Carlyle's blankets* which with the pretty pink border would have a rather dashing effect I imagine!

Today we have a most violent frost—every thing covered with ice—but I look out upon [it] with a surpri[si]ng indifference considering the horrible suffering which I have had from the winter of late years— My chest is evidently quite sound again, and I may not die of consumption after all—as I confidently anticipated at one time—but after all what does it signify which malady one dies of—to die of *old age* is as bad a way of it as any other—

My husband is writing an article with such a vengeance that I hardly get twenty words of him thro'out the day—it is a wonder he has not put himself off sleeping with it; but he has been having much more quiet nights since he came home— He professed to be greatly tormented in the first nights by *fleas*!—but I incline to think it had been only the ghosts of those we slew at *newby*— Any how I have heard no more of this entirely novel disturbance—

Helen goes on very comfortably—much more in her element than when you saw her— [S]he speaks from time to time of the puddlement at newby with a sort of sacred horror which is really edifying— It is a great mercy for me that I have the like of her that I can keep, and who likes to stay with me— I should be very solitary in the house if I were as at one time always changing a bad scrog [broken branch] for a worse—

Thank you for your letter, dear—*this* is not an answer to *it* but only an acknowledgement of the *good*[.] I will write again presently—when I am more at leisure—for today is *washing* day when I need to be more 'Studious of household good' than on other days of the week, and besides I have to write some consolation to my Mother who is again in a mess with her maids love-affair—but I did not wish to lose a post in telling you that everything had come safe— [L]ove to all

affectionately yours /

Jane Carlyle

A kiss to Jamie if he will take it from me—

To Grace Welsh, Chelsea, 23 February 1842

I am continuing to mend. If I could only get a good sleep, I should be quite recovered; but, alas! we are gone to the devil again in the sleeping department. That dreadful woman next door, instead of putting away the cock which we so pathetically appealed against, has produced another. The servant has ceased to take charge of them. They are stuffed with ever so many hens into a small hencoop every night, and left out of doors the night long. Of course they are not comfortable, and of course they crow and screech not only from daylight, but from midnight, and so near that it goes through one's head every time like a sword. The night before last they woke me every quarter of an hour, but I slept some in the intervals; for they had not succeeded in rousing *him* above. But last night they had him up at three. He went to bed again, and got some sleep after, the 'horrors' not recommencing their efforts till five; but I, listening every minute for a new screech that would send him down a second time and prepare such wretchedness for the day, could sleep no more.

What is to be done God knows! If this goes on, he will soon be in Bedlam; and I too, for anything I see to the contrary: and how to hinder it from going on? The last note we sent the cruel woman would not open. I send for the maid, and she will not come. I would give them guineas for quiet, but they prefer tormenting us. In the *law* there is no resource in such cases. They may keep wild beasts in their back yard if they choose to do so. Carlyle swears he will shoot them, and orders me to borrow Mazzini's gun. Shoot them with all my heart if the consequences were merely having to go to a police office and pay the damage. But the woman would only be irritated thereby into getting fifty instead of two. If there is to be any shooting, however, I will do it myself. It will sound better my shooting them on principle than his doing it in a passion.

This despicable nuisance is not at all unlikely to drive us out of the house after all, just when he had reconciled himself to stay in it. How one is vexed with little things in this life! The great evils one triumphs over bravely, but the little eat away one's heart.

[no signature]

Figure 5: Samuel Laurence, *Jane Baillie Welsh, Mrs Thomas Carlyle* (1838), Carlyle House, © National Trust Images

4

'Alone, Alone in the World': 1842–1843

Out of nowhere, Grace Welsh died of a stroke on 25 February 1842, aged only sixty.

'The strongest natures', Froude suggested as regards Jane's reaction to her mother's death, 'suffer worst from remorse.'[1] *We have few letters from her in the immediate aftermath, but Mazzini witnessed her devastation. 'Madame Carlyle', he told his mother,*

> is very sad, firstly, as is natural, at the loss of her mother; then because she remains alone, alone in the world: she has no children; her husband is good, but like all such writers, he lives only in ideas, in his own books, in short in the brain more than in the heart.[2]

In March Jane returned heartbroken to Chelsea from Liverpool—where she had broken down, halfway to Templand, having been told her mother was unwell—accompanied by her cousin Jeannie ('Babbie'), who became a surrogate younger sister, companion and confidante while Thomas wound up his mother-in-law's property (glad perhaps to be away from home and his struggles with the Cromwell project). At a distance, however, he made a series of typical blunders: one involving another proposed resettlement at Craigenputtoch, the second to do with giving Jane's father's desk to his brother Alick, for whom Jane had never cared. (In the end that desk would come to Cheyne Row: see 9 August 1865, below.) His side of the correspondence suggests that their relationship hit a low point as a result; his mistakes also produced in her an absolute, even defiant, commitment to life at her home in Chelsea. She would not revisit Scotland for eight years.

By early May he was home, and in August they wisely took separate holidays: Thomas to the Low Countries, Jane to the Buller family in Suffolk. In October Jeannie returned to Liverpool, and one of Jane's most important correspondences began, though it would cool in time as a result of what Jane saw as Jeannie's neglect after her marriage in 1853. Though Thomas visited various East Anglian sites associated with Cromwell, progress was nowhere to be seen and the end of the year

1. John Clubbe (ed.), *Froude's Life of Carlyle* (London, 1979), 404.
2. Rosemary Ashton, *Thomas and Jane Carlyle: Portrait of a Marriage* (London, 2002), 229.

found them bunkered down in Chelsea: Jane suffering her normal suite of influenzas, Thomas battering his head against a biographical brick wall. In the new year of 1843 he temporarily abandoned Cromwell and completed the compelling curate's egg, Past and Present. It would be his most important contribution to the 'Condition of England' debate, and mark his final arrival on the literary scene—not that Jane paid it much mind.

The next major household event was a visit from Geraldine Jewsbury, whom Thomas invited for two or three weeks but who stayed for five, from early February on. Jewsbury behaved presumptuously and made eyes at Thomas with the reverse of success. Husband and wife alike were glad to see the back of her, but her friendship with Jane recovered, not least because up in Manchester she helped Jane rescue Elizabeth and Juliet Mudie, daughters of a deceased Scottish author who had fallen on hard times in London. At around this time Thomas first became involved with Lady Harriet Baring: wholeheartedly representative, as Jane would point out, of the 'do-nothing' ruling class Thomas had excoriated in Past and Present. Astutely enough, Jane recognised Baring as an 'Intellectual Circe' who had managed to seduce male Victorian intellectuals from Mill to Thackeray by virtue of her commanding but flattering personality. In late May, accordingly, Jane paid a visit. 'I liked her on the whole,' she told Babbie:

> —she is immensely *large*—might easily have been one of the *ugliest* women living—but is almost beautiful—simply thro the intelligence and cordiality of her expression— I saw nothing of the impertinence and hauteur which people impute to her—only a certain *brusquerie* of manner which seemed to me to proceed from exuberant spirits and absence of all affectation— She is unquestionably very clever—just the wittiest woman I have seen—but with many aristocratic prejudices—which I wonder *Carlyle* should have got over so completely as he seems to have done—in a word I take her to be a very loveable spoilt Child of Fortune—that a little *whipping*, judiciously administered would have made into a first rate woman— (*CL* 16: 184)

The joking attitude would return to haunt her in future years.

In July Thomas escaped once more, to South Wales and thence to Annandale. He would return in October, and his absence gave Jane an opportunity to indulge her love-hate relationship with No. 5 and the tradesmen who were employed to renovate it. (Rent from Craigenputtoch had reverted to Thomas since Grace's death, so the financial case was made for the work.) In August she could stand it no more and—after a day-trip to the East End to hero-worship the Irish evangelist of teetotalism, Father Theobald Mathew—took the opportunity to visit the Isle of Wight with Edward Sterling to visit John, then living at Ventnor. Typically, she never made it but after a few days ran back to Chelsea from Ryde, not least to supervise the alcoholic Helen Mitchell and the infestation of the mattresses that had broken out in her absence. Thomas's satisfaction with the Cheyne Row makeover on his return was grudging, to put it mildly, and 'the old eternal story commenced again' of settlement somewhere, anywhere, free of noise and disturbance. Enter the builders once more at the end of October, with plans for insulation, ventilation and remuneration. Thomas picked up the fight with Cromwell, and Jane had the relief of an anarchic Boxing Day party with Dickens in the spotlight. Another year was done.

To Eliza Aitken (née Stodart), Chelsea, 3 June 1842

My dear Eliza

I *know* that I wrote *part* of a letter to you some few weeks ago—immediately after receiving your last—but whether I finished it, and sent it off or whether it shared the fate of many others of my late undertakings and came to an untimely close, I cannot remember, tho' it were to save my life!— From this you may infer that my memory is tolerably bad—indeed all about me has been tolerably bad this long while—and I do not feel as if I could ever gather myself up into the old state again in this world.— Parted as I had been from my Mother so many years and with so many new objects of interest about me it was not to have been foreseen that her loss could have so completely changed the whole face of my existence—indeed I had never thought about losing her—her life seemed always better than my own,— What I had thought about, and always the longer the more anxiously, was getting her beside me again that I might show her more love and care in her old age than in the thoughtlessness of my heart I had done heretofore— And she had promised me not to keep me unquiet by passing any more winters in that lonely place [Templand]— Had just promised me that 'if it pleased God we should meet this summer, it should be all arranged according to my wish'— So many fine schemes I had in my head for her future comfort!—too late—for her death was already on her and I did not know it— She had taken every pains and forced those about her to take every pains to keep me in ignorance of her state—'a journey at that season would be so dangerous for me.'— All her last weeks seemed one continued thought about *me*—to ward off anxiety from me while she lived and to soften the shock for me should she die— [I]n a letter she wrote to Dr Russel—after many directions about what was to be done for me if I *must* be sent for[—]

she concluded with these words which stick for ever in my heart—'for Jeannie must be saved in *every* way—or there is much to be dreaded'— And when the first stroke came upon her, Margaret Macqueen being by—she uttered no thought for her own future[,] only in sinking down exclaimed 'I am dying Margaret! Oh my poor Jeannie'— On the Saturday I received a letter from her—tender and cheerful as all her late letters had been— She had written the day before[,] she said[,] and had nothing new to tell me—but as there was no post in London on Sunday if I was kept waiting till Monday I 'would be making myself uneasy again'!—and at the time I read that letter she was already dead!— On the Monday came no letter from her as promised—but one from the Dr stating her to be dangerously ill—yet not precluding all hope—for he feared the blow for me altho at the time he wrote he had no hope himself— [O]f course I set out by the next Railway train—not despairing—Oh no—or I *could* not have gone— I thought I had little hope—but when all hope was taken from me I found that I had had much. You know the rest— I travelled all night in the cruellest suspense and arriving in Liverpool in the morning was told that my uncle and Walter were already gone—to her funeral!— Oh Bess is it not a wonder that I kept my senses— I am better in health now—but still very feeble and nervous—and so sad!— Oh there is such a perpetual weight on my heart as I cannot describe to you— I feel as helpless and desolate as a little child turned adrift in the world! *I* who have so many friends!—but what are friends?— What is a husband even compared with ones Mother?— Of *her* love one is always so sure!—it is the only love that nothing—not even misconduct on our part can take away from us—. If the letter I began went to you, I have said all this before—for it is the only sort of thing I have to say to anyone—and accordingly I write none at all except to the few whose sympathy I have perfect confidence in—

When shall I see you again? here I mean—for I do not think I shall ever have the heart to set foot in Scotland any more— Alas Alas What a changed Scotland for me—a place of graves—

My Sweet little Cousin Jeannie [Welsh] is still here with me—a comfort so far [as] any companionship *can* be a comfort to me—

Write to me dear Eliza and do not mind my silences That I have thought of you much during *this time* is a sufficient proof of the constancy of regard

Ever your affectionate / Jane Carlyle

❧

To Margaret Welsh, Chelsea, 15 July 1842

My dear Maggie,

It was a good thought in you to send me the little purse—and I feel very grateful to you for it— This last birthday was very sad for me as you may easily suppose—very unlike what it was last year and former years—and I needed all the heartening kind souls could give me—but by your kindness and that of others the day was got over with less of a foresaken feeling than could have been anticipated. Only think of my husband too having given me a little present! he who never attends to such *nonsenses* as birthdays—and who dislikes nothing in the world so much as going into a shop to buy anything—even his own trowsers and coats; so that to the consternation of Cockney-tailors *I* am obliged to go about them— Well he actually risked himself in a Jewlers shop and bought me a very nice smelling-bottle!— I cannot tell you how *wae* [sad] his little gift made me as well as glad—it was the first thing of the kind he ever gave me in his life— [I]n *great* matters he is always kind and considerate, but all these *little* attentions which we women attach so much importance to he was never in the habit of rendering to any one—his up-bringing and the severe turn of mind he has from nature had alike indisposed him towards them—and now the desire to replace to me the irreplacable makes him as good in *little* things as he used to be in great—

Helen's[3] box arrived this morning—so like a Templand box!—alas alas—those preserves— I had thought about making some all this time—and never could bring myself to set about it—it was not only to *make* them but to *learn* to make them for me—and I had finally settled it with myself that I must be stronger before I did such out of the way things— So that in every way Helens present is welcome—most of all welcome for the kind consideration it shows for my helplessness and the quantity of really disagreeable labour she has imposed on herself for my sake— Give her my kindest love and say I will write in a day or two to herself— I have been meaning to write to her every day this week back, but the pigs have always run thro' the good intertention— Jeanie expresses surprise at the fancy of 'sending coffee to Chelsea'— but for my share I find the '*fancy*' extremely *reasonable*—considering that when I was in Liverpool I *brought* coffee from there to Chelsea— and a very good speculation it turned out—[4] Thank my Uncle for his

3. A parcel from cousin Helen Welsh, daughter of Uncle John of Liverpool—who seems to have added a 'golden kiss', probably a sovereign, to the package.

4. There is nothing absurd about coffee coming from Liverpool; even today that port (alongside Tilbury, in London) is the main point of entry to the UK for unroasted beans.

golden kiss— I am thinking seriously what to do with it—as I *never eat snaps* [gingerbread biscuits]—and besides would rather invest such an amount of capitol in some-thing of a permanent character that might remind me of him more agreeably than by an indegestion—but for my life I cannot fix upon any thing that I *need*—and to buy some-thing that I feel to be superfluity is so little in my way!— I think I shall let it lie in the purse for good luck till winter, and then buy something particular cozzy to put about my throat— [. . .]

We went down the water last night to take tea with the Chaplain of Guy's Hospital[5]—found him and his wife in the country and had to return *tea*less—rather belated and extremely cold—the consequence of which *betise* [folly] is that today I am hoarse—with a soreish head and soreish throat—so you will excuse my horrible writing

God bless you all— Ever your affectionate Cousin
Jane Carlyle

To Jeannie Welsh, Chelsea, 25 November 1842

There *is* some paper in the house today—but I absolutely *dare* not go in for it—so let us be thankful for the unfailing tho' rather prosaical resource of the Butchers book! My Darling Babbie: the 'moral satisfaction' I have in you is great! almost my only '*unmitigated* satisfaction' (as Sir R Peel[6] would say)—in the present existing state of my affairs— 'The *trail* of the *Serpent*'[7] is over all else that pretends to give me comfort or pleasure!— My Aunt Anne[8] writes to me,—as if it were great *news*— that 'happiness is not to be found in this world! it was not Gods purpose with us in sending us into it'! '[G]ood gracious!' have not I known that much for upwards of a quarter of a century and put it into a formula too for my own behoof; before *she*,—wise woman as she now thinks

5. Frederick Denison Maurice (1805–1872), academic, theologian, originator of working men's colleges, and Christian Socialist. He would later be depicted alongside Thomas in Ford Madox Brown's epochal Victorian painting *Work* (1865). Guy's is at Southwark, on the Surrey bank of the Thames, four miles downriver from Chelsea.
6. Robert Peel (1788–1850), Byron's school friend at Harrow and British Prime Minister 1834–1835 and 1841–1846, founder of the Metropolitan Police and the modern Conservative Party. The expression is inimitably Parliamentary, of just the kind the Carlyles would pick up from speech reports in the newspapers.
7. Thomas Moore, 'Paradise and the Peri', from *Lalla Rookh* (1817), 207.
8. One of the 'Edinburgh Aunts', sisters of Jane's father.

herself,—had discovered that 'Gods purpose in sending us into *it*' was *not* to run after 'the *fashion*,' a seeking of *happiness* in the very lowest walk where it could be imagined findable— It is not *happiness* which I ask of Heaven, however much I might *like* to have it (in conjunction, I believe with all my fellow-mortals, even the most philosophical—if they would but speak without cant)[;] THAT I agree to the impossibleness of, and should be a fool therefore if I did not leave it out of my prayers—but what I *do* ask of Heaven, and with ever increasing earnestness, and ever increasing protest against the 'lions in the way'[9] is *calm*—let me be sad as death if God wills it so—but let me be left in peace with my sadness!—*that* it seems to me one has a right to demand of one's fellow creatures—especially of those who profess to have our wellbeing at heart, and the unnecessary griefs which *they* cause us look to me not so much of God's sending as of the Devils! Oh but I am wrong in taking this view of the matter,—these every-day highly superfluous worries and tribulations are a part of our allotted trials, as well as the inevitable irremediable bereavements and afflictions—granted they *are* a part—but a part to be struggled against—protested against—only *submitted* to because one cannot help oneself— Why otherwise should God have planted in our hearts a sense of *justice* and of self-*preservation*? Meanwhile I have swallowed a Sedliz powder[10] which as yet has had no beneficial results— A vision of a teacupful of soup crossed my mind—but Helen was ironing and I would not trouble her to make it for me— Helen however seeing me look ill, of her own accord *broiled* and brought up (with a little air of self-complacency which it would have been a thousand pities to dash) a morsel of mutton! as opposite a thing to the tendencies of my 'interior' at the moment, as could have been hit upon by the wit of cooks! [H]owever like a simpleton I eat it to please her and now I am wishing 'the devil had flown away with it'— I am not *well* certainly, but so long as I *keep on my legs*, and have nothing that needs to be *taken care of* I should be thankful— I have no cough only a perpetual dull headach of now a fortnights standing—very bad in the mornings and evenings and less so during the middle of the day— It seems to make no difference in it what I do or abstain from doing—it would be worse for me if it hindered me from writing— Fontenelle,[11] I think it

9. Proverbs 26: 13.
10. 'Seidlitz powders', named after a village in Bohemia: a combination of tartaric acid, potassium sodium tartrate and sodium bicarbonate widely employed in nineteenth-century Europe as a laxative.
11. Bernard Le Bovier de Fontenelle (1657–1757), Enlightenment-era philosophical explicator.

was, who observed in speaking of Hell that 'he *flattered himself* one would get *used* to it'—it rather makes against this theory of the force of custom, that I still make such an outcry about headach, for certainly I have had opportunity enough to 'get used to it'— For the rest the weather has been more adapted for Ducks, or the Witches of Macbeth[12] than for a delicate female like me— I went out a little yesterday however between two showers—and made excellent use of my time— I was not absent an hour and a half in all and in that brief space I executed a scold on Mr Boulter—shopped to the amount of Sixpence—made three new acquaintances and did three good actions! I should have returned then with a comfortable sensation of *virtue* you will say— Alas no I returned cold and wearied, and forlorn— On the whole the pleasures of *benevolence* between ourselves, are not a whit less visionary than other sublunary pleasures—at least I find them so— There *is* a moment of moral satisfaction in putting a starved old woman into a warm flannel petticoat but one reflects the next instant—'of course she will pawn it'—and so on of every thing else of the sort one attempts in the way of *charity*— That you may not be forming too magnificent an idea of my 'good actions' of yesterday I must tell you, that they cost me *in all* only half a crown, and wet feet. Some nights ago Carlyle in one of his dark walks along the Kings road[13] observed a 'remarkably decent even *dignified* looking woman' sitting on some steps with a baby in her arms—'if he saw her again he would give her a penny'— [H]e did see her again the following night and gave her not only a penny but three halfpence— The next night also she was 'still there with the same *sad, calm,* look'[.] He addressed her and found her pretty deaf—she professed to be a soldier's widow— [T]hat night he 'had not a penny' so he told her to come down to me and I would give her some old clothes— I am sure he thinks I can *invent* old clothes—for it was only a few days before I had given all the duds I had to the widow of that pale faced street-sweeper in the Kings road now relieved from street sweeping for ever more— The woman arrived next morning at ten oclock—strongly perfumed with gin!—a decent looking woman nevertheless—and if a poor wretch have no fire—no warm breakfast—and for three farthings can get gin enough to both *warm* and *strengthen* her, who shall say that her taking it is a *fatal* sign of her—not I!—so in spite of the *questionable* smell I entered on a searching examination of her claims to my assistance. She told me she was the daughter of a Hotel keeper in Dublin, had eloped from a

12. 'When shall we three meet again / In thunder, lightning, or in rain?': opening lines of Shakespeare's tragedy, intoned by three witches.
13. In effect the high street of Chelsea, running south-west from Sloane Square more or less parallel with the Thames.

boarding school with her soldier husband at fourteen—had never since been taken the smallest notice of by any of her relatives—her Parents had died—her husband had died and here she was a beggar—with three children—a boy of twelve who had been taken into the Chelsea *Institution* for soldiers orphans[14]—a girl of six and the baby at her heart— She 'never went to see her son—for fear of disgracing him among his companions—he did not know what was become of her—but she lived here for the sake of knowing herself near him'— All very touching—*if true*— 'She could *sew* perfectly well could do any work she was put to— but none was to be had'— I *did invent* some clothes for her—among the rest a most *massive* petticoat out of the old floor-cloth!!—gave her a shilling and promised to enquire about her at the address she gave me— And accordingly, yesterday, I set forth on that errand—when it occurred to me that the truth of her story was to be got better from her son (if she had one) at the Institution than at her lodgings where they tell lies for one another.— I addressed myself to the bookkeeper who discovered in his Ledgers the name—John Wood—and took the trouble to bring the boy for me into his private room—a dear little fellow full of spirit and intelligence—but the terrified expression of whose face at being brought in to me gave me a mournful idea of his young experiences of his fellow creatures— He looked as if he thought I *must* be come to tell him his Mother was hanged— His answers to all my enquiries were clear as spring-water—he had seen his Mother three weeks ago! she lived in Union Street! his Father died six years ago! there was no baby! (a borrowed baby!) his Mothers Mother was alive! he had an uncle in Smithfield![15]—in short on a basis of truth I had been amused with a whole superstructure of lies—and the woman was just an inveterate, never-do-well!— I patted his head, gave him a shilling for his fright— and inwardly resolved to take some further charge of the son since nothing could be done for the mother— And there you see how imprudent it is to enter on a long story!—with limited time and limited paper—such histories are only for being *chattered* by the fireside[.] So I spare you my other *good actions* hoping that I may do some more another day— [. . .]

—Deariest babbie! I sometimes wish I had you here just to assure me by your contented looks that every thing in and about this establishment is not actually but only Cromwellianly fallen into a state of *detestableness*

14. The Royal Military Asylum for Children of Soldiers of the Regular Army, founded in Chelsea in 1803 and in 1909 relocated to Dover as the Duke of York's Royal Military School.
15. Union Street is a major thoroughfare in Southwark; Smithfield a tenth-century meat market still held on site in the City of London, near St Paul's.

disgraceful to hear tell of—and then again I thank heaven that you are *not* here— 'Night must it be 'ere Friedland's star can burn'[16]—and so is it for me tho' no Friedland!— [*S*]*upport*, tho' most soothing at the moment, only weakens me in the long run, when I have much to bear. When I feel myself quite, quite ALONE, with only *myself* to rely upon—then I am true to myself!—at least have been hitherto—but the petting and consideration I have of late been used to once more has revived the *leaning* tendency of my earlier days—and I feel dreary and helpless as in the *first* *un*learning to be a much-made-of Only Child— In a few weeks it is to be hoped 'the winter of our discontent'[17] being fairly set in, I shall have wrapped myself in my fur-mantle of imperturbability, and be living on my own individual resources—such as they are!— Happily one does not live for ever—nor even very long! [. . .]

Your own heart's-sister J. C.

To Jeannie Welsh, Chelsea, 9 March 1843

Dearest

I was very disappointed yesterday forenoon, when no letter arrived from you—and over and above, a little out of humour—but my humour was quickly restored to its natural calm, by what was meant to aggravate it. The fussy officiousness and superfluous enthusiasm with which Geraldine [Jewsbury] struck into the concern, wondering how it ever should happen that 'any one whose letters I was at the pains to wish for should not feel it worth the pains to write' &c &c produced a speedy reaction in your favour, just as the wife who getting herself beaten by her husband—fell foul of the stranger who interfered in her behalf—demanding [']what it was to *him* if her husband chose to beat his own wife'?— After dinner came the parcel—truly a beautiful and most luxurious wrapage! but in spite of my admiration of it, I did not willingly leave off shaking it, and shaking the books, in hopes that a letter would fall out— 'Perhaps, I said[,] the letter will be coming by tonights post'—and at this same moment Helen who had come in without my noticing

16. Wallenstein, Duke of Friedland, is the eponymous hero of Friedrich Schiller's three-part *Sturm und Drang* drama (1797–1799), concerning a general who rebels against Emperor Ferdinand II during the Thirty Years' War. See *Wallenstein's Death*, scene 10; like Friedland, Jane can only be herself when the day is done.

17. 'Now is the winter of our discontent / Made glorious summer by this son of York': opening lines of Shakespeare's *Richard III.*

her, my attention being absorbed in the shawl, put the letter into my hand—*then* finally my contentment was complete! When I had finished reading it I put on the shawl[—]drew the delicious little hood over my head—and stretched myself on the sofa to be supremely comfortable— I had been in the forenoon to the Chinese exhibition[18]—which like all *exhibitions* had tired me dreadfully— I was soon asleep— Carlyle was stretched on the green chair and two others—he had yesterday finished his book![19] he also slept profoundly—as he had good right to do— Geraldine makes herself a bed with the *priedieu*—chair and a sofa cushion and the hearth rug—*every day* after dinner—and sleeps like a person under the influence of liquor—or drugs—a singular phasis of a young lady— [Y]esterday evening she was stretched out and sound as usual!— Into this enchanted looking room walked Garnier—considerably distracted—singling out me to chatecise he asked 'why do you *tender* yourself in this way? or are you really not well?'— Geraldine who had got on her end, and always bursts out of sleep into volubility—poured forth a torrent of words a[bout] 'the poor creature having been to that *confounded* Chinese exhibition &c &c'—but she was cut short by Garnier's uplifting his two hands, and saying to me with an affectation of dismay—'Oh my goodness! how fast that Lady does talk! it is quite impossible for me to follow her! Mrs Carlyle is she a relation of yours'?— She pretended to be vastly amused—and vastly amused with the quizzing which he carried on the whole evening—but I believe she had her own private misgivings about it! After tea Carlyle and Garnier went down to smoke—and in the interim a gentleman sent in his card— Helen whispered it was the gentleman of next door[20]—and that you may understand all the awfulness of this announcement for me— I must tell you that Carlyle had yesterday put into effect his long matured purpose of trying the fair musician with a letter! I was out at the time and did not see it—but he gave me to understand that it was of the most chivalrous discription, professing his conviction that 'a young beautiful female soul working in the most beautiful element that of *music* would not willingly give annoyance to any fellow worker'!! &c &c &c— What he required of her practically to do—or rather to not do was to refrain from playing all days of the year till after two oclock!!!—a modest request to a young lady whose whole existence

18. 'The Chinese Collection', assembled by the American businessman Nathan Dunn, was exhibited at St George's Place, Hyde Park Corner, in spring 1843. After reappearing in London at the time of the Great Exhibition of 1851 it was sold off at auction.
19. Proofs, I assume, of *Past and Present*, published the following month.
20. The Lamberts, residents of No. 6, two of whose daughters played the piano, much to Thomas's exasperation.

seems to be in practicing!— I feared 'the gentleman next door['] must be come to make *a shine* [scene]. But the first glance at him as he entered, hat in hand, reassured me— He lookd at me most benignly from head to foot—sat down on the chair I motioned him to and then observed 'We have had a delightful day Mam'!— I myself led the conversation to the piano—saying that I understood my husband had been invading his house today with a most unheard of remonstrance—but the amiable gentleman would not let me finish—he bewailed the annoyance his daughters must have given us—bewailed our patience in having suffered so long without protest—would do unheard of things to spare us in future—the piano should be drawn into the middle of the floor—the *top* should never be opened—there should be no playing in forenoons unless when the mistress came on Wednesdays—and if *she* could possible change the hour it should be done—in short there never was such a complaisant gentleman as 'the gentleman of next door' since this world began!— When Carlyle came he seemed ready to fall on his knees before him to implore his forgiveness for having daughters who played on the piano— I assure you we were quite melted by his superhuman politeness and he seemed to find himself quite melted by our greatful sense of it—and he staid talking—till suppertime!—and then there was such a shaking of hands—and repetition of civil speeches on both sides— [N]obody knows what he can do till he tries! the putting down of a piano under such circumstances would have seemed desperate even to me!— Today the *faintest* sound of it was heard as if for trial for about a minute—it was hardly audible— Heaven knows how they have deadened the sound— So pray my dear have a fly at your chimney cans [pots]!—that is an insupportable thing and ought not to be tolerated for twentyfour hours—

Geraldine goes on Saturday thank heaven— I did not absolutely give her notice—but I took precious good care to avoid uttering a word that could be a second time misconstrued into an invitation to stay longer.— On monday she said 'I *must* write to that *horrid* Mrs Green[21]—to say when I am to pay her the long visit—[s]he wanted me before tomorrow evening for a music party'— [T]he '*horrid* Mrs Green['] you should know is a pretty, gentle—rather silly—but very innocent and goodnatured looking young woman who has shown her first and last a deal of kindness—and who when she came here the other day was caressed and flattered all over by Geraldine—just as she caresses and flatters *me*! before my face too—but *that* I *think* was an oversight, she

21. Jewsbury's friend, resident in St John's Wood, a middle-class suburb some four miles to the north of Chelsea.

afterwards bethought herself of—certainly it was a sad oversight, for the credit of her *sincerity* considering the atrocious things she had said to me of the poor young woman— I was reading when she began to speak of her visit to her— I turned over a leaf and made no answer— She scribbled a few lines—then looked up to me pen in hand—and asked—'well! *when*?—will you tell me *when* you would have me go'?— I answered dryly—'surely it is for *you* to decide on the *when* not for me'—and continued my reading—she wrote a note naming Saturday then handed it to me to read— I glanced it over, and giving it back said merely—'it seems all quite right'!— This I think was the next thing to 'giving notice'!—but indeed I am sick to death of her—and I have not her gift of showing kindness where I feel only annoyance and disgust— Your own JC [. . .]

To Thomas Carlyle, Chelsea, 7–8 July 1843

Dearest

I *take time by the pig-tail*[22] and write at night—*after* post-hours—during the day there is such an infernal noise of *pumice-stone*—diversified with snatches of 'wild strains'—the youth who is scraping the walls, (—as if it were a hundred knife-grinders melted into one)—consoling himself under the hideous task by striking up every two minutes '*the Red-cross Knights*—' or [']*Evelyn's Bower*' or some such plaintive melody, which after a brief attempt to render itself predominant dies away into an unintelligible whimper— Yesterday forenoon Mrs Chadwick came—and had just seated herself on the sofa beside me and was beginning to set forth amiabilities; when bang, bang, crash, screech, came the pumice-stone over the room—door—to the tune of 'Oh rest thee my darling

Thy sire is a Knight &c &'

making us both start to our feet with a little scream—and then fall back again in fits of laughter— Then the stairs are all flowing with white-wash—'and altogether' when I fancy *you* here 'in the midst of it,' I do not know whether to laugh, or to cry, or to shriek— But it will be a clean pretty house for you to come home to—and should you find that I have exceeded by *a few pounds* your modest allowance for painting

22. That is, not by the forelock.

and papering; you will find that I have *not* been *thoughtless* nevertheless, when I show you a document from Mr Morgan[23] promising to 'idemnify us for the same in the undisturbed possession of our house for five years'!—a piece of paper in fact equivalent to a lease of the house for five years 'with the receprocity all on one side'—binding him and leaving us free—'such a thing' old Sterling said who attended me to *Popes head ahoy* 'as no woman but myself would have had the impudence to ask, nor any *lawyer in his senses* the folly to grant'— I do not see but we might get a lease of the house after all for as long as we pleased—if *I* went about it, instead of the voluptuous Perry[24]— Mr Morgan said he rather thought *he* had the first claim on the property himself and that 'it was a pity but he had *seen me* sooner'—at all events as it stands at present—should the woman die tomorrow they cannot raise the rent on us or turn us out without remunerating us for our outlay—and *that* was really as much as I could in my conscience insist on—seeing that we have the house so very cheap—and that Mr Morgan had been *till he saw me* quite indifferent whether we kept it, at the present rent, or not— But this was one of those remarkable instances of *fascination* which I exercise over gentlemen of 'a certain age.' [B]efore I had spoken six words to him it was plain to the meanest capacity that he had fallen over head and ears in love with me—and if he put off time in writing me the promise I required, it was plainly only because he could not bear the idea of my going away again!—no wonder!—probably no such beatific vision as that of a *real, live woman*, in a silk bonnet and muslin gown, ever irradiated that dingy dusty law-chamber of his and sat there on a three-feet-high stool—since he had held a pen behind his ear—and most certainly never before had either man or woman in that place addressed him as a human-being—not as a lawyer—or he would not have looked so struck dumb with admiration when *I* did so.— For respectability's sake I said in taking leave that 'my husband was out of town or he would have come himself'— 'Better as it is' said the old gentleman 'do you think I would have written to your *husband's* dictation as I have done to *yours*'?— He asked if your name were John or William—plainly he had lodged an angel unawares[25]— By the way—

23. A lawyer in the City, representing the owners of No. 5, with offices at 3 Pope's Head Alley, Cornhill. 'Ahoy' seems to be a joke of Jane's.
24. John Perry, local estate agent, who might have acted for the Carlyles in Jane's stead; 'voluptuous' must be a private joke.
25. Hebrews 13: 2: 'Be not forgetful to entertain strangers: for thereby some have entertained angels unawares.' The lawyer has no idea that his client's leaseholder is a famous British intellectual; the name means nothing to him.

that other *angel* is becoming a bore[26]— Charles Barton with whom I dined at Sterlings in returning from Popes head a-hoy—told me that he had been making quite a sensation in Berlin and been invited to a great many places on the strength of *The French Revolution*— He (Charles B) was asked to dine with him—that is, 'with Thomas Carlyle author of the French Revolution,' at the Marquis of Westmorland's— 'Is *he* here' said Charles—'I shall be delighted to see him I know him quite well'—and accordingly on the appointed day he 'almost ran into the arms of the announced Thomas Carlyle—*and then retreated with consternation*.' It was so far good that he had opportunity to disabuse *these* people at least—by declaring 'THAT was not Thomas Carlyle at all'! But is it not a shame in the creature to encourage the delusion, and let himself be fêted as a Man of Genius when he is only a 'crack-brained enthusiastic.' Charles walked home with me and told me of a great many domestic grievances—amongst the rest that the poor Maurices have lost *the whole* of Annie's fortune by America![27]— This is a secret however— [A]nother thing about the Maurice's affected me strangely—the new baby is perfectly healthy and well formed—but it never ceases from *sobbing and sighing*—not like a baby but like a grown person!—the Dr imputes it to the Mother's suppressed grief—and says the habit will *wear off*—

I have awoke at four every morning since you went away—and the night before last I slept just *half an hour* in all—it is always the effect of finding myself *in a new position*— When the work people come at six I get up, which makes a prodigiously long day—but I do not weary—having so many mechanical things to do—this morning I took—or rather failed to take the showerbath—I pulled with concentrated courage and nothing would come—determined not to be quite baffled however, I made Helen pour a pitcherful of water on me instead— [. . .]

Saturday [8 July]

When one gets up at six and 'is always *virtuous*'; it *does* look so long till post-time!— But I have your letter, now, and have been to Regent Street too—altho it is still but one oclock and a regular rainy day!— Sterling came to ask if I wanted any thing, on his way early to the club—so I told him to take me up—and *drop himself at the club*—and I would fetch the carriage home—acceded to—in spite of the discontents occasioned

26. This was a member of Edward Irving's London congregation: 'long a double-ganger of mine', according to Thomas. Clearly the name 'Thomas Carlyle' is recognised by *some* people. John Fane, 11th Earl of Westmoreland, was resident minister of the British Government in Berlin: used to networking, no doubt.

27. For Frederick Denison Maurice see 15 July 1842; Anna Barton married Maurice in 1837 and would die in 1845; her sister had died earlier in the year. The details of the financial loss remain mysterious.

by Popes head alley!— Well the beast of an Umbrella-man simpered and bowed and told endless great lies, and, plainly had—utterly *forgotten* the whole transaction![28] I recalled it to his mind 'emphatically enough' especially the fact of his having received payment for an article which he had failed to send and seemed to be never intending to send— He promised for tonight and I left him with a look—'significative of much'![29] Never mind dearest—the poor little umbrella is only the more precious to me for the difficulty of getting it—

If you have not that sea-bathing lodging I am afraid these good lean people will soon weary you— Well! you cannot come back here just now at all rates—*that* is flat— What think you of going to this Forster[30]— Here indeed you would not '*come out strong*' under the existing circumstances—it is only I who can be '*jolly*'[31] in such a mess of noise—dirt, and wild dismay! I said to the Lad in the lobby this morning who was filling the whole house with '*Loves young dream*'—'how *happy* you must feel—that can sing thro' that horrible noise you are making'!— 'Yes, *thank you mam*' says he—'I am happy enough *so far as I knows* but I's always a-singing anyhow!—it sounds pleasant to sing at one's work—does'nt it Mam?' 'Oh very pleasant' said I quite conquered by his simplicity 'but it would be still pleasanter, for me at least, if you would sing a song from beginning to end—instead of bits here and there'— '*Thank you* Mam' says he again—'I will try'!—but he does not succeed— [. . .]

There now I *must* stop I dare say I have wearied you— God keep you Dear Be quite at ease about *me*

Ever your J C

To John Welsh, Chelsea, 18 July 1843

Dearest, dear, only Uncle of me!

I would give a crown that you could see me at this moment, thro a powerful telescope! you would laugh for the next twelve hours—I am

28. Thomas had ordered an umbrella before leaving town, which the supplier had failed to deliver.
29. A Thomas-ism that Jane employed remorselessly.
30. Not their London friend John Forster, but William Edward Forster. They would eventually meet him in 1847, in Derbyshire. (See Characters and Correspondents.)
31. See Dickens' *Martin Chuzzlewit* (being serialised as Jane wrote), chapter 5, where the hero's infuriatingly optimistic servant Mark Tapley speaks of his ambition to find a position in life sufficiently miserable that to be 'jolly' in it would be praiseworthy.

doing the rural after a fashion so entirely my own! To escape from the abominable paint-smell and the infernal noise within doors; I have erected *with my own hands* a gipsey-tent in the garden, constructed with clothes-lines—long poles and an old brown floor-cloth!—under which remarkable shade I sit in an arm-chair, at a small round table—with a hearth rug for carpet under my feet—writing materials sewing materials—and a mind superior to Fate!— The only drawback to this retreat, is its being exposed to 'the envy of surrounding nations'[32]—so many heads peer out on me from all the windows of *the Row*—eager to penetrate my meaning!— If I had a speaking-trumpet I would address them once for all—'Ladies & gentlemen, I am not here to enter my individual protest against the progress of civilization!—nor yet to mock you with an Arcadian felicity which you have neither the taste nor the ingenuity to make your own!—but simply to *enjoy nature* according to ability, and to get out of the smell of new paint! So pray you, leave me to pursue my innocent avocations, in the modest seclusion which I covet'!

—Not to represent my contrivance as too perfect, I must also tell you that a strong puff of wind is apt to blow down the poles and then the whole tent falls down on my head!—this has happened once already since I began to write—but an instant puts it all to rights again—Indeed without counteracting the indoors-influences by all lawful means I could not stay here at present without injury to my health which is at no time of the strongest—our house has for a fortnight back been a house possessed with seven devils!— A painter, two carpenters a paper-hanger, two non-descript apprentice-lads and '*a spy*'—all playing the devil to the utmost of their powers—hurrying and scurrying 'up stairs down stairs and in my Lady's chamber'![33] affording the liveliest image of a sacked City! When they rush in at six of the morning and spread themselves over the premises, I instantly jump out of bed and 'in wera [very] desperation' take a shower-bath. Then such a long day to be virtuous in! I make a chair and sofa covers—write letters to my friends—scold the work people, and suggest improved methods of doing things—and when I go to bed at night I have to leave both windows of my room wide open—(and plenty of ladders lying quite handy underneath) that I may not as old Sterling predicted 'awake dead' of the paint— The first night that I lay down in this open state of things, I recollected Jeannies house-breaker-adventure last year, and not wishing that all the thieves who *might* walk in at my open windows should take me quite unprepared, I laid my policeman's-rattle and my dagger

32. A journalistic cliché of the period, used ironically or otherwise with respect to the glorious British constitution.
33. Lines from the eighteenth-century nursery rhyme 'Goosey Goosey Gander'.

on the spare pillow—and then I went to sleep quite secure— But it is to be confidently expected that in a week more things will begin to subside into their normal state—and meanwhile it were absurd to expect that any sort of *Revolution* can be accomplished with *rose-water*[34]

There!—the tent has been down on the top of me again but it has only upset the ink—

Jeannie appears to be earthquaking with like energy in Maryland Street—but finds time to write me nice long letters nevertheless, and even to make me the loveliest pincushion for my birthday—and my birthday was celebrated also with the arrival of a hamper into which I have not yet penetrated. Accept kisses *ad infinitum* for your kind thought of me[,] dearest Uncle. I hope to drink your health many times in the Maidera[35] when I have Carlyle with me again to give an air of *respectability* to the act— Nay on that evening when it came to hand, I was feeling so sad and dreary over the contrast between this 14th of July—alone—in a house like a sacked city—and other 14ths [birthdays] that I can never forget—that I hesitated whether or no to get myself out a bottle of the Maidera there and then—and try for once in my life the hitherto unknown comfort of being dead-drunk[.] But my sense of the respectable overcame the temptation— I am so thankful to hear such comfortable accounts of you from Helen—whom you are to kiss one dozen of times and thank in my name for her welcome letter—I will write to herself very speedily—

My husband has now left his Welchman and is gone for a little while to visit the Bishop of St Davids[36] Then he purposes crossing over somehow to Liverpool—and after a brief benediction to Jeannie passing into Annandale— He has suffered unutterable things in Wales from the want of any adequate supply—of tea! the *Spooney* [noodle]! For the rest his visit appears to have been pretty successful—plenty of seabathing—plenty of riding on horseback—and of *lying under trees*!— I wonder it never enters his head to lie under the walnut tree here at home—*it is a tree*!—leaves as green as any leaves can be even in South Wales!—but it were too *easy* to repose under that—if one had to travel a long journey by railway to it—then indeed it might be worth while!

34. A proverb coined by the French Enlightenment historian Jean-François Marmontel (1723–1799) as regards the French Revolution and quoted many times since, not least by Byron in Italy.

35. A fortified wine from the Portuguese Atlantic islands, properly called Madeira; like Iberian port and sherry (from which Ruskin's father made his fortune), hugely appreciated by the English middle and upper classes.

36. Britain's smallest city, in Pembrokeshire, south-west Wales. Thomas's 'Welchman' is the solicitor Charles Redwood, a tiresome admirer whom he nonetheless visited occasionally on his escapes from London.

But I have no more time for scribbling just now—besides my pen is positively declining to act— So God bless you Dear and all of them— Ever your affectionate / Jane Carlyle

To Thomas Carlyle, Pier Hotel, Ryde, 9 August 1843

Dearest—

Here I actually am—and so far as has yet appeared, 'if it had not been for the honour of the thing' I had better have staid where I was— The journey hither was not *pleasant* the least in the world, what *journey* ever was or shall be pleasant for poor me?— But *this* railway seems to me particularly *shaky*, and then the steamboating from Gosport,[37] tho it had not time to make me *sick*;—the water moreover being smooth as the Thames—still it made me as perfectly *uncomfortable* as need be—a heavy dew was falling—one could not see many yards ahead—every body on board looked peevish— I wished myself at home in my bed—

We reached Ryde at eight in the evening—and the second Hotel being filled, had to take up our quarters for that night at the first—which 'is the *dearest* Hotel in Europe'—and the Hotel in Europe so far as I have seen, where there is least human comfort— I had to make tea from an urn the water of which was certainly *not* 'as hot as one could drink it'—the cream was blue milk—the butter tasted of straw—and the 'cold fowl' was a *luke-warm* one, and as tough as leather— After this insalubrious repast which the Stimabile, more easily pleased than I, pronounced to be 'infinitely refreshing by Jove'!—finding that beyond sounding the depths of *vacuum* there was nothing to be done that night I retired to my bed—the window looked out over house roofs and the sea so I hoped it would be quiet—but alas—there was a dog!—such a Devil of a dog! uttering a volley of loud barks about once in the five minutes—and rousing up what seemed to be a whole infinitude of dogs in the distance! Of course fevered and nervous as I was at any rate from the journey—I could not sleep at all— I do not mean that I *slept ill* but I have absolutely *never been asleep at all the whole night*! so you may fancy the favourable mood I am in towards Ryde this morning! I feel as if I would not pass another night in that bed for a hundred pounds!—nor

37. Town on the western side of Portsmouth Harbour, Hampshire, and once the point of departure for the ferry to the Isle of Wight, a few miles off the mainland. Jane's destination was the seaside town of Ryde, popular in the Victorian era, on the north-eastern end of the holiday island.

shall I need— Clark[38] has been out this morning to seek *a lodging* and has found one he says very quiet—quite away from the town— If I cannot sleep *there* I will return to my own red bed as fast as possible— I did not bind myself for any specified time,— To Helen I said I should most likely be back in three or four days—but in my private mind I thought it possible I might make out a week— It was best however to let her expect me from day to day—both that she might get on faster with her work—and that she might suffer less from her apprehensions of thieves for she flattered herself nobody would know I was gone before I should be returned [. . .]

And now let me tell you something which you will perhaps think more *questionable* than the placing of the Mudie girls—a little piece of *Hero-worship* that I have been after— My 'youthful enthusiasm' as John Sterling calls it is not extinct there, as I had supposed—but must certainly be *immortal*! Only think of its blazing up for—*Father Mathew*![39]— You know I have always had the greatest reverence for that Priest—and when I heard he was in London—attainable to me, I felt that I *must* see him—shake him by the hand—and tell him I loved him considerably!— I was expressing my wish to see him to Robertson[40] the night he brought the Ballad collector—and he told me it could be gratified—quite easily— Mrs Hall had offered *him* a note of introduction to Father Mathew, and she would be pleased to include my name in it—'fix my time then'—he was administering the pledge all day long in the Commercial Road[41]— I fixed next evening— He (Robertson) called for me at five—and we rumbled off in [an] Omnibus all the way to *Mile end*—that hitherto for me unimaginable goal!—then there was still a good *way* to walk—the Place was a large piece of waste ground boarded off from the Commercial road for a Catholic cemetery— I found 'my youthful enthusiasm' rising higher and higher as I got on the ground and saw the thousands of people all hushed into awful silence; with *not a single exception* that I saw—the only *religious* meeting I ever saw in Cokney-land which had not plenty of scoffers hanging on its outskirts.— [T]he Crowd was all in front of a narrow scaffolding from

38. A valet of Edward Sterling's.
39. The Catholic priest Theobald Mathew (1790–1856) enrolled nearly half the Irish population under the banner of total abstinence in the mid-1840s; his visits to Liverpool, Manchester and London were similarly messianic.
40. John Robertson, friend and sub-editor at the *Westminster Review*. The 'Mudie girls' were four young women the Carlyles had aided in poverty earlier that summer.
41. The Commercial Road runs east from Whitechapel High Street on the edge of the City out towards the old docklands of Limehouse and Canary Wharf. Mile End is to its north: East London 'Cokney-land' by definition.

which an American Capt[ain] was then haranguing it—and Father Mathew stood beside him so good and simple looking!— Of course we could not push our way to the front of the scafold where steps led up to it—so we went to one end—where there was no steps or other visible means of access—and handed up our letter of introduction to a Policeman—he took it and returned presently—saying that Father Mathew was coming.— And he came—and reached down his hand to me—and I grasped it—but the boards were higher than my head—and it seemed that our communication must stop there— But I have told you—I was in a moment of enthusiasm— I felt the need of getting closer to that good man— I saw a bit of rope hanging in the form of a festoon from the end of the boards— I put my foot on it—held still by Father Mathews hand—seized the end of the boards with the other—and in some to myself, up to this moment, incomprehensible way—flung myself *horizontally* onto the scafolding at Father Mathew's feet!!— He uttered a scream!—for he thought (I suppose) I must fall back—but not at all— I jumped to my feet—shook hands with him and said what?— 'God only knows'— He made me sit down on the only chair a moment, then took me *by the hand* as if I had been a little girl and led me to the front of the scafold to see him administer the pledge—from a hundred to two hundred took it—and all the Tragedies and theatrical representations I ever saw melted into one could not have given me such emotion as that scene did— There were faces both of men and of women that will haunt me while I live—faces exhibiting such concentrated wretchedness—making, you would have said, its last deadly struggle with the powers of darkness— [T]here was one man in particular with a baby in his arms—and a young girl that seemed of the 'unfortunate' sort[42]—that gave me an insight into the lot of humanity that I still wanted—and in the face of Father Mathew when one looked from them to him, the mercy of heaven seemed to be laid bare— Of course I *cried*—but I longed to have laid my head down on the good mans shoulder and taken a hearty cry *there* before the whole assembled multitude!! He said to me one such nice thing— 'I dare not be absent for an hour' he said 'I think always if some dreadful drunkard were to come! and me away; he might never muster determination perhaps to come again in all his life, and *there* would be a man *lost*'!

I was turning sick and needed to get out of the thing—but in the act of leaving him—never to see him again thro all time most probably—*feeling* him to be the very best man of modern times (*you* excepted)—I had another movement of youthful enthusiasm—which you will hold

42. That is, a prostitute.

up your hands and eyes at— Did I take the pledge then?— No— I *would* tho', if I had not feared it would have been put in the newspapers!— No—not *that*—but I drew him aside—having considered if I had any *ring* on—any *handkerchief*—any anything that I could leave with him in remembrance of me—and having bethought me of a pretty memorandum book in my reticule—I drew him aside and put it into his hand—and bade him keep it for my sake, and asked him to give me one of his medals to keep for his!—and all this in tears and the utmost agitation!!— Had you any idea that your wife was still such a fool! I am sure *I* had not— The Father got thro the thing admirably—he seemed to understand what it all meant quite well—inarticulate tho I was— [H]e would not give me a common medal but took a little silver one from the neck of a young man who had just taken the pledge for example's sake, telling him he would get him another presently and then laid the medal into my hand—with a solemn blessing— I could not speak for excitement all the way home,—when I went to bed I could not sleep—the pale faces I had seen haunted me—and Father Mathew's smile—and even next morning I could not any how subside into my normal state until I had sat down and—written Father Mathew a long letter—accompanying it with your *Past and Present*!!! Now my dear if you are ready to beat me for a distracted Gomeril [simpleton]—I cannot help it—all *that* it was *put into my head to do— Ich könnte nichts anders*[43]

When you write just address to Cheyne Row—I cannot engage for myself being here twentyfour hours longer—it will depend on how I sleep tonight—and also a little on when I find Elizabeth Mudie will be needed in Manchester— I must be back in time to get her clothes gathered together—

Bless you always—love to them all

Your J C

I began this at the Hotel—but it has been finished at our lodging which looks quiet and comfortable so far—

To Jeannie Welsh, Chelsea, 17 August 1843

My Child

The sympathy that is between thee and me has something of—what shall I say—supernatural in it. Morally and materially we go on at this

43. See Martin Luther's famous statement of faith before the Diet of Worms, 1521, answering charges of heresy: '*Hier stehe ich, Ich kann nicht anders*': 'Here I stand; I can do no other.'

distance in the beautifulest fellowship of worries—first heart-worries that cannot be put on paper—then household-worries from cleanings &c—and finally indignant worries with one's maid—during the last week I have been exercising a quantity of philosophy that will never be known or estimated '*here*-down,' in merely abstaining from taking a poker and killing Helen for the woe she has brought me—

But to start fair— After I wrote to you last I was really very ill— I did not get over my horrid Ryde expedition so easily as I expected— I had a spell of headachs and the most extraordinary aches in my limbs as well making it imperative on me for one day to keep my bed— Well[:] I had got on foot again, Carlyle had begun to *talk* of coming home— I must wind up my fag ends of radical reform and get in readiness for him—and just when I was sitting down to breakfast with a feeling of the necessity of despatch making me rather flighty—says Helen 'My!— I was just looking up at the corner of my bed this morning, and there ye ken what should I see but two *bogues* (*anglicê* [in English] bugs!) I hope there's nae mair'! 'Good god said I you hope? It will be a precious affair if you have let bugs into your bed again after the fright you got five years ago'!

And off I ran to investigate with my own eyes—I had *killed* two in the first instant—and on pulling the bed separate I saw—oh heaven and earth plenty of 'little *beings*' (as Mazzini would say) moving—I told her so in despair— But now she considered her honour concerned—went and investigated after me and returned very angry to tell me 'there was not a single *bogue* there—SHE had looked and there was nothing of the sort[']— [N]eedless to argue with a wild animal—so there was nothing for it but to have back Pearson[44] and get the bed taken down—[w]hich Helen *left* me to do with him myself, going out messages during the time and staying—that she might not be *openly* proved in the wrong— It was just as well for plainly she would have been an insecure hand to have delegated such a critical business to— We found them as Pearson phrased it 'pretty strong' and the slaughter was a thing to make ones blood curdle to think back on. With my own hands I threw some twenty pails of water over the kitchen floor to drown any who might attempt to save themselves—and all the bed was then flung piece by piece into water and steeped for several days—and emboldened by my former victory I do opine that there is no bogue alive therein[.] But in the course of my bug investigations I had made another discovery[:] the woolmatrass under her was absolutely alive with moths threatening soon to eat up the whole house—so all that had to be pulled in pieces and washed and boiled and put in

44. The Carlyles' builder and carpenter; see 2 and 25 October 1843, below.

again—and then I could not rest till I had all the other beds taken down and looked into—all except my own—in which so long as I am not *bitten* I may be perfectly sure there is no shadow of a bug— A simpler way would have been to have gone and slept in them all by turns but that idea was too horrible to me.

So you may figure what a week I have had—for seeking after bugs and slaying them is a mission that cannot be delegated— I have been up at seven every morning and not in bed til twelve—and have never got half done that I proposed to do in the morning— So you may figure that when the letters that must be written to the master of the house were written I had little faculty never to speak of time remaining—the idea of his arriving at home after such a time consumed in brightening the outside of the platter and finding me in a beastly mess of this sort being an idea that has chased me all thro the day and even haunted my dreams—

Surely some time again we shall be at leisure Babby!— It does not look like it yet—[. . .]

I have a hundred things to tell you some of them much more poetical than what I *have* told—but it is midnight and I am dead weary—and if I do not go to bed I shall put myself entirely off my nights rest which I need of all things

The quantity of needlework too that I have done! the beautiful house that I have maid—for absolutely nothing at all so far as money is concerned! If I had you now to shew it you all and then kiss you—after twenty times what a difference

Your own / Jane C

The garters![45] never once thanked you for them— Ah—but they had passed away from me! Only think I gave them to Darwin and said you worked them for him and the poor man blushed up to the eyes and so will you at hearing of it—never mind I put it all to rights after I told him you had worked them for me who cannot wear that sort and that I could not have them wasted on anybody *you* did not care for—[h]e declared he should be *delighted* to receive them—! [. . .]

45. In this case what Victorians called 'hose supporters', worn below the knee to keep up socks, not stockings; but still intimate enough items of apparel to cause embarrassment between the sexes, clearly.

To Jeannie Welsh, Chelsea, 2 October 1843

D'abord [First], you *are* an angelical Babbie; to make me never a reproach for my silence—never a reproach for anything!— I am sufficiently conscious without being told, of the imperfection of my actual manner of being; but I console myself with the reflection that, if not *inevitable* absolutely, it is at all rates the *very natural* reaction against the outrageous activity and universal benevolence which I have been carrying on for the last two or three months— My husband has been returned this fortnight back, and since then I have not written to you—have not written to anyone—have not *done* anything except occasionally mend my stockings and read in the dreamy novels of the Gräfin Hahn Hahn (Countess cock cock! What a name![)] She is a sort of German George Sand *without the genius*—and *en revanche* [on the other hand] a good deal more of what we call in Scotland *gumtion*— A clever woman really—separated from her husband of course—and on the whole very good to read when one is in a state of moral and physical collapse[46]— For the rest nothing can exceed this great City in these weeks, for absence of all earthly objects of interest!— Even Darwin has been gone for a month!—the last to go— But I had the pleasure of meeting him yesterday in Cadogan Place[47] having returned the night before. To give you the most striking illustration that occurs to me of the desert-state of things; I saw the other day a little girl of six years old playing her hoop in the centre of Piccadilly!! a cab *did* come at last and as nearly as possible ran over her—but skipping from under the horse's belly, literally, she recommenced her hoop-playing, with the same assiduity as before

And within doors is not a whit more gay I can assure you than without— Carlyle returned, as usual from his journeyings in quest of health, as bilious and out of sorts as he went away— Blue pill

46. The *CL* note cannot be improved upon: 'Ida, Countess von Hahn-Hahn (1805–1880), German author of lyric verse and novels, acquired her hyphenated dual name by marrying 1826, a cousin of the same name, from whom she separated, 1829. She published several volumes of lyrics, 1835–1837, and then a series of social novels dealing with contemporary aristocratic society, especially with passionate, emotionally dissatisfied women, 1838–1846. After the revolutions of 1848 she changed her views of society; became a Roman Catholic, 1850; founded, 1854, a convent in which she lived till her death.'

47. Sloane Street runs north from Sloane Square towards Knightsbridge, and Cadogan Place is a long residential garden square on part of its eastern side. The garden itself is closed to the public. Piccadilly Circus was built in 1819, connecting Regent Street with Piccadilly; it still serves as a transport node between London's West End and the suburbs of Knightsbridge, Belgravia, Kensington and Chelsea further to the west. The London 'season' ran from late October to June, while Parliament was in session; outside that period the West End was drained of its upper-class citizens and could be quiet, indeed.

with castor-oil 'and the usual trimmings' had to be taken at the very out-set[,] then by the time the distress of *that* was over it was time to be feeling the intolerable influences of—London!— The house was approved of as much as I had flattered myself it would be—and between ourselves he would have been a monster if he had not exhibited some admiration more or less at my magnificent improvements affected at such small cost—*to him*— The upstairs room is now a really beautiful little drawingroom with a sofa—easy chair—ottoman—cushions—stools—every conceivable luxury!—all covered—and all the chairs covered also—with a buff and red chintz made by my own hands!!!— Mrs Carlyle's picture is over the mantle-piece—but then yours and my uncles are on the mid-wall with Jean Paul between[48]—and you cannot think how beautiful you both look on the pretty new paper—

All this and his own bed room new carpeted and smartened up amazingly—to say nothing of the old big press in the china closet transformed by the female genius into a glorious resplendent chinese-cabinet! could not fail to yield him 'a certain' satisfaction and obtain me some meed of praise—but—alas alas—never can one get out of the shadow of that *but*!—but—after two or three days he began to find that 'there was no getting on in that up stairs room for want of the closet or some equivalent to fling ones confusion in—'!!—'best to accumulate no confusion' said I— 'Oh there must be a place for keeping all sorts of papers for *a year* or so, till one has made up ones mind what to burn and what not'! This was a first ground for quarrel with the room—and then—oh then—one day when he had been home about [a] week Miss Lambert took a fit of playing—the *first*—but that only made it the more intolerable—for he had fallen into a false security thro her prolonged silence— [T]he next day again she played half an hour in the morning which was sufficient to set all his nerves up for the rest of the day—and it was solemnly declared that 'no life of Cromwell or any other book could ever be written alongside of that damnable noise'— Then Mr Chancellors cock had awoke him he said at six for two mornings[49]—(he had not however come down to breakfast till ten) and 'that bedroom was uninhabitable'— 'Could one get a piece of ground to build *some crib of a* house upon at the Isle of Whight did I think?'— In fact just all the old eternal story commenced again!— I must fetch back Pierson

48. The imposing portrait of Thomas's mother (1842) by Maxwell of Dumfries is still in the Carlyle house in Cheyne Row, as is the portrait of Jean Paul Richter (1763–1825), German Romantic novelist, and the portraits of John and Jeannie Welsh by the Carlyles' Italian friend Spiridione Gambardella.

49. Owned by a stabler at No. 1, George Chancellor.

to *consult* about the possibility of excluding noise—&c &c in the mean while— Accordingly Pierson was here yesterday—kept in consultation for *three* hours! the whole result being plenty of *possibilities*—and a positive order for a pair of window boards to be all stuffed with cotton! to fasten on the back windows or the front (viz in *your* room) at pleasure—and as these will prevent the sleeping with windows *open*—zink pipes are to be introduced thro the walls to let in a sufficiency of fresh air! You are to observe by the way that it is only when the windows are wide open that this distant cock ever makes itself heard and—that the simple expedient which Pierson suggested—of *shutting the windows* and *opening the door* would have solved the problem as effectually and much more cheaply than all this apparatus of stuffed shutters and zink pipes! But then if the shutters make even the front room quiet enough for *him* to sleep in—and the zink pipe brings in air enough for *him* to breath; the piano-problem is also solved!—for his present-bedroom where alone the piano noise is not clearly audible is to be converted into his study—the partition taken down between the two front rooms—that the *two* four posted beds may have room to stand up *there*! until we can get a lease of the house (which is not procurable) and then a *silent* room—*twenty feet long*—*lighted from above*—is to be built on the roof!!!— So here is a quite other prospect than that of quiet order which I was looking forward to for the next twelve months at least! And I assure you it is with a heartrending sigh that I resign myself to the thought of lifting and altering all the carpets again, before they have been well down and having carpenters plasterers and white washers as before—besides the inconvenience of having ones spare room as it were annihiliated—for could *you* for instance sleep in a doublebedded room with Carlyle? However there may be many plans, before the definitive one gets *carried into effect*—and anyhow I cannot help it—and at least as Darwin says I 'have always the consolation of knowing that he will need some *new* arrangements in six months or so'!— But indeed Babbie if you saw how pretty the upstairs floor is in its actual state and knew all the toil and scheming I had in bringing it into such order you would not wonder that I am fretted— Your room too with the blue carpet from his bedroom (his had got the drawingroom one) and the position of the bed altered looked so like the Templand bedroom—all the little things in it arranged as they were *there*—that one could almost deceive oneself into its being the same—[a]nd all this to be overturned— Well Well I cannot help it and what *is* the use of talking—*such* woes are but very petty ones after all!—[. . .]

How strange it is for me to fancy you all in Scotland—my uncle in Edin!—strange and sad— I feel so as if I should be there too—to welcome you—and yet I would not be there for the world— (I have no faith in Dr Abercrombie—my Father considered him a sort of quack who got on chiefly by psalm singing and praying with sick old Ladies but he has seen plenty of practice—and every vote about *diet* is in my uncles case worth going out of the way to get—in fact is I really suppose the only medical prescription that can be impressed on him with any utility—) Give Helen a hearty kiss for me—and tell her that I love her all the same as if I were writing to her every day— I will never never as long as I live forget her kind and considerate management for me under circumstances in which not mere kindness and judgement but a sort of loving inspiration was needed to do all so well as she did it god bless her[50] and all of you my Child write to me quickly again your own J C—

To Jeannie Welsh, Chelsea, 25 October 1843

I entreat Miss Babbie that you would devote ten minutes of your valuable time just to certify me that you are alive and whether you be returned to Liverpool— To be sure you may think in a commercial spirit (wholly unworthy of you) that whilst your last long letter from Helen[s] burgh remained unanswered I could not have any desire to know about you—at all rates if I had any such desire that I did not deserve to have it gratified—but I have my own idea babbie that if a Radamanthus[51] had to administer justice in this case—he would pronounce unmitigated sentence on *you*, whereas *me* he would find 'guilty under *extenuating circumstances*' and commute my sentence to a one-farthing fine— When that letter arrived hoping that my troubles would pass over with the blue pill—I was already up to the ears in them. Pearson with his troop of incarnate fiends carpenters bricklayers whitewashers plasterers has already spread themselves *per ogne dove* [everywhere]—and Helen, at sight of such unexpected finale to her cleaning labours had been struck with a temporary ideocy—so that I had to follow her about and supply her with wits as well as with active help at every turn, and with such heart as you can imagine—besides having to ward off the deluge of confusion from the man himself—who conducted himself on the occasion much like a half-conjuror— [F]inding that he had not the

50. Jane's cousin Helen Welsh had helped clear her mother's house after her death.
51. Mythological son of Zeus and Europa, and king of Crete; so just a judge that he was assigned the same function in the Underworld.

counter-spell to allay the storm which himself had raised he raged and lamented and all but rent his garments and tore his hair—[52] The front-bed-rooms were to have been thrown into one in TWO days according to Pearson—in *ten* days the workmen had finished there!— [T]hen the room had to be instantly fitted up for Carlyles sleeping room—at least so long as the people should be breaking out a chimney and instituting a small fire place in his dressingroom, which last plan had dawned on his mind as the probablest escape from the piano forte— [A]nother *week* they were messing *there*—Carlyle unable to sleep in the new room—not for noise—his *stuffed* window shutters fastened on with as many screws and bolts as if they were for the windows of a mad house almost wholly exclude all noise from the street—but merely from the nervousness always incident with him on 'finding himself in a new position'— There were wanderings about during the night—fires kindled with his own hands, bread and butter eaten in the china-closet!—all sorts of what shall I say—strange things upon my honour done—and I all the while lying awake listening with a bouncing heart but *afraid* to meddle with him—even to offer any assistance—then the sort of days sure to follow that sort of nights! I will not try to describe—to have overlived them was botheration enough,—no sooner were the workmen out of the dressing room than back he must be moved bag and baggage into his old bedroom—and at this point of the business I caught a fine rheumatism in the back of my head and shoulders—in consequence of spending a whole forenoon in papering the broken parts of the plaster and all the afternoon of the same day in nailing carpets—*that* is a thing that Helen *can not* do—and the hands of me are absolutely blackened and coarsefied with the quantity of it I have had to transact this season— To make the mess still thicker the dining-room grate which you may remember was a perpetual source of execration was finally voted insupportable for another twentyfour hours—another must be got—and then—as all our things are never to be made like other peoples but on some superior plan of our own—the new grate—with cover of dutch tiles—needed ever so much of the chimney to be pulled down and a man building and plastering at it for two days and a half— [O]f course all the carpets and furniture of that beautifully clean room had to be removed also— [Ten] days ago I nailed down the carpets of *it*—and readjusted the things[,] and today I have nailed down all the stair and passage carpets—at last!— [T]here is still a good piece of work for me in the front bedroom which will be all the fitter for your

52. This is the 'sorcerer's apprentice' story of the hapless assistant unable to control the powers he evokes, which first appeared in Goethe's ballad 'Der Zauberlehrling' (1797).

and our visitors reception in consequence of what it has undergone—but if he had only allowed me to do these things when I was about it in the summer it would have spared a world of fash [bother]—and such a sickening feeling towards 'household good' as I do not remember ever in my life before to have experienced— I am physically ill of the long continued discomfort and the cinderella labours in which I have had to put forth the activity of a maid of all-work—along with improvisation and inventive-faculty of a woman of genius— The fact is I have spoiled Mr C—I have accustomed him to have all wants supplied 'without visible means'[53]—until he has forgotten how much head and hands it takes to supply the common resource of a good round outlay of money[.] When one had not any money—it was all well—I never grudged my work—but now that we have enough to live on it would be good sense in him to say 'get in a carpenter to nail your carpets' and a few other such considerate suggestions— [N]o matter—I shall get my hands kept clean and put into mitts for a time so soon as I have patched together a carpet for the new bedroom—and will be on the sofa by heaven for two weeks and read french novels!

It was not that I was so *eternally* in motion from morning till night that I could not write to you—one can always find a half hour during which it is possible to sit still if one looks for it but my temper was so bad that I could not compose it to write even to you—and as I have said my health has been bad as well as my temper—indeed these two things with me pretty invariably go with one another—

I will tell you of all the rest—that is about people &c &c next time— Write you little false hearted gipsey— Love to them all Ever your affectionate / Jane Carlyle

❧

To John Welsh, Chelsea, 28 November 1843

Uncle dear! How are you? I kiss you from ear to ear—and I love you very considerably; '*hopping to find you in the same.*'

The spirit moves me to write to you just at this *unlikeliest* moment (for *my* spirit is a contradictory spirit) when the Influenza has left me with scarce faculty enough to spell words of more than one syllable[.] I caught the horrid thing a week ago—by Destiny—thro no indiscretion of my own—which is a consolation of a certain sort—for it does form

53. 'Without visible means of support': a legal definition of vagrancy in Victorian Britain.

a most '*aggravating*' ingredient in ones suffering to be held *responsible* for it, to be told, 'this comes of your going to such a place, or doing such a thing—if you had taken *my* advice &c &c'! But this time I had been going nowhere—doing nothing in the least degree questionable—the utmost *lark* I had engaged in for months being to descend at *Granges* (Babbie knows the place) in the course of my last drive with old Sterling and there refresh exhausted nature with a hot jelly and *one* modest sponge-cake! It would have been no harm I think had the Influenza taken, instead of temperate me, a *personage* who *sat* on the next chair to us at the said Grange's[54] and before whose bottomless appetite all the surrounding platefuls of cakes disappeared like *reek* [smoke]! His companion who was *treating* him finally snatched up a large pound-cake cut it into *junks* [thick pieces] and handed him one after another on the point of a knife till *that* also had gone *ad plura* [in addition]— [T]he *Dog*(!) for it was with a dog that I had the honour of lunching that day; appeared to consume poundcake as my Penfillan Grandfather[55] professed to eat cheese 'purely for *diversion*'!— By the way it must have been a curious sight for the starved beggars who hang about the doors of such places to see a *dog* make away with as much *cake* in five minutes as would have kept *them* in *bread* for a week or weeks! bad enough for them to see human beings neither bonnier, perhaps, nor wiser, nor, except for the clothes on their backs, in any way better than themselves eating hot jelly and such like delicacies while they must go without the necessaries of life—but *a dog*!—really *that* was stretching the injustice to something very like *impiety* it strikes me. I should like to know the name of 'the Gentleman as belonged to that *dog*'—he seemed by his equipments and bearing a person holding some rank in the world besides the generical rank of *fool*; and should one find him some other day maintaining in Parliament that 'all goes well'—it would throw some light on the worth of his opinion to know that HIS *dog* may have as much pound-cake at Grange's as it likes to eat!

That however was the last social fact which I witnessed having been since laid up at home; and part of the time in bed.— I do not know why the solitude of a bedroom should be so much more solitary than the solitude of other places—but so I find it— When my husband is at work I hardly ever see his face from breakfast till dinner, and if it rains or

54. A famous confectioner's at 176 Piccadilly, also mentioned by Byron in his satire *The Blues* (1821). Pound cake is one made up of 'a pound each' of its major ingredients: butter, flour, sugar, etc.

55. Jane's correspondent was her mother's brother; Jane's paternal grandfather was also called John Welsh, 'of Penfillan', in Dumfries.

often even when it does not rain; no living soul comes near me to speak one cheerful word—yet so long as I am in what the french call my 'room of reception' it never occurs to me to feel lonely—but send me to my bedroom for a day to that great red bed in which I have transacted so many headachs so many *influenzas*! and I feel as if I were already half buried!— Oh so lonely! as in some intermediate stage betwixt the living world and the dead! I sometimes think that were I to remain there *long*, I should arrive in the end at prophecying like my great great Ancestors![56]— *That* solitude has such a power of blending Past, Present, and Future, Far and Near all into one confused jumblement—in which I wander about like a disembodied spirit that has put off the beggarly conditions of Time and Space—and *that* I take to be a first development of the Spirit of Prophecy in one!

The letters of Babbie used to be no small comfort to me when I was ailing—but Babbie since she went to Scotland has had other things to do it would seem than writing to *me*— Babbies beautiful constancy in writing has like many other beautiful things of this earth succumbed to the force of circumstances! Ah yes! what *young Lady* can withstand the force of circumstances? *Circumstances* are the young Lady's *Destiny*!—it is only when she has lived long enough to have tried conclusions with the *real* Destiny that she learns to know the difference and learns to submit herself peaceably to the one and to say to the other—that humbug *force of circumstances*—'but I WILL! *Je le veux, moi* [*I* want it, *me*]!'— Oh it is the grand happiness of existence when one can break thro one's *circumstances* by a strong *will*, as Samson burst the cords of the Philistines! Is n't it Uncle?— *You* should know if any man does!—you who are—permit me—I mean it entirely in a complimentary sense—so very *very* wilful! But as for my sweet Babbie her volition is not yet adequate to breaking *the pack threads of the Lilliputians*—never to speak of *Cords of the Philistines*![57] And meanwhile what can one do for her, but just what poor Edward Irving counseled certain Elders to do—who once waited upon him at Annan to complain of the backslidings of their minister and ask his (Edwards) advice under the same. Edward having listened to their catalogue of enormities, knit his brows, meditated some moments and then answered succinctly: 'my good friends you had best *pray for him to the Lord*!'

56. Yet another John Welsh, 'of Ayr' (1568?–1622), who married the daughter of the founder of Presbyterianism, John Knox, and who was a preacher in his own right; in point of fact not related to Jane.

57. For the binding of Samson see Judges 15: 12–14. In the first part of Jonathan Swift's *Gulliver's Travels* (1726) the eponymous hero survives shipwreck on the shores of Lilliput, whose citizens are one-tenth his size. Terrified by his gigantism, they tie him down in his state of exhaustion with cables that to him are like cotton threads.

My American was immensely pleased with your reception of him— *that* is the only American whom I have found it possible to be civil to this great long while— Oh such a precious specimen of the regular Yankee I have seen since![58] Coming in from a drive one forenoon, I was informed by Helen, with a certain agitation, that there was a *strange gentleman* in the Library, 'he said he had come a long way and would wait for the Master's coming home to dinner and I have been,' said she 'in a perfect fidget all this while for I remembered after he was in, *that you had left your watch on the table*!' I proceeded to the Library to inspect this unauthorized Settler with my own eyes—a tall, lean, red-herring-looking man *rose from Carlyles writing table which he was sitting writing at*, with Carlyles manuscripts and private letters all lying about—and running his eyes over me from head to foot—said; 'Oh—*you* are Mrs Carlyle are you?'— An inclination of the head—intended to be hauteur [haughtiness] itself—was all the answer he got— 'Do you keep your health pretty well Mrs Carlyle'? said the wretch, nothing daunted—*that* being always your regular Yankees second words— [A]nother inclination of the head even slighter than the first— 'I have come a great way out of my road' said he '*to congratulate Mr Carlyle on his increasing reputation*, and as I did not wish to have my walk for nothing I am waiting till he come in—but in case he should not come in time for me, I am just writing him a letter here at his own table as you see[,] Mrs Carlyle'! Having reseated himself without invitation of mine I turned on my heel and quitted the room determined not to sit down in it while the Yankee staid— But about half an hour after came Darwin and Mr [Hensleigh] Wedgwood and as there was no fire in the room below they had to be shown up to the Library where on my return I found the Yankee, still seated in Carlyles chair, very actively *doing*, as it were, the honours of the house to them!! And there he sat, upwards of another hour—not one of us addressing a word to him—but he not the less thrusting in *his* word into all that was said— Finding that I would absolutely make no answer to his *remarks* he poured in upon me a broadside of positive questions— 'Does Mr Carlyle enjoy good health *Mrs Carlyle*?'— '*No*!'— [']Oh he doesn't!— What does he complain of *Mrs Carlyle*?'— '*Of everything*.'! 'Perhaps he studies too hard—does he study too hard *Mrs Carlyle*?' '*Who knows*'?— 'How many hours a day *does* he study *Mrs Carlyle*?[']— 'My husband does not work by the clock'— And so on— his impertinent questions receiving the most churlish answers—but

58. The first 'regular Yankee' is Le Baron Russell, who alongside Ralph Waldo Emerson had helped popularise Thomas's works in America and who visited John Welsh in Liverpool on his way home; the second is (mercifully) unidentified.

which seemed to patter off the rhinoceros hide of him as tho they had been sugar-plums! At length he declared that Mr Carlyle was really very long of coming, to which I replied that it would be still longer before he came— Whereupon having informed himself as to all the possible and probable Omnibuses he took himself away leaving my two gentlemen ready to expire of laughter and me to fall upon Helen at the first convenient moment for not defending better 'the wooden guardian of our privacy'[59]

But really these Yankees form a considerable item in the ennuis [vexations] of our mortal life. I counted lately *fourteen* of them in one fortnight!—of whom Dr Russel was the only one that you did not feel tempted to take the poker to— If Mr Carlyle's '*increasing reputation*' bore no other fruits but *congratulatory* Yankees and the like I should vote for its proceeding to *diminish* with all possible despatch!—[. . .]

And now dear Uncle if I have not wearied *you* I have wearied *myself*—which is not at present hard to do—for altho' the worst of my cold is over, I suppose; I am as weak as a sparrow—

I wish I knew how *you* exactly are—and what that little demoralized Babbie is doing—for altho' she has left my last letter unanswered for nearly three weeks I cannot help still retaining a certain tenderness for her—

God bless you all—

Ever your affectionate

Jane W. Carlyle

Carlyle is over head and ears in Cromwell—is lost to humanity for the time being—

To Jeannie Welsh, Chelsea, 28 December 1843

A thousand thanks my darling for your long good Christmas-letter and also for the *prospective footstools*. Anything like a *worthy* answer you have small chance of getting from me to day or any day *this* week; I have just had to swallow a bumper of my Uncle's Madeira—(which *is* capital drink!) to *nerve* me for writing at all! A huge boxful of dead animals from the Welshman arriving late on Saturday night together with the visions of *Scrooge*—had so worked on Carlyles nervous organization that

59. A preposterous image for a door in Alexander Pope's prose satire 'Peri Bathous, or the Art of Sinking in Poetry' (1728).

he has been seized with a perfect *convulsion* of hospitality,[60] and has actually insisted on *improvising two* dinner parties with only a day between— Now the *improvisation* of dinner parties is all very well for the parties who have to *eat* them, simply, but for those who have to *organize* them and *help to cook them c'est autre chose ma chere* [that's another thing, darling]! I do not remember that I have ever sustained a moment of greater embarrassment in life than yesterday when Helen suggested to me that '*I* had better *stuff the Turkey*—as she had *forgotten* all about it'! *I* had never *known* 'about it'! but as I make it a rule never to exhibit *ignorance* on *any* subject '*Devant les domestiques*' [in front of the servants] for fear of losing their respect—I proceeded to *stuff* the Turkey with the same air of calm self dependance with which I told her some time ago, when she applied to me, the whole history of the Scotch-free-church dissentions—which up to this hour I have never been able to *take in*![61] 'Fortune favours the brave'—*the stuffing* proved pleasanter to the taste than any stuffing I ever remember to have eaten—perhaps it was made with quite new ingredients!—I do not know!—yesterday I had hare-soup—*the* Turkey—Stewed mutton—a bread pudding and mince-pies—with Mrs Allan Cunningham Miss Cunningham and Major Burns (son of the Poet) to eat thereof[62]— On Monday hare soup—roasted-*welch*-mutton stewed beef ditto pudding ditto pies—with Robertson, and John Carlyle, and *the disappointment* of Darwin—and all *that* day, to add to my difficulties, I had a headach—so bad that I should have been in bed if I had not had to stay up to help Helen—whose faculties get rusted by disuse— On Tuesday evening I was engaged to assist at Nina Macready's birthday party—but felt so little up to gaities on the Monday that I had resolved to send an apology *as usual* When voila—on the morning of the appointed day arrives a note from Mrs Macready *imploring* me almost with tears in its eyes not to disappoint

60. For the Welshman see 18 July 1843, above. Ebenezer Scrooge is the miserly anti-hero of Dickens' *A Christmas Carol*, published four days earlier, who has clearly motivated Thomas to celebrate the season.

61. Jane would not be the first or the last person to be confused by Scottish Protestant ecclesiastical history. In 1843 the Free Church of Scotland split off from the Church of Scotland in the so-called 'Disruption' that Helen Mitchell wants to have explained. In 1900 the Free Church joined the United Presbyterian Church to form the United Free Church, which in 1929 mostly rejoined the Church of Scotland once more, though the 'Wee Frees' did not follow suit and in 2000 eventually formed the Free Church of Scotland (Continuing).

62. Allan Cunningham (1784–1842), Scottish poet and London acquaintance of Thomas's from the early 1830s. Robert Burns' son is probably Major James Glencairn Burns (1794–1865); see 'Major Burns', below. Burns had twelve children that we know of with various women; few survived into adulthood.

her and her 'poor little daughter' by sending an apology!—that a well aired BED was prepared for me &c &c— [T]his forestalling of my cruel purpose was successful— I felt that I *must* go *for once*—so after spending the day in writing—not to *you*—but to people who, not having the reason you have to believe in my love, needed more than you to have a visible sign from me—I dressed myself and sat down to await *the fly*— 'My dear['] says Carlyle 'I think I never saw you look more bilious[;] your face is *green* and your eyes all *blood-shot*'! fine comfort when one was about to make—public appearance! 'the first time this season'— In fact I was very ill—had been *off* my sleep for a week and felt as if this night must almost *finish* me— But little does one know in this world *what* will *finish* them or what will *set them up* again. I question if a long course of mercury would have acted so beneficially on my liver as this party which I had gone to with a sacred shudder! But then it was the *very* most agreeable party that ever I was at in London—everybody there seemed animated with one purpose to make up to Mrs Macready and her children for absence of 'the tragic actor'[63] and so amiable a purpose produced the most joyous results— Dickens and Forster above all exerted themselves till the perspiration was pouring down and they seemed *drunk* with their efforts! Only think of that excellent Dickens playing the *conjuror* for one whole hour—the *best* conjuror I ever saw—(and I have paid money to see several)—and Forster acting as his servant!— This part of the entertainment concluded with a plum pudding made out of raw flour raw eggs—all the raw usual ingredients—boiled in a gentleman's hat—and tumbled out reeking—all in one minute before the eyes of the astonished children, and astonished grown people! [T]hat trick—and his other of changing ladies pocket handkerchiefs into comfits [sweets]—and a box full of bran into a box full of—a live-guinea-pig! would enable him to make a handsome subsistence[,] let the book-seller trade go as it please! Then the dancing—old Major Burns with his one eye—old Jerdan of the Literary Gazette, (escaped out of the Rules of the Queen's Bench for the great occasion!) the gigantic Thackeray &c &c all capering like *Mænades*!![64]

63. Her husband, William Macready (1793–1873), actor and theatre-manager, on tour in the United States.

64. William Jerdan (1782–1869), editor of this literary review, 1817–1850; he had a legal background and perhaps this brought him into the orbit of one of Britain's great appeal courts. 'Gigantic' Thackeray was six foot three when the average Victorian male was around five foot five and the average female around five foot. (His great admirer, Charlotte Brontë, was four foot eight.) The Maenads were female followers of Dionysus, the Greek god of intoxication. Daniel Maclise (1806–1870), Irish artist and illustrator of some of Dickens' fiction. The rape of Sabine women: an atrocity in mythic Roman history, painted on countless occasions by neoclassical artists.

Dickens did all but go down on his knees to make *me*—waltz with him!— But I thought I did my part well enough in talking the maddest nonsense with *him*, *Forster* Thackeray and Maclise—without attempting the Impossible— [H]owever *after supper* when we were all madder than ever with the pulling of crackers, the drinking of champaign, and the making of speeches, a universal country dance was proposed—and Forster *seizing me round the waist*, whirled me into the thick of it—and MADE me dance!! like a person in the tread mill who must move forward or be crushed to death! Once I cried out 'oh for the love of Heaven let me go! you are going to dash my brains out against the folding doors'! to which he answered—(you can fancy the tone)—'your *brains*! who cares about their brains *here*? *let them go*!' In fact the thing was rising into something not unlike the *rape of the Sabines*! (*Mrs Reid* was happily gone some time) when somebody looked at her watch and exclaimed 'twelve o'clock'! Whereupon we all rushed to the cloak-room—and *there* and in the lobby and up to the last moment the mirth raged on— Dickens took home Thacke[ra]y and Forster with him and his wife 'to *finish the night* THERE!['] and a *royal* night they would have of it I fancy!—ending perhaps with a visit to the watch house.[65] After all—the pleasantest company, as Burns thought, *are* the *blackguards*![66]—that is; those who have just a sufficient dash of blackguardism in them to make them snap their fingers at *ceremony* and 'all that sort of thing.' I question if there was as much witty speech uttered, in all the aristocratic, conventional drawingrooms thro out London that night as among us little knot of blackguardist literary people who felt ourselves above all rules, and independent of the universe! Well and the result?— Why the result my dear was, that I went to bed on my return and—slept like a top!!!! Plainly proving that *excitement* is my *rest*! To be sure my head ached a little next morning but the coffee cleared it—and I went about the dinner for Mrs Cunningham without much physical inconvenience.

See what a letter I have written!—and such writing!—but I must stop now for the post hour is at hand.— [. . .] Your own / J C

65. That is, the police station.
66. Perhaps Jane is thinking of Robert Burns' anarchic 'cantata', 'The Jolly Beggars' (1785), which ends: 'A fig for those by law protected! / Liberty's a glorious feast! / Courts for cowards were erected, / Churches built to please the priest.'

To Martha Lamont, Chelsea, 29 December 1843

Dear Madam

My husband's excessive occupation at present affords a pretext which I gladly avail myself of to write my own thanks for your book sent me thro him. Remembering the *real* interest with which I read your *Gladiator* I shall fall to this new book with good hope; so soon as I have finished Harriet Martineau's *Life in the sick Room* which came to me exactly in the same moment and which, for old friendship's sake, I could not but read first.[67]

Thanks also for having said a word in season to my husband on the heterodox state of his opinions respecting us women. That he thinks us an inferior order of beings—that is, an order of beings born *to obey*; I am afraid there is not the shadow of a doubt!—not that he is in the habit of promulgating such opinion with any offensive clearness. He never almost speaks about *women in the abstract*, and for this and the other *concrete woman* I have heard him express a very passable admiration: but this reticence—I should say from his practice—proceeds not from any misgivings on the question of our inferiority, nor yet from any delicacy towards *our* feelings; but simply and solely from that self-complacency of full conviction which finds its natural expression *in silence*. Just as nobody thinks it worth while to call peoples attention at midday to the fact of its being daylight!— Never mind!— As Napoleon said at St Helena when they *would* make him into *General Buonapart* 'They may *call* me what they like[,] they cannot hinder me *being* what I *am*!'— So these arrogant *men* may please themselves in their ideas of our *inferiority* to their hearts content; they cannot hinder us in *being* what we *will* and *can* be. Oh we can afford very well to laugh at their *ideas*, so long as we feel in ourselves the power to make slaves, and even fools of the wisest of them!—

If you are ever in London be sure to come and see us; for I have a presentiment that I should like you considerably. [I]n which case tho 'I am not the rose—have only lived beside the rose'[68]—you will certainly like *me*—for all my experience has gone to prove that human sympathy is invariably two-sided.

67. Liverpool-based Irish novelist Martha Macdonald Lamont (1803–1878) published *The Gladiator, a Tale of the Roman Empire* in 1840; her *Impressions, Thoughts, and Sketches: During Two Years in France and Switzerland* was published in 1844. Harriet Martineau's book of essays on being a patient—believing herself incurably afflicted with a tumour of the uterus—was published in 1844: Jane must have been sent an advance copy.

68. A well-used quote the origins of which are disputed: whether from Chaucer's translation of the thirteenth-century *Romaunt of the Rose*, or from the French Romantic writer Benjamin Constant.

I have relations in Liverpool and go there at rare intervals; should you be still in Liverpool at my next visit I shall make a point of finding you—

Meanwhile till further acquaintance believe me yours

with sincere esteem / Jane Carlyle

My husband would send his kind regards if he were not upstairs over head and ears almost to the drowning point in a Life of Cromwell which he can make no sort of sense out of—as yet—

Figure 6: Francis Holl, *Lady Harriet Baring, first wife of the Hon William Baring, later Lord Ashburton* (nd), Carlyle House, © National Trust Images

5

The Onset of Lady Harriet: 1844–1847

For Thomas these years mark the final completion of the Cromwell letters and speeches project, progress with which was agonisingly slow ('frightful' was his word) up to its completed first draft in August 1845 and beyond, as the book made its way through the publishers and the printers. For Jane there were two new patterns in her existence—which reached a nadir in the spring of 1846, when insomnia and depression made her fear for her sanity at a time when various of her acquaintances were self-evidently deranged.

We associate Jane with her native Scotland on the one hand and her adopted Chelsea on the other. But during this period and beyond it we find her often enough between those two extremes, in the industrial north of England. Her uncle John Welsh, a copper founder in Liverpool, often hosted her there on her trips from south to north, and London acquaintances such as Geraldine Jewsbury and Harriet Martineau had northern roots, also. In June of 1844 she visited her Liverpool family, but went to stay the following month with a friend of Geraldine's: Elizabeth ('Betsy') Paulet and her Swiss businessman husband Étienne. Originally, Geraldine, Elizabeth and Jane had planned to cooperate on what would become Geraldine's first novel, Zoe—which Jane edited and carried to its eventual publisher in early 1844 (see 29 February 1844). For three summers in a row ('44, '45 and '46) she stayed with Paulet at Seaforth House, in the seaside village of that name at the mouth of the Mersey inlet. In Liverpool in 1844 she also met Harriet Martineau's brother James (1805–1900), Professor of Mental and Moral Philosophy and Political Economy at the Unitarian Manchester New College. In the summer of 1846 she went on from Seaforth to visit Geraldine in Manchester itself, where she visited factories and met engineer and philanthropist Joseph Whitworth (1803–1887), radical poet Samuel Bamford (1788–1872) and Corfiote businessman Stavros Dilberoglue. In the summer of 1847 she and Thomas toured the Derbyshire Peak District and visited another such northerner, William Edward Forster, Quaker and woollen manufacturer in Rawdon, Yorkshire, before staying with Elizabeth Paulet's brother in Barnsley.

These gulps of fresh air—outside the boxes of marriage and family alike—were all the more important because between them Oliver Cromwell and Lady Harriet Baring (Harriet Ashburton when her husband succeeded to that baronage in 1848) drove Jane almost to her wits' end during this period. The Lord Protector, she told cousin Jeannie in February 1845 (CL 19: 26), made the '(moral) atmosphere within doors [. . .] far too sulphury *and* brimstoneish*' for comfort, and all she could hope for where he was concerned was to see him finally out of the house. But Lady Harriet was (she felt) an enemy deep within her marriage, whose company her husband demonstrably and unapologetically preferred to her own. (In her, Virginia Surtees astutely remarks, Jane 'found herself supplanted in those intellectual qualities in which she had expected to excel'.*[1]*) Jane no doubt knew enough to know that there was nothing sexual in Thomas's fixation on this mannish and imperious hostess. ('My sovereign lady', he called her; 'Daughter of Adam most beautiful', amidst other cringeworthy appellatives.) But sexual infatuation might at least be somewhat outside a husband's control, whereas the howl of pain at his conscious desertion of her still echoed ten years later, in Jane's journal of October 1855 that is discussed in Chapter 8.*

As we saw in the previous chapter, Thomas first met this 'masterly coquette' (CL 18: 163–4) in March 1839, and became a Bath House regular in 1842,[2] *a year or so before Jane even met her. On 16 November 1845 (below) she was comparing the Barings' Hampshire country house unfavourably with Seaforth; by February 1846 she was trying to put a brave face on things: 'I* love *her now as much [as] I* admired *her in the beginning' (CL 20: 119). But it wasn't true; and by the time she left Chelsea for Seaforth in July 1846 she and Thomas were at breaking point on the issue, perhaps as the very outcome of her efforts to ingratiate herself with the enigmatic lady at her various country houses in the spring. 'Certainly we have never before parted in such a manner!' Thomas blindly wrote on 6 July: 'And all for,—literally,—Nothing!' (CL 20: 220). 'The annals of insanity contain nothing madder', he wrote to her in Manchester, 'than "jealousy" directed against such a journey as I have before me today' (CL 21: 14): on holiday with the Barings to Scotland, that is. On 7 November Jane was still reporting to Helen Welsh (CL 21: 86) that 'her Ladyships will is become the law of this house!—even her* whims *are as imperative as the ten commandments!' Yet all the while the conventions had to be obeyed, and Jane had again and again to accompany Thomas on visits to Bay House, Addiscombe and The Grange as if all was well. In the end, the Victorian wife could do nothing other than buckle under.*[3] *No wonder she speaks to Robert Scot Skirvington, below, of her 'dissolving views' of herself; or that she essentially went to*

1. Virginia Surtees, *Jane Welsh Carlyle* (Salisbury, 1986), 184.
2. The Barings'/Ashburtons' London residence, on Piccadilly in the West End; demolished in 1960.
3. Each of the contributors to this 'unhappy triangle', Rosemary Ashton suggests (*Thomas and Jane Carlyle: Portrait of a Marriage* (London, 2002), 271), 'was to blame in some degree'. 'Carlyle was selfish and acted, for such an honest man, in self-deceiving bad faith. Jane was excessively sensitive and excessively punitive. And Lady Harriet was either surprisingly insensitive or actually malicious.'

bed for the entire month of December 1846, ostensibly in reaction to servant dramas ('Kirkcaldy Helen' having quit the post in September), but probably as a symptom of depression. In the summer of 1847 Dr John diagnosed a tumour in her throat: she did not tell Thomas. Her letters hide far more than they reveal, yet they are a sign of life, too. 'Oh Babbie,' she wrote to Jeannie Welsh in September 1843 (CL 17: 134–5): 'I am horribly sad always at the bottom of my heart—my external life is all smoothed over again, and flows on noiselessly enough—but underneath!' But in time there would be a second Lady Ashburton—Louisa, not Harriet—who would be Jane's particular friend and surrogate daughter, and would heal some of the wounds her predecessor had inflicted.

To Geraldine Jewsbury, Chelsea, 29 February 1844

Dearest Geraldine

If my sympathy could do you the least good; you have it 'hot and hot'—nobody can appreciate the utter wretchedness of all *that* better than I! Sick selves; sick *helps*— Ach gott [O Lord]!— But the sick going out in a cab to seek their dinner! *there* is a cut beyond even *me*! We have sometimes gone *without* dinner in this house for want of somebody to cook it—and once when Helen had lain all day on the floor dead-drunk, and I could not go on doing her work without victual; I went in all simplicity to a neighbouring cookshop and brought away a *quarter of a pound* of cold beef in a piece of grey paper! But mounting with Carlyle into a cab, and driving off madly to repair exhausted nature at the house of a friend is *a new idea for me*, which I shall bear in mind for future emergencies! The very day I last wrote to you, finding *after I was in it* that I might take [Edward] Sterlings carriage to the Strand, I drove to Chapman & Halls and presented myself to these Dignitaries, without either M.S. [of *Zoe*] or *Credentials* but on what Mrs Mudie would call 'the broad basis' of my own feminine merits! You may think that it was taking my hens to market in a rainy day, going with my *feminine merits* to an old dingy bookshop in the Strand— But trust me for always knowing where and when I can turn my *womanhood* to account—*that* I believe is an instinct which every woman beyond the rank of an idiot brings into the world with her— Mr Chapman[4] had been several times to this house on

4. For Edward Chapman (1804–1880), partner in this prodigious publishing house, see Rosemary Ashton, *142 Strand: A Radical Address in Victorian London* (London, 2008); No. 142 was Chapman's home, No. 186 the office Jane visited.

business with my husband—and on my husbands invisible hours had been shown in to *me* as a substitute—and on these occasions he had—*blushed* as if he were going to break a bloodvessel! and I having a great feeling for blushing men (when they are not sheepish withal) treated him with 'a certain' marked politeness— So I said to myself thou hast thrown thy bread on the waters and shallt find it after many days.[5] Accordingly I asked not for Messrs Chapman and Hall—but for Mr Chapman and was told—that his Sister was just dead and he could not be seen—but that Mr Hall was forthcoming— I had chosen precisely the wrong moment— However to come away with nothing whatever accomplished was contrary to my nature so I requested to see this Hall—and a poor little insignificant spectacle it was! Sterling having followed me into the shop, not choosing that he should hear me talking *business-like*[,] I requested to be taken into a private room and the small Hall with a look of considerable perplexity bowed me into his dark *Sanctum* where stood to my consternation poor Chapman leaning on the mantlepiece and all bewept! the large face of him absolutely swollen with weeping—however such is the ennobling power of a deep grief that he received me this time without any embarrassment but with the air of the most perfect Gentleman, and it was to him that I addressed myself after all— I told him my own impression of your book, the impression which it had made on two men of cultivated minds,[6] and my husbands idea of your general tallents 'tho he had not had time to spare from Cromwell to inspect this particular manifestation of them. ['] And moreover I told him you were a sister of Miss Jewsbury—but very unlike her—and to my thinking a person much more likely to suit our *existing* public taste—on which Chapman surprised me by saying 'Oh he remembered you perfectly he had seen you one day in my house'—tant mieux [so much the better]— The result of this first visit was a promise from both Partners to 'give the *MS* their *most serious consideration*'— I did not however send it to them immediately—judging that it would be better to wait a little till Chapman should have got thro' the sad cares of his Sister's funeral and be a little more in a condition for giving 'serious consideration' to any earthly thing— Meanwhile I got a note of *general recommendation* from Carlyle—which I am sorry I did not keep a copy of for your *amusement*— He had not read this M.S.

5. Ecclesiastes 11: 1.
6. George Lillie Craik, co-author of *The Pictorial History of England*, and Edward Sterling, 'The Thunderer' at *The Times* (see below). 'Miss Jewsbury' was Maria Jane Jewsbury (1800–1833), popular poet and Christian moralist, who died of cholera in India while married to an East India Company chaplain.

himself, he said but 'a friend of *mature years* (that's me!) quick insight and *sufficiently impatient temper* had read it all thro even in its *Manuscript* state and without a single expression of weariness—but with apparent interest and pleasures, a fact which of itself said much he considered to its credit.' To this note I added a repetition of my own favourite opinion, backed with that of the Thunder of the Times and the Author of the Pictorial history of England—and having tied up all this along with a kind message to Mr Chapman not as a Publisher but a *Man* and the *Corpus delecti* ['fact of the crime': the MS] itself of course. I left it at the shop on Saturday last—and am now waiting with my 'sufficiently impatient temper' for their answer.

I wish *something* would really prosper in my hands—just to show me that I am not like Mazzini under *a fatality*.

Oh Geraldine have you been reading the daily papers last week? If so you could not miss a *crim con* process which filled many columns of them for four successive days.[7] But little would you think of the downright *agony* of suspense in which *I* was watching its progress— I neither a *principal* nor even a witness! I was not when this infernal prosecution was first started a friend of Mrs Fraser's— She called on me at my first coming to London with her 'handsome husband' but they were just newly married then and she looked so happy so *triumphant* over her bad bargain that I did not take to her—never returned her call—refused their invitation to dinner—and there our intercourse terminated— John [Carlyle] afterwards became intimate with her at Munich where her husbands extravagance compelled them to reside for several years—and from him I had heard much of her virtues as a Mother and *housewife*—and Carlyle who dined with them after their return to this country had also a good opinion of her—and was very sorry for her when after a horrid course of dissipation and extravagance her husband finally deserted her some two years ago—about a month before the birth of her last child! When this Process came to light Carlyle and John were both *certain* of its atrocity and that the poor woman had *done nothing*—for me after such treatment I should have

7. The legal euphemism for the civil offence of adultery in the Victorian age was 'criminal conversation' (the tort would be abolished in 1847). William Fraser (1805–1852) was a literary editor who had published some of Thomas's early essays. Having used up his wife's income he was declared bankrupt, egregiously abandoned her to the care of his friend, William Bagley, and in the fullness of time brought this suit against her in part at least on the basis of his wife calling Bagley 'my dear', as Jane herself often called *her* male friends. The case (in which Dr John gave medical evidence) was dismissed, but the double standard being what it was—the fourth estate repeatedly referred to Fraser as 'the handsome husband'—the damage was done to Mrs Fraser's reputation.

stood up for her whether I believed that she had *done anything* or no—in fact I have quite made the case *my own*— '*Esprit de Corps* my Dear'? says Carlyle— *Before* her acquittal I sent her a message by John that I begged permission to come and be of some comfort to her—and on Saturday I went to see her—perfectly indifferent in the warmth of my indignation how many people might *cut* my acquaintance in consequence. Had you found her as I did—stretching out her arms to me from her bed, with a burst of hysterical weeping—so pale and wasted and nearly out of her wits you could hardly have resisted the temptation to go off and assassinate the wretch of a husband on the spot— I fear she will never be herself again in this world—tho the verdict was in her favour it appeared to be due to the Jurys detestation of her husbands conduct rather than to their conviction of *her* innocence and this is the public feeling about it—for *me* I solemnly believe her innocent—but *that* as I have said would hardly have increased my sympathy with her.

I was to have gone again on Tuesday to have staid the whole day[,] and Carlyle had generously promised to come and fetch me back—but she was quite light in the head on Monday—and continues in a dreadful way— She has a young lady staying with her—and her Sisters and intimate friends adhere to her and believe in her thank God— I will do all I can to console her—but it is so little! for I fear after all his diabolical usage and this infernal climax to it, she is still *in love* with her own husband! several things she said to me the other day left that impression on my mind—and that sort of feeling makes a woman eternally irrevocably *a victim*—

I have been very ill again myself—but I have no more time for writing—

God bless you Your affectionate / JC

To Thomas Carlyle, Liverpool, 17 July 1844

Dearest, most punctual Good! May your shadow never be less! One letter to console me on my arrival, another on getting out of bed this morning! I am more content with you than I choose to express—for fear of your getting vain upon it and giving yourself *airs*! Today's letter kept me laughing all the way thro—a signal triumph of Genius, as I had not slept till four in the morning! Noises?— No—nothing but my own '*Interior*' to blame for it!

My last letter was cut short by Mrs Paulet and Geraldine entering with a riding habit— You felt no misgivings over my concluding words?— In that case you have nothing of the Prophetical in you— Lend me all your ears and I *will* 'hasten to the catastrophe'[8]— Being equipped in the most approved Amazonian fashion I was led forth to my horse; the whole house even to 'pup' (the youngest Child) turning out to see what they called '*the procession*'—and a dashing *procession* truly it was going to have been; The groom who was to follow me on one of the carriage-horses (besides the eldest boy on his poney) having turned out *the whole pack* of spotted Dalmation dogs to my honour and glory! and there were they all (*five* in number) barking, capering, leaping up and *biting at the horse's neck* after the manner of that species of dog![9] While I was still seeking in my consternation words of polite protest against this riotous cortège [train of attendants] Mrs Paulet suggested that 'the dogs had better be put up' very much to the disappointment of the groom, who made no haste to obey, till I peremptorily declared I would not ride a step with them. It was these very spotted dogs, if you remember, who tormented the carriage-horses into running off with us before— Well! they were *eventually* got housed; their '*owls*' beating all '*organs*' hollow![10] And when the coast was clear of them I had time to look at my steed— [T]he inspection was far from satisfactory—it was a beautiful animal with *blood* enough and to spare—but its manner of tossing its head and foaming at the mouth appeared to me 'significative of much'!—and in spite of my dislike to be taken for a coward I again asked Mrs Paulet if she were *perfectly* sure that it was *quiet*. 'Oh not a doubt of it! it was Julia Musprat's Horse—and she exercised it every day'—so I mounted with a modest trust in Providence— [T]he saddle, an old one of Mrs Paulets, pleased me as little as the horse—it seemed made with a view to one's sliding off.— 'Now my dear for god's sake do get to the catastrophe'!— Well! with the long-legged boy on his small poney by my side, and the groom on his carriage-horse behind I moved off, thinking in my own mind; 'decidedly I *will* not go far—neither far nor fast'— So soon as we got within sight of the Musprat-house my steed 'felt it his duty to intimate' to me that he liked that road the best; and a stout debate ensued between us, which after various circumvoluings and questionable conduct on his part, ended in his giving up *that* point and allowing himself to be guided towards the shore—not however without

8. A Thomas-ism for getting to the point of a story, used in *Sartor Resartus* and elsewhere.
9. The Dalmatian had its origins in the Balkans, but was bred up in England during the Regency. The breed has a pronounced guarding instinct, which makes it loyal to its owner and indifferent to others besides. It was often used to guard horses, stables and coaches in the period.
10. Dickens, *Martin Chuzzlewit*, chapter 49, in which the alcoholic district nurse Mrs Gamp and her associate Betsy Prig go over the case history of a certain Mr Harris, who could not tolerate his first newborn's crying until the doctor told him the child's '[h]owls was organs'.

symptoms of that 'subdued temper' which Darwin so justly detests. But no sooner did he feel the sand under his feet, than at one *bound* he set off like an incarnate Devil—and I found myself *run-away-with* beyond all controversy—not like Attila Schmelzle '*at a walk*'[11]—but at full race-course gallop! Would he run on till I became dizzy and fell off and got my brains kicked out with his heels? or would he turn sharp up some back road to his own stable and dash me against some gate or stable-door?— I could not predict 'the least in the world,' and I was extremely anxious to know—meanwhile I had the sense not to irritate him by any vain efforts at pulling up—and the *luck* to keep my seat—heaven knows how on such a saddle, and all out of practice as I was! Among the innumerable thoughts that passed thro' my head during this devils-race was the thought of your last advice 'not to be getting into any adventure with wild horses at Seaforth,' and I could have cried if there had been convenience for crying—but there was none—and so I rushed along with dry eyes and closed mouth, until, as happened to *you* on a former occasion, the Demon of a brute was stopt by 'an arm of the sea'!—*There* was an adventure for your poor necessary evil![12] which could you have seen thro 'a powerful telescope' the groom would not have been the only person that 'trembled all over'[.] When he overtook me he was as white as milk—and heartily approved my determination to risk myself no further— He proposed to put the sidesaddle on *his* mare, for whose good temper he said he 'could answer with his life'— So I got upon the carriage horse next—rode on to the Bootle post office with the letter for *you* which I had all the while in my breast, and then came home at a decent butter-and-eggs trot rather gratified than otherwise to observe the loss of the grooms hat and other difficulties which even *he* had to struggle with on the back of *Miss Julia Musprat's horse*!—Decidedly, thought I 'Miss Julia Musprat' must be a first rate horse-woman! Perhaps no better than myself after all, for the horse—was none of Miss Julia's! turned out to have been 'Mr Richards[']'[13]—sent as a credit to the Musprat-stables, instead of the one asked for,—tho it had once run away with a Miss Roberts before, and nearly finished her!!—Can you fancy people doing such things?— Poor Mrs Paulet was almost at the crying when she found how it had all been. However *thanks* God I was not even made *stiff* by the business only a little nervous—

Mrs Ames's musical *soirée* in the evening—in a small room—with every breath of air excluded did me far more mischief— Still I do not

11. The tale 'Army-Chaplain Schmelzle's Journey to Flaetz', by German Romantic author Jean Paul Richter (1763–1825), had been translated by Thomas.
12. One of Thomas's pet names for Jane.
13. Julia and Richard Muspratt were son and daughter of an important Lancashire chemical manufacturer: the first to industrialise the production of alkalis.

regret having gone to see how they ack [act; behave] in the various places— Most of the company were Unitarians[,] the men with faces like a meataxe—the women most palpably *without bustles*[14]—a more unloveable set of humanbeings I never looked on— However I had a long rather agreeable talk with James Martineau the only 'Bae-ing I could love'— of the whole nightmare-looking fraternity— HE is a man with 'a *subdued temper*' or I am greatly mistaken but he is singularly in earnest—for a Unitarian—bold enough to utter any truth THAT HE HAS in season and out of season—and as affectionate-hearted *as a woman*—(I use the common form of expression without recognising the justice of it)

My Seaforth visit—in spite of cold and all the rest of it, has been a great success— I have sworn everlasting friendship with Mrs Paulet— we suit each other perfectly—neither of us have been rash in coming to this conclusion—and now that we *have* come to it—I feel confident that we shall be each others dearest *friend* as long as we both live.

My reception here [Maryland Street] was so cordial that it almost reconciled me to the difference of *atmosphere*—My Uncle not the least *ecstatic* among them— Still I desire to be home now—and shall go to Manchester God willing on Saturday—(Geraldine waits at Seaforth for me) and back to my own Good in the beginning of the week—on Tuesday perhaps but I will not fix the day positively till I get there— I have promised to visit Mrs Darbyshire who is fallen deeply in love with me and I with her *to a moderate extent*[.] She reminds me somewhat of poor Mrs Sterling only much more cultivated and less given to *talk*. But I must not write here all day Good— You sent me two most welcome letters old Betty and Mrs Russel— Mazzini wrote to me the other day that he had sent your letter in the Times to his Mother and that she had written him 'a long letter full of the most *fervid* gratitude that ever woman tried to express'— Poor fellow he is much to be sympathized with just now

Your own

J C

I shall perhaps have no time to write tomorrow[;] Walter Mac is going to take me to THE RACES!!! Not on horseback in a carriage

14. A waist-level undergarment on the rear, designed to support the shape and weight of Victorian dresses, and producing an exaggerated posterior thereby. Unitarians were notoriously austere in terms of all social habits, fashion included. James Martineau was Harriet's brother. Jane refused ever to wear either the bustle or the equally impractical hoop-shaped skirt-reinforcer, the crinoline.

To Jeannie Welsh, Chelsea, circa 29 August 1844

Dearest

You may well say *in this instance at least* that while others talk I act—

Certainly I have been *acting*—with a vengeance!— You will wonder if I have not become insane myself when I tell you the *sequel*—would to Heaven I could call it *the solution*!— Last Sunday evening Carlyle and I had just finished an early dinner preparatory to setting off on a Cockney-Sunday-excursion to the Regent's Park to be helped out with tea at Mrs Macready's—when I heard a gentleman's voice at the door inquiring for *me*— I had heard that voice only once before in my life but I recognized it instantly as Sir Alexander Morison's[15]— What on earth had brought so busy a man to my own house?— Was he come to tell me that *He* had committed *suicide* or *escaped*!— I rushed up stairs to him as white as milk—tearing my muslin gown by the way to an extent that would have tried even the temper of Ann Jane— With an impassive air, that operated like a shower-bath on me at the moment, the good old Doctor delivered me a letter from my friend—stating that he had 'appeared before the Committee on the previous day['] been pronounced *cured* and now only waited till some friend should '*take him out*'—a formality it seemed which could not be dispensed with— Would I *send some one*— I told Sir Alexander of course that I would come myself next morning if C could not leave his work— But what then?—suffer him so soon as I had emancipated him to rush out into space under the first excitement natural to recovered liberty—and without either money or plan from all I could learn— The thing was not to be thought of—so when Sir Alexander asked 'but where will he go'? I looked imploringly at Carlyle who, good as he always is on *great* occasions, said directly 'Oh he must come *here* for a while till he sees what is to be done next'— And so it was settled and I had no difficulty in bringing *himself* to [']consent to the arrangement.' Thro unavoidable hindrances I was obliged to spend nearly *the whole day* in the Lunatic Asylum and a *happier* day I hardly ever past in life— At seven at night I landed him here in a *fly*[16] and here

15. Scots-born physician (1779–1866) who moved to London in 1808 and began a long-standing interest in the treatment of mental disability, being appointed visiting physician to Surrey asylums in 1810. There is a remarkable portrait of him at the National Gallery of Scotland by Richard Dadd (1817–1866), the prodigious miniaturist painter, hospitalised at Bethlem and Broadmoor after killing his father in a psychotic fit in 1843. Morison was looking after the Carlyles' long-suffering German friend, Richard Plattnauer.
16. A two-wheeled light carriage with a roof, for local transport, hired at a livery stable; the predecessor of the hansom cab, which became the taxi of nineteenth-century London. Jane mentions them frequently.

he has been ever since and will be for some time yet— Whether it be the consciousness of having done a good action—or that he discovers a faculty and nobleness of character in him, which he had before not allowed himself opportunity to discover; I cannot say—but the fact is that Carlyle seems to take to him most *lovingly* and shows him the uttermost kindness!! Still I have much to keep me anxious for not only does his future lie most perplexedly before us but—whatever the Drs and Committee have judged—*I* do not consider him by any means *sane*— He is horribly excitable—and has many wild whims in his head which might at any moment by injudicious treatment, be exploded into madness— And his whole bearing and manner of speech is quite changed—*for the better*— [S]o far as that goes—never did he seem half so clever or noble or highbred—but this very superiority alarms one— I know that *I* can keep him from any new crisis so long as he is beside *me*—my influence over him is without limit—but then he cannot be *always* with *me*—and I tremble at the thought of what will become of him when left to himself— God knows—perhaps I frighten myself needlessly and his present state is but the *natural* consequen[ce] of the past five weeks—

Mrs Buller is worrying herself to death with the fear of his killing me—in these days of *insane* murdering just as [Francis] Jeffrey used to warn me against William Glen[17] but no madman will ever hurt a hair of *my* head—I have too much *affinity* with them—

You will understand how it is not easy for me to write in these days— There is still a deal of writing to be caried on with the Marchioness—the Authoress of *The City of the Sultan* and others[18]—which is merely *boring me* without doing the slightest practical good to *him*—and then Lord bless you he has torn all his linen entirely to rags—as he did all the ropes they bound him with— It is somewhat awful to hear him say in the midst of a calm tete a tete [conversation]—such a thing crossed his mind when they were 'carrying him to such a place *in chains*'—or when they had chained him down on the floor of the [']*House of Correction*'!— He remembers accurately every thing that happened only fancys that *he* was all the while quite in his right mind and merely that the other people were 'so *stupid*'— But I was saying his clothes are all in rags and as I have constituted myself his sister for the present I am

17. A Scots-born London acquaintance of Thomas's, confined to a Glasgow asylum in the early 1830s.
18. Lady Mary Herbert (1813–1892), wife of the 2nd Marquess of Ailesbury. *The City of the Sultan, and Domestic Manners of the Turks* was published by Julia Pardoe (1804–1862) in 1837, after her travels in the Middle East with her father; it was a popular success and helped to change British attitudes to Turkey and Islam. She also wrote on Portugal and Hungary.

kept very busy repairing them— What things I have done for him to be sure! in the way of *familiarity*— Poor poor Soul his body is still all lacerated with those infernal chains—and Sir A Morison assured me that had any judicious Dr or friend been beside him at the commencement nothing of all that need ever have been!

But there is his rap at the door so I must conclude for the present—

I cannot help regretting that monster was *not* hanged in spite of all my sympathy with his children—[19]

Love and kisses to all

Ever your affectionate /

Jane Carlyle

To Helen Welsh, Chelsea, 12 November 1844

Dearest Helen

If your letter had not been so long or so amusing, if it had been in fact less 'creditable to your head and *hort*'; the chances are it would have been answered sooner. I should have flashed you off a few lines 'at the earliest opportunity'—but being a meritorious letter; I wished as poor William Gibson used to phrase it, 'to make a suitable *return*'—and for *that*, one has to await the 'convenient season.' Thus you see my dear young Lady there is always 'something very particular' occurring '*here down*' (*qui giù*) to prevent virtue having its 'own reward'! There is one touch in your letter which has filled me with genuine admiration— you were not at all aware I dare say (for merit is ever *unconscious*) when you historically mentioned the fact; of the importance I was likely to attach to it, and the favourable inferences I should draw from it respecting the general state of your soul. You said that on being told how Margaret had poured boiling soup 'all over her'—you *ran for cotton*, and THEN down stairs &c &c— Now *that* is what I call having ones wits about one, that is really being a *useful* member of society. There is not one of a hundred young Ladies who would have *run for cotton* FIRST, who would not have run to see the state of the accident first—and so lost time which is always precious but never so precious as in cases of burning— I make you my compliments on your calm ready helpfulness my gentle cousin— [I]t would be well if there were more of that sort

19. Obscure; but the mother of Margaret, the Liverpool Welshes' housemaid (see next letter), had been murdered.

of helpfulness circulating in this *fussy* little world. And when I meet with an accident—'happen a misfortune' as my first London servant used to say—I hope you may be at hand to help me—you—with your '*little* cry and *much* WOOL'![20]

If I had not been very busy in these weeks, I really think I should have been tempted to send for sixpenny-worth of Arsnece [arsenic]—and put myself out of pain— Everlasting rains—the air a solution of soot—the universe one abominable '*Clart*' [mud]—no possibility of taking outdoors exercise, and no faculty of *sleeping* without it— And every body that comes in, sworn (one might think) in a general conspiracy, to tell one something tragical or disagreeable— I really do think sometimes that a sort of things occur to ME which occur to noone else, at least they occur with a *frequency* which has no parallel[.] *There* is another of my intimate acquaintance gone mad!—madder than twenty March hares—and as if *I* must needs be mixed up with all the madness that occurs in my sphere—*the idea* of her *Monomania* is, that her husband is *my Lover*!!— The poor creature (Mrs Anthony Sterling)[21] has done nothing—absolutely nothing—these many years but read *novels*—and now I suppose we are witnessing the *consummation* of her futile existence!— It is more than a fortnight ago, that hearing accidentally she was *ill*, I put on my things like a good Samaritan[,] and went off in the rain, to see whether I could be of any help— The servants looked *strange* at me—the Master looked *strange*—the whole house had an atmosphere of *strangeness*, which puzzled my unsuspecting mind— Anthony shut the door of the Library cautiously on himself and me—and then told me his wife was 'out of her wits simply and shortly'— 'Good gracious! I asked do you seriously mean that she is gone mad'?— Yes said he—[']she is at present in a decided state of Monomania—which the Drs say the slightest contradiction may drive into *Hysterical phrenzy*'— [']Monomania? said I and what is her particular *idea*?'— Her 'particular idea' said Anthony with all the *military* composure in the world, 'is, that I have fallen in love with *you*—that *you* are a dreadful person—and that I ruin myself in making you presents'!— Actually the poor wretch was raving one day about his (Anthony's) having *given me my new dining room carpet and new piano*— 'She was sure it was *he*'!!! and all these base visions growing out of the one poor little fact of her husband's having once given me a *crockery jug*!! You may fancy if I sat very comfortable in

20. The proverbial expression is 'great cry and little wool': to make a mountain out of a molehill.
21. Charlotte, wife of John Sterling's brother Anthony, eldest son of Edward (the 'Stimabile') and wife Hester.

my chair after this *revealation*[.] He offered me wine, which I declined tho really *needing it*—as I also declined his offer to send the carriage home with me; tho' I should have been the better of that too— [I]n short I conducted myself like an angel of *discretion*, and *came away* with all despatch—but MY *discretion* never succeeds[:] the unhappy woman was told by one of John's children that I had been there, and forthwith fell into the *Phrenzy* which the Drs apprehended— For several days the poor Husband's state was truly pitiable—he could not leave her room a moment without her shrieking out that he was 'going to walk with Mrs Carlyle'—and flinging the *poker* all about— At last she suddenly took a violent *dislike to him* and would not suffer his presence, which was so far good— He still keeps her in his own house—but shut up with *three* experienced attendants in a part of the house which is *boarded* off from the rest with improvised planks—lined with *flock* to prevent her noise being heard. It is very horrible—she is sometimes like to lay all waste[22] and has to be put in a straight waistcoat— I wish she had chosen one of her maids or some other of her *friends* than *myself* to be jealous of—almost *anybody* would have been more feasable— Nevertheless Anthony tells me this jealously has been an affair of some standing—tho' neither of us can recall a single circumstance that could have given a rational or even irrational ground for it— Meanwhile it is slightly annoying to have ones name uttered *in shrieks*, before assembled Drs and servants—and coupled with the most ignominious epithets. Happily I never liked her much, so that I can bear her misfortune *like a christian*—and her madness is of such a very repulsive sort that one cannot feel any *tender* sympathy with it— [F]ancy the meanness of the creature— On the night after my visit—Carlyle went up 'to speak a word of comfort to poor Anthony' and she being not yet *boarded off*—nor contradicted in any of her caprices—sent her own maid *to listen all the while at the Library door to hear what Carlyle and her husband were saying of her*!!

Curiously enough—another married Lady of my acquaintance[23]—*not* mad—has just at this moment—misfortunes never coming single—taken up a rabid jealousy of poor innocent *me*! Has done such absurd things in evidence thereof and made her husband do such absurd things that *even Carlyle* 'has no longer a doubt of it'[.] He Carlyle is making himself very merry at what he calls '*the judgement* come upon me' and calls me oftener than 'Jane' or 'my Dear' '*Destroyer of the peace of families*!'

22. Ambiguous; *OED* has 'lie all waste' as 'to remain in an uncultivated or ruinous condition', and 'lay waste' as 'to devastate, ravage'. Both make sense in context.
23. Elizabeth ('Bessy') Fuller, married writer and political secretary Arthur Helps in 1836; they had a son in 1843.

This morning as I was sitting only half-awake over my coffee, he suddenly exclaimed—'just to look at you there, looking as if butter would not melt in your mouth, and think of the profligate life you lead'! As John Carlyle would say 'it is *very* absurd'!— He John Carlyle is expected to arrive here this evening— God's will be done!— [. . .]

And now with kisses world without end to all and several—I bid you adieu

Your affectionate cousin

Jane Carlyle

Send this letter on to Babbie—she has not had many lately—nor long ones—and I forgot to tell her of Mrs Anthony Sterling

To John Welsh, Chelsea, 13 December 1844

My dearest Uncle

I write to you *de profundis*—that is to say from the *depths* of my tub-chair, into which I have migrated within the last two hours out of the still lower depths of my gigantic red bed, which has held me all this week—a victim to 'the inclemency of the season'! Oh uncle of my affection such a season! did you ever feel the like of it? *Already* solid ice in ones waterjug!—'poor Gardiners all *froz* out' and Capt Sterling going at large in a *dress of skins*, the same that he wore in Canada! I tried to make head against it by *force of volition*—kept off the fire as if I had been still at 'Miss Hall's' where it was a fine of sixpence to touch the hearthrug,[24] and *walked*, walked, on Carlyles pernicious counsel—(always so for *me* at least) to '*take the Bull by the horns*' instead of following Darwin's more sensible maxim: 'in matters of health always *consult your sensations*.' And so 'by working late and early I'm come to what ye see'! in a tub chair—a little live bundle of flannel shawls and dressing-gowns—with little or no strength to speak of, having coughed myself all to fiddle-strings in the course of the week! and 'in a dibble of a temper' if I had only any body to vent it on!

Nevertheless I am sure 'I have now got the turn' for I feel what Carlyle would call '*a wholesome desire*'—to smoke! which cannot be gratified—as C is dining with Darwin—but the tendency indicates a return to my normal state of health. The next best thing I can think of is to write to *thee*;—beside one's bedroom-fire, in a tub-chair, the

24. An Edinburgh school Jane had attended, 1817–1818.

family-affections bloom up so strong in one!— Moreover I have just been reading for the first time Harriet Martineau's outpourings in the Athenaeum[25] and '*that* minds me' as my Helen says that you wished to know if *I* too had gone into this devilish thing— Catch me! what I think about it were not easy to say, but one thing I am very sure of, that the less one has to do with it the better—and that it is all of one family with witch craft—demonaical possession—is in fact the selfsame principle presenting itself under new scientific forms and under a polite name. To deny that there is such a thing as animal magnetism, and that it actually *does* produce many of the phenomena here recorded is idle—nor do I find much of this, which seems wonderful because we think of it for the first time, a whit more wonderful than those Common instances of it which have never struck us with surprise, merely because we have been used to see them all our lives— [E]very body for instance has seen children thrown almost into convulsions by some one *going thro the motions* of tickling them! Nay one has known a sensitive Uncle shrink his head between his shoulders at the first *pointing of a finger towards his neck*!— [D]oes not a man *physically tremble* under the mere *look* of a wild beast or fellow man that is stronger than himself— [D]oes not a woman *redden all over* when she feels her lovers eyes on her— [H]ow then should one doubt the mysterious power of one individual over another!—or what is there more surprising in being made *rigid* than in being made *red*? in falling into sleep than in falling into convulsions? in following somebody across a room—than in *trembling* before him from head to foot?— I perfectly believe then in the power of magnetism to throw people into all sorts of unnatural states of *body*—could have believed so far *without* the evidence of my senses, and *have* the evidence of my senses for it also— I saw Miss Bölte magnetized one evening at Mrs Buller's by a distinguished Magnetiser who could not sound his *hs*, and who maintained nevertheless that mesmerism 'consisted in moral and intellectual superiority—' [I]n a quarter of an hour by gazing with his dark animal-eyes into hers, and simply holding one of her hands, while his other rested on her head he had made her into the image of death—no *marble* was ever colder, paler, or more motionless, and her face had that peculiarly beautiful expression which Miss Martineau speaks of—never seen but in a dead face or a mesmerized one— Then he played cantrups [tricks] with her arm and leg and left them stretched out for an hour in an attitude which no awake person could have preserved for three minutes. I touched them and they felt horrid—stiff as iron—I

25. *Letters on Mesmerism* (aka 'animal magnetism') published in the venerable Victorian annual and in book form in 1845.

could not bend them down with all my force—they pricked her hand with the point of a penknife[—]she felt nothing—and now comes the strangest part of my story— The man[,] who regards Carlyle and me as Philistines[,] said, '*now* are you convinced?' 'Yes said Carlyle there is no possibility of doubting but that you have stiffened all poor little Miss Bölte there into something very awful'— 'Yes said I pertly but then she *wished* to be magnetized[;] what I doubt is whether anyone could be reduced to that state *without the consent of their own volition*[.] I should like for instance to see anyone magnetize ME!' 'You think I could not'? said the man with a look of ineffable disdain— [']Yes said I—I defy you'!— 'Will you give me your hand MISS'? 'Oh by all means' and I gave him my hand with the most perfect confidence in my force of volition and a smile of contempt— [H]e held it in one of his and with the other made what H Martineau calls some '*passes*' over it—as if he were darting something from his finger ends— I looked him defiantly in the face as much as to say, you must learn to sound your HS Sir before you can produce any effect on a woman like *me*! and whilst this or some similar thought was passing thro' my head—flash—there went over me from head to foot something precisely like what I once experienced from taking hold of a galvanic ball—only *not nearly* so violent— I had presence of mind to keep looking him in the face as if I had felt nothing and presently he flung away my hand with a provoked look, saying 'I believe you would be a very difficult subject, but nevertheless if I had *time* given me I am sure I could mesmerize you[;] at least I never failed with any one yet.' Now if this destroyed for me my theory of *the need of a consenting will*—it as signally destroyed *his* of *moral and intellectual superiority*—for *that* man was superior to *me* in nothing but animal strength as I am a living woman![26] I could even hinder him from *perceiving* that he had mesmerized me by my moral and intellectual superiority! Of the *clairvoyance* I have *witnessed* nothing—but one knows that people with a diseased or violently excited state of nerves can see more than their neighbours. When my insane friend was in this house he said many things *on the strength of his insanity*—which in a mesmerized person would have been quoted as miracles of clairvoyance— Of course a vast deal of what one hears is humbug—this girl of Harriets seems half diseased—half makebelieving— I think it a horrible blasphemy they are there perpetuating in *exploiting* that poor girl for their idle purposes of curiosity! In fact I quite agree with the girl that had this

26. Some readers may find this uncannily reminiscent of Jane Eyre's climactic conversation about sexual equality with Mr Rochester in Charlotte Brontë's novel (published three years later), chapter 23.

Mrs Winyard lived in an earlier age of the world she would have been burnt for a witch—and deserved it better than many that were—since her *poking* into these mysteries of nature is not the result of superstitious ignorance but of *educated* self-conceit. In fact with all this amount of belief in the results of Animal magnetism I regard it as a damnable sort of tempting of Providence which I 'as one solitary individual['] will henceforth stand entirely aloof from— And now having given you my views at great length I will return to my bed and compose my mind.

Love to all—thanks to Helen—with tremenduous kisses

Your devoted Niece

Jane Carlyle

that wretched little Babbie does not write because I owe her a letter—a letter from her would have been some comfort in these dreary days of sickness but since she has not bestowed it I owe her the less thanks—

To Jeannie Welsh, Chelsea, 29 December 1844

Oh Babbie! my dear Babbie! I am thoroughly ashamed of myself— Carlyle put my letter of yesterday in the post office on his way to the Bank— On his return from that august place he proceeded to pull out *your* pocketbook full of [bank]notes—and while counting them, said to me, 'You told Jeanie how much I was pleased with her gift? it is really very pretty and *convenient*—poor little Babbie! it was very kind of her to take so much trouble for her Parent'!— My whole answer was 'Oh mercy'! 'Mercy What' said he— 'Why I [Jane] did not say a single word about the pocketbook'!— 'That was certainly a most extraordinary piece of negligence' said he with such a *grave* look!— 'Will you take THE TROUBLE to thank her for it now then by the very next post'— I was vexed enough at myself without *his* being cross about it— [T]he fact was, not only the pocket-book but the *man* had entirely got themselves crushed out of my head by the confusion I was in yesterday—confusion of soul I mean—to be sure ones soul *ought* to be above its *circumstances* ought to keep *calm*—whatever else— [W]ell I made amends by being very calm last night or rather this morning under circumstances of the most astounding nature— About one in the morning not having been yet asleep and being as is common with me just now extremely *fidgety* I gave my large square pan of hot-water a peevish push with my foot, which sent it right over the bed!—where by the sound it gave in falling I knew that it had broken in pieces—and all the hot water flooding my carpet!—perhaps penetrating the parlour ceiling! and having turned into *ink* in the process (as had once before happened to me) dripping down on my span [perfectly] new brussels carpet beneath! Distraction was in the thought— I sprang over the bed and rang my bell furiously—twice to bring up Helen—who however being in bed did not see any propriety in coming tho' I might have been *dying* for anything she knew— Carlyle however who was still below, reading, came with 'a certain' deliberation—and found me standing in my night clothes with the fragments of crokery and a lake of water at my naked feet— So soon as I had light I got all the towels in the room and flung them down into the lake—and then got down on my knees to soak it up— Carlyle went like a sensible man for his bason and large sponge—and fell to it more effectually with that[,] ordering *me* into bed— [B]ut alas when I turned to go, I found my nightshift all dripping!—had to take another un-aired from the drawer! and after I was in bed found that it had 'most *mistairously*' got wetted also— Carlyle brought me *his small* bottle—and once more all was quiet—except *my heart* which went on at a fine rate for hours—

Today of course I have more cold—but not so much as was to have been anticipated— I asked Helen when she came in in the morning if she had not heard the bell, 'Oh heard it?' said she 'how could she miss hearing it?' And why then did not she come?—'before she had *got her clothes on* she heard Mr Carlyle go up—so she *thought that I had fainted*— and since he was there there could be no use for *her*'!

Cool!—and not over-logical— But she will make up for it by *going into fits* the next time that I *faint in the day time* [. . .]

And now dear Babbie forgive me all my enormities and believe me ever your

Affectionate Cousin /
Jane Carlyle

To Jeannie Welsh, Chelsea, mid-April? 1845

Dearest Babbie

I said that I would write yesterday *god willing* but god was *not willing* and the manner of it was thus— [O]n the preceding night I had *five grains of mercury* (!) introduced into my interior *by mistake*—instead of *one half grain* the quantity I am in the habit of taking at one time—and which is quite enough '*for anything*'— So much for my husbands *false refinement*! I had been wretchedly bilious for some days and sent him to Alsop's for *my* blue *pills*—he also being in the practise of getting pills there—of *five grains*—which he swallows from time to time 'in werra desperation' (as you know) and in fellowship with an ocean of Castor oil—[27] [T]he pills came and I swallowed one; merely wondering why they had sent me only *three* instead of my customary *dozen*—but ten minutes after when I became deadly sick I understood at once how it was[.] Carlyle frankly admitted it was quite likely there had been a mistake—'when he went into the shop a gentleman was with Alsop and he *did not like* to say *send the blue pills for Mrs Carlyle* but said instead send the blue pills *for our house*[']— Alsop of course had prefered the *masculine gender* as grammatically bound to do—and so was *delicacy* another person's 'own reward'[.] All yesterday I was sick enough you may fancy—for I felt too weak to deliver myself from the confounded stuff thro a great doze of physic—I thought it safest to let it work away there in the unfortunate *interior* of me until it had its humour out— Carlyle comforted himself and tried to comfort *me*, by suggesting that 'it might possibly do me a *great deal of good* in the long run'! It may be 'strongly doubted' (as they say in Edinr)— [A]nyhow it has not begun to do me good *yet*—for today I am still passably *sick* and the pill and the new onslaught of frost at the same moment are making me as miserable as Mrs Anthony Sterling (my only enemy) could wish! But I write not to seem a promisebreaker, so long as I can help myself—

Well my Dear just think of my having had a dinner-party last Sunday! the botheration of which was in fact the cause of feeling the *besoin* [need] of blue pill—John Fergus and Miss Jessy[28] were in town and Carlyle asked them 'quite promiscuously' to dine— Miss Jessy 'had a cold' but John would come 'with pleasure'— I was very much shocked—*under the circumstances*—but proceed to meet the emergency as I best could—schemed *a dinner*, had the ingredients provided—and asked Darwin *for party*— The *acceptance* of Darwin arrived on

27. Here are the Carlyles coping 'manfully' with what would appear to be chronic constipation—the source of which is unclear, though their diet was woefully short of fresh fruit and vegetables. 'Blue pills' are a combination of calomel (mercuric chloride) and some sweetening agent to help the medicine go down; and the proportion of the active agent in the pill (the 'doze' as Jane calls it) was mostly anybody's guess (half a grain or five, as Jane records). It was a powerful cathartic, but loaded with dangerous side-effects, being a mercuric compound. The oil derived from the castor bean is far less dangerous and was used almost religiously by Victorian families, especially on their children, in the hope of keeping them 'regular'. The Carlyles' experience (like Charles Darwin's) demonstrates that none of these remedies, patent or otherwise, did any good.
28. Brother and sister; old acquaintance from Kirkcaldy; see Pepoli in Characters and Correspondents.

Saturday along with John Fergus's *excuse*— He had bethought him, like a good soul as he is, that I was not well enough to be plagued with a dinner and so, on the plea of next to nothing, he wrote that he could not come to dine but that he and Miss Jessy would come in the evening—if I would not give myself the smallest trouble for them— [T]he *trouble* alas was already under way—the dinner had been *got in*[29] and Darwin asked and coming—so 'who was to be got to meet Darwin?'—'perfectly unnecessary to get anybody' said I—but no[,] Carlyle had a fixed idea of *giving a dinner*—exactly at the wrong moment—and so at ten oclock of Saturday night Helen was despatched with an invitation to Arthur Helps—worse and worse—for Arthur Helps *does his* dinners in immense style—and the idea of dining him was rather awful for me— He accepted *of course*—then people came without intermission from one oclock on Sunday until the dinner hour five—so that I could not so much as get the room cleared for the dinner table to be set out *until half an hour after Darwin and Helps were come to eat their dinner*[,] and at the last moment Carlyle invited John [Carlyle] and *Monkton Milnes* of all people in the world to stay and assist at the dinner which seemed never likely to be served up!! I was never so nearly upset by a household-complication in my life before and how Helen got thro with it even with the aid of *Martha* (!) I have no comprehension— [E]verybody did get dined at last better or worse—and the novelty of *the style* I dare say rather charmed Milnes and Helps[,] blasés on *fine* dinners[.] Certainly Milnes tho I have seen him give himself the most insolent airs at great peoples tables was modestys self here— And as Carlyle feeling the whole thing to be his own most voluntary act *talked* like an Angel—and there was always my uncle's *Madeira* excellent;— whatever else might be humanly imperfect—the whole thing went off like a sort of firework—crackers of wit exploding in every direction— Darwin spoke only in epigrams—Carlyle in flights of Genius—Milnes in poetical paradoxes—Helps in witicisms, rather small, but perfectly well turned—and John Carlyle did his best to ressemble *Solomon*[30]— As for myself—you may fancy what the preliminary fret made of me!— Shu-ping-sing[31] was a *spooney* in comparison—every opening of my lips

29. It was quite normal in the period to have 'takeaway' delivered from local food outlets; but Jane might be referring simply to the ingredients. She could cook for herself and Thomas when necessary, but a larger group might have required outside resources.
30. The legendary king and prophet of Jewish and Islamic faiths alike, son of David, builder of the First Temple at Jerusalem, wealthy, wise and powerful beyond words. See 2 Samuel, 1 Kings, 2 Chronicles.
31. See Thomas to Jane of 11 August 1831, on Jane's 'prophetic faculty', comparable it seems with the ability of a hero in Chinese fiction to see 'almost through millstones'.

was sensibly felt—and Miss Jessy must have gone away with the feeling that she had seen for the first time in her life a woman of superhuman intelligence! Pity that one can only be superhumanly intelligent, in *dadding* [leading] one's nerves *a-breed* [abroad]!— I went to bed feeling a decided tendency to *fly*—and lay *the whole night thro* without *once* closing my eyes— By breakfast time I had got instead of the inclination to fly, a horrible headach—and so I have been bilious ever since—and needed blue pill—and got it!

There is no paper in the house so I am writing on backs of notes—and have written already more than seemed possible when I commenced— I have something to tell you—what shall I say—strange! upon *my* honour—but not at this writing for several reasons— Love to all—kisses especially to my Uncle—

Ever your own /
J C

❧

To Mary Russell, Chelsea, 12 July 1845

My dearest Mrs Russell

I wonder how you are all going on at Thornhill—it is so long that I have had no news of you. Do write—there is nothing you ever tell me that is not deeply interesting; there is not a tree or a stone about Thornhill that I should not like to hear about, never to speak of the *people*!—

For us here; we go on in much the old fashion—my Husband always *writing*—I always *ailing*—which is perhaps the most laborious business of the two, tho' yielding less result— I was confined four months to the house during winter and spring, taking care of a cough—but it went when the warm weather came— Since then however I have never felt to have got back even my usual limited amount of strength and spirits—so I am going to try what people call 'a change'— My Husband is going to Scotsbrig so soon as his weary book is completed which he expects will be in the course of next month—and he has been very urgent on me to go to Scotland also, and even without waiting his time which will be rather late in the season. But I do not fancy the object of my going from home would be attained by encountering so much painful emotion as a visit to a country made so desolate for me would excite. I have tried to bring my mind to it—but it will not do— So I am going to Liverpool some ten days hence—and then to Seaforth[,] a place in the neighbourhood belonging to a favourite friend of mine—where I enjoy the inestimable advantage of being *let alone*— My uncle and Jeanie start for Helensborough again on the first of August and would have had me go *there* with *them*—but on one hand there was the sea voyage which occasions me such horrible suffering that only the hope of seeing my Mother at the end of it ever could make me undertake it—or if I went by land I must have passed thro Dumfriesshire—stayed some days at Scotsbrig—and the notion of all that was too sad— If there were any positive duty to be accomplished by going to Scotland I hope I would not be so weak as to let the pain of it withhold me— But going there merely to recover my *strength* and *spirits*!— No no it would be labour worse than lost.

I had my Uncle Roberts eldest Son[32] here for two or three weeks lately— He wrote me a letter about 'natural affection' and all that sort of thing, which was taking me on my weak side—and as he stated moreover his intention of coming to see London—I was simple enough to invite him *unknown* and *unseen* to take up his quarters here,—tho pretty well aware in the secret of my heart that the sudden development of his '*natural affection*' for me had just this for its object, to get himself invited— And so he came and in my life I was never more thankful when a visit ended—for a young gentleman full of selfcomplacency, and Edinr logic, and without the faculty of being *still* for two minutes of his existence together was no joke in a household like ours. He is not a bad fellow at heart nor stupid—but he has grown up in the idea that he cannot possibly be de trop [superfluous] in any environment—and that *his pleasure* is to be the law of the Universe—so far as he can make it so—and *his opinion* the dominant opinion of the times! Then he was out and in—in and out; at all hours, like a *dingledoozy*![33]—sightseeing—alas—by night as well as by day—and taking it as the most natural thing that *I* should sit up for him night after night till two in the morning—while he frequented the Houses of Parliament the Theatres and what not! Oh Heaven defend me thro all coming time from young gentlemen educated in Edinr who come to London to see sights! Hating *sights* myself I have no sympathy with the passion some people put into seeing them.

I saw a very curious sight the other night, the only one I have been to for a long while—viz: some thousands of the grandest and most cultivated people in England all gazing in ecstasy, and applauding to death,

32. John May Welsh (1824–1856), son of Jane's paternal uncle Robert (1786–1841). He had been studying law at the University of Edinburgh, and would be admitted to the Faculty of Advocates in 1846.
33. Scots, with multiple spellings: a lit stick waved in the air, as children do, to form an arc of light; metaphorically a busy person.

over a woman, not even pretty, balancing herself on the extreme point of one great toe, and stretching the other foot high into the air— Much *higher* than decency ever dreamt of! It was *Taglioni* our chief dancer at the Opera,[34] and this is her chief feat[,] repeated over and over to weariness—at least to my weariness—but Duchesses were flinging *bouquets* at her feet—and not a man (except Carlyle) who did not seem disposed to fling *himself*. I counted *twentyfive* bouquets!—but what of that? the Empress of All the Russias once in a fit of enthusiasm flung her diamond bracelet at the feet of this same Taglioni— 'Virtue its own reward' (in *this* world)? *dancing* is and *singing*, and some other things still more frivolous—but for *virtue*?—'it may be strongly doubted' (as Edinr people say to every thing one tells them.)

Monday is my birthday—how fast they come these birthdays of mine! and how little are they marked by any good done— *I* cannot even balance myself on the point of my great toe!—but *that* perhaps is not much to be regreted!— I send rememb[rances] for Mary and Margaret—for Mary *tea*—to Margaret perhaps you had better give the money in case she might like some other little thing better—[35]

God bless you dearest Mrs Russell—you and all that belong to you—my gratitude for your kindness to my beloved Mother in her last days is as strong now as it was in the first moment I read that letter in which *she* so touchingly expressed *her* gratitude to you and your husband— May your kindness to her be returned to you when you most need it!

Ever affectionately / Yours
Jane Carlyle

To Thomas Carlyle, Seaforth, 5 August 1845

No letter today— Well I had one *yesterday* which was more than bargain— [O]nly think; your Saturdays letter lay all thro' Sunday at the little postoffice within five minutes walk of me!— Letters seldom arrive at this house unless brought by Mr Paulet; so that it is not a *rule*

34. Madame Marie Taglioni (1804–1884), Swedish-born but of Italian descent; great Romantic ballerina credited with being the first to dance *en pointe*, as Jane bluntly describes it. Legend has it that a group of Russian admirers paid a large sum for a pair of her used ballet shoes in 1842, and had them cooked and served with a sauce.

35. Mary Mills and Margaret Hiddlestone, erstwhile servants in Grace Welsh's household.

to *send* to the postoffice and I, having no idea of a house in which the post office plays so insignificant a part, never thought of asking: had they sent?—but when no letter came at eleven, took it for granted there was none. I even walked to the postoffice myself afterwards with my own letter and put it in without inquiry—so it was produced on the *Monday*, an unexpected blessing.

I go on beautifully here—sleep, and eat, and am '*happy*'—to a *certain* extent— I fancy that being very much *made of* agrees with my constitution— I have not had a headach since I arrived or any sort of illness, except yesterday morning a fit of *sickness* which made my life from five in the morning till ten—what Mrs Ames in her Italian journal[36] calls the road from Genoa to Pisa[:] 'one *succession of Interests*'— [*E*]*very* quarter of an hour I found myself fainting away and the bell in the room is—broken! Finally Mrs Paulet sent the maid to see what was come of me—and then herself brought me tea—which put me all to rights—and to guard against such extremities of fate for the future 'the great Saloon *alarm-bell*' was brought and set down at my bed side where it still stands, exploding me into laughter as often as I look on it— I imputed the small *crisis* to a dreadfully long walk which I had taken the day before— [H]aving put my letter to you in the post office, I strolled on solitary, in a spirit of adventure, to try whether I could not *get up a sentiment*, more or less, towards *Nature*. [A]nd 'I came and I came till I came to' a little boy—seven years old—herding cows—and—smoking a pipe! I asked him *when* he learnt to smoke, and he answered that *he did not remember*! then I asked him how I could get back to Seaforth without going the same road I had come—and he gave me long most uncockneyecal directions which landed me at a Seabathing village called *Crosby*[37] and from Crosbey I had still to walk some three miles to Seaforth— [W]hen I got within sight of it I saw the children on the leads playing the part of Sister Ann[38]—and the moment they discried me '*coming*' they rushed off to relieve the anxieties of the rest, who had been kept waiting dinner for me, more than an hour—for we dine here at two—*sans facons* [unceremoniously]—have tea at five and supper at half after nine— [Y]esterday Mrs Ames came to dinner and staid till this morning— She sung me delightful songs from Don Giovanni while

36. Never published, it seems.
37. Coastal town in Merseyside, north-west of Liverpool, twinned perhaps unexpectedly with the Italian pleasure-isle of Capri, but with its own fine views of the Irish Sea.
38. 'The leads': the house roof, often sheeted with that pliable and rust-proof metal. Anne is the sister of the apparently doomed bride in 'Bluebeard', sent up to the roof by her to look for the arrival of her brothers to save her life: 'Anne, sister Anne, do you see anyone coming?'

Mrs Paulet and Geraldine *rubbed my feet*!!— My dear I wish YOU would *take a notion* to rub my feet! it is so soothing to the feelings— Mrs Ames told me that James Martineau in one of his sermons had said; 'it has been observed by the wisest man and profoundest thinker of the age—that'—'someething very *Carlyleesque*'—she did not remember what—but that the hearers might be in no doubt as to [what] *the man* meant he went on 'and if this has been *Carlyles* experience what must it have been for others'? Geraldine came yesterday afternoon—looking even better than when in London—and not '*triste*' [sad], as Robertson expected, by any means. She has brought a good stock of cigarittos with her—which is rather a pity—as I had just begun to forget there was such a weed as tobacco in the civilized world— She is very amusing and good-humoured—*does* all '*the wits*' of the party—and Mrs Paulet and I look to the *Pure Reason* and *Practical Endeavour*!!! I fancy you would find our talk as '*amusing*' as Dr Julius found my marmalade[39]—that is, if you could *assist* at it in a *cloak of darkness*—for one of the penalties of being 'the wisest man and profoundest thinker of the age' is the royal one of never hearing the plain 'unornamented' truth spoken—every one striving to be wise and profound *invita natura* [without help from nature] in presence of such a one and making himself as much as possible into his own likeness— And this is the reason that Arthur Helps and so many others talk very nicely to *me* and *bore you* to distraction—with *me* they are not afraid to stand on the little 'broad basis' of their own *individuality*—such as it is—with *you* they are always balancing themselves like Taglioni on the point of their moral or intellectual great toe! If *I* were going 'at *my* age and with *my* cough' to take up a '*mission*'—it would be the reverse of Fanny Wrights—[40] [I]nstead of boiling up *individuals* into *the species*—I would draw a chalk circle round every individuality and preach to it to keep within *that*, and preserve and cultivate its identity at the expense of ever so much lost giltlacker [gilt lacquer: gold coating] of other people's *isms*— But I forget that Robert is going to town so soon as I have finished—the post here being already missed— Mrs Paulet talks of our all going over to Holywell to spend a day with her mother— I for one am quite willing— What an amazing feeling it must have been for that mother to see all her children so soon as they came to the years of

39. Thomas's letter to Jane of 22 May 1825 mentions encountering this physician and prison reformer from Hamburg in Edinburgh, 'who almost embraced me as a father, because I had written a Life of Schiller and translated a novel of Goethe's' (*CL*). Clearly he got to sample Jane's home-made marmalade.

40. Frances D'Arusmont, *née* Wright (1795–1852), Dundee-born but long a resident of the United States, freethinker, socialist, abolitionist, feminist and so forth: a proponent of universal egalitarianism. Robert, next line, was the Paulets' servant.

reflection dash off into *new religions*— Mrs Paulet a freethinker—Julia a roman Catholic—Emma an *emancipated Evangelical*—writing books to show the evils of Sectarianism and how all christians should meet together 'on the broad basis' of *Crayst*—Rebecca a strong Church of England Woman—Caroline adhering alone to Wesleyan methosim[,] Noedes[41] an Epicuraean Philosopher[,] and Frank a Unitarian minister!!! A hen beholding her brood of ducklings take the water were a feeble comparison for such a case as poor Mrs Newton's— Suppose a hen to see one day her brood all take wing[,] one to water another to air another to fire! what a cruel surprise! [. . .]

What '*babbles*' I am writing God bless you dearest

Your own

Jane

❦

To Thomas Carlyle, Chelsea, 1 October 1845

Well! now I am subsided again—set in for a quiet evening—at leisure to write, and with plenty to write about[.] I know not how it is; I seem to myself to be leading a most solitary and *virtuous* and eventless life here at this *dead* season of the year; and yet when I sit down to write, I have so many things to tell always that I am puzzled where to begin! Decidedly, I was meant to have been a subaltern of the Daily Press—not 'a Penny-Lady,' but a Penny-a-liner[42]—for it is not only a faculty with me but a necessity of my nature to make a great deal out of nothing!

To begin with something I have been treasuring up for a week (for I would not hollo till we were out of the wood) *I have put down the Dog!*— 'The Dog?—wasn't he put down at Christmas—with a hare?'— [I]t seemed so, and 'we wished we might get it'! But on my return, I found him in the old place, at the back of the wall, barking 'like—like—anything'! 'Helen!' I said, with the calmness of a great despair, 'is not

41. Robert Nodes Newton, linen manufacturer and Wesleyan minister, son of Elizabeth Newton, Mrs Paulet's mother. His sister Emma was the author of *Difficulties of a Young Clergyman in Times of Division* (1844) and *The Modern Unbelievers* (1847; see 12 June 1848, below): a family of strong and divergent views, clearly, in a peculiarly Victorian manner—like Fanny Wright.

42. 'In Scotland the "Penny Ladies" (extraneously so called)', Thomas comments characteristically (*CL*), 'were busy, "benevolent" persons; subscribers of a penny a week for educating, &c. &c., not with much success.' A penny-a-liner was a journalist paid on the basis of column length and nothing else.

that the same Dog'? 'Deed is it!' said she 'and the whole two months you have been away its tongue has never lain!—it has driven *even me* almost distracted'! I said no more; but I had my own thoughts on the subject—*poison*!—a pistol-bullet!—the Metropolitan Police!— One way or other that Dog—or *I*—must terminate! Meanwhile I went on cleaning with what heart I could.— 'My Dear—will you hasten to the catastrophe!'— I *am* hastening—slowly!—*festina lente* [hasten slowly]—bless your heart 'there's nothing pushing—the rowans are a in the loft'—for this night!—[43] Well! it was the evening after John's departure—I had been too busy all day to *listen*—the candles were lit, and I had set myself down with my feet on the fender to enjoy the happiness of being *let alone*, and to—bid myself 'consider.' 'Bow-wow-wow,' roared the Dog and 'dashed the cup of fame from my brow'!— 'Bow-wow-wow' again and again, till the whole Universe seemed turned into one great Dog-kennel! I hid my face in my hands and groaned inwardly, 'Oh Destiny accursed! what use of scrubbing and sorting?— All this availeth me nothing so long as *The Dog* sitteth at the Washerman's gate!' I could have burst into tears; but I did not! 'I was a republican before the Revolution, and I never wanted energy'![44] I ran for ink and paper, and wrote

'Dear Gambardella
'You once offered to shoot
'some cocks for me; *that* service
'I was enabled to dispense with;
'but now, I accept your devotion.
'Come, if you value my sanity—and

But here 'a sudden thought struck me'— He could not take aim at the Dog without scaling the high wall—and in so doing he would certainly be seized by the Police— So I threw away that first Sybillan Leaf,[45]

43. 'Saying', Thomas notes (*CL*), 'of my indolent sister-in-law, brother Alick's wife, on one occasion. "Rowins" are wool completely carded [combed], ready for the [spinning] wheel when it comes down from "the loft".' *OED* records Jane's spelling, not his. Jane's 'a' is the Scots and northern form of 'all', normally spelt *a'*: as in Burns' 'A man's a man for a' that'.
44. The proud claim of Girondin Charlotte Corday, on trial for assassinating radical French-Revolutionary journalist Jean-Paul Marat—with a knife, in his bath—in 1793. Thomas had told her tale in *The French Revolution*: 'Hapless beautiful Charlotte; hapless squalid Marat!', and so forth.
45. The legendary and fragmentary *Sibylline Books*, recording the various prophecies of these various female prophetesses, scattered around ancient Greece. 'Spelt from Sibyl's Leaves' is a famously dithyrambic sonnet by Victorian poet and Jesuit Gerard Manley Hopkins.

and wrote another—to the Washerman!—once more!— I offered him 'any price for that horrible dog—*to hang it*'—offered to 'settle an yearly income on it; if it would hold its accursed tongue'— I implored, threatened, imprecated! and ended by proposing that in case he could not take an immediate final resolution; he should in the interim 'make the dog dead-drunk with a bottle of Whiskey which I sent for the purpose'! Helen was sent off with the note and the whiskey—and I sat all concentrated, awaiting her return as if the fate of Nations had depended on my diplomacy—and so it did—to a certain extent!— [W]ould not the inspirations of 'the first man in Europe'[46] be modified for the next six months at least by the fact, who should come off victorious, I or the Dog! Ah it is curious to think how *first men in Europe* and first *women* too are acted upon by the inferior Animals!

Helen came—but even before *that*, had 'the raven down of Night'[47] smoothed itself in heavenly silence! God grant this were not mere accident! Oh no! verily it was not accident!— The washerman's two daughters had seized upon and read the note—and what was death to *me*, had been such rare amusement to *them*, that they 'fell into fits of laughter' in the first place; and in the second place ran down and untied the dog—and solemnly pledged themselves that it should 'never trouble me more'! At Christmas they 'had sent it into the Country for three months, *to learn to be quiet*'—and then chained it in the old place— Now they would take some final measure— Next morning came a note from the Washerman himself—written on glazed note-paper, with a crowquill—apologizing—promising—he could not put it away entirely as it is 'a great protection' to him and '*belonged to a Relation*' (who shall say where *sentiment* may *not* exist?) but he 'had untied it' and would take care it gave me no further trouble—and he 'returned his grateful thanks for *what as been sent*'[.] It is a week ago, and one may now rest satisfied that *the tying up* caused the whole nuisance—the Dog is to be seen going about there all day in the yard, like any other Christian Dog—'carrying out' *your* principle of *Silence* not merely '*platonically*' but *practically*— [S]ince that night, as Helen remarks, 'it has not said one word'! So 'thanks God' you shall have quietude to return to!—

I took tea with [Edward] Sterling on Monday night—walked there and he sent the carriage home with me. It is very difficult to know how to do with him— He does not seem to me *essentially mad*—but rather

46. Originally an honorific awarded to French Enlightenment author Voltaire (1694–1778); some of Thomas's admirers were happy to apply the expression to him, much to his and Jane's amusement.
47. Milton, *Comus*, 250–1.

mad with the apprehension of madness— A state of mind I can perfectly understand—moi— He forgets something[,] Anthony's name; for example, or mine, or how many children he has, and then he gets into a rage that he cannot recollect, and then he stamps about and rings the bells and brings everybody in the house to 'help him to remember'—and when all will not do; he exclaims—'I am going *mad* by God'! and then he *is* mad—as mad as a March hare.— *I* can do next to nothing for him beyond cheering him up a little, for the moment. Yesterday again I went a little drive with him—of course not without Saunders as well as the Coachman— He told me that when he heard I had written about him he 'cried for three days'[.] Anthony's desertion seems the central point around which all his hypicondrical Ideas congregate— Anthony has never written him the scrape of a pen since he left him insensible at Manchester *nor ever written about him* so far as himself or his Manservant knows—

Yesterday I had a call from—Nell Gwyn of all people in the world!—[48] She came with Elizabeth Pepoli—having 'long desired my acquaintance'—and if she had gone on *desiring it* to the end of the chapter it would have been 'probably just as well'—for we are not in each other's line the least in the world— Howsomeclever—as *Miss Wilson* says she is *now* 'in unexceptionable society' and never '*did* anything improper'[,] only *looked* improper— [T]here is no great harm done by my having been *too* charming in the Macready's box—I can return her call, *in course of time*—refuse her invitations—and so 'do her neither ill nor gude.'

Who else have I seen—? nobody else I think except Mazzini, whom I was beginning to fancy the Jewess must have made an *enlevement* [kidnapping] of— [A]nd *enlevé* he had been, sure enough—but not by the Jewess—*by himself*—and only the length of Oxford or rather he meant to go only the length of Oxford—but with his usual practicality let himself be carried sixty miles further—to a Place he called *Swinton*(?)—[49]

48. Not the legendary actress of the Restoration stage and mistress of Charles II, but Jane's nickname for Susanna Arethusa Milner-Gibson (1814–1885), avid society hostess, feminist, supporter of Italian nationalism, spiritualist, mesmerist and so forth. A 'great dimpling-baby in miniature' according to Jane in a letter to Jeannie Welsh of 4 September 1842. 'Miss Wilson', I take it, is Harriette Wilson (1786–1845), prodigious woman of affairs (with the Duke of Wellington among many others), who liked to present herself 'without regrets' but also (somehow) blamelessly in her famous *Memoirs: Written by Herself* (1825).

49. Swindon, largest town in Wiltshire, made by the railways in the nineteenth century. The hapless Mazzini missed his connection and ended up there, thirty miles southwest of Oxford.

Then; that the journey back might have also its share of misadventure, he was not *in time* to avail himself of the place he had taken 'in the Second Class'—but had to jump up 'quite promiscuously' beside 'the Conductor'—where he had 'all the winds of Heaven blowing *on* him and *thro* him'—the result 'a dreadful cold'—*dreadful* it must have been when it confined *him* to the house— [M]eanwhile he had had—two other declarations of love!! they begin to be as absurd as the *midges* in Mr Fleming's '*right* eye'— 'What! more of them?'— 'Ah Yes! *unhappily*!—they begin to—what shall I say?—rain on me like *sauterelles* [grasshoppers]!' One was from a young Lady in Genoa, who sent him a bracelet of her hair (the only feature he has seen of her) and begged 'to be united to him—in *plotting*!'— 'That one was *good* upon my *honour*'— 'And the other'? 'Ah!—from a woman here—*married* thanks God—tho to a man fifty years more old—french—and *sings*—the other *played*—decidedly my love of music has consequences'! 'And how did *she* set about it?' '*Franchement* [frankly]—thro' a mutual friend—and then she sent me an invitation to supper—and I returned for answer that I was going to Oxford—*where I still am*, and will remain a long long time!' *Emancipation de la Femme*! one would say it *marches* almost faster than Intellect!— And now if *there* be not chatter enough for one night!— I have a great many *half moons* and *stars* to cut in paper before I go to bed— '[F]or what purpose'? *That* is my *secret*, 'and you wish that you could tell!'

Good night—Schlaf wohl [sleep well]

J C [. . .]

To Jeannie Welsh, Bay House, Alverstoke, Hampshire, 16 November 1845

Dearest Babbie

I must not leave you so good a pretext for not writing to me as doubt about my actual address— Of course a letter addressed to Cheyne Row would be sent after me even to Timbuctoo—but these simple ideas are slow of suggesting themselves to those who find the state of uncertainty favour their natural tendency to sit still, with their hands gracefully crossed in Indian-God-like adoration of the Force of Circumstances— Know then, to leave you without excuse, that I am *here*—very accessible to letters—and much in want of them—here being—Bay House—a large fantastical looking New Building on the shore of the Sea & belonging to Lord Ashburton but made over for this winter to Lady

Harriet—[50] It is not *in* the Isle of Wight as I had fancied but opposite to it— I dare say it is a charming place in Summer but in winter all that body of cold water which immense ranges of windows look out on makes me feel like William Gibson 'rather chilly'—and then the gardens about it have lost their bloom for this year and the *woods* are as yet prospective—more like nursery-grounds than anything else— Inside, it is warm enough and magnificent as money and taste can make it— Carlyle and I have *two* rooms which I stipulated for before I would undertake to come at all—and the first principle of living comfortably in another persons house is granted one amply viz: one is 'well let alone'—may do as one likes within reasonable limits— But the grand happiness of friendly intercourse—viz: leave to be 'as ugly and stupid and disagreeable as one likes'[,] *that* of course is out of the question here—*tanto peggio per me* [so much the worse for me]! My cold thanks God was considerably abated before I left home—and is no worse for the 'fine change' (as Helen would say)—and I was cut out of my complication with Mrs Paulet in the most unexpected manner— As I had feared just when we were on the eve of setting off they arrived in London for the Operation!—giving me just twelve hours notice— I was in the horriblest *quandary*; to go away and leave them alone there with their troubles was impossible for me—to renounce the visit here equally *impossible*—in another sense— I meditated a sort of compromise between the two impossible—to let Carlyle go without me and follow in a week or two—but the following morning in rushed Mrs Paulet fresh and rosy like a lump of coral and told me they were all to go back the road they had come that very day—the eyes were not ready to be operated on. Instead of sympathizing in their provocation I was heartily thankful that all that money had been spent and trouble undertaken for no end— [B]y the time they return I hope that I also shall be returned—in a month or six weeks she said— Lady Harriet insists we are to stay here 'all the winter'—to stay 'till parliament meets in February'—but I fancy Carlyle's need to be ugly and stupid and disagreeable without restraint[,] never to speak of my own, will send us back to London in a month or so—

I feel as if I should get on here in an even, middlingly pleasant sort of a way. I am not in the horribly excitable state I was in when I went to

50. Built for Alexander Baring, 1st Baron Ashburton, by architect Decimus Burton in 1832 at Stokes Bay, Alverstoke, Hampshire, opposite the Isle of Wight. (Not to be confused with the Ashburtons' *other* Hampshire mansion, inland: 'The Grange'.) In 1863 it was sold to the Admiralty for use as a college for naval cadets, and it still serves as part of an 'academy school'.

Addiscombe—[51] I take things now very calmly—almost coolly— Lady Harriet seems a woman of *good sense* and perfect good breeding—and with a person of that sort one need not, unless one be a fool oneself have any *collisions*— [A]t the same time she seems to me so *systematic* and *superior* to her *natural feeling* that however long and pleasantly I may live beside her I am sure I shall never feel *warm affection* for her nor inspire her with warm affection—her intercourse will remain *an honour for me* never be a heartfelt delight—as it might be if she were as loving as she is charming—and Bay House will consequently not suit me so well as Seaforth House—

Plattnauer returned from Germany some weeks ago—*not changed* the least in the world—except that he is now entirely in his natural senses— He had in rummaging in a Cabinet of his Brother in law come upon all my letters about his madness!! read them—and even 'taken a copy of one of them'— [H]is vexation had been considerable—especially over my 'excessive eagerness to have him kept in Germany for the rest of his life'—but he spoke even of this *contretemps* with a courtesy and justness which proved as much as anything his sane state of mind— [H]e brought me a beautifully embroidered card case from his Sister—it might have been done by Titania Queen of the Fairies![52]

And now it will behoove me to go and dress for dinner—at *seven* in these days instead of *four*[,] Lady Harriets usual hour—but after tomorrow thank goodness we are to return to christian habits— A Mr Senior who is here causes the present formalities [. . .]

love and kisses to all of them—no—only to my Uncle—the rest are undeserving of remembrance

Ever yours

J C

To Helen Welsh, Addiscombe, Surrey, 24 April 1846

Dearest Helen

I would have answered your letter in the *enthusiasm of the moment* if the moment had not been between needed for more practical purposes.

51. 'Ashburton House', the Ashburtons' country residence in leafy Surrey, nine miles south of London's West End and therefore more easily accessible from the capital (see next letter); it was demolished in 1910, but Ashburton Park still exists in the commuter-belt suburb. The Baring family's colossal wealth is reflected in their owning three places in the country as well as one in town.
52. From Shakespeare's *A Midsummer Night's Dream*.

There was much to be put straight on my return *morally* as well as *materially*, and I had not even my *normal* amount of force either moral or material to bring to the work: for the excitement of a houseful of the most exciting and excited people during the last ten days had been a prodigious overbalance to the '*pure* air' and other advantages of Addiscombe. The more I see of aristocratic life, the more I wonder how people with the same system of nerves as oneself, and with the same human needs, can keep themselves alive in it—and *sane*! Lady Harriet especially, who is the woman of largest intellect I have ever seen—how *she* can reconcile herself to a life which is after all a mere dramatic representation, however successful, fills me with astonishment and a *certain* sorrow. But like the pigs they 'are used to it' and nobody, I fancy knows till he try how difficult it is to tear himself loose from the network of Lilliputan packthreads in which our nobility grow up from their earliest days. [A] *poor* woman has enough of serious occupation cut out for her by the nature of things—sometimes *more* than is good for her—and therein lies *her* grievance— [W]e in *our* sphere have also something given us to *do*—how far it may suit our taste is another question and a secondary one—we see at least how our activity may be turned to account better or worse. [B]ut a great Lady—should *she* take a notion to wrap herself in a blanket and go to sleep like *Beauty* for a hundred years; what would stand still that needs to go forward?—only herself!— [A]nd should she take the better notion to put away Great-Lady-things and lead a rational useful life how is she to set about it? how extricate herself from the imposed *do-nothingism* of her *position*?— As Lady Harriet herself once said to me 'one would have to begin by quarrelling with all one's husbands relations and one's own'—a beginning that one may be excused for finding rather questionable!— No! it is not *easy* for a Great Lady in these days to be anything but 'an ornament to Society in every direction,' and *that* her Ladyship succeeds in being—to perfection! The old illustration of the camel passing thro' the eye of a needle[53] still holds good— Let those who are not in the camels shoes, among whom are you and I, be thankful—tho' cooks may sometimes give one a deal of trouble—and holed stockings may accumulate into a small Ben Lomond while one is away on a visit—and other the like nuisances render ones carreer of household activity often enough anything but a *pleasurable* one!— Now, what has tempted me into this moral-essay style, I have not the slightest conception!— [W]hen I sat down to write I did

53. Matthew 19: 24: 'It is easier for a camel to pass through the eye of a needle, than for a rich man to enter into the kingdom of God.' Ben Lomond is a Scottish peak on the eastern shore of Loch Lomond.

not feel at all *preachingly*-disposed[.] But I am in the habit of letting my pen go its own way, and this is the way it has gone.

The Cromwell-turmoil is again subsiding and the second edition will be out in a few weeks. '*Thanks* God'! And now I hope we shall really be done with that man! if he had been my Husband's Own Father he could not have gone thro' more hardship for him! We have lived 'in the valley of the shadow'[54] of Cromwell now, as of Death, for some three years— But every thing comes to an end if one have patience— What is to come next Heaven knows— We have been enquiring all about for houses in the country—without, it seems to me, much chance or even *much intention* of a practical result— Sometimes—in desperately bilious days Carlyle speaks of returning to Scotland and living *there* 'in seclusion for his few remaining years'— I do not look for much practical result to *that* idea either— Still this perpetual talk of moving takes away all ones pleasure (such as it was) in Chelsea— I feel myself no longer in a *home* but in a *tent* to be struck any day that the commanding officer is sufficiently bilious. When the warm weather comes and it is coming fast—the present restlessness will mount into a crisis of some sort—a journey somewhere— But as yet I do not see a fortnight before my nose. [. . .]

What is Jeanie about with Andrew Crystal?—[55] I do not like these dawdling courtships at all—in the Laird of Noloss's phraseologhy 'they are a great off-put of time.'[56] If people do not know what they would be at in Love they may depend on it what they *call* love is no authentic love or it would tell them. The most important thing that has happened to me since my return has been the gift of a splendid indian scarf (from Lady Harriet) almost '*too* splendid *for any thing*'— But I was greatly pleased with it because of its being the facsimile of one she had got for herself— She rails at *sentiment* and never puts any into her *words* but it peeps out often enough in her *actions*. She would not put an *affectionate* sentence in her letters for the world but she will put *violets*—leaves of the *flowers one likes*—sometimes sends me envelopes by post containing nothing else!! What a contrast I often think betwixt that woman and Geraldine! the opposite poles of woman-nature!

I wish you would go oftener to Seaforth— Mrs Paulet is a *real* woman full of kindness and a sort of dreamy intellect—whom you would get to like—and she is much disposed to like *you*. She is full of *bashfulness* little as she *looks* it, and does not know how to accommodate herself to *young*

54. Psalms 23: 1–6.
55. She would marry him in 1853 and lose contact with Jane thereafter.
56. 'Off-put': northern English and Scottish idiom for 'waste'; particular source untraced.

Ladies but such a young lady as you might find it easy enough to accommodate yourself to *her.* When I hear the talk of the women that come about you in Liverpool I have often thought what a godsend for you a *friendship* with a woman of Mrs Paulets *natural* character and speculative turn of mind might be— You would soon find, if you took to studying her, that her disorderly housekeeping and all that first shows itself make a very small fraction of the whole woman— Kisses without number to my uncle

God bless you and all of you
Ever your own
Jane Carlyle

To Jeannie Welsh, Chelsea, 19 May 1846

Dearest Babbie

Few deaths could have surprised me more than Mr Liddle's; he had so little the look of one born to die young! I can well believe that all who were in habits of intimacy with him will long mourn the loss of such a cheerful kindly soul. For me; I am got to that with it now, that I can no longer feel sorry for the one who *dies* but only for the friends he leaves behind to miss him— One escapes so much suffering by dying young!—all the good one *could possibly* have enjoyed in longer life is not it seems to me to be put in the balance against the evil which one *must necessarily* have suffered. Surviving one after another of all one loved—one after another of all one's beautiful illusions and even most reasonable hopes, surv[iv]ing in short one's original self!— You cannot understand yet how life may grow to look no such blessing—even for those who have no claim to be considered exceptionally unfortunate— [L]ong may it be before you feel this as I do! it is a weary, dreary feeling, almost making one regret the feelings of acute sorrow out of which it grows— And yet it is well to be prepared for it—that one may have it in as gentle a degree as possible by beginning early to pitch ones hopes from the world rather low—and by laying in as many good thoughts and good actions as one possibly can to look back upon for comfort, when one ceases to feel any comfort in looking forward. I have not got into a Socinian[57] zeal for the

57. Like Unitarianism, Socinianism is an anti-trinitarian Christian belief developed in the seventeenth century; it upholds the mortality of Adam and Eve (the Tree of Knowledge notwithstanding) and limits God's omniscience: so, one might say, a more *morally* centred system of belief than, say, Catholicism.

'pleasures of a good conscience' tho' the foregoing sentence might lead you to that idea— I do not pretend to know by experience what the '*pleasures of a good conscience*' may really be—but I fancy them like all other *pleasures* that I *have* experience of, a feeble refuge against the pressure of existence as it hardens gradually into old age—stript of *all* its early poetical illusions. [B]ut without any Socinian selfconceit I *may* say to you, of my own knowledge, that the natural sadness of the latter part of ones life may be cruelly *embittered* by the reflection, that ones best years, which might perhaps have produced something good have been suffered to run to waste, fertile only of tares[58] and nettles!— But enough of moralising—

I have not been well—as Mrs Paulet said—but not more ill than when Mrs Paulet spread such fine news of my improved looks!— People must talk—about other peoples looks and much else that comes readiest—but what they say *for talkings sake* is not worth a minutes recollection[.] Ach gott! how little even those who like one *divine* of one's actual state!—unless one *put oneself into words* and hardly even then, can the generality of one's friends tell whether one is glad or sorrowful—feeling pain or pleasure!— I called at the Macreadys the other day—in a humour that a person under sentence of death need hardly have envied— For days and weeks a cheerful feeling had not been in my mind—but of course one does not make calls to show oneself as *a spectacle of woe*— I talked talked—about the feats of Carlyle's horse &c—and they laughed till their tears ran down[.] *I* could not *laugh*—but no matter—perhaps my own gravity made the things I was saying only more amusing by contrast. By and by Mrs Macready who is in the family-way began to talk of the dreadful 'depression of spirits' she occasionally laboured under— 'Ah said I, everyone I suppose has their own fits of depression to bear up against if the truth were told'— 'Do you say so' said Miss Macready— 'Oh no surely!—some people are never out of spirits—*yourself* for example I really believe you do not know what it is to be ever sad for a minute!!! one never sees you that you do not keep one in fits of laughter!' I made no answer—but congratulated myself on having played my part so well— I wish I could find some hard work I *could* do—and saw any sense in doing— If I do not soon it will be the worse for me—

Meanwhile all *around* me goes on as usual— C is just getting done with *his* work—speculating about 'where to go'— The usual people come about; but seldomer I think—seeing that I am less disposed to amuse them— [N]ew people come—but I have lost my talent for 'swearing everlasting friendships'— All my talents seem to be going one after another—

58. The parable of the wheat and the tares (weeds) is at Matthew 13: 24–43.

Did I ever tell you that Plattnauer had gone quite mad again—committed follies rather dangerous—for her sacred Majesty the Queen—and finally been obliged to leave the country— I hear he is in Paris—still *at large* the very man for *actually* shooting Louis Philipe!—[59] God grant he may not come back here anyhow—he had become *really dangerous* and what I considered worse to tolerate—a dreadful *bore* from his fatuous vanity—

God bless thee Babie love me while you can
Ever your affectionate
Jane Carlyle [. . .]

To Thomas Carlyle, Seaforth, 14 July 1846

Oh my dear Husband Fortune has played me such a cruel trick this day!—but it is all right now! and I do not even feel any resentment against fortune for the suffocating misery of the last two hours. I know always, even when I seem to you most exacting, that whatever happens to me is nothing like so bad as I deserve— But you shall here all how it was—

Yesterday in coming back from the Post office where I had gone myself with the letter to you, my head took to aching and ached ached on all day in a bearable sort of fashion till the evening when Geraldine came over from Manchester—and the sudden bounce my heart gave at sight of her finished me off on the spot— I had to get myself put to bed and made a bad wakeful night of it—so that this morning I was nervous as you may figure—and despairing of all things—even of the letter from you that I expected so confidently yesterday.

*Encourage*ment came however from a quarter I was little dreaming of— [*B*]*efore* the post time—before I was dressed in fact—heaven knows how she had managed it—there was delivered to me a packet from—Bolte! at Cambridge!—a pretty little collar and cuffs of the poor things own work with the kindest letter—after all my cruelties to her!— Well I thought if *she* can be so loving and forgiving for me—I need not be tormenting myself with the fear that *he* will not write today either— And I put on the *collar* there and then, and went down to breakfast in a little better heart— At ten—the post hour[—]I slipt away myself to the post

59. Louis Philippe reigned as the penultimate king of France from 1830 to 1848. On 16 April a former guardsman had tried to shoot him; someone else would make the attempt on 29 July. (He survived seven such attempts in all.) He was forced to abdicate in 1848, the 'Year of Revolutions', and spent the rest of his life in the relative safety of Surrey at Queen Victoria's invitation.

office but was '*detected*' by Betsy [Paulet] and Geraldine who insisted on putting on their bonnets and accompanying me— I could well have dispensed with the attention—however I trusted there would be a letter and their presence would only hinder me reading it for a little— And *two* were handed out which I stretched *my* hand to receive—both for Betsy!— *None* for *me* the postmistress averred!—not a line from you on my Birthday—on the fifth day! I did not burst out crying—did not faint—did not *do* anything absurd so far as I know—but I walked back again without speaking a word, and with such a tumult of wretchedness in my heart as you who know me can conceive— And then I shut myself in my own room to fancy everything that was most tormenting— Were you finally so out of patience with me that you had resolved to write to me no more at all?— [H]ad you gone to Addiscombe and found no leisure *there* to remember my existence?— Were you taken ill so ill that you *could* not write? that last idea made me mad to get off to the railway and back to London— Oh mercy what a two hours I had of it!— And just when I was at my wits end, I heard Julia crying out thro' the house—[']Mrs Carlyle Mrs Carlyle! Are you there? here is a letter for you!' And so there was after all!—the Postmistress had overlooked it—and given it to Robert when he went afterwards not knowing that we had been. I wonder what *love-letter* was ever received with such thankfulness!— Oh my dear I am not fit for living in the World with this organisation— I am as much broken to pieces by that little accident as if I had come thro an attack of Colera or Typhus fever— I cannot even steady my hand to *write* decently— But I felt an irresistible need of thanking you by return of post— Yes I have kissed the dear little cardcase—and now I will lie down a while and try to get some sleep—at least to quieten myself will try to believe—oh why can I not believe it once for all—that with all my faults and follies I *am* 'dearer to you than any earthly creature'— I will be better for Geraldine here she is very quite and nice become—and as affectionate for me as ever

Your own /
JC

To Helen Welsh, Chelsea, 29 September 1846

Dearest Helen

Two letters for one is a windfall that never came to me out of Maryland Street before—and claiming double thanks—for the *novelty* of the thing as well as for its *generosity*.— I would have written sooner if I had had anything *pleasant* to say: but to tell you that I was down at *Zero* again, seemed a thing there was no haste about communicating— C came home wearied and gloomy—with no work to fall to—nothing to do but ray out darkness on all *my* human attempts at occupation or amusement—and these alas! are never so energetic now-a-days that they should make any long stand against that sort of thing. C should have had 'a strong-minded woman' for wife, with a perfectly sound liver, plenty of *solid fat*, and mirth and good humour world without end—[60] [M]en do best with their opposites. *I* am too like himself in some things—especially as to the state of our livers[—]and so we aggravate one anothers tendencies to *despair*! But there is no altering of all that now—nothing to be done but make the best of it—which I candidly confess I am far from doing— I do *try* however to the best of my humble ability—and having found small profit hitherto in mending and tinkering at my *soul*, I am for the moment modestly directing my faculties to the repairing of my *body*—trusting that the soul may be ultimately reached thro' that outwork. Every morning I take the shower-bath—quite cold—and three pailfuls of it! The shock is indiscribable! and whether it strengthens or shatters me I have not yet made up my mind! but at all events when I have taken it; I feel to have accomplished a very decided act of *volition*—and *that* makes my *moral* blood circulate a little[,] however it may be with the physical! Then I *eat* all that ever I can and drink *bottled porter*—not so good as *yours* by any means—but tolerable—and I *walk* as if the Devil were in me—and so, I fancy he *is*—six and seven miles in the day on an average! I also try to be 'neither *solitary* nor *idle*'—which old Burton recommends as the grand cure of 'melancholy'—[61] Still I must not put too much reliance on these laudable efforts.— Whenever one gets into the self-complacent idea of being able to *put down Destiny* by *one's own Deserving*—then, if ever, is one sure of being 'made to *eat dirt*'—more of it than one has the power of digesting.

I was wondering one day what effect a great *practical* misfortune would have on me—for instance being burnt out of house and home and reduced to *work* for my bread[;] and twenty four hours after Providence kindly gave promise of gratifying my curiosity—in a small way—prepared as pretty a *little* practical misfortune for me as one could have imagined!

60. Is Jane thinking of Lady Harriet? A 'strong-minded woman' if ever there was one, with plenty of 'solid fat', to boot.

61. Excellent advice, however hard to follow, from Robert Burton's seventeenth-century treatise, *The Anatomy of Melancholy*.

Helen came with tears in her eyes and smiles on her lips to tell me she was going away! Never could such news have found me less prepared for it—or less disposed— Her conduct has been so exemplary of late that, I saw no more danger of *needing* to put her away, and her attachment to me seeming greater than ever, and her matrimonial chances none to speak of, I had no apprehension of her going of her own accord. But Helen also, insignificant as she looks has a *Destiny*!—is liable to great Events!—and what is most extraordinary of all is going to be an exceptional instance of *virtue* really *getting* its own reward! At least one hopes so!— A Brother in Dublin—a pushing sort of fellow—has got into trade on his own basis—manufactures *coach-fringe*[,] for which there is immense consumption at present on the Railways, and so well has he prospered (by his own showing) that he has now three hundred girls in his employment—a *genteel house* and plenty to keep it with! *Himself* however (for I saw him the other night) remaining a particularly *ungenteel* man. He never did anything for Helen hitherto beyond calling on her for a *quarter of an hour* when his business brought him to London—never gave her to the value of a farthing in his life—tho sometimes asking her if she would like that he brought her a poplin gown!! 'Dont you wish you may get it!'

Now however he is seized with a sudden fit of brotherly love and invites her 'to come and be his housekeeper and MISTRESS' and she has of course accepted at the first word— I wish it may end well for her—the man looks to me a flustery incredible sort of man—and very selfish[,] with the two black eyes set close together in his head!— His conduct hitherto has been so unbrotherly!—that I cannot help fancying he merely wants a *good servant* in Helen on his own terms— Then he may marry shortly—and turn her adrift—tho he does *promise* in that case to 'settle a handsome provision on her.' [B]ut *will* he?— On the whole I wish for her own sake that Helen had taken a little time to investigate and reflect. It is not I however, who having a manifest interest in retaining her can urge prudence with any effect—so go she must and take her chance. 'Poor thing,['] says C, perhaps she may get married to some decent man in Dublin and become Mother 'of a mighty nation'[62]—the last part of the possibility I should think in the highest degree improbable! Meanwhile I have written in the first rush of the business to Mrs Russel to see if there be any chance *now* of getting Margaret Hiddlestone[63]—also to Betty in Edinr to ask if she knows anyone to suit me—and also to Susan Hunter (Mrs Stirling) in Dundee who once

62. Oft-repeated expression; Genesis 18: 18.
63. See 12 July 1845, above.

offered should I be in need to look out for me in that region— *Somebody* I shall get— It will be a while any how before another can suit me as well as this one who has been with me ten or eleven years—but as John Carlyle says 'there is no use in rebelling against Providence.' You may believe I am rather unsettled for the moment— Nor do I know more of our *own* plans than when I left you— Lady Harriet is not returned and nothing has been said about Alverstoke— But all will arrange itself by and by better or worse—and sometime either in winter or spring *you* will come and help to cheer me up.

I had a letter from Jeanie on Saturday—relating a horrid story of a boiling showerbath— Certainly Maggie must in some previous state of existence have given serious offence to the Spirit of Fire! I never heard of any one so constantly getting scalded.

My great love to my Uncle— Will you get him the *Memoirs of Lady Hester Stanhope* to read—[64] I have just finished the book (in three volumes) and am sure it would amuse him—a kiss to Mary ever your / affectionate Cousin

Jane Carlyle

❧

To Robert Skirving, Chelsea, 11 May 1847

MY DEAR—ROBERT,[65] then, since you protest against 'Sir' and 'Mr'

When your letter came I was in the country, for a week; and my maid, after her fashion of doing precisely what she is told to do—neither more nor less—kept all my letters during that time lying on the table *here*, I, in the unbounded confidence of my nature, having given her no *express injunction* to forward them. Since my return *two days* ago, the head of me has been 'too bad *for anything*' (as the Lancashire phrase is), aching in fact as if it were about giving birth to a young '*Sin*' or young '*Wisdom*,'[66] all thro' having come part of the way by steamboat in a straw bonnet that cost *two shillings*. I give you these particulars,

64. Lady Hester Stanhope (1776–1839) was an intrepid and significant traveller, explorer and archaeologist, especially in the Middle East: 'The Queen of the East' according to the narrator of George Eliot's *Daniel Deronda* (1876). Her *Memoirs* appeared in two instalments in the late 1840s.

65. Robert Scot Skirving (1821–1900), nephew of the eccentric Haddington friend Mary Scot: see 20 April 1831, above.

66. Just as Sin emerged from Satan's head in Milton's *Paradise Lost*, Book 2, so Athena, goddess of wisdom, was born from the forehead of Zeus in Greek myth.

that you may see I have lost no time that could be helped. To-day I am rather better, and write to you the first thing I do. I am glad that you are coming to London, especially since you have got over the crisis of 'detestability.' It would have gone against my feelings to have detested you, and I could not have helped it had I seen you in your 'first pangs of finding'—that is to say *fearing* 'you were to be nobody and nothing.' One only begins to be really *something* after those pangs have been happily transacted; it is a sort of moral *cutting of one's teeth.*

My No. is 5, and my street spells itself *Cheyne* Row; and there is even, contrary to London etiquette, a brass plate with the name upon the door. A Chelsea omnibus will bring you within a gunshot for *sixpence*, or you may come by steamboat at the easy rate of *twopence*! If with all these helps you fail to arrive at me with perfect easy you must be the stupidest of mortals. When you come, let it be early; after one, everybody here goes out to call for everybody, everybody wishing to find everybody 'not at home.' How you will *like* me when you see me heaven knows. *Realised ideals* are always dreadfully precarious. Nor do I remember the least in the world what sort of a sketch of myself I gave you in '41. Most likely it was wide of the mark; would depend more on *how I had slept* the previous night than on 'the fact of things.' My views of myself are a sort of 'dissolving views,'[67] never the same for many minutes together. To-day, for example, I find myself horrid—in a second epoch of detestability. Our next-door neighbour having given a ball last night, the noise of which thro' the thin partition kept me awake till six in the morning; and so to-day I am in a state of 'protest and appeal to Posterity'[68] against everybody and everything, myself included. Will you tell your Father that one day not long ago, in a roomful of people, Frank Charteris[69] happening to name your Father, *apropos* of something about farming, I shouted out in the joyfullest tone, 'Oh, dear me!' which caused quite a sensation?

My kindest love to your Mother and Aunt. How I should like to see them all again! I often meditate going to survey once more with bodily

67. Contemporary 'magic lantern' shows often exhibited 'dissolving views', in which one projected image gradually faded to be replaced by another: day for night, for example, or summer to winter in a given scene.
68. The weekly paper, *The Examiner*, which had a theatrical interest via its connection with Leigh Hunt and William Hazlitt, discussed Shakespeare on 26 March 1842 in terms of his prodigious modernity. 'In the construction of all his plays,' the paper suggested, 'not seldom in the mere stage directions of the scene, we find as it were his protest and appeal to posterity.'
69. Deputy lieutenant of Haddingtonshire and MP for the region 1847–1883, later 10th Earl of Wemyss. He was a supporter of the National Portrait Gallery in London, as was Thomas.

eyes what is still all vivid enough in memory; but when it comes to the point my courage fails me: and so,

Yours with great faith,
JANE CARLYLE

To Helen Welsh, Chelsea, 5 July 1847

Dearest Helen

It was thro a special interposition of Providence under the simple form of *Reflection* that you did not receive a letter from me yesterday dated *3 o'clock* of Saturday morning! What sort of letter it would have been, written at *that* hour—in my night-clothes of course—and with dreadful goings on in my 'Interior'—also of course, may be more easily imagined than told!— *Reflection* however suggested, after I had opened my blot-book and dipt my pen in the ink, that if I could not sleep, nor even lie like a Christian in bed, I should abstain at least from aggravating my nerves still further by so exciting an occupation as writing always is to me, *with the house all to myself*— Needle-work—some dull book would answer better— I could not find any needle-work suitable for being done in one's night shift—so I remained till *six* in the morning down stairs having risen in despair of sleep at two, reading first Segur's *Campaigns of Napoleon*, and then Douglas Jerrald's newspaper—[70] I then returned to bed sick and weary, envying the birds who had been singing for hours—and slept—a few *minutes*—beautiful work—

I have been worse than usual all last week and do not seem tending to betterness this week— Perhaps the *iodine* of which I had been taking daily (by Johns order) for a fortnight *ninety* drops (!) at three takings, had got to disagree with me—[71] Anyhow I gave it up on my own judgement—leaving the dumpling to its fate for the present— John

70. Louis Philippe, Comte de Ségur's *History of the Expedition to Russia, undertaken by the Emperor Napoleon in the year 1812* was published in 1825; Douglas William Jerrold (1803–1857) was a successful London dramatist of the 1820s who later moved to journalism, above all in the humorous weekly *Punch*. His eponymous *Weekly Newspaper* was nowhere near as successful. Dickens was a pall-bearer at his funeral.

71. Iodine was isolated from seaweed in 1811 and was used thereafter as an antiseptic and a dietary supplement (with no particularly clear purpose in Victorian times). It can have allergic reactions and affect the thyroid gland for good and evil: Jane's 'dumpling' is in her throat, we notice. Perhaps it was a blessing that Dr John was a hit-and-miss prescriber, not given to persisting with anything.

approved my doing so—when I told him—but *all* Johns prescribings are on the pattern of that one recorded by his Sister Mary when her children had the measles[:] 'You had better give them some *senna—or perhaps you had better not*'— The lump has got no larger—neither is it perceptibly diminished[—]and as it gives me no pain and no inconvenience the least in the world beyond that of having to wear something round my throat it may stick there till it grow more formidable and then I will consult some *regular* Dr—

If it had not been for my plenty of headaches; I would have sent you sooner, for the benefit of my Uncle chiefly, a penny-a-line account of the Grand-Duke's visit to Cheyne Row—and now it looks an old story, and I cannot get up even penny-a-line-steam about it— Here however is *the* fact of the business— Saturday gone a week the Secretary announced in *official* style, that 'his Royal Highness Reigning Duke of Saxe Weimar'[72] would call for Mr Carlyle next day at twelve *if convenient*— and received of course an affirmative reply— On Sunday morning I *dusted all my little things* very accurately—put clean water to some flowers I already had—saw that Anne bloomed out into her best gown—(for Anne unless expressly ordered would not dress herself *out of the usual time* for Queen Victoria, never to speak of a foreign Highness—) and then— I walked off into space!

Had I staid at home I was going to have felt myself in a '*false position*'—either I must have been put *au secret* [in solitary confinement] in my own house—or invited down to my own sitting room, as an ineffable condescension—and I did not feel any *besoin* [need] of the *condescension* of anybody— With Carlyle it was all right—the Prince had to do with *him*—and the visit was honourable to both parties—but *I* should only have embarrassed his Highness and he me—and so I went up to Mrs Buller's— She insisted on my staying till her driving hour, when she would take me home— I came in half an hour after the dinner hour expecting to be reproved—but C's first words were 'you have just missed these people by ten minutes'!— 'From twelve till twenty minutes after five'? What a frightful royal visit I thought; but it had not been so bad as that— At twelve the little Secretary had arrived 'all in a sweat' to say the Queen Dowager (*our visitors* Aunt) had insisted on his going to Church with her!! So it was hoped an hour or two later would make

72. Strictly speaking not the reigning Grand Duke of Saxe-Weimar, Karl Friedrich, but his heir apparent, Karl Alexander (1818–1901). Goethe was long resident in the court at the Thuringian city of Weimar, so the Duke would naturally be interested in his leading British disciple. 'Ann' is Anne Brown, maid at No. 5 since the end of 1846, on the departure of Kirkcaldy Helen.

no difference— About four they came[:] that is to say the Prince his Chamberlain and Secretary in a handsome open carriage with two servants behind, who excited Ann's admiration by their 'genteel dress— plain black coats, blue breeches, and white silk stockings— Nothing the least *fine* about them except their—*gold garters*!' Another thing seemed to have struck her rather forcibly— 'So soon as the carriage stopt the Prince took off his hat and then all the rest did the same—and at going away they all remained bear headed till the Prince put on *his* hat after he had sat down in the carriage'[.] And all this uncovering of heads I really believe Ann considered honour paid to—her Master!— In which blessed illusion I allowed her to remain, as a new reason for cooking his chops to the best of her power!— C liked the Prince very well—but who would not like a Prince that comes to pay one a morning visit,— [H]e is only some four or five and twenty—very handsome C said, 'with beautiful blue eyes'[,] 'extremely aristocratic looking'—(who is to look aristocratic if not Kings and Queens?)—'the most dignified German' C had ever seen[.] '*More* dignified, than Plattnauer,' I asked— 'Why—no—the indistructable dignity of Plattnauer *in all sorts of coats* is what one *never* sees the like of.' When they arrived C was doing a *Yankee* of all things—introduced by Emerson, but he had him up stairs and dismissed him summarily—with apologies— [T]he Yankee[73] loitered, and seemed to think it strange that *he* should not be invited to assist at the interview—

When C came down to the low room he found his Highness *standing* with the other two men. He apologised for *intruding on his retired habits* &c &c then said looking about that he could fancy himself at home in Weimar here; so many reminiscences of Goethe and of Germany:— then he went about looking at the various portraits of Goethe and finally seated himself on the sofa and *invited* C to be seated— *That* was one of the prospective etiquettes that scared me *out*—having to *stand* till I was permitted to sit down on my own chair!— He staid some hour and quarter talking 'intelligently enough' and being talked to I imagine *emphatically* enough— He invited C to Weimar—promised to show him various things—promised to send him a scarce book they had talked of—begged that 'he would not forget him'—(how touching! and I should think *superfluous*) and then went in peace—

I have heard nothing of Geraldine for many days[.] She is very busy finishing her book down there—[74] By the way I had to write to Mrs

73. Possibly, *CL* speculates, Ebenezer Rockwood Hoar (1816–1895), predictably enough from Concord, MA. Literate at the age of four and a freshman at Harvard aged fifteen, Ebenezer entered the law and then politics, serving eminently in both in progressive causes.

74. Her novel, *The Half Sisters*, concerning illegitimacy, published 1848 (see 12 June 1848, below).

Paulet the other day that I must have back my miniature— When she got it I told her it was C's property—but a chance of he would remember any thing about it till after my death when she was to be sure and restore it— *You* had one picture of me already and if she *liked* to have the keeping of it I thought it better there than here in a dark box—But C happened to ask where it was and much displeased at its being at Seaforth 'where it would be either lost or spoilt like every thing else' and desired I should immediately write for it so I have written and desired her to take it to Maryland Street—that you may send it by the first person you know of coming to London— [. . .]

Pray send this letter on to Babbie—I will write to herself in a day or two—about the Bazaar—[75]

Ever your affectionate /
J C

To Thomas Carlyle, Chelsea, 2 October 1847

'Thanks God'! Dear, I write from *home* again! I arrived yesterday much in the state I expected, with a racking headach and face-ach, but also with a little 'Monarch-of-all-I-survey-feeling,'[76] which was compensation '*for much*'! In my life, I think, I never did so enjoy *giving orders*, and being *waited upon* as last night! and being asked *What I would like to take* and *getting it*! And thanks to the 'considerable mass of poridge' which John inculcated; I had some sleep, and to day I am quite free of headach—and the face-ach is greatly diminished, and I had very nice coffee *in bed*, and a fire to dress at, and in short I feel in a state of *luxury* perfectly indescribable!

Your letter last night too was a most agreeable surprise—*two* letters in one day!—*that* I was not exacting enough to have ever looked for!

Lady Harriet spoke of writing to you one of these days— On Monday she comes to town, to go to the Grange[77] on Tuesday—perhaps— for 'if Charles Buller come from Cornwall on Monday he might like

75. A Victorian charitable institution, bazaars were often held to support worthy causes via the sale, mostly, of women's craft ware, homewares and the like. This was perhaps such an event for the benefit of poor Italians in the capital organised, needless to say, by Mazzini.
76. William Cowper, 'Verses Supposed to be Written by Alexander Selkirk' (1782). (Selkirk was the original inspiration for Defoe's Robinson Crusoe, so the proverbial phrase is strictly accurate.)
77. The Ashburtons' third country house, after Alverstoke and Addiscombe, at Northington, near Winchester in Hampshire: a Greek Revival edifice still in the Baring/ Ashburton family.

one day at the Cottage before they go'—in which case they would put off going to the Grange till Wednesday— Or perhaps, 'if Mr Baring wants *two* days in London' Lady H would come up with him on Monday and go somewhere (Lord Grey's I think) over Tuesday— At all events the Grange after Wednesday seemed her probable address.— Sometime in November she expected to be in town for a week—and after Christmas she wished us to go to Alverstoke— She has got a grey spanish horse, looked up for her by Mr Fleming, and a new riding habit and beaver [helmet] and is 'going to ride *quick* now.'

The Coachman has made a new epigram about you— He was backing out Mr Baring in trying to persuade her Ladyship to ride the Cangaroo— 'Good gracious,' said Lady H, do none of you remember how it behaved with Mrs Carlyle? *She* could not ride it!' 'Pooh! pooh!' said the old humbug[:] 'Mrs Carlyle could have ridden the horse perfectly well, it was not *the horse* Mrs Carlyle was afraid of[;] what she was afraid of was *Mr* Carlyle!'

Well—if the coachman dont appreciate you here is 'a young heart' that does, 'Immortal one!'— The note I send is accompanied by a blood-red volume entitled *Criticisms.*[78] I have looked at *the gratitude* in the preface— A very grand paragraph indeed about 'the magnificent— *Trench*! and the *collossal Carlyle*; one of whom reminds us of some gigantic river, now winding &c &c; the other of some tremendous being struggling with mighty power &c &c'[.] A very tremendous blockhead does this writer *remind* us of!

I can tell you next to nothing of Mazzini— After I had been at home a week I sent him simply my *visiting card*!! which however he immediately replied to in person—but when he arrived I had already fallen ill—was just going to bed in a fainting state, and could merely shake hands with him and bid him go away— [H]e sent to ask for me two or three days after, and a week after he came—one evening when John was here—who kept him all the time talking about Dante—and in an hour I was wearied and sent them away together. That is all I have seen of him—and all he got opportunity to tell me of 'our things'[79] was that

78. A collection of literary and religious essays (1847) by John William Lester (1826–1876). Lester waxes lyrical about Thomas in his preface: a 'tremendous being struggling with mighty power, now standing amid thick darkness, and now beneath the sublime radiance of universal sunlight', and so forth. Richard Chevenix Trench (1807–1886): poetic disciple of Wordsworth and religious disciple of bishop Samuel Wilberforce (cruelly nicknamed 'Soapy Sam' by some). In typical Victorian fashion Lester seeks to situate his contribution, mindfully, between the religious (Trench) and the sceptical (Carlyle).

79. A Mazzini-ism, referring to his activities in Italian nationalism.

he had been for weeks expecting private information that would take him away at an hours notice—but that now there seemed no prospect of anything immediate taking effect[,] and on the tenth October he would go to Paris for a month and 'into the Valley of Madame Sand'[.][80] I asked if he had meant to put himself at the disposal of the Pope?— 'Oh no' he said[,] what he aimed at was 'to *organize* and *lead* an expedition into Lombardy which would be *better than being an individual under the Pope*'—in which words seemed to me to lie the whole secret of Mazzinis *failed life*!

I send some cigar-lights which I begged from Anthony Sterling before I took to bed—and forgot all about them—you push the small end into the point of the cigar till the thick end is on a level with the leaf and then rub it like a match on the rough of the box— And now I have pretty well tired myself— Kind regards to the others

Ever faithfully /
Yours JWC

To W. E. Forster, Chelsea, 28 October 1847

> 'If W. E. F who went by rail to Leeds on Saturday night will return to the house he started from; no questions will be asked & every exertion made to meet his views: If this appeal to his feelings fail to move him; let him send back to his afflicted friends the key of the linen chest.'

Dear William

The above was written to send to the Times; but I bethink me, an advertisement will cost five & sixpence, a letter only a penny, & so I take the cheaper course. Why don't you write to me for God's sake? (*that* is not swearing is it?) I should hardly have looked for a letter from you in such a press of business & other things; had it not been for the *fact of the key*—but why dont you send back my key? I fancy there must be some

80. Mazzini got to Paris on 17 October and visited the freedom-loving French novelist George Sand (1804–1876) thereafter. His mission was to encourage the 'Young Italy' movement in France. Some Italians felt that the future of unity lay with Pope Pius IX; others, like Mazzini, Cavour and Garibaldi, thought the reverse—as did Pius himself, who turned increasingly conservative and reigned until 1878.

new worry to have driven that out of your mind, not that I have *wanted* the key—anymore than if it had been the key of Blue Beard's closet—but *you* did not know whether I should want it or not, & *you* are always so considerate. Pray write me two lines just to quieten my imagination which has a faculty of self tormenting that beats the world.

Emerson is here has been here since Monday night[.] I have seen him 'face to face & (over-) soul to (over-) soul'[81] & (I may just as well 'speak the truth & chance the Devil[']) I do *not* like him the least bit! C. says he is a 'most polite & gentle creature—a man really of a quite *seraphic* nature'; & all that may be true, at all rates C has good cause to say it; for Emerson with a tact as laudable as prudent avoids all occasions of dispute, & when dragged into it, by the hair of his head, so to speak he receives the most provoking contradictions with the softness of a feather-bed—*gives* under them for the moment & so, no 'dreadful collision' takes place, such as I was looking for. But with his *politeness* & tolerance, *my* approbation ends. The man has no '*natur*'[82] about him, his geniality is of the *head* not the *heart*—a theoretic systematic geniality that (as Mazzini would say) 'leaves me *cold*'[.] In fact you can get no *hold* of him—nor yet feel *held* by him—his is neither *impressive* nor *impressionable*[:] a sort of man I cannot get on with, *that*! His very face is *two* or rather ½ a dozen faces! that change into one another like '*dissolving views*'[.] [H]e has one face—young refined almost beautiful, radiant with '*virtue its own reward*' and another that is old hatchet-like; A crotchety, inclusive, like an incarnation of one of his own poems. Wh[ich]ever way you take him he slips thro' your fingers, 'like water that cannot be gathered[']'[83]—fine pure spring water, but water all the same[.] C. & he will end I predict in disliking one another pretty well tho' C. under the first restraining grace of hospitality & *a certain* regard to consistency makes the best of him as yet, altho' the other (in confidence with me)

81. 'The Over-Soul' was a central essay of Emerson's (1841), blending any number of religious and philosophical traditions in pursuit of both an expanded notion of human spirituality and an underlying existential unity in which to situate it: Platonic, Neoplatonic, Hindu and/or Swedenborgian.
82. It is hard to say here whether Jane refers empirically to 'nature' (human nature, for example), or to the complex system of ideas developed by Friedrich von Schelling (1775–1854) out of Johann Gottlieb Fichte (1762–1814) about the status of nature within and outside human consciousness: the tradition of *Naturphilosophie*, which Thomas would certainly have understood, itself related to the transcendental idealism of Immanuel Kant (1724–1804), which in turn fed into Emerson's thinking. (But Dickens often spells 'nature' as 'natur', too.)
83. A sub-biblical form of words recorded in Scottish sermons of the 1830s, to say that not all church teaching faded away in such a fashion; that some of it did remain, in the minds of its hearers, and so forth. Jane inverts the sense.

calls C. 'a good child(!) in spite of his love of *the positive*, the *practical*, wh must be very astonishing to all who have learnt to know him thro' his Books.' [V]ery astonishing indeed thou American *Seraph*! & you will find many things to astonish you on this side the atlantic 'I guess'!— I never saw better come of men who wait upon what is called *elevation*. [You]r *elevated* man *par excellence* is always, as far as my experience goes[,] a sort of moral *reed*—has run all to hight without taking breadth along with him— Oh give me *Naetur Natur*! nobody is loveable without *that*; however he may 'strike the stars with his sublime head'[84]—nor turns to any good practical acc[oun]t— I am rather satisfied that he is going away tomorrow night to commence his orations in the north— He will return to London when the town fills, to lecture here—but *then* I fancy he will go into *lodgings*— I hope you will decide for London; if it can be done without hurt to yourself, what a blessing you would be to *me*! Verily I feel quite SCHWESTERLICH [sisterly] towards you. That journey into Yorkshire was a modern version of Saul going out to meet his Father's asses & finding a Kingdom.[85] I went to seek the *picturesque* & found *you*—& catch me losing you again!— Dear Wm Edwd you are worth a cartload of Emersons & so God bless you with *calm* & all good things

Ever yr true friend /
Jane Carlyle

84. Horace, *Odes*, I. i. 35.
85. 1 Samuel 10.

Figure 7: Robert Scott Tait, 'Nero' (1855), Thomas Carlyle Papers, Rare Book & Manuscript Library, Columbia University in the City of New York

6

The Widening Circle: 1848–1851

As regards the world at large this three-year period is known first and foremost as one of Continental revolution—including the publication of Marx and Engels' Communist Manifesto, in German, in London, in 1848. The Carlyle circle generally welcomed the ejection of the French 'sham king', Louis Philippe; hoped for the ejection of the Austrians from northern Italy; sympathised up to a point with the sufferings of the Irish (where Thomas toured for a second time in July 1849); and kept a nervous eye on the situation at home, where Chartism reached a high water mark in April 1848, with a huge rally and a petition to Parliament. But as in the 1790s Britain seemed immune to revolution, and reform continued to manifest itself, however slowly.

But there was a revolution of another sort, too: the rise of the novel as the supreme literary manifestation of the age in the aftermath of Romanticism. Thomas generally took only a skimming interest in such books, even when published by friends like Dickens and Thackeray—though he provided a good deal of moral support to Elizabeth Gaskell when she sent him her 'Tale of Manchester Life', Mary Barton, in November 1848. But Jane was an avid reader of novels, good, bad and indifferent, and we can see them entering her life in droves at this time. Her demanding friend Geraldine Jewsbury had sent her the draft of her second novel, The Half Sisters, in September 1847, and Jane assisted with its progress right up to publication in March the following year. (The book was dedicated to her and Elizabeth Paulet.) In that same month she read Emily Brontë's Wuthering Heights, after a request she made to John Forster on 26? February: 'Have you the other novels of the Currell [Currer] Bell people?— I should like them any time*—', Jane Eyre being the only Brontë stablemate available at that time. In December of that year Thackeray sent Vanity Fair to No. 5, and in 1849 the Carlyles came by David Copperfield, issue by issue. In November 1849 Jane read Charlotte Brontë's Shirley, and on 12 June 1850 she and Thomas were present at a famous soirée hosted by Thackeray to introduce its painfully shy author to literary London. On 8 September 1850 she could record her dissatisfaction with Charles Kingsley's Chartist novel Alton Locke in a letter to Thomas (CL 25: 201): 'It will surely be gratifying to you, the sight of your own name in almost every second page! but for* that*; I am ashamed to say, I should have broken down in it a great way on this side of the end!'*

Had Thomas read Jane Eyre and Wuthering Heights, there is every likelihood that he would have associated their 'unfeminine' depiction of romantic passion with the equally incandescent and prodigious French novelist George Sand (1804–1876) and what, in a disapproving unpublished essay on her written in 1848, he called 'Phallus-Worship'. Jane read George Sand unapologetically—even borrowing her novels from the London Library (though on one occasion she used Erasmus Darwin's name on the reader's slip). Geraldine Jewsbury clearly modelled herself on Sand, right down to the cigar-smoking, and Mazzini in fact sent Sand a copy of Geraldine's first novel, Zoe, in 1845. Another friend (and partner of George Eliot), George Henry Lewes, was a profound admirer, too, and sent the Carlyles his two Sandian homage-fictions, Ranthorpe, and Rose, Blanche, and Violet, in 1847 and 1848 respectively. Though Jane found the second novel 'execrable' and 'silly', Carlyle read them for Lewes's sake; they proved his theory that, morally speaking, the world was going to hell in a handcart to a tee. Indeed, as his 'Phallus-Worship' essay suggested, the negative elements of the 'Year of Revolutions' could in part be laid at George Sand's door. 'These universal suffrages, national workshops, reigns of fraternity, and generally red or white republics with their fraternities and phenomena', he wrote, 'are to me very mainly a George-Sand novel come forth from the land of dreams, intending to enact itself as a fact under this sun.'[1]

The vagueness and the note of confected outrage in this association of realist fiction with political reality demonstrates Thomas's increasing intolerance during this period, especially in his eight serially published Latter-Day Pamphlets of 1850, the rhetorical overdrive and manic dystopianism of which made liberal-minded friends like Edward Fitzgerald, W. E. Forster, Mill and Thackeray react in disbelief. The eight essays haunt his reputation to this day, and whereas it is unlikely that Jane would ever have gone so far as Thomas into the sphere of anti-democratic vituperation, she certainly shared his callous attitude to prison reform (see 7 January 1851, below). Yet the very next year he would publish perhaps the gentlest of all his books, the Life of his friend John Sterling. Even there, however, the mournful note hovers not over a literary talent snuffed out too soon, but over a talent misdirected into the realm of literature: weak and useless in his view. The Carlyles could appreciate a virtuoso like Chopin (lover of George Sand, as it happened), but that was because he was a musician, and Franco-Polish to boot, who made no claim on social reality and could be petted as an exotic: what Virginia Surtees calls their 'aesthetic appetite' was sadly limited.[2] *The irony being that Thomas's most profound influence was probably on the Victorian novelists more than any other group: Dickens and Eliot, in particular. (Dickens dedicated Hard Times to Thomas, and A Tale of Two Cities is substantially derived from his French Revolution.)*

1. Fred Kaplan, '"Phallus-Worship" (1848): Unpublished Manuscripts III—A Response to the Revolution of 1848', *Carlyle Newsletter*, 2 (1980), 22.
2. Virginia Surtees, *Jane Welsh Carlyle* (Salisbury, 1986), 134.

In other respects the Carlyles' lives carried on in much the same groove. The crisis of 1846 did not recur; relations settled somewhat; visits to the Ashburtons, long and short, were welcomed by Thomas and tolerated by Jane. Her health was somewhat better, though there was another cold in the winter of 1849 and an accidental injury to her shoulder the following winter. (Thomas was oblivious to both.) Even 'Kirkcaldy Helen' returned to the stage in October 1849, finally to be dismissed for incurable drunkenness in March 1850. In the summer of 1849 they took separate holidays in the north, and Jane returned to Scotland for the first time since her mother's death—including a performance from her as a revenant at Haddington, recorded in a journal she entitled 'Much Ado About Nothing'. There was another serious tiff in the aftermath, when Thomas went off for another Highlands holiday with the Ashburtons without his wife. Best news for her was a December 1849 present from Stavros Dilberoglue in Manchester: a loyal and endearing Maltese-cross she named Nero, whose companionship became essential to her in the ten years to come.

To Thomas Carlyle, Chelsea, 17 January 1848

Well, Dearest, I have written what I have written,[3] and what I have written I will keep to; If I am spared on foot till Thursday I will go on Thursday, and accept the consequences—if any. This time; I am under engagement to go, and it is pitiful to break one's engagements for any thing short of necessity. But I will never, with the health I have, or rather, have *not*, *engage* to leave home for a long fixed period another winter.[4] One of the main uses of a *home* is *to stay in it*, when one is too weak and spiritless for conforming without *effort* to the ways of other houses. Besides is not *Home*—at least, was it not 'in more earnest Times' 'the Womans proper sphere'?— Decidedly; if she '*have nothing to keep her at home*'—as the phrase is—she should *find something*—'or *die*'! *That* is my idea in these days of solitary musing. *Amusement*, after a certain age is *no go*, even when there are no other nullifying conditions; it gets to be merely *distraction*, in the Gambardella-sense, between which and distraction in the general sense there is but a thin partition, so thin that one can hear thro' it, whenever one likes to *listen*, the clanking of chains and shrieking of 'Mads,' as plainly as I am hearing at this moment the Chambers-piano-forte—oh yes—I had found out *that* 'by my own smartness' *before*

3. John 19: 22.
4. That is, to visit the Ashburtons at one of their 'places in the country', for Thomas's pleasure and benefit rather than her own.

I took to reading on Insanity. To be sure it is hard on flesh and blood, when one 'has nothing to keep one at home,' to sit down in honest life-weariness and look out into unmitigated *Zero*; but perhaps it 'would be a great advantage' just to 'go ahead' in that—the barefaced indigence of such a state might drive one—like the Piper's Cow[5]—to '*consider*,' and who knows but, in considering long enough, one might discover what one 'has wanted' and what one 'wants'—an essential preliminary to *getting it*! Meanwhile here is Hare's Sterling-book come for you—late—for Miss Wynne[6] had read it four days ago—and 'with the *Publishers* compliments.'[7] No copy had been sent to Anthony [Sterling] when I saw him! he had bought it, and said if *you* did not feel yourself bound to place his Brother in a truer light *he* must attempt it himself. I will take the book to Lady Harriet or send it. The letter you sent was from Bölte. Maggie [Welsh] writes to me this morning that the talk of [business] failures in Liverpool is now given place to talk about *robberies*, that you 'cannot at night walk thro' a quiet street without imminent risk of being not only knocked down and robbed, but beaten into the bargain.['] [. . .]

John is to dine with Darwin today, so I shall not have him in the evening. He has been very kind—coming *early* every evening and reading to me when I could bear it— Miss Wynne was here two hours on Saturday, and kissed me when she went away—*that* was nothing, but, having done it, she *blushed* up to the very roots of her hair, and *that* was lovely! My head aches a great deal—which is natural—for, except the first night after you went, I have slept little—some three hours a-night and that in small pieces—but I am able to lie quite peaceable, *without reading*— [. . .]

We have rain today and a good deal of wind—

'And now to Father son and *T'olly Goast*'—for my head will stand no more writing

yours faithfully /
Jane W. C.

---

5. Oft-repeated, from the folk ballad 'The Tune the Old Cow Died Of': 'There was an old man, and he had an old cow, / But he had no fodder to give her, / So he took up his fiddle and played her the tune— / "Consider, good cow, consider, / This isn't the time for the grass to grow. / Consider, good cow, consider."'
6. Charlotte Williams-Wynn (1807–1869), traveller, diarist and spinster friend of Carlyle connections such as F. D. Maurice and Karl August Varnhagen von Ense.
7. John Sterling's *Essays and Tales*, edited by Julius Hare; Sterling had died in September 1844. The inadequacy of Hare's introductory memoir would inspire Thomas to write his *Life of John Sterling* (1851).

To Lady Harriet Ashburton, Chelsea, 11 June 1848

My dear Lady Harriet

Mr C must make you the *Report* of Lecture 3d;[8] for this one 'tacked on' to *The Sublime* rather than to *The Ridiculous*, and my memory (more shame to me!) is retentive of only the Ridiculous in human speech. He (my Husband) likened the former Lecture to the Tune of '*Over the Water to Charlie*,' as he had once heard it played on an indifferent fiddle; the last was more in the style of '*With one consent let all the Earth*' played on a (barrel-)organ; or of that mystical *Fantasia* on the violincello with which Albert in the last chapter of *Consuelo thrills* the two Artist-souls who had come from remote lands and up a steep mountain to ask him for '*The Solution*.'[9] The audience were quite charmed; so beautiful it all *sounded*, so profound, and lofty, and prophetic! but ask any one of them, or the man himself, what that tongue-*sonate* '*wished of you*,' and the answer could only be; 'Dont know the least in the world[']; further than, that you should 'prick the slumberous side of the Giant who dwells in the unseen—the Angel who stood by God in the day of Creation—and stimulate *Him* (the Giant—the Angel) into all-searching, all-pervading activity,' said *Giant* or *Angel* having been *precised* as '*The Instinct* within us—that *first Look* of the Soul into every object.' By all which, if he meant to say in plain English, that it would be well we should *give more heed to our instincts*, I, for one, whatever *the fish* or *flower* may do, most cordially 'think along with him.' On the whole we shall none of us be wiser for the Lecture I fear, but they amuse, and can do no possible harm—'*a song of triumph*'—over *no* victory—*voila tout* [that's all]!

The new-charmed Duchess has not come again—has found, it would seem, something more unintelligible for her elsewhere. Lady Byron sat in her place, pale and transparent as a wax candle[.][10] Ah!—I recollected how I once walked half an hour, to and fro, in the rain, before an Edinr Book-shop; to catch sacred glimpses of—that woman's *skirts*! and I sighed, that 'the rude hand of Time' should have so effectually 'swept *the down*' (as a Lady once said to me) 'from *the cheek* of my beautiful enthusiasm.'

8. By Emerson, that is, speaking in London: 'Tendencies and Duties of Men of Thought'. The second was on 'Relation of Intellect to Natural Science'.
9. Not from George Sand's novel *Consuelo* (1843), in fact, but *The Countess of Rudolstadt* (1844), chapter 41.
10. Harriet Elizabeth Georgiana (*née* Howard), Duchess of Sutherland (1806–1868), friend of Queen Victoria and abolitionist. Anne Isabella Noel Byron (*née* Milbanke), 11th Baroness Wentworth and Baroness Byron (1792–1860), the poet's wife 1815–1816 before his departure from England amidst the scandal generated by their separation.

Miss Wynn told us in returning from the Lecture that Lord Sligo in his capacity of Special Constable had 'seized two cart-loads of arms'—probably some old *brace* of pistols—and that the *Rising* was looked for today instead of tomorrow—but I hear only church-bells, no *Tocsin*—[11] She told us too, what you have perhaps heard, that a gentleman (?) went up to Milnes in the House of Commons, and said he understood that he (Milnes) now sent his *washing* to Mrs Cuffy; but that there was *so little of it*, and what *was*, so *thoroughly soiled*, that poor Mrs Cuffy was frantic. And Milnes had 'taken this joke very much to heart.' If I were Milnes, I would call out a few of these Jokers and shoot *one*, at least, dead—for the example's sake. [. . .]

Emerson is dining here today and a Welshman whom Mr C once staid three weeks with, and my Brother in law—and they are now looking for tea I suppose—[12] [T]he dinner *went* off charmingly—well-cooked and well-waited—and what is of more enduring interest to my household good my maid has persuaded me that her two 'accidents' really were accidental, and stays under the condition that *I* am to regulate her intercourse with her Lover according to my own ideas of *propriety*.

What a letter! Ever yours / JWC

❧

To Lady Harriet Ashburton, Chelsea, 12 June? 1848

My dear Lady Harriet

Since your note arrived at breakfast; I have enquired out, seen, and taken the particulars of *two* possible scullery-maids,[13] and as it is now only twelve of the clock I may come on the traces of some more of them in the course of the day.

No 1 is a large, *strapping* young woman, with a physiognomy that hovers betwixt sense and *softness*—'will be three and twenty next

11. England was in the middle of a series of protests by the Chartist movement, seeking political reform such as universal (male) suffrage. The authorities prepared, but no alarm bell of revolution (tocsin) sounded in the end. William Cuffey was a Chartist leader arrested and tried for insurgency and arson; an MP at Westminster has made a nasty joke about Monckton Milnes' sympathy for the movement—alluding, apparently, to his slovenly dress habits.
12. For Charles Redwood, see 18 July 1843, above. Fellow diner is John Carlyle.
13. The scullery is the room in a large house in which crockery, cutlery and cooking utensils are stored and cleaned—by the scullery maid, who might well want to upgrade her skills in the kitchen as a cook.

September'—has lived three years with a family in Upper Cheyne Row—single servant there—*not* liable to *colds*—can have a good character from her present mistress who 'has known her from a child'—'is *not afraid of work*'—'is *leaving*, of her own accord, *for the heaviness of the work*['](?)—has in fact already *left officially*, another servant being come in her place; but her mistress 'let her stay, doing needle-work till she find a place to suit her[']—'has no objection to live in the country all the year round or for any number of years round[']—'rather *prefers* the country'—had 12£ of wages where she is—would prefer the situation of scullery maid 'in a *high* family' to any other situation being 'desirous to *get on* into *cook*'—is not, I think, without promptings of ambition. Finally No 1 is, *Irish* and thinks no shame of herself for *that.*

No 2 is less in stature—considerably—upper half of her face cheery and intelligent—under half *questionable*; a mouthful of teeth slightly projecting *to one side* give it something of a shilly-shallying [irresolute] look— She is two and twenty—is single servant at No 10 of this street—went there in room of a Sister who fell sick, and her sister having died, had stayed on ten months without having intended it—is leaving now of her own accord having '*strong inclinations for cooking*' and her present mistress doing all the cooking herself—would like of all things the place of scullery-maid 'in a *good* Family,' where she could 'learn something'—has had eight pounds a year of wages where she is; but would 'expect a *bit more* if she went into a *good* family'—'can have a satisfactory character from her present Mistress and can assure me that she is very *respectably connected*'—no objections to the country, 'Oh no indeed!'—'rather likes *heat*' (this taste was elicited by my question; if she were strong enough for hot kitchen-work?) No 2 has every drop of blood in her *English*

Both these Damsels will seek no further, till I have heard whether you would like either or both of them sent to Bath House for further investigation. If I hear of any other more promising I will write again.

I enclose a letter from India which contains some rather interesting details of English Life at Loodiana. The Writer is a beautiful little deaf Lady who bestowed herself and fortune on that Capt Mackenzie who was, after Lady Sale, our greatest Afghanistan *Lion.*[14] I never saw such an instance of a woman loving a man 'for the dangers he had

14. Helen Mackenzie, who accompanied her husband on military service in Ludhiana, in the Punjab, northern India. Florentia, Lady Sale, was a civilian swept up in the disastrous retreat from Kabul of 1842 (without her husband), during the First Anglo-Afghan War, and was held captive with her daughter till her rescue, by Sir Robert Sale himself at the head of a troop of cavalry—a tale of love, endurance and courage if ever there was one.

passed'—[15] The moment Capt M. began his *Tale*, which he had to tell over at least *once* in every company; the little deaf wife, however occupied elsewhere, seemed to know by instinct, and would hasten towards him, and sit down with her ear within two inches of his mouth, and exhibit all the different phases of emotion which his narrative could possibly have excited in her at the first hearing—and all this without the least affectation in the world I really believe— [S]he always struck me as a most sincere, natural little woman. I send too a note of female criticism on *the Halfsisters* which Lady Ashburton may perhaps like to read, as one small evidence that *all* my friends who think and write upon *woman* are not so entirely immoral after all! it is from a sister of Mrs Paulets, Emma Newton, who wrote a book in one volume called *the Unbeliever.*

Ever faithfully / JW Carlyle

To Helen Welsh, Chelsea, circa 16 July 1848

My dearest Helen

I am not going to write you a long letter today— I slept ill, and have already exhausted myself in writing trumpery notes of the *inevitable* sort—besides a little letter to Walter—but I have already let myself be hindered thanking you for your kind remembrance of me and my poor birth-day too long. (Oh why do *some* of us give ourselves the trouble of being *born*?)—and if I do not take the present hour perhaps tomorrow will bring another rush of visitors and such like consequences of *The Fall*[.] Thanks then for the beautiful sleeves and the as beautiful letter—the sleeves almost *frightened* me for a moment, for there seemed to be some touch of witch-craft in them— I had got home a new black-silk *polka spencer*![16] (God help me!) from the dressmaker—and she had made the sleeves half-short—and at the *very instant* your packet came, I was sitting looking at it '*in a state of mind*' (Capt [Anthony] Sterlings phrase) saying to myself 'Oh dear me I must make white sleeves for it, the first thing, and how am I to shape them'?! Certainly there are secret affinities in people and things that no mortal will ever get to the bottom of!

15. Shakespeare, *Othello*, I. iii. 167.
16. The two words mean the same thing, more or less, in fashion terms: a close-fitting lady's jacket; but 'polka' suggests woollen fabric and (possibly) Polish origin.

I have been very *gay* of late weeks! Nobody unless the paralytic Miss Chorley,[17] I should think, has been going more *resolutely* a-head in 'the gaities of the season' *so-called*—with *my body*—that is to say, for my soul has been at quite other work—

We dined at Mrs Nortons one day![18] We grow very *compatible* dont you think?— Well she is a beautiful witty graceful woman—whatever else, then a dinner at the Macreadys where was Count D'Orsay! and old Lady Morgan 'naked as robins' half way down—age seventy five!—and Lady Duff Gordon and an american Mrs Jay[.] (I must tell you something of *her*—a friend of Lady Harriets had her at dinner—and after they had gone up to the drawing room, invited her *selon les regles* [according to the rules] to go to a bedroom[19]— '[N]o indeed' said Mrs Jay with a Lady's maid air and tone which I can give you no notion of—'no indeed—in *our* country we never think of such a thing!— *We consider such practices extremely injurious*! just twice a day we retire for *that purpose* and never oftener, unless when we are in the family-way'—!! You may figure how the *English* Lady of Rank stared! Tell my uncle this tho '*decency forbids*'[.)] Then we had another dinner at the Procters—where were Adelaide Kemble and her husband—and a morning music party at Lady Eddisburys—'the beautiful Mrs Stanley'—that was—Darwins '*Moonface*'— Young girls—*very* young and pretty—sang with the self-possession of Grisis[20] to an immense concourse of Ladies and (more to the purpose) of *young marriageable Lords*[,] one of whom (Lord Dufferin) said to me—'a charming way of passing a morning this!—and such a capital thing—don't you think for *curing* them of all sort of shyness'? Decidedly!— There was one girl a real beauty—the daughter of Sir *James* Graham—about seventeen—with the most innocent modest *face* in the world and there she stood with her face to the company—trilling and quavering *with the smile* of a consumate Opera singer![21] It seemed to me really *bad* all this!

17. An old acquaintance; Lancastrian, friend of Elizabeth Gaskell, crippled by spinal disease around this time.
18. Caroline Elizabeth Sarah Norton (*née* Sheridan; 1808–1877), granddaughter of playwright Richard Brinsley Sheridan and important campaigner for women's marital rights in terms of child access and property on the basis of her own cruel experience. She lived apart from her husband from 1836 on. Sydney, Lady Morgan (1781–1859), novelist and travel-writer; Lucie, Lady Duff-Gordon (1821–1869), authority on modern Egypt; Hannah Augusta McVickar, wife of American jurist and abolitionist William Jay.
19. Presumably to make use of a chamber pot, if required after a long dinner.
20. Giuditta and Giulia Grisi, Italian opera singers of renown at the time.
21. Probably Mabel Violet Graham, later Duncombe, Countess of Feversham (1833–1915).

But I went to hear Chopin[22] too—once in private and once at a morning concert[;] and Chopin has been *here*!! I never heard the piano played before—could not have believed the capabilities that lie in it— Quantities of more things of the same nature I have *done*—I was going to say *in my sleep*—but *in a bad dream* were nearer the truth.

The one earthly thing that I have been getting any real satisfaction out of has been something very far away from all that—the wise and valourous conduct of General Cavaignac—and the admiration he has won from all parties— If I had been his Sister I could not have watched his progress with more interest—[23]

Anne has had no more 'accidents'—and I suppose may hold out a while longer—but it is an inconvenient item in a servant having a prospective Husband to fall back upon in all emergencies.

And now I must I really make an end—
Love and a kiss to my Uncle
Ever your affectionate
Jane Carlyle

To Helen Welsh, Chelsea, 20 January 1849

Dearest Helen what a shame! The only real business I have, '*here down*,' (as Mazzini used to say) seems to be writing to the people who like to hear from me—and see how I bestir myself in *that*! The fact is; nobody that is much caring to do ever the 'things that they *ought* to do,'[24] and even the things they *intend* to do should live in London—even on the most domestic principles; there being here a *parti pris* [preconceived opinion] on the side of *the pigs* to 'Run thro'' all ones 'best laid schemes':[25]

22. Frédéric Chopin (1810–1849), Romantic composer and virtuoso pianist, lover of George Sand, and victim of tuberculosis, who left Paris during the 1848 revolution for London, where he gave several concerts in the great private houses of the capital. After his last ever performance in November he returned to Paris, where he died in October 1849.
23. This is General Louis-Eugène Cavaignac (1802–1857), *de facto* president of France from June to December 1848 and younger brother of the Carlyles' friend Godefroi Cavaignac (see Characters and Correspondents). He stoutly defended democratic processes and gave way to Louis-Napoleon Bonaparte in an election some of his supporters suggested he could annul.
24. 'A General Confession' in the *Book of Common Prayer* of the Church of England: 'we have done those things which we ought not to have done'.
25. Robert Burns, 'To a Mouse': 'The best laid schemes o' Mice an' Men / Gang aft agley'.

I have been interrupted dreadfully these two weeks, but the wonderfulest '*go*' of all has been a *child*![26] Yes indeed! I have had a child—to keep,—to sit at meat with, and *sleep* with (good God!) and dress dolls for, and wash and comb and all that sort of thing—and also (—most fatiguing of all—) to *protect* it from Mr C who gave manifest indications of a tendency to wring its neck! Where did I pick the creature up?— Ah my Dear! the creature picked up *me*—'quite promiscuously'— I went some six weeks ago to call at the Macreadys—and dined at the childrens dinner and was reminded that I had a Godchild, *by seeing it.* Not one godmotherly thing had I ever done towards that child! and really it was a Godchild to be proud of. So now I took it on my knee and kissed it and, like a fool; asked 'will you go with *me*?' I should like it very much said the Child. '*That she would*' said the Mother; 'and you need not be afraid of her misconducting herself for she is a good child'— I saw the thing had been taken *on the serious* so I backed out of it as well as I could, 'Some time we shall see!—when I come again *with a carriage*.' Well! ten days ago I went there again with Anthony Sterling—and was asked gravely by the eldest daughter if I 'meant to take Jane Lydia back with me'? 'She had never ceased talking about *her visit* since I had been there.' I was in for it! so I said 'not today'; (it was necessary to prepare C's mind as well as my own) 'but if her Mother would bring her any day she liked to name I should do my best with her'— So Saturday was named—and the little creature delivered over to me in a transport of joy, (hardly mutual) to stay as 'long as I could be troubled to keep her'— I modestly suggested that three days and three nights—just the time that Jonah was in the whale's belly[27]—would probably be enough of it for *her* as well as for me—and the Mother went and I remained alone—with a child of six years—very *stirring* and very small and delicate! [D]uring the first day I 'ran horses' at her bidding, and performed my new functions with a determined energy—but the night came, I durst not put her to sleep in the spare room—for fear of her crying in the night—and awaking Mr C, and being herself very miserable[;] so after infinite perplexity in getting off her clothes (all *sewed* together) I laid her in my own bed, where she soon commenced—singing!— [A]fter an hour's waiting upon her I left her still awake—when I went up again she was asleep but lying right *accross* the bed—at twelve I placed her properly, and went into bed myself; but of course not to sleep: all night long she pitched into my breast with her active little heels—and when she awoke at seven and threw her arms about my neck calling out 'Oh I

26. Lydia Jane Macready, who died aged sixteen in 1858.
27. Jonah 1: 17.

am so glad to be here!' I had not once closed my eyes and in this state to have to wash and dress her and play at horses again! [I]t was a strange and severe penalty for being a Godmother— [N]ext night I put her in the spare bed at all risks—with a good fire and trusted in Providence—and she did very well there—but I had got some cold by the job and the idea of being *laid up* in such a cause after having got so far thro' the winter on foot was very vexatious so I kept the house a few days and when the childs time came Anthony Sterling took her home for me!! I have a great quantity more to tell you about this '*go*' and other things—but Mr C has been bothering ever since I began to write about helping him to pack a boxful of old clothes and things for Scotsbrig—and in an hour I have to be off to Mrs Buller so I will finish this letter to Babbie—God bless you all your affectionate

Jane Welsh

To Jeannie Welsh, Chelsea, 27 February 1849

Dearest Babbie

I have so much to tell and so little time to tell it in that I don't know where to begin—besides I have forgotten in the, 'hubbub wild and dire dismay['][28] of late days where I left off in *my life*—that is to say the history of my life—outwardly speaking—but certainly when I wrote last I was not gone nor meaning to go to Hedly—so I shall begin with that—Mr C surprisingly invited himself to Hedly (Capt [Anthony] S[terling]'s country place) incited thereto by the charming description given of it by John Carlyle, who had gone down with Capt S for a couple of days—a beautiful country mansion, with 'fresh air,' and horses to ride, and no *woman* in the house, or servant of any sort indoors, but one old Scotch Cook—taking care of the premises in the absence of Mrs Sterling and the children now settled at Knightsbridge— [A]ll *that* had charms for Mr C—[a]nd there being nobody in town just then that he cared to stay for—he proposed to go down with Anthony on his next weekly visit to the place— [B]ut Anthony had no notion of having *him* without *me*, and Mr C himself thought I should go, to 'keep Anthony off him and let him enjoy *the perfect* silence'— (As if *that* man *could* enjoy or yet *endure* perfect silence for one week!)— I liked the idea of going; but would not agree till I had written to Mrs Sterling about it, and asked *her* to go too!

28. Milton, *Paradise Lost*, ii. 951.

It was all very well to tell me she was fast going mad again, and that it was determined she should *never* go back to Hedley[.] All that was no concern of mine no reason that I should cause her annoyance— So I wrote and she answered me in the friendliest manner—without mentioning the thing to her Husband—declining to go to Hedly 'from the shades of which she was too happy to have just escaped' but 'seeing no earthly reason why I should not go with Mr C and Capt Sg[.'] I was so glad after, that I had, as Mr C phrased it, 'completely attended to *the three thousand punctualities* with her,' for if I had not; I could not have felt sure the irritation of our settling such a thing without her knowledge had not hastened the final explosion of the fit of mania hanging over her the last six weeks— It exploded *before* our visit took place—for a *fortnight* she was in a strait-waistcoat occasionally; but is now more quiet tho' still confined to a room with two mad-nurses. She has shewn no dislike of *me* this time—on the contrary seems to want to make *me* a party against her Husband—poor thing. But all this of *her*, is nothing new now— Her Husband takes it, as a matter of course—and tries to keep 'never minding'— We went to Hedly on Tuesday gone a week, meaning to return on Friday—but the curious Gipsy life we led, on a *basis* of all the comforts and luxuries of civilization—answered so well that on Friday I came to town with Anthony (who had to go and speak with Mad-doctors) leaving Mr C in perfect bliss—*if solitude* BE *bliss*—and having provided changes of linen &c returned next morning to remain till Monday—[29] It was the most successful visit I have made for long— Anthony and I laid the table set wax candles &c &c[;] the old woman cooked out of sight what victuals were not brought ready from London—and Mr C let himself be *waited upon* by us with an amiability. Then He had four riding horses which he might by turns gallop to death—and I had a pony which took me as fast as Anthony could *walk* at his head, over all the beautiful hills in the neighbourhood—and we sat and smoked *in the carpenters shop* Capt S has fitted up for himself—and I learned to *turn* and shoot with a bow—and shot—*myself* in the cheek!—as a green mark can testify to this hour: and indeed indeed—I felt very like little Macready on its late three days visit to myself—with no end of wishes and whim and a childish surprise and felicity to find them all immediately gratified.

Monday came however—and we *must* return— [T]he Ashburtons were to come to town that day, and we were to dine at Bath House Tuesday— We drove to our own door where Mr C and the luggage

29. The speed with which Jane is able to come and go suggests this is Headley in Surrey, on the North Downs near Box Hill, surrounded by heathland.

were to be deposited, I going on to Knightsbridge with Anthony to settle about a Governess for him— But Mr C knocked in vain for a good while and we were speculation about breaking in at a window, and storming at Helen for having gone out when she knew we were coming[,] when the door opened to a twentieth blow and an apparition presented itself which I shall remember as long as I live. There stood Helen—her mouth all over blood, her brow and cheeks white with chalk from the kitchen floor—like an excessively *ill got up* stage-ghost! her dark gown—ditto—her hair hanging in two wild streams down her neck—her crushed cap all awry—and on her face a hideous smile of idiotic self-complacency!— Nothing *could* be more drunk! We ordered her down stairs but she refused to be '*used in that way*'[.] So Mr C had to drag her down—and leave her on the kitchen floor. I walked off, with the *sublime calm* which always comes to me in purely *material* trouble, followed by Anthony to Mrs White to tell her to come to the rescue— [W]hen we came in Mr C was on his knees lighting the parlour fire— Anthony then drove off coolly remarking—that 'as I seemed to have affairs of my own to attend to he could not expect me to come and settle his'— Mr C retired to his study— [T]here was no fire in the kitchen either— Mrs White lighted one and proceded to get dinner cooked while the little beast stormed at her for 'daring to do *her* work.' I tidyed things up stairs— The whole house was beastly— [S]he had been—drunk every day of our absence and having *drinking parties* in the house— That it escaped being either burnt or robbed is a miracle— [A]bout five in the afternoon—(we came at one)—she got her legs and rushed out into space for more drink—staggered home at ten and fell insensible on the kitchen floor—she had had *half a pint of rum*, and a quart of ale—in addition to the *half pint of gin* she had taken in the morning— Mrs White got her into bed with difficulty, took away by my desire all combustibles and bolted her in (as she believed). I was to open the outer door to Mrs White at seven in the morning[,] and barred and chained it for the night as usual— When I came down at seven the bars and chain were all undone and there was a sound as of an animal rolling on the kitchen stairs— The little beast had been out! with a bonnet and shawl on the top of her nightclothes and had more drink— [A]t night she got her senses again—and was told by Mrs White that she must get ready to leave the house next day— *I* would not see her at all— Providence under the form of Miss Bolte had sent a most promising looking servant here the very day we came home— Miss Bolte knew nothing of the exigency but this servant 'had come in her way and she could not resist sending her to me, to see if the sight of her would not tempt me to put away that dirty little Helen'— Did you ever know such luck? I liked the girl—found her character satisfactory and engaged her to come as soon as I could get the little beast out of the House— She tried her old despair and tears upon me—but in vain this time—I had found her a shocking dirty stupid servant ever since she came and now I knew why—she had been all the time partially drunk— When I was not to be moved by tears she took to bed, and swore she would not go—I told her thro Mrs White—that I would take her at two on friday in Capt S's carriage to the house of her dearest friend—who lives at Cambden town and has a room to let, or I would put her on board a Kirkaldy steamer and pay her expences—whichever she liked— [I]f she insisted on lying in bed I would send for a Police man and have her taken to the Station— She saw there was no irresolution more[,] rose and dressed herself—and agreed to go to Cambden Town[.][30] I spake hardly ten words to her all the way—explained the circumstances to the woman of the house—put two sovereigns into *her* hands, that she might pay herself the present shelter afforded her—and came away desiring never to see her Helen again in this world—she may go to the Devil her own way—I have bothered myself enough in trying to hold her back— The new servant came on Saturday—and bodes well to be an immense blessing to us.— And now tho' I have not told you half what I had to tell I must make an end for the present—and try to walk off the headach I got at a dinner at Thackerays last night where *you* were not

love to them all / Your affectionate J Carlyle

To Jeannie Welsh, Chelsea, 15 June 1849

Dearest Babbie,

I have been putting off writing from day to day, in expectation of having either to notify to you my final death and burial, or some energetic resolution taken to deliver myself 'out of this'— You are to know that with the first warm days back came my *sickness* with all its hideous accompaniments, depression of spirits, incapacity of exertion, &c &c &c—enough to make a woman poison herself if she had only the courage; for I can never join in with the high flown twaddle about killing oneself being '*a piece of cowardice*'—

30. Camden Town, then a working-class suburb, two miles north of the West End.

John [Carlyle] who was still here, seemed quite hopeless of any remedy, *did* prescribe *vitriol* before breakfast[31]—thought blue pill might be '*no harm*'—but evidently considered that nothing remained for me but *patience*—while *I* again was of opinion that I had *exploited* patience quite long enough. In fact *this* is the only remnant of health and sanity I find in myself, a *certain* beginning of *Volition*—a *perception* almost amounting to a *feeling* (and feelings with me become determinating fast enough) that I must not sit here *suffering* and doing nothing earthly else, thro' all this summer as I did thro all the last;—must *stir*, in short, under my burden—if it were only turning it from one shoulder to another— If change of air, or the mere movement do not help, I *know* by experience that getting one's *vicious circle* of ideas broken up by the necessities and contingencies of movement is better for me than either blue pill or *vitriol before breakfast*— And so—I must *try to try* this remedy—

Mr C has been talking for many weeks of a tour in Ireland[;] sometimes it seemed quite near at hand, and then again fell back into the vague—and when the idea of going somewhere myself came into my mind I postponed the practical consideration of it till he should have fixed his time for going—or decided he was not to go at all— There will be some difficulties about leaving the house with this new maid who is very trustworthy but dreadfully timorous, and hating loneliness—but one cannot sit *always* taking care of ones maid-of-all-work— So I must just risk the driving her into giving warning—tho she is the very nicest servant I ever had. Once I thought, if Mr C went; to stay still here, and ask Helen [Welsh] to bear me company—and that would have been very nice for her and me if—I had been in tolerable bodily case—but as it is I could not make her visit a bit more agreeable to her than the last was—and should be losing an opportunity of making *myself* a little more fit for the place I still hold among the Living— Now for the *where*?—*that* is just the difficulty— Bölte is strong for me going with *her* to Germany, and she would be a capital person to travel with[,] combining the *protecting* powers of a *man* with the nursing ones of a *woman*—but travelling with any comfort in foreign countries is expensive (tho Mr C would give me whatever money I ask for) and I fear the fatigue of *such* a 'stirring up' would extinguish me altogether—if *that* be a thing to be *feared*! Invitations I have in plenty—to Rawdon[,] Seaforth[,] Barnsly[32] &c—but I

31. This sounds dramatic, but green vitriol is just hydrated iron sulphate. Its medicinal qualities were discussed in ancient times, and its major modern use is in iron deficiency. It is on the World Health Organization's list of essential medicines, but what it could do for Jane in this instance is unclear. Another of Dr John's shots in the dark, it seems.
32. Homes of W. E. Forster, the Paulets and Robert Nodes Newton (in Barnsley, in West Yorkshire, as is Rawdon).

could not properly stay long at Rawdon with no woman in the house— and Seaforth!— I have had enough of Seaforth!— Scotland poor old Scotland! am I *up to that*? If I were only *once there* I fancy that were the best place for me— It would do me good to see Haddington, and the house I lived in and my Father's grave, and all the old faces that are still extant—and to see Walter and you in that unknown Scotch home[33]— for I suppose you would take me a little while?—the Liverpool people are not going down *very* soon are they?—*then*, there would be enough without *me* to complicate your difficulties— Write me how it is, whether Walter and you would really like me to come—that is to say—for I don't doubt the *affection* the least in the world—whether there would be houseroom for me—whether your own arrangements would not be interfered with &c— The worst thing in going to Scotland is, that if there; Mr C's relations would feel it to be extremely unkind should I not visit *them*[,] and going into Dumfrieshire looks quite horrible for me somehow— But if I look at all lions in all ways; I shall never move a step but just sit still in Cheyne Row and die 'the death of Jenkins hen'[.][34] So I shall try to think nothing about Dumfrieshire till I have your answer at all events—

I could not have managed to write so long and apparently purpose-full a letter if I had not been less *sick* for some days back—whether it be the cold weather, or a dozen of *Quinine* powders[35] I have swallowed on *my own prescription*—having found them lying in my toilette drawer (!) and thinking that *if* they did not do harm, they might perhaps do good!! and that anyhow they would be well used up!—the fact is certain that I have *seemed* to get more good of them than of any medicine lately given me.— What a discovery it would be *any thing* to stop that horrid sensation of dying always— But enough of *moaning* for once— Write presently

Your affectionate
Jane W Carlyle

33. In Auchtertool, near Kirkcaldy, Fife.
34. That is, of boredom (coterie speech).
35. Quinine—which historically is associated with the treatment of malaria, but is now mostly used with lupus and arthritis—was first derived from the Cinchona tree in Peru in 1820 and, like iron sulphate, is on the WHO's list of essential medicines. Again, Jane's self-prescribing from the dressing-table drawer hardly suggests an informed purpose.

To Thomas Carlyle, Ben Rhydding, Yorkshire, 20 July 1849

Oh my dear! I have been '*packed*'[.][36] The Dr proposed to 'pack' me, for courtesy, and I for curiosity accepted[,] so at six in the morning, just when I had fallen into sound sleep; I was roused by a bath-woman coming to my bedside, in a huge white flannel gown, and bidding me turn out! I got on to the floor in a very bewildered state, and she proceeded to double back one half of my bed clothes and feather-bed, spread a pair of blankets on the matrass; then a sheet rung out of cold water; then bid me strip and lie down, I lay down and she swathed me with the wet-sheet like a mummy, then swathe me with the blankets, my arms pinioned down, exactly in fact like a mummy[,] then rolled back the feather bed and original bedclothes on the top of me, leaving out the head—and so left me—for an hour—to *go mad* at my leisure!— I had no sooner fairly *realized* my situation—of being bound hand and foot under a heap of things, than I felt quite frantic, and cursed my foolish curiosity, and made horrid efforts to release myself—thought of *rolling* to the bell and ringing it with my *teeth*, but could not shake off the feather bed!—did ultimately get one of my hands *turned round*—and was thankful for even *that* change of posture— Dr Nichol says the bath-woman should have *stayed* with me during the first 'pack' and put a wet cloth on my head—that it was the blood being sent to my head that 'caused all this wildness'— [W]hatever it was; I would not undergo the thing again for a hundred guineas[.] When the Bath-woman came back at seven I ordered her to take me out instantly— 'But the Dr'?— [T]he Dr I told her had no business with *me*, I was not a patient— 'Oh! then you have only been *packed* for *foon*, have you?'— 'Yes—and very bad fun'! [S]o she filled a slipper-bath to 'put me to rights again'— and I plunged into *that* so soon as I was set loose, and she plashed pitcher after pitcherful of water on my head—and this shall be the last of my water-curing—for the present. I feel quite shattered still, with an incipient headach[,] and am wishing much that Forster would come, and take me back to Rawdon—

I suppose Forster has sent you a Bradford paper containing the report of our meeting for 'Roman Liberty'— It went off very successfully *as a meeting*, but did not bring in to Forster all the 'virtue's own reward' he anticipated—and he was out of humour for twentyfour hours after— His speech was long-winded, not good, and his delivery the worst in

36. The Yorkshire village of Ben Rhydding was known for its Hydropathic Establishment, which opened in 1844. The 'Dr' must be William Macleod, manager of the premises. Discipline was certainly maintained, with prayers being read in the drawing room each day, after breakfast.

nature— The *people* (*il populo*) often cried '*Time—time*'! to him—and once they cried 'sweet soap'!—the yorkshire for 'soft sawder'—[37] In fact the Bradford *Gentlemen* on the platform were like Bess Stodart's legs 'no great things'—but the Bradford *men*, filling the Hall to suffocation, were a sight to see!—to cry over 'if one liked'!—such ardent, earnest half intelligent, half-bewildered countenances! as made me, for the time being, almost into a *friend of the species* and advocate for *fusion de biens*[.][38] And I must tell you—'I aye thocht meikle [thought much] o' you'; but that night I 'thocht mair [more] o' you than ever'— A man of the people mounted the platform and spoke—a youngish, intelligent looking man, who alone of all the Speakers seemed to *understand* the question, and to have *feelings* as well as *notions* about it—he spoke with a heart-eloquence that '*left me warm*'— I never was more affected by public speaking— When he ceased I did *not* throw myself on his neck and swear everlasting friendship, but I assure you, it was in *putting constraint on myself*, that I *merely* started to my feet and shook hands with him— [A]ll the *Gentlemen* immitated my example and shook hands with him—then 'a sudden thought' struck me; *this* man would like to know *you*—I would give him my address in London—I borrowed a pencil and piece of paper, and handed him my address—when he looked at it he started as if I had sent a bullet into him—caught my hand again, almost squeezed it to 'immortal smash,' and said; 'Oh! *it is* your Husband!—Mr Carlyle has been my teacher and Master—I have owed everything to him for years and years'!— I *felt* it a credit to you really to have had a hand in *turning* out this man—was prouder of that heart-tribute to your genius than of any amount of Reviewer-praises or of aristocratic invitations to dinner— Forster had him to breakfast next morning— I shall have

37. The *CL* note is excellent: 'The meeting to persuade the govt. "to protest on behalf of the British nation, against any further foreign interference with Rome's freedom and independence" was initiated by Forster, held in Temperance Hall, and reported by the *Bradford Observer*, 19 July. The hall was crowded with "a large body of operatives" and a "numerous sprinkling of middling classes." JWC and Elizabeth Paulet were mentioned as on the platform; Forster spoke at length about papal misgovernment, after which the *Observer* gave up detailed reporting, and left out the interruptions, as his speech was "chiefly a recapitulation of recent events."' In February 1849 republican forces had taken control of the Papal States of Italy during the Pope's absence. In June French forces ('foreign interference') laid siege to the city to restore papal authority, and a month later all was over. Mazzini was involved (of course) in various negotiations, and the drama (witnessed by the author at first hand) is drolly captured in Arthur Hugh Clough's poem *Amours de Voyage* (1858). 'Soft sawder' is a colloquial form of 'soft *solder*', meaning 'exaggeration'.
38. 'Communal ownership': one of the proto-Communist ideas of French social theorist Henri de Saint-Simon (1760–1825).

plenty of things to tell you when we meet at leisure—if I can only keep them in mind—but in this wandering-jew[39] life I feel no time on hand ever for going into particulars

Today I am pretty well finished off for all practical purposes, by that confounded *pack*— My head is getting every moment hotter and heavier—and the best I can do is to get out on the hillside and think of nothing!— Lucas's[40] Father and Sister are here genteel Quakerly people—very lean—

After Monday address to Auchtertool Manse Kircaldy[.] I wish to heaven I were fairly there—I could almost lose heart, and turn, and go back to London—but I *will* go— [A]s I used to say when a little child and they asked if anything was too hard for me—'Me can do what me's bid'— The difficulty is still chiefly to *bid myself*—and I *have bid* myself go to Scotland—

Mrs Paulet is asleep on a sofa beside me—so young and pretty and happy looking—I wonder at her—

God bless you Dear—when I have 'some reasonably good leisure'[41] again, I will write you better letters, and more legible ones when I get a decent pen— If you saw the stump I am writing with you would be filled with admiration of my superiority to circumstances— God bless you—all to be said worth the saying lies in *that*—

Your affectionate / Jane W C

Journal, 'Much Ado About Nothing', 2 August 1849

On Tuesday 24th July 1849, I left Rawdon after breakfast, and at five of the afternoon reached Morpeth;[42] where I had decided to pass the night. William Forster escorted me thus far, and stayed to start me by the 2 o'clock train next day;—out of pure *charity*, having adopted Donovan's[43] theory of me, that I am wholly without *observing Faculty*,

39. A medieval tale, of a Jew who abused Christ on his way to crucifixion and was fated to walk the earth for ever after.
40. Frederick Lucas (1812–1855), 'Catholic editor, Irish M. P., poor soul!' according to Thomas (*CL*). He founded *The Tablet*, Britain's second-oldest weekly magazine (after *The Spectator*), devoted to Catholic issues. His father, Samuel Hayhurst Lucas, was a London corn-merchant and Quaker.
41. 'Cromwell', notes Thomas (*CL*).
42. Market town on the River Wansbeck, Northumberland.
43. Thomas notes 'a quack Physiognomist &c. of the time' (*CL*): Cornelius Donovan (1820–1872), founder of the London School of Phrenology.

with large *Reflectiveness* turned inward;—a sort of woman, *that*, ill adapted for travelling by railway, alone, with two boxes, a writing-case, and carpet-bag. Anyhow, I was much the better of such a cheerful companion; to stave off the nervousness about Haddington; not to speak of the *material* comforts,—a rousing fire, brandy-negus[44] &c,—which he ordered for me at the Inn, and which I should not have had the audacity to order on my own basis.

After a modest dinner of chops and cherrytart; we walked by the River-side in a drizzling rain (*that* was at *my* suggestion); then back to the Phenex for tea, chess, and speculative talk till midnight: when I went to bed expecting no sleep to speak of, and of course slept unusually well; for the surest way to get a thing in this Life is to be prepared for doing without it,—to the exclusion even of *hope*.

Next morning was bright as diamonds, and we walked all about the Town and neighbouring Hights; where, rendered unusually communicative by our isolated position, I informed William Edward that my maternal Grandmother was 'descended from *a Gang* of Gipsies,'—was in fact grandniece to Matthew Baillie who '*suffered* at Lanark,'—that is to say, was *hanged* there,—a genealogical fact Forster said which made *me* at last intelligible for him,—'a cross betwixt John Knox and a Gipsey how that explained all.'— By the way, my uncle has told me since I came here, that the wife of that Mathew Baillie, Margaret Euston by name, was the original of Sir W Scott's *Meg Merrilies*.[45] Mathew himself was *the last of the Gipsies*,—could steal a horse *from under* the owner, if he liked, but left always the saddle and bridle; a thorough *gentleman* in his way, and sixfeet four in stature!

But to go back to Morpeth, we again dined at the Phenex; then Forster put me into my carriage, and my luggage in the van and I was shot off towards Scotland; while himself took train for—*Ireland*!

From Morpeth to Haddington is a journey of only four hours; again 'the wished for come too late'! rapidest travelling to Scotland now, and no *home* there any more!

44. A drink made of fortified wine or brandy mixed with hot water, sugar and sometimes a spice. The Phoenix was an eighteenth-century hotel and public house on Bridge Street, Morpeth, long since disappeared.

45. Matthew Baillie was indeed a 'Gypsy king' in eighteenth-century lowland Scotland, who was imprisoned but not hanged. His wife Margaret Yowston was transported for theft in 1732. Meg Merrilies figures in Scott's *Guy Mannering* (1815). Jane also (erroneously) claimed descent from the Scottish Presbyterian preacher John Knox (1524–1572).

The first locality I recognised was the *Peas Bridge*:[46] I had been there *once* before, a little child, in a postchaise with my Father; he had held his arm round me while I looked down the ravine; it was my first sight of the Picturesque, *that*, I recognised the place even in passing it at railway speed, after all these long long years.

At the Dunbar station an old Lady in widow's dress, and a young one, her daughter, got into the carriage which I had had so far all to myself; a man in yeomanry uniform waiting to see them off. 'Ye'll maybe come and see us the *morn's nicht*?' said the younger Lady from the carriage. '*What* for did ye *no* come to the Ball?[']' answered the yeoman, with a look 'to split a pitcher'? The young Lady *tchick-tchicked*, and looked deprecatingly, and tried again and again to *enchain* conversation; but, to every thing she said, came the same answer; '*what* for did ye *no* come to the Ball?'— The poor young Lady then tried holding her tongue; her lover (only her *Lover* would have used her so *brutally*) did the same; but rested his chin on the carriage-window to scowl at her with more convenience. The interest was rising; but one could see who of them would speak first. 'Oh!' broke out the young Lady, 'I'm just mourning!'— '*What for*?'— 'Oh just *that* Ball!'— '*What for* then did [ye] *no* come?' growled the *repeating decimal*; 'I waited an *oor* for ye!' and he got his upper lip over the strap of his cap and champed it—like a horse!— Squeal went the engine; we were off; the young Lady '*just mourned*' for a minute or two, then fell to talking with her Mother; for me, I reflected how 'the feelings were just the same there as here,' and the Devil every where busy!

Before these Ladies got out at Drem, I had identified the pale, old, shrivelled widow with a buxom bright-eyed rosy Mrs Frank Sheriff of *my* time.[47] The Daughter had not only grown up but got herself born in the interval. What chiefly struck me, however, indeed confounded me, was to be stared at by Mrs Sheriff as a stranger, or even *foreigner*! (for, when I asked her some questions about the road, she answered with that compassionate distinctness which one puts on with only *foreigners*—or *idiots*.) I began to think my precautions for keeping *Incognita* in my native place might turn out to have been superfluous.

One of these *precautions* had the foolishest little consequence. In leaving London, I had written the addresses for my luggage on the

46. *CL* gives us all the details: 'JWC went by rail from Newcastle to Tweedmouth (opened 1847), by ferry to Berwick, then on the North British Railway's main line N from Berwick (opened 1846) to Edinburgh, which had a branch from Longniddry to Haddington. The gap at Berwick was bridged, Aug. 1850. Pease Bridge, nr. Cockburnspath, Berwickshire, built 1786 over a large ravine, is 300 ft. long and 127 ft. high.'

47. Helen Walker married Haddington neighbour of the Carlyles, Francis Sheriff, in 1806.

backs of other peoples visiting-cards; 'without respect of persons';—a stupid practice when one thinks of it!—but at Morpeth I removed three of the cards, leaving one to the carpet-bag; carpet-bags being so confoundable; I was at the pains however to rub off *my own* name from *that* card, which, for the rest, happened to be Mrs Humphrey St John Mildmay's. Well! at Longniddry, where I had to wait some fifteen minutes for the cross-train to Haddington, '*there came to pass*' a *Porter*! who helped me with my things, and would not leave off helping me—quite teazed me in fact with *delicate attentions*. At last he made me a low bow and said he was 'not aware that any of the family were in this quarter.' I believe I answered; '*quite well I thank you*'; for I was getting every instant more *excited* with my circumstances. He shut the carriage-door on me, then opened it again and said with another low bow; 'Excuse me, Mam but I was in the service of the Brother of Mr Humphrey St John Mildmay.' I am positive as to my answer this time, that it was; '*Oh thank you No! I am quite another person*!'

A few minutes more and I was at the H[addington]. Station; where I looked out timidly, then more boldly, as my senses took in the utter *strangeness* of the scene; and luckily I had '*the cares of luggage*' to keep down *sentiment* for the moment. No vehicle was in waiting but a dusty little Omnibus licenced to carry—*any number*, it seemed! for on remarking there was no seat for me I was told by all the *Insides* in a breath; 'never heed! come in! *that* makes *no* difference!'— And so I was trundled to *The George Inn*, where a Landlord and Waiter, both strangers to me, and looking half-asleep showed me to the best room on the first floor—a large old-fashioned, three windowed room, looking out on *The Fore Street*—and, without having spoken one word, shut the door on me, and there I was at the end of it!—actually in the George Inn, Haddington, alone, amidst the silence of death!

I sat down quite composedly at a window, and looked up the Street,—towards our old House; it was the same street, the same houses; but so silent,—dead,—*petrified*! it looked, the old place, just as I had seen it at Chelsea in my dreams—only *more* dreamlike!— Having exhausted that outlook, I rung my bell, and told the silent Landlord to bring tea, and took order about my bedroom. The tea swallowed down; I notified my wish to view 'the old church there,' and the keeper of the keys was immediately fetched me. In my part of stranger-in-search-of-the-Picturesque, I let myself be shown the way which I knew every inch of,—shown 'the school houses,' where myself had been *Dux*,—'the play-ground,[']' 'the *Bool*ing green,'—and so on to the church-gate, which so soon as my guide had unlocked for me, I told him he might wait—that I needed him no further.

The Church-yard had become very full of graves. Within *the Ruin* were two new *smartly got up* tombs; *His* [her father's] looked old, old; was surrounded by nettles; the inscription all over moss; except *two lines* which had been quite recently cleared.— [B]y *whom*? who had been there, before *me*, still caring for *his* tomb after 29 years? The old *Ruin* knew, and could not tell me! that place *felt* the very centre of eternal silence—silence and sadness world without end! When I returned to the sexton, or whatever he was, he asked would I not walk thro the church; I said yes, and he led the way, but without playing the Cicerone [guide] any more; he had become pretty sure there was no need. *Our* pew looked to have never been new-lined since *we* occupied it; the *green* cloth was become all but *white* from age! I looked at it in the dim twilight till I almost fancied I saw my beautiful Mother in her old corner, and myself a bright-looking girl in the other! it was time to 'come out of *that*'! Meaning to return to the Churchyard next morning, to clear the moss from the inscription; I asked my conductor where he lived—with his key. '[N]ext door to the house that was Dr Welsh's[']; he answered, with a sharp glance at my face; then added *gently*; 'excuse me mem for mentioning that, but the minute I set eyes on ye at the George, I *jaloosed* [suspected] it was *her* we all looked after whenever she went up or down.' 'You won't tell of me?' I said crying, like a child caught stealing apples; and gave him half a crown to keep my secret, and open the gate for me at eight next morning. Then turning, up the waterside by myself, I made the circuit of *The Haugh*, *Dodd's Gardens* and *Babbies Butts*—the customary evening walk in my teens; and except that it was perfectly *solitary* (in the whole round, I met just two little children walking hand in hand, like the *Babes of the wood*) the whole thing looked exactly as I left it 22 years back![48] the very puddles made by the last rain I *felt* to have stepped over before.— But where were all the living beings one used to meet? What could have come to the place to strike it so dead? I have been since answered; the railway had come to it, and ruined it. At all rates 'it must have taken a great deal to make a *place* so dull as that!'— Leaving the lanes I now went boldly thro' the streets, the thick black veil, put on for the occasion, thrown back; I was getting

48. Again *CL* has the details: 'The Haughs, Dod's Gardens, and Babbie's Butts (now "the Butts")—still identifiable—lie on JWC's walk from her former home, round by the riverbanks to the rear of St. Mary's, a partly ruined abbey church (12th or 13th cent.) known as "the Lamp of Lothian." After restoration, 1811, it had a central tower and five bays of the nave in use as a parish church, but the rest was ruinous, including the E end where JWC and her father are buried, now enclosed. St. Mary's, reroofed today, is used as the parish church.'

confident that I might have ridden like *the Lady Godiva*[49] thro Haddington, with impunity,—so far as recognition went.— I looked thro' the sparred [fastened shut] door of our old coachhouse, which seemed to be vacant; the House itself I left over till morning, when its occupants should be asleep. Passing a Cooper's-shop which I had once had *the run of*, I stept in and bought two little *quaichs* [drinking cups]; then, in the character of the travelling Englishwoman, suddenly seized with an unaccountable passion for wooden dishes, I questioned the Cooper as to the *Past and Present* of his town.[50] He was the very man for me, being ready to talk the tongue small in his head about his town's-folks, men, women, and children of them. He told me amongst other interesting things, that 'Doctor Welsh's death was the sorest loss ever cam to the Place';—that myself 'went away into England and—died there!' adding a handsome enough tribute to my memory—'Yes! Miss Welsh! he remembered her famously,—used to think her the *tastiest* young Lady in the whole Place—but she was very—not just to call *proud*,—very *reserved in her company*.'— In leaving this man, I felt more than ever like my own gohst; if I had really been *walking* after my death and burial, there could not I think have been any material difference in my sensations.

My next visit was to the front gate of the Sunny Bank, where I stood some minutes, looking up at the beautifully quiet House; not unlike the 'outcast *Peri*' *done into prose*.[51] How would my old godmother and the others have looked, I wondered, had they known who was there, so near them? I longed to go in and kiss them once more, but positively *dared* not; I felt that their demonstrations of affection would break me down into a torrent of tears, which there was no time for; so I contented myself with kissing—the *gate*(!) and returned to my Inn, it being now near Dark.

Surely it was the silentest Inn on the Planet! not a living being male or female to be seen in it except when I rung my bell, and then the Landlord or Waiter (both old men) did my bidding promptly and silently and vanished again into space. On my reentrance I rung for candles, and for a glass of sherry and hot water; my feet had been wetted amongst the long grass of the churchyard, and I felt to be taking cold; so I made myself negus as an antidote, and they say I am not a *practical* woman! Then it struck me; I would write to Mr Carlyle,— one more letter from the old place, after so much come and gone.

49. Eleventh-century wife of the Earl of Mercia who, legend tells, rode naked through the streets of Coventry to protest her husband's taxation.
50. Alluding to Thomas's book with that title (1843).
51. Thomas Moore, 'Paradise and the Peri', from *Lalla Rookh* (1817).

Accordingly I wrote till the Town clock (the first familiar voice I had heard) struck eleven, then twelve, and near *one* I wrote the Irish address on my Letter and finally put myself to bed—in the George Inn of Haddington, good God!— I thought it too strange and mournful a position for ever falling asleep in; nevertheless I *slept* in the first instance; for I was 'a-weary a-weary,'[52] body and soul of me! But, alas! the *only noise* I was to hear in Haddington '*transpired*' exactly at the wrong moment; before I had slept one hour I was awoke by—an explosion of cats! The rest of that night I spent betwixt sleeping and waking, in nightmare efforts to 'sort up my thoughts.' At half after five I put my clothes on, and began the business of the day by destroying, in a moment of enthusiasm—for *silence*—the long letter 'all about feelings' which I had written the night before. Soon after six I was *haunting* our old house, while the present occupants still slept.— I found the garden door *locked*, and *iron staunchions*,—my Heavens!—on the porch and cellar windows, 'significative of much!' [F]or the rest, there was a general need of paint and white wash: in fact the whole premises had a bedimmed melancholy look as of 'having *seen better days*.' It was difficult for me to realise to myself that the people inside were only *asleep*—and not *dead*—*dead since many years*. Ah! one breathed freer in the church-yard, with the bright morning sunshine streaming down on it than near that (so-called) habitation of the Living! I went straight from the one to the other. The gate was still locked; for I was an hour before my time; so I made a dash at the wall, some seven feet high I shoud think, and dropt safe on the inside—a feat I should never have imagined to *try* in my actual phase, not even with a mad bull at my heels, if I had not trained myself to it at a more elastic age. Godefroi Cavaignac's '*quoi donc je ne suis pas mort?*[']' crossed my mind but *I* had none of that feeling ['what then; I'm not dead!']—*moi*,—was *morte* enough, I *knew*, whatever face I might put on it[,] only, what one has well learnt one never forgets.

When I had scraped the moss out of the inscription, as well as I could with the only thing in my dressing case at all suited to the purpose, namely *his own* button hook with the mother-of-pearl handle, I made a deliberate survey of the whole church-yard, and most of the names I had missed out of the *signboards* turned up for me once more on the *tomb-stones*. It was strange the feeling of almost *glad* recognition that came over me, in finding so many familiar figures out of my childhood and youth all gathered together in one place. But still more interesting for me than these later graves were *two* that I remembered to have

52. A refrain from Tennyson's 'Mariana' (1830): 'She said "I am aweary, aweary / I would that I were dead!"'

weeped little innocent tears over before I had a conception what real weeping meant,—the grave of the little girl who was burnt to death, thro' drying her white muslin frock at the fire, and that of the young officer (Rutherford) who was shot in a duel. The oval tablet of white marble over the little girl's grave looked as bright and spotless as on the first day—as emblematic of the child existence it commemorated; it seemed to my somewhat excited imagination that the youthfulness and innocence there buried had impregnated the marble to keep it snow-white for ever!— When the sexton came at eight to let me in, he found me ready to be *let out*. 'How in the world had I got in?'— '[O]ver the wall.'— 'No! surely I couldn't mean *that*?'— 'Why not?'— 'Lordsake then, cried the man in real admiration, there is *no end* to you!'—

He told me at parting, 'there is *one* man in this Town, Mem, you might like to see—James Robertson. Your Father's old servant.' Our own old Jamie! he was waiter at *The Star* good gracious! had returned to Haddington within the last year. 'Yes indeed'—I said, 'he must be sent to me at the George an hour hence, and told only that *a Lady* wanted him.'

It was still but eight o'clock, so I should have time to look at Sunny Bank from the *back* gate, and streamed off in that direction; but passing my dear old schoolhouse, I observed the door a little a-jar, walked in and sat down in my old seat; to the manifest astonishment of a decent woman who was sweeping the floor. *Ach gott! our* maps and Geometrical Figures had given place to *Texts from Scripture* and the foolishest *half-penny pictures*! it was become an *Infant School* Good God! and a *Miss* Alexander was now Teacher where Edward Irving and James Brown had taught!— Miss A and her Infants were not, it seemed early risers; their schoolroom after eight oclock was only *being swept*; it was at *seven* of the morning that James Brown once found *me* asleep there—after two hours hard study—asleep betwixt the leaves of *the Great Atlas*, like a *keep-lesson* [pupil's book mark]! but 'things have been all gone to the Devil ever since the reform-bill'; as my Uncle is always telling us.[53] The Woman interrupted her sweeping to inform me amongst other things that it was 'a most terrible place for dust'; that 'a deal was put into *Bairns* now, which she *dooted* was *wastewark*'; that 'it was little one got by *cleaning after them*,' and 'if her Husband *had his legs*, they might *have* the school that liked'

Not the vestige of a Boy or even of a *girl* was to be seen about the *Grammar* School either; *that* school, I afterwards heard from Jamie 'had

53. Since the Representation of the People Act of 1832, which reorganised Parliamentary constituencies to disenfranchise 'rotten boroughs' and extended male suffrage in Britain, but actually also formally excluded women voters in British law for the first time.

gone to just perfect nonsense'— 'There was a *Master* (one White) but no *scholars.*['] 'How *is* that, I asked; *are* there no children here any longer?' 'Why its not altogether the want o' children' said Jamie, with his queer old *smudge* of inarticulate fun, 'but the new master is *rather* severe,—*broke the jawbone of a wee Boy*—they tell me; but indeed the whole place is sore *gone down.*' I should think so! But I am not gone to Jamie yet; another meeting came off before that one.

Sunny Bank looked even lovelier 'in the light of a new morning' than it had done in the evening dusk. A hedge of red roses in full blow extended now from the House to the gate; and I thought I might go in and gather one without evoking any—Beast. Once inside the gate I passed easily to the idea of proceeding as far as the back door, just to ask the servant how they all were, and leave compliments without naming myself; the servants only would be a-stir so early. Well! when I had knocked at the door with my finger 'sharp but mannerly'; it was opened by a tidy maidservant exhibiting no more surprise than if I had been the Baker's boy!— Strange, was it not, that *anybody* should be in a calm state of mind, while *I* was so full of emotions? Strange that the Universe should pursue its own course without reference to my presence in Haddington!!— 'Are you Ladies quite well': I asked nevertheless. 'Miss Jess and Miss Catherine are quite well; Miss Donaldson rather *complaining*; you are aware Mem that Mr Donaldson is dead?'— 'Oh dear yes!' I said, thinking she meant Alexander. 'At what hour do you Ladies get up?' 'They *are* up Mem and done breakfast, will you walk round to the front-door?'— Goodness gracious! *should* I 'walk round,' or not?— My *own* nerves had got braced somewhat by the morning air; but *their* nerves—how would the sight of me thus '*promiscuously*' operate on *them*? 'You had better go round and let me tell the Ladies,' put in the servant, as if in reply to my cogitations; 'what name shall I say?'— 'None, I think, perhaps my name would startle them more than myself; tell them; *someone they will be glad to see.*' And so, flinging the responsibility on *Providence*, who is made for being fallen back upon in such dilemmas, ('Providence must have meant me to see them in raising them out of bed so betimes!'), I did 'go round,' with my heart thumping, 'like,—like,—like—*anything.*'

The maidservant met me at the front-door and conducted me to the Drawingroom, where was—nobody; but on a table lay a pile of *black*-bordered note-paper which explained to me, that it was Mr Donaldson of London who was *dead*; the last Brother—dead in these very days! I wished I had not come in; but it was out of time now.— The door opened and showed me Miss Catherine changed into an *old* woman, and showed Miss Catherine *me*, changed into one of—*a certain* age!

She remained at the door, motionless, speechless, and *I* couldn't rise off my chair, at least I didn't; but when I saw her eyes staring 'like watch-faces,' I said, 'Oh Miss Catherine don't be frightened at me!'— and then she quite *shrieked* 'Jeanie! Jeanie! Jeanie Welsh! *my* Jeanie! *my* Jeanie!'— Oh mercy I shan't forget that scene in a hurry! I got her in my arms and kissed her into her wits again; and then we both cried a little—naturally—; both of us had had enough since we last met to cry for. I explained to her 'how I was *situated*,' as Mr C. would say, and that I was meaning to visit them after—like a Christian; and she found it all 'most wisely done—done like my own self.'— Humph!— Poor Miss Catherine! its little she knows of my own self's and perhaps the less the better! She told me about their Brother's death, which had been sudden at the last. Supposing me still in London as usual, and that in London we hear of one anothers deaths; they had been saying it was strange I did not write to them and my Godmother had remarked; 'it is not like her!'—just while I was standing at their gate most likely; for it was 'the evening before, about dark,' they had been speaking of me.

But again the door opened and showed Miss Jess— *Ach*!— She had to be *told* who I was, and pretty *loudly* too; but when she *did* take in the immense fact, oh *my*!—if she didn't '*show feeling enough*' (her own favourite expression of old!)— Poor Jess after all! We used to think she *showed* even more *feeling* than she *felt*, and nothing came out on the present emergence to alter our opinion of her. But enough—*the very old*, it seems to me, should be admitted, by favour, to the privelege of *the Dead*,—have '*no ill*' spoken of them, that can possibly be helped.

My 'Godmother' was keeping her bed 'with rheumatism' and grief; as I 'would *really* come back soon' it was settled to leave her quiet. They offered me breakfast,—it was still on the table: but '*horrible was the thought*' to me! It was all so solemn and doleful there that I should have heard every morsel going down my throat! besides I was engaged to breakfast with *myself* at *the George*. So, with blessings for many days, I slipt away from them like a knotless thread.

My friend the Cooper, espying me from his doorway, on the road back, planted himself *firmly* in my path: 'if I would just comple*mennt* him with my name, he would be *terribly* obliged; we had been *uncommon comfortable* together, and he *must* know what they called me!'— I told him, and he neither died on the spot nor went mad; he looked pleased and asked how many children I had had. *None*, I told him. 'None!' (in a tone of astonishment, verging on horror) 'None at all! then what on the Earth had I been *doing* all this time?' 'Amusing myself,' I told him. He ran after me, to beg I would give him a call on my return (I had spoken of returning) 'as he might be making something, belike, to *send* *south* with me, something *small* and *of a fancy sort, liker myself* than *them* I had bought.'

Breakfast stood ready for me at the Inn and was discussed [consumed] in five minutes. Then I wrote a note to Mr C, a compromise betwixt '*all about feelings*' and '*the new silent system*'—of the *Prisons*.[54] Then I went to my bed room to pack up. The Chambermaid came to say a *gentleman* was asking for me. 'For *me*?' 'Yes! he asked for THE *Lady stopping here*.' (no influx of company at the George it seemed) 'Did you see him' I asked, divining Jamie, 'are you sure it is a *gentleman*?['] 'I am sure of his being *put on* like one.' I flew down to my parlour, and there was Jamie sure enough! Jamie to the Life! and I threw my arms round his neck, that did I— He stood quite passive and quite pale with *great* tears rolling down; it was minutes before he spoke, and then he said only, low under his breath; 'Mrs—Carlyle!' So nice he looked, and hardly a day older, and really as like 'a Gentleman' as some Lords; he had dressed himself in his Sunday Clothes for the occasion, and they were capital good ones. 'And you knew me, Jamie, at first sight,['] I asked?— '*Toot! we* knew ye *afore* we seed ye.'— 'Then you were told it was me?'— 'No! they told us just we was to speak to a Lady at the George, and I knew it was Mrs Carlyle,'— [']But how *could* you tell, dear Jamie?' 'Hoots! *who else could it be*?'(!) Dear funniest of created Jamies!— While he was ostler at the Black Bull Edinr; 'one of them what-ye-call *Bagmen* [salesman] *furgottet* his patterns' at Haddington and he (Jamie) was 'sent to take them up[']; and falling in talk with *him* of *the Star*; it came out there was no waiter, 'and so in that way,' said Jamie, 'we came back to the old place.['] He told me all sorts of particulars 'more profitable to the soul of man' than anything I should have got out of Mr Charteris[55] in three *years*, never to say 'three weeks.' But 'a waggon came in atween ten and eleven and he must be stepping west.'— '[H]e was glad to have seen me looking so (dropping his voice)—*stootish*!' (I saw him, from the Omnibus, after, unloading the waggon, in his workday clothes, almost on the very spot where, for a dozen years, he had helped me in and out of our carriage!)

And now there only remained to pay my bill and await the Omnibus[.] I have that bill of 6/6 in my writing case; and shall keep it all my days; not only as an eloquent memorial of human change—like grass from graves and all that sort of thing; but as the first Inn bill I ever in my life contracted and paid *on my own basis*.

54. A cruel innovation introduced at Coldbath Fields Prison, Clerkenwell, London, in 1834, and described by Thomas in his essay 'Model Prisons'; demolished in 1929.
55. See 11 May 1847, above.

Another long look from the George Inn window,—and then into the shabby little Omnibus again; where the faces of a Lady next me and a gentleman opposite me tormented my memory without result.

In the railway carriage which I selected, an old gentleman had taken his seat, and I recognised him at once as Mr Lea—the same who made the little obelisk which hangs in my bedroom at Chelsea. He had grown old like a golden pippin [apple], merely *crined* [shrunk], with the bloom upon him. I laid my hand on his arm, turning away my face, and said, 'Thank God here is one person I feel no difficulty about.' 'I don't know you,' he said in his old blunt way, 'who are you?'— 'Guess!'— 'Was it you who got over the church-yard wall this morning? I saw a stranger-lady climb the wall and I said to myself that's Jeanie Welsh!—no other woman would climb the wall instead of going in at the gate—*are* you Jeanie Welsh?[']

I 'owned the soft impeachment';[56] then such shaking of hands! embracing even! But so soon as things had calmed down a little between us; Mr Lea laid his hand on my shoulder and said *as if pursuing knowledge under difficulties*, 'now tell me, my Dear, why *did* you get over the wall instead of just asking for the key?'

He spoke of William Ainsleys death; I said I had never known him, that he went to India before I could remember. 'Nonsense,' said Mr Lea; 'not remember William Ainsley? Never knew William Ainsley? What are you thinking of? Why; didnt he wrap you in a shawl and run away with you to our house *the very day you were born*, I believe?[']— I said it might be very true but that the circumstance had escaped my recollection. Mr Lea was left at Longniddry where he came daily, he said, to bathe in the sea. What energy!

While waiting there for the train from London, I saw again my Lady and Gentleman of the Omnibus and got their names from Mr Lea; they were not people I had ever visited with, but I had been at school with them both; We passed and repassed one another without the slightest sign of recognition on their side.

George Cunningham too was pacing the Longniddry-platform, the Boy of our school who never got into *trouble* and never helped others out of it,—a slow bullet-headed boy who said his lessons like an eight-day clock and never looked *young*; *now*, on the wrong side of forty it might be doubted if he would ever look *old*. He came up to me and shook hands, and asked me by name how I did, exactly as tho' we met *on change* every day of our lives! To be sure I had seen *him once* since we were at school together, had met him at Craik's some twelve years ago.— Such as he

56. Richard Brinsley Sheridan, *The Rivals* (1775), V. iii.

was; we stood together till the train came up, and 'talked of geography, politics, and *natur.*'

At Edinr Jeanie's sweet little face looked wildly into the carriage for me, and next minute we were *chirping* and *twittering* together on the platform whilst the eternal two boxes writing case and carpet-bag were being once more brought into one focus.— 'Look look Cousin' said Jeanie[,] *there* are people who know you!' and looking as I was bid; who but the pair who had accompanied me from Haddington were standing, with their heads laid together, and the eyes starting out of them *me*-ward! The Lady the instant she saw I noticed them sprang forward extending her hand; the Husband 'emboldened by her excellent example' did the same; they were 'surprised,' 'delighted,' everything that could be wished; 'had not had a conception of its being me till they saw me *smiling*'— 'Eh Sirs!' said my Mother's old nurse to her after a separation of twenty years [']there's no a *featur* o' ye left, but just *the bit smile*!'

I will call for these Richardsons when I go back to Haddington; I liked their *hop-skip-and-jump* over Ceremony—their oblivion in the enthusiasm of the moment that we had '*belonged to different circles*' (*Haddingtonly* speaking)

And now having brought myself to Edinr and under the little protecting wing of Jeanie, I bid myself adieu and 'wave my lilly hand'— I was back into the Present! and it is only in connection with the Past that I can get up a sentiment for myself— The Present Mrs Carlyle is what shall I say?—*detestable*—upon *my* honour!

Auchtertool Manse
2d August

❧

To John Carlyle, Chelsea, 10 December 1849

My dear John

I ought to tell you that I am *about* again—that is to say when it does not rain—and that again is to say at rare intervals— The weather is in fact detestable—but it will mend in time—which cant be said of all the detestable things one knows.— The chief news to tell you is that I have got a dog!—and can hardly believe my senses!— I should never have mustered courage to risk such a great step, had not Dilberoglue the Greek I know in Manchester, having heard me talking about my wish for a dog which was merely a 'dont you wish you may get it'? actually, on his return to Manchester, set about seeking one and fired it off at me by railway—and so well has he sought and found, that here is a little dog perfectly beautiful and *queer*looking, which does not *bark* at all! nor whine, more than if it were deaf and dumb!! it sleeps at the foot of my bed without ever stirring or audibly breathing all night long and never dreams of getting up till I get up myself—it follows me like my shadow and lies in my lap—and at meals when animals are apt to be so troublesome it makes no sort of demonstration beyond standing on its hind legs![57] Not only has Mr C no temptation to 'kick his foot thro it' but seems getting quite fond of it and looks flattered when it musters the hardihood to leap on *his* knee[.] So *this* is one small comfort achieved for it *is* really a comfort to have something alive and cheery and fond of me always there— My fear now is not that Mr C will put it away but that I shall become the envy of surrounding dog-stealers! Anthony Sterling says 'it is much too valuable a dog not to get itself stolen fast enough'— Well! I can but get a chain to fasten it to my arm and keep a sharp look out—

My cold is away again—but oh dear! 'my interior' is always very miserable—and nothing that I do or forbear seems to make the least difference— The worst is the dreadful pressure on my faculties—there *are* kinds of illness that one can *work* under—but this sort of thing that *I* go on with makes every thing next to *impossible* for me—

Mr Neuberg is always lamenting your absence—he comes occasionally and plays chess with me, and I generally beat him— What is it that makes that man so heavy?— [H]e is clever and well informed and wellbred and kind and has even some humour and yet—when he goes away every time I yawn and yawn and feel so dished!

No thoughts of coming back yet? I miss you very bad

Mr C bids me tell you to cut out his 'trees of Liberty' from the Nation and send it back—

Ever yours lovingly

Jane W C

Kindest regards to your Mother and Isabella and Jamie— I don't think you will get so well on with your translation [of Dante] there as here—

57. Nero seems to have been a Maltese-cross. In her journal of 24 November 1855 Jane describes Ruskin's reaction (*CL* 30: 224): 'Nero had been washed and combed for the occasion [of Ruskin's visit], and had curled himself very winningly on the party coloured round cushion with his head pillowed on an end of my red shawl. "Look" I said to Ruskin, "Isn't he beautiful so?"— "Very" said Ruskin with grave emphasis— "very beautiful indeed! I find just one—I can hardly call it a *fault*, but one objection to that dog; which is, that one never *can* tell which is head and which is his tail."'

To Thomas Carlyle, Chelsea, 29–30 January 1850

Dear Master

I take the liberty to write to you myself, my Mistress being out of the way of writing to you she says, that you may know Columbine [the cat] and I are quite well and play about as usual. There was no dinner yesterday to speak of; I had for my share only a piece of biscuit that might have been round the World, and if Columbine got anything at all, *I* didn't see it. I made a grab at one of two 'small beings' on my Mistress's plate, she called them Heralds of the Morn; but my Mistress said 'don't you wish you may get it?' and boxed my ears. I wasn't taken to walk on account of its being wet, and nobody came but a man for 'burial rate,' and my Mistress gave him a rowing because she wasn't going to be buried here at all— Columbine and I don't mind *where* we are buried.

This is a fine day for a run, and I hope I may be taken to see *Mohe* and *Dumm*— They are both, nice well bred dogs and always so glad to see me, and the parrot is great fun when I spring at her, and Mrs Lindsay has always such a lot of bones, and doesn't mind Mohe and Dumm and me eating them on the carpet; I like Mrs Lindsay very much!

Tuesday evening

Dear Master

My Mistress brought my chain, and said 'come along with me,' while it shined, and I could finish after— But she kept me so long in the London Library[58] and other places that I had to miss the post. An old Gentleman in the Omnibus took *such* notice of me! he looked at me a long time and then turned to my Mistress and said '*sharp*; isn't He?'— And my Mistress was so good as say; 'Oh yes!' and then the old Gentleman said again, '*I* knew it!—easy to see *that*!' And he put his hand in his hind pocket and took out a whole biscuit—a *sweet* one—and gave it me in bits— I was quite sorry to part from him; he was such a good judge of Dogs. Mr Greig from Canadagua and his wife left cards while we were out—Columbine said she saw them thro the blind and they seemed nice people.

Wednesday

I left off last night dear Master to be washed—this morning I have seen a note from you which says you will come tomorrow. Columbine

58. Alongside the National Portrait Gallery, the London Library in St James's Square (established in 1841) is Thomas's greatest non-literary gift to the British nation. The British Library was in existence, but did not lend; nor was the network of public lending libraries yet established. Its first collection of 2,000 books was selected by future Prime Minister William Gladstone, John Stuart Mill and (irrepressibly) Mazzini.

and I are extremely happy to hear it; for then there will be some dinner to come and go on—being to see you so soon no more at present from your

obedient little dog

Nero

❧

To Helen Welsh, Chelsea, 4 July 1850

Dearest Helen

I heard from John that you were bound for Auchtertool yesterday or today, and I wished to send you a letter of goodby—which having failed in; I now change it into one of welcome— John would tell you I was extremely well—extremely gay—rushing after *ball-dresses*, good Heavens! and you would believe of all that as much as your credulity could take in— I am *rather* less sick and sleepless than I was last year at this time, but still consuming a quantity of inward suffering, which as I know John has no remedy for it I did not feel any call to trouble him with—especially as during the month he staid here, he seemed incapable of fixing his attention on anything for two seconds together—and it hurts ones *sensibility* to make complaints and be asked a minute after some question proving that not a word of them had been *heard*— So finding him in *that* line this time, I immediately adapted myself to it—and held my peace in every thing but the trivialities of the hour—

For *company*—I have indeed had more than enough of *that* of late weeks—not a day, hardly an hour of repose—so many strangers from foreign parts introduced to Mr C, and so many old friends of my own from a distance coming and going till the house has got to look like a Hotel with this only difference that no charges are made for the 'entertainment to man and beast'

The Bath House Ball threw me into a perfect fever for one week—as I had got no dress for it; not understanding that I was to go—but Mr C was 'quite determined for once in his life to see an aristocratic Ball and if I chose to be so peevish and ungracious as to stay away there was no help for me'— I pleaded the want of a dress—he 'would pay for any dress I chose to get'; and then I fell back on the horror of *stripping* myself, of 'being bare'—at my age after being muffled up so many years! and that if I didn't I should be like no one else—to which he told me angrily—'true propriety consisted in conforming to other peoples fashions!!! and that Eve he supposed had as much sense of decency as I had and *she* wore no clothes at all!!!' So I got a white silk dress—which first was made high and longsleeved—and then on the very day of the ball was sent back to be cut down to the due pitch of indecency!— I could have gone into *fits* of crying when I began to put it on—but I looked so astonishingly well in it *by candle light*, and when I got into the fine rooms amongst the universally *bare* people I felt so much in *keeping*, that I forgot my neck and arms almost immediately— I was glad *after* that I went—not for any pleasure I had at the time being past dancing, and knowing but few people—but it is an additional idea for life, to have seen such a party—all the Duchesses one ever heard tell of blazing in diamonds, all the young beauties of the season, all the distinguished Statesmen &c &c were to be seen among the six or seven hundred people present—and the rooms all hung with artificial roses looked like an Arabian Nights entertainment— [W]hat pleased me best was the good look I got *into the eyes* of the old Duke of Wellington—one has no notion, seeing him on the streets what a dear kind face he has— Lady Ashburton receiving all these people with her grand-Lady airs was also a sight worth seeing— On Saturday I went to Addiscombe with a party of *boys* and *girls* and returned on Monday night[.] Mr C and Thackeray came to dinner on Sunday but had to return at night every room being taken up— I cant imagine why Lady A always asks *me* to help her with these flirting young ladies and gentlemen[;] I feel more disposed to wring their necks than take part in their riotous nonsense.

Now; all is changed in *that* quarter by the death of Peel—[59] Lady A was deeply attached to him—she is off into the country again to escape parties; came here on her way, all in tears, and asked Mr C to come by himself *this* week—as one asks the Clergyman when one is in affliction!— [I]ndeed this death has produced a greater dismay than any public event of my time. Not only among his own set but crowds of working people pressed round his house all the time of his illness demanding news which a Constable lifted above their heads tried to make heard in vain—and written paper bulletins were finally hoisted up to be read by the crowd from hour to hour— Mr C is mourning over him as I never saw him mourn before—went today to look at the house where he lies dead!—

But no impression lasts long in London society—in a few weeks they will all be visiting and 'making wits' again as if nothing had happened—

59. See 25 November 1842, above. Peel's death aged sixty-two was sudden; he was thrown from a horse on Constitution Hill, near Hyde Park in London, and suffered the broken collarbone so often associated with riding, which in his case ruptured his subclavian blood vessel.

I have seen little of Geraldine she comes pretty often but has always engagements to hurry her away— She has sworn friendship with Fanny Lewald the German Authoress who is also lionizing in London at present—and gives me much of her semi-articulate company— I also met Jane Eyre (Miss Bronte) one night at Thackerays[:][60] a less figure than Geraldine and extremely unimpressive to *look at*—

Write to me how you feel after your journey—John wrote that you seemed to him much better than last year—kindest love to them all and kisses to my Uncle

ever your affectionate

J C

To Thomas Carlyle, Addiscombe, 3 October 1850

I have put a lucifer[61] to my bedroom fire, Dear, and sat down to write but I feel more disposed to lay my head on the table and cry. By this time I suppose you are at home—returned after a two months absence—arrived off a long journey—and I not there, nobody there but a stranger servant, who will need to be told everything you want of her, and a mercy if she can do it even then! The *comfort* which offers itself under this last innovation in our life together (for it is the *first* time in all the twenty years I have lived beside you that you ever arrived at home and I away) is the greatest part of the grievance for my irrational mind— I am not *consoled* but '*aggravated*' by reflecting, that in point of fact you will prefer

60. A famous literary event of 12 June during Charlotte Brontë's first visit to London. *CL* reprints Thackeray's daughter's recollection from her *Chapters of Some Memoirs* (1894): 'a tiny, delicate, serious, little lady, pale, with fair straight hair, and steady eyes [. . .] dressed in a little barège dress with a pattern of faint green moss [. . .] It was a gloomy and a silent evening. Everyone waited for the brilliant conversation which never began at all. Miss Brontë retired to the sofa in the study, and murmured a low word now and then to our kind governess [. . .] The room looked very dark, the lamp began to smoke a little, the conversation grew dimmer and more dim, the ladies sat round still expectant, my father was too much perturbed by the gloom and the silence to be able to cope with it at all.' Brontë's worship of Thackeray made the evening doubly uncomfortable; his wife had been committed to an asylum, and Brontë dedicated the second edition of her novel—with its famous 'madwoman in the attic'—to him, which made gossip prick up its ears.

61. A primitive form of match, pre-dating the safety match we know today, and depending on the pyrophoric qualities of 'white phosphorous': a highly toxic element that caused dreadful diseases in its manufacture, and was only internationally prohibited in 1906.

finding 'perfect solitude' in your own house, and that if I were to do as nature prompts me to do, start off home by the next train, I should take more from your comfort on one side than I should add to it on another: [b]esides being considered *here* as beyond measure ridiculous. Certainly this is the best school that the like of me was ever put to for getting cured of every particle of 'the finer sensibilities'

Mrs Henry Taylor[62] was in London yesterday at 'Virginia Pattle's' marriage and saw my maid, on business of her own, and brought back word from her that you were coming last night—and the shouts of laughter, and cutting 'wits' with which my startled look and exclamation 'Oh gracious'! were visited when the news was told me as we sat down to dinner were enough to terrify me from '*showing feeling*' for twelvemonths to come— Mrs Henry Taylor shan't *snub* me however—I am quite as clever as her any day of the year and am bound to *her* by no ties human or divine—and so I showed her so plainly that I was displeased with her impertinent jesting at my expence that she made me an apology in the course of the evening.

And now what is to be done next? You say, stay where I am as if you were not— [E]asily said but not at all easily done— It is quite out of the question my remaining here till the 20th—the day Lady A has appointed for the term of my visit—doing nothing—and thinking of *you* at home with that inexperienced girl!— *Who* cares one doit for me here, that I should stay here; when you who still care a little for me—more anyhow than any other person living does—are again at home? and what good can 'ornament and grandeur' and 'wits' and 'the honour of the thing' do to my health when 'my heart's in the Highland's my heart is not here'!—[63] Oh dear certainly not— I shall keep to my original programme and come home after a fortnight, *that* will be next Wednesday when you will have had plenty of time to *subside* from your jumbling, and will have exhausted all Emmas powers of cooking—unless you are savage enough to *wish* not to see my face till the 20th and honest enough to tell me so—or unless you prefer to accept the invitation which Lady A is again writing to you to come here after you are rested— You would be bored here just at present, with Henry Taylors solemn fatherhood, and the much talk and bother about the children— But the Taylors depart[,] sucking baby and all, on the eighth—and after that I hear of no one coming but Thackeray and Brookfield, and Lady Montague, George Bunsen and Colonel Rawlinson are coming but only for a day

62. See 11 August 1837, above. Henry Taylor's wife was the Hon. Theodosia Alice Spring Rice, daughter of the 1st Baron Monteagle of Brandon.

63. Robert Burns, 'My Heart's in the Highlands'.

or two— *Do* Dear 'consult *your* authentic wish' whether you will join me here or have me back there— [W]hich ever way of it you like best I shall like best—upon my honour— The only very good reason for my staying till the 20th, viz: to be 'another woman in the house' as Lady A said, while men visitors are here in Lord A's absence[,] is done away with by the fact of Lady Montagues coming and Miss Farrers being to stay till the 19th— [B]y going next Wednesday I shall not put Lady A about then the least in the world— [A]t the same time—*you* might be better here perhaps till the 20th than in London—as Lady A says you should have this bedroom which is quiet enough—at least will be— when the Taylor children have ceased to 'run horses' over head, and shall have your dinner by yourself at what hour you please— And so I will now go and try to walk off the headach I have got by—what do you think?—*crying* actually!— [P]rosaic as this letter looks I have not somehow been able to 'dry myself up' while writing it— I suppose it is the *compress* put on me in the drawingroom that makes me bubble up at no allowance when I am alone

Ever your
J C

[. . .] I have been to seek my letter out of the box that I might append a most needful piece of information— I trust still in time the key of the wine cellar and of the sideboard drawer where there is some brandy and sherry and lump sugar are in the uppermost of your small drawers in the Library—and the key of *that* under the slide of the old ink-stand

To John Welsh, Chelsea, 7 January 1851

dear, estimable Uncle of me!

Have you been reading Thackerays Pendennis?[64] if so you have made acquaintance with *Blanche Amory*, and when I tell you that my young lady of last week, is the original of that portrait, you will give me joy that she, Lady's maid, and infinite baggage is all gone! Not that the poor little 'Tizzy' (Theresa Revis) is *quite* such a little devil as Thackeray who has detested her from a child has here represented—

64. Thackeray's semi-autobiographical novel of 1848, with a remarkable depiction of male adolescence. Blanche Amory is one of his amoral man-eaters (like Becky Sharp in *Vanity Fair*): a vamp whom Pendennis survives to find true love. Theresa Revis served as model for both Blanche and Becky.

but the looks, the manners, the wiles, the *Larmes* [tears] 'and all that sort of thing['] are a perfect likeness— [T]he blame however is chiefly on those who placed her in a position so *false*, that it required extraordinary virtue not to become false along with it— She was the only *legitimate* child of a beautiful young 'improper female' who was for a number of years Arthur Bullers mistress—she had *had* a husband[,] a swindler— [H]is Mother took the freak of patronizing this mistress, saw the child and behold it was very pretty and clever. Poor Mrs Buller had tired of parties, of Politics, of most things in Heaven and earth: 'a sudden thought struck her,' she would *adopt* this child; give herself the excitement of *making a scandal* and *braving public opinion*, and of educating a flesh and blood girl into the Heroine of the three volume novel which she had for years been trying to *write*; but wanted perseverance to elaborate!— The child was made the idol of the whole house—even Charles did whatever she pleased—her showy education was fitting her more for her own Mothers profession than for any honest one—and when she was seventeen and *the novel* was just rising into the interest of *love-affairs*—a rich young man having been refused—or rather *jilted* by her—Mrs Buller died—her husband and son being already dead[,] and poor Tizzy was left without any earthly stay and with only 250£ a year to support her in the extravagantly luxurious habits she had been brought up in— She has a splendid voice and wished to get trained for the Opera— Mrs Buller's fine Lady friends screamed at the idea—but offered her nothing instead—not even their countenance—[H]er two male-guardians, to wash their hands of her resolved to send her to India to Sir Arthur Buller, whose wife hated her—naturally—being the child of her husbands ci-devant [former] mistress— To India she had to go however; vowing that if their object was to marry her off—she would disappoint them, and return 'to prosecute the Artist Life'— She produced the most extraordinary *furor* at Calcutta, had offers of Sudor Judges[65] and what not? every week—refused them point blank, terrified Sir Arthur by her extravagance, tormented Lady Buller by her caprices, 'fell into *consumption*'—for the nonce—was ordered by the Doctors back to England! and to the dismay of her two cowardly guardians arrived here six months ago—*with her health perfectly restored*! But her Indian reputation had preceded her and the fine Ladies who turned their backs on her in her extreme need now invite a girl who has refused Sudor Judges by the dozen— She had been going about from one house to another, while no *home* could be found for her! The Guardians had a brilliant idea— 'Would *we* take her'?— Not for her

65. Senior judges in British India.

weight in gold I said—but I asked her to spend *a day* with me that I might see what she was grown to, and whether I could do anything in placing her with some proper person— The result of this invitation was that alarming arrival bag, and baggage on newyearsday! She has saved us all further speculation about her however by engaging herself to a Capt. Neale (from Ayrshire) who came home in the ship with her and seems a most devoted lover— SHE 'does not love *him* a bit' she told me—'had been hesitating some time betwixt accepting him, or going on the stage, or drowning herself—' I told her her decision was good, as marrying did not preclude either 'going on the stage' at a subsequent period, or 'drowning herself'—whereas had she decided on the *drowning*; [']there could have been no more of it'— I have my own notion that she will throw him over yet; meanwhile it was a *blessed calm* after the *Fly* rolled her away from here on Saturday— 'Oh my Dear!' Mr C said 'we cannot be sufficiently thankful!!'— [I]ndeed you can have no notion how the whole routine of this quiet house was tumbled heels over head— It had been for these three days and three nights *not* Jonah in the whale's belly—but the whale in Jonah's belly![66]—that little creature seemed to have absorbed this whole establishment with *her*self—

There is a long story for you! which perhaps you cant take any interest in— I am sure however you would be amused with an account of our visit, the other day, to Pentonville Prison[67]—if I had left myself time and breath to tell it— 'Oh my!' (as old Helen used to say) 'How *expensive*'! Prisoners costing 50£ a year each!— [Y]ou may fancy their accomodations are somewhat remarkable— In each cell I saw a pretty little corner cupboard—on one shelf of which was *the dressing apparatus* a comb and brush and *small tooth comb*! laid on a neatly folded-up towel—a shaving jug *with mettle top* on one side, an artistic soap box on the other!— In one cell I remarked a blue tassell with a bit of steel chain attached to it hung from a brass nail— 'What *is* the use of that tassell' I asked the Inspector— 'That tassell Mam—why—that tassell is—a *fancy* of the Prisoner's own!—we allow them to have their little fancies!'— They all wear masks when in each others presence—that should they afterwards meet in society their feelings may be spared—they have such charming *bath rooms*(!)—each man has a good sized

66. Jonah 1–2.
67. Still in operation in the London borough of Islington, 'The Ville' opened in 1842, on the 'separate system' of silence and solitary confinement. Conditions were physically better than in the antiquated jails of the eighteenth century, but the regime took a psychological toll on inmates. Still, the prison was a model for the British Empire and beyond. A recent British minister of justice has described the institution as a 'dramatic example of failure'.

court all to himself to run about in for an hour at a time—and while we were there they all 'went to school' with books and slates under their arm—*masked*!!— If any man wants to have the comforts of life, and be taught—and 'have his fancies' let him rush out and commit a felony!— We went to hear their religious teaching in the Chapel— An under Chaplain stood on the Altar with a bible in one hand and a red book (like a butchers) in the other[;] he read a passage from the bible then looked in the red-book for *the numbers* (they have no *names*) whose turn it was to be examined— [F]or instance he read about the young man who came to Jesus and asked what he should do to be saved—then after consulting the red book he called out 'Numbers *32* and *78*, what shall I do to enter into eternal life'?— 32 & 78 answered, the one in a growl the other in a squeal, 'sell all that thou hast and give to the poor'—[68] Now, my blessed Uncle did you ever hear such damned nonsense? If a grain of logic was in the heads of 32 and 78, mustnt they have thought; Well what the devil are *we* taken up, and imprisoned and called criminals for; but just, because *we* take this injunction seriously, and *help* YOU to carry it out, by relieving you of your watches 'and other sundries'—

I should tell you too that each prisoner has a bell in his cell!— [O]ne man said to some visitor 'and if I ring my bell a fool answers it'!

Uncle dear, good night— If you and I were the Government wouldn't we sweep such confounded humbug out of creation

Ever your affectionate

Jane Carlyle

Love to the children

To Thomas Carlyle, Manchester, 12 September 1851

There never was such a Postman! His morning delivery varies from nine till half after ten! Yesterday it was half after ten when he brought your letter;—after I had lost all hope of it, and was beginning to think; could it be that you were fallen ill?—and, with this incipient fear threatening to spoil my day's *lark*, was stepping into a cab, according to programme to be ultimately conveyed by railway 'thro the prettiest scenery in all Lancashire' to Burnley— When I had read the letter I wished that I had not been going for an hour at least that I might first have written to Blanche—but a carriage, or to speak with truthful modesty, an old

68. Matthew 19: 21; Mark 10: 21; Luke 18: 22.

gig was to be in waiting for us at the Burnley Station, and a dinner waiting for us, a mile or two beyond—so without disappointing and provoking various persons, there was no delaying—and as we did not get home till eleven at night the letter to Blanche has only got written this morning.— (Oh these pens of Geraldines!) I have begged her however to answer by return of post— As it is now so near upon her marriage—(on the 22d Lady Stanley said it was to come off) I judged it best to express the strongest doubts of its being convenient for them to receive us for even the shortest number of *days*—but offered to come over, *without luggage*, and spend a part of a day with them if they had still leisure to see us on that principle— It is possible they may have their house full of the mutual relations—and if otherwise they can renew their invitation—but it was best not to put *them* to the awkwardness of saying they did not want us at this time—

I am very sorry to hear of your rushing down into coffee and castor [oil] so soon—and an amount of *smoking* I dare say!— [F]or me; I can tell you with a little 'proud Pharasee' feeling,[69] that I have not—'what shall I say?'—swallowed a pill since I left Malvern!!!—and I am alive, and *rather well*— But then my life otherwise is so very wholesome—nice little railway excursions almost every day—nice *country* dinners at two o'clock—everybody so fond of me!—and Geraldine guarding me from all sorts of 'mental agony with my own inside,' telling me Tales of Manchester life—much better than her novels—*rubbing my feet* at every leisure moment and taking as much fond trouble with me as if I were her own little red infant—

It is great fun too visiting these primeval Cotton spinners with '*Parlour kitchens*' and bare-headed servant maids—so overflowing with fervent hospitality—and in the profoundest darkness about my Husband's 'Literary reputation'— I have a great deal to tell about these people but it is needless to waste time in writing that sort of thing— But one thing of another sort, belonging to our *natural sphere* I must tell you so long as I remember—that Espinasse has—renounced his allegiance to you![70] When his Father was in London lately, he (the Father[,] anything but an admirer of yours) was greatly charmed to hear his son declare that he had 'quite changed his views about Carlyle—and was no longer blind to his many and great faults' whereon the Espinasse Father in a

69. Luke 18: 11.
70. Francis Espinasse (1823–1912), of French heritage but Edinburgh-born. Jeffrey and Wordsworth both warned him against a literary career, but he persisted, with Thomas's support, as a freelance critic. In later life he would publish biographies of Voltaire and Renan.

transport of gratitude to Heaven for a *saved* 'insipid offspring' pulled out—a five pound note! and made Espinasse a present of it— Espinasse, thanking his Father, then went on to say that, 'he no longer liked *Mrs* Carlyle either—that he believed her an excellent woman once—but she had grown more and more into Carlyle's likeness, until there was no enduring her'! The Father however did not again open his purse!— Store Smith,[71] who was present, is the authority for this charming little history—which has amused Espinasse's enemies here very much—

Mrs Gaskell took Geraldine and me a beautiful drive the other day 'in a friends carriage'— She is a very kind cheery woman in her own house but there is an atmosphere of moral dullness about her, as about all Socinian women— I am thinking whether it would not be expedient however to ask *her* to give *you* a bed when you come—she would be 'proud and happy' I guess—and you do not wish to sleep at Geraldine's—besides that mine is the only spare-room furnished— The Gaskell house is very large and in the midst of a shrubbery and quite near this—

Kind love to your Mother and the rest— I had a parcel of letters from Chelsea—round by Liverpool—where Mary had coolly kept them three days— Miss Farrer, Mrs John Stodart and the marriage cards of Mr and Mrs John Allan Braun— Heaven knows who these are!—the post mark was Rothsay—

Nero is the happiest of dogs[;] goes all the journeys by railway— *smuggled* with the utmost ease—and has run many hundreds of miles after the little Lancashire birds—

'Oh *my*'! your old gloves *have* come home with their tails behind them![72] I found something bulky in my great-coat pocket the other night when I put it on, and pulled out—the gloves! You must have placed them there yourself—for there was also a mass of rolled up paper for *pipical* purposes—

Ever yours /
Jane W Carlyle [. . .]

71. John Stores Smith, *littérateur* and biographer of French-Revolutionary statesman Mirabeau.
72. As in the nursery rhyme 'Little Bo-Peep', who lost her sheep, 'And doesn't know where to find them; / Leave them alone and they'll come home, / Wagging their tails behind them.'

To Thomas Carlyle, Chelsea, 1 October 1851

Alas! your letter, which came on the Monday morning in due course, couldn't get itself so much as *opened* till late at night! I was all that day in bed again with a raging headach, only lifting my head to—what shall I say?—*retch*! When Anne told me there were three letters, I asked if one of them were from you, and that demonstration of interest was just the most I was *up to* for the moment. Really Nero makes a capital little nurse! he never left me for an instant, except for *inevitable purposes*, and these he transacted with a despatch! for the rest; he warmed my feet and my back by turns, licked my face, and once was so overpowered by his feelings that the consequences, had I been of superstitious turn, might have proved fatal!—for he laid his little head on my breast and set up that peculiarly dismal, preternatural howl which is said to portend 'a death in the family'— I assure you I remained amazed for a moment as in presence of the Infinite! the effect was more startling than you can well conceive!— The newspapers too failed of getting sent that day; there being no one to address them—yesterday however I made them ready so soon as I got up, and wrote a short business note to John, and *began* to write a letter to you—but I was still so weak and *fluttery* from all that pain that I felt I had best desist, in case of accidents[,] and I spent the day purposely in doing as nearly as human faculties could accomplish it—*nothing at all.* About nine at night the two Triumvirs Mazzini and Saffi came,[73] and found me emancipated from combs, with my hair all down!— I had tried to gather myself up and escape, on hearing a knock but failed— Saffi is a very gentlemanly, grave, sincere looking young man—with an unfortunate habit of tumbling over the fire irons— He does this, Mazzini says, wherever he goes—not once—but three or four times at one visit— [L]ast night he restrained himself on account of my weak nerves, and did it only *twice*. I have had the quietest time since you went—'chiefly *sewing* Mr Carlyle'— I have finished my *dressing gown* and 'other things too'— My visitors are extremely few and those who do come are not always let in— Dr Samuel Brown[74] had tea given him one night, for the sake of dear old Haddington—for himself he strikes me as 'the thinnest

73. Count Aurelio Saffi (1819–1890) had served with Mazzini (and Carlo Armellini) as an interim 'triumvir' in republican Rome in 1849, and was in exile in the aftermath. He married an Englishwoman and would late in life take up a professorship at the University of Bologna.

74. Samuel Morrison Brown (1817–1856), born in Haddington, was both dramatist and chemist: author of a tragedy on Galileo (1850) and *Lectures on the Atomic Theory* (1858).

of men'—a sort of shoemakers awl in human form— [T]he night after he was here I dreamt that I saw *a Head*, with HIS eyes peering out of it on all sides, moving along the floor, and while I looked at it with a mild wonder, it dropt down thro a trapdoor!— My Imagination you see is still lively—at nights— Mr Neuberg came according to appointment to take me to the Exhibition and I went and staid—just five minutes[.] It was too dreadful!— Darwin came another day in the same intention, but I made him drive me instead to different shops where I had wants— There was a letter on Saturday from the new Lady Airlie[75]—requesting me to thank you for her book—not feeling up to addressing 'the great Man' herself— She writes pleasantly and hopefully—'feels, she says, as if she could be very happy there, and feels *strong to do all she is appointed to*[']—(Alas!)—'Airlie is kinder than words can say'!— So are they all generally speaking in the first week!

There are no letters for *you* of any moment— Two shilling Yankee ones *returned*—after thro the Postmans help taking 'a peep into their inside'—[76] Anne is out for a holiday for once in her life—and I have her daughter to 'do for me'— When I made her the offer she curtsied and said 'well Mam—if you have no objections I think I really *should* like to go and see—the *Tower*![']'[77] I was quite glad she had the sense to prefer the good old tower to the Crystal Palace[.] I called at the Chorleys door on Saturday— Mr & Miss 'as well as could be expected[']— It was the day I had Darwins carriage

Ever faithfully yours
J W C

75. See Characters and Correspondents. Carlyle had sent her mother a copy of his *Life of John Sterling* before its publication on 11 October.

76. Jane was reluctant to shell out a shilling each for letters from unknown American admirers, with her experience of the breed at first hand at No. 5.

77. The Tower of London, six or seven miles downriver from Chelsea. Tourists had visited it since Tudor times, and numbers greatly increased during the nineteenth century, despite the opposition of none other than the Duke of Wellington, who wanted it maintained as a barracks. Indeed a ticket office was constructed on site in this very year. Far more ephemeral was the 'Crystal Palace' constructed in Hyde Park to house the Great Exhibition of May–October; it was reconstructed on Sydenham Hill, south London, but was destroyed by fire in 1936—the local football team's name is all that remains by way of memorial.

To Lady Airlie, Chelsea, 15? October 1851

Dear Lady Airlie,

Since the day that I left you in the *trousseau-room* at Alderley,[78] I have written some *fifty* letters, I should think,—more or less *flowingly*,—to correspondents old and new; how comes it then,—I wish some Clairvoyant, or Physiologist, or other exceptionally deep-knowing human Being would tell me:—that to *you*, who have been oftener and more kindly in my thoughts than some of these others, & to whom moreover I had *promised* to write soon, no letter should have yet got itself written by me?— I have given myself a variety of reasons for this silence, some absurd enough to make a cat laugh—but the most reasonable reason, and the only one that will bear being offered as an excuse is this. I find myself *in a false position* with you as a correspondent! Don't misunderstand me; I do not mean that you being a brilliant young Countess, and I a poor Philosopher's elderly wife, there should be thro' *that* any *difficulty* in our writing to one another. My life has been too much made up of *strong contrasts* that I should feel the external discrepencies between us at all perplexing for me at this date—but the *false position* which *bothers* me is an accident, produced by *your* lovely enthusiasm, by your—what shall I say? *passion* for *genius* and *wisdom* and 'all that sort of thing'! My Husbands writings and speech have found a quick response in *your* noble nature—you feel enthusiastically grateful to *him* for giving you high aspirations, and strengthening you for *good*. And therein you do well; People who elevate and strengthen us in this modern world being so woefully scarce; one can hardly be *too* grateful to that man or woman who does us that benefit or even *honestly strive to do it*. But *you* go further—by the transfiguring light of your 'beautiful enthusiasm' you contrive to see a sort of a *Teacher* even in *me*!—not because you ever heard any *wisdom* from *me*, or have any ground for believing me wise, the least in the world; but just because I am Mr *Carlyle's Wife*!— Now this is what I mean by being in a false position towards you—I am here receiving a *certain* sentiment of consideration from you, which I feel to be given me *on false pretences* and not feeling in myself—loving you as I do—the straightforward virtue to wholly disclaim it; I should like to keep up your *illusion of Faith*, so flattering to me, by writing you, not such offhand letters as I write to others, and as nature prompts me to write, abounding in nonsense rather than in sense, but instead, little exquisite

78. Lady Airlie was the daughter of Edward Stanley, 2nd Baron Stanley of Alderley, in Cheshire, north-west England. The nineteenth-century Alderley New Hall was seriously damaged by fire in 1931 and all but abandoned, until Imperial Chemical Industries adapted it to house research in 1950.

sheetfuls of—what shall I say?—*female Carlyleism*! I should like—but no good ever comes of trying to pass for wiser or better than one is—and in any case the thing is frankly *impossible* to me. So I have decided on making you this little foolish avowal once for all—and writing henceforth, so long as you choose me to write, on the veracious principle of having no wisdom of my own 'to speak of'! [. . .]

Mr C made out his visit to the Ashburtons at Paris but it seemed to be rather a failure— Lady A confined indoors with cold all the while, and Mr C ruined in *his sleep*, by a beautiful *Time piece* in his bedroom which 'struck even the half hours'! and by the want of '*a four posted bed*' &c &c. He returned after a week in a most *domestic* frame of mind, bringing little Nero *a homage* of a new collar and leading string!— The Ashburtons are now at the Grange— Lady A kindly invited me there for three weeks along with the Taylors—but but—I confess to finding the Taylors too *boring*,[79] for being lived in the same house with a second time! Besides I had been *about* so long! and my soul as well as my household affairs, were getting out of order and needing to be sorted up,—

Do write to me and tell me how you pass your time, everything about you will be always interesting for me— Yours affectionately

Jane Carlyle

79. See 18 September 1838, above. The passage of thirteen years had not improved their social interest.

Figure 8: Lynton Lamb, chapter illustration to Thea Holme, *The Carlyles at Home*, chapter 9, 'Money' (1965), © Oxford University Press

7

'The New-Modelling of our House': 1852–1855

The Lady Harriet issue continued like an ulcer in Jane's life, and her suffering came to a head in her journal of 1855 (to be discussed in Chapter 8). But another storm cloud was in the offing, though initially only the size of a fist. Thomas's biography of Frederick the Great stirred in the darkness in the spring of 1852, produced a tour of Germany in the summer of that year, became the object of apparently endless vacillation thereafter until 1854, and was eventually completed in six volumes only in 1865, the year before her death. 'The Valley of the Shadow of Frederick', as Jane would refer to the project, was opening up.

Like Lady Harriet, the all-unwitting Prussian emperor would put pressure on the Carlyles' relationship. But now was the time for the third member of their ménage à trois almost to have Jane and Thomas part company with it, rather than each other. After fifteen years of peace and quiet, for the most part (spring cleans notwithstanding), No. 5 Cheyne Row suddenly took on an existence of its own, like a gigantic poltergeist. Frederick and No. 5; No. 5 and Frederick: it seemed the two projects were determined never to make peace with each other, and to exasperate the two people who tried to exist between them.[1]

The story started innocuously enough, when husband and wife signed a thirty-one-year lease in July 1852, an act of commitment that (understandably) inaugurated a major renovation lasting until December. Water was laid on to the house, cisterns were installed, and a tap as well as gaslight introduced to the kitchen. The library was entirely modernised to function also as a drawing room. None of this could Thomas tolerate, and he escaped the builders and the London heatwave in Scotland, suggesting that Jane accompany him on a Frederick-related tour of Germany, which she wisely declined. Before he left for the Continent Thomas wrote a letter of 13 August (in reply to hers of the tenth, below) which, in retrospect, seems innocently but fatally provocative. There is the customary prevarication about Frederick ('Nor do I care much for quitting even Frederic; *really at heart I do not*

1. See Thea Holme, *The Carlyles at Home* (London, 1965; 2002), chapter 6, 'The Soundproof Study'.

much love him: yet perhaps I could *write a goodish kind of Book upon him'), and then another suggestion:*

> I am sorry to hear of your one good worker being still busy in my room; that surely must be the smallest of his 'paintings,'—paintings not the thing most necessary there! However, I leave it all to Goody, I do loyally; and foresee that, one way or other, she will actually make a nice thing of it: she never failed yet, the shifty little creature. But are you putting some clothes-shelves, some Press, or an apparatus for convenient stowage of clothes? Think of that, my ingenious Goody; do not desert me there! I thot once of *shelves* with a door at the left-hand corner of the fireplace: wd that do anything? The 'thot' was cursory, and I pretend only to state the want; by no means to provide for it;—is not that ingenuous? One other thing tell me, and no more: *Has* Morgan put in that *Hole* in the cornice; that ventilating cavity, I mean, which is to shut and open from the upper window? If he have forgotten—! But he cannot have forgotten; nor will Goody permit him. Fergus told me, Cubitt's plan now is, simply to put a hole *thro'* the wall above each window; hole free into the air, with a *lid* at the inner end of it whh you can open or shut with a string. Nothing better; not even my own plan, tho' perhaps as good.— (*CL* 27: 225)

If ever there was a man constitutionally incapable of planning a renovation, surely that man was Thomas Carlyle, with his 'thots', his holes and his Heath Robinson lids on strings. All these suggestions he left in the hands of Jane and Messrs Cubitt (Thomas and William), before disappearing to Germany to return in mid-October. The Cubitts, it should be noted, were no cowboy outfit. Thomas (1788–1855) was a master builder of renown: he built Belgrave Square, Eaton Square, Tavistock Square, Gordon Square, a part of Buckingham Palace, Osborne Palace on the Isle of Wight, and Polesden Lacey, in Surrey. (Nor did the royal connection end at Buckingham Palace: he is the great-great-great-grandfather of the present Queen Consort.) It is hard to imagine either him or his brother (who built Covent Garden) taking a personal interest in Thomas's cornices.

Be that as it may, in April 1853 workmen were back, hanging wallpaper and fitting bookshelves. In May the work seemed finished, just in time for the authorities to dig up the street to run a sewer from Kensington to the Thames Embankment. In June the painters were back once more, to finish around mid-July, when Jane escaped to Liverpool and to Moffat, in Scotland, to visit Dr John and his new wife Phoebe (a wealthy widow with four sons). On the eighteenth of that month, however, Thomas re-entered the fray, writing to Jane from Chelsea with a wholly new idea:

On one point I expect to surprise you: A Cubitt Builder is actually coming here [. . .] to give me an exact survey, with exact estimate (*time*, money &c) of an impenetrably *deaf* apart[men]t up aloft! I hardly think I shall dare to *build* just yet, after all. But these summer noises, in some of my neuralgic moods, drive me upon such speculations. I still hope and believe *you* will, in some magnanimous day, undertake the Ronca poultry [at No. 6]; yes you will: really we should then be very well as we are; a nice *house* as need be! However, the man shall estimate. (*CL* 28: 209)[2]

The Cubitts assured Thomas that an entirely soundproof attic study could certainly be installed, and work began on 11 August (quote, £169). On 2 September the attic floor (joists, beams and so forth) were done—though in the meantime the housemaid had run off with an Irish builder. On 14 October Thomas wrote to John from the shelter of the Athenaeum club on Pall Mall:

Our new apartment is nearly clear of its carpenters for a week past: an Irish labourer is at present washing out the floor &c: but the papering or even painting is impossible owing to moist plaster; the place will certainly not be habitable till spring: much if I can occasionally smoke in it with comfort. For it is yet far from completely *deaf*; and I foresee considerable higglings on many sides before it can be perfect. (*CL* 28: 290)

In November Jane declared 'the silent room is the noisiest in the house' (CL 28: 318), and in December the painters returned. Only on 14 March 1854 was the study finally papered, but on 24 November workmen were back for another week, and Thomas reported to his sister Jean:

Meanwhile I have carpenters again upon me; grate-smiths &c,—to rage for two days yet, like the sack of Babylon (or the taking of Sebastopol, if it *were* taken)! On deciding for a *carpet* (when the cold weather came, and 'drugget' wd no longer do) I perceived, more glaringly than ever that my new floor had been all made of *green wood* (an incredible fact, but not an uncommon one here); that a pennypiece could be introduced anywhere between the planks, and that torrents of cold were pouring in *there*,—as the one fruit I had got from my 'ventilating trunks' &c &c. Closing my *lips* (for what good is there in talk)

2. The Roncas, Thea Holme tells us (*The Carlyles at Home*, 59), were 'a feckless Irish-Italian family [. . .] with "mechanic sons-in-law" who hammered and sawed in the back garden while female members of the tribe dragged out large washing-tubs and strung lines of laundry from wall to wall'.

> I had to decide on mending this misery;—and so for a week I am banished again, and sit inconveniently down stairs, my Books &c inaccessible and the house not pleasanter than common!— (*CL* 29: 206)

In this chaotic atmosphere it is hardly surprising that distress spread from the house to the household: on 12 February 1855 Jane wrote her pseudo-parliamentary letter of protest, 'budget of a Femme incomprise' *(below); in August she visited Rottingdean near Brighton in search of a place in the country (a plan abandoned by the end of the month); and on 25 October a cistern overflowed, flooding two rooms (though Jane entertained visitors throughout). Ever the irrepressible fixer-upper, on 26 November Thomas wrote to Erasmus Darwin to ask a favour: 'I think I have heard you say Professor Newman [Latin, University College London] has a Stove in his Library or Writing room? It has become evident to me I must either have one here very soon, or else quit the apartment for one of more comfortable temperature.' Could Erasmus visit the professor to see the stove in operation? 'I will not stir in the matter (at* caulking *my room &c) till I hear from you' (CL 30: 120).*

Parts of the human fabric were giving way, as well. In 1853 Jane's correspondence with Jeannie Chrystal (née Welsh; 'Babbie') came to an end in a sense of neglect; in October of that year her 'only uncle of me', John Welsh, died in Liverpool; in December Welsh's daughter Helen and Thomas's mother Margaret died, too. The ménage was closing in upon itself. We shall return to the matter of Jane's health in Chapter 9, but her physical condition was clearly deteriorating at this time, too: we only have to compare two portraits from London's National Portrait Gallery—Samuel Laurence's oil portrait of her from 1852, and William Jeffrey's carte-de-visite of 1862—to see a woman much older in expression and appearance than her sixty years should suggest.

To Calliope Dilberoglue, Chelsea, 8 January 1852?

Oh Heavens! How beautiful! *You*—the shirt—the whole thing! It is not in mere terrestrial prose that one should acknowledge such a gift; one's thanks should be a new '*Song of the Shirt*'[3] as bright and glowing as the other was dark and dreary—if only I had any power of Song left

3. The key protest poem of the era, 'The Song of the Shirt' (1843) by Thomas Hood (1799–1845) depicts the cruelty of the piece-work garment trade: 'Stitch! Stitch! Stitch! / In poverty, hunger, and dirt, / And still with a voice of dolorous pitch / She sang the "Song of the Shirt".'

in me!—but—alas! Let me keep my thanks then until we meet dear Calliope, and give you them in a kiss, which may be made poetical in any degree according to the sentiment one puts in it— But the shirt— when I had shaken it out, and hung it over a chair, and gone some steps back to look at it; it seemed to me in its glistening loveliness an emanation from the Moon, fallen on this lower Earth! 'What a beautiful thing' said Mr Carlyle 'is it for sleeping in'? the question awoke in me some practical considerations as to the wearing it— Be kind enough to tell me; am I to wear it on the outside of my gown and to let it hang loose, or to tie it round the waist with a cord? or how?—for with Heavens blessing I *will* wear it come what come may!— I *will* astonish the finest Ladies in London with my bit of 'Orientalism'[4]—my glistening shirt out of the Moon! Only I should wish to wear it in right fashion—so you must do me the further kindness to teach me the right fashion—

How glad I am that you have made such progress in English—for now we shall understand each other when we meet, all the difficulty, I think, lay in the want of a mutual language— I meant to write a long letter when I began, but a tiresome Lady came and sat an hour and has run me close on our post-time. And I would not miss another post in announcing the safe arrival of your work— Will you give my kindest remembrance to your Mother. I have forgotten quite the few words of greek which she taught me— To your Brother I will write soon—

All good be with you dear Calliope—
Ever truly yours /
Jane Carlyle

To Joseph Neuberg, Chelsea, 16 July 1852

Oh dear Mr Neuberg! Did I ever tell you of the Annan Baillie who when his health was drunk at a public dinner, and he had risen to speak, could find no words to express his feelings but 'Oh Gentlemen! I am *but* a MAN! of like form and passions with yourselves!' If I did not say the same words, or some words very like them on receiving your birthday cup it was only because you were not there to hear! Upon my honour I was never more surprised in my life or more *touched*! tho' I have a natural tendency to being *touched*—*moi*! Your remembrance of

4. An older word than we perhaps imagine; *OED* records its first use in 1747.

my poor little Birthday for so long a time and at such a distance, made visible and palpable for me in the form of that most beautiful of cups, was indeed something to stand amazed before 'as in presence of the Infinite'! and something for which to thank my husbands friends '*the Gods*'—something to almost reconcile me for the moment to the questionable fact of having been verily BORN!—thanks then to Joseph and Rosetta—the heartiest thanks! And they are to know that their poetical intention was punctually and safely 'carried out'—the cup and saucer were placed in my hands on the 14th, and without crack or damage of any sort. And now while I write I have those lovely mountains before me and wish myself there[5]—but alas! the German project lies buried for the present under a chaos of pulled down chimnies and *partitions*, clouds of lime dust and crash, as of Doom! the thermo[me]ter all the while at 80 in the shade, and Mr C still 'hanging on by the eyelids' (as sailors say) to his usual life of *study with dignity*![6] For we have taken a lease of this house for thirty one years! (*that* should serve our time I think!) and are what Mr C called 'getting it made habitable,' at our own expence. Did you ever have a house pretty well *gutted* and try to *live* in it while *gutting*? If not, you can form no adequate idea of the 'hubbub wild and dire dismay'[7] in which we have for already one fortnight lived, moved, and NOT had our being and which looks not unlike lasting for six months, instead of the six weeks, the Architect deluded us with! Mr C's *patience*, which, as you may have remarked, is not by any means his most *conspicuous* virtue, has found its limit within the last few days, and he intends bolting to Scotland on Wednesday next. [B]ut I—I am a *woman*,—and if a woman dont bring patience into the world with her 'the Destinies' teach it to her *gratis*. So I am peaceably awaiting in this '*belly of Chaos*' as Jonah *awaited* in the Belly of the whale[8]—my presence here being indispensable for getting these sublime *improvements* done to our mind. When Mr C is gone to Scotland I may possibly go out to *sleep*—in Darwin's empty house or somewhere—for I am finally reduced to *one* hour of sleep on the strength of Morphia! but by day I need to furnish commonsense to the bricklayers and carpenters &c and have besides a change of servants to transact next week. My old woman having decided that she 'would like to do nobodys bidding, but live in a cottage of her own in the country'— So should I!—but 'don't I wish

5. Apparently the cup depicted the 'Seven Mountains' (or *Siebengebirge*) near Bonn, Germany. 14 July was Jane's birthday.
6. Cicero (106–43 BC), his speech, 'For Cestius'.
7. Milton, *Paradise Lost*, ii. 951, and (next line) Acts 17: 28.
8. Jonah 1.

I may get it?'— The German project is not however renounced— only last night Mr C was talking about my 'getting things in progress' to go with him to Germany in the end of August or beginning of September— You had best write him another *heartening* letter about it—it would be so pleasant to leave this '*belly of Chaos*' and climb with you and Rosetta those mountains on my cup!

For the rest I am hardly so sickly this summer as usual, in spite of the frightful heat; and the *material* row has been complicated by no great *moral* shocks— Nero has not been once stolen since you saw him—he improves in sense and all engaging qualities—tho for the moment I confess he is sulking about a new white cat that has been given me— I took it in my lap to see how he would feel, and his manifestation of jealousy exceeded my most sanguine expectations—he retired under the sofa and neither coaxing nor cake could persuade him out; to all my blandishments he answered with an angry growl, and when I put in my hand to pull him out he retired further in, and went thro the form of *snapping* at it—and this mood held out for an hour or two after I had sent the cat from the room— I have just got a new M.S. from Geraldine Jewsbury[,] a story called *The Adopted Daughter* written for some *little* girls' *series*—and it is extremely gracefully and graciously done I think;[9] and does her more credit then her novels of 'power and passion'— Your Brother would tell you that he saw us for a few minutes—I think he speaks english *worse* every time I see him. He promised to come and spend a day on his return— I speak german a great deal now having a german friend who knows no English, and whom I see very often—but Oh such german! it will do your heart good to hear it when I come—if I come—with love to Rosetta ever affectionately yours

Jane Carlyle

To John Carlyle, Chelsea, 27 July 1852

My dear John

You will like to hear 'what I am thinking of Life' in the present confusion. Well then; I am not *thinking* of it at all but *living* it very contentedly. The tumult has been even greater since Mr C went than it was before; for new floors are being put down in the top story and the noise

9. Geraldine Jewsbury, *The History of an Adopted Child* (1852): the first novel to treat the issue.

of *that* is something terrific. But now that I feel the noise and dirt and discord with my own senses only and not thro *his* as well, it is amazing how little I care about it. Nay in superintending all these men I begin to find myself in the career open to my particular talents,[10] and am infinitely more satisfied than I was in talking '*wits*' in my white silk gown with white feathers in my head, at soirees at Bath House 'and all that sort of thing.' It is such a consolation to be of some *use*, tho' it were only in helping stupid carpenters and bricklayers out of their *impossibilities*, and at all rates keeping them to their work, especially when the *ornamental* no longer succeeds with one so well as it *has* done! The fact is I am remarkably indifferent to *material* annoyances, considering my morbid sensitiveness to *moral* ones. And when Mr C is not here recognising it with his overwhelming eloquence, I can regard the present earthquake as something almost *laughable*. Another house-wife trial of temper has come upon me since Mr C went, of which he yet knows nothing, and which has been born with the same imperturbability— He told you perhaps that I had got a new servant in the midst of this mess—a great beauty, whom I engaged because she had been six years in her last place, and because *he* decidedly liked her physiognomy[.] She came home the night before he left— It was a rough establishment to come into, and no fair field for showing at once her capabilities; but her dispositions were perhaps on that account the more quickly ascertained. The first night; I came upon her listening at the door, and the next morning, I came upon her reading one of my letters! and in every little box drawer and corner I found *traces* of her prying— It was going to be like living under an Austrian Spy[;][11] then because she had no regular work possible to do, she did nothing of her own accord that was required— Little Martha who was here in Anne's illness, and whom I had taken back for a week or two, was worth a dozen of her in serviceableness, the little cooking I needed, was always 'what she hadnt been used to where she lived before' and for that or some other reason detestable— I saw before the first week was out that I had got, a helpless, illtrained, low minded goose, and this morning the last day of the week I was wishing to Heaven I had brought no regular Servant into the house at all just now, but gone on with little Martha.— As there was not work enough for *half a one* never to speak of two, I had told little Martha she must go

10. Napoleon's famous boast, that under his rule, 'la carrière est ouverte aux talents', he being a model case.
11. Austria had a widespread and fairly well-deserved reputation in the post-Napoleonic world for its legions of spies throughout its Empire: especially in restless zones like Italy.

home tonight— I would rather have sent away the other, but she had waited three weeks for the place and couldn't be despatched without a months warning, and besides I felt hardly justified in giving her no longer trial. Figure my satisfaction then, when on my return from taking Mazzini to call for the Brownings the new servant came to me with a set face and said, 'she had now been here a week and found the place didnt suit her—if it had been *all straight* perhaps she could have lived in it but it was such a muddle and would be such a muddle for months to come, that she thought it best to get out of it'— I told her I was quite of her opinion and received the news with such amiabity that she became quite amiable too and asked 'when would I like her to go.' '*Tonight*, I said. Martha was to have gone tonight, now you will go in her stead and that will be all the difference'!— And she is gone!—bag and baggage! we parted with mutual civilities and I never was more thankful for a small mercy in my Life— And the most amusing part of the business is that altho taken thus by surprise, I had, before she left the house— engaged another servant! By the strangest chance Irish Fanny who has always kept on coming to see me from time to time and is now in better health, arrived at teatime to tell me she had left her place— I offered her mine which she had already made trial of and she accepted with an enthusiasm that did ones heart good after all those cold ungrateful English wretches— I stipulated however that she should not come for a month[,] Little Martha being the suitablest help in the present state of the family[.] Little Martha is gone to bed the happiest child in Chelsea at the honour thus done her; 'I would have told you Mam, she said, the very first day that girl was here that she wasnt fit for a *genteel* place like yours! And Im sure she isnt so much older than *me* as she says she is'!

Oh such a fuss the Brownings made over Mazzini this day![12] My private opinion of Browning is, in spite of Mr C's favour for him, that he is nothing or very little but 'a fluff of feathers'! *She* is true and *good*, and the most *womanly* creature! I go to Sherborne on Friday to stay till Monday. It is a long fatiguing journey for so short a time—and will be a sad visit, but *she* wishes it—and now good night—

With kind regards to all affectionately yours / Jane W Carlyle

12. Robert and Elizabeth Barrett Browning were both pronounced Italophiles, and lived there from the time of their marriage (1846) to her death (1861); above all in Florence and Venice.

To Thomas Carlyle, Chelsea, 5–6 August 1852

You recollect Dear that Macready told me of *two* routes;[13] recommending that by Frome as the quickest and least fatiguing: so I rendered myself at the Paddington Station on Friday morning, with my night things in a bag on one arm, and my 'Blessed' in a basket on the other. HE [Nero] gave me no trouble—kept himself hidden and motionless till the train started, and then looked out cautiously, as much as to say 'are we safe?' The journey to Frome was quite a *rest* after that mornings work—(carrying down all the books from the top landing place into the back parlour)! And I descended from the train quite fresh for the thirty miles by coach— But when I inquired about the coach to Sherborne I was told there was none!! a coach passing thro' Sherborne, passed thro Frome, without coming to the Station, at eleven in the morning—three hours *before* the time we were at! no other since many months back! My first thought was; what a mercy *you* were not with me! my next, that the Macreadys could not blame *me* for keeping them waiting—and then I '*considered*'—like the piper's cow—and *resolved*—not to stay all day and night at Frome, but to take a Yeovil coach which started at five, which could take me, I was told, to a way-side Inn within eight miles of Sherborne, and there I hoped to find a fly—'*or something*'! Meanwhile I would proceed to the town of Frome, a mile from the station, and get something to eat and even to drink; 'feeling it my duty' to keep my heart up by all needful appliances. I left my little bag at the Station where the coach came, and set my dog quite free, and we pursued our way as calmly and naturally as if we had known where we were going. Frome is a dull dirty looking place full of Plumbers, one could fancy the Bennet controversy[14] must have been a godsend to it— I saw several Inns, and chose *The George*, for its name's sake— I walked in and asked to have some cold meat and a pint bottle of Guiness's porter! They shewed me to an ill-aired parlour and brought me some cold Lamb that the flies had been buzzing round for a week—even Nero disdained to touch it!— I eat bread however, and drank *all* the porter!

13. Jane dashed to the market town of Sherborne, north-west Dorset, to see her dying friend, Catherine Macready, wife of actor-manager William, via Frome (thirty miles to its north-east) in Somerset. Paddington is the London station serving western counties. Yeovil is only five miles due west from Sherborne.

14. The Reverend William James Early Bennett (1804–1886) left his Church of England parish in Knightsbridge, west London, in 1851 because of concerns raised about his stress on church ritual, in particular the ancient Catholic doctrine of the 'real presence' of Christ in the service of the Eucharist. He became vicar of Frome and served there until his death. Like many West Country towns, Frome was a centre for Protestant nonconformity, too: so the complacent agnostic Jane meets below speaks of going 'to neither one nor other of them', Congregationalist or Church of England.

and, 'The *cha-arge*' for that feeble refection was—2 / 6d! Already I had paid one pound eight and 6 sixpence for the train—it was going to be a most unexpectedly costly journey to me! But for *that* reflection I could almost have laughed at my forlorn position there. The Inn and Town were 'so disagreeable' that I went presently back to the station prefering to wait *there*. One of the men who had informed me about the coach came to me as I was sitting on a bench and remarked on the beauty of the scene, especially of some scarlet beans that were growing in *his own* piece of garden— 'Ah'! he said 'I have lived in London and I have lived abroad—I have been here and there, backwards and forwards, while I was in service, *with them as never could rest*; but Im satisfied now, that the only contentment for Man is in growing his own VEGETABLE'! 'Look at them beans' he said again—'Well! tomorrow they'll be ready and I'll be pulling them, and boiling them, and—eating them! and *such* a taste! No agriculture like *that* in Piccadilly!' Then he looked sympathisyingly at *me* and said—'Im going to get you something you'll like—and that's a glass of cool, fresh, clear water![']—and he went away with a jug to his garden and fetched some water from a little spring well—and a great handful of mignionette—[15] 'There! there's something sweet for you, and here's splendid water!—that you wont find the like of in Piccadilly.' I asked him how it was going with Mr Bennet? 'Huh! I hear no complaints! but *I* goes to neither one nor other of them and follows my own notions! *I* finds agriculture the thing!' He would have been worth a hundred pounds to Dickens that man! I had *the coach* all to myself for a while, then a young gentleman got in who did exactly the right thing by me, neither spoke to me nor looked at me—till we stopt at Castle Carry (*Yeovil* pronounced Youghel?— *Castle Carry*? I grew quite frightened that I had been somehow transported into Ireland!)[16] There the Young Gentleman went into the Inn and said to me first, '*Excuse the liberty I take in asking*; but—*would* you take anything—a little wine and water'? I thought *that* very *polite*; but I was to meet with 'something more exquisite still' before I got to Sherborne. At the Sparkford Inn[17]—eight miles from Sherborne—I got out and asked had they a *fly*— '*Yes*! but one of its wheels was broken and it was gone to be mended'! Had they any other conveyance that was *whole*—a gig, or cart? 'Yes they

15. The tall and fragrant flowering plant, *Reseda*, much favoured by the Victorians in countering city smells.
16. Castle *Cary* (pronounced to rhyme with 'mary') is a town a few miles north-east of Yeovil; Castle *Cahir* (pronounced 'care') in County Tipperary, Ireland, was taken by Cromwell in 1649 during his Irish campaign.
17. Still in existence in the village of that name, halfway between Castle Cary and Yeovil, and due north of Sherborne.

had a nice little gig and I should have the loan of a cloak to keep me warm'—(the evening was rather chill)— So I went in—and sat down in a parlour where an old gentleman was finishing off with cheese and bread. He soon made himself master of my case, and regretted he was not going back to Sherborne that night, as then he would have taken me in *his* carriage—and presently he offered something else more practical, viz: to try to recover my parasol (my Mother's, the one she bought with the Sovereign you gave her, and which I had got new covered) left stupidly in the roof of the coach, and never recollected till the coach with its four horses had thundered past the window! If the Landlord would tell the coachman about it next day, and get it there, he, the old Gentleman, would bring it to Sherborne House. I went into the Lobby to tell the Landlady, some five or eight minutes after the coach had started, and told her in presence of a gentleman who was preparing to start in a *barouchette* with two horses—[18] He looked at me, but said nothing—and a minute or two after I saw *him* also drive past the window. Some twenty minutes after; I started myself, in a little gig, with a brisk little horse, and silent driver— Nothing could be more pleasant—than so *pirring* [whirring along] thro' quiet roads in the dusk—with the moon coming out— I felt as if I were *reading about myself in a Miss Austin novel*! But it got beyond *Miss Austin* when at the end of some three miles before a sort of Carrier's Inn, the gentleman of the barouchette stept into the middle of the road, making a sort of military signal to my driver, which he repeated with impatience when the man did not at once draw up!— I sat confounded—expecting what he *would* do next. We had halted; the gentleman came to my side, and said exactly as in a book 'Madam! I have the happiness of informing you that I have reclaimed your parasol and it is here in my carriage ready to be restored!' 'But how on earth'? I asked— 'Madam I judged that it would be more with yourself, than to trust to its being brought by the other gentleman— So I just galloped my horses, overtook the coach as it was leaving this court, reclaimed the parasol, and have waited here—knowing you could take no other road to Sherborne—for the happiness of presenting it to you!—(to an ostler) bring the parasol!' It was brought and handed to me—and then I found myself making a speech in the same style, caught by the infection of the thing. I said; 'Sir! this day has been full of mischances for me, but I regard this recovery of my parasol so unexpectedly as a good omen, and have a confidence that I shall now reach my destination in safety— accept my thanks tho' it is impossible to give any adequate expression to my sense of your courtesy'! I never certainly made so long and

18. A four-wheeled light carriage with a collapsible leather hood.

formal a speech in my life! And how I came to make any thing like it I cant imagine unless it were under mesmerism! We bowed to each other like first cousins of Sir Charles Grandison[19]—and I *pirred* on— Do you know that gentleman? I asked my driver[.] 'Never saw him before'— I found Sherborne House without difficulty—and a stately beautiful house it was and a kind welcome it had for me— The mistake had been discovered in the morning and great anxiety felt all day as to my fate—

I was wonderfully little tired and able to make them all (*her* too) laugh with my adventures— But I must positively interrupt this penny a lining and go to bed— It is true TO THE LETTER all I have told. My two days at Sherborne House were as happy as could possibly be with that fearfully emaciated dying woman before my eyes. They were all doing their best to be cheerful[,] herself as cheerful as the others. She never spoke of her death except in taking leave of me; when she took my head in her hands and kissed it and gave me her solemn blessing and asked me to come again, with *you*, to see William and the children when *she* should be gone— *That* was a dreadful trial of my composure[.] I am so glad I went[—]it pleased her and all of them so much! The journey back by Dorchester went all right—and was less expensive, for I came by the second class, so saved the nine shillings my *gig* had cost me. It was a weary long way however—from a quarter before nine till half after seven flying along in one shape or other—with only ten minutes delay—(at Southampton)[.][20] My only *adventure* on the road back was falling in with a young *Unfortunate Female* in the Chelsea boat, the strangest compound of Angel and Devil that I ever set eyes on, and whom, had I been a great, rich Lady, I should decidedly have—brought home to tea with me, and tried 'to *save*'! The helpless thought that *I* had nothing to offer her INSTEAD alone prevented me— I could not leave her however without—speaking to her!—and my words were so moving,—thro my own emotion,—that she rushed from me *in tears* to the other side of the vessel. You may feel a *certain* curiosity to know what I said. I hardly recollect—something about 'her Mother, alive or dead—and her evident superiority to the life she was leading.' She said '*do you think so Mam*['], with a look of bitter wretchedness and forced gaiety that I

19. The eponymous hero of Samuel Richardson's epistolary novel of 1753, much admired by Miss Austen: an impossibly noble and high-minded gentleman, who rescues the heroine from one of Richardson's amoral rakes. A dull version of *Clarissa*, for many readers.

20. Sherborne to Dorchester is twenty miles due south; Dorchester (Dorset) to Southampton (Hampshire) is fifty miles due east; but from there Jane could travel the seventy-five miles to London on the London and Southwestern Railway, up to Nine Elms on the southern bank of the Thames, for a boat upriver to Chelsea.

shall never forget— [S]he was trying to *smile* defiantly, when she burst into tears and ran away.

I dont know very well where to direct to you now—it is long since I got your last letter—on Sunday at Sherborne—but one is not always in the humour for writing letters, and then it is best *not to write* them.

Friday morning

If you are at Scotsbrig, tell John I was very glad of *his long*(!) kind letter on my return, and will answer it when I have heard from Miss Macready to whom I wrote immediately on receiving it.

I made a frantic appeal to the workmen the other day, since when we have been getting on a little more briskly— The *spokesman* of them, a *dashing* young man, whom you have not seen answered me—'My *dear*(!) Madam! you must have *patience*! indeed you must! it will be all done—*some day*!' Mr Morgan has been 'down with Mr Helps'—came at last the day before yesterday—'told a flattering tale'[.][21] I have one really capital, swift, and thorough workman the Painter who is now painting in your bedroom— *He* is from Newcastle on Tyne— [T]hanks God!—I am not at all troubled with the smell down here—nor even in my bedroom; with the windows open—which they would be, were no painting going on—the weather is most lovely,—'*Monsieur* Le *Thermometre*' pretty generally at 70. My health continues wonderfully good— The day after my return from Sherborne I thought, in the afternoon that I was in for a bad headach—and lay down on the sofa with a wet cloth on my head—to endure—in five minutes I went to sleep amidst the raging noise— Martha coming into the room without having awoken me, 'did not know whether I was asleep or in a faint I looked so dead'—and went away without ascertaining!! half an hour after I awoke out of this *deep* sleep, unprecedented in my history; the headach quite gone—and my *memory* quite gone! for some ten minutes[.] Then it came gradually back and I went out for a walk quite well—

Today I dine at the Brookfields—for what poor Helen used to call 'a fine change'

And now to Father Son and Tally Gohast.

Ever yours affecty / Jane W C [. . .]

21. A popular and dismal air by Giovanni Paisiello, published in England in 1830: 'Hope told a flatt'ring tale / That joy would soon return', and so forth.

To Thomas Carlyle, Chelsea, 10–11 August 1852

Oh my Dear! What a comfortless letter! In your last from Linlathen you said you were 'decidedly better,' and now you seem to be again '*all nohow*'! I hope it has only been the fag of the journey. Dont fret about the house; it is getting on pretty fast now, and *will* be satisfactory when finished. For my part I am got quite used to the disturbance, and begin to like the what shall I say?—*excitement* of it—to see something *going on* and to help its going on fulfils a great want of my nature! I have prevented so many mistakes being made, and afforded so many capital suggestions, that I begin to feel rather proud of myself, and to suspect I must have been a *Builder* in some previous state of existence. The Painter is my chief delight, he does his work so *thoroughly*; he is only in your bedroom as yet, but he has rubbed it all down with pumice stone till it looks as smooth as paper. And I have never been at all inconvenienced by any smell!— Perhaps the house may be *habitable* a week or two sooner than I guessed, tho' I hardly think the workmen will be fairly out of it sooner— I shall 'see my way' better next week— The weather is capital for drying both paint and plaster—that is one blessing! My *half* of the low room is kept always tidy—the bedding, and tables with their legs in the air, as if in convulsions which show themselves *above* the screen often make me laugh— When the noise is *very* great I *practice* on the piano! I do quite well in short, and dont see how I can be spared till things are done to my mind, and the chaotic heaps of furniture restored to their proper places[.] Decidedly nobody but myself can do *that*.

I found your letter today on my return from Tavistock House where I had gone to see Forster.[22] He is staying there *for a change* in the absence of the Dickenses— I had promised the Macreadys to go and tell him about *her* [Catherine], and found no time till today. I went by the boat to Paul's warf, like a goose, and found myself so far off my destination![23] Besides, a violent thunder shower fell just as I set my foot on land, and having on a pair of those *cheap* boots I bought a *stock of*—(chiefly paper Mr Carlyle!) [m]y feet were wet thro in two minutes— I went into a shop and bought a pair of stockings, then on till I found a good looking shoeshop and bought a pair of *real* boots[,] left my dripping stockings and paper boots with the Shoemaker, requesting that when they were dry—and not till then—he would pack them up and send them to the care of Forster—and so proceeded on my long walk dry-shod—

22. The Dickens family lived at Tavistock House, in the Bloomsbury square of that name, from 1851 to 1860, and Charles wrote *Bleak House*, *Hard Times* and *Little Dorrit* there; his friend John Forster was staying there while the Dickenses were in Kent. The building was demolished in 1901.
23. From Chelsea to Bloomsbury one must head east, but Jane has overshot by two miles, to St Paul's in the City.

[C]leverly managed dont you think 'regardless of expense'? Forster was very glad to see me, he is a *little* less helpless—but still on fish diet— I got into a Holborn omnibus after, which left me at the top of Regent Street, and then I went to Verey's and had—a beautiful little mutton chop! and a glass of bitter ale![24] That is the sort of things I do!— It was my second dinner at Vereys, *meat dinners* at home are as nearly impossible as can be—and one sleeps ill on tea dinners[.] [T]he *chaarge* at Vereys is very moderate and the cooking *perfect.* [F]or my dinner and ale today I paid one and five pence. The day I went to the Foundry I dined at a clean looking shop in the Strand, where I had half a roast chicken (warm very small indeed) a large slice of warm ham and three new potatoes for one shilling! It amuses me all that; besides keeping me in health and for the outrage to '*delicate female'ism* I am beyond all such considerations at present. However I see single women besides myself at Vereys—*not* improper—governesses and the like— And now goodnight I am off to bed

Wednesday

Ah! it is a tempting of Providence always, to congratulate oneself on the weather! Today, it 'is pouring hale water' (as Helen used to say) and has so poured all night— If it weren't for the paint and plaster's sake I should have no objection. I called at the London Library yesterday on my way home—to get Me de Staals Memoires for Count Reichenbach[.][25] Mr Donne never comes out of that end room seemingly— Mr Jones was 'absent three days for a little pleasuring'— The tall young man was on the eve of his departure—had 'found, on trial of six years, that the place didn't suit him'— He was going to embark in a silk manufactory at Derby—'a very good opening indeed.'

Mrs Humphrey Mildmay,[26] did I tell you, left your books and a *Card* for me, *just before leaving town*— Dilberoglue might surely call that

24. Verrey's on Hanover Street, off Regent Street, was something of an institution at the time, founded by a Swiss and, it has been said, the first French restaurant in London—though Jane orders an impeccably English dinner.

25. Marguerite Jeanne Cordier de Launay, Baronne de Staal (1684–1750), author of a famous set of *Mémoires*, published in 1755, recounting a chequered and passionate life around the French aristocracy. Donne was one of the London librarians. German politician Oskar von Reichenbach (1815–1893), who exiled himself to London after the events of 1848, was married to Hedwig Plattnauer, sister of the Carlyles' mad friend; they emigrated to the US in 1853.

26. Marianne Frances Harcourt-Vernon (1814–1873), second wife of Humphrey St John-Mildmay (1794–1853), partner in Barings and future governor of the Bank of England; Humphrey's first wife had been the 1st Baron Ashburton's daughter, which probably explains his success as a merchant banker. The Farrers are Mary, mother of two daughters, Annie Louisa and Mary, of whom the former was the Carlyles' closest acquaintance: as Thomas told Dr John on 11 September 1848, 'a rather pretty, rather reasonable, and most cheerful and agreeable young soul' (*CL*).

'*glorious* prudence'!— Nevertheless she might have safely relied on her own powers of *boring* me—and on *my* general indisposition to *intrude*! god help us! I dont know of any fine people remaining except the Farrers who cant get away for fear of their house being robbed. Mazzini was here on Sunday morning and made my hair stand on end with his projects— If he dont be shot, or in an Austrian Fortress *within the month*!; it will be more by good luck than good guiding. I rely on the promise 'God is kind to women fools and drunk people.'

Kind love to your Mother and all of them— After going all that way to Sherborne for *two* days, who knows whether I shant run to Scotsbrig for two days, and see her when she is not thinking of me— Ever yours

J W C

If you wont go to Germany alone, and dont much like the notion; is there no little lodging to be got by the sea side within reach of Scotsbrig butter and eggs for two or three weeks—for *yourself* I mean—

To Thomas Carlyle, Moffat, 8 July 1853

And my letter must be in the Postoffice before *one* o'clock! 'very absurd'!—and I have had to go to Beattock in the Omnibus with my cousin Helen to see HER off for Glasgow—and am so tired!— Dont wonder then if you get a 'John's letter' from me also.[27] The most important thing I have to tell you is that you could not know me here as I sit from a red Indian! that I was kept awake the first night after my arrival by a—*Hyæna*! (yes upon my honour! and *you* complain of a simple *cock*!) and that yesterday I was as near as possible for giving occasion for the most romantic paragraph of the 'melancholy accident' nature that has appeared in any newspaper for some years! But first of the Hyæna. [O]n my arrival I found an immense caravan of Wild Beasts pitched exactly in front of this House and they went on their way during the night and the animal in question made a devil of a row— I thought it was the Lion roaring but John said 'no—it was ONLY the Hyeana'! I rather enjoyed the oddness of having fled into the country for 'quiet' and being kept awake by *Wild Beasts*! Well having got no sleep the first night owing to these Beasts and my faceach—I felt very bothered all Wednesday, and gladly accepted Johns offer to tell you of my safe

27. Jane was visiting Moffat House, in the Dumfries spa town of that name, where brother John now lived with his wife Phoebe. A 'John's letter', Thomas tells us (*CL*), was 'Too brief generally'.

arrival, meaning to write myself yesterday—but it was settled that we should go yesterday to see St Mary's Loch and the Grey-Mares Tail—[28] [W]e started at nine of the morning in an open carriage—'the Dr' and Phoebe, a tall, red-haired young woman with a hoarse voice, who is here on a visit ('the Bridesmaid' she was)[,] my cousin Helen & one little boy and myself—the other two boys preceding us on horseback. It was the loveliest of days and beautifuler scenery I never beheld; besides that it was full of tender interest for me, as the birth place of my mother—no pursuit of the Picturesque had ever gone better with me till, on the way back when we stopt to take a nearer inspection of the Tail— The Boys had been left fishing in the loch of the Lows—John and Miss Hutchison had gone over the hills by another road to look at Loch Skeen and were to meet us at The Tail[,] so there was only Phoebe Helen and I went up to the Tail from underneath— We went on together to the customary point of view and then I scrambled on by myself (that is with Nero) from my habitual tendency to go a little further always than the rest— Nero grew quite frightened and pressed against my legs and when we came close in front of the Waterfall he stretched his neck out at it from under my petticoats and then barked furiously—Just then I saw John waving his hat to me from the top of the hill—and *excited* by the grandeur of the scene I quite forgot how old I was[,] how out of the practice of 'speeling [climbing] rocks,' and quite forgot too that John had made me take the night before a double doze of morphia which was still in my head making it very light—and I began to climb up the precipice!!— [F]or a little way I got on well enough but when I discovered that I was *climbing up a ridge* (!)—that the precipice was not only behind but on *both sides* of me—I grew, for the first time in my life that I remember of, *frightened—physically* frightened— I was not only afraid of *falling* down—but of losing my head to the extent of *throwing* myself down— [T]o go back on my hands and knees as I had come up was impossible—my only chance was to look at the grass under my face and toil on till John should see me— I tried to call to him but my tongue stuck fast and dry to the roof of my mouth— Nero barking with terror and keeping close to my head still further confused me—John had meanwhile been descending the hill; and holding by the grass [we] reached one another. [H]e said hold on—dont give way to panic I will stand between you and everything short of death— We had now got off the ridge onto the slope of the

28. The Grey Mare's Tail is a precipitous waterfall below Loch Skeen in the Moffat Valley: 'Lofty cataract in the green wilderness left altogether to itself,' Thomas notes (*CL*); 'the most impressive I ever looked on.' St Mary's Loch is a remarkably still and sheltered lake fifteen miles north of Moffat; the Loch of the Lowes is adjacent to it.

Hill but *it* was so steep that in the *panic* I had taken my danger was extreme for the next quarter of an hour— [T]he bed of a torrent had been for a long time the object of my desire— I thought I should stick faster there than on the glassy slope with the precipice at the bottom of it[,] but John called to me that 'if I got among those stones I should roll to perdition'[.] He was very kind, encouraging me all he could—but no other assistance was possible— In my life I was never so thankful as when I found myself at the bottom of that hill with a glass of water to drink— None of them knew the horrors I had suffered—for I made no screaming or crying—but my face they said was *purple* all over with a large black spot under each eye—and today I still retain something of the same complexion and I am all of a tremble, as if I had been on the rack—

It is a lovely place this—and a charming oldfashioned house with 'grounds' to the back— It is comfortably but plainly and old-fashionedly furnished—looks as if it had been stript of all its *ornamental* details—and just the *necessaries* left— There is a cook housemaid and Ladys-maid and everything goes on very nicely— The three boys are as clever well behaved boys as I ever saw and seem excessively fond of 'the Doctor'— John is kind as kind can be and seems to have an excellent gift of making his guests comfortable— Phoebe's *manner* is so different from mine—so formal and cold, that I dont feel at ease with her yet— [S]he looks to me like a woman who had been all her life made the *first* person with those she lived beside and to feel herself in a *false position* when she doubts her *superiority* being recognized— [S]he seems very content with John however and to suit him entirely— My hand shakes so you must excuse illegibility[;] I dont know yet when I am to go to Scotsbrig

[no signature]

To Thomas Carlyle, Scotsbrig, 20 July 1853

I dare say you have thought me very neglectful Dear in not writing yesterday, to give you news of your Mother; but there was nothing comfortable or even positive to be said yesterday, and to torture you at a distance with miserable uncertainty seemed a cruel attention. Thro' Saturday and Sunday your Mother continued much the same as I found her on my last coming. Too weak and frail to be out of bed; but without pain or sickness—for the rest perfectly clear in her mind, and liking us to be in the room talking to her. During the Sunday night, she became very restless and about seven on Monday morning she fell into a state which was considered by all here, the *Minister* included, to be the beginning of the end— There was no pain no struggle— She lay without sense or motion, cold and deathlike, hardly breathing at all— The Minister prayed without her hearing him— John and Mary were sent for with scarce a hope that they could arrive in time and all of us sat in solemn silence awaiting the end— Had it come thus, you would have had no cause to lament Dear, a more merciful termination there could not have been to a good Life. But after lying in this state from seven in the morning till a quarter after two in the day—she rallied as by miracle—Jane was wiping her lips with a wet sponge when she (your Mother) suddenly took the sponge out of Jane's hand and sponged her face all over with her own hand then she opened her eyes, and spoke quite collectedly as if nothing had happened; nor has she ever shown the least consciousness of having come thro' that fearful crisis. When John and Mary arrived together at a quarter after four, not expecting to find her alive they found her a *little* weaker perhaps, but not otherwise worse than when they left her. She talked a good deal to *me* during the afternoon, said you had been as good a son to her as ever woman had—'but indeed they had been all good bairns—and Isabella puir bodie, was guy distressed hersell and it was just to say, that Isabella had been often kind to her, extrordnar kind—and was ay kindest when they were alain thegither, and she had none else to depend on.'— *That* I can well believe!—and very glad I was to have those kind words to carry to Jamie and Isabella— Isabella had been crying all morning; for since Jane came your Mother had hardly spoken to her. When I left your Mother that night[,] she said in a clear loud voice 'I thank ye most kindly for all yeer attentions'— 'Oh if I *could* but do you any good[,]' I said. 'Ye *have* done me good—mony a time,' she answered. I went to bed to lie awake all night listening for noises—John slept in the midroom— But the light of a new day found your Mother better rather than worse— It was more the recollection of the state in which she *had been* than her actual state that kept us in agitation all yesterday— [O]ne thing that leads me to believe her life will be prolonged is that she recovered out of *that* crisis, by the *natural* strength that was still in her[;] she must have been *much* stronger than anyone thought to have rallied after so many hours of such deathlike prostration—*entirely of herself.* She had been in the habit of getting what seems to me perfectly extraordinary quantities of wine, whisky and porter[,] exciting a false strength not to be depended on for an hour— Of late days this system has discontinued and she takes now only little drops of wine and water two or three times a day and about the third of a Tumbler of guiness' porter at night. The day that John was sent for last week he told me himself she had 'a *bottle* of wine (strong greek wine) a quarter of a bottle of whisky (25 over proof) besides a tumbler of porter!'— A life kept up in that way was neither to be depended on nor I should say to be desired— Now she is living on her own strength such as it is and you may conceive what irritation is removed—

I dont know whether it is to be considered lucky or unlucky that I came at this time— Of course I give as little trouble as possible and make myself as useful as possible— And I feel sure that *Jamie* and *Isabella like* me to be here even under these sad circumstances—and that the sight of me coming and going in her room does your Mother good rather than harm—and then I shall be able to answer all your questions about her when I come back, better than the others could do by letter. For the rest; I doubt not I am in *John's* way, and perhaps a little in *Jane*'s, as I absolutely decline entering into her *views* of Jamie and Isabella—who as I told herself had never either of *them* said to me one unkind word about *her*. As for Mary she is the same kindly soul as I knew her at Craigenputtoch— Jamie was to have driven me over to the Gill on Monday and instead the empty gig was sent to bring Mary here— She ran out of the house to meet *me* and was told her Mother was at the point of death— She is still here but goes home tomorrow I believe, and John goes back to Moffat today— He will probably be down again tomorrow— It is a comfort to himself to come—but he can *do* nothing—no Dr *can* do anything against old age—which is your Mothers whole disease—

I shall be home one of these days[;] any little spirits for visiting and travelling that I had left are completely worn out by what I have found here. I only wait till things are reestablished in a state in which I can leave with comfort—

I have just been to see if your Mother had awoke— She has slept two hours— I asked her if she had any message for you—and she said 'none I am afraid that he will like to hear—for he'll be sorry that Im so frail'— She had had some chicken broth— I will write after tomorrow—and I beseech you not to be fancying her ill off in *any* way. She has no pain, no anxiety of mind—is more comfortable really, lying in bed there 'so frail,' than we have often seen her going about after her work. She is attended to every moment of the day—gets every thing she is able to take— No one can predict as to the length of her life after what we saw on Monday—but there is *nothing* in her *actual* state or appearance to make it impossible or even improbable that she should live a long time yet—

I would much rather *not* have written today—but I judged that my silence might alarm you even more than the truth told you— I like few things worse than writing ill news

Ever affly yours /

J W Carlyle

I had a very kind letter from Jeannie Crystal[29] pressing me to go there for a week or two—but as I have said I am quite out of heart—I have had no sleep the last *two* nights and shall get none *now* probably till I am in my own bed at Chelsea

It is quite *affecting* Jamie's *devoted* attention to me— If I am but out one half an hour for a walk he will follow me to my bedroom—no matter how early in the day, carrying (very awkwardly you may be sure) a little tray with a decanter of wine—(*not* the 'greek wine' but wine bought for me by himself) and a plateful of shortbread—Nor can anybody be more heartily and politely kind than Isabella has been to me

My remembrances to [housemaid] Fanny—

To Charles Redwood, Chelsea, 25 December 1853

My dear Mr Redwood

It falls to me—this time to acknowledge with thanks the arrival of your never-failing Christmas gifts—since it falls to me—alas—to eat them 'all to myself' (as the children say)![30]

Mr Carlyle and I were on a visit at Lord Ashburtons which commenced on the 4th of December and was to have lasted till about newyears day. But last Monday I was despatched to London about certain—*Cocks*! and a *Macaw*! which you have perhaps heard of—'the great first Cause least understood'[31] of that 'Silent apartment' which Mr C built this summer at an outlay of some 200£[.] The Silent Apartment having proved a complete failure[,] having proved in fact *the* apartment most accessible to sound in the whole house (no wonder! having 14 air-holes in frank and free communication with the before

29. Jeannie Welsh ('Babbie'), from Liverpool; now married and living in Glasgow. Their vivid correspondence would now run dry.

30. For Redwood, see 18 July 1843, above. As a Welshman he had sent Jane some lamb to eat: see below.

31. Alexander Pope, 'The Universal Prayer', deistically addressed to 'Jehovah, Jove, or Lord', all being ultimately names for the same invisible supreme being.

and behind!)[,] it became imperative, that unless we were both to be landed in Bedlam[—]*he* thro' these Demon-birds and I thro their effects on *him*—some thing else should be done of real efficacy—*Poisoning* them was his fixed idea; but *that* I held him back from all I could—especially at this time of the year when the newspapers have no *debates* to fill *their* pages,[32]—such a recourse would have been questionable. It was finally settled we should try to *take* the house no 6 ourselves for three years and eject the present occupants—*if we could*—and to achieve *this* I was sent to Chelsea 'quite promiscuously'— To be in time for the Xmas term, the utmost despatch was needed— The fine people at the Grange, were greatly *amused* as well as astonished to see a Wife sent off from the midst of Xmas festivities to consult with house agents and house owners— But Mr C was quite right in insisting 'She can do it better than I'— Decidedly he had neither the temper nor the dexterity(!) to bring this romantic undertaking to the happy issue *I* have brought it to— For I not only *got* the house but got rid of it when gotten, and by the potency of a notice to quit got rid of the whole lot of birds in consideration of a present of 5£—and have my neighbour *legally* bound at this moment 'not to keep or allow to be kept on these premises any birds *or other nuisance* under penalty of 10£ and a notice to quit'— I will *tell* you someday how I managed it— Meanwhile I am here still, all alone—with painters (of the Silent apartment) in the house creating an atmosphere! Mr C receiving from Scotland daily letters about his Mother's increasing weakness, felt when left behind at the Grange that it would be much more suitable he should go to Scotland and see her once more than stay on amidst these festivities[,] and so he came to town last Wednesday and started for Scotsbrig on Thursday night. I was very urgent to hurry him off, since he WAS going; for fear of his finding his Mother no more— I know what *that* is!—dashing along a railway in agonies of impatience and uncertainty to be told at the end 'your Mother is dead'— I have had a few lines from him to say he had found her still alive and glad to see him—tho in the last stage of weakness—

Dear Mr Redwood, my penmanship is not always so bad as this— But I have been so excited the last week—I cant even *write* as usual— I

32. As Parliament was on its winter break the newspapers would be short of news, and would pick up on local scandal. The 'Xmas term' is a legal date by which tenants can be given notice of eviction and new rents established. The Carlyles contacted the estate agent managing No. 6 and via his good offices threatened the Ronca family with eviction if birds continued to offend, having paid them £5 to get rid of the ones they had; a far better solution than becoming landlords in their own right.

have dined on your mutton today and shall grow fat on all these nice things— Thank you heartily for him and for myself

Truly yours /
Jane Carlyle

To Thomas Carlyle, Chelsea, 27 December 1853

Oh my Dear! Never does one feel oneself so utterly helpless as in trying to speak comfort for a great bereavement. I will not try it. Time is the only Comforter for the loss of a Mother. One does not believe in Time while the grief is quite new. One feels as if it could never be less and yet all griefs, when there is no *bitterness* in them, are soothed down by Time. And *your* grief for your Mother must be altogether sweet and soft. For you must feel that you have always been a good son to her, that you have always appreciated her as she deserved, and that she knew this, and loved you to the last moment. How thankful we may be that you went when you did, in time to have the assurance of her love surviving all bodily weakness, made doubly sure to you by her last look and words. Oh what *I* would have given for *last words*; to keep in my innermost heart all the rest of my Life—but the words that awaited *me* were; 'your Mother is DEAD'!— And I deserved it should so end— I was not the dutiful child to my Mother that you have been to yours.

Strange that I should have passed that Sunday in such utter seclusion here—as if in sympathy with what was going on there.

It is a great mercy you have had *some* sleep. It will surely be a comfortable reflection for you in coming home this time, that you will look out over a perfectly empty hencourt,—part of it even already pulled down, as all the rest, I dare say, will soon be. There are cocks enough in all directions, as poor Shuttleworth remarked; but none will plague you like these which had become a fixed idea, and a question, shall I, a man of Genius, or you 'a sooty washerman' be master here? If you would like to know the ultimate fate of the poultry; it was sold away to a Postman, who has 'a hobby for fowls,' in Milman's Row.[33] I let them make what profit they could of their fowls—for we had no *right* to deprive them of them—only the right of hummanity to have the people forced to do us a favour voluntarily for a suitable compensation. I am on terms of good

33. Local street of low repute, given over to second-hand clothes stores and poor-quality housing.

neighbourhood now with all the Roncas except the old Laundress herself—who 'took to her bed *nearly mad*,' the married daughter told me, 'at *lying under a penalty*'— 'She must leave the place' she said—'her husband would sooner have died than broken his word, *when he had passed it* and to be bound under a penalty'!! I got quite sorry for the people so soon as I had got them in my power, and have done what I could to sooth them down.

Chorley has just brought me my money—how absurd to plague you about *that* at such a moment. He came after your second letter of today—(the one I should have had last night came at nine—the second at 2) and told me very kindly to say all that was kind from him. He would not write, for 'nothing could be written.' I am glad to hear poor Jane is gone Home—

My love to Jamie and Isabella who are now all that remain beside you I suppose— Come the end of the week or stay a little while— Do whatever best suits yourself[.] You will be welcome or I can await

Ever yours /
JWC

To Isabella Carlyle, Chelsea, 28 August 1854

Oh my dear Isabella what a horrible thing! I do not know if *he* have written to you himself. I write in case he has not, to tell you that Mrs John died on Saturday night at nine o'clock— After finishing my letter to you, I was on my way to some warm baths in this neighbourhood, to take one, feeling very unwell, and my friend Geraldine who was with me, having insisted a warm bath would do me good, when Dr Carlyle jumped out of a cab that met us, to say he had been going to our house to say that Phoebe had just been delivered of a dead child— [T]he whole thing had passed over in ten minutes— Dr Rigby was leaving the house when the nurse ran after him to say she was sure Mrs C was in labour—he returned and the child was already half born— She was 'doing well' John said and leapt into his cab again and drove home. I came home to tell Mr Carlyle then I went and had the bath and then I went to bed to keep quite still— [B]etween 8 and 9 Marianne Mrs John['s] maid was shown up to my bedroom— She had come to see if I could give them 'a quantity of napkins'—they had not any of the necessary linen at all—a boxful all ready packed had been left at Moffat!! and here were they as ill off as the poorest people!— She said her mistress had had a dreadful flooding [uterine haemorrhage] which if Dr Hunter had not been at hand to stop would have carried her off[,] but now she was all right— I sent for Geraldine Jewsbury to take Marianne to a shop where everything needed could be got ready made—for among us all we could not raise as many things as would be needed— They had been gone about a quarter of an hour when Mr Carlyle came into my room crying out 'Oh my Dear! my Dear! what a thing![']— I said 'She is dead!'— 'Yes she is dead'!— Just in the brief time of her maid's absence who had never left her all the week the poor woman had expired— She was lying quite quiet when something came over her like a return of the fits with which her illness began—it never came to a fit exactly but her breathing became weaker and weaker till it ceased— [A] woman who had gone up from here with some sheets she had been washing in a hurry for them, had brought the news— Mr Carlyle went up immediately and did not return till about 12 when he brought John to sleep here. He continues to sleep here but is at his own lodging during the day— [T]he funeral is to be on Wednesday. [T]he poor baby who was to have been put under ground the night of its birth to be buried now with its mother— It was a large fine Baby Marianne told me—a boy and 'so like the Doctor'— All this horrible tragedy resulting[,] Dr Rigby is perfectly sure[,] from the fright she got on the railway, three days before the fits began— Oh if they had only been poor people, with no time or money for racketting about, she might have born him a living son and they might have been very happy over it. He is in a strange stupified state—indeed we are all quite stunned. When Dr Rigby came a little after nine for the fourth time that day, thinking after the flooding had been stopt she might still recover, he almost fainted with the shock of being told she was dead.

I suppose the Dr will be about here for some time settling their affairs. What he will do after I cant think—thrown all at sea again[,] without so much as a house of his own for a fixed point—

I will write again when I have anything to tell that Jamie and you may care to know—I feel so sick and nervous that I can settle to nothing

God keep you both

Affectionately yours /

Jane Carlyle

Nothing can be more kind and gentle than Mr Carlyle is with John

To Thomas Carlyle, Chelsea, 12 February 1855

BUDGET *of a Femme incomprise* [misunderstood woman]

I dont choose to *speak* again on the *Money Question*. The 'replies[']' from the Noble Lord[34] are unfair, and unkind, and little to the purpose. When you tell me I 'pester your life out about money'—that 'your soul is sick with hearing about it'—that I 'had better make the money I *have* serve, at all rates—hang it!—let *you* alone of it'; *all that* I call perfectly unfair, the reverse of kind, and tending to nothing—but disagreement—

If I were greedy, or extravagant, or a bad manager; you would be justified in 'staving me off' with loud words: but you cannot say *that* of me (whatever else) cannot *think* it of me! At least I am sure I never 'asked for more'[35]—to myself—from you or anyone—not even from my own Mother—in all my life; and that, thro' six and twenty years, I have kept house for you, at more or less cost according to given circumstances, but always on less than it costs the generality of People, living in the same style.— What I should have expected you to say, rather, would have been; 'My Dear! you *must* be dreadfully hampered in your finances, and dreadfully anxious and unhappy about it, and quite desperate of *making it do*; since *you* are "asking for more"! Make me *understand* the case then. I can and will help you out of that *sordid* suffering at least. Either by giving you "more," if that be found prudent to do; or by reducing our wants to within the present means.' *That* is the sort of thing you would have said, had you been a perfect man. So I suppose you are not a perfect man. Then; instead of crying in my bed half the night after, I would have explained my *Budget* to you in peace and confidence. But *now*; I am driven to explain it on paper, 'in a state of mind'! *driven*; for I *cannot*, it is not in my nature, to live 'intangled in the details.' And I *will* not! I would sooner hang myself—tho' 'pestering you about money' is also more repugnant to me than you dream of.

You 'dont understand why the allowance which sufficed in former years no longer suffices'?

That is what I would explain to the Noble Lord if he would but—what shall I say?—*keep his temper.*

34. Jane is couching her entire protest in terms of a debate in the House of Lords, with vocal interruptions from the benches ('Hear, hear' and so forth), and in which members address each other as 'my noble Lord': a debate, that is, about the Budget, such as takes place once a year in the Palace of Westminster.
35. Perhaps Jane is remembering the eponymous hero's pathetic request at meal time in the workhouse in Dickens' *Oliver Twist* (1838): 'Please sir, I want some more.'

The Beginning of my Embarrassments, it will not surprise the Noble Lord to learn—since it has also been 'the beginning of' almost every human ill to himself—was *The Repairing of the House*. There was a *destruction*, an *irregularity*, *an incessant recurrence of small incidental expenses*, during all that period, or *two* periods; thro which I found myself, in September gone a year, *ten* pounds behind, instead of having some pounds saved up toward the Winter Coals.— I could have worked round 'out of that' however in course of time; if habits of *unpinched* house-keeping had not been long taken by *you* as well as myself; and if new unavoidable, or not to be avoided; *current* expenses had not followed close on those incidental ones.— I will show the Noble Lord, with his permission, what the new current expenses *are* and to what they *amount, per annum*. ('*Hear*'! '*Hear*'! and cries of '*be brief*')

1st We have a Servant of 'higher grade,' than we ever ventured on before. More expensive in *money*. Ann's wages are *sixteen pounds* a year; Fanny's were *thirteen*;[36] most of the others had *twelve*. And Ann never dreams of being other than *well fed*; the others *scrambled* for their living out of ours. Her regular *meat*-dinner at one o'clock, regular allowance of butter &c adds *at least three pounds* to the *years* bills. But *she* plagues us with no fits of *illness* nor of *drunkenness* no *warnings* nor complainings; she does perfectly what she is *paid* and *fed* to do. I see houses not so well kept, with 'Cook' 'Housemaid' and 'Manservant.' ('*Question*'!) Ann is the *last* item, then, I should vote for retrenching in. I may set her down, however, at *six additional pounds*.

2d We have now *Gass* and *Water* 'laid on,' both producing an admirable result. But betwixt 'water laid on' at *one pound sixteen shillings* per annum, with *shilling* to Turncock, and water carried at fourpence a week, there is a yearly difference of nineteen shillings and fourpence; and betwixt *gass* all the year round, and a few sixpenny boxes of *lights* in the winter, the difference may be computed at *fifteen shillings*. These two excellent innovations, then, increase the yearly expenditure by *one pound fourteen and fourpence*. A trifle 'to speak of'; but you, my Lord, born and bred in thrifty Scotland must know well the proverb 'Every Little maks a Mickle [more]'—

3d We are higher *taxed*. Within the last eighteen months there has been added to the *Lighting Pavement and Improvement Rate ten shillings*, yearly; to the *Poor Rate one pound*, yearly; to the *Sewer Rate*

36. *CL* illuminates: 'Fanny had run off with one of the Irishmen at work on TC's new room, Sept. 1853. Anne succeeded her, Nov. 1853.' Anne would stay with Jane for five and a half years, but was dismissed in March 1858, to be succeeded by Charlotte Southam (Chapter 8).

(one cannot mention *it* without a curse) *ten shillings*, yearly[;] and now the doubled *Income Tax* makes a difference of *five pounds sixteen shillings and eightpence*, yearly. Which sums added together amounts to a difference of *seven pounds sixteen shillings and eightpence* yearly! On Taxes which already amounted to *seventeen pounds twelve shillings and eightpence*! 'There need be no reflections for want of *Taxes*!'

4th Provisions of all sorts are higher priced than in former years. *Four shillings* a week for bread, instead of *two shillings and sixpence* makes at the years end a difference of THREE POUNDS EIGHTEEN SHILLINGS! *Butter* has kept all the year round twopence a pound dearer than I ever knew it, instead of (fresh) at the cheapest season, salt 8 instead of a shilling. On the quantity we use, two pounds and a half per week, quite reg'lar—there is a difference of TWENTY-ONE SHILLINGS AND EIGHT PENCE, by the year.— *Butcher-meat* is a penny a pound dearer; At the rate of a pound and a half a day, *bones* inclusive (no exorbitant allowance for three people), the difference on that at the years end would be TWO POUNDS FIVE SHILLINGS AND SIXPENCE.— *Coals*, which had been for some years at twenty one shillings per ton, cost this year *twenty six* shillings; last year twenty nine—bought judiciously too! If I had had to pay fifty shillings a ton for them, as some housewives had TO, god knows what would have become of me! (Passionate cries of 'question'! 'Question!') We burn, or used to burn (I am afraid they are going faster this winter) *12 tons* one year with another. *Candles* are rizz. Composites a *shilling* a pound, instead of *tenpence*, dips eightpence instead of fivepence or sixpence; of the former we burn three pounds in nine days the greater part of the year (you sit so late), and of dips two pounds a fortnight on the average of the whole year. Bacon is twopence a pound dearer, soap ditto, Potatoes, at the cheapest, a penny a pound instead of three pounds for twopence. We use three pounds of potatoes in two days, neat. Who could imagine that, at the years end, *that* makes a difference of fifteen shillings and twopence! on ones mere potatoes! Compute all this, and you will find that the difference on *provisions* cannot be under TWELVE POUNDS in the year.

5th What I should blush to state, if I were not *at bay* (so to speak) [.] Ever since we have been in London *you* have, in the handsomest manner, paid the winter butter with *your own money*! tho' it was not 'in the bond.'[37] And this gentlemanly proceeding on your part, till the butter became uneatable, was a good TWO POUNDS saved me.

37. Shakespeare, *The Merchant of Venice*, IV. i. 262.

Add up these differences

	per annum	£	s.	d.
1st	Rise on *Servant*	6	0	0
2d	Rise on *Light and Water*	1	14	4
3d	Rise on Taxes	7	16	8
4th	Rise on Provisions	12	0	0
5th	Cessation of Butter	2	0	0
		29	11	0

and you will find a total of *twenty nine pounds eleven shillings.* My calculations, I think, will be found quite correct; tho' I am not strong in arithmetic, never could learn *the multiplication table* in my life.[38] But I have '*thochtered*['] all this well in my head; and *Indignation* make a sort of arithmetic as well as *verses*![39]

Do you finally understand why the allowance which sufficed formerly no longer suffices? and pity my difficulties instead of being angry at them?

The only thing you can reproach me with—*if you like*—is, that, fifteen months ago, when I found myself, already in debt and everything *rising* on me, I did not fall at once to *pinching* and *muddling* as when we didn't know where the next money was to come from; instead of 'lashing down' at the accustomed rate, nay, expanding into 'a regular servant.' But you are to recollect that when I first complained to you of the '*prices*,' (at Addiscombe it was); you said, quite goodnaturedly; 'Then, you are coming to Bankruptcy are you? not going to be able to *go on*, you think? Well, we must come to your assistance, poor *Crittur*; you mustn't be made a Bankrupt of!'— So I kept my mind easy, and *retrenched* in nothing; relying on the promised 'assistance.' But when 'Oh! it was lang o'coming, lang o'coming!' and my arrears taking every quarter a more alarming cipher; what *could* I do but put you in mind? Once—twice; at the *third* speaking, what you were pleasantly calling 'a *great heap of money*,' *fifteen pounds* (well wanted) was—'what shall I say?'—*flung* to me. Far from *leaving anything*, to meet the increased demand of another nine months; this sum did not clear me of *debt*—not by *five pounds*.— But from time to time, encouraging *words* fell from the Noble Lord; 'No! you cannot pay "the double-income-tax"; *clearly*! *I* must pay *that* for you.' And again; 'I WILLA burn as many "coals" as I like! if you "*can't*" pay them somebody must!' All resulting however, thus far, in '*don't you wish you may get it*?'— Decidedly, I should have needed to be

38. Untrue; as a child Jane was as talented a mathematician as a Latinist. See 11 January 1857, below.
39. Juvenal, *Satires*, i. 79.

more than mortal, or else a 'born *Daughter* of Chaos,'[40] to have gone on without attempt ever made at ascertaining what *coming to my assistance* specifically meant? whether it meant 15£ without a blessing, once for all? and if so, what retrenchments were to be *permitted*?

You asked me at last money-row, with 'withering sarcasm;' 'had I the *slightest* idea what amount of money would *satisfy* me? Was I wanting *fifty* pounds more? or *forty*? or thirty? Was there any conceivable sum of money that could put an end to my eternal botheration?'— I will answer the question as if it had been asked practically, and kindly.

Yes! I have the *strongest* idea what amount of money would 'satisfy' me. I have computed it often enough as I lay awake at night; and 'didn't I wish I might get it?'— [I]ndeed, when I can't sleep now, it is my 'difficulties' I think about, more than my sins; till they become 'a real mental agony in my own inside!'— The above-named sum 29£, divided into quarterly payments would *satisfy* me. (With a *certain* parsimony about *little* things; somewhat less might do.) I engaging my word of Gentlewoman, to *give* back at the year's end, whatever portion thereof any diminution of the *Demand* on me might enable me to save.

I am not so unpractical, however as to ask for whole 29£, pounds, without thought or care where it is to come from. '*I have settled all that*' ('derisive laughter' and 'Hear'!)—so that *nine* pounds only will have to be *disbursed* by you, over and above your long-accustomed disbursements ('Hear,' [']Hear'!)— You anticipate perhaps some draft on your waste-paper basket! No, my Lord! It has never been my habit to interfere with your ways of making money, or the rate which you make it at; and if I never did so in *early years*, most unlikely I should do it *now*! My *Bill of Ways and Means*[41] has nothing to do with *making* money, only with disposing of the money made. ('Bravo!' 'Hear'!)

> 1st Ever since my Mother's death, you have allowed me for Old Mary Mills *three pounds* yearly. [S]he needs them no more [d. 1854]— *Continue these three pounds*, for the House.
>
> 2d Thro' the same long term of years; you have made *me* the handsomest Xmas and Birthday presents; and when I had purposely disgusted you from *buying me things*, you gave me at newyear—5£. (Oh I knew the meaning of that 5£ quite well.)

40. Robert Burns, 'Ode to the Departed Regency-Bill—1789', 1.
41. The UK Parliamentary website is helpful: 'Ways and Means resolutions are used by the Commons to give consent to parts of a Bill that will involve taxes or other charges being made on the public. They are usually approved without debate after a Bill has passed its Second reading; an exception being the annual Finance Bill whose ways and means resolutions are debated after the Budget statement and agreed before the Bill is introduced.'

GIVE *me* NOTHING; neither money nor money's worth! (I would have it so *anyhow*) and *continue the 5£* for the House.

3d Ever since we came to London you have paid some two pounds (I guess) for *butter*—now become uneatable— *Continue that two pounds*, for the House; and we have already *ten* pounds which you can't miss not having been used to have them.

4th My allowance of 25£ is a very liberal one; has enabled me to 'spend freely' for *myself*; and I don't deny there is a pleasure in *that*, when there is no Household *crisis*; but with an appalling *deficit* in the House exchequer it is not only no pleasure, but an *impossibility*.— I can 'keep up my dignity' and my wardrobe, on a less sum—on 15£ a year.— A silk *dress*, a 'splendid dressing gown,' a Milliner's bonnet the less! what signifies that at my age?— Nothing!— Besides I have had so many 'gowns' *given* me, that they may serve for two or three years; By then; God knows if I shall be *needing gowns* at all! So deduct *ten* pounds from my personal allowance and *continue that*, for the House.— But why not transfer it *privately* from my own purse to the house one[,] and ask for only 19 pounds? It would have *sounded* more modest—'figured' better!— Just because 'that sort of thing' dont please me! I have *tried* it, and found it a bad '*go*'—a virtue *not* 'its own reward'! I am for every herring to hang 'by its own head,' every purse to stand on its own bottom. It would worry me to be thought rolling in the wealth of 25£, when I was cleverly making 15 *do*, and investing 10 in *coals* or *taxes*. Mrs Brookfield is *up* to that sort of self-sacrifice thing, and to finding compensation in the sympathy of 'many friends' and in smouldering discontent, with 'William' *for having no intuition* of *her maganimity*. I am *up* to neither the magnanimity, nor the *compensation*. But I am *quite up to* laying down ten pounds of my allowance, in a straightforward, recognised way; without standing on my *toes* to it either. And what is more I am determined upon it. *Will not* accept more than 15 pounds in the present state of affairs.

There only remains to disclose the actual state of the Exchequer. It is empty *as a drum*! ('*sensation*'!) If I consider 29 more pounds indispensable (things remaining as they are) for the coming year, beginning from the 22d of March;—it is just because I have found it so in the year that is gone. And I commenced *that*, as already stated, with *ten pounds* of arrears. Now, you 'assisted' me with 15 pounds, and I have 'assisted' *myself* with *ten* pounds—*five* last August which I took from the *Savings Bank*, and the *five* you gave me at newyear, which I threw into the coal account. (Don't suppose, 'if thou's i' the habit o' *supposing*' that I tell you this in the *un*devout imagination of being *repaid*; by all that's *sacred* for me—*the memory of my Father and Mother*—(what else can an 'irreligious creature' like me, *swear* by?) I would *not* take back that money, if you *offered* it, with the best grace, and had picked it up in the Street! I tell it you simply, that you may see I am not so dreadfully *greedy* as you have appeared to think me—latterly.— Setting *my ten pounds*, then, against the original arrears, with *fifteen* pounds in 'assistance' from *you*; it would follow from my own computation, that I should need *fourteen pounds 'more'* to clear off arrears on the weekly bills, and carry me on, paying my way, till the 22d of March (next quarter-day). ([C]ries of '*shame*'! and '*Turn her out*'!) I say only, '*should need*.'— (Your money of course is *yours*, to do as you will with—) And, that I *would like* to again 'walk the causway, carrying my head as high as—' Mr Allan, the upholsterer! 'owing no man anything'[.] And, that *dearly I would like* to 'at all rates let YOU alone of it'; if I knew who else had any business with my housekeeping, or to whom else I could properly address myself! I cannot address *myself* to myself for the moment; as what with that expensive, most ill-timed Dressing-gown, and my *cheap*, illtimed *chiffonnière*, and my halfyears bills to Rhind and Catchpole;[42] I have only what will serve me till June come round.— If I were a man, I might 'fling the gauntlet to Society, join with a few brave fellows, and rob a Diligence [stagecoach].' But my sex 'kind of' debars me from *that*!— Mercy! to think there are women, your friend Lady Ashburton for example ('*rumeur*' and '*sensation*') I say, *for example*; who spend not merely the 'additimental' pounds, I must make such pother about; but *four times my whole income* in the *Ball* of *one* night! and none the worse for it; nor anyone the better!— It is—'what shall I say?'—*curious* 'upon *my* honour!' But just in the same manner Mrs Freeman[43] might say; 'to think there are women, Mrs Carlyle, for example, who spend *three pounds, fourteen shillings* on one dressing-gown! and I with just *two loaves* and *eighteen pence* (from the Parish) to *live* on, by the week!' There is no bottom to such reflexions; the only thing one is perfectly sure of is 'it will come all to the same ultimately.' [A]nd 'I can't say I'll regret the loss of myself—' for *one*!

I subjoin a schedule of Expenses on the last 50 pounds, *before beginning to eat* &c—that you may just see what remained for *living, washing, candles*, and all the *odds* and *ends* of housekeeping, for *three months*—in *London*!

42. William Rhind, lace manufacturer and dressmaker, on Sloane Street; Misses Elizabeth and A. Catchpool, dressmakers, Cavendish Square. A chiffonier is a small sideboard.

43. Occasional cook at No. 5.

Also account of the *25£ check* you gave me to pay your own bills with—inclosing the balance, every shilling.

'I add no more; but remain, dear Sir, your / Obedient humble Servant'

Jane Welsh C [. . .]

❧

To Thomas Carlyle, Chelsea, 14 August 1855

No Dear; I dont take to *your* seabathing place, because I have a place of my own in view! Positively I fancy I have found the *Coming cottage*! I am just going off to consult [Robert] Tait about it. And at all events you must go and look at it with me next Monday, before we incur any lodging-expenses—which would be best laid out on a place 'all to oneself.'

I took such an amount of air and exercise yesterday as would have DONE FOR most nine-teenth century *females*! Started at eight, by the boat, with a good tide and was at the station a quarter before nine.[44] Was quite well situated in my open carriage and reached Brighton without the least fatigue. *Bathed* the first thing; and then walked along the shore to a little Inn I had been told of by Neuberg and Ballantyne; as a charming quiet place 'for *even* Mr Carlyle' to stop at; found it, of course, noisy dirty not to be even *dined* at by Mrs Carlyle—and walked on, still further along the cliffs, to a village I had SEEN ON THE MAP, and was sure must be very retired. The name of it is Rottingdean. It is 4 miles *at least* from the Brighton Station. I *walked* there and back again!! and in the last two miles along the cliffs I met just ONE man! in a white smock! Thus you perceive the traveller expences to one of the quietest sea villages in England is just per boat & third class train 3/10d!. [A] convenient locality for one's cottage at all rates. The place itself is an *old sleepy* looking little village close on the sea, with simple poor inhabitants. [N]ot a trace of a Lady or gentleman bather to be seen!— In fact except at the Inn there were no lodgings visible. I asked the maid at the Inn, 'was it always as quiet as this?'— '[*A*]*lways*,' she said, in a half whisper, with a half sigh,—'a-most *too*

44. Chelsea steamboat to London Bridge station, thence (third class) to Brighton and on to the village of Rottingdean, now adjacent to the Brighton and Hove conurbation. All this in search of an escape to the country which the couple had often (ultimately unrealistically) entertained.

quiet!'— Near the Inn, and so near the sea you could throw a stone into it, are three houses in a row—the center one old—quaint, and empty[45]—small rooms but enough of them—and capable of being made very livable in at small cost—and there are *two* 'decent women' I *saw*, who might either of them be trusted to keep it— But I should fill sheets with details without giving you a right impression—you must just go and *look*. I returned to Brighton again—after having dined at the Rottingdean Inn on two fresh eggs a plateful of homebaked bread and butter, and a pint bottle of *Guiness* (ch*aa*rge 1/6d)— I walked miles up and down Brighton to find the Agent, for that cottage— did finally get him by miracle—name and street being both different from what I set out to seek—and almost committed myself to take the cottage for a year at 12£ (no taxes or rates whatever) or to take it for 3 months at six pounds— However I took fright about *your* not liking it,—and the expences of furnishing &c &c—on the road up—and wrote him a note from Alsops shop that he might not refuse any other offer and hold me engaged till you had seen and approved of it. If Tait shared *this* cottage and went halves in the furnishings it would cost very little indeed— My only objection to it this morning, is that one might not be able to get it *another year* and then what would be done with the furniture? But oh what a beautiful sea! blue as the Firth of Forth it was last night!— I lay on the cliffs in the stillness, and looked at the 'beautiful Nature' for an hour and more, which was such a *doing* of the picturesque as I have not been up to for years. The most curious thing is the sudden solitude beggining *without gradation* just where Kemptown [central Brighton] ends— It is as if the Brighton people were all *enchanted* not to pass beyond their peir—

One can get any sort of Lodgings *in Brighton*— I brought away the card of one—very beautiful, and clean as a pin where the *Lady* 'received no *dogs* nor *children*'—'dogs she did *not* dislike, but she dreaded their fleas.' An excellent sitting room and bed room 30/— sitting room and two bedrooms 2£—but then they are such rooms as one has at home not like Eastbourne! But Brighton is Brighton— Rottingdean is like a place in a novel. I *am* stiff today.— I had to walk to St Pauls last night—after all my walking—before I got an omnibus and then from Alsop's home—and last night the results of Cremorne in the Kingsroad were what shall I say?—*strange* upon my

45. Presumably, Prospect Cottage, Aubrey Cottage and North End, the first two of which would eventually be owned by the Pre-Raphaelite painter Edward Burne-Jones (1833–1898); inspiration for his granddaughter Angela Thirkell's memoir, *Three Houses* (1931). 'Alsops shop', below: chemists on Sloane Street.

honour![46] First I heard a measured tread[,] and then out of the darkness advanced on me eight soldiers carrying high over their heads a bier! on which lay a figure covered with a black cloth all but the white white face! and before I had recovered from the shock of that—some twenty yards further on behold precisely the same thing over again!

I asked a working man what had happened— 'It was a great night at Cremorne—storming of Sebastopol—30 or forty soldiers were *storming*, when the scafolding broke, and they all fell in *on their own* bayonets! The two who had passed were killed they said and all the others hurt'— But a sergeant, whom I accosted after, told me there were none killed and only three hurt badly.

Lord Goodrich[47] had your *Zouaves* and it is come back with a farewell note to *me* from the Lady[,] and Lady Sandwich brought on Sunday *anecdotes Germanique*— Is that one of the books you had lost? Your silent room is swept and the books dusted—

I am making shocking writing but my pen is horrid— My mind in a frightful hurry—and my hand very unsteady with yesterdays fatigues—

A letter from you was eagerly asked for last night—but it came this morning— Those Cows must have been Philistines in some previous in some previous [*sic*] state of existence

Ever yours /
JWC

Journal, 21 November 1855

21st *O me miseram*! [misery me] Not one wink of sleep the whole night thro'! so great the '*rale mental agony in my own inside*,' at thought of that

46. Cremorne Gardens were a pleasure ground on the Thames at Chelsea; they were painted on numerous occasions later in the century by American artist James McNeill Whistler (1834–1903). An original pair of gates is all that remains, just off Cremorne Road. A group of soldiers drawn from the Household regiments, the Royal Artillery and the Grenadier Guards were re-enacting the famous Siege of Sevastapol from the Crimean War (1853–1856) to a packed house when the accident occurred, causing about twenty injuries.
47. Frederick John Robinson, 1st Viscount Goderich (1782–1859), Whig politician, briefly Prime Minister in 1827–1828; later president of the Royal Society of Literature, 1834–1845. Thomas mentions 'some French booklet' on the topic of the famous Franco-Algerian light infantry troops. The other book is possibly the anonymous *Anecdotes Relative to our Affairs in Germany* (1762), which was in Thomas's library. He had written to complain of local cattle keeping him awake at night.

horrid *appealing*! It was feeling like the ghost of a dead dog that I rose and dressed and drank my coffee, and then started for Kensington. Mr C said 'the voice of honour *seemed* to call on him to go himself'; but either it did not call loud enough or he would not listen to that Charmer. I went in a cab to save all my breath for the *appealing*. Set down at 30 Hornton Street I found a dirty private like house, only with *Tax Office* painted on the door. A dirty woman-servant opened the door and told me the Commissioners would not be there for half an hour, but I might walk up. There were already some half-score of *men* assembled in the waiting room—among whom I saw the man who cleans our clocks, and a young Apothecary of Cheyne Walk[. A]ll the others, to look at them, could not have been suspected for an instant, I should have said, of *making* a hundred a year—never to say more— Feeling in a false position I stood by myself at a window and '*thought shame*' (as children say). Men trooped in by twos and threes till the small room was pretty well filled; at last a *woman* showed herself. 'O MY![']' Did I ever know the full value of any sort of woman, as *woman*, before! By this time some benches had been brought in, and I was sitting nearest the door. The woman sat down on the same bench with me, and, misery acquainting one with strange bedfellows, we entered into conversation without having been *introduced*, and I had 'the happiness' (as Allan termed it) of 'seeing a woman *more* miserable than myself'! *Two* more women arrived, at intervals[:] one a young girl of Dundee (!) 'sent by my Uncle that's ill'[,] who looked to be always recapitulating inwardly what she had been told to say to the Commissioners: the other a widow, and such a goose poor thing! *She* was bringing appeal against—no overcharge in her individual paper—but against *the doubling of the Income Tax*! 'She had payed the double tax *once*,' she said, because she was told they would take her goods for it if she didn't—and it *was* so *disgraceful* for one *in a small business* to have her goods taken; besides that it was *very* disadvantageous! but now that it was come round again she WOULD *give up*.' She seemed to attach an irresistable pathos to the title of '*widow*' this woman—'and me a *widow* Mam!' was the winding up of her every paragraph! The men seemed as worried as the women, tho they put a better face on it, even carrying on a sort of *sickly* laughing and bantering with one another. '*First-come* Lady'! called the Clerk, opening a small side door & *I* stept forward into a *grand peutêtre* [great perhaps]. There was an instant of darkness while the one door was shut behind and the other opened in front; and then I stood in a dim room where three men sat round a large table spread with papers, one held a pen ready over an open ledger[,] another was taking snuff—(and had *taken* still worse in his time, to judge by his shaky dazed appearance). The third who was plainly the cock of that Dungheap was *sitting for Rhadamanthus*. A Rhadamanthus *without the justice*. 'Name'?—said the horned-owl-looking individual holding the pen.— 'Carlyle'— '*What?*'— 'Ca-r-lyle'—seeing he still looked dubious, I spelt it for him C-a-r-l-y-l-e. 'Ha'! cried Rhadamanthus, a big bloodless faced insolent looking fellow[,] 'What is this? Why is Mr Carlyle not come himself? Didnt he get a letter, *ordering* him to appear?— Mr Carlyle wrote *some nonsense* about being exempted from coming and I desired an answer to be sent; that he *must* come—*must* do as other people. [']— 'Then sir,' I said, 'your desire has been neglected, it would seem— My Husband having received no such letter—and I was told by one of your fellow commissioners that his (Mr Carlyles) personal appearance was not indispensable'— '*Huffh! Huffh*! What does Mr Carlyle mean by saying he has no income from his writings, when he himself fixed it in the beginning at a hundred & fifty?'— 'It means sir, that in ceasing to *write* one ceases to be paid for writing—and Mr Carlyle has published nothing for several years.' 'Huffh! Huffh! I understand nothing about that'— 'I do[,'] whispered the snufftaking Commissioner at my ear— 'I can QUITE understand that a Literary man does not always make money— *I* would *take it all off*—for *my* share—but (sinking his voice still lower) I am only *one* voice here and *not* the most important.' 'There' said I handing to Rhadamanthus Chapman & Halls account[48]—'that will prove Mr C's statement'— 'What am I to make of that? Huffh! we should have Mr Carlyle here to *swear* to this, before we believe it.'— 'If a gentlemans word of honour written at the bottom of that paper is not enough; you can put *me* on my oath. *I* am ready to swear to it.'— *You*! 'You indeed! no no! we can do nothing with *your* oath.'— 'But sir I understand my Husbands affairs fully better than he does himself.'— '*That I* can *well* believe!—but we can make nothing of *this*'; flinging my document contemptuously on the table.— The horned-owl picked it up, glanced over it, while Rhadamanthus was tossing papers about and grumbling about 'people that wouldnt conform to rules' then handed it back to him saying deprecatingly[,] 'But sir this is a very plain statement.' 'Then what has Mr Carlyle to live upon? You dont mean to tell me he lives on *that*'? pointing to the document— 'Heaven forbid, sir—but I am not here to explain what Mr Carlyle *has to live on*; only to declare his income from Literature during the last three years.' 'True,

48. Rhadamanthus, wise king and incorruptible judge of mythic Crete; Chapman and Hall, one of the greatest Victorian publishers (see 29 February 1844, above): Carlyle, Dickens, Thackeray, Trollope and Elizabeth Barrett Browning were all handled by them. Now it is an imprint owned by Routledge specialising in mathematics and statistics—which would make Thomas (not to mention the author of *Hard Times*) smile if he knew.

true'! mumbled the '*not* most important voice' at my elbow, 'Mr Carlyle I believe has landed income.'[49] 'Of which,' said I haughtily, for my spirit was up, [']I have fortunately no account to render in this kingdom, and to this board'— 'Take off—fifty pounds—say—a hundred— take off a hundred pounds' said Radamanthus to the horned owl— 'If we write Mr Carlyle down at *a hundred and fifty* he has no reason to complain I think! there—you may go!—no no! Mr Carlyle has no reason to complain!'— *Second-come* woman was already introduced, and I was motioned to the door; but I could not depart without saying; that 'at all events there was no *use* in complaining, since they had the power to enforce their decision.'

In stepping out into the open air, my first thought was what a mercy Carlyle didn't come himself!— For the rest, tho it might have gone better I was thankful it had not gone worse. When one has been threatened with a great injustice, one accepts a smaller as a favour.

After walking home with the news of my half-success, I walked to Regent Street! for buttons— The fever from want of sleep is as good as ablebodiedness for *some* purposes. Sat a while with Geraldine— Went back to spend the evening with Geraldine, when Mr C set forth for Bath House. Her Ladyship [Ashburton] in town for two days.

49. Thomas did get £210 a year rent from the house and land at Craigenputtoch in 1852.

Figure 9: Robert Scott Tait, 'Study, Chelsea' (1857), Thomas Carlyle Papers, Rare Book & Manuscript Library, Columbia University in the City of New York

8

'More than One Place at a Time': 1856–1859

If No. 5 Cheyne Row dominated the period covered by the previous chapter, Jane's grief and desperation regarding Thomas's desertion of her for Lady Harriet spilled over powerfully into the journal she started at the end of that time, on 21 October 1855:

> 22d I was cut short in my *Introduction* last night by Mr C's return from Bath House. That eternal Bath House! I wonder how many thousand miles Mr C has walked between there and here, put it all together? setting up always another mile-stone, and another, betwixt himself and me! Oh, good grasious! when I first noticed that heavy yellow House without knowing or caring to know who it belonged to, how far I was from dreaming that thro' years and years I should carry every stone's weight of it on my heart! (*CL* 30: 200)

His frequent late-afternoon departure from his study, past her very door in the drawing-room without so much as a by-your-leave—and the thought that after a hard day's work on the ghastly Frederick he preferred Lady Harriet's company to her own for the purposes of mental refreshment—must have been agonising for a sensitive person who had supported Thomas's career before its very beginning. But it must be said: out of her sense of desertion Jane also acquired and exhibited an ironical and belittling hardness, particularly as regards Thomas in front of guests, and he was a sensitive person, too. And Jane seems to have been self-medicating with large amounts of morphine, which may have made her incommunicative—though he should have paid more attention to her deteriorating medical condition, which alarmed many of her friends in this period. His behaviour is not incomprehensible, though it is deeply regrettable. Ruskin's 1885 recollection of the couple at this time is bleak, indeed: 'there was never the slightest look of right affection,' he told Charles Eliot Norton, and he 'rarely attended to a word she said'.[1]

1. John Lewis Bradley and Ian Ousby (eds.), *The Correspondence of John Ruskin and Charles Eliot Norton* (Cambridge, 1987), 488. Her journal entry dated 26 June 1856 is the one concerning 'blue wrists', mentioned in the Introduction—evidence it seems of physical violence from her husband. The entry was cut out from the journal but not by Thomas: probably by his niece Mary Aitken Carlyle, many years later, to protect her uncle.

There is nothing surprising, then, in a noteworthy feature of what the editors of the Collected Letters call Jane's 'Miscellaneous Writings' (gathered together in CL 30). I mean a pronounced nostalgia (from the Greek: nostos*: 'return home', and* algia*: 'pain'; first used in English in 1756) for her pre-marital youth in Haddington, when her father and not her husband was at the centre of her universe. We have seen this already, in her 'Much Ado About Nothing' journal of August 1849 (Chapter 6), recording her revisitation of her childhood home, half in the hope of remaining anonymous (and therefore free to gratify herself: 'I let myself be shown the way which I knew every inch of,—shown "the school houses," where myself had been* Dux*') and half in the hope of being recognised (and thus reclaimed, as she was by numerous locals). At the core of that visit was her father's grave ('the very centre of eternal silence'), which she cleaned with his own button hook out of her dressing case. Then there was the miraculous resumption—'the very puddles made by the last rain I* felt *to have stepped over before'—and the peculiar recovery of youth which had her jumping over a church wall, much to the sexton's amazement. But there is the humiliating note of reality, too, when the village cooper asked her how many children she had: '*None, *I told him. "None!" (in a tone of astonishment, verging on horror) "None at all! then what on the Earth had I been* doing *all this time?"'*

In October 1852 the theme returns, in her autobiographical sketch 'The Simple Story of my own First Love', which has its origin, she makes clear, in Thomas's scepticism about the centrality of love in human existence, as set forth in Thackeray's latest novel, The History of Henry Esmond. Here is Jane, 'going ten', 'a girl so renowned for her eyelashes, her Latin, and her wit', and the possessor of 'manifold fascinations, personal and spiritual', being disregarded by a 'Stranger Boy' from a military family which moves on from Haddington, leaving her bereft—for a while, at least. There is plenty of irony in the presentation, but that is not all. The urge to recapture is present, too: 'Curious! that recalling so many particulars of this old story, as vividly as if I had it under an opera-glass; I should have nevertheless quite forgot—the Boy's first name!' The nostalgic lens 'vividly' crosses the gulf of time; the irrelevancies disappear; but the image of the 'Dancing-school Ball' and the impolitely uncongenial partner is intensely, iconographically complete: 'a Boy of twelve, or perhaps thirteen, tall for his years, and very slight,—with sunshiny hair, and dark blue eyes,—a dark blue ribbon about his neck, and grey jacket with silver buttons.'

In the 1855–1856 journal the blend is the same, of a powerfully evoked present-day existence—'Answered a note from Ruskin. Went and sat an hour with Lady Sandwich[.] Bought coffee at Fortnum & Mason's and took a book at the London Library (a novel. Cooper's Pathfinder*— I ought to be ashamed of myself, but I'm* not.*)'—interspersed with reflections channelled in child-like verse (5 November: 'Alone this evening. Lady A. in town again, and Mr C of course at Bath House'):*

When I think on what I is,
And what I use to was;
I 'gin to think I've sold myself
For very little *cas*. [cause?]

Or (7 November: 'Oh my Mother! Nobody sees when I am suffering now; and I have learnt to suffer "all to myself." From only childness to that is a far and a rough road to travel!'):

Oh little did my mother think,
The day she cradl'd me,
The Lands I was to travel in,
The Death I was to dee!

On 25 April 1856 one of her many old flames, the now plump and stuffy sculptor George Rennie, came to call at No. 5; she sprang into his arms and 'kissed him a great many times': 'Oh it has done me so much good this meeting!' she wrote: 'My bright, whole-hearted, impulsive youth seemed conjured back by his hearty embrace for certain.' But the previous winter had taken its toll: 'The evening devoted to mending; Mr C's trousers among other things!' she noted on 31 October. '"Being an only child" I never "wished" to sew mens trousers—no never!' 'Today [11 November] has been like other days outwardly— I have done this and that and people have come and gone—but all as in a bad dream.*' And such are the related themes in this chapter overall, as Jane's focus shuttles between London and Scotland, the halfway houses of Liverpool, Seaforth and Yorkshire now mostly closed to her by the passage of time. And then, all unexpectedly and aged only fifty-two, Lady Harriet died in May 1857 and that particular cycle of unhappiness was at an end, though the scars would take time to heal.*

To William Allingham, Chelsea, 23 February 1856

Dear Mr Allingham

I like your idea. It is original; and like the notes of the nightingale 'touching and strong.'[2] I shall bear it in mind for my own use. Now and then I have met with a person '*here down*' (as Mazzini calls it) whom absence did not sweep from my recollection, and to whom, in some dreamy moment I should have liked to say, 'I remember you; do *you* remember *me*?' But it never occurred to me to *do* this, tho' so extremely easy to be done! without having gone thro' the *slow* preliminary to a regular friendly correspondence and to regular friendly correspondences, indeed to *regular anything* I have a sacred horror of committing myself— This sort of impulsive irregular thing suits me exactly; so I thank you for your letter and answer it with right good will.

2. From Thomas's translation of Goethe's *Wilhelm Meister's Apprenticeship*: see *Works*, 22: 23.

What you say of Ruskins book[3] is excellent. 'Claret and buttermilk' till one don't know which is which! But what *could* be expected from a man who goes to sleep with, every night, a different Turner's picture on a chair opposite his bed 'that he may have something beautiful to look at on first opening his eyes of a morning' (so his Mother told me)[.] Mrs Ruskin I suppose was not beautiful *enough* to open one's eyes on the first thing; and, *hinc illae lachrymae* [hence those tears]![4] you see Millais (I dont know how to spell him) and she *have* married—you wouldn't believe me, I have heard of her several times since her marriage, from people who had seen her in Scotland—one said she looked 'sad'; another that she looked '*cross*'; another that she kept Millais in order; and another that she was 'in an interesting situation.' As for Ruskin; I never saw a man so improved by the loss of his wife! He is amiable and gay, and full of hope and faith in—one doesn't know exactly *what*—but of course *he* does. Twice last summer he drove Mr C and me and *Nero* out to his place at Denmark hill,[5] and gave us a dinner like what one reads of in the *Arabian Nights*, and strawberries and cream on the lawn; and was indulgent and considerate for even *Nero*! and I returned each time more satisfied, that Mrs Ruskin must have been hard to please. One feels always, one could manage other women's husbands so much better than they do—and so much better than one manages one's own husband!

We lived in the same house with Alfred Tennyson lately—at Lord Ashburton's in Hampshire—and he read *Maud* and 'other poems' aloud to us—and was much made of by all the large party assembled there. He seemed strangely excited about *Maud*—as sensitive to criticisms on it, as if they were imputations on his honour—and all his friends are excited about *Maud* for him! and an unknown Cambridge gentleman wrote to Mr Carlyle to ask him to be so good as inform him what was

3. Ruskin, *Modern Painters*, III (1856); the expression is a shrewd one as regards Ruskin's style, passionate and mellifluous by turns.
4. Euphemia ('Effie') Gray (1828–1897) married Ruskin in 1848, but their marriage was unconsummated for reasons that remain mysterious: in the resulting annulment proceedings Ruskin spoke of her bodily deformity; later he insisted that she had married him not for love but for money. In any event, she went on to marry the Pre-Raphaelite painter John Everett Millais in 1855, one year after the annulment on the grounds of incurable impotence, and they went on to have eight children together. She is depicted in Millais's *The Order of Release* (1853).
5. The Ruskin family's home in the Camberwell area of south London, with which he identified passionately and which he left only in 1872 to move to the Lake District. It was demolished in 1947, but there is still a Ruskin Park in the neighbourhood.

his opinion of *Maud*!!! You may imagine how Mr C would toss that letter into the fire, sending a savage growl after it![6]

Dear Mr Allingham be a Poet by all means, for you have a *real* gift that way; but for Gods sake beware of becoming too caring about whether your gift is *appreciated* by 'the million'—of Jack asses. The nightingale dont trouble itself about *appreciation*—and sings none the worse for that.

I can't tell you how glad I was that you got back to humdrum *work*, yielding you *visible means* and not overworking your nervous system.

I never thanked you for the book of poems you sent me—the custom of this house is to send away the books of poems that come, to the first person one can think of that 'cares for that sort of thing'[.] When I tell you that your *Day and Night* songs, were not sent away; but on the contrary placed in my little private bookcase, in my own room, and still stand there; you will perceive they must have had some peculiar charm for me—either of merit or of affection—or of both together.

Mr C says there is nothing of the least moment in the 4 vol edition of his Cromwell that is not in the 3 vol and supplement one—

As to the atlases he does not discommend Brewer for he never heard of it before. But he thinks *Arrowsmith's Gen' Atlas*—the best little atlas he ever saw. Also *Walkers England* is very good, and the *Govt map of Ireland* (4 pieces) excellent. And now good by dear Mr Allingham—and as a German friend of mine wrote to me from America the other day 'a serene mind to you in the new era'!

Very sincerely yours
Jane Carlyle

6. The Carlyles' almost complete indifference to poetry notwithstanding, Thomas and Jane both liked Alfred, Lord Tennyson (1809–1892), whose collection *Maud, and Other Poems* (1855) was his first since becoming poet laureate on the death of Wordsworth in 1850. On 31 January 1845 Jane wrote to Helen Welsh about a visit from Tennyson when Thomas was out (*CL* 19: 17): 'The only chance of my getting any right good of him was to make him forget my womanness—so I did just as Carlyle would have done had he been there; got out pipes and TOBACCO—and brandy and water—with a deluge of tea over and above,— The effect of these accessories was miraculous—he professed to be ashamed of polluting my room[,] "felt" he said "as if he were stealing cups and sacred vessels in the Temple" but he smoked on all the same—for three mortal hours!—talking like an angel—only exactly as if he were talking with a clever man—which—being a thing I am not used to—men always adapting their conversation to what they take to be a womans taste—strained me to a terrible pitch of intellectuality— When Carlyle came home at Twelve and found me all alone in an atmosphere of tobacco so thick that you might have cut it with a knife his astonishment was considerable!'

To Thomas Carlyle, Haddington, 8 August 1856

I got here last night about seven. The carriage was waiting for me at the Station; but this time *empty*—no kind Miss Kate in it[7]—we came in at the back gate, and when we turned round the house I saw Miss Jess—or rather I saw *a face*—or rather *eyes* straining at the dining room window with a look I shall remember while I live. The next moment I was in her arms, and then my 'god mother' tottered *blindly* forward and took me in hers and the two dear old women clasped and kissed and wept over me, both together—and called out 'Jeanie Jeanie'[—]'Oh my own bairn'!—'my Angel'!! and ever so many beautiful names.— Mrs Donaldson and Miss Eliza, had kindly retired to their own room, that the meeting might transact itself in peace. A beautiful *tea* was waiting on the table—all so pretty, and calm, and good!— [I]t looked like one of those entertainments spread for the good boys that 'went out to *poos* [poose: push] their fortune' in my Godmothers fairy Tales[,] and my Godmother herself like the Good Fairy—so *little*— Oh so little she has grown! and her *face* so little and so round and so sweet!— And Miss Jess has been transformed by Kate's death into an active self forgetting Providence for the older and blinder sister—she waits upon her, cuts her bread into mouthfuls, is gentle and thoughtful for her, *reads aloud to her* (Miss Donaldson tells me), she herself being about eighty. [A]nd instead of complaints about her own ailments—it is all now 'poor Jean' and 'the loss she had in Kate'— The *hearts* of these two old women are as fresh as gowans [daisies]. It is like being pretty well up towards Heaven, being here. And what a house! so quiet and clean, and so perfectly the same as I knew it thirty years ago!—the same papers the same carpets the same everything that I made acquaintance with when I was a child, in perfect condition still.

I expect to *sleep* in my great comfortable fourposted bed—now that the first exciting night is over—and shall stay till the middle of next week I think. My Aunts were extremely kind, and expect me to make *them* a long visit on my return—but that is not possible, on account of the gass in my bedroom at Morningside, and the public road passing the window, where carts grind from three in the morning— Besides that I *like* being at Auchtertool, and they want me there for all the time I *can* stay— Everybody is so kind to me—oh so kind! that I often burst out crying with pure thankfulness to them all—

7. See Donaldson in Characters and Correspondents: old friends of her mother. For her Morningside paternal aunts, below, see Welsh in Characters and Correspondents. 'Betty' is Elizabeth Welsh. Jane's other Scottish destination is her cousin Walter Welsh at Auchtertool, Fife, near Kirkcaldy.

Betty said yesterday, speaking of the Photograph I had sent her, the one with the bonnet and the dog—and which together with yours she has got handsomely framed and keeps in a *pocket-handkerchief in a drawer*!—'It has a look o'ye—but I dinna ken what that white thing is aboot the face,'— 'That is the white roses of my bonnet Betty.' 'A weel! a weel! *May be sae*—but as ye wur kindly sending me yer pictur, Dear, I wud hae liket better ye had goten't dune wi yer bare pow![']— I promised her one with the bare pow [head]—but said 'you know it is a shame for me to be without a cap or a bonnet at this age'— 'Ay, Ay, I dar say—its no very richt—but ye ken Bairn ye was nae brocht up to dou just like ither folk—at aa rates I'll hae the *bare pow* if ye please: *tho' I wudna be thocht ower greedy*!!['] Dear Darling old Betty—she gets no rest night or day for that poor specter of a son—and it looks to me he may live for years in this suffering hopeless state— And the husband tho' a good enough man in his way—sober and laborious and all that—has not the refinement or the spirituality of Betty and can be but a sorry comforter to her in her sore trouble. She called me back as I was coming away yesterday—to say 'Dear—wull ye tell Miss Donaldson—for Im sure it ill please her to hear it—that the Bishop is rale gude to us—puir auld *manny*'!

I had two bathes in the sea—neither did me any good but harm—the first a great deal of harm, by ill luck—

Just the day after I wrote I had had no bathing; Walter took me to Aberdower and I was to partly undress and get a bathing gown at Aberdower House[8] wher Mrs Major Liddle lives— She gave me the key of the park that Maggie and I might walk thro it to the shore—but the key proved a wrong one[,] and as there was no time to return for the right key I proposed to Maggie to leap from the top of the wall which was only high on the off side— She positively declined—and we were at a fix—when a working man passing I called to him and asked him to catch us in leaping— He took me between his big thumbs—one on my *left* side and the other, alas, on my *right breast*—that unlucky breast I am always hurting!— *There*! I thought to myself as I found my feet—'*there* is something to serve me for six weeks again!' I suffered a good deal for the first two or three days and lost my just recovered sleep— It (the pain[)] is going off however, tho still a nuisance especially when I use my right arm—remember *that* in estimating the virtue of this very long letter—

I inclose a note from Lady A[shburton] which was forwarded to me here this morning—

8. Next to Aberdour Castle at the seaside village of Aberdour in Fife.

I am not sure where to address but as one letter was sent to Scotsbrig I had best send this one to the Gill

Yours faithfully /

J W C

❧

To Robert Tait, Haddington, 12 August 1856

My dear Mr Tait

I do think you are the kindest man alive! Thank you with all my heart for the beautiful little photographs— If you only knew how they are valued here!

Your letter was forwarded from Auchtertool to this place, my little Birthplace, god bless it!— I came to stay three days, but the three days had to turn to ten—the dear old ladies I am staying with *cried* so when I spoke of going yesterday. Oh how I should like to show you these old Ladies! the one eighty the other eightysix—and they are as clear minded and warmhearted as ever they were in their lives—and look so pretty! like the *good Fairies* they used to tell me about when I sat on their knees a pretty while ago!—and their house reminds me of the 'beautiful house among trees' that the 'good boy'—who 'sent to *poos* his fortune[']' (in their Tales) arrived at always—and where in all comfort and stillness he found 'every thing on earth that he needed'— Oh Mr Tait! these dear old women are a rehabilitation of old age for one after the horrid *guys* [frights] in London!—after having been familiarized with that disreputable old age that dies its hair and bares its neck and arms and seeks '*distraction*' at Parties!

Do you *know* I think dear old Scotland so much better in every respect than 'the south' that I should like to come back to it for altogether—and have you and two or three more London people come to stay with me in the summer—

What on earth does one get by living amidst all that dirt and dearth and din but sick nerves and weariness and vexation of spirit!

I was grown as cold and hard as a stone, with continued pressure of ill health and worry— Now I am so *soft* that I fall a-crying twenty times aday with sheer gratitude to everybody for making so much of me!!

Yours affly /

Jane W Carlyle

❧

To Mary Smith, Chelsea, 11 January 1857

Dear Miss Smith,

This time you come to me as an old acquaintance, whom I am glad to shake hands with again. The mere fact of your being still in the same position after so long an interval, and with such passionate inward protest as that first letter indicated, is a more authentic testimony to your worth, than if you had sent me a *certificate of character* signed by all the clergy and householders of Carlisle! So many talents are wasted, so many enthusiasms turned to smoke, so many lives blighted, for want of a little patience and endurance! for want of understanding and laying to heart that which you have so well expressed in these verses—the meaning of *the Present*![9]—for want of recognising, that it is not the greatness or littleness of 'the duty nearest hand,' but the spirit in which one does it, that makes one's doing noble or mean!

I can't think how people, who have any natural ambition, and any sense of power in them, escape going *mad* in a world like this, without the recognition of that! I know I was very near *mad* when I found it out for myself (as one has to find out for one-self *everything* that is to be of any real practical use to one). Shall I tell you how it came into my head? Perhaps it may be of comfort to you in similar moments of fatigue and disgust.

I had gone with my husband to live on a little estate of *peat* bog, that had descended to me, all the way down from John Welsh, the Covenanter, who married a daughter of John Knox.[10] That didn't, I am ashamed to say, make me feel Craigenputtock a whit less of a peat bog, and most dreary, untoward place to live at! In fact, it was sixteen miles distant on every side from all the conveniences of life—shops and even post office!

Further, we were very poor; and further and worst, being an only child, and brought up to 'great prospects,' I was sublimely ignorant of every branch of useful knowledge, though a capital Latin scholar and a very fair mathematician!! It behoved me in these astonishing circumstances to learn—to *sew*! Husbands, I was shocked to find, wore their stockings into holes! and were always losing buttons! and I was expected to 'look to all that!' Also, it behoved me to learn to *cook*! No *capable* servant choosing to live at 'such an out of the way place,' and my husband having 'bad digestion,' which complicated my difficulties

9. 'The Present': one of Smith's poems, eventually published in *Poems. By M. S.* (1860), dedicated to Jane.
10. In fact Jane was descended from Elizabeth Knox's brother-in-law, David Welsh, of Colliston near Craigenputtoch.

dreadfully. The bread, above all, brought from Dumfries, 'soured on his stomach,' (Oh, Heavens!) and it was plainly my duty as a christian wife to bake at home!

So I sent for Cobbett's 'Cottage Economy,'[11] and fell to work at a loaf of bread. But knowing nothing about the process of fermentation or the heat of ovens, it came to pass that my loaf got put into the oven at the time *myself* ought to have put into bed, and I remained the only person not asleep, in a house in the middle of a desert! *One* o'clock struck, and then *two*, and then *three*; and still I was sitting there in an intense solitude, my whole body aching with weariness, my heart aching with a sense of forlornness and degradation. 'That I who had been so petted at home, whose comfort had been studied by everybody in the house, who had never been required to do anything but *cultivate my mind*, should have to pass all those hours of the night in watching *a loaf of bread*! which mightn't turn out bread after all!'

Such thoughts maddened me, till I laid down my head on the table, and sobbed aloud. It was then that somehow the idea of Benvenuto Cellini,[12] sitting up all night watching his Pericles in the oven, came into my head; and suddenly I asked myself, 'After all; in the sight of the upper powers, what is the mighty difference between a statue of Pericles and a loaf of bread, so that each be the thing one's hand hath found to do? The man's determined will, his energy, his patience, his resource, were the really admirable things, of which the statue of Pericles was the mere chance expression. If he had been a woman, living at Craigenputtock, with a dyspeptic husband, sixteen miles from a baker, and *he a bad one*—all these same qualities would have come out most fitly in a *good* loaf of bread!'

I cannot express what consolation this germ of an idea spread over my uncongenial life, during five years we lived at that savage place; where my two immediate predecessors had gone *mad*, and the third had taken to drink!

But here am I beginning on a third little sheet and you are waiting for my opinion of the verses! If you knew how completely I have lost all taste for poetry (so called), you would not have appealed to *my* judgment of all peoples! Indeed, I should need to have been a poet

11. William Cobbett (1763–1835), gadfly journalist, agrarian politician and farmer, published this immortal self-help book in 1821, with the aim of assisting 'the Affairs of a Labourer's Family'.
12. Benvenuto Cellini (1500–1571), prodigious Renaissance goldsmith and sculptor, described the casting of his statue of mythic hero Perseus (not the Greek politician Pericles) with the head of Medusa in his classic autobiography, completed in 1563.

born, to have continued writing or reading anything in verse, in the valley of the shadow of Mr Carlyle's denunciations of verse! I suppose, too, as one gets old, one naturally falls back on plain prose. But since you have asked my opinion, it would be discourteous to refuse it, even on the plea of incompetence.

I have read these verses very carefully several times over, and what I feel about them is that they are full of *thought* and *sense*, and deficient in *music*. They give me the impression of thought put into verse by *force of will*, rather than from a natural *taste for singing itself.*

My husband once asked Monkton Milnes why he put what he had to say into rhymes, 'instead of JUST SAYING IT.' The answer was—'Why you see, a very little thought goes so much further in verse!' Now, it seems to me, that *you* do not lie under that general exigence of modern poets, driving them on expedients to make a little thought go further than its natural length. There is more thought in the verses you have sent me, than might be elaborated into a long prose essay—more thought than in several volumes of poems, lying about on drawing room tables. But it is hurt rather than shown to advantage by the versification, which is hard and stiff—in a word, *unmusical.*

I should hardly have trusted my own judgment in such a matter, if Mr Carlyle had not confirmed it. I read the verses to him, having first given him my notions about them, and he said—'Well, they are just what you said. The young lady has something in her to write, but she should resolve on sticking to prose.' That from him was rather high praise, I assure you.

Yours truly, /
JANE W. CARLYLE

To George Lillie Craik, Chelsea, 5 May 1857

'*Ill*'? dear Mr Craik! I should think so! When, in the memory of man, was I ever *well*? And didn't I tell you in my last letter, that I was confined to the house with a protracted cold, which I had no expectation to shake off till warm weather come? I put it to you as a man of veracity and candour if warm weather have come yet! I am not however *so* ill as I was; my cough is all but gone[,] I get about half instead of a tithe of the sleep *normal* to Human beings, and I eat certainly as much as Nero eats, or rather, *is allowed to eat.* When the Eastwind has blown itself out, which wont be (Mr C's tailor says) till 'the 26 of June'; I expect to be 'about' to more or less purpose.

Et tu Brute![13] Oh how *could* you fill so much of your paper with the *Life of Miss Bronte*[,] a topic I have got to almost scream at the first word of![14] I am so sick of Mrs Gaskell, Miss Bronte poor thing, and all that 'day of (literary) small things'![15] I dont think I am malevolent the least in the world, I cant usually *be at the trouble* to hate people enough to wish them ill; but upon *my* honour it was with a sensation wonderfully like pleasure, that I heard from dear old John Richardson two days since, a prosecution is commenced against Mrs Gaskell by '*that woman*' whom she has so needlessly, indelicately and cruelly gibbeted. Who the Devil wanted to know the amours of a low scamp like young Bronte? And who constituted Mrs Gaskell the avenging Deity of public morals? Is no woman to be obscure enough for escaping the prying eyes of bookmakers and penny a liners? I am so glad Lady Scott has had the courage to step forward and say; 'you mean *me*, and you *lie*.' And I hope Mrs Gaskell will be made to know that 'A Nemesis' may 'follow' a woman in Paternoster Row as well as in Mayfair[.][16] Sir George Stephen who has undertaken the prosecution has telegraphed to Rome, where Mrs Gaskell, having thrown her poisoned shaft in to 'that woman's' heart and life (she thought) had gone to disport herself with her two daughters, leaving *her* Husband (this Rhadamantha [judge] of conjugal life) to nurse the younger children and keep the house, as he has to do one half the year! And desired Mrs Gaskell to come home and defend herself against the charge of defamation— Lady Scott denies the whole

13. 'You, too, Brutus?': the famous accusation Julius Caesar makes of his assassin in Shakespeare's play, III. i. 77. Elizabeth Gaskell's biography of her friend had been published in March and caused a sensation. One of its revelations was that Charlotte's brother Branwell's life had been ruined by an unnamed lady: in fact Mrs Lydia Robinson (whose son Branwell had tutored in 1843, and with whom he became infatuated), now remarried as Lady Scott—who threatened Gaskell with legal proceedings on grounds of defamation. Sir John Richardson was a parliamentary legal authority and old friend of the Carlyles.
14. Jane had certainly kept up with the Brontës. It seems she read *Jane Eyre* and *Wuthering Heights* ('the Currell [Currer] Bell people' as she calls Charlotte and Emily in a letter to John Forster of 26? February 1848), and *Shirley* in the winter of 1849, writing to Jeannie Welsh on 6 November, 'you see I get the credit with certain CRITICS IN STYLE of writing these Jane Eyre books myself—and I was curious to see whether the new one was up to my reputation!' She makes no mention of *Villette* (1854), which is a shame. Charlotte was no longer 'Miss Brontë' at the time of her death; she had married her father's curate, Arthur Bell Nicholls, in 1854 and died tragically of hyperemesis gravidarum in March the following year.
15. Zechariah 4: 10.
16. Paternoster Row, near St Paul's Cathedral, ancient centre of the English book trade. In the first edition of her biography Gaskell had written, of Branwell Bronte (d. 1848): 'He died! she [Lady Scott] lives still,—in May Fair', the fashionable area of London's West End.

accusation and declares Mr Bronte to have been *mad* and a great liar— Her [first] Husbands will, she says, contained no mention of Bronte whatever—and he left his fortune to her without a single condition. I am the readier to believe the poor woman innocent or at least nothing like so bad as Mrs G has painted her; because I have had the evidence of my own senses that Mrs G speaks too fast, and nothing she narrates is to be wholly relied on— The novel writer tendency to dramatise everything, the desire to *ingratiate* herself as a popular Lioness, and (I think) a natural deficiency of *precision* both in her thoughts and feelings make her *I have found* a person rather dangerous to associate with.

As for Whitty, I think he needs to be covered up, and *left to stand*— like a barrel of gooseberry wine—till he settles and clears— I do dislike that sort of *working drummly* [murky] *stuff*; however much spirit there may be in it—[17]

I am anxiously looking for Georgina's Book— *She* wont empty her mind out, dregs and all, in that nasty impertinent fashion but will pour off the wine clear, I expect— [. . .]

Love to the girls
Yours affly /
Jane W Carlyle

To Mary Russell, Chelsea, circa 18 May 1857

Dearest Mary

I have been long in answering your dear letter; If you saw Lady Ashburton's death in the newspapers you would partly guess why; that I was shocked, and dispirited, and feeling *silence* best. *But* you could *not* guess the *outward* disturbance consequent on this event! The letters and calls of inquiry and condolence that have been eating up my days for the last two weeks! distressingly and irritatingly— For it does not require any particular accuteness to detect, in this fussy display of feeling, more impertinent curiosity than genuine sympathy. *Some* Ladies (of her circle) who never were here before, have come, out of *good* motives, talking to us as *her* friends, out of regard for her memory— But

17. Probably *Friends of Bohemia, or Phases of London Life* (1857) by Edward Michael Whitty (1827–1860), a satirical potboiler about his journalistic experiences. He emigrated to Melbourne to edit *The Argus* soon after and died there. Craik's daughter published her first novel, *Riverston*, in October.

the greater number of these *condolers* have come to ask particulars of her death (which we were likely to know) and to see how we, especially *Mr Carlyle*, were taking her loss![18]

At no moment since the time she was first declared in danger could her death have come with more shock. Lord Ashburton had just been here for a week, making preparations for her immediate return to England, and he represented her as 'progressing most favourably'[.] Sir James Clark who had been to Paris to see her said the same. Lord A was to have gone back to Paris on the Sunday but on Saturday he got a letter from *her*, telling him to go to St Leonards and take a house there: 'that she might be at the seaside, *if she liked*, during September'!—[19] He went and took the house, and so did not get to Paris till the Monday; when she had been *dead* two hours! I never heard of so easy a death! She was dressing about four o'clock, felt faint and called for Dr Rousse (her private Dr) [. H]e told her, in answer to her question; 'what is this'?—'You are going to faint, it is nothing; you mustn't mind these faintnesses'! He put his arm round her to support her, she clasped her hands over his other arm, leant her forehead on his shoulder, gave a sigh, and was dead!

Last Tuesday Mr C went to the Grange to be present at her funeral— It was conducted with a sort of royal state, and all the men, who used to compose a sort of *Court* for her, were there; *in tears*! I never heard of a gloomier funeral.

All this has kept me from getting the good I expected from the change of weather. My cough is entirely gone; but I am weak and nervous to a degree! and driving out thro' these stifling streets puts no strength into me. I long to be far away— I feel as if one long breath of pure scotch air would cure me!— The German scheme is fallen entirely into abeyance— Mr C has commenced printing the first two volumes of

18. Jane's close friend Ellen Twisleton, *CL* tells us, 'spent an hour with JWC on the day of Lady Ashburton's funeral. She wrote to her sister, 14 May: "[S]he was so unhappy, I dreaded to leave her to herself." On the way to Cheyne Row, she had seen Jane Brookfield: "I shrunk back in the carriage, feeling as if it were too much to bow to her, even,—when she bent forward, & gave me a bow, with such a broad smile as if we had met at a dinner! & in all my life I never saw her with a more cheerful & serene expression. And two hours after, I left Mrs Carlyle—so pale—so wretched, hardly able to speak without crying;—& there were the two friends (the true and the false as Edward said curtly,) & poor Lady Ashburton had not the gift to see them as they were. I couldn't be convinced, after that look, that Mrs B. has a heart,—except for her own interests. I do so pity the Carlyles [. . .] London will never be anything like the same to them, again."' It is hard to believe there was not some relief for Jane, alongside the pain.

19. St Leonards-on-Sea, just to the west of Hastings, Sussex: a new town in the early 1800s, it rapidly became popular as a holiday destination with royal connections and a train connection to London. In years to come Jane would recuperate there after her Cheapside accident of 1863.

his Book, and it will be a *year* he says before they are ready. 'How was it then' I asked last night, 'that you spoke of being done with them, in *two months*; telling me I *must make haste and get well*, to go to Germany'? Oh, said he, 'one talks all *sorts* of things!'— '[B]ut, said I, that was a talk that cost me three nights sleep, and ever so many days of anxious uneasy thought'! 'Bless me!' he said, quite astonished; 'I said all that *chiefly by way of cheering you up*'!!! Oh men! men!, how stupid you are in your dealings with us poor egg-shell wretches! There is no fear of Germany then for a year anyhow!— And he will be too busy for going from home at all, if he can possibly stand the heat in Town. So that I fancy I shall be at liberty to regulate my own goings according to my own will; which however is hampered enough by many considerations;—chiefly that of *his* solitude and tendency to overwork himself when left in the house alone— For his material comfort Ann can care as well as I, now; the only difference being in our scales of expenditure—and even that is not exorbitant. It will be no kindness to him however, in the long run, to leave untried any feasible means of strengthening myself before the winter returns, to take me by the lungs; and certainly *getting out of this* and breathing fresh air awhile, under favourable *moral* circumstances, would be the most feasible means of all! No where could I be so well, and content, I think, as with *you*; And if I could go to *you* for a fortnight or so, without travelling further, and making more visits; I would say at once your kind invitation is *believed in* and accepted! But there are so many, in Scotland, who have always been kind to me, and whose kindness I would not for the world seem insensible to, who would be grieved and angered if I should be in Scotland without going to see them; and that sort of knocking about, as I experienced last year, is more than I have either strength or spirits for in my *normal* state; After this long illness and confinement to one spot and one circle of ideas, I shudder at the bare notion of going over the ground both material and emotional that I went over last year! But it is time enough to be making up ones plans— In the meantime I am going for a week to Easthampstead Park (the Marquis of Downshires)—almost immediately. But these great grand Country Houses are not the places nature prompts me to take my sick nerves and bad spirits to! especially when I am not going as a sort of animated, still wholly *irresponsible carpet-bag*, with Mr Carlyle's name on it; but on my own basis! The Marchioness of Downshire is an acquaintance I have made, *myself*, in a romantic sort of way—and not one of the flattering consequences of *his* celebrity.[20]

20. Caroline Frances Stapleton Cotton (b. 1815), wife of Arthur Hill, 4th Marquess of Downshire, an Irish peer with an English seat at Easthampstead Park in Berkshire: a house demolished and replaced with a Jacobean Revival building (still standing) in 1860.

She has been very kind to me all winter, coming to see me, and sending me game and beautiful flowers; and for weeks before they left London, hardly a day had past without her daughter or boys coming to ask for me. She is a most lovely, *natural* woman; and so when she insisted it would do me good to go to this place of theirs I assented; hoping Mr C would come too, and help me thro' it; but he is too busy and so I find myself engaged to a piece of work that I wish to Heaven were well over! I have quite forgot how to *dress for dinner* and all that sort of thing!

I have not made a single call *yet*; but when I have finished this letter I am going off in a cab to call for the old Countess of Sandwich (Lady A's Mother). (She said yesterday she would like to see me) and I tremble at the prospect! Her daughter and she could never live together without misunderstandings and disagreeableness; but now the poor old woman thinks of her and talks of her as 'such a kind daughter as never lived'! 'Would have given *her* anything she had in the world'!— Dear! Dear! When I think of the dreadful hard things I have heard Lady Ashburton say of her Mother, at all times and always; how am I to join in, about her kindness to that Mother! in a way to please the beautiful mystification of the Mother-heart!

I send you some poems—amongst which you will find *some* to like— God bless you my darling! Kindest love to your Husband. I was so very thankful to hear of your improved sleep.

Affectionately yours /
Jane W Carlyle

To Thomas Carlyle, Morningside, Edinburgh, 24 August 1857

Oh my Dear! What a magnificent Book *this* is going to be! The best of all your Books! *I* say so who *never flatter*, as you are too well aware; and who am 'the only person I know that is always in the right'![21] So far as it is here before me; I find it forcible, and vivid, and sparkling as *The French Revolution*, with the geniality, and composure, and finish of *Cromwell*—a wonderful combination of merits! And how you *have*

21. Jane has advance proof sheets of the first two volumes of the *History of Friedrich II of Prussia, Called Frederick the Great*, which would be published in 1858 and earn Thomas the princely sum of £2,800. It would be 1865 before the enterprise was complete. It was Adrienne de Noailles, Marquise de La Fayette, wife of the American Revolutionary and French Revolutionary hero (1757–1834), who told her husband she was always right.

contrived to fit together all those different sorts of pictures, belonging to different Times, as compactly and smoothly as a bit of the finest mosaic! Really one may say of these two first Books at least, what Helen said of the letters of her sister who died—you remember? 'So *splendidly* put together; one would have thought that HAND couldn't have written them!'

It was *the sheets* that hindered me from writing yesterday; tho' I doubt if a letter posted at Morningside (the Scotch *Campo Santo* ['holy field': cemetery][)] yesterday (Sunday) would have reached you sooner than if posted today. Certainly it is a Devil of a place for keeping the Sunday, this! Such Preaching, and Fasting, and 'Tooting and Praying' as I was never before concerned in! But one never knows whence *deliverance* is to come any more than *misfortune*! I was cut out of all, or nearly all my difficulties yesterday—by the simple provedential means of—a *bowel complaint*! It was reason enough for staying away from Church; excuse enough for declining to be read to; and the loss of my dinner was entirely made up for, by the loss of my appetite! Nothing could have happened more opportunely! Left at home with Pen (the cat) when they had gone every one to their *different* 'Places of Worship'; I opened my desk to write you a letter. But I would just take a look at *the sheets* first. (Miss Jess [Donaldson] had put a second cover on the parcel, and forwarded it by railway on Saturday night; and I had not been able to *read* then, by the *gass* light, which dazzles my eyes. It is one of the little peculiarities of this house that there isn't a *candle* allowed in it of any sort, wax, dip, moulded or composite!) Well I took up the sheets, and read 'here a little and there a little,' and then I began at the beginning, and never could stop till I had read to the end, and pretty well learnt it by heart. I was still reading when Church came out, and so my letter got nipt in the bud. If it is so interesting for *me*, who have read and heard so many of the STORIES in it before, what must it be for others to whom it is *all* new? the matter as well as the manner of the narrative? Yes, you shall see it will be the best of all your books!—and small thanks to *it*! It has taken a *doing*!

I suppose you are roasting again. *Here*, there has been no such heat since I came north, as in the last three days—mercury at 75 in the shade yesterday. But there is plenty of EAST wind to keep one from suffocating—provided one can get it without the dust— I used to fancy Piccadilly dusty! but oh *my*! if you saw the morning-side Road! Here has been Anne to ask, '*when* will you be ready to go Jeanie'? we are for Edinr (in the Omnibus of course) to call for Mrs George Welsh's Sisters— And I am hardly begun! But I have nothing to tell that wont keep. Oh, wont you put a picture of *Triglaph* (on his tail) in the book?— And that dear brave old Barbarossa, one wants so much to embrace him, and lay one's cheek on his beard![22]

I must tell you a compliment paid me, before I conclude— A Lady I hadnt seen for twenty years came to call for me— 'You were ill I heard,' she said, 'Ah yes—it is easy to see you have suffered!—*an entire wreck*, like myself'—then, looking round on my three Aunts [Welsh]—'indeed like all of us'!!

Yours affectionately / Jane W Carlyle [. . .]

❧

To Thomas Carlyle, Sunny Bank, Haddington, 30 August 1857

Thanks! you are really a good correspondent—*considering*. Wherever I have been, praises have been showered on your 'punctuality in writing'—your 'attention to me' &c &c. But it isn't 'with the reciprocity all on one side'! tho' nobody praises *my* punctuality in writing—*my* attention to *you*!— Oh my Dear! I was prettily frightened in finishing up my last letter! I had reason to believe I was taking 'A COLD' (in *my* emphatic sense of the word!) and what was to become of me? how was I to get home? Worse and worse I grew all the evening, my skin burning and violent pains in my face and back! By a decided inspiration of Nature, I asked Miss Jess to give me a *stiff* little tumbler of Hollands Toddy!!![23] I drank it off, and retired to bed, while the *intoxication* lasted; fell into the soundest, longest sleep I had had for some years! and got up next morning as well as ever!

But how I wish now, I had my long journey safely over! If I could only like 'the Princess of China' (in the Arabian Nights) be carried thro the air, asleep in my bed, and set down on the roof of my own house![24] I fear far more the journey back than I did the journey hither. I seemed *then* to have nothing to lose— [*N*]*ow*, I am so desirous, (God knows,

22. The Triglaph was the grotesque god of an anti-Christian set of peoples of the Baltic, the Wends, who invaded German lands in the early medieval period: 'like a triple porpoise under the influence of laudanum', according to Thomas (*CL*). Frederick Barbarossa (1122–1190), Holy Roman Emperor, King of Germany and Italy: greatest of the medieval emperors, with his famous red beard. All background, however remote, to Frederick the Great's arrival on the German scene.
23. 'Dutch gin with hot water and sugar' (*CL*).
24. 'The Story of Prince Camaralzaman and the Princess Badoura', in the great Middle Eastern narrative collection *One Thousand and One Nights*, of special importance to Western writers in both the Enlightenment and Romantic eras.

for your sake as well as for my own) to take back my little gains of strength, and sleep, and cheerfulness unbroken in upon by any exposure or fatigue. Oh Dear! that one should ever live to have to bother so much about *oneself*! I have been considering about making two days of the journey, and would do it, if I could find a travelling companion, or had any *known* house to put up at in the road. But all alone in a Railway Hotel! no amount of *Hollands*, I fancy, could put me to sleep in that circumstance!

Well—no more about it just now, for I haven't yet fixed my day! haven't been *up to* speaking of it! It takes more courage than I have always at hand now a days, to answer the pleadings of these dear old old women with; '*I must*' '*I will*'!

Meanwhile I am reading *the sheets* to them—*they* most likely will not live to see the finished Book— You never saw more *ardent* listeners! My Godmother with her head bent forward, hearkening with her blind eyes as well as her ears, might sit for a picture of *Attention*! And every now and then one or other asks some question, or makes some remark that shows how *intelligently* they listen[.] Miss Jess said one good thing, 'To look merely to the *wording*, it is so *brief* so *concise*, that one would expect some obscurity in the narrative or at least that it would need a great effort of attention to understand it; instead of which the meaning is as clear as glass.' [A]nd Miss Donaldson said—

'I see more than ever in this, my Dear, what I have always seen in Mr Carlyle's Books; and what I think distinguishs him from all the Writers of the present day; a great love of Truth—and *what is more* (observe the fine discrimination!) *a perfect detestation of Lies*!'

I was afraid having to read in a voice so high pitched, my reading would not do justice to the thing[,] but—Miss Donaldson asked me last night 'My Dear, does Mr Carlyle read—what he writes to you bit by bit'? 'Oh dear no!—he does not like reading aloud.' 'Then I suppose you read it often over to yourself? For I was noticing that in reading those sheets, you did it so—so—*natural like*; just as if it was coming out of your *own* head!'

You may well say what a letter of Lord Ashburtons! Curious! that man seems in a general way so sweet-natured; and yet the only sentiment I ever see him express in a *real human* way is *anger*! Several times, for moments, I have seen him really, *humanly* angry (tho' *shriekily* and *hysterically* enough) but all the rest of his sentiments (his grief included) seem no more *really* HIS than the sentiments of Macbeth are William Macready's[;] indeed not so much! He plays the part of *his own Life* like a *third rate* actor who cant identify himself for a moment with the feelings he has got to express—unless you make him *angry*!

Poor little Mrs Royston!— I am sure Chancellor's Dunghill is concerned in this! Mrs Royston herself has never had a weeks health in that house. And the Hazzlets were always ill in it and left it on account of the Dunghill—[25] It is a shame that, with so much fuss making about drainage, such a thing should be permitted— I am quite sure its mischief reaches in hot nights to [our] own house— I was dreaming last night about going to some strange House—among strange people—to make representations about *cocks*! I went on *my knees* at last, *weeping*, to an old man with a cast metal face and grey hair, and while I was explaining all about how you were an author and couldnt get sleep for these new cocks, my Auditor flounced off, and I became aware he was the man who had three serpent-daughters and kept people in glass bottles in Hoffmans Tale![26] I forget his name—but knew it well enough in my dream— [A] kiss to Nero—

Yours ever JWC

To William Dods, Chelsea, 19? September 1857

My dear 'William Dodds'

Nature prompts me to write you a letter, 'all out of my own head' (as the Children say); to thank you for the good you did me the other morning—more, I dare say, than you proposed to yourself: for you not only smoothed my journey to London, as by magic; but you diffused some sunshine on my *Life-journey* at a point where it was drowned in tears. Decidedly; you played the part of *Deus ex machina*[27] that morning, as successfully as on that other morning, long, long, long ago; when you lent me your white, cotton stockings, good God!

How well I remember it! and what a morning to be sure! all glancing like diamonds, and smelling of hawthorn and sweet briar, with the dew on them!— Don't you find this Earth has changed its face amazingly for the worse, since then; especially in the *mornings*; before breakfast has put a little life in one?— Ach! It was in 1814 that Arcadian transaction of the cotton stockings! I cannot get the date forgotten; for it stands

25. George Chancellor operated a local stable, which generated manure. Mrs Royston of Cheyne Row had caught typhoid from her husband, according to Thomas, 28 August. William Haylett Royston was a stationer and bookseller of Old Broad Street, in the City.
26. For Archivarius Lindhorst in Hoffman's 'The Golden Pot', see 29 August 1837, above.
27. 'God from the machine'; a deity descending to the stage at the denouement of a classical play to resolve issues and avoid a tragedy. Jane is remembering a morning of her schooldays in Haddington, and two schoolmates, too.

written, after my name and designation, in your hand-writing, on the rim of my mathematical-instrument-case[.] I will show it you, if you like, when you come to see me.

You may be sure I lost neither myself nor my luggage with Mr Trotter for escort. At Dunbar he got his ticket exchanged for a first class one; and from that moment, 'stuck closer' to me 'than a Brother'! Had I been a box of gold-dust with thieves lying in wait for it; or an Infant, with no capacity except to suck; I couldn't have been kept more in his eye or more assiduously tended! Good innocent Man! And I to have gone and forgotten him out and out! Really, as much a stranger he was for me, when you brought him up and he stood there in his shoes, as if he had dropt that moment, full-grown, out of the Moon, and his name along with him! He asked if I recollected his 'stealing a piece of jasper' from me; which he afterwards got cut into a seal? Oh no! not even *that*! But had he been in the way of getting *above* me in the class; *shouldn't* I have remembered him with a *vividness*!—as I have always remembered *Tom Dodds* whom I only got the better of '*by one*'!— My utter oblivion of him proves, I think, that dear Mr Trotter must have been, as a boy, 'a considerable of a dunce'!

I 'drew out the cushion' (as you directed) and lay most of the way at full length—a great mitigation of my fatigues[.] Pray, did you find out that property of the cushions 'by your own sharpness'? They *look* as immovable as Arthurs Seat![28]

On the whole, I suppose one should be thankful for the convenience of being shot, as out of a cannon, from Scotland to London 'in no time'— ([M]y handkerchief when taken out of my reticule at Cheyne Row still wet with tears shed at *Haddington*! Think of *that*! all the way from Haddington to Chelsea travelled over, before tears had time to dry on a bit of cambric!) Still it seems to me always a sort of travelling, *that*, more suitable to the Infernal Regions, than to Beings of flesh and blood, with sense of hearing, and not damned—yet!

I heard from Miss Jess Donaldson that your Wife 'called next day,' to tell them of my having an escort to London— I *knew* it already, without being told; as well as if I had seen her, thro *Prince Ahmed's* wonderful Telescope, or in the little mirror *Beauty* got from the *Beast*,[29] put on

28. An ancient (extinct) volcano that dominates the skyline seen from central Edinburgh, and above all from its castle; the name is obscure, but may be related to King Arthur of legend.

29. The first in 'The Story of Prince Ahmed and the Fairy Paribanou' in *One Thousand and One Nights* (which also features a flying carpet); the second in Jeanne-Marie Leprince de Beaumont's version of the fairy story, where Beauty can see her father returning home heartbroken in a magic mirror at the Beast's castle. The wishing cap features in the Renaissance German story of Fortunatus, and allows its wearers' desires to come true.

her bonnet and shawl, and take the road to Sunny Bank, and go in. Because, you see; it was exactly what a kind-hearted thoughtful woman would be certain to do; and when I kissed your wife at parting, it was exactly because I had seen in her these qualities, in a high degree.

Please tell her with my love; I hope she will go often to my dear old friends. They are not without people enough 'dropping in' to call; but people who drop in to call are not invariably good company; when one happens to have some sense and feeling!— I often pitied them from my heart, straining their poor deaf ears, to hear stuff I should have been ashamed to talk to my dog! and they so *wise* and good! Your Wife appreciates them as I do, and sympathizes with their earnest, saddened manner of being. I perceived *that*, in the little talk I had with her alone. So it would be a comfort to me, in thinking about them, at this impracticable distance, to hear they saw *her* very often.

Oh Heaven! what a pity it is, one cannot live in more than one place at a time! or that there is not now a '*flying carpet*' or a '*Wishing Cap*' to be had for love or money! But for *that*; I would spend at least one hour at dear old Sunny Bank (hang its new name!) every day of my life.

Well! there is no truer proverb than that 'two afflictions make a consolation.' For example, the affliction of not being able to live in *two* places at the same time is quite consoled for me just now, by this other affliction of being hardly able to live at all! I have gone and taken a shocking bad cold again—and am '*suffering* MARTYRS' (as a foreign friend of mine [Etienne Paulet] says)

Speak of *remorse*! Had I made one crash of the whole *ten commandments* I couldn't feel more downhearted than this feverish *cold* is making me! It all comes of a 'delicate attention' of my Husbands—what he calls 'letting in a little fresh air on you, my Dear'!—(in point of fact keeping me always in a violent draught.) There are many ways of killing a wife besides those that appear in Police Reports. But the absurdity here is that my Husband really wishes me to live!—

Kind remembrance to *your* wife— Yours affectionately Jane Welsh Carlyle

To Agnes Howden, Chelsea, 23 November 1857

There's a good Girl! And thank you!— I choose the present moment for answering; as it is the most improbable I am likely to find! for I have the same sort of defiant pleasure in going in the teeth of probability that

I used to have in going in the teeth of a high wind— I am pressed for time, having an appointment two miles off at one o'clock; my attention is distracted by a man painting beside me, and talking;[30] my nerves are all in a flurry from a recent fright; and Mr Carlyle has just brought me an impossible glove to mend! What more would I have?—

But *the fright*?—gracious goodness, the fright is worth telling about!— I have a servant [Anne] whom, during five years that she has been with me, I had never seen in a hurry, or excited, or deprived of her presence of mind. What then was my astonishment when she rushed into the drawing room last night, with her head *tumbled off* (as at first it looked to me) and carrying it in her hands!! and crying wildly 'Oh Mam! I must go to a Doctor! (scream) my ear my ear! (scream) an *animal* has run into my ear!!' She was holding down her head as low as her waist, her cap off, her hair flying, and her hand pressed to her right ear. I sprang forward and pulled her fingers from her ear which was full of blood. 'What *animal*?' I gasped. 'Oh I think it is a black beetle!!'— and the screams went on, and she declared the beetle was 'running up into her brain.' Her ignorance of anatomy was very unfortunate at the moment! I called up Mr Carlyle, for I had lost all presence of mind as well as herself— He took it coolly, as he takes most things; 'Syringe it,' he said; 'syringing will bring out *any amount of black beetles*!!'— There is an apothecary at the bottom of our street; I threw a table cover about her, and told her to run to him; and I begged Mr C to go with her, as it was a dangerous thing for *me* to go out in the night air. 'Go with her?' he said; 'What good could it do *my* seeing the Beetle taken out of her ear?'— But I had read in a newspaper not long ago of a man killed, by some insect creeping into his ear; and how did I know the apothecary was not an ass, and might spoil her hearing for life with probes and things—if indeed she did not die of it,! or go raving mad, as I should do in her place I thought!

I paced up and down the room for some ten minutes like a wild animal in its cage; then put on a cloak and bonnet and rushed after her—Mr C running after *me*, to pull me back. When I arrived in the man's little surgery; I found poor Ann covered with soapsuds, and comparitively calm; and the beetle (it actually was a black beetle) extracted piecemeal (with a probe)— 'There might be a leg or so left' he said; but he would syringe the ear again in the morning— She would not go back to him this morning however; the rushing sound being gone,

30. This is Robert Tait, painting his photographic *Chelsea Interior* picture of the parlour at No. 5 with Jane, Thomas and Nero, which still hangs at the Carlyle house. Tait obsessed over it for months, and made something of a nuisance of himself, accordingly.

and the deafness remaining being owing she thinks to the ear being swelled from the rough treatment it got. I was better pleased that this man should not *probe* any more— If she does not hear with it tomorrow I will send her to a regular Surgeon. Meanwhile I feel as if I had been pounded in a mortar, with the fright of the thing, and have narrowly missed a cold, for I *coughed* half the night. But that is passed off thank god. I am so afraid of another seven months confinement!

I liked to hear of your Halloween—my ideas of Halloween are all connected with Maitlanfield. I always spent it *there* as far back as I recollect. Have ducked for apples and burnt nuts in that very kitchen of yours![31]

If Mrs Skirving wants to escape money disaster and all sorts of disaster, she should replace little Ann Camerons poor little white marble tablet in the Churchyard![32] I could not have confidence in my Fortunes, with such a thing in my cellar. Could you?— I should like ill to be the wife of a speculator just now! Mr C has or *had* some money in America— He *doesn't recollect how much*! and doesn't feel even a natural *curiosity* what is become of it!!— I have never heard a word out of his head about it except to say *once*, 'I suppose *my* money will have gone in the crash, and poor *Buttler* (the gentleman who invested it for him) will be very sorry!'— Being a Philosopher's wife has *some* advantages!— I never think about money myself beyond what serves my daily needs—but if *he* werent of the same mind I might be made sufficiently uncomfortable about it.

And now good luck to you— Remember me to them all— I owe your sister in law a letter, which she shall get some day—

Yours affly / Jane W Carlyle

To George Eliot, Chelsea, 21 January 1858

Dear Sir

I have to thank you for a surprise, a pleasure, and a—*consolation* (!) all in one Book! and I *do* thank you most sincerely. I cannot divine what

31. Maitlandfield House, Haddington, was built in the mid-seventeenth century and bought by Agnes and Thomas Howden (see Characters and Correspondents) in the 1840s; Jane must have known the Maitlands, the previous owners, in her youth. The house still stands, and is a hotel.

32. Margaret Skirving, Haddington local and probably the mother of Robert Skirving, to whom Jane wrote on 11 May 1847, above. *CL* suggests that Ann Cameron's tombstone was in the cellar of Agnes Howden's brother's house, and that he had promised to erect it in the garden in memory of the girl, killed in a fire.

inspired the good thought to send *me* your Book; since (if the name on the Title Page be your real name) it could not have been personal regard; there has never been a *George Eliot* among my friends or acquaintances.[33] But neither I am sure could *you* divine the circumstance under which I should read the Book, and the particular benefit it should confer on me!— I read it—at least the first volume—during one of the most (physically) wretched nights of my life; sitting up in bed, unable to get a wink of sleep for fever and sorethroat; and it helped me thro that dreary night, as well—better than the most sympathetic helpful friend watching by my bedside could have done!

You will believe that the book needed to be something more than a 'new novel' for me; that I *could*, at my years, and after so much reading, read it in positive torment, and be beguiled by it of the torment! that it needed to be the one sort of Book, however named, that still takes hold of me, and that grows rarer every year—a *human* book—written out of the heart of a live man, not merely out of the brain of an author—full of tenderness and pathos without a scrap of sentimentality, of sense without dogmatism, of earnestness without twaddle—a book that makes one *feel friends*, at once and for always, with the man or woman who wrote it!

In guessing at why you gave me this good gift; I have thought amongst other things; 'Oh, perhaps it was a delicate way of presenting the *novel* to my Husband, he being over head and ears in *History*.'— If that was it; I compliment you on your *tact*! for my Husband is much liklier to read the *Scenes* on *my* responsibility than on a venture of his own— Tho', as a general rule, never opening a novel, he has engaged to read this one, whenever he has some leisure from his present Task.

A severe Influenza, which fell on me the same day I had the windfall of the book, and from which I am but just *beginning* to recover, must excuse the tardiness of my acknowledgments.

I hope to know someday if the person I am addressing bears any resemblance, in external things to the Idea I have conceived of him in my mind—a man of middle age—with a wife from whom he has got those beautiful *feminine* touches in his book—a good many children—and a dog—that he has as much fondness for as I have for my little Nero! for the rest—not just a Clergyman; but Brother or first cousin to a Clergyman!— How ridiculous all this *may* read, beside the reality!

33. Eliot's first substantial work of fiction, *Scenes of Clerical Life*: a group of three novellas, each featuring a clergyman, it was well received and assumed to be the work of a country parson such as those depicted. (One even went so far as to volunteer himself as the author.) In her journal of 8 January Eliot recorded, 'I ordered copies to be sent to the following persons—Froude, Dickens, Thackeray, Tennyson, Ruskin, Faraday [. . .] Mrs Carlyle.' Jane is astute about the book's 'feminine touches'; other readers discerned those, too.

Any how; I honestly confess I am very curious about you—and look forward with what Mr Carlyle would call 'a good, healthy, genuine desire' to shaking hands with you someday— In the meanwhile I remain your obliged

Jane W. Carlyle

❧

To Charlotte Southam, Bay House, Alverstoke, Hampshire, 5 August 1858

Oh, little woman! little woman! I wonder how you get on there [Cheyne Row], all by yourself, in that 'highly *genteel* seven-roomed House' (as the retired Cheese-monger would describe it!) If you hadn't made 'ducks and drakes' of your opportunities; and, when I was ready to teach you to *write*, and you had time to learn, preferred sitting drearily at the upstairs window looking out into the street; you might by this time have been *up to* writing me a nice little letter; to your own honour and glory! as well as to *my* peace of mind; seeing that I can't help making myself anxious about you; when day after day passes, and I hear nothing from home—not a word either from you, or the dog, or the sparrow!

I am much better since I came here— Indeed this life is the very wholesomest that could have been cut out for me! Sea-air blowing round me day and night—a drive in an open carriage every day—nothing to do 'about dinner' except *eat* it! perfect comfort, without too much ceremony; and kindness without fuss!— [A]ll this considered; you won't expect me home on *Saturday*! not a bit of me!— I will write to Mr Larkin to take you money for another week.

And I entreat you to find new work for yourself! that you mayn't, in my absence, scrape acquaintance with a certain person [the Devil] who, I told you, was 'always at the elbow of an idle girl'!— And that I may see cause to commend your diligence when I return! Tell Nero, with my dear love, that I fervently hope he is not overeating himself! And to the Sparrow give, in my name, a good-sized worm![34]

God keep you a good girl!

Yours kindly, /

JANE CARLYLE

❧

34. Jane adopted odd pets and wild animals frequently; on 23 July 1845, for example, she wrote to Thomas in Chelsea (*CL* 19: 106), 'Will you tell Helen to be sure to give *the leech* water *every day* and keep it out of the Sun.'

To Henry Larkin, Bay House, Alverstoke, Hampshire, 6 August 1858

My dear Mr Larkin

Will you give my Charlotte the half-sovereign on Saturday—I am not coming for some time yet. The place suits me famously! and already I both feel and look quite different from the '*Seedy Party*' that took leave of you at Chelsea! I get some *human* sleep here, and no longer *cough* at all in the *evening*, and very little at any time. I have a long drive in an open carriage every day; and every day eat *two* dinners!—one at half after one, and the second at eight! this system answers perfectly!

But oh Mr Larkin!—my watch!— If it didn't go and stop, at a quarter to five, the very first morning!— I tried every persuasion to make it go on again, but beyond *nine* it positively would not go!— I now for the first time see the sense of those Great *Bells* which make such a devil of a row in aristocratic Houses. They are in aid of visitors whose watches refuse to go! If it were'nt for 'the getting up Bell,' and 'the breakfast Bell,' and 'the servants' dinner-Bell,' and 'the Lunch Bell,' and 'the dressing-Bell,' and 'the dinner Bell,' I dont know what would become of me! for to *tell the time* by *feeling*, in a strange house thrown loose from ones home habits and occupations is quite beyond me!

Mr Carlyle is still in the vague about Germany. His going will depend, I think, on Lord Ashburtons success in looking up 'a man with a yacht'!

I had a fine sail in Portsmouth Harbour the other day, and went on board The *Urgent*, and got two *splatches* (scotch) of brown paint on my new dress!— There are *Forts* here, and a *camp*, and every thing a reasonable woman could desire![35]

Remember me kindly to your mother— yours most truly

Jane W Carlyle[36]

35. There were no fewer than six forts in the Portsmouth area, five of them built recently in response to the sabre-rattling of Napoleon III, by turns first president and last monarch of France, and nephew of Napoleon Bonaparte. Browndown Army Camp at Stokes Bay was there for the same reason. HMS *Urgent* was a troopship.

36. *CL* gives us Mr Larkin's side of this little story: 'Reading this pleasant little letter, at once suggested to me to give her an equally pleasant surprise in return. So I wound up my own watch, packed it carefully in wadding in a little box, put the key inside, and upon the watch a slip of paper on which I had written, "Please wind me up!" This I posted, together with a letter; picturing to myself what her surprise would be, but little thinking how deeply she would feel such a simple act of playful goodwill.'

To Henry Larkin, Bay House, Alverstoke, Hampshire, 9 August 1858

Oh my dear Mr Larkin, upon my honour I all but burst into tears (!) this morning, at your kindness! and I astonished the company at breakfast, by the new views of the world it had given me! It was impossible to keep one's stand on Misanthropy in the face of that watch! 'Excuse me,' said a Lady-visitor to the mistress of the house, who had taxed her with not returning her salutation on entering the room, 'I was so confounded at hearing *Mrs Carlyle* say, "It was a *good* world," that I quite forgot myself!'

It came to hand *going*, the watch! and I wound it up immediately. It gave me such an odd feeling of *aliveness*, that ticking away amongst cotton, all along the rail from London to here; I felt inclined to say to it, 'How do you do? dear little thing,' and to expect an articulate answer.

I am all the more thankful for it, that the Bells were no longer to be trusted. On Sunday morning I sat reading, wearying for my breakfast, till a House-maid bounced in with dust-brush and pitcher and the usual &c.'s. I stared, and so did she. 'It is not time to go down, is it?' I asked. 'Oh yes, Mam, breakfast must be nearly over!' 'But only *one* Bell has rung yet.' 'Yes, but *that* was the Breakfast Bell; no Prayer-Bell rings on Sundays!' And so I had to go down to reproaches on my laziness, accompanied by the coldest tea and the toughest toast!

We have the loveliest weather here, and I flourish 'like the green Bay Tree,'—unhappy simile![37] I have been once to 'The Island,' (as they say here), and am going again. We have a Lady in the house, who, tho' the oldest of us, has an untiring love of 'expeditions,' and in *her* hands we are safe from stagnation at all rates. To-day, after luncheon, she is going to take me on board *The Renown*.[38] It is the gayest country place. A quarter of a mile off is a field all covered with snow-white canvas Cones; which, in my simplicity, I took at first for the most stupendous gipsy-encampment. But it is a regular *Camp*, where some two thousand soldiers idle about. Then, just outside the gates, a grand new Fort is building, the most interesting peculiarity of which is, that the guns of it, if ever they are fired, *must* smash right through this House.

I am not going home this week either. So that blessed Dog must just console himself with the Sparrow! When I do return, it is possible I shall soon start off again! as soon as I have got clean ribbons to my bonnet,

37. Psalms 37: 35. 'The Island' is the Isle of Wight, just across the Solent.
38. Many naval battleships have borne this name: this was a recently commissioned screw steamer, sold to the Prussian Navy as a training ship in 1870, and broken up in 1892. She arrived at Spithead on 24 June and Admiral Fremantle hoisted his flag aboard on this very day.

and a few other feminine necessities supplied. It is very dreary spending one's life coughing alone, in that House of Cheyne Row, with which I have hardly any associations that are not saddening, or worse!—*very* dreary!— And why should I do it? When I am not needed for '*The Cares of Bread*' (as Mazzini calls Housekeeping), or the cares of *Buttons* or of *mislaid papers*! Whether Mr C goes to Germany or not, I dont think he will be home till October— So I have still a good few weeks in which to 'wander at my own sweet will'![39]

If all have gone right Mr C is at this hour showing the Lions (or rather, the *Lambs*) of Dumfries to Lord Ashburton!— Lord A had arranged to leave London tomorrow morning, with his eldest Sister, for the Highlands; '*Consequently*' he took a sudden whim to start from London today and spend an evening and morning with Carlyle at Dumfries, leaving his Sister to proceed to Glasgow, with the house Doctor!! He is perfectly charming that man, for giving those about him a never flagging series of surprises!—

I continue to improve in health—hardly *cough* at all now—and have bloomed out into the most captivating head-dresses—'regardless of expence'! I hope to return to London with such a look of *living*, that no man will dream of kissing me into a fright; however dramatical his *line*!

Love to your Mother— And to all your family remember me—and believe in my gratitude and affection—Jane Carlyle [. . .]

To Janet Pringle, Chelsea, circa 23 November 1858

My dear Mrs Pringle

With a great effort I got up to breakfast this morning, the first time for a fortnight, having again my *cold*; and by the disheartening light of a London Fog, I perceived one letter on the table for me, black edged—which proved to be an announcement of your Uncle's death![40] His poor Wife who seemed so fond of him! I feel *very* sorry for her,—if my sorrow could but do her any good! which it can't! I remember when I was there you considered his Life a precarious one; but he *looked* so hale and hearty,—was so full of kindness, and fun, and life, that day we dined with him, that the news of his death has shocked me more than my

39. Wordsworth's famous sonnet, 'Composed upon Westminster Bridge'.
40. John Hunter and wife Catherine, of Bennan, Tynron, near Thornhill, Dumfries; he died of liver disease.

slight acquaintance with him seems to make natural.— Do write when you can find time, and tell me if his death was sudden, and what was his malady, and how his wife bears it. And, when you find a fit opportunity, give her my kind regards, and tell her I have a grateful remembrance of *his* and her kindness to me, and sincere sympathy with her affliction.— Oh Dear! what a comfortable, hospitable cheerful House Bermin looked to me that day! And what fun we made about 'Aunt Kates' puff-paste, and all that—and now—!

I have been expecting and wanting a letter from you. Plenty of people are kind to me here—very kind; but when one has found a place so good and pleasant for me as Tynron was, one likes to attach a thread (like little Tom Thumb) to the bushes along the road! in plain prose one likes to keep up ones relations with those who made it so pleasant. [. . .]

It is rather vexatious, don't you think, to have gone and laid myself up so early in the winter? It was Lord Ashburton's *Picture* that was the innocent ostensible cause![41] I told you I think of the beautiful Picture of little Friz and his Sister Whilelmina which Lord A *would* give me, and which I had no place for in all my house, unless I removed the great Bookcase from the Drawingroom to the room below. It was sent on his return to London exactly at the wrong moment, when the weather had become intensely cold. At least at the wrong moment when there was a remarkably impatient Husband in the case! I would have let it stand on the parlour floor, for my part, until there was fitter weather for a household Earthquake. But every day Mr C suggested; 'My Dear when are you thinking of &c' 'Is the paper made yet for that wall?' 'Are you *never* going to &c'? till mortal patience could stand it no longer! and I sent for the Carpenter and the paper hanger, and the staircase window had to be taken out; and all the doors flying, and myself flying—to direct blockheads for a whole day. So at night I went to bed in a high fever—quite another sort of 'fever' from any *you* ever saw me in!—and for three successive nights I never closed my eyes, and was in agonies of face ach &c &c— And now I am shut up for six months I expect with my *cough* and all the rest of it. But the cough is not so bad as last year, and I have more *strength* to bear it. Thanks to Bay House and Lann Hall! Pity there is no sunshine in this world without shadow! That Picture is very charming to look at from my sofa; but *such* a cold is a heavy price for the pleasure!— I remember as if it were yesterday travelling all night in a post chaise with my Mother and an old East Lothian Farmer, who was going to meet my Father at Craigenputtoch, and advise about

41. Antoine Pesne, *The Little Drummer* (1714), depicting Frederick the Great as a child. Whereabouts now uncertain, though many prints exist.

drains. My Mother and I were to be dropt at my Grand Fathers, I was mad with joy to go on my *first* journey, but oh so *sick* in a close carriage always! one minute I was chattering like a magpie, the next vomiting out of the window! In the course of the night I lay down at the bottom of the chaise, my head on my Mothers knees and whimpered and moaned. The old Farmer got tired of me—naturally—and said with a certain sharpness, words that cut into my small heart with a sudden mysterious horror! 'Little girl,' he said, 'don't you know that there is no pleasure to be had in this world without pain!' No! I didn't know it! But it was dreadful to hear[,] for somehow I thought he who was *old* must be speaking truth. And I believed him, all in shrinking from him as a sort of cruel ogre! That was *my* initiation into the dark side of Life[.] What was yours?

Now good night— Love to the Boys[.] Is the nursemaid gone to fulfill her Destiny?

affly yours /

Jane C Welsh—

Oh! I mean Jane W Carlyle

To Mary Carlyle Austin, Chelsea, mid-January 1859?

My dear Mary,

My *speechless dismay* yesterday on the arrival of your box might be reproduced, with grand effect, on the stage of one of the minor theatres!

First I must tell you, that ever since your promise of '*fresh eggs*' reached Mr C; it had been, not absolutely *only*, but without exaggeration—*the only pleasant* idea of his mind! '[I]n a few days there would be Gill Eggs to one's breakfast, Thank God!' And in the meantime, his chronic discontent with his *fried bacon*, with his *Yarmouth bloaters*,[42] because *they* were NOT fresh eggs was gradually rising to phrenzy pitch! And in the same ratio intensified itself his scorn of my stupidity in not being able to discover *fresh* eggs *here* 'at any season of the year!' and his sacred horror of badness of egg-arrangements generally!! I had been listening to every van that passed our house, for two days; in trembling hope it would stop and '*fresh* eggs' issue from it! Yesterday, being fine,

42. The bloater is a cold-smoked herring, perennially associated with the Norfolk port of Great Yarmouth; a form of kipper, but lighter in flavour, smoked whole, and sometimes jestingly referred to as a 'Yarmouth capon'.

a fine bright sunshine, before the frost and snow that were on the road; I went out for a little walk. On my return, while standing till the door was opened, I noticed the door steps all *trickled over* with a thick buff colored fluid! 'What *can that* be!' I asked at Charlotte the moment she appeared— 'Come in— Oh do come in out of the cold Mam,' said she coaxingly, and you shall know all about it!— [']In the first place *There*!' she said, pointing to what shall I say? the ruins of a Box on one of the passage chairs! '*That* is the box you were expecting; and *People have been into it*, and they say lots of the eggs are smashed; but it's *my* opinion they have taken them! Master came down, and told the man; he had better in Future read the address on boxes *before* breaking into them! as if *that* would bring back *the eggs, now*!' At last I got the state of the case out of her: The Carrier who brought the box from the railway had left it by mistake at 5 Cheyne Walk—and the man of that house, who must be not the master, but in to keep it (from Mr C's observation of his appearance) 'being expecting something himself'—proceeded to knock the lid in pieces, and finding what he did *not* expect, looked at the address, tied all up anyhow and nohow, and brought it here—marking his way with dripping of Egg, as, of yore, dear little Thom Thumb marked *his* with bread crumbs![43] Now my opinion is, 'the man' had done nothing very heinous. It was the carrier who had the blame. Tell me how many eggs you put in. I took out, *whole*, precisely 2 dozens—but from the fact that only *four* of these were in the first lair, and that the hay was quite soaked, I infer there must have been nearly as many again. What a cruel pity! Charlotte's notion that the man had 'taken a *rare lot* to himself' was founded on the fact that there was only *one* broken empty shell amongst the hay! still the hay was saturated with egg, and the man had not thought it necessary, I suppose, to put back the broken shells he would first take out; besides the 2 dozen of eggs, there were 4 magnificent fowls, and a tongue—(I wish it were an inspired one!)—was that right? I am so sorry about the eggs—for *your* disappointment and Mr C's—more than for my own—*that tongue* will for many days leave *me* nothing

43. The tale of Tom Thumb the miniature boy is told in many different versions in English folklore. In one, little Tom tries to mark his way home from the woods by leaving a trail of breadcrumbs, but the birds eat them. Lost, he is forced to spend the night at a giant's house, who later pursues him wearing the famous 'Seven League Boots'. The egg saga ran and ran, as Austin sent eggs no fewer than three times. On 7 February Jane reported 'certainly two thirds of that first lair [layer] of eggs had to be lifted with a spoon'; on 17 February 'The eggs actually arrived last night! A complete success this time! for there was not a single egg broken, or so much as cracked!' Austin clearly sent a beef tongue, too, which keeps Jane happy at breakfast. (For 'inspired' tongues, see Acts 2: 1.)

to wish for to my breakfast!— I think the box had been loosened by the *division*; and so the poor dear inestimable eggs had taken to polkaing on the road! besides perhaps *the man* DID break a few himself, before he was sensible what kittle [delicate] ware he had to deal with! that is a less intolerable supposition than the one of his having *eaten* them!

Oh my Dear! My Dear, what a Devil-to-pay time of it we have just now!— The new volumes don't seem in the way to being done a whit easier than the former ones![44] and meanwhile the Books and papers that are '*lost*' every day—'*irretrievably lost! swept away into the abyss*! Oh CON-FOUND it! *No man was ever so situated*!![''] and the book or paper missing, lying all the while before his nose! My Dear! I assure you it is enough, combined with the dark winter weather, and 'the general pressure of things,' to make one invest a sixpence in arsenic! If one hadn't enjoyed the advantages of a presbyterian education![45] As an old rheumatic beggar-man said in his last illness, to our white-neckclothed Curate, 'I don't think I shall *regret the loss of myself*!' 'A very incomprehensible speech' said the Curate—[b]ut I understood it perfectly well. Especially when Mr C. is in a phase of 'losing things,' and *tearing about*; and CONFOUNDING it! It is to be hoped these eggs (the whole ones) and these prize-fowls may have a calming influence on his 'Interior'! A hundred thanks Dear! Kindest regards to Jamie and all the girls and the nice wee boy.

Your Affectionate
Jane Welsh Carlyle

To George Eliot, Chelsea, 20 February 1859

Dear Sir

I must again offer you my heartiest thanks. Since I received your *Scenes of Clerical Life* nothing has fallen from the skies to me so welcome as *Adam Bede, all to myself*, 'from the Author.'[46]

44. Volumes 3 and 4 of the interminable *Frederick*, eventually published in 1862 and 1864.
45. Presbyterianism is a branch of the Protestant faith having its origins in sixteenth-century Scotland and its star performer in John Knox, much influenced by Swiss theologian Jean Calvin. The church has always placed a huge emphasis on education, which has permeated Scottish culture at large.
46. A powerful follow-up to Eliot's first book, this classic novel, set in her English Midlands, had many reviewers pondering the author's gender.

My Husband had just read an advertisement of it aloud to me, adding; '*Scenes of Clerical Life*? *That* was *your* Book wasn't it?' (The '*your*' being in the sense not of possession but of prediliction) 'Yes,' I had said, 'and I am so glad that he has written another! *Will* he send me this one, I wonder?'—thereby bringing on myself an utterly disregarded admonition about 'the tendency of the Female Mind to run into unreasonable expectations' when up rattled the Parcel Delivery cart, and, a startling double-rap having transacted itself, a Book-parcel was brought me. 'There it is!' I said, with a little air of injured innocence triumphant!— 'There is *what*, my Dear?'— 'Why, *Adam Bede* to be sure'!— 'How do you know?' (I had not yet opened the parcel) 'By *divination*.'— 'Oh!—Well!—I hope you also *divine* that *Adam Bede* will justify your enthusiasm now you have got it'!— 'As to *that*' (snappishly) 'I needn't have recourse to divination, only to natural logic!'— Now; if it had turned out *not* Adam Bede after all; where *was* my 'diminished head' going to have hidden itself?—[47] But Fortune favours the Brave! I had foretold aright, on both points! The Book was actually *Adam Bede*, and *Adam Bede* 'justified my enthusiasm'; to say the least!

Oh yes! It was as good as *going into the country for one's health*, the reading of that Book was!— Like a visit to Scotland *minus* the fatigues of the long journey and the grief of seeing friends grown old, and Places that knew me knowing me no more! I could fancy, in reading it, to be seeing and hearing once again a crystal-clear, musical, scotch stream, such as I long to lie down beside and—*cry* at (!) for gladness and sadness; after long stifling Sojourn in the South; where there [is] no *water* but what is stagnant or muddy!—

In truth, it is a beautiful most *human* Book! Every *Dog* in it, not to say every man woman and child in it, is brought home to one's 'business and bosom,'[48] an individual fellow-creature! I found myself in charity with the whole human race when I laid it down— [T]he *canine* race I had always appreciated—'not wisely but too well!'[49]—the *human*, however,—Ach!—*that* has troubled me—as badly at times as 'twenty gallons of milk on one's mind'![50] For the rest; why you are so good to *me* is still a *mystery*, with every appearance of remaining so! Yet have I lavished more childish conjecture on it than on anything since I *was* a child, and got mistified about—a door (!) in our dining-room. What *did* that door

47. Milton, *Paradise Lost*, iv. 35.
48. Francis Bacon, *Essays* (1625), dedication.
49. Shakespeare, *Othello*, V. ii. 344.
50. *Adam Bede* itself, chapter 32.

open into? Why had I never seen it opened? Standing before it, 'as in presence of The Infinite,' I pictured to myself glorious possibilities on the other side, and also horrible ones! I spun long romances about it in my little absurd head! I never *told* how that door had taken hold of me, for I '*thought shame*'; it was a curiosity too sacred for speech! But I lay in wait to catch it open some day; and then I somehow—forgot all about it!—till long after (a year or so) that the recollection of my door-worship occurred to me 'quite promiscuously,' and in the same instant, the whole fact as to the door smote me, like a slap on the face! It was a door into—*nothing*! Make-believe! *There* for uniformity! Behind it was bare lath and plaster; behind that the Drawing-room with its familiar tables and chairs! Dispelled illusion no. 1! and epitome 'of *much*!' (as Mr Carlyle might say)[51]

Perhaps *could* I penetrate my little mystery of the present date; I should arrive at the same sort of lath-and-plaster results! And so—I give it up; just 'taking,' gratefully and gladly, 'the good the Gods (under the name of George Elliot) have provided me.'[52]

Now, Heaven knows if such a long letter to read be not illustrating for *you* also 'the tendency of the female mind to run into unreasonable expectations'! But just consider! Is it possible that, with my opportunities, I should not know perfectly well, what a 'distinguish-Author' *does* with letters of compliment *that bore him*; either by their length or their stupidity? He lights his pipe with them, or he makes them into spills [lighters]; or he crushes them into a ball, and pitches them in the fire or waste-paper basket; does anything with them *except read them*! So I needn't take fright about having *bored* you; Since, long before it came to that, I should have, or shall have been slit up into spills, or done good service in lighting your pipe! It is lawful for *Clergymen* to smoke, I hope,—for their own sakes? The newspaper critics have decided you are a Clergyman, but I don't believe it the least in the world. You understand the duties and uses of a Clergyman too well, for *being* one! An old Lord, who did not know my Husband, came up to him once at a Public meeting where he had been summoned to give his 'views' (not *having* any) on the 'Distressed Needle Women,' and asked; 'pray Sir, may I inquire, are *you* a Stock-Broker?'— 'A Stock-Broker! certainly not!'— 'Humph! Well I thought you *must* be a Stock-Broker; because, Sir, you

51. It is interesting here to see Jane favouring Eliot with example after example of her and Thomas's 'coterie speech' that the novelist could not possibly share: as if this person, whom she does not know at first hand, was a personal friend.
52. Dryden, 'Alexander's Feast, or the Power of Music', 106: 'Take the good the Gods provide thee!'

go to the root of the matter.'—[53] If that be the signal of a Stock-Broker I should say you must certainly be a *Stock Broker*, and must certainly not be a *Clergyman*!

Respectfully and affectionately yours, whatever you be
Jane W. Carlyle

❧

To Mary Russell, Chelsea, 26 October 1859

Dearest Mary

If you but knew how I have been situated! (my Husbands favorite phrase) First I arrived so tired! Oh so dead tired! Notwithstanding that I actually summoned nerve to put in effect my often cherished idea of sleeping at York (half way) *alone*—in *an Inn*! Odd! that I should never at this age have done that thing before, in my life! except once when after an absence of eighteen years I spent a night *Incognita* [unknown] in the George Inn of Haddington! where I *could* not feel myself a mere traveller. It was a proof that my nerves were stronger—if not my limbs—that I really '*carried out*' the York speculation, *when it came to the point*. It would certainly have been again a failure however, but for a Lady in Fife telling me of a comfortable Inn to stop at. I was to ask on getting out of the carriage 'was any porter from Mrs Scawins [the landlady] here?' Which I had no sooner done, than the name Scawen was shouted out in the sound of '*Sowens*'! to my great shame!— I feeling as if everybody knew where I was going; and that it was my first adventure of the sort!! But I was comfortably and quietly lodged—no bugs—no anything to molest me—only that the tumult in my own blood me kept awake all night— So that I arrived here as tired next evening, as if I had come the whole road at one horrid rush—

53. Eliot may indeed have been using Jane to get to Thomas. *CL* quotes a note she sent her publisher, William Blackwood, with Jane's letter, on 24 February: 'I want the philosopher himself to read it because the [Thomas's] pre-philosophic period [. . .] lay among the furrowed fields and pious peasantry. If he could be urged to read a novel! I should like, if possible, to give him the same sort of pleasure he has given me in the early chapters of *Sartor*, where he describes little Diogenes eating his porridge on the wall in sight of the sunset, and gaining deep wisdom from the contemplation of the pigs and other "higher animals" of Entepfuhl.' As for Eliot's identity, *CL* also has this: 'A notice in the *Scotsman*, 10 Aug., read: "The great 'Adam Bede' secret is at length thought to be discovered, and the author is [. . .] simply a Miss Mary Ann Evans, already known in this strong-minded generation as the translator of Strauss's 'Life of Jesus.'"'

And I hadn't much time allowed me to rest: for tho' Charlotte had got down all the carpets, there were still quantities of details for *me* to do; before Mr C came. And he staid only a week behind me—

When the house was all in order for him; my cares were destined to take another turn—even more engrossing. Just the night before his arrival, Charlotte went to some shops, taking the dog with her, and brought him home in her arms, all crumpled together like a crushed spider, and his poor little eyes protruding, and fixedly staring in his head! A Butcher's cart, driving furiously round a sharp corner, had passed over poor little Nero's Throat! and *not* killed him on the spot! But he looked killed enough at the first. When I tried to '*stand him* on the ground' (as the servants here say) he flopped over on his side quite stiff and apparently unconscious![54]

You may figure my sensations! And I durst not show all my grief; Charlotte was so distressed and really could not have helped it!— I put him in a warm bath—and afterwards wrapt him warmly and laid him on a pillow—and left him; without much hope of finding him alive in the morning.

But in the morning he still breathed, tho' incapable of any movement: but he swallowed some warm milk that I put into his mouth— About midday I was saying aloud 'poor dog—poor little Nero!,' when I saw the bit tail trying to wag itself!— And after that, I had good hopes— In another day he could raise his head to lap the milk himself— And so by little and little, he recovered the use of himself—but it was ten days before he was able to raise a *bark*—his first attempt was like the *scream* of an infant!

It has been a revealation to me this of the strength of the throat of a dog!!— Mr C says if the wheel had gone over *anywhere else* it would have killed him! A gentleman told me the other night that he once *saw* a fine large dog run over—the great wheel of one of Pickford's[55] heavy-laden vans went over *its* throat!! And the dog—just rose up and shook itself!! It next staggered a little to one side and then a little to the other, as if drunk—then it steadied itself, and walked composedly home!

54. *CL* has Thomas's recollection: 'Poor little foolish faithful dog! it killed him after all; was never well again. He died in some four months [. . .] with a degree of pitying sorrow even from me, which I am still surprised at. The wreck of poor Nero, who had to be strychnined by the doctor, was, and is still, memorable, sad and miserable to me, the last nocturnal walk he took with me, his dim white little figure in the universe of dreary black, and my then mood about "Frederick" and other things.'

55. A transport and storage company with origins in the early seventeenth century, and the proverbial removalist in the British imagination, earning a mention in Dickens' *Our Mutual Friend*.

When I was out of trouble with my dog, I had time to feel how very relaxing and depressing the air of Chelsea was for me—as usual—after the bracing climate of Scotland. I was perfectly *done*, till Mr C insisted on my setting up the carriage again, and providence put me on drinking water out of a '*bitter cup*'—that is a new invention, very popular here this year! A cup made of the wood of Quassia which makes the water quite bitter in a minute—of course a chip of quassie put into water would have the same effect, but nobody ever bid me take that![56] I thought for three or four days that I had discovered the grand panacea of Life! I felt so hungry! and so cheerful!! and so active! But one night I was seized with the horridest cramps!—which quite took the shine out of quassia for me—tho' I dare say it was merely that I had quite neglected my bowels I haven't had courage to recommence with the 'bitter cup'—but it will come! Meanwhile I am pretty well over the bilious crisis that has befallen; to 'remind me that I *am but a woman*'! and a very *frail* one—(I mean in a physical sense!)

How pleasant it will be to think of you at that pretty Holmhill![57] tho' one will always have a tender feeling toward the 'old rambling house' where we have had such good days together— But the other place will be for the good of your health as well as more agreeable—when you have once got over the pain of *change* which is painful to good hearts, altho it may be joyful enough to light ones—. It will also be a comfort to my mind to think of the drawing room getting papered all with *one sort of paper*!— God bless you love to your Husband

J W Carlyle [. . .]

56. *Quassia amara*, or bitter-ash, a bush from tropical South America: key ingredient in Angostura bitters, and used by the Victorians for stomach complaints and fever.

57. Mary's husband, Dr Russell, had retired from practice in the nearby village of Thornhill, Dumfries.

Figure 10: Unknown, 'Photograph of Jane Carlyle' (nd), Thomas Carlyle Papers, Rare Book & Manuscript Library, Columbia University in the City of New York

9

The Rehabilitation of the Flesh: 1860–1862

Perhaps this is the place to reintroduce some remarks from the Preface, made by the foundational editor of these letters, Charles Richard Sanders, as regards Thomas, Jane and their letters:

> Like one of Carlyle's heroes, Dr Samuel Johnson, they led lives and made statements that were commentaries on the art of living. Though they did not perfect this art, they experienced many hours of a very rare quality as recorded in the letters; and fortified and illumined by extensive reading, they observed the lives of those around them and evaluated their own experiences from day to day while at the same time they were writing letters which recorded their conclusions. Hence it is possible for us to read the letters not merely for the pleasure that they bring to us but also for what they may teach us about the most difficult and the greatest of the arts.

It is a bold claim, but perhaps this chapter bears it out particularly well. Jane's letters here may not be 'commentaries on the art of living' if that suggests some sort of philosophical position or conscious point of view. They are anti-Archimedean commentaries of the kind we associate with art rather than knowledge, and with experience as it is felt before it is reflected upon. And they are the more remarkable in that they are delivered during a time in the author's existence when life might have seemed to be ebbing from her.

If we review the period 1859–1862 from Jane's perspective her struggle with poor health, mental as well as physical, dominates the landscape. The invaluable chronologies attached to the Collected Letters allow us to summarise the process. In February 1859 Jane started taking whisky at night, to help her sleep but also to evade 'insane thoughts'; in March she complained of weariness, and in April she had a severe cold and was too ill to write ('the worst cold I have ever seen her have,' Thomas told Ruskin on the 19th). By May her doctor was visiting her daily and in June she declined a wedding invitation on grounds of ill health. A Scottish summer holiday (as so often) saw a recovery: she even took to riding a donkey. But autumn saw her suffering from insomnia as usual. Her winter was not too bad, but in May 1860 she fell and broke a rib; in August she complained of 'nerves' and insomnia; in September she was bedridden by influenza, and experienced a hacking cough even after recovery. A cold persisted into January 1861, and even her summer was afflicted, though she got to Ramsgate despite bad health. Another cold descended in November, and she reported herself 'room-fast [. . .] bed-fast'. The following month she complained of weakness and restlessness and was self-medicating (I assume with morphine) to prevent what she called 'dangerous excitement'. The New Year of 1862 found her 'weak as water' and writing to Charlotte Cushman on 31 January to apologise for being out of touch. 'I will not go back upon the causes of my long silence,' she wrote: 'It is enough to have been four months ill *and shut up in two rooms; without "renewing grief" by details of one's fit-for-nothingness; so soon as ever one has recovered* a certain *use of one's tongue and pen!' (see below). There was recovery again, but by June ill health prevented her from writing much at all. In August she bruised her foot, but still managed to get away to Scotland, and by October 1862 she was bathing in the sea with friends at Dover.*

But poor physical health is one thing. In an age where understanding of mental concerns was primitive, to put it mildly—as we have seen in the cases of Richard Plattnauer and Charlotte Sterling—Jane's only avenue was self-expression and her only curative apart from drugs was sympathetic understanding of the kind her husband could not offer. On 25 June 1858 she wrote to him that 'to see you *constantly discontented and as much so with* me *apparently with all other* things, *when I have neither the strength and spirits to bear up against your discontent, nor the obtuseness to be indifferent to it,* that *has done me more harm than you have the least notion of' (CL 33: 252). (Thomas's reply (CL 33: 261) was typically beside the point: 'to tell you the truth, your anger at me [. . .] was itself sometimes a kind of comfort to me: I thot, "Well, she has strength to be cross and ill-natured at me; she is not all softness and affection and* weakness*!" On the whole it will now be better.') On 9 July 1858 she warned him again that 'My constitution is completely worn out—my nerves, my spirits worn out!' (CL 34: 23). Still: there was a capacity for relief, if not recovery. On 17 August of that same year she wrote to a friend from the Ashburtons' Bay House that 'I have recovered the highly useful faculties of sleeping and eating, and quite ceased to cough; and life is no longer the horrid nightmare I had been feeling it for many months', a viewpoint from which Cheyne Row seemed 'something compounded of a Hospital a Prison and a Madhouse!' (CL 34: 133–4). Back in Chelsea, she told the second Lady Ashburton in February 1861, '[N]othing can be more dull—not to say dismal,—than the life we lead! And if it were only* dull*! but there is an amount of worry, to temper the dullness, which begets many floating notions of—*suicide*!' (CL 37: 128). At the end of 1862 she wrote to her sister-in-law Mary—her husband's sister, that is—that 'I sometimes feel as if I should like to—run away! But the question always arises: where* to*?' (CL 39: 7).*

The period is marked by a parallel source of unhappiness and a parallel source of renewal. Jane lost many friends during the period, to death, disaffection or the normal passage of time. Primus inter pares, the little dog Nero; but also Geraldine Jewsbury (temporarily), Mazzini, Lady Sandwich, her new young Bostonian friend Ellen Twisleton, George Rennie (whom she nursed on his deathbed), Jess Donaldson, Robert MacTurk, Countess Pepoli, Arthur Hugh Clough, Kate Stirling and Elizabeth Barrett Browning. Yet there were additions and replacements, too, often among young women: John Forster's wife Eliza; a one-time housemaid, now married to a doctor, Bessy Blakiston; and Lady Airlie, Lady Louisa Ashburton, Kate Stanley, Mary Carlyle Austin, the actress Charlotte Cushman, the novelist Margaret Oliphant, Mary Russell and Caroline Davenport Bromley. The capacity to make and build these new relations, and to take a maternal interest in the younger women and their children ('me whose lines have always been cast in Babyless Places'), suggests that the art of life was something Jane was still bent on practising in her way, against all odds. So, in another way and from a different perspective, does her valiantly unscientific response of 28 February 1860 to the publication in November the previous year of Darwin's Origin of Species—never a book likely to enthuse either her or Thomas (there is a copy in his library, unannotated, which says it all):

> But even when Darwin, in a Book that all the scientific world is in ecstasy over, *proved* the other day, that we are all come from shell-fish! it didn't move me to the slightest curiosity whether we are or not! I did not feel that the slightest light would be thrown on my practical life for me by having it ever so logically made out, that my first ancestor millions of millions of ages back had been or even had *not* been an oyster! It remained a plain fact that I was no oyster! nor had no grandfather oyster within my knowledge and for the rest, there was nothing to be gained for this world or the next by going into the oyster-question till all more pressing questions were exhausted! (*CL* 36: 53)

The letters in this chapter, set against the background of physical and mental struggle I have described, prove that Jane was indeed no oyster. 'Practical life' and its 'pressing questions' could never be confronted by adopting the position of Alexander Pope's 'cockle-kind'. That having been said, when Lady Ashburton sent her an invitation in March 1863 to witness the marriage of the future Edward VII to Princess Alexandra of Denmark, she declined outright, saying she had too much of 'the Great Original Oyster *in me' to 'get up a sentiment or even a sensation about that "procession"!'*

❧

To Lady Airlie, Chelsea, 28 November or 5 December 1859

Heaven bless you my Lady! and bless *It*!—the new 'little Bundle of flannel,'—little 'armful of joy,'—Baby that I divined by my own sharpness, while yet in a most incipient state! What do you think? this is the *third* Baby deduced by me,—who have no personal experience in Babies,—and rightly deduced, from a—*Yawn*! Gracious! I hope no young Lady, that is to say no unmarried Lady will ever have the idea to yawn in my presence, for I should hardly now be able to pass over such fact without inferences!

The present Lady Ashburton is far *past* yawning! has indeed—(so Lord A wrote to his Brother Frederick Baring, who had not had a scrape of a pen from him since the marriage,)—has indeed 'passed the critical point at which *the dear* Girl had miscarried hitherto.' *Twice* she had miscarried, Lord A told my Husband, 'with the simple ingenuousness of a young Boy' (these were Mr C's words). [A]lso Mr C said, that Lord A, to do him justice, seemed 'extremely anxious that the thing *should get itself born this time*; much more out of anxiety about his wife's health, than from any selfish notions about an heir!' In fact Lord A and Mr C talking together on this subject, with their mutual 'simple ingenuousness' must be something grand to hear!

Anyhow I am glad they (the Ashburtons) have given up their projected visit to the Francis Barings[1] and the '*pauvres Enfants*,' [poor children] till the important Child is fairly confectioned and 'in arms.' That '*Heir*' looks to me *up* to most things that Heirs do in French novels; and it would have been so easy to give the young Lady a *fall* or a *fright* when one had her under one's own roof!

When are you coming to London, I wonder? I am confined to the house as usual with a bad cold, and the dear little woman who nursed me angelically in my last illness is away in Florence. I am asked to go to the Grange 'to be made strong'!! One must go some time—if we all live;—so, 'as well soon as syne.'[2] But I shudder at the idea of a first visit there, under such changed circumstances. The very fact, that the new Lady seems to wish to be as kind to me *as the other was*, constantly

1. Lord Ashburton's brother and his heir (1800–1868), who would succeed as third baron on Ashburton's death in 1864. Ashburton's only child by Lady Harriet, a son, died in infancy in 1830. Perhaps Francis was rendered apprehensive by his brother's speedy remarriage to a woman of child-bearing age, Lady Louisa; but this child would be a girl, Mary Florence. Byron's heir apparent at the time of his marriage—which produced only a daughter, Ada—was his cousin George, who lost no time in aiding and abetting Lady Byron in her separation from the poet: from sincere motives regarding her wellbeing, no doubt.
2. 'Syne': 'since'; 'sooner rather than later' might be an English equivalent.

reminds me of the other, and that *this* is not *she*! My dear Lady!—*You*!—Don't go and die! and get replaced! I should *hate* your successor and be horribly ungrateful for any attentions she might show me!

My poor little dog—*my* substitute for a little bundle of flannel,—being in a musing and trustful state of mind on his return from Fife, got run over by a Butchers Cart— Ach! Yes! the wheel passed over his poor little neck! and he was brought home to me in the arms of the sobbing Charlotte, all huddled up like a crushed spider, and the eyes all but started out of his head! For a week he was despaired of; but my loving cares prevailed to restore him to what an old Lady of my acquaintance would call his 'frail usual' (she is always writing to me—I am THANKFUL to say I am in my frail usual!). Since then however his incipient Asthma has developed itself at a fearful rate— The dog doctor has now ordered him to keep the house all winter if he wouldn't die—so the choice is to die of Asthma or Indigestion. Meanwhile I have made him a little warm coat, which gives him the looking of an inchanted human being! and I devote myself to soothing his sufferings! Poor little dog after all!

I end as I began with God bless you my Lady—

To see your handwriting warms my blood always—

Yours faithfully

Jane Carlyle

no feathered things please! to us they are not worth the carriage which is heavy from [so] long a distance.[3]

To Lady Louisa Ashburton, Chelsea, 16 January 1860

Dear Lady Ashburton

The worst of that Arabian-Nights-Entertainment sort of thing is that, coming back to one's ordinary Life, one finds it has gained immeasurably in dinginess and dulness!

Our ordinary Life recommenced at Waterloo Station; where I had to leave off thinking about The Grange, and its *goings on*, and about *you* and your adorable kindness; that I might seek and identify our various luggage; which Mr C insisted was 'hopelessly engulphed in the Belly of

3. Lady Airlie is asked not to send game (pheasants, grouse and so forth) from her castle in Angus, north of Dundee; both animals were in season at the time of writing, and the Carlyles could find no use for such foodstuffs. See 12 February 1860, below.

Chaos'!—where it might have remained, for any step that *he* would stir in the matter!—

Then followed the drive in a rickety bad-smelling street-cab, thro' fog and mud; justifying Mr C's exclamation: '*Ough*! my Dear! This is a *terribly clarty* [dirty] City we are come back to!'

When we stopt at our own door; my heart was going 'like-like-like-*anything*!' about the wee sick Dog. Would he be still among 'the Living and Loving'—*Dogs*? Would he be able to raise one bark of welcome?

The door was opened;—no bark! My eyes plunged into the lobby; no Dog!— 'Is he dead'? I asked at the Servant [Charlotte]; and, simultaneously with the question, came the answer: 'Oh Mam! *He* is a little better!'—

Was it a sin and a shame to say—'Thank God?'—whether or not; I said it!

Poor little Creature! he had hurried to the bottom of the stairs, to receive us '*avec explosion*'[4] (no doubt), and there, had been seized with a paroxysm of coughing! and the more he tried to express his joy, the more he couldn't do it!— Apart from violent emotions however, he really seems less suffering; certainly not requiring to be poisoned—just yet!

I tell you about my Dog, knowing that you also had a dog, and believing that one's dog makes all dogs *touching* for one!

For the rest; having come back to a 'clarty City' is nothing like so bad as having come back to *Frederick the Great*! You can't imagine what it is to have to pass one's days in the Valley of the Shadow of that dead man! I am sure he is taking many years of life out of me, as well as out of his Historian! Better be an 'owl in Desert'[5] at once and cry to-hoo! to-hoo! than have an articulate speaking tongue in ones head and next to no opportunities of using it!

Just now especially—since my return from the Grange—I am tempted to fall back on what Mr C calls 'the *one* happiness of Life—the great Charm of *Home*—unbounded freedom to be as ugly and stupid and disagreeable as ever one likes'!— But I doubt if Woman can ever appreciate that freedom as man does; besides,—'*Don't she wish she may get it?*'

Now, I am not expressing myself like a reasonable woman for I have not had to leave all the good of the Grange behind

'*For some one else to find*'!—

I have brought back with me the picture of it and of the life carried on in it, retouched and brightened up in my head; and have brought

4. Not a French idiom, but something Jane had picked up from a French play: 'excitedly', perhaps?

5. Psalms 102: 6.

back with me loving and trusting feelings towards *you*, my Lady, which are a pleasant wonder to myself! so set had I been on never caring for you the least bit! having got it in my head that it would be a sort of infidelity, a sort of disloyalty to ever care for another Lady Ashburton than Her who had shown me so much kindness and exercised so much influence over me, during some fourteen years!

It was a narrow ungenerous idea; as if one's human heart were like the stone house one lived in, laid out in a certain number of rooms of certain dimensions! I have overcome it or rather *you* have overcome it—to my great relief!

This is a delicate topic to engage in with *you*; but you encouraged me by saying the first word; with a noble frankness which touched me more than I can express!—

—And so—at parting—I made you that proposal, meaning every syllable of it; and hoping that, by its *audacity* if nothing else, you might be surprised into bearing it practically in mind.

Lord Ashburton did not say good by to me!— When I saw him going off before our departure, I took one step to run after him, and tell him I had been very happy—then suddenly I 'thought shame'—and slunk back to my seat—

Mr C was again, at breakfast this morning, lyrically recognising your 'recklessness,' and wondering how you were!— If he were your monthly Nurse he couldn't be more interested than he is in your 'getting successfully thro' the thing'!!

God bless you—sincerely yours / Jane W Carlyle

To Lady Louisa Ashburton, Chelsea, 12 February 1860

My Dear Lady,

Have you ever noticed how long—preternaturally long—the time looks, when one had been thinking and feeling more than usual in it, even without changing of place or interrupting of one's outward routine?

I have just been making an experience of this.. . . It wasn't much 'to speak of.' A small tragedy—very small—and yet, more heart-rending than some grander ones.

My little dog had become rapidly worse, till 'common humanity required that he should be made away with,' I was told. 'My Dear' (urged Mr C.) 'it is an Act of Roman Virtue that is demanded of you;

and so (!) you surely will not shrink from it!'—as if Acts of Roman Virtue were among the simplest ordinary obligations on a nineteenth Century Scotchwoman!—and I who have no taste at all for Roman Virtue—oh, *any* other sort of virtue rather than that! Indeed I have never been able to understand what these old Romans could be made of, or to altogether believe in them. The appeal to any latent Roman Virtue in *me* found nothing to act upon. But the intervention of my Doctor, who happened to call, was more effective. He told me the little creature was suffering dreadfully, and would suffer still worse if he lived;—that keeping him going on so was 'a bit of selfishness' he wouldn't have given me credit for. And then he asked, suppose he himself should come some day when I was out—in a week or so—and give the poor dog something to put him out of pain *in one moment*, 'without hurting him the least[']; would I be very angry? Of course I burst out crying which meant consent. He had said 'in a week or so,' but *that*, I knew, was merely to put off apprehension, and accordingly, the very next day, the Dr in driving past our house, seeing the Drawing room windows open, supposed me gone out; and was half way up stairs, when we met each other face to face. He was for retreating, good kind man; but I felt, '*the sooner the better*,' the sight of my little dog following one about, trying to discharge his bits of duties the same as ever, in spite of his agony of breathlessness; with my knowledge that he was about to *die*—to be *poisoned*; that the *reward* about to be given him, for his lifelong devotion—the *only* reward that *could* and *ought* to be given him, was—prussic acid![6] Oh it was too horrible, could not be ended too soon. So I called him (the Dr) back, and said *now* was no worse than any other time would be, and bade Charlotte take my little dog away. I *could* not lift him to put him into her arms, but I kissed his poor little head. And *He licked my cheek*.

Then I ran and shut myself into my bedroom, and flung myself down and cried—as I hadn't cried since I was a girl.

My Dr kept his promise, the little creature died in *one moment* (Charlotte said) without a struggle. Fortunately Mr Carlyle was himself entirely upset by little Nero's death; so that he could not *lecture me* on my 'excessive grief,' his 'own heart being' (as he expressed it) 'quite *unexpectedly* and *distractedly* torn to pieces by the misery of the thing.'—His lyrical recognition of 'the poor little creature's docility, and loyalty, and sense of duty, and *manifold undeniable* merits,' interrupted more than once by downright human *tears*, might have seemed to some people a

6. Hydrogen cyanide, derived from the pigment Prussian blue in the early eighteenth century, now mostly used in mining and electro-plating. In its gaseous form it was the active agent in the Nazis' Zyklon-B[lau] extermination agent.

fall from his (Mr C.'s) philosophic heights. But for me, I liked him for it more than for all the philosophy that ever came out of his head.

Now, however, already, he speaks of 'poor Nero' very composedly. And Charlotte, who went about, the first two days, with her face swollen and red with weeping, on the third day recovered her prettiness and cheeriness. Only myself whom the little creature belonged to, and whom he loved before everybody and everything else, only *I* am still horribly sad and *perplexed*. For, what is become of that beautiful, engaging little *life*, with its '*manifold undeniable virtues*' (as Mr C said)? Could these be extinguished, abolished, annihilated by some drops of Prussic Acid? Is *that* credible? Is Prussic Acid more powerful than qualities which, found in a *Human Being*, the self same qualities—we call *divine*, *immortal*? 'I cannot make myself believe that,' I said the other day to Lady William Russell;[7] and *she* whom people call 'so Worldly,' (I could never see why), answered—'But why *should* you make yourself believe it, my good Lady? Who does believe it? *I* don't.' And then she gave me her ideas about the *Future* of dogs, which, if not particularly well founded, were so poetical and so sympathetic to me, that I was tempted to jump up and kiss her. Luckily I didn't; for it would have given her a dreadful fright.

All my other visitors have spoken odiously on what they call my 'little bereavement.' They don't conceive what pain they give me. Three several men, the only men I am intimate with here, offered one after another to 'give me *another little dog*.' And two women, of the sort called 'full of sensibility,' inquired if I had 'had him *stuffed*?' 'I wonder you didn't' said one of them plaintively, 'he would have looked *so* pretty in a glass case in your room, and still been quite a companion to you.' Merciful Heavens! If one lived in what Mr Carlyle calls 'a sincere age of the world,' wouldn't one take such a Comforter as *that* by the neck and pitch her out at the window?

The frank indifference of one's fellow-creatures, that is a common complaint. But it is not *that* one suffers most from; their so called sympathy is often far worse to bear.

But why, you think, in the name of wonder, do I write always to *you*, my Lady? I know well enough why. It is because the Heavenly kindness in your eyes and voice, when we talked about my little dog at the Grange, has come back to me many times since, and *magnetises* me into these strange confidences. But understand, I have no expectation that you should *answer* such a letter as this. If you read it to an end without

7. Lady Elizabeth Anne Russell, *née* Rawdon (1793–1874), wife of Lord George Russell, and mentioned in Byron's *Beppo* (1818), as a woman 'whose bloom could, after dancing, dare the dawn'. She was always called 'Lady William', for reasons that are obscure.

protest it is as much as could be asked. Someday however when you have much leisure perhaps you will write me two or three lines, just to say how you feel, and when you come to Town, and how the dear wee Baby is. [. . .]

I have so many things to thank you for, my Lady, that I really don't know where to begin—or end. All that game, that unfailing Addiscombe hamper. 'My Heavens!' (as Lord Ashburton used to say, as often as Mr Carlyle says 'Ah me!') what *am* I to do with it all?

Ever yours, /

J. W. CARLYLE

To William Dods, Chelsea, 6–7? October 1860

Good morning! I couldn't desire a finer day to write to you on! Soft sunshine, bracing air, and everything as clear as a bell!— Besides, it is more than time you should be written to; dont you think?— I think so; at the same time, I feel no need—not the least in the world to begin with apology! when one has been true to a childish affection thro' a tolerably long life time—has kept on caring for a man (or perhaps I should say rather a *Boy*) some twenty years long, without once seeing him, or exchanging words with him,—nothing to remind one of him except old memories in one's own heart; one must surely have earned in the opinion of *that* man (or *Boy*) at least, a faith in one's *constancy* (whatever else) which nothing one may do after, or may fail to do, can shake!— Is it not so?— If, by ill luck, you should never set eyes on me again, never get the scrape of a pen from me again; you should know *now*, all the same, should you not? that so long as you had not heard I was *dead* or *out of my wits*, I should still have my affection of long ago for you—only without the *longagoness*; alas!—

For myself, I am always heartily glad of any outward, visible signs of remembrance from those I love; but I dont *depend* on the outward and visible signs for belief in the remembrance!— *That* comes to me by—*divination*!—a faculty, inherited from my Great Ancestor John Welsh The Covenanter,[8] and worth all my other faculties put together—in

8. *CL*: 'JWC wrongly claimed descent from the Protestant reformer John Knox (1505–1572) through his son-in-law John Welsh (1568–1622)'; see 11 January 1857, above. The Covenanters were seventeenth-century Protestants who supported the separate Presbyterian Church of Scotland in the face of English interference in church matters. Many sacrificed their lives in the ongoing struggle.

matters of feeling; which are indeed a woman's most important matters on this Earth!— Yes! you may smile at my pretending to preternatural powers; but, it is as true as you live, that my *Divination* never misleads me, while my *Understanding* makes a fool of me every day of my life! so I trust and have trusted and will trust in this my preternatural heritage! whatever anyone may think or say!

Sunday

At the bottom of last page an interruption occurred—providentially—as I seemed about to lose myself in metaphysics of The Imagination!

Poor absurd George Conningham; I couldn't have believed it possible beforehand, that an announcement of *his* death would have made me quite sorrowful for a whole day!— When he came to see me a year ago, I had a presentiment he would soon die. His whole nature seemed changed; grown tender, affectionate, sentimental even! he that had used to be a perfect little *marble* of self conceit and self-love! And he told me, I remember, with a solemnity which *now* seems no longer ridiculous that he had had 'a monition' to go and 'see my face once more.' [I]n fact my 'APPARITION had *stood over him in his study at Windermere* one evening' &c &c! All that *now* is sad—not laughable to recall; as indicating morbid action of the Brain.[9]

Dear William Dods! how few besides yourself are left me of those I began Life with! Should I not draw nearer to you, and hold you faster, as the night closes in on my early Life, and one after another of my early companions disappear in the darkness![10] Oh if it were not for *you*—still living—and caring for me, more or less—I couldnt bear to think of Haddington—with Sunny Bank passed into other hands!— But thank God, anyhow, that bag of vanity and vulgarity, Stuart Donaldson, did not purchase it! It would have been enough to have made the House *haunted*, such a representative of my beloved old friends!—

The wretches! to leave the print of Mr Carlyle and all those awful photographs of ME to be sold by Auction! I hope you got the print? I shall like better to know it in your house than in any other—and as for the photographs, I *think* you would have sufficient feeling for me to *burn* them? There was a picture of our room too, done by Sir Anthony Sterling, whose *likeness* of me was so unlike that I covered the face with a photograph! producing a most ghastly result!— Did you become the generous purchaser of *that* master-piece also? If so, oh do burn it!—

9. George Cunningham (1802–1860), geographer, lived at Elleray Bank above Windermere in the Lake District. Designed by the great Victorian architect Alfred Waterhouse, the house still stands, subdivided into flats.

10. Jean and Jess Donaldson ('these dear women', below), George Rennie and Robert MacTurk, all deceased since March. Stuart was nephew of the Donaldsons.

No No! I would not care to have the shawl and brooch *now*, if I could get them for the asking!— Coming with 'airs' from Miss Jess's drawer, the things would have been prized, as sacred relicks—but, desecrated by the covetous hands and eyes of the Craven Hill Donaldsons,[11] I would rather be without them. If I *needed* any visible thing to put me in mind of the life-long motherlove of these dear women for me; I have on my finger day and night a little old diamond ring they gave me eight years ago! I may look at *that*, and think it a fit memorial of their love—; without a flaw, and not to be dimmed by time! and Miss Jess placed it on my finger herself, with a living kiss.— God keep me from having any more to do with the Craven Hill Donaldsons! They are a bad lot!—

You asked was there anything you could put aside for me that I would like. Yes—I would like some flower or shrub out of the garden—if you could find one able to live in my soilless and airless bit of ground. Would *hawthorn live* here do you think? If it *would*; I should dearly like a little hawthorn seedling from Sunny Bank! The smell of hawthorn reminds me always of the gladdest, loveliest time in my life; when I went about 'at my own sweet will' jumping over ditches—or into them!— But *is* there any hawthorn at Sunny Bank? If not—there is, or was, plenty about 'Babbies Butts'?[12] I should like it from that locality quite well—and you might send me something else—of a hardy nature—from the Sunny Bank garden with some moss about the root, the thing could come safely by post— That Jessamine [jasmine] you saw covering half the Garden wall, came by post—originally.

After my abrupt return from Cheshire, and renunciation of a sight of Dumfrieshire; that wretch of a man did not come home till three or four weeks later! Had never intended sailing from Thurso to London direct; and considered I ought to have known that *by instinct*! So I had plenty of time to make the necessary preparations and to transact a bad Influenza, over and above.— I am now getting back my strength—or, as Jackie Welsh of Haddington expresses herself, 'am *happy to say* I am in my *frail ordinar*'—after having taken iron enough, to have made—what shall I say?—*a small saucepan* in my stomach!

And now I want to know, how are you, and your 'nice wife'? Consider how deathly silent Haddington must be for me *now*, unless *you* give it a voice! and how heavy that silence must lie on my heart, being the foolish, clinging, back-looking heart it is!

11. Stuart Donaldson's mother and sisters, resident in Craven Hill Gardens, Bayswater, west London.

12. A path in Haddington; see the 'Much Ado About Nothing' journal of 2 August 1849.

And so God bless you both—
Ever affectionately yours
Jane Welsh Carlyle [. . .]

To Lady Airlie, Chelsea, 24 October 1860

Bless you 'Oh Lady fair'—and dear!— The sight of that dashing handwriting of yours is to me always 'a good joy'—as of old were the sight of 'daisies' and 'sky *so* blue!' to Leigh Hunt's children! I *do* wish you had been at Alderley when I was there—tho' I candidly own that without you I enjoyed my visit extremely— In the first place it came off at the moment when I was just recovered from something of the nature of nervous fever; so that the mere greenness and quietness of Alderley Park were in themselves delightfully soothing to my wearied brain! And then those 'Bright Young Beings' (as Mr C calls your siserts) were so kind to me, and so charming; that I felt quite humanized, *for the time being*!—underwent what the St Simonians[13] called (for I suppose *they* are now in the past tense) a 'Rehabilitation of the Flesh'—believed once more in youth, and young hopes, and aspirations, and all that poetical sort of thing, which I lose sight of at Cheyne Row, and hardly think of even as a myth! And then Lady Stanley too was so kind to me and so charming! In the Country she always looks to me like an escaped Bird; The natural woman in her comes out *there* in a way quite refreshing to see! She is not made, your Mother, for being caged up in a London circle—she is too *large* for it and too *real*! I assure you I came away with the warmest, gratefulest feelings towards them all—even the white dogs were parted from with regret; for they too had been good to me; besides being very pretty.

I saw your Mother and Sister at Dover Street, on their way to Bath; your Sister having written to tell me they were there. Mr Carlyle called the day after me, and what do you think he said?— It was at night—hours after his return—he had been lying on the sofa—asleep, I fancied. And he suddenly broke out in a tenderly reproachful tone; 'These people dont like *me* nearly as well as I do *them*!' 'What *people*? I said,

13. Followers of Claude Henri de Rouvroy, Comte de Saint-Simon (1760–1825), whose thought combined socialism and Christianity, and also celebrated the body for its own sake rather than as an appendage of the soul. Thomas and Jane held him in high regard in their younger days.

what on Earth are you talking about'?— 'The Stanleys I mean—I dont think they care a bit about me!— I was far gladder to see them today than they were to see me!'— 'Well, I said, I dare say Lord Stanley cares nothing about you—but I am sure Lady Stanley does—she has always professed to do so, and I am sure she is *sincere* in whatever she *says*'— 'Ah—h— Well—I—I *used* to think *she* liked me very well—but *today* she didn't seem to care *rigmarree* [rigmarie: coin of low value] for me!'— '[A]nd I am sure Miss Stanley likes you; only *she* is very undemonstrative.' I went on comforting him!— But he turned over on his side, and murmuring—'I don't believe any of them like *me* half as well as I do *them*'—went to sleep again! You can't appreciate the singularity of this *human* outburst of Mr C's unless you had had *my* opportunities of observing how he never troubles his head whether people '*like* him' or not!

The fact is,—as to the nonappearances of *liking*,—that he has been very bilious since he came home, seeing every thing *in black*— I dare swear nothing was missing in his reception at Dover Street but poor Lady Stanley's accustomed good health and liveliness.

I am going off to lunch with Miss Farrer, and help her to entertain Syme the Edinr Surgeon! In a moment of enthusiasm she had begged of him to stop in London on his way to some patient in Devonshire; that he might examine Lady Tierney, about whom she was in a dreadful fright, poor Soul! And now Lady Tierney declines being examined by *him*, and he is to have luncheon instead. That poor woman has a dreadful life with that idiot Husband of hers! And when he dies, as he is expected to do this winter, you will see, she will be an inconsolable widow![14] Women always suffer more in losing a husband who has wholly depended on them, and painfully occupied every moment of their lives, than in losing one whom they have been 'at ease in Zion'[15] beside, and had no bother at all with— I have seen this more times than I can count! One of the loveliest women I ever knew was promised at fifteen, by a mercenary Brute of a Mother to a little fat vulgar rich man who was taken by the poor childs Beauty.[16] Bred up in a scotch Wilderness the

14. Annie Louise Farrer (1818–1910), friend of the Ashburtons; her elder sister, Mary, had married the baronet Matthew Edward Tierney in 1855. He would indeed die this year. James Syme (1799–1870), eminent Edinburgh surgeon.
15. Amos 6: 1.
16. Helen Grierson (1789–1862), mother Frances Davis Sibbald (*née* Bontein), husband William Grierson (1772–1852), merchant from Dumfries. The 'scotch Wilderness' is Johnstone, Dumfries; the 'Town' is Haddington; and the son was Thomas Boyle Grierson (1818–1889), founder of the Thornhill Institute and its Museum, by all accounts a decent man. As Jane points out, she is on the verge of a novel here.

girl had seen no men to compare him with,—was grateful for the trinkets and 'sweeties' he gave her,—and when her Mother accepted him for her, hadn't courage to say *no*. A year or two later, when transplanted to a Town, where there were numerous men, she was claimed by her Betrothed whom she had not seen in the interim, and was horror-struck at his fatness and vulgarity— [A]s for his riches, having taken, poor girl[,] to thinking and writing Poetry, they (the riches) were no consolation whatever— So she wept, and remonstrated, and postponed,—did every thing except what she ought to have viz: kick her foot thro' the whole '*burble*' [problem]— She had a very nice conscience *unfortunately*, and they persuaded her it would be dishonourable to fling the man over, and moreover he worked on her timidity by threatening to 'prosecute' her and publish her child-letters to him!! So after some five years of vain struggle to get out of the thing, she let herself be married to the odious little man. And from the day she married the brightness went out of her face for ever!— Well—(what a long story I have got into!) She did all her duties of Wife,—obeyed him at a word, studied his humours, was gently impassive to his ill temper and vulgarity. But for the rest, she looked *dead* and *buried*! Her voice sounded always as if it came from a great distance—nothing seemed ever to amuse, or please; or pain or excite her. Beautiful as she was she gave one the sensation of a nightmare dream. People tired of trying to be any comfort to her, and, she was left to the seclusion she courted—with nothing to live for, that any one could see, but one horrid little son—whom she indulged to the foolishest lengths. Her Husband seemed to weary of her deadness and lived much away from her— She never said an unkind word of him, or a complaining word of herself—*but* it was easy to see she loathed him, and was slowly *dying of him*. This was the state of things when the Husband's 'affairs' went to the dogs, and himself was struck with paralysis in consequence, or at least in sequence. Then the true woman in her rose up tender and strong! She devoted herself to nursing the helpless little (now old) man who had been the curse on her young Life. *Slaved* to supply him with the comforts he could no longer afford, shook off her long lethargy to cheer him up—was nurse, servant, comforter Guardian angel to him for three years—till he died—and then one saw another instance of what I was remarking— Her grief was near killing her!! The Doctor, who was present when the miserable wretch of a Husband expired, told me he had never seen a woman suffer so terribly on a similar occasion—that *he* felt 'perfectly ashamed of himself' for the thoughts in his own breast, about how happy she *ought* to be to be rid of him! And I *know* she perfectly loathed the man when she was forced to marry him, and all the years she lived in affluence with him, and up to the time that he became a helpless, mad-tempered, disgusting burden on her!— Nor was it only *at first* that she regretted him— When I saw her in Dumfrieshire *two years* after his death; she told me with a look of inconsolable woe—that there could be no mistake about, that 'her Life on Earth was darkened for ever—and that she lived on merely in the one hope of being reunited to Mr Grierson in Heaven'!

I said to the Dr above mentioned [Russell]: 'good gracious! If it were possible for her to conceive Mr Grierson *in Heaven* one might have thought she would almost have wished to go to *the other Place*.' But he answered very sensibly, 'a woman always regrets the man who *gave her plenty to do*—and God knows she had a busy time of it, while she had him paralysed on her hands and no money in the house'! Have you read this far? Since I don't write Novels, I may be permitted to tell a true story, by way of safety valve may I not—otherwise such a long yarn in a *letter* is inexcusable.

Of course I did not fill all this paper *before* lunchtime with Miss Farrer— I left off and began again after tea at home

Lady Tierney *did* 'see' Syme and well that she did; for he has made her mind quite easy, the 'lump' in her side is nothing he says of the least moment, a mere enlargement of a particular bowel—which will probably go away as it came—insensibly—and at all events can do her no harm while it lasts.— What an unspeakable relief for her—and for her sister too poor soul! Even *I* feel immensely relieved—I have such poignant pity for people with 'tumours'— Will you write to me again—and will you please to believe me always your sincerely attached wellwish[er]

Jane W Carlyle

To Margaret Welsh, Chelsea, 8 December 1860

Dearest Maggie

Having made no sign of myself for the last month; you may be fancying I have succumbed to the general doom; seeing that it has been 'the gloomy month of November, in which the People of England hang and drown themselves'!— But I am neither hanged nor drowned *yet*; (in virtue perhaps of being born in *Scotland*) only, all my energies having been needed to stave off Suicide; I had none left for letterwriting. It is now December, and the suicidal mania should have passed off; but I can't see much difference between *this* December and the gloomiest November on record! the fog and the mud and the liquid soot (called *rain* in the language of flattery) have not abated. And the blood in ones veins feels as thick and dirty!— But shame of my silence must serve instead of inspiration, impossible under the circumstances! and you, dear good little Soul, as you are, will not be critical!

In the first place you will be glad to hear I am '*about*,' anyhow. Except for one week that I had to lie on the sofa on my back with *Neuralgia*, (differing in nothing so far as I can see from the old fashioned 'Rheum*atiz*') I have not been *laid up* since you heard of me[,] and I have had a great fret taken off me, in the removal of that vulgar conceited woman [servant: 'Tall Charlotte'], and the restoration of little Charlotte [Southam]. Upon my word; I havn't been as near what they call '*happy*' for many a day; as in the first flush of little Charlotte! She looked so bursting with ecstasy as she ran up and down the house, *taking possession*, as it were of her old work—and as she showed in the visitors, (not *her* business; but she *would* open the door to them all, the first time; to show herself; and receive their congratulations) that it was impossible not to share in her delighted excitement!

Most of the people shook hands with her!, and all of them said they were 'glad to see her back![']— I had trusted that she would, *in time*, *humanize* the other girl and that the two would be good friends when the other girl got over the prejudices the woman who had left had inspired her with! But it needed no time at all! Sarah was humanized, and the two sworn friends in the first half hour!! In the first half hour Sarah had confided to Charlotte that if I hadn't given the tall Charlotte warning, *she* (Sarah) would have given *me* warning. She disliked 'tall Charlotte' so much!

It is now three weeks since the new order of things; mistress and maid have subsided out of the emotional state, into the normal one; but are still very glad over one another; and if the work of the house does not get done with as much order and method as under the tall Charlotte; it is done with more *thoroughness* and infinitely more heartiness and pleasantness[,] and the 'bread-puddings' are first rate! Sarah's tidiness and method are just what was wanted to correct little Charlotte's born tendency to *muddle*; while little Charlottes willingness and affectionateness warm up Sarah's drier more selfish nature. It is a curious establishment with something of the *sound* and character of a *nursery*! Charlotte not nineteen till next March and Sarah seventeen last week! And they keep up an incessant chirping and chattering and laughing—and as both have remarkably sweet voices it is rather pleasant to hear! The *twoness* is no nuisance to me *now*.— As neither of them can awake of themselves, I dont know what I should have done about THAT: hadn't Charlotte's friends come to the rescue! an old man who lodges with

Charlottes 'Mother' (*aunt*) raps on the kitchen window till he wakes them every morning at *six* (!) on his way to his work, and Charlotte's 'Father' (uncle) raps again on the window before seven, to make sure the first summons had been attended to!!—to say nothing of an ALARM which runs down at six, at their very bed-head, and *never* is heard by either of these fortunate girls!— So I dare say we shall get on as well as possible—in a world where perfection is not to be looked for!

I shall be glad to hear that *your* domesticities are in as flourishing a state!

I hope we shall go to the Grange by and by, and make a longer visit than last year. It is such a good break in the long dreary Chelsea winter! and stirs up ones stagnant spirits, and rubs up ones manners! But Mr C won't stay *anywhere*, if he can't get work done—and tho Lady A *says* he shall have every facility afforded him for working I don't know how that will be when it comes to be tried. I never *saw* any *work* done in that house!— Meanwhile I have sent an azure blue moiré [rippled silk] that Lady Sandwich gave me last Xmas day to be made *in case*. [. . .]

Your affectionate /

J W Carlyle [. . .]

To Kate Stanley, Chelsea, 28 December 1860

Darling!

What a bright, good thought of yours, to write me a Xmas letter! Bless your little Heart and all it cares for!

I think there must have been spiritual magnetism at work; more or less. For *I* had been wanting to write to *you*, for a good while back; to tell you a 'Tale of Horror' about the Canary! and should have anticipated your letter; but that the end of the year brings me always such a heap of letters to be written *in the Course of Nature*, and little parcels to be made up for old friends [in] the North, which (*not* the friends but the parcels) have come, by length of habit to be a sort of moral necessity. Then these duties (such as they are) have this year had to be 'pursued under difficulties'—a severe cold; involving confinement to the house. For the first touch of frost as usual knocked me over—like a nine-pin!

I am pretty well thro' my Labours of—what shall I say? *Love*? (Well I suppose so!)[—]now however. Besides all the letters and parcels already sent; I have *three* long letters already written for Newyears morning, and some half dozen Books made ready for the Post! That is what I call '*taking time by the forelock*,' a rule of conduct strongly impress[ed] on me at an early age by the Frontispiece to one of my Story-Books. It represented (or meant to represent) an excited Boy, crossing *the page* with long strides, and pulling after him, by a tuft of hair on the forehead (the rest of the head being bald as an ivory ball), a lean ill conditioned looking old Man (*Time*); while the Boys other hand carried, (*with ostentation*) a sealed letter.

But you are thinking all the while; 'what *is* it about the Canary?— Has *the Cat*—?'—*Eaten* it; you would ask; and the question is by no means an irrelevant one!— No—my Dear! your Canary is not quite eaten; but I am bound to say; no other Canary past, present, or to come, ever had such an affair with a Cat, and came out of it *without being eaten*. Nor could this one, unless *your* Guardian Angel, or mine, or the Canary's own had worked a miracle on its behalf!

The Cat had taken to *studying* the Bird, at its first elevation, with a degree of interest that made one's blood run cold! so I had sent for the Carpenter, and made him suspend the cage from the Drawing-room ceiling with a pully and brass chain. That done, I had no misgivings about leaving the Two alone together; having no idea what a Cat, under the influence of strong desire was *up to*! Returning from my walk one forenoon I was met at the door by Charlotte in the wildest excitement! 'Oh! she said, *whatever* do you think the Cat has gone and done?'— 'Eaten my Canary'? I answered, with calm desperation,— 'NO! FAR WORSE'! 'She must have sprung off the little table on to the cage, and dragged it down, for the chain is lying in a hundred pieces! and the table is tilted over, and broken in two! and oh! Lady Airlie's basket is broken to shivers! and the *ferns all about*! and the glass cover is broken to shivers! and every thing is all over the carpet'!— 'And the Bird safe?'— 'Well yes—tho' the cage door was wide open, she hadn't staid to eat it! The noise of the *lead* and everything falling must have frightened herself; for I met *her* rushing down the stairs, as *I* ran up at the row'!

What a mess when I entered the Drawing room! for 'the Row' had just come off, and nothing was cleared away yet; the cage on its side still, on the floor; the table in two separate pieces; the carpet strewn with earth, and ferns, and bird seed, and water, and fragments of earthen ware, glass, brass-chain &c &c! and amidst all the Bird hopping about rather grave, but otherwise 'as well as could be expected.' I was very sorry about my ferns; for they too were a sort of live pets, and had been given me when I was confined, spring gone a year, by Lady Airlie.

The Cat probably *had* not only frightened herself, but hurt herself, in the general crash of doom she had unexpectedly created. For she had rushed right out at the back door, and never showed herself for 24 hours after, tho a most domestic cat in general,

Relying (Ah too much) on the analogy between feline fools and human ones, I hoped Experience would have taught this individual fool wisdom! So did not at once send the Canary out of the House; seeing that the Cat herself could not be put away—for both practical and sentimental reasons. [O]n the practical hand, We are never catless for a single week but hosts of very little mice troop in to us, out of the drains. Not only does this Cat keep us free of the mice, but she is cleanly, and moral, and honest—except under the temptation of a live Bird. Then, on the sentimental hand; was she not loved by my little Dog, as tho' she had been his own Sister or wedded Wife? stirring him up to games of romps in his old age, and the chief delight of his old age! For *his* dear little sake, I couldnt put her away!

So a second time I sent for the carpenter; and had the cage fixed up against the window shutter at the very top—the brass chains of the present day, being it seems (as Mr C says) '*like every thing else*, an article that the man who made them ought to have been hanged for'!

The cat pretending to take no further notice of the Bird, I thought she had made up her mind that attempts on its life were not only perilous but hopeless, but one night while I was saying something to Charlotte, She suddenly Sprang at *one perpendicular leap* to the cage and hung on to it with her claws!! I couldnt have believed in such a leap if I hadn't seen it! I flung my sofa cushions at her, and screamed, and frightened her into dropping down. But I kept the poor Bird under lock and key, after that, till I found her a safer home.

Miss Farrers Bird had escaped out of the window one day, and its pretty cage was swinging empty, so I sent the poor thing there, where it is now enjoying a life without shocks! I was very sorry to part with the Bird but should have been far sorrier to have it *eaten*.

The Downshire Story is equal to the 'Six-black-crows' story. I was like to cry about it while I was believing it. It seemed such a fatality that a kindhearted simple, straightforward man like Lord Downshire, should be always happening to kill somebody! And poor Lady Alice was too young and pretty to be thought of without emotion as having occasioned a murder.[17]

You have heard perhaps how the story arose?

A Miss Russell who was yachting with the Downshires, wrote to her family here, amongst other news, that Earl (one of the Party) had

17. A piece of Victorian 'fake news', involving Arthur Hill, 4th Marquess of Downshire, cruising in the Mediterranean, who (it seems) found his daughter Alice romantically positioned with the yacht's skipper and threw him overboard to drown. A journalist at *The Guardian*, it seems, had misinterpreted the expression 'thrown overboard': the skipper had just been dismissed.

been making such a fool of himself—'*looking so spooney* at my Lady, that my Lord had finally wearied of him, and *flung him over* at Civitta Vecchia'— This repeated magnified itself into '*flung him overboard*'[.] Then the *Dramatic Personae* in the *Spooneism*(!) were changed from Lady D and Major Earl into Lady Alice and the Skipper (a worthy plain old sailor of sixty!)—a Mr Hammond mentioned the improved report to Azelio who said, 'Oh yes it had been *officially* communicated to *him* from Naples'—whereupon Mr Hammond made an *official despatch* of the news to Lord Cowley at Paris! And now they talk of prosecutions— But I dare say it will all end in that dear, good, Savage (Lord Downshire) thrashing somebody (Azelio perhaps) within an inch of his life! They say Mr Hammond called Azelio to account for his words, and Azelio simply *denied* that he ever said '*officially* communicated.'

And now I see it is within a few minutes of posttime. I must wind up abruptly—

I dont think anyone, even Mr Carlyle, could be disinclined towards worked [embroidered] Slippers—provided the Lady who worked them was young and charming. But I will frankly tell you that of *three* pairs of slippers worked for him in my time, not one was ever worn!— Two came made up, and the third pair he had made up by his own shoemaker, and all three pairs were too short for him. So he has it now a *fixed* idea in his head, that it is an inseparable fault in *worked slippers* to be *too short*.

My kindest regards and the best of good wishes to Lady Stanley and your sisters and self

Affectionately yours /

Jane Carlyle

Remember me to the white Dogs

To Thomas Carlyle, Ramsgate, 6 August 1861

Very charming, doesn't that look with sea in front as far as eye can reach?— And *that* seen (the East Cliff) you needn't wish to ever see more of Ramsgate![18] It is made up of narrow, steep confused streets, like the worst parts of Brighton. The shops look nasty, the people nasty, the smells

18. Tourist coastal town of East Kent, one of the 'Cinque Ports' of south-east England; the ancient fishing community lay between two cliffs, East and West. Within fifteen years of Jane's letter an obscure young Dutchman, Vincent van Gogh, would take up a post as a teacher in the town; he appreciated the views of the sea. Broadstairs, below, is a similar town, two miles to the north.

are nasty! (spoiled shrimps complicated with cess-pool!)— Only the *East Cliff* is clean, and *genteel*, and airy, and *would be* perfect as sea-quarters, if it weren't for the noise! which is so extraordinary as to be almost laughable!

Along that still looking road or street between the Houses and the Gardens, are passing and repassing from early morning to late night *Criers* of Prawns, Shrimps[,] Lollipops, things one never wanted, and will never want, of the most miscellaneous sort, and if that were all! But a Brass Band plays all thro our Breakfast, and repeats the performance *often* during the day, and the Brass Band is succeeded by a Band of Ethiopians,[19] and that again by a Band of female fiddlers!, and interspersed with these are individual Barrel organs[,] individual Scotch Bagpipes, individual French Horns!—

Oh Lord it is—'most expensive!'—and the night noises were not to be estimated by the first night!— These are so many and frequent as to form a sort of *mass of noise*—perhaps *easier* to get some sleep thro' than an individual nuisance of cock or dog— There are *hundreds* of cocks! and they get waked up at, say, *one* in the morning! by some outburst of drunken song or of cat-wailing! and never go to sleep again (these cocks) but for minutes!—and there are three Steeples clocks, that strike *in succession*—and there are doors and gates that slam—and dogs that bark *occasionally*—and a *saw-mill*—and a *Mews* [stables] and—and—in short, everything you could wish *not* to hear!—and I hear it all, and am getting to *sleep in hearing it*!! the bed is so soft and clean! and the room so airy!—and then I think under every shock, so triumphantly; 'crow away'—'roar away'—'bark away'—'slam away'—you 'cant disturb Mr C at Cheyne-Row'—that can't you!—and the thought is so soothing I go off asleep—*till next thing*! I might try [G]eraldines room but *she* has now got an adjoining Baby!— Yesterday we drove to Broadstairs—a quieter place but I saw no *lodgings* that were likely to be quiet—except *one* villa at *six guineas a-week*—already occupied!

I sleep about—in intervals of the Bands—on sofas—during the day—and am less *sick* than when I left home, and we get good enough food *very* well cooked—and I dont repent coming on the whole— Tho' I hate being in Lodgings,—in strange places I saw the Bains, and saw Mrs George before she left—

[no signature]

19. Not authentic Africans, but British musicians from hither and yon, in 'blackface'; a common phenomenon at the time.

To Mary Carlyle Austin, Chelsea, 27 December 1861

My dear Mary

I should like to put my arms round your neck and '*give you a kiss for it*' (as the children say; in the fond idea, poor things, that their kisses are recompense for everything and anything!— And perhaps *their* kisses are; when bestowed on—the Fathers and Mothers of them)!— Anyhow I should like to give *you* a good kiss! and would trust, in Providence, and long experience of your goodwill, for your taking it and returning it with the old heartiness!

Yes! My dear! I could give you the warmest of *kisses* still; but I cannot write you much of a *letter*! and if it werent that the safe arrival of a present should always be notified by return of post; that the kind sender may not be left with misgivings as to its fate; I should put off writing a little while; till I had gained 'more power to my elbow,' and shaken off the languor and dullness produced by eight weeks confinement to the house, and a good deal of suffering, and the 'calming' medecines given me, which have 'calmed' me down to something in the nature of a dead fish!

For the rest; except that I was ill, and would much rather have been well; these eight weeks have passed rather peaceably, for myself and others— I was never as well attended to in illness since I lost my Mother; nor did the House ever go on as comfortably in *my* illness since I knew it—as just on this last occasion. I have got two such good clever Maids— A Welch cook (age 20—and *Roman Catholic*!) & a Hampshire Housemaid (age 18 and *Wesleyan Methodist*!)[20] I haven't had a thing to find fault with while I have been laid up— Nor Mr C either which is still more extraordinary! And I have had very much to congratulate myself, and thank God for—in their kind attentions—so seldom to be met with from servants at the present day! My young Methodist especially, with *her* warm heart, her unobtrusive piety, her clear, open mind and pleasant manners is a comfort to live beside! She brings Mr C *any* Book he wants from the Library!—*in any* language! and *valets* him to perfection! and does all his complicated 'little *jobs* of *sewing*'—with an intelligence that often strikes me as superhuman! I could tell you many amusing things of these girls— But I so soon get tired with writing—or reading—or *doing* any earthly thing. Indeed my Dr forbids me all activity beyond '*eating* and TRYING to sleep!' [. . .]

Affectionately Yours
Jane Welsh Carlyle

20. Margaret Sullivan was actually from Limerick; Maria Chamberlayne came from The Grange.

To Charlotte Cushman, Chelsea, 31 January 1862

My Dear! My Dear! I want to put my arms round your neck, and give you—oh! such a good kiss! And then,—if you can stand that sort of thing, once in a way,—I should like to lay my head on your shoulder and take a good cry! *That* is how natu[re] prompts me to acknowledge your dear letter, and dear newyear's tokens,—with a good kiss and a good cry; rather than with any written sentences that my poor nearly extinct Brain can cobble together in these Hard Times! (I am so worn out and disheartened with long illness and confinement to two rooms!) But alas Dear! The 'gods,' however entreated, will not 'annihilate Time and Space, to make two Lovers happy'![21] *That* has been clearly ascertained some time since! And so, *faute de mieux* [for want of better] I must have recourse to *writing*, 'under difficulties['] and that without further delay, on penalty of passing for both fickle and ungrateful; when—God bless you!—I am as far as possible from being either! and as unwilling as possible that such an idea should be entertained of me—by *you*!

Mrs Dilberoglue, being the precisest and faithfulest of dear little 'Goods,' would do infallibly what she promised, nay volunteered to do, namely, '*explain* to Miss Cushman all about it'—'*It*' meaning my happiness at having a letter from you,—my true Scotch-woman impatience to make 'a *suitable return*,'—and then my illness—the extreme weakness and nervousness which made any—the least—use of my *head* intolerably irksome besides being especially prohibited by my Doctor;—*all that* the little *Good* was to 'explain'! and trusting that she did so with her accustomed accuracy and lucidity, I will not go back upon the causes of my long silence; It is enough to have been *four months ill* and shut up in two rooms; without 'renewing grief' by details of one's fit-for-nothingness; so soon as ever one has recovered *a certain* use of one's tongue and pen!

But if I shut down the lid and turn the key on my sick room tribulations; what is there left out of these weary four months to tell you? *This*—first and foremost; that I am not a bit cooled on the sudden affection I took for you; and believe it to be one of those Elective Affinities[22] on which one does not cool—*ever*! I have seen you twice—that's all! and already you are mixed up with my life like an old friend! Something new and good *in* my life—not outside it! I look forward with pleasure to seeing you again; but, without seeing you without interchanging words with you, it is a pleasure to know of you in the same world with me.

21. Alexander Pope's essay 'Peri Bathous, or the Art of Sinking in Poetry' (1728), chapter 11.
22. Goethe's novel *Die Wahlverwandtschaften* (1809), commonly translated under this title, involves four aristocratic souls and their emotional inter-relations; but the English term in fact derives from chemistry and the 'preference' of some substances for some others.

The influence of a strong, brave, loving true woman may be felt at any distance, I firmly believe, without outward visible sign. And then Dear, you are come to me just at the right time!—to be a consolation as well as a possession! For, of late years, it had been all loss, loss with me! Never gain! One Friend after another out of 'dear old Long Ago,' that had cared for me and that I had cared for all my Life had gone to their rest, leaving me so lonely on the Earth! *Playing at Friendship* with the new people I was thrown amongst; and so discouraged in my secret heart that I despaired of both my chances and my ability to ever make myself a *new real* Friend!— My Heavens! when I went to Barnesbury Park that day to see *you*; how very very little I dreamt of jumping into your arms! and 'swearing eternal Friendship,' like any boarding-school girl! But it was all right! After so many months and after *a severe fit of illness* (which I take to be the best possible test of realities and shams) I feel no misgivings about that somewhat german-looking transaction![23] rather compliment myself on having so much *Life* left in me after all! and on having turn[ed] it to such account!

My *Life* has been making another *pronunciamento* [declaration] with which I could throw you into fits of laughter, if I had you beside me! My Dear! I have had a fearful row with Geraldine Jewsbury! which has made 'pigs and whistles' of that everlasting friendship! and

'Like cliffs that have been rent asunder
A dreary sea now flows between!'[24]

I should be more overpowerd with grief than I am, (in fact I have shown an insensibility unexampled!) had the cliffs been rent by *one* explosion; but the rent has been the gradual work of many years, and the cliffs were only of *sand* or some loose material to begin with! I do think that sort of emotional woman, all 'finer sensibilities' and no feeling, all smoke and no flame is one of the most intolerable inventions of Civilization, should be put down by act of Parliament; and prayed against in all Churches!

You asked for Mrs Hawk's (Madame Venturi's) address.[25] After the *7th* of January (she wrote to me) I was to address *Emilia Venturi nata*

23. 'Germane' rather than 'German': children of the same biological parents; closely related.
24. Coleridge, 'Christabel' (1798), 422–3. She and Geraldine would patch things up in time.
25. Emilie Venturi (*née* Ashurst; 1821–1893), translator of Mazzini, painter and essayist. She married Italian nationalist Carlo Venturi after obtaining a divorce in 1861. It seems a wager from Jane encouraged her to write her only novel, *The Owl's Nest in the City* (1876), under a male pseudonym, to demonstrate that a woman *could* write an unsentimental book. Later she would introduce Thomas to his Chelsea neighbour, James McNeill Whistler, who painted his portrait: *Arrangement in Grey and Black No. 2* (1873), now in the Kelvingrove Gallery, Glasgow.

Ashurst poste restante Milan[.] She had been living up to that date in some rooms of an old Château, near Brescia, dismantled and unfurnished, in the midst of all sorts of inconveniences and discomforts; waited on by a girl of the Country whom she named *Bare* legs (as Mr Carlyle would say 'significative of much!'[)] But caring for none of these things—very fond of her new Husband I think and very happy with him!—happy as a young girl!—and with a touching air of consciousness that not *being* a young girl she has no claim to that sort of happiness and no sure hold of it! She writes to me 'I am so glad you like Charlotte Cushman, she is a dear good noble soul!'

Aren't you glad we are not to be natural enemies? It would have been so absurd that way as well as so vexatious!! When will you come? And how long will you stay?

I cannot put into words how touched I was by your newyears bouquet, and the *little* scarfs! I took them not only as tokens from *you* but as omens of a fortunate year; and—next day I had a relapse and was thrown into bed again for a fortnight!!

Does your friend remember me? I do her—and offer her my kind regards and just one word more and the paper is full. Please love me ever so much but *dont* flatter me for it makes me '*think shame*'! Yours faithfully and affectionately Jane Carlyle

To Mary Russell, Chelsea, 23 February 1862

Oh my Dear what a horrid thing! It still makes my flesh creep all over, whenever I think of it!—and I think of it—a great deal oftener than there is occasion for! since, thank God, he is now on foot again! But—I have SEEN *that Safe*! I can appreciate to the full, the crash of *it's* lid, smack down on human fingers!— Mercy! what a piece of capital good stuff *the* Dr must have been made of originally, that his fingers should have stuck together thro' such an accident instead of being all pounded into *mush*! *That* is not what surprises me most however, in the business! What surprises me most is, that the Dr, *being a Dr*, and a good, skilful one, should have gone about after, braving such a hurt, as tho' he had never in his life heard of lockedjaw,[26] or gangrene, or fever! I dont wonder that you were terrified! I wonder rather that you are not, now when your nursing is no more, needed, in a brain fever yourself! The

26. A symptom of a tetanus bacterial infection of a wound.

longer I live, the more I am certified that *men*, in all that relates to their own health, have not common sense! whether it be their Pride, or their Impatience, or their Obstinacy or their ingrained Spirit of Contradiction that stultifies and misleads them—the result is always a certain amount of idiocy or distraction, in their dealings with their own bodies! I am not generalizing from my own Husband. I know that *he* is a quite extravagant example of that want of common sense in bodily matters, which I complain of. Few *men* (even) are so lost to themselves as to dry their soaked trowsers on their legs! (as he does) or swallow five grains of mercury *in the middle of the day*, and then walk or ride three hours under a plunge of rain! (as he does) &c &c[.] But *men* generally—all of them I have ever had to do with—even *your* sensible Husband included you see!—drive the poor women who care for them to despair; either by their wild impatience of bodily suffering, and the exaggerated moan they make over it, or else by their reckless defiance of it, and neglect of every dictate of Prudence! There! you may tell the Dr what I say! It wont do him the slightest good against *next time*; but it is well he should know what one thinks of him! that one does not approve of such costly heroism at all!

I have nothing new to tell you. Which is lucky. As the things that have *happened*, this long time back, have been of a disastrous sort.

I go out now occasionally for a drive—walking tires me too much—I have even been twice out at dinner last week! and was at a *Wedding* besides!!! The two dinners were of the quietest; at the one (Miss Baring's) nobody but Lord Ashburton who had come up from the Grange for a consultation—at the other (Lady Sandwich's) nobody but the Marchioness of Lothian, who having lived thirty years in Scotland is as good as a Scotch woman. But the wedding was an immense affair! It was my Dr's little Daughter who was being married after a three years engagement, and as soon as she was engaged she had made me promise to attend her wedding. I had rather wished to see a Marriage *performed* in a *Church* with all the forms—the *eight* bridesmaids &c &c— But I had renounced all idea of going *to the church*—for fear of being laid up with a fresh cold, and meant to attend only the breakfast party after—in which I took less interest. But imagine how good the people here are to me. Our Rector in whose church (St Luke's) the marriage was to take place, being told by his wife, I wished to go, but *durstn't* for fear of the coldness of the Church, ordered the fires to be kept up from Sunday over into Tuesday morning!! besides a rousing fire in the Vestry where I sat at my ease till the moment the ceremony began— I was much pressed afterwards to acknowledge how superior the English way of marrying was to the Scotch and asked how I had liked it. I said my feelings were very mixed—'*mixed*?'

the Rector asked—'mixed of what?[']' Well I said, 'it looked to me something betwixt a *Religious Ceremony* and a—*Pantomime*!'— So it is!— There were 44 people at the breakfast!

Countess Pepoli has rallied quite wonderfully. I forced myself to pay her another visit last week—and was rewarded by finding her less ungenial and aggravating. Erasmus Wilson told her Servants she could not possible recover—a good many weeks ago—but London *Great* Doctors make the wonderfullest blunders!— Poor Mrs Twisleton is suffering less for the time being

I hope you wont be long of writing as I shall feel anxious to know for certain that the Dr goes on well and that *you* have not fallen quite ill

Your ever affte /

J W Carlyle

To Thomas Carlyle, Sidney Villas, Dover, 1 October 1862

I may take a reasonable sheet of paper, Dear, for besides being not 'too tired for writing' I have abbundance of *time* for writing[,] '*the Larks*'[27] being *all* far up, out of sight beyond the visible sky! looking for *me* there!— My journey was successful, and I stepped out at Dover worth 'half a dozen of' the woman I left Chelsea & curious what a curative effect a rail-way journey has on *me*, always while *you* it makes pigs and whistles of! Is it the motion? or is it the changed air?—'god knows'!

The first thing that befell me at Dover was a disappointment. [N]o Larks waiting! not a feather of them to be discovered by the naked eye! The next thing that befell me was to be deceived, and betrayed, and entirely discomfited by—a sailor! After looking about for the Larks, some ten minutes and being persecuted as long by pressing proposals from Cabmen and omnibus conductors, I was asking a porter how far it was to Sidney Villas. [T]he Porter not knowing the place, a sailor came forward and said *he* knew it—that it was 'just a few steps,' I 'would be there in a minute if I liked to walk' and *he* 'would carry my trunk for me!' And without waiting to have the question debated he threw my trunk over his shoulder and walked off. I following, quite taken by assault!

27. Jane was visiting her friend Caroline Davenport Bromley (1820–1891), whom she met through the Ashburtons in the summer of 1862, and whom she nicknamed 'the flight of sky-larks', for reasons that remain obscure. Bromley normally lived at Wootton Hall, Staffordshire, and had come to Dover for some sea air.

And we walked on—and on and oh *on*—such a distance—certainly *two miles* at least! the sailor pretending to *not hear*, every time I remonstrated assuring me 'I couldnt find a prettier walk in all Dover than this!'— [A]t last we reached 1 Sidney villa and when I accused my sailor of having basely misled me, that he might have a job—he candidly owned: 'Well, things are dear just now—and few jobs going'!! wiping the sweat from his brow at the same time, and looking delighted with the shilling I gave him! I thought it was all gone to the Devil together, when the man who answered the bell denied that Miss Bromley was there! On cross questioning however he explained that she *did* reside there; but was not at home[,] was 'gone to the railway to meet a Lady'! and his eye just then squinting on my portmanteau, he exclaimed with sudden cordiality—'perhaps you are the Lady!' I owned the soft impeachment, and was shown to the bedroom prepared for me—[a]nd have washed and unpacked. Meanwhile Miss B's maid who had gone to one Station, while Miss B went to the other, to make sure of me, returned, and gave me a cup of tea, and then went off to catch the poor dear Larks who was waiting for me at a *wrong* station! There being a *third* Station (the one, at which I landed)! It hadn't occurred to either mistress or maid to ask at *which* of the three Stations the *three* o'clock train stopt.[28]

Larks come! With feathers all in a fluff! 'So dreadfully sorry' &c &c, dinner not till 7—and to be enlivened by the presence of Mr Brookfield, whom she had met while looking for *me*.— '7'! and I had only *one* small cup of tea and *one* slice of etherial bread and butter. But we 'must make it do'![29]

This house is within a stone cast of the sea, and also alas of the *pier*. So that there is as much squealing of children at this moment as if it were Cheyne Row[,] nothing but a white blind to keep out the light of a large window— But with shutters, and stillness and all possible furtherances I was finding sleep impossible at home; so perhaps it may suit the contradictory nature of the animal to sleep *here*, without them!

Now upon my word this is a fairly long letter to be still in the *first* day of absence!!

It will at least show that I am less ghastly-sick and with less worry in my bits of bowels, than when I left in the morning

Yours anyhow

J W Carlyle

28. That is, Dover Town, Dover Pier or Dover Priory.

29. Charlotte Brontë, *Jane Eyre*, chapter 8.

To Lady Airlie, Chelsea, 10 November 1862

Darlingest of Ladyships! What a nice, dear letter you sent me! and so soon!— Decidedly, you are good!—good as gold, *when you follow just your own inspirations*!— And I should be a wretch if I were long of answering this time! should be (as Mr C might say) 'a vile off-scouring of Humanity, only fit to have a red-hot poker run thro' me, or a torrent of red hot shot poured into my belly'!!! Yes! *that* is the *style* Mr C is rioting in, since the Novr fogs set in! I don't mean his style in addressing myself—better *not*; I can tell him!—but his style in speaking of the *greater* number of his Contemporaries who have risen to 'office'—or power or distinction of any sort 'on the shoulders of a pack of braying jack asses (the Public)'— I don't know whether or not people *breakfast* in Pandemonium, but if they do; I think it must be very much like our breakfastings in Cheyne-Row—'the blackness of Darkness'[30] outside; and inside, red-hot pokers, and red-hot shot, and every description of red-hot thing, flashed (figuratively) before ones eyes!— Ah you are happy who have not to pass in London 'that gloomy month of November, in which the People of England hang and drown themselves'! Still happier perhaps in having that blessed power of reaction which comes of Youth, and Health, and a whole Heart!

The last week has been a little enlivened for me by almost daily visits at Bath House; where the Lord and the Lady [Ashburton] were going on like two buckets at a well in point of health[31]—and their journey postponed until today. They were to start this morning at ten finally—but I shall not be sure, till I have been up and seen the gates closed.

They were very urgent that Mr C and I would go with them or to them for two or three months. I should have liked it so much! I who was never out of this Island! But until that weary Book is done; an invitation to spend three months in Paradise even would be declined by Mr C as an 'impossibility.' Oh what a dreary winter is before me! hardly a soul here that I care for! Countess Pepoli dead, dear clever little Mrs Twisleton dead, Lady Sandwich dead, almost all the rest gone away, not to return till the winter is past and gone. And the winter, it is inferred from premature Robin-red-breasts—multitudinous 'red-rowans'[32] &c—will be a long and severe one. I begin to regret that I declined the offer of a certain Lady Holmes, wife of the Governor of Guiana, to present me with 'a pair of lovely green parrots' and 'a little monkey of a most affectionate disposition'! With such animal resources to fall back upon I might have

30. Jude 1: 13.
31. Empty and full: taking turns at being ill.
32. *Sorbus acuparia*: the mountain ash shrub or tree, a heavy fruit on which was often taken as the sign of a cold winter to come.

fronted the winter with less *apprehension*, [b]ut if there is one thing on earth Mr C detests more than a parrot, it is exactly a—monkey!

Are you one of the prejudiced people who hate Mazzini? If not, I will send you, to read, a little book of his on *Duty*, which has just been translated into English. There was never a greater Fanatic than Mazzini! but also there was never a man more maligned! For example; *there* is a whole public of 'braying jack asses' accusing Mazzini of urging on the Mountebank Garibaldi to that mad expedition against Rome.[33] And I *know*—knew it from Mazzini's own lips, *three weeks* BEFORE Garibaldi landed on the main land that Mazzini considered his enterprise 'perfectly ruinous'—had implored him to desist from it—and had written to him that he (Mazzini) would come and join him if he made the country rise—would come and join him because he was bound to him; but—that he would 'come, with a DEAD HEART'! All *that*, he said to me a month before [A]spremonte and he wrote to me, in Scotland; 'I go in two days—*knowing* that I go, merely to involve myself in the ruin which Garibaldi has prepared for us all.'

You did not say if you liked Mr C's photograph— Surely I did not omit after all to send IT? Tell me if I did; and the stupidity shall be immediately made good. Read *Lady Audleys Secret*[34]

yours with true love
Jane Carlyle

33. In his 'Expedition of the Thousand' (1860), the Italian patriot Giuseppe Garibaldi (1807–1882) had successfully uprooted the Bourbon monarchy in the Kingdom of the Two Sicilies (Sicily and Calabria) and allied it with the Kingdom of Sardinia to build the Italian state. But the Pope and the Papal States would remain a powerful obstacle to unification until 1870. In August 1862 Garibaldi (without the support of senior leaders such as Mazzini) led a small army of volunteers out of Calabria towards Rome to break the deadlock; his venture was arrested at the Battle of Aspromonte of 29 August.
34. The scandalous mother of the 'sensation novel' by Mary Elizabeth Braddon (1835–1915). Critic Elaine Showalter summarises it to perfection: 'Braddon's bigamous heroine deserts her child, pushes husband number one down a well, thinks about poisoning husband number two and sets fire to a hotel in which her other male acquaintances are residing.'

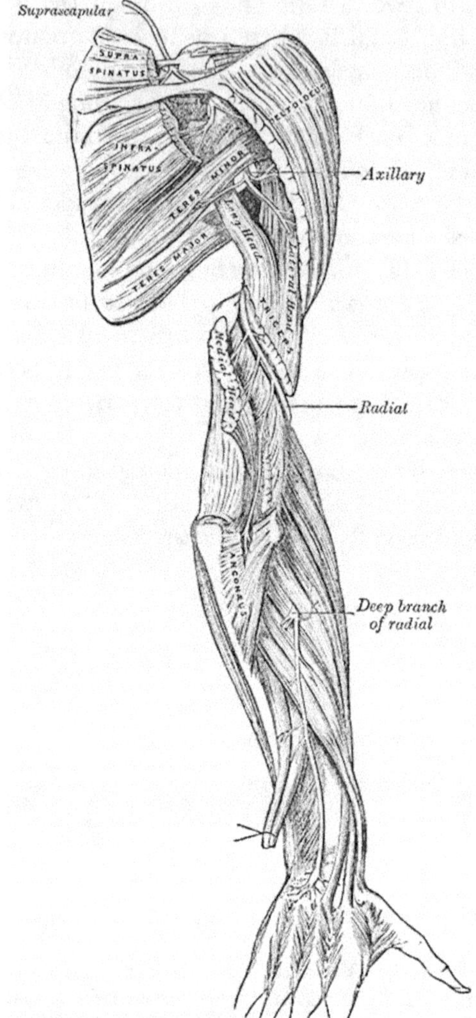

Figure 11: Henry Gray, *Anatomy Descriptive and Physical*, 21st edition (1924), 'The Suprascapular, Axillary, and Radial Nerves', The British Library Board

10

The Accident in Cheapside: 1863–1864

On 22 September 1863 Jane fell in the street, either avoiding a cab while waiting for a bus, or seeking a cab: accounts vary. On 13 October she wrote to her aunt Grace Welsh (see below):

> I was plashed down on the pavement of *St Martin le Grand* (five miles from home) on my left side (the arm of which couldnt break the fall)—and hurt all down from the hip joint so fearfully and on the already lamed shoulder besides—that I couldnt stir, but had to be lifted up by people who gathered round me (a Policeman among them) and put into a cab—

St Martin's Le Grand is a short street that runs south from the Museum of London to St Paul's, and Jane was there to visit a cousin, Mary Godby.[1] *She had suffered from 'neuralgia' (or perhaps rheumatism) in her left arm for two months or so, and couldn't break her fall, as she describes.*

The injuries she sustained are vague, but the result was some weeks of really agonising pain in her leg (which abated by 19 October) and ongoing pain in the originally affected shoulder and arm: no suggestion, it seems, of broken ribs or collarbone. 'Lacerated sinews' was the medical expression she reported on 13 October (see below). But in late November the situation became worse again: she was confined to bed, and the pain in her arm persisted at a high intensity. No fewer than three doctors came to consult: her Chelsea local, Dr Barnes; a Harley Street eminence, Dr Richard Quain (President of the Royal College of Surgeons, 1868); and the husband of Bessy Barnet, Jane's first servant at No. 5, Dr Blakiston, now practising in St Leonards-on-Sea in Sussex. By the end of December she was on

1. *CL* has a note alongside Jane's letter to Mary Russell of 5 July 1857: 'Mrs. Godby was the widow of "an important Post-Official, once in Edinburgh" who came to "London a year or two ago" (from 1863) with her children to "a fine situation as 'Matron of the Post-office Establishment' [. . .] in St. Martin's-le-Grand"; she may already have been living in London. According to TC, JWC and she often visited each other (Carlyle, *Reminiscences*).'

high doses of morphine (twenty-five drops a day)[2] *for the pain—though Thomas told John he hated 'all druggings and opiate abominations'—and (perhaps as a side-effect of the drug) came to dread insanity so much that she implored Thomas not to commit her. (On 28 February 1865 she confessed to Mary Russell that she had asked Quain to end her life.) It would be nine months before she recovered, a process we can chart fairly well by her ability to continue her correspondence, increasingly restricted to the inner circle of family and Mary Russell (whose own husband was a doctor in Dumfries). In October and November 1863 we have about a dozen letters a month from her; in December and January none; in February 1864 one (ordering house coal from a local supplier); in March three, in April six, in May six, in June three, in July fifteen, and in August 1864 twenty-nine. There were evident fears for her life in the three or four months after the accident—fears all the more distressing because her condition was so hard to diagnose.*[3]

On 2 January Thomas wrote to Louisa, Lady Ashburton, that 'We (that is, she) are still in very great distress' and that the various opiates she was being prescribed were 'refuges of lies'. On 13 January he told Lady Stanley, 'I never saw her (nor indeed anybody) in such suffering, and continual misery night and day'. On 27 February he told his sister Jean, 'It is certain she is very much quieter *than formerly (some weeks ago); but whether by exhaustion of strength, abate[men]t of the disease, or use of opium, I cannot with my whole industry in the least convince myself. She is very low; speaks little, and only about* one *stern release as the alone possible for her.' Cousin Maggie Welsh came down from Liverpool to nurse and on 8 March it was decided to take Jane to the Blakistons' in St Leonards for a change of scene and air—her bedroom at No. 5 having become oppressive to her. On 25 March she told her old school friend William Dods that 'I fear the last is near'. By the middle of April, fearing that she was an imposition—but also exercising some independence—she moved into a house at 117 Marina at St Leonards (a Grade II listed building even now).*

Thomas and Jane's 'Titanesque power of making mountains out of molehills' was noted in the Introduction: 'like two Othellos bellowing about life and death over the dropping of a handkerchief'. But Margaret Welsh was less of a hyperbolist, and she reported to Jane's women friends in the spring of 1864 in ways which, however short of diagnostic detail, suggest that there was nothing of the molehill or

2. The relation of Victorian dosages to modern ones is hard to establish. In modern practice twenty drops of morphine amount to 1ml, and each ml contains 10mg of raw opium: so each drop contains 0.5mg of the drug. And a safe dose for an adult seems to be five to ten drops two to three times daily: not so far off Jane's dosage if the measures were alike. But opium should be prescribed for as brief a period as possible, and 'drops' are entirely different things given the nature of the fluid and the construction of the pipette. We perhaps could not call Jane an addict, exactly; but she was certainly a user during quite long periods in her later life. The comparison with Coleridge springs to mind.
3. The early improvement in the 'lacerated sinews' of her leg suggests an injury in the hip of that kind. By contrast the long-lasting pain in her arm, unresponsive to analgesics, perhaps points to neuritis: specifically, a peripheral mono-neuropathy of the axillary nerve.

the handkerchief about Jane's sufferings at this time. (Her letters are reprinted in CL.) Maggie told Lady Ashburton on 6 February that 'today she is really very *poorly, suffering very great pain, & she looks, I think, very poorly indeed'; on 17 February she reported, 'For the last week she has not been suffering the weary, & sometimes intense, nervous pain nearly so much; this* must *be an improvement; for that constant suffering was most wearing out.' On 7 March she told William Dods, 'I grieve to say that my Cousin Mrs Carlyle is still very ill. The doctors are most anxious for her to go to the seaside, as they appear to think that a Change of air & of scene may do great good when many other things have unfortunately failed.' Jane was transported to the coast in a hideous invalid carriage, and ten days later Maggie told Maria-Louisa Stewart Mackenzie, 'She is certainly in every respect stronger than when we came, but she herself says that she has suffered for so long now that she feels as if she had but little courage or hope to aid her recovery.' On 8 April she had better news for Lady Louisa: 'Dr Blakiston considers her to be very* much better; *she is able to drive out once every day & often she goes twice, & is up all the day, at least moving about now & then & resting on the sofa.' But on 24 April news for Thomas was bad again: 'I can only give you a very poor account of my Cousin today I am sorry to say. She was very poorly all day yesterday & went to bed as soon as she came in from her drive. This morning she went out for an hour but she felt so ill when she came home that she said she could not sit up & has been in bed all the afternoon.' (In mid-May, it must be noted, Thomas packed up his books and himself relocated to St Leonards, to be nearer to her in her desperation.) Friends made the pilgrimage to Sussex to see her, but she was too ill to be visited. By 31 May she spoke to Mary Russell, psychosomatically, of an 'everlasting torture in my womb', which suggests an almost complete prostration, mentally as well as physically.*

On 12 July Jane's old instinct for the north kicked in and she set out with that most uncongenial of fellow travellers, John Carlyle, for her beloved sister-in-law Mary Carlyle Austin at The Gill, Dumfriesshire; then ten days later to the Russells at Holm Hill, where, as summer gave way to autumn, she came off opium, her condition finally abated, her appetite returned, and her depression began to recede. It would be 1 October before Thomas and No. 5 would see her again—to take up a redecorated bedroom and resume her old life.

❧

To Mary Russell, Chelsea, 27 January or 3 February 1863

Dearest Mary

You thought I must be *ill* that I did not write; and now that three days have brought no answer to your inquiry, I shouldn't wonder if you are thinking I must be *dead*!

I am only very *stupid* Dear! uncommonly stupid! not to have learnt, by this time of day, to write off a few lines, when I am hindered by business, or illness, or anything, from writing a good long letter— But there I go on, from day to day, holding my peace, because the *season is not convenient* for saying *all* I want to say—leaving my friend to frighten herself at getting no letter at all, just because nothing would content me but that she should get a good long one!— I really must try ammend this stupidity, the result in part of having lived and learnt to write letters, long before the era of Rowland Hill[4]—when the postage of a letter from London to Scotland was fourteen pence halfpenny and to be paid by the *receiver*; so that nobody with a conscience would have dreamt of dispatching letters of only a *few lines*!

Yes, Dear, you were quite right in thinking things must be wrong with me; when YOU were so long of hearing. And if you were to guess far into next week, *you* wouldn't guess *what* the matter has been! The first thing to imagine, in the course of nature, especially in midwinter, is, that I have been ill. And in truth I have been far from well—with my old *sickness* very bad on me, and a weary pain in my back besides; a thing I never had before. But it hasnt been the winter that has hurt me—indeed we have had *no* winter here yet! only fine spring-like weather, in which even I couldnt manage to be laid up with my usual cold. The illness I have had, and am still having has been caused, palpably enough, by a mental shock which struck me deadly sick at stomach, and struck the pain into my back, in the first moment of it; And tho' my mind has recovered its balance, these consequences still remain.

One expects to hear of something sentimental, romantic, at least exciting; when anybody speaks of having had a great mental shock. My Dear! lower your expectations, bring them down to the level of the meanest prose!— For what I have to tell you is again about—my Servants!!! But take up the Servant as a human being—a fellow creature—and read my paltry tale as a phsycological illustration; and it *is* enough to throw one into a fit of misanthropy—besides making one sick at stomach and breaking one's spine in two!

When I wrote last, I was looking forward to better times below stairs. The new cook [Mary] seemed a decent young woman, not bright or quick; but who would, with a little teaching and a good deal of patience be made to *do*— 'Flo' [Florence] was clever, and assiduous, and thoughtful and helpful. [T]he only thing to be guarded against with *her*, was the

4. Rowland Hill (1795–1869) was the key campaigner for a reform of the British postal service, father of the uniform penny post and the postage stamp (1840)—above all, the famous 'Penny Black', which could become a rival form of currency in itself, as below.

tendency to praise and pet her overmuch, and so—spoil her; as I had spoilt Charlotte [Southam]! But I was helped in *that* by the want of personal *attraction* for me in the Child. There was something dry and hard, something *unyouthful* in her manner, and voice, which coupled with her extraordinary cleverness and assiduity, sometimes reminded me of the '*Changelings*' in Fairy Legends.[5]

Well! As the days went on 'a change' seemed to come over 'the Spirit of' the new Cooks 'dream.'[6] She grew more and more gloomy, and sullen, and indifferent; till she grew exactly into her Scotch predecessor *translated into English—minus* the utter blockheadism!!! I was careful to make no remarks on her before Flo; but Flo was constantly *blurting out* aggravating instances of negligence and disagreeableness on the part of the new comer. At last one day my dissatisfaction reached a climax; and I told this Mary, that I perceived she would not suit, and that I thought it best to tell her so in the first month. And again my weary Spirit was wandering thro' space in Search of a Cook, beset by far greater difficulties than '*Celebs in search of a Wife*'[.][7] The only person that looked delighted was Flo, as delighted as she had looked when I gave Elizabeth warning [in 1862].

Next day I was just putting on my bonnet to go out on this miserable search, when the Cook said to me; she thought it very strange to be *going* in this way! that she had 'never gone out of any place before in less than a year at the least.' 'Whose fault is it?' I said— 'Do you consider it *possible* for me to keep a woman, who shows no sort of interest in doing or learning the work she has undertaken to do here'?— 'Well said the woman, with a half sob, I am aware I have made myself very disagreeable; but it wasnt easy, to be good tempered and to try to please; with Flo, every time she came down stairs telling me the dreadfulest things that you said of me, and of every thing I did'!!![:] 'that I was "nothing but a stupid dirty maid-of-All work, fit for nothing but a Tradesman's house where I could get tumbling about among a lot of rough workmen"—and Oh far worse things than that!'— [A]stonishment took away my speech for a moment; I had not said ONE WORD of the woman to the Child—knowing that she carried every thing to her Mother.

5. In which a strange child is smuggled into an unsuspecting family, with ruinous results; the largest such instance in English literature is probably Heathcliff in Emily Brontë's *Wuthering Heights* (1847).
6. Byron, 'The Dream' (1816).
7. *Coelebs in Search of a Wife* (1809), a novel by Christian moralist Hannah More (1745–1833) in which a high-minded young man seeks a wife who can live up to his mother's exacting standards. See 10 July 1841, above.

I rung the bell for Flo.— 'What is all this, I asked that you have been telling Mary—as said of her by *me*?' 'Well Mam said Flo very red, *I couldn't help it*! Mary was always asking me what you said about her—you *know* you *were* Mary! (like a viper); and I was *obliged* to tell her *something*'! 'You were *obliged* to invent horrible lies, were you?'— 'If I didn't tell her something, Mam, she wouldnt leave me alone'!— 'Oh you wicked girl!' burst in Mary, 'What was I asking you when you tried to set me against the Place and the Mistress from the first night I entered the house'!— 'I said Flo—I only repeated what Elizabeth said!['] 'And the Mistress would be a little surprised, said Mary, if I were to tell Her what you told *Me*!'— 'Oh I will tell her myself,' said Flo; '*if you please* Mam, Elizabeth said, a woman that was her fellow-servant in Scotland, told her before she came here that you were a She-devil! And Elizabeth said *that* tall chair (pointing to a *prie Dieu*) was *for strapping you to, when you were mad*!!!'— It was at this point that the sickness came into my stomach and the pain into my back! 'Good God' I said, when I could speak, [']is it possible that you who have lived beside me these two months, who have never got a cross look or harsh word from me who have *seen* my behavior to that very Elizabeth, could say the like of this?' 'If you please Mam it wasn't me that said it, it was Elizabeth'! 'Oh you lying bad girl' broke in Mary. [']I see it all now! that you were set on driving me out of the place, and I shouldnt wonder if you did the same by Elizabeth.'

The same thought had just flashed on myself. It was from the day Maria left and *this child* came, that Elizabeth began to grow, from a mere obedient blockhead, into a sullen, disobliging, blockhead, seeming to rather take pleasure in poisoning Mr C than not!

In *her* case there wasnt even *invention* needed. The imp had only to do what I was constantly warning her against viz: to *repeat* the strong things Mr C said of Elizabeths cookery and self generally, to drive the woman to fury, and make her the unbearable creature she became!

—Flo seeing herself unmasked began to cry very hard—repeating again and again, 'you will never be able to bear me again, I know! I *have been so treacherous*! You were so kind to me! and I was so fond of you! and I have been so very treacherous oooh-oooh oo—oh.'— I didn't know what on earth to do— I didn't feel justified in turning her off on the spot—[a]nd to keep her was like keeping a poisonous viper at large in the House— The only thing I was clear about was to withdraw my warning to Mary, whose behaviour had been sufficiently excused by the influences acting on her. Flo's Mother, hearing of the row came over to try and shift the blame on Mary— I rung the bell and said to Mary, 'Mrs Morrison has accusations to make against you Mary—you had better hear them yourself, and answer her—as I know nothing about it.'— And then ensued an altercation, between the two women, (while I sat with my feet on the fender and my back to them) in which Mrs Morrison came by the worse; having only drawn out a *fuller* statement of Flo's horrid conduct. She went away imploring me to 'try her (Flo) a little longer—it would be a lesson she would never forget &c &c'[.] And I said 'she can stay—for the present, till I see what comes of her.' But three days after the Child herself said 'I can never be happy here after having been so treacherous and I had better go away.' I am glad you think so I said so the sooner you go the better today if you like—and in an hour she was gone! My paragone little Housemaid! Three days after she came over—tears all dried—looking hard and bold, to ask me to 'see a Lady' for her. 'What sort of Character do you think I can give you I asked—'— 'Well! said the Child[,] I have *told a few lies* and I *have been treacherous*; but that is ALL you can say against me'! The dreadful child!

I saw a girl [Lizzy], that I thought would suit me, the same day Flo left; but she couldn't come for a month, and her Aunt who wished me to wait for her, offered to come and help Mary—till the girl was free— So I have a great jolly clever elderly woman in the kitchen except for the two last days of the week when she is engaged elsewh[ere]—and Mary does nicely up stairs— This woman is a capital Cook and I almost wish the present arrangement, tho' an expensive one, could last—now that I have got used to the big woman, who 'thoroughly understands her business'— But she has a Husband and couldn't stay with me in permanence

Now; do you wonder I fell ill?— (Think of Mr C's impatience as a running accompaniment to all this disgusting worry!)

Marion's[8] announcement was vexatious enough—but there was no '*treachery*' to turn your heart upside down.— Still I am very sorry she has taken such a whim in her head; for she saved you a deal of trouble—and your establishment was all so *settled* looking—that I often envied you in my own changings

You have plenty of time before you to look out; that is one comfort; and another is, taking a new servant in the country where she is known is not such a leap in the dark as taking a Town one; and the greatest comfort of all is; *your* Husband is not so awfully impatient as some people's Husbands, and is a help to you rather than a hindrance in difficulties! But I shall be very glad when you can tell me you have heard of somebody likely to suit—

8. Mary Russell's servant, planning to emigrate to America.

Lord Ashburton's convalesence is at a stand— I have never been able till lately to feel the hope of him that Mr C and others felt—and now the accounts are ominous again—

I have written all this at intervals—my back aching too bad for sitting straight up long together

Write to me soon— I *need* a letter—

I owe your Husband sixpence—please give him these six Stamps—they were left out of my letter to him by mistake

God bless you both

Your ever affectionate

Jane Carlyle

To Charlotte Southam, Chelsea, 29 March 1863

Little Woman!

It was a nice thought in you to send the violets. A kind little practical thought!—just like my little Charlotte in her *good* Time; when she was a bright, loving girl, full of aspirations after knowledge and refinement,—before she had become stubborn and callous on my hands and taken up with people and things unworthy of her,—quite beneath the sphere in which Nature, by endowing her so richly with taste and intelligence, seemed to have appointed her to 'live and have her Being!'[9]— Oh child! child! you have no idea of the disappointment, the heart-sorrow you caused me! I had set so much love on you, and so much hope! So much permanent good was to have come out of our chance-relation for both of us! And all ending in a mere vulgar common-place disruption betwixt *Mistress* and *Maid*!—in a mere vulgar common-place attempt on both sides to '*better oneself*'!—no!—not ending all and absolutely in that!— There are the *violets*!—and this letter!—so much (alas! how small a thing!) saved from the wreck of my sentimental venture!

Do you know the violets found me breakfasting in bed, (the first and only time I have breakfasted in bed these twelve months!) and their sweet smell reminded me somehow of your kind nursing in my long Influenza. No one has nursed me as kindly and as cleverly since!

9. Acts 17: 28. Charlotte left in May 1861, going to work for the Marquess of Camden in his country house in Kent.

I was so sorry for your Mother's terrible loss! it has told on her looks poor woman! I hope you write to her often and are all the comfort you can be to her.

Ever affectionately yours,
JANE W. CARLYLE

❧

To Grace Welsh, Chelsea, 13 October 1863

Thank you a thousand times dearest Grace[10] for your long most moving letter. It is not because of it, that I write today, for I was meaning to write today at any rate; indeed *it* rather makes writing more difficult to me; I have cried so over it, that I have given myself a bad headach in addition to my other lamings— But a little letter I *will* write by todays post and a *bigger* one when I am more able—

I wrote a few lines to Mrs Craven in answer to her announcement of that dear girls angel death— I told her of my accident, and was trusting to *her* telling you: but as I told *her* I had kept you in ignorance of it in the beginning lest Elizabeth and you and Ann with your terrible experience of such an accident might be alarmed and distressed for me more than (I *hoped*) there would prove cause for—she thought perhaps I wished you to remain unaware of it, even when I reported myself progressing more favourably than could have been predicted. I need not go into the *how* of the fall. I will tell you all 'particulars' when I gain more facility in writing—enough to say that exactly this day three weeks, I was plashed down on the pavement of *St Martin le Grand* (five miles from home) on my left side (the arm of which couldnt break the fall)—and hurt all down from the hip joint so fearfully and on the already lamed shoulder besides—that I couldnt stir, but had to be lifted up by people who gathered round me (a Policeman among them) and put into a cab— *Elizabeth* can fancy my drive home—five miles—and the getting of me out of the cab and upstairs to bed! Wasn't I often thinking of *her* all the time? 'My' Dr came immediately; and found neither breakage of the leg nor dislocation—but the agony of pain he said would have been *less* had the bone broken— I thought of Elizabeth, and doubted *that*!

10. This is Jane's paternal aunt in Morningside, Edinburgh, not her mother, dead twenty years. Mary Craven was Jane's cousin, daughter of her paternal uncle Robert; her sister Grace Dobie had died of pulmonary tuberculosis on 2 October.

Still for three days and three sleepless nights it was such agony as I had never known before— After that the pain went gradually out of the leg unless when I moved it—when the bedpan was pushed under me &c &c! But the arm with its complication of sprain and neuralgia has given me a sad time—till these last two days that it has returned almost to the state it was in before the fall. [A] week ago Mr Barnes made me get out of bed for fear of 'a bad back' and sit *on end* on a sofa in my bedroom[,] like *Miss Biffin*—(the little egg-shaped woman that used to be *shown*)[11]—and two days ago he compelled me to *walk a few steps*, supported with his arms—and to do the same thing at least twice a day[.] It has been a case of what they call 'lacerated sinews,' and he said the tendency of the muscles was to contract themselves after such a thing, and if I did not force myself to put down my foot now and then, I should never be able to walk at all! Such a threat and his determined manner enables me to make the effort which COSTS! I can tell you[.] But at whatever cost of pain and nervousness, I have today passed thro' the door of my bedroom (which opens into the Drawing room luckily), using one of the maids as a crutch. So you see I am already a good way towards recovery—for which I feel every moment deep thankfulness to God— To have experienced such agony and to be delivered from it comparatively—makes one feel one's dependence as nothing else does!

For the rest as dear Betty [Braid] is always saying 'I have mony mercies'— My Servants have been most kind and unwearied in their attentions—my Friends more like Sisters or Mothers than commonplace *friends*— Oh I shall have such wonderful kindnesses to tell you of when I can write freely— [M]y third cousin Mrs Godby and several others wished to stay with me—but the '*nursing*' I *needed* was of quite a menial sort— I should still have sought it from my servants, and a Lady nurse would only have given *them* more to do, and been dreadfully in the way of Mr C— [M]y great object, after getting what *waiting* on I absolutely needed[,] has been that the usual quiet routine of the house should not be disturbed around Mr C—who thinks, I am sure, that HE has been victimised *enough* in having to answer occasional letters of enquiry about me!! And now I must conclude—for the present [. . .]

11. Sarah Biffen (1784–1850), born with no legs and only tiny arms, who learned to paint with a brush in her mouth. Only three feet tall, she was exhibited as a curiosity until she was rescued by the Earl of Morton, who got her art lessons, but she ended her life in poverty on a royal pension.

A hearty kiss to each of you— Be sure to send me the copy of Graces words to her Mother— Oh poor Souls! What woe and what mercy!

Your loving niece/

Jane W Carlyle

❧

To Isabella Simmonds, Chelsea, 27 November 1863

Dear Pet! I am not the least well! and should just about as soon walk overhead into The Thames, as into a Roomful of People!— At the same time I wish to pay my respects to the Baby on this her next grand performance after getting herself *born*! and to place in her small hands a *talisman* worthy of the occasion, and suitable to a Baby born on 'All Saints Day'—(whatever sort of day *that* may be!)[12]

As I shouldn't at all recommend running a long pin into the creature; I advise YOU to wear the brooch in its present form till the Baby is significantly hardened from its present pulpy condition, to bear something tied round its throat, without fear of strangulation! And then you may remove the pin, and attach the talisman to a string, in form of locket. But what *is* it? 'what does it *do*'? (as a servant of mine once asked me in respect of 'a *Lord*';)[. W]hat it *is* my Dear, is an emblematic mosaic, made from bits of some tomb of the Early Xians—and representing an Early Xian device—[t]he greek cross the palm leaves and all the rest of it!— [W]orn by the like of *me*, I dare say it would have no virtue to speak of—but worn by a Baby born on *All Saints day*—! it must be a potent charm against the Devil and all his works one would think!—for it is a *perfectly authentic* memorial of the Early Xians.

I hope you didn't go and drop the '*Jane*' after all!— Bless you—and IT

affectionately yours

Jane Baillie Welsh Carlyle!

❧

12. Celebrated on 1 November in Catholic and Protestant churches alike, this feast celebrates *all* the saints, known or unknown. It is associated also with the departed, as it falls the day before All Souls' Day. In a larger sense it celebrates the necessary connection between Christians in heaven ('triumphant') and those on earth ('militant').

To Lady Louisa Ashburton, St Leonards, 25 March 1864

Oh my Darling! My Darling! I have only been told now— The Dr ordered it should be kept from me till this morning.[13]

Oh God Comfort you! if ever there was a man ready to pass from this sorrowful earth to be an angel in Heaven it was he! My spirit flies to your dear side, while my poor body is chained here with a cruel malady that I believe will prove fatal; tho the Drs hold out hopes still— Oh God! it is among the few things for which I pray to be spared in life a little longer, this that I might prove to *you* my love and gratitude.

Oh do not forget me and may your kindness to me help to warm your own sad heart.

Ever your affectionate Jane Carlyle

To Thomas Carlyle, St Leonards, 19 April 1864

It is no 'morbid despondency'[14]—it is *positive* physical torment day and night—a burning throbbing maddening sensation in the most nervous part of me ever and ever— How be in good spirits or have any hope but to die!

When I spoke of going home it was to *die* there, here were the place for *living*—if one could!

It was not *my* wish to leave here. It was the Blakistons *own* suggestion and wish that we should get a little house of our own. I have rather wondered at the short time their benevolence has held out but it is natural as not even the honour of a *cure* is to be gained for all their pains!

Oh have pity on me— I am worse than ever I was in that terrible malady

I am yours as ever
Jane Carlyle

13. News, that is, of Lord Ashburton's death on 23 March, at The Grange, aged only sixty-four.
14. Jane is responding to Thomas's tactless report from Chelsea (18 April) that various medical authorities were putting her sufferings down to psychosomatic causes: '*morbid* imagination', as he was told (*CL*).

To Mary Russell, St Leonards, circa 31 May 1864

Oh my dearest Mary—your kind invitations to Holmhill draw tears from my heart. Alas my Darling you have no idea I perceive of the critical, miserable state I am in— Mrs [Jean] Aitken knows nothing of it—and Dr Carlyle about as little— The Drs, who have attended me, themselves have been at a nonplus— You speak of *my* '*arm*'—my arm is nothing in it now—for months my arm has been all right—the misery has been a more terrible thing, an everlasting torture in my *womb*—it is not a cancer or any such thing—the Drs say, only a nervous affection—but all the same the suffering attending it is beyond all words to tell.

It is a degree less since I came to this house but still sufficient to keep me in wretchedness day and night

I am very weak—can hardly walk across the floor—but that is partly because of pain and stiffness in my legs which Dr Blackiston imputes to supposed GOUT![15] God help me whatever it is—

I have hardly a hope of recovery—but they tell me I am too dispondent.

It was cruel in Maggie Welsh to leave me in such a state[16]—but the Mary Craik I have got in her stead is much more to my taste—a kind useful modest girl—

Oh *my* Mary shall I live to see your dear face again?— God only knows— I am *very* miserable

love to the Dr / Your own friend Jane Carlyle

To Thomas Carlyle, The Gill, 15 July 1864

Oh my Dear! I am quite as amazed as you to find myself here! so promiscuous! I had given up all idea of Scotland when I left St Leonards—felt neither strength nor courage for it—but postponed *projects* till I saw what lay for me at Palace Gate House—[17]

15. A variety of inflammatory arthritis in the joints, typically the legs, related to uric acid in the blood, often associated with diet—and drinking habits, too. It hardly seems to fit Jane's complaint.
16. Margaret, Uncle John's daughter, rushed back to Liverpool to nurse her dying nephew. Mary Craik was daughter of George Lillie Craik (see Characters and Correspondents), and came down from Belfast to help; she was in her mid-thirties, hardly a girl.
17. Jane had fled St Leonards to her sister-in-law Mary, at The Gill in Dumfriesshire (via Eliza and John Forster in London), which Thomas describes (*CL*) as a 'poor but ever kind and generous *human* habitation, [. . .] a small farmhouse, seven miles beyond Annan, twenty-seven beyond Carlisle, eight or ten miles short of Dumfries'. On 21 July she went on to the Russells at Holm Hill, where affection and medical attention would accompany each other. Meanwhile the Larkin family had moved in from No. 6 Cheyne Row.

I found there much kindness, and much STATE, and a firm expectation that I was merely passing thro! and if they had wanted me ever so much to stay; there was not a bed in the house fit to be slept in—from the noise point of view!— Cheyne Row full of Larkins and my old room in the same state—horrible was the idea to me!— The Blunts perhaps out of town— London very hot!

I *did* sleep some *human* sleep in my luxurious bedroom, all crashing with wheels—but only the having had NO sleep the night before made me so clever!

I could not have slept a *second* night—no—there was nothing to be done but what I did!—turn that second night to *use*!—travel thro' it—and not try for any sleep until there was some chance of getting it!—[T]hat night on the road was nothing like so wretched as those nights at [St Leonards] Marina— I drank four glasses of champagne in the night—!! and took a good breakfast at Carlisle— John was *dreadfully* ill-tempered— We quarrelled incessantly—but he had the grace to be ashamed of himself after, and apologize—[18] [*O*]*n* the whole it was a *Birthday* of *good* omen my horrible ailment kept off as by enchantment!—

Mary is all that mortal could wish as hostess, nurse and Sister—She has had something of the sort herself and her sympathy is INTELLIGENT—

I am *gone in* for milk diet took porridge and buttermilk, *in quantity* last night!!!! and slept with few awakings all night—had a tumbler of new milk at eight and *got up* to breakfast at nine!!!

I am very *shaky* you will see; but oh so thankful for my sleep and *ease*—would it last!

John went to Dumfries yesterday afternoon—and all who had been about me being gone; I felt like a child set down out of arms—but am contriving to *totter* pretty well so far— John was to be here today some time— I am very sorry for you with those idiot Servants—

18. John's side of the story (14 July) is in *CL*: 'We were fortunate enough to get a compartment to ourselves all the way to Carlisle last night, & Jane stood the journey quite well, suffering much less than she has often done of late from one night of sleeplessness. Mary had a comfortable carriage to meet us with at Cummertrees [station two miles south-east of The Gill]. The rooms here look very nice & tidy. [. . .] Jane looks better today than I have seen her since April—partly perhaps owing to her having accomplished the long journey so successfully. Let us hope that she may now make more rapid progress, & let us also be thankful that she has got through last night's fatigue so satisfactorily. [. . .] Mrs [Eliza] Forster had provided Jane with sandwiches sherry & champagne for the journey when I went to Palace Gate House last night; & all were very useful in making her journey comfortable.' Few would blame Jane for being tetchy, given her condition.

Mary proved herself of no earthly use to me; besides being sulky and conceited— Mary Craik is your only present stay—kiss her for me! dear kind good girl. I will write to *her* next— I am so sorry at having had to leave her in such a mess

James Austin had *already* got a nice carriage for *Mary* to drive me about in!! Oh they are so kind! and so *polite*!

Your own— / J W C

❧

To Thomas Carlyle, Holm Hill, 23 July 1864

I find if I do not write today no letter will reach you till Tuesday— So just two lines to say I have arrived safe and got your note.

They met me at the station [Cummertrees] and are kind kind—as indeed many are—John offered to accompany me here but I declined— I have not had so much pleasure in him as to prolong our intercourse a moment beyond what I could help—

He has been very hard and cruel—and *mean* inconceivably! but THAT, is HIS OWN affair! Fancy him telling me in my agony yesterday that 'if I had ever DONE anything in my life, this would not have been! that no *poor* woman with *work* to mind had ever had such an ailment as this of mine since the world began!!!'—

I am not so ill today but *that* was of course—movement—change—change—! and I have but one wish—to *stay still*— I slept last night the FIRST part of the night—and awoke at *four*—better than the other way of it lying awake till morning

Oh my Dear I think how near my Mother I am!—how still I should be laid beside *her*!— But I *wish* to live—for YOU—if only—I could live *out* of torment—

Yours affly / Jane Carlyle

❧

To Thomas Carlyle, Holm Hill, 8 August 1864

Again the enforced silence at the end of the week has been an advantage.

If I had written to you on Saturday what a letter it would have been! For my wakefulness had reached a height! Friday night had been the counterpart of the preceding night:—about half an hour of *partial* unconsciousness, after seven in the morning.

Still I was not the least *tired*; only wild, and the *irritation* dreadful, so I took to bed in the afternoon. Something I said about my bowels, which I had assured Dr R[ussell] all this time were in a charming state, put him on ascertaining with his own eyes and the result was a discovery that I was excessively *bilious*, and needed four grains of blue pill!! (He wouldnt have me take one of Dr Balkiston's mild compound articles)—and he was justified by my *falling asleep* soon after, and sleeping thro' the whole night!! I woke some twenty or thirty times—but just to think; 'Oh God! what a mercy this is!' and go to sleep again. Much bile was got rid of yesterday, and I was sanguine enough to expect another such night— But not so— [L]ast night I lay awake, very restless till half after two—then I took a glass of wine, and calmed down into what I call *waking sleep*, which continued till seven. How it will go on I cannot predict I only feel sure if I had tried narcotics on the top of all that bile, it must have produced a brain fever—and also; that until this terrible wakefulness of the last two months is quenched, there can be no REAL basis for hopes of recovery— Oh my Dear! I am very weary! My agony has lasted long!

—I am tempted to take a 'long cry *over myself*'—and no good will come of *that*! I will go and get ready for my drive.

Yours for ever / Jane W Carlyle

❧

To Thomas Carlyle, Holm Hill, 19 August 1864

Dearest

There is a question I have meant to ask in every letter for some time back, and which has always been put aside, and 'eventually' forgotten till the letter had been posted. *What became of our kitten*? Was it left with anyone 'in particular' at St Leonards? or was it brought back to Chelsea? Surely Mary Craik would secure its Future?

Something occurred here last evening between the hours of 8 and 9, which produced an extraordinary sensation! Mrs Russell has not got over it yet! My Dear, I LAUGHED!!! 'the first time I had laughed since I came'! And it was no feeble attempt; but a good loud hearty laugh!— Perhaps you will wonder what could have produced an effect so startling? The cause was a nothing—Mrs Russell had been telling of a row Mrs Ewart at Nith Bank had had with her servants. Hearing some disturbance in the room where her Maids slept, she got out of bed to see what it was, and found a stranger man in one of their beds. 'Only think what a terrible thing! said Mrs R—and a *great big* man!'— 'My Dear,' said the Dr in his quiet, dry way; 'would it have been any better had it been a LITTLE man?'— I don't know why this tickled me so much—but I *laughed*; and if I had *cried* I couldn't have surprised them more—or so much!

Along with Forsters letter to *you*, there is come this morning a kind little letter from Forster to *me*. Nobody else has written to me for long[,] which makes me feel sometimes as if I were officially dead. Curious that Geraldine [Jewsbury], above all, who made more protestations of undying love to me than all my other friends put together, does not see what '*a bad* EFFECT' such inconstancy would have *in a* NOVEL!

Again I have not lain awake all night; tho', for the rest, my sleep was as little satisfactory as *sleep*, at all, could well be. The blue pill has done 'neither good nor ill' this time, I think. Perhaps because I had not such dreadful need of it!

You are quite right about Mary—honesty and frugality are her ostensible virtues. She has some *latent* ones besides, especially good-heartedness—but these are sadly overlaid with a constitutional apathy, and a morbid self-conceit.

I read in *Forster's Essays* the other day a charming paragraph about *Frederick*. After telling the story of Frederick making Zeitern add a line to his letter to his wife, to the effect that 'next day at two o'clock he would be *dead*[,]' Forster remarks; there are people who have called in question the *truth* of this incident; but it accords so well with the cruel tyrannical disposition of the man, that if it did not actually take place it might have done so!![19]

There—you have a long letter today, tho' I am rather *shaky*—for you will get no more till Tuesday— Your ever affte

Jane W Carlyle

I hope Mary is shaking my *furs*—to keep the moths off. If she knows where to find my shawls[,] let her shake *them* too

19. Hans Joachim von Ziethen (1699–1786); it is unclear as to whether this is John Forster (Dickens' friend) or Friedrich Förster (biographer of Frederick), but the important point is that Jane is taking an interest in the world outside, in Thomas's work, and in her winter clothes (in summer). In her next letter she seeks Eliza Forster's help to plan home-decorating.

To Eliza Forster, Holm Hill, 29–30 August 1864

Dearest Mrs Forster

Such is the severe observance of the Sunday in these regions that the letters posted in the South on Saturday are detained at Carlisle till monday; and so I have your letter only today. And I couldn't make up my mind about the paper till after post time. I have now come to the conclusion that the pattern I return will do for both the Drawing room and bed room (with closet)[.] There is a striped white one among the patterns marked 'for Drawingroom' which I like better, that is, think prettier—but one must study a certain consistency, and I fancy that one would be too *fine*, for a room with otherwise no pretensions to finery. I do not admire any of the borders—the one I return is the best—but rather too marked a contrast I think.

I have written to Mr C to tell him you would be down upon him with a paper-hanger! So as soon as perfectly convenient, you will perhaps be so kind as call at Cheyne Row, and explain to the maids about clearing out the first floor,—remembering always that they are to be addressed as perfect idiots; and ascertain from *them* and Mr C *when* the Man may come. And oh please get the man to be speedy—so that Mr C may not be fidgited with him too long. [A]nd Oh tell the maids, when the rooms are done they must not go rubbing against the clean paper with their dirty Crinolines!— It wont be necessary to paper *behind* the large Picture, which would involve *its* being taken down— Bid them cover it with a sheet.

I am so glad to hear of Mr Macready's visit. It seemed such a pity that old and dear friends should be parted before the time

I have been very poorly for some days—but I hope it is only an accidental worseness.

Thank you very much / Affectionately yours

Jane Carlyle

Tuesday—

I have opened my letter to say that the paper hanger had better *wash* the paint (doors &c) in the rooms. The maids couldnt do it properly without my direction.

Also. I have changed the *border*[;] this one will suit the yellow doors better than the purple & gold pattern

I had no wink of sleep last night but instead horrible neuralgic pains; so today I am very wretched

To Thomas Carlyle, Holm Hill, 29 September 1864

This, then, is to be my last letter from *Here*! *Where* will the *next* letter be from? or will there *be* a *next*? Blind Moles! with our pride of Insight too! we can't tell even *that much* before-hand!

If I had trusted *my* power of divination yesterday, I should have renounced all hope of seeing you this week. I had to go to bed at five in the afternoon in a sort of nervous fever from want of sleep. *The irritation* too unbearable! That clammy, deathly sweat, in which I had passed the previous night, as if I had been dipped in ice-water! then placed under a crushing weight of frozen blankets, seemed to have taken all warm life out of me. So I gave up, and went to bed. At night I took one of Dr Blakiston's blue pills. (The larger doze had ceased to be beneficial)—and—*about* twelve I fell asleep thank God! and went on sleeping and waking till halfpast seven! It was *healing* sleep, besides being a good deal of it! My first reflection this morning was; 'And there are Beggars, nay there are Blackguards, or Both in one, who get every night of their lives far better sleep than even this, which is such an unspeakable mercy to *me*!['] Ach! it is no discovery, that much in this world quite surpasses one's human comprehension!

I have been thrown out of my reckoning. I had calculated that on the principle of a bad night and a *less bad*, the less bad would fall tonight, and I should have some sleep in me to start with. But TWO waking nights coming together changes the order; and *to night* in the course of nature (second nature) no rest is to be expected!

Tell Mary I now take coffee to breakfast, (John takes tea) and to have a little cream in the house that one may *fall soft*.

And now goodby till we meet oh that I had been a day and night—(and the night a good one) in the House! no mortal can imagine the thoughts of my heart in returning *there*,—where I was *buried* from! And my life still unrenewed!—*only* the hope, often overcast, that it is in the way of being renewed.

Your ever affte / Jane Carlyle

My little maid asked me this morning, when about to draw on my stockings: 'what d'ye think? wouldn't it be a good thing to have the taes (toes) clippet again, afore ye gang away?' I shall so miss that kind thoughtful girl!

❧

To Mary Russell, Chelsea, 3 October 1864

Oh my Darling! my Darling! God for ever bless you! You, and dear Dr Russell, for your goodness to me, your patience with me, and all the good you have done me! I am better aware *now* how much I have *gained* than I was *before* this journey—how much stronger I am, both in body and mind, than I was on my journey *to* Scotland. I felt no fatigue on the journey down, but I made up for it in nervous excitement! On the journey *up*, all my nervousness was over when I had parted with *you two*! Even when arrived at my own door (which I had always looked forward to as a most terrible moment, remembering the hearse-like fashion in which I was carried away from it) I could possess my soul in quiet, and meet the excited people who rushed out to me, as gladly as if I had been returned from any ordinary pleasure-excursion! Very *excited* people they were! Dr C had stupidly told his Brother he might look for us about ten, and as we did not arrive till half after eleven, Mr C had settled it in his own mind, that I had been taken ill somewhere *on* the road, and he was momentarily expecting a Telegram to say I was dead. So he rushed out in his dressing gown, and kissed me and *wept* over me as I was in the act of getting down out of the cab! (much to the edification of the neighbours at their windows, I have no doubt) and then the Maids appeared behind him, looking *timidly*, with flushed faces, and tears in THEIR eyes! and the little one (the cook) threw *her* arms round my neck, and fell to kissing me in the open street; and the big one (the House maid) I had to kiss, that she might not be made *jealous*, the first thing! They were all astonished at the improvement in my appearance. Mr C has said again and again, that he would not have believed anyone who had sworn it to him, that I should return so changed for the better. Breakfast was presented to me, but tho' I had still Holm hill things to eat I had not my Holm hill appetite to eat them with. All Saturday there was nothing I cared to swallow but Champagne (Lady Ashburton had sent me two dozen first rate, in the winter.) So I took the Blakiston bluepill that first night instead of the next as Dr Russell had advised and oh such a heavenly sleep I had! awoke only twice the whole night! It is worth while passing a whole night on the railway to get such blessed sleep the night after! Last night again I *slept*—not so well as the first night, of course; but wonderfully well for *me*. [A]nd this morning my breakfast was not contemptible. But it is a great hardship to have lost my warm milk in the morning— I thought by paying an exorbitant price, it might have been obtained;—but no! the stuff offered me yesterday at eight oclock, was impossible to swallow!— And my poor 'Bowels' perfectly bewildered by all the sudden changes put on them, don't seem to have any clear idea left, when to 'act' or when to let it alone! so I am driven back into the valley of the shadow of *pills*!

I had a two hours drive yesterday in Battersea Park and Clapham Common.[20] When one hasn't the Beauties of Nature, one must content oneself with the Beauties of Art.

Today my drive must be townward—so many things wanted at the shops! There is hardly a dish or kitchen utensil left unbroken—all broken by '*I-can't-imagine-who-did-it*—' Still it might have been worse—there seems to have no *serious* mischief been done.

Wasnt it curious to have your eternal [Dr] 'Simpson' given me for fellow traveller? I *might* have *consulted* him at the Carlisle Hotel, with perfect convenience had I wished it! But oh my Dear! *No*! That man's appearance inspired no particle of confidence! Your own Drs sensible candid face was worth a hundred such faces as Simpsons, boiled down into *one*— And he has no more human feeling, that man, than a pig! I could infer so from his way of talking about that poor Mrs Baird.

Now I must stop; for I have to '*consider wi' mysell*,' like the Piper's Cow, and make out a list of what I am to buy at the shops—before my *Fly* comes.

Oh my Darling if I might continue just as well as I am *now*! But that is not to be hoped! Anyway I shall always feel as if I owed my life chiefly to your Husband and you, who procured me such *rest* as I could have had nowhere else in the world / your own / Jane W C

To Mary Russell, Chelsea, 31 October 1864

Dearest

I sent you today the fullest accounts of that wretched Müller trial;[21] and meant to supplement the newspapers with a letter. But a Madman (our former letter-Carrier for twenty years) was let in to me, under the mixrepresentation that he had recovered his senses, and remained the

20. The first just over the Thames from Chelsea, the second a mile or two beyond it, due south.
21. Franz Müller (German tailor), tried for the murder of Thomas Briggs (London banker) on 9 July on a train to the north London suburb of Chalk Farm; the case preoccupied the press because of transport security but also because Müller had made his escape to New York before being arrested by the long arm of the law. He was hanged on 14 November. The carrier is John Piper, husband of Susan, confined to the Hanwell Lunatic Asylum in Ealing, west London.

whole hour between my leaving my bed-room and going out in the carriage; consulting me about getting a divorce from his wife, whose 'long tounge' was enough to 'make him commit suicide.' I began to feel as if a corner of Dr Russells mantle had fallen on me!— Poor man! he was a solid, industrious, religious obliging creature—till five years ago when he became '*filled with Devils*' (as he *says* himself) and attempted his Life in a most strangely shocking manner. [A]nd he told me today that twice since then he had tied himself by the neck at Hanwell. Not a pleasant morning-visitor! especially after 'a bad night,' and with a threatening of sore-throat. I took THAT yesterday, and thought I was *in* for a severe cold—but I am better rather since my drive; which was long today and in the *country*. Yes! my Dear I saw fields of *sheep*[,] not white but dirt-colour, and also, I saw a field with a charming lot of little black pigs in it! I am not tied to *two hours* now for my drive, which was long enough to stay out in a '*Fly*' costing as it did six shillings! I have now set up a nice little Brougham, or *Clarence* (as *you* call it)[22] all to myself—with a smart grey horse and an elderly Driver (in Mr C's old brown surtout ['above everything': overcoat]!!![)] I was at half a dozen coachmakers yards seeking that carriage!! examining with my own eyes, on my own legs!! of course I took *advice* as to the *outside* quality. Mr Farie and the Livery-Stable Man who has kept Mr C's horse these dozen years both approved my choice and considered it a great bargain—*sixty pounds* and perfectly new, and *handsome* in a plain way. It needs no unbleached linen to protect it, being dark blue morocco and cloth inside, which wont dirty in a hurry, and it is all glass in front like Mrs Ewart's! so you will see finely about you when I drive you to see the lions here [at London Zoo]— That prospect is one of my pleasures in the new *equipage* [means of transport]! I have nothing to show you like the drive to Sanquhar [Dumfriesshire], but *the Parks* here are very beautiful, and I never drive thro' them now, without fancying *you* at my side, and seeing them with *your* fresh eyes!

Mr C expects to actually finish his Book about new-year—and then, please God that I keep well enough for it, we go to Lady Ashburton at a new place she has got in Devonshire[23]—where it will be warmer than

22. A Brougham was a carriage with either four wheels and four seats, or two wheels and two seats; a Clarence was always four and four. This was Jane's great treat in her later years, as a form of exercise and distraction. The 'Livery-Stable Man' is John Silvester, who would become her driver. Thomas noted, after Jane's death (*CL*): 'She had infinite satisfaction in this poor gift; was boundlessly proud of it, as her husband's testimony to her; believed it to be the very saving of her, and the source of all the health she had, &c. &c.'

23. Seaforth Lodge, Seaton, Devon, built in 1864.

here, and evidently I can't have too much change!— [W]hen we come back and the weather is fit for the journey the Dr and you *must* come!

It has been moist even rainy of late and *damp* seems to suit me worst of anything. My appetite defies quinine, to bring it back! and the IRRITATION has been more distressing. Still I am no worse on the whole than when I left you. And I force myself to take always the new milk, and the custard at twelve. There is a weighing machine at our Green Grocers at the bottom of the Street; but I *dare not* get myself weighed!

I dont like *that* photograph of Mary at all— The crinoline quite changes her character and makes her a stranger for me— I want the one that is as I have always seen her a sensible girl with *no* crinoline— I would like best if she would get herself done for me as she is on washing mornings— in the little pink bedgown and blue petticoat. I send a shilling (in stamps) for the purpose— But don't force her inclinations in the matter—

My friend Mr [John] Forster was at Müller's trial the last day—saw him receive his sentence, and said he behaved very well. When the sentence was pronounced he merely bowed to the Judge and walked away with the Turnkey. But at the little door leading down from the Court he stopt and said to the Turnkey he wished to say a few words to the Judge, and the Turnkey led him back, and he said something which could not be heard, on account of his keeping his hand at his mouth—to steady it— Forster said the only sign of emotion he had given all thro the business was a quivering of his lips. When told to speak out, he removed his hand and said courteously to the Judge 'I have had a most fair Trial! but I cannot help saying *some* of the worst things said by the witnesses against me are gross falsehoods.' Then he seemed to break down and hurried out.

I am certain, had it not been that every Juryman felt his personal safety on the railway compromised by the acquittal of this man, he would not have been condemned to Death on the evidence. It is clear to everybody he had no *premeditation* of murder and that Mr Briggs *threw himself* out of the carriage, and *probably* caused his own death thereby. The poor wretch returning from his visit to his 'Unfortunate,' having *taken a second class* ticket, had seen Mr Briggs with his glittering watch chain get into the first-class carriage and jumped in after him, thinking that chain would take him to America. It was to take him to a far other land!

Curious that he got off that night without the discovery of his ticket not being second class. The Train had been very late, and contrary to all use and wont the tickets were not asked for in the carriages. [. . .]

Your loving / Jane Carlyle [. . .]

To Mary Craik, Chelsea, 28 November 1864

Oh little Woman! Little Woman! How could you have the face to tell me, that you 'are not much of a letter-writer[']—*me*, who, for weeks and weeks together, saw you letter-writing, 'late and early,' as if you had been a Secretary of State! and saw the *packets* you sent off by every post, as bulky as the Proof-sheets of a novel! Oh! Oh! never make lame excuses my Dear! Enough to say, you had not felt to have anything to write to me, in particular; or enough to say just nothing at all about it but when the Spirit *did* move you, then rush right into the middle of Things!

As I shall do now. My Dear the most extraordinary things have Come to pass in this House! Things to make you, and my Cousin Maggie, and Mrs Blakiston, and myself, all 'hide our diminished heads'[24] as good house-wives, and women of discernment!— Before you ceased your kind ministrations here—you made an effort to rid the House of Helen, and consign Mr C wholly to the slow, but trustworthy and attached Mary. But in the uncertainty as to when I should return, and in what state I should return, Mr C thought it best to struggle on as well as he could with the incorrigible Helen; threatening once a day at least, to 'fling her out into the Street,' but never doing it! So on my return, the same *Two* received me; Mary running out to embrace me in the open Street, and crying for joy to see me 'so like myself again.' When I had rested, and to my own astonishment as well as the astonishment of Mr C and everybody, found myself even better than I had been in Dumfriesshire, and capable of looking after my own affairs; I *did* look after them, tried for two or three weeks patiently and strenuously to manipulate Helen into a bearable Housemaid, and failing utterly, gave her warning[. N]ot only there was no getting her to do her work like a civilized being but the destruction and waste in the House for all which she got the blame was intolerable. Imagine *four* pounds of fresh butter at 20 pence a-pound consumed in the kitchen weekly! and half a pound of tea every four days!! It was too disgusting! So in spite of her extreme unwillingness to go, I engaged a woman of fifty (a widow) to be Cook & *Housekeeper* and, Mary having shown such incapacity for *ruling*[,] was to try if she could *obey*, in the position of Housemaid & *Ladys maid*. This being settled, Mary got leave to go into Cambridgeshire (to see her Father 'who had been dangerously ill') for a week before Helen left and the new Cook came. Mrs Southam [Charlotte's mother] (who *sat up* with me all the last winter) was brought to assist Helen in Mary's absence. Mary had not been gone two days, when I was taken with a violent feverish cold; and in the first worst stage thereof I got a '*moral shock*,' which affected me exactly like a blow with a stick on the pit of my stomach! making me *retch*

24. Milton, *Paradise Lost*, iv. 35.

for half an hour, and so sick that for six and thirty hours I could swallow nothing but a tablespoonful of brandy in water!

This was the shock— Mrs Southam being at my bedside, giving me some tea, said abruptly: 'Helen tells me you are parting with her Mam?'— 'Yes, said I, and full time, she is a most unsatisfactory servant'— 'Well— you know best Mam! But—I never like to see the innocent suffering for the guilty'!— '*Who* is innocent? and *who* is guilty I asked in amaze; what *are* you talking about?'— 'Well Mam, said the woman, it is pretty well known in the neighbourhood, and you are sure to find it out *some* time, and then you would be angry at me if knowing it I had not told you'— 'Out with it for God's sake!' 'It is *Mary* Mam! Mary is just the worst girl that ever was in your House! While you were putting such trust in her, she was deceiving you in every way, and laughing at you for being so blind!! All the time you were ill, and all the time you were in Scotland she was having constant men in the House! fed at your expense! and even since you came home *The Father of her Child* has pretty well *lived* here.'— 'The *Father of her Child*?' I repeated aghast— 'Yes; she bore a child in this house, soon after Mr Carlyle returned from St Leonards, while Mr Carlyle was sitting at tea with Miss Jewsbury!!! There wasn't a rag of clothing prepared for the Child. [A] woman was brought by Helen at two in the morning, and carried *It* away in one of your blankets! But you will now understand the disappearance of all your small napery (!) and all the butter and tea and things that you complained of, and that were laid to Helen'!

Yes my Dear! this 'insipid offspring'[25] was born on the 29th of July three days after you left!! It is all true!— I said to Mrs Southam 'Oh it is the treachery, the deceit that grieves me; I could have forgiven the *baby*, *that* might have been weakness *inexperience*'— 'Well said Mrs Southam "inexperience" it couldn't be; for it was her SECOND!!'— Every *particle* of this I have had corroborated on undoubted authority! with oh such sickening details!

When the wretched little animal returned from Cambridgeshire, where she had gone to place her child with a married Sister; never going to her Father's at all! she drove up in a cab, at broad midday, with the Ex Boots[26] (aged twenty) and was taking him in, to have his dinner comfortable, as usual; but Helen met her at the door with the wages due to her, and the news that 'it was all found out'!— She looked horrified for a moment; and then said; 'I knew I should be found out *some* time, altho' the Mistress *is* such a simpleton!! and I don't care! I can get a

25. A characteristic expression Thomas used of the children whose birth he was obliged to record in *Frederick*.
26. The bootboy, or 'Boots', was the lowest rank of male household servant, normally a boy or teenager.

place without a character from *Her*! Come along *Ben*! Get in!'—and the two remounted into the Cab and drove off—*Devilward*!

Helen was kept on another month on trial, in the new conditions; with a superior servant over her; but it won't do! and we are to part tomorrow—in perfect good humour! A woman of eight and twenty comes as Housemaid, of good family, and a good phisiognomy except for a too plaintive droop at the corners of her mouth.

I have stood all this upturning wonderfully. Indeed I am not at all 'nervous' now tho' the *special misery*, is not altogether gone—and tho' my back is still so weak that I can walk no better—hardly so well—as at St Leonards!

I have got a nice little Brougham 'all to myself' (as the children say) and a smart grey Horse, and a Paternal almost grand-paternal Coachman![27] And I drive, in all weathers, from two to three hours daily; so I dont much miss the use of my *legs*—or rather *Back*—

People were so adorably kind to me when I reappeared! I never got myself so kissed and cried over in all my life! and that sort of thing does me no harm now—rather it does me good! So you may conceive how wonderfully rehabilitated my nervous system is! I don't *sleep* yet like the rest of the world; but a degree better than in Dumfriesshire and several degrees better than at Marina [St Leonards]. Oh Heavens! I shudder when I look back!

Mr C is extremely pleased to have me back, and in a comparitively efficient state! He hopes to finish his Book about new years day and then we propose going to Lady Ashburton in Devonshire. There is no one 'with me'— My Aunt in Law Mrs George Welsh wished to come; but I did not feel to need anyone *in* the House with so many visitors[.] Thanks to your Father love to him and Georgina Your ever affectionate / JC

To John Stodart, Chelsea, 2 December 1864

'Dear John'

I have been all my life under a fatality—I mean one particular fatality—this namely; to leave undone the things which I ought to have done;[28] not thro' laziness, nor forgetfulness, nor perversity,—the common reasons for human short-comings; but from a wish and intention to do the thing which I ought to do impossibly WELL!

27. Bellona the mare, and Silvester the coachman: see next chapter.
28. The 'General Confession' from the *Book of Common Prayer* of the Church of England.

So it has been in acknowledging your letter and photograph. I should have done so in a reasonably short time, had not the idea come to me, to enhance my letter and make, what they call in Scotland 'a suitable return,' by inclosing a photograph of myself, which you had not seen, and which would please you (I was sure) 'for reasons which it may be interesting *not* to state'! This 'touching' likeness, however, was not in my possession, but in the Artist's; and altho' I have applied for it several times, my *fatality* has hitherto prevented my getting it; so I wait no longer, in case you begin to think ill of me, which at this time of day,—after so many years of generous faith—it would be a pity and a shame to do!

Ah yes! I have been dreadfully ill! I did not know that Life had in it such possibilities of suffering! For nearly a year I was in constant torture, in constant terror that the torture would drive me *mad*, in constant expectation of Death as the only deliverance! And here I am after all, not only alive, and sane, but in rather better health and spirits than I had been for long, before my illness! I have done a good many strange things in the course of my life but this *recovering* is the strangest thing of all!

Not that I am to be called *well* even now—my Back is so weak that I cannot walk six yards without being ready to sink, and I feel a constant tendency towards going on all fours! But then it is so long ago since I was *well* that I dont remember the least in the world how it felt! and so don't pine after it!

For the rest, I am not unhappy; I believe in the Doctrine of *Compensations*.[29] It is a nuisance to be unable to walk; but it is pleasant to have a nice little Brougham 'all to oneself' (as the children say) and to drive wherever one will three hours, in all weathers, every day of one's Life! Then the People are so unspeakably kind to me since my return to the Land of the Living! I was never so kissed and cried over in all my life as in the first weeks after my Home-coming. *Men* even, that I had not supposed to care twopence for me, clasped me to their 'manly breasts,' and kissed me, and cried over me like—like anything!— And my own Husband shared in the general enthusiasm and was become so *considerate*! Bless him! He never bids me ring the bell now, without saying; 'Oh I beg your pardon! I *forgot*'!

Dear John! do you *never* come to London now? I wish you would! I should like to see you again in this world; true friend that you are—in spite of all your perverse ways!

God bless you. It is my hour for driving, and I live like an eight-day-clock

Yours ever affectionately
Jane Welsh Carlyle

29. As stated by Emerson in his essay 'Compensation', in *Essays* (1841).

Figure 12: Samuel Laurence, *Jane Baillie Carlyle (née Welsh)* (1852), © National Portrait Gallery, London

11

'I Want *so* Much to *Live*': 1865–1866

Frederick was finally finished in January 1865 and published in March. Whether it was worth the suffering it caused is hard to say. Certainly it is somewhat reminiscent of Rossini's catty remark about Wagner's operas, with their 'wonderful moments separated by terrible half hours', in which Thomas presents the abysmal quality of his sources as an index of intellectual futility rather than gets on with his story—itself of limited interest to non-German readers (admired as it was by Thomas Mann). The book as a whole was last in print in 1930, and even Ruskin's behemoths, Modern Painters (1843–1860) and Fors Clavigera (1871–1884), probably have more to offer the modern reader, overall.

But the nightmare was over and relief set in, to be accompanied in due course by moods of post-natal depression and fitfulness. Jane's overall health improved, though punctuated by colds: she could walk more and enjoyed her long London afternoon drives in the carriage Thomas had bought for her. But her arm remained stiff and sore and eventually she had to train herself to write with her left hand as her neurological problems moved into her right arm and hand. In March 1865 she and Thomas even went so far as to holiday together, at the dowager Lady Ashburton's seaside place, Seaforth Lodge, near Seaton, east Devon (still standing, but subdivided into flats). Her capacity for revival glowed out as she wrote to Mary Russell on 10 March:

> When we started on Wednesday morning, with, on my part, no sleep 'to speak of'—and five hours of railway before us, besides a carriage drive after, my mood was of the blackest. But George Cooke was at the Station to look after our luggage, and, halfway, the Sun broke out, and it was new Country for me, part of the way, and very beautiful; and the sheep, bless them! were not only *white* as milk, but had dear wee lambs skipping beside them! And the river, that falls into the Sea near here, was not muddy and slugish; like all the rivers (very few indeed) I had seen since I left dear Nith [Dumfriesshire]; but clear as crystal and bright *blue*![1]

1. This is the River Axe, flowing south-west down from Dorset, of scientific interest because of its aquatic life, unshaded character and stable bed: features that might promote the aqueous clarity Jane speaks of.

> And, at the end, such a lovely House, on a high cliff, overlooking the bluest sea! and such a lovely and loveable Hostess!— So truly the latter end of that woman was better than the beginning! (*CL* 41: 184)

And when Thomas went off to Scotland soon afterwards in the old style, leaving Jane in charge of plumbers and painters in Chelsea, he sincerely missed her and was delighted when they met up north of the border. (Jane returned to the Russells at Holm Hill.)

In August she was back, getting better, driving daily, and reshelving Thomas's books, brought down from the abandoned attic study to make room for servants' quarters. Yet another new housemaid, Jessie Hiddleston, was installed alongside the cook, Sarah Warren, but predictably enough the pair failed to get on. Jane also visited her friend Miss Davenport Bromley (the 'flight of larks') in Folkestone, on the Kent coast. In November Thomas was elected Rector of the University of Edinburgh, gratifyingly defeating Benjamin Disraeli 650 to 300; he planned to give his inaugural on 2 April, and collapsed into a state of pre-lecture nerves as in days of old. Jane, meanwhile, was taking up her ancient set of cudgels to deal with neighbourhood noise. The sense of history repeating or reasserting itself was palpable in a brilliantly novelistic letter to Mary Russell of 26 January 1866, concerning a cook, his son and daughter-in-law, their daughter and a footman. In that same month she threw out a line to Geraldine Jewsbury: 'You "are wanted"*—not by the Police but by* me*! I want you every day and all!' In March she even took on a new pet dog, Tiny (the gift of Miss Davenport Bromley): Nero redivivus. In the event Thomas's lecture was 'a perfect Triumph', as his friend John Tyndall (up there for an honorary degree) was kind enough to cable to Jane directly after the ceremony, and No. 5 and its environs exploded genteelly in unpondered celebration: Sarah Warren in particular by frying lots of food.*

The three-week period from the beginning of April and the letters it contains are peculiarly moving because of the note of harmony they sound, with barely a hint of irony. (That irony never entirely deserted her, of course, or she would not be who she was: on 10 April she told Thomas, 'a pity if he have taken the habit of being worshipped *[in Edinburgh]! for he may find some difficulty in keeping it up,* here*!'; CL 43: 175.) 'If we could only sleep Dear,' she wrote on 4 April, 'and what you call "*digest*"; wouldn't it be nice?' Sleep and digestion—the ability to relax and the ability to let things take their course in a more general sense—had evaded them for nearly forty-five years; but they would come for Jane when she died quietly in her carriage on a spring afternoon of 21 April 1866. The following day Thomas wrote to her old school friend, William Dods, to complete the circle he had innocently broken to form the new one of their marriage. 'Long ago', he wrote,*

> it was her covenant with me that she was to lie beside her Father in Haddington Churchyard; and, within these two years, she repeatedly made me promise that I shd write at once to you,—who wd

immediately, for her sake, undertake all the arrang[emen]ts. In perfect faith I write accordingly.

She was buried according to plan four days later.

❧

To Sarah Warren, Seaforth Lodge, Seaton, Devonshire, 27 March 1865

Dear Mrs Warren

We have made out our visit, you see, with greater deliberation than I predicted, in leaving! Not that Mr Carlyle has *not* talked of *being off* '*this very day*,' every morning after a restless night! And he has had too many of these; since his habits have been turned all heels over head, and there has been no punctual Mrs Warren at hand to *measure* out his dinners!— So I have been in constant uncertainty all the time; and no woman living hates uncertainty more than I do! It would spoil my pleasure in Heaven itself!

Tho' I am in no haste to go, then; and never wearying of either the *Sea* or Lady Ashburton; still it is a sort of a melancholy satisfaction to know, that our departure is finally *fixed* for Saturday next.— When, I hope to find you well, and glad to see us! And to find the kitchen smartened up, and the cistern cured of leaking!

I dont know yet what hour we shall arrive; but it will probably be in time for a late dinner. Mr C likes mutton-broth after a journey, and *I like—nothing*!! so I can dine with *Him* that day. And you must get in things for Sunday; but I need not be telling *you* what to do; for, thank God, you have *sense*; which is not so common a qualification as one might think! Oh dear me! there hasn't been a day here, that I have not wished I could have brought one half of you with me, and left the other half to take care of the House! The times and times I have been put into a rage is quite disgraceful!

Please tell the Postman of our coming; in time to prevent his sending off the letters that may come on Saturday.

Good by! / Yours kindly

Jane W Carlyle

I dont forget, that I only left money up to Wednesday. But what you after need till Saturday had best be put down in the Bills as I have no means of sending money from here except in a letter, which wouldnt be safe

❧

To John Ruskin, Holm Hill, 15 July 1865

Oh how delightful! My dear Mr Ruskin! That nice long letter and lovely little Book— Imagine! they came to me the first thing on my Birthday morning! Came with all the charm of a Birthday present!— You once gave me strawberries and cream on my Birthday—do you remember? (I have never seen such strawberries and cream since! nor have I had any such pleasant Birth-day since! but all have passed in pain and sorrow!) I like the Book and letter far better however, because these will *keep*! And being superstitious a little, as a Scotch woman ought to be, I draw ever so many good omens from the Book and Letter beginning a new year of Life for me! One piece of good I clearly divine therefrom; that *you* are not going to forget poor me in the pressure of your avocations and *distractions* but will care for me, and give me flowers now and then, as long as I last!

What a talent for naming you have!

Of Kings Treasuries!
Of Queen's Gardens!

The names lift me already into the sphere of the Arabian Nights![2]

Please tell your Mother how much I am obliged to her for her call, altho' I was so unlucky as [to] miss it. And you may add, if you like, that I am sure she would not dislike me if she knew me: for, the only time I ever saw her, I felt to *take to Her* very much, because she said no superfluous or insincere word! And I have always found that those I take to at first sight take to me sooner or later if they give themselves a fair chance.

I cannot understand your persistence in forgetting Mrs Hawks (Madame Venturi)![3] She is to my mind perfectly charming! If you knew the romantic thing she once did for love of you, it would fix her in your mind for ever!

'My lamed hand'! Alas no! It is not with *that* I write. *That* is quite past making any sort of writing whatever! It is too painful to attempt using *it* at all. So I have had to learn to write with my *left* hand, which protests against the unwonted exaction in taking every now and then the Cramp!

2. Ruskin published these two lectures as *Sesame and Lilies*: an important statement on the nature and duties of men and women, focusing (first) on the education of men and (second) on the vital duty of women in fact to judge and direct masculine behaviour in a man's world. The texts are more politically complex, therefore, than they are sometimes taken to be.
3. See 31 January 1862, above. I do not know what 'romantic thing' Venturi did for Ruskin.

I hope to get home on the 24th or 25th.
Yours affectionately /
Jane Carlyle

I saw Mr Carlyle yesterday[,] entirely sick of '*Solitude*' which he has got to call '*Stagnation*'! He is about to start on further travels.

To Thomas Carlyle, Chelsea, 27 July 1865

'All goes well' *still*, Dearest. And this time nothing serious is *manquing* [lacking]

The second night, as I expected, I slept 'beautiful'! *Three hours* without a break to begin with!— When I woke from *that* I not only didnt know *where* I was; but didnt know *who* I was!!! As I got out of bed (by force of habit) to look at my watch; I was saying to myself 'It can't be *me* that has made this fine sleep! I MUST BE SOMEBODY ELSE'!!! It was a full minute, I am sure, before I could satisfy myself that I hadn't been changed into somebody else! Then I slept piecemeal till seven o'clock, when I was startled erect by what seemed the House falling! Jessie came at my call, looking very guilty, and explained that it was she, who had been coming down stairs very softly for fear of waking me, and having new shoes on had 'slid and sossed down on her back'! Just opposite my bedhead— Luckily she was none the worse for the fall. A greater contrast than that young woman is to Fanny [dismissed in June] cannot be figured! So quick so willing so intelligent: Never needs to be told a thing twice! and so warmly *human*! My only fear about *her* is that she will be married-up, away from me![4] Mrs Warren calls her 'My Dear' and they get on charmingly together.

The person who addressed the newspaper to you at '*Coming Trees*'[5] was Fanny[,] who had called to ask if I would '*See* a Lady' for her: and Mrs Warren being busy asked *her* to address the newspaper.

On Tuesday Bellona,[6] who had been warned a week before, came round at one, and after some shopping I called at Grosvenor Street and found Miss Bromley at home. A satisfaction which I owed to the

4. Jessie Hiddlestone did marry, after Jane's death in 1866.
5. Cummertrees: village in Dumfriesshire where a train station opened in 1848, and thus a connection for the Carlyles' Scottish friends and families. 'See a lady' means provide a reference.
6. Mare to Jane's carriage; Jane is speaking of her as if the horse kept appointments.

youngest of the three Pugs 'Jocky,' who was 'suffering from the heat'! She was delighted to see me: most anxious I should come to her at Folkstone! and told me to my great joy, that Lady A[shburton] had NOT started on the 21st, wasnt going till Thursday (today)—was staying at Bath House—but gone that morning to Bath for one day. I left a card and message at Bath house on the road home. Yesterday (Wednesday) I drove to Bath House the first thing; when I went out at one; and found the Lady looking lovely in a spruce little *half mourning* bonnet![7] and so loving! and she *would* 'if it was within the bounds of possibility' come to me in the evening 'between ten and eleven.' [A]nd I went in *her* carriage with her (my own following) to Norfolk Street (Mrs Anstruther's) to see Baby who is going with her mother to Germany after all— I left her there, and got into my own carriage and went and bought my Birthday present—with the sovereign—at least I laid out fifteen shillings of it.— [O]n what?— My Dear! The thing I bought was most appropriate and rather *touching*! I drove to the great shop in Conduit Street, where the world is supplied with 'Trusses' 'Laced Stockings'—and mechanical appliances for every species of human derangement—and bought a dainty little *Sling* for my arm!! The mere ribbon round my neck hurt my neck and drew my head down. This fastens across the back and is altogether a superior contrivance! I dont believe in Dr Russells prediction any more than you do! At all rates there was *no call on him* to *state* so hopeless a view of the question! when I was not asking his opinion at all! It could do no *harm* to leave me the consolation of hope! But I WILL hope in spite of Him! Indeed it seems to me that ever since he said I should never get the use of my hand nor get rid of the pain there; that a Spirit of protest and opposition has animated the poor hand and set it on trying to do things it had some time ceased from doing!!

And Lady A did come last night[.] Came at half after eleven! and staid till near one! Mrs Anstruther was left sitting in the carriage and sent up to say 'it was on the stroke of twelve'— And then with Lady A's permission I invited her up—and if it had not been for her I dont think Lady A would have gone *till* daylight! She said in going 'My regards—my—*what* shall I send to *Him* (you)—' 'Oh, I said send him a kiss!'— '*That is just what I should like* she said but would he not think it forward'— 'Oh dear! not at all' I said— So you are to consider yourself *kissed*—

7. Lord Ashburton had died at The Grange on 23 March 1864, the same age as the century. Mrs Anstruther is Lady Louisa's sister, and 'Baby' the Ashburtons' daughter, Mary Florence.

I am going up to Bath House *now*— She goes [to Wiesbaden] at night

Lady Stanley writes to ask how I am and to beg that you will come *that* way.

What a long letter!

I ought to have said that all this did not give me a *bad* night— Of course I did not sleep as on the preceeding night but better than I *ever* did at Holmhill—and the pain in my arm is really less since I came home—

Yours affly /
Jane Carlyle

❧

To Thomas Carlyle, Chelsea, 9 August 1865

Again you have had no letter Dear! But, in compensation, all the ink-spots are out of your writing table!! Had It been going straight to any Literary Museum, I shouldn't have meddled with the INK, which Hero-worshipers might have regarded with a *certain* adoration; but for your *own* use, I thought you would like it better *clean*! It has never been cleaned, that poor table, since I used to do all the Housemaid work myself [at Craigenputtoch]! And it is a wonder of Heaven that I should be up to such work again—after all! and I cannot better express my thankfulness than in *working* while I may! So I fastened on that table after breakfast this morning, and rubbed at it the whole time till the carriage came at two! Of course Jessie could have waxed and turpentined the table better than me; but no one but me, I flatter myself could have shown the patience and ingenuity necessary for extracting all that ink!—

You will infer that I am going on well as to my arm, my sleep, and all that. I have really had not *one* downright *bad* night since I came home—except the first. The pain is almost entirely gone out of my arm and hand. But the stiffness continues—and is easy to bear! I *can* use some of my fingers—a little. I am now writing with the lamed [right] hand! But I cannot *take hold*; nor could I raise my arm to my head if it were to save my life.

If it were not that almost everybody I know is 'out of Town['] I should rather regret having promised to go to Folkstone on Monday. But it is to be hoped that the Sea breezes will blow the dust of those Books off me! Two of the Pug-Puppies and their amiable Mama have been placed 'at Hampstead for change of air'; and only Spark and the youngest [Jocky] accompany us to Folkstone.

Another proof of wellness I am going *alone*! I find I can now do everything, in dressing, with my left hand, except twisting up my back hair and putting the comb in; and Miss Bromley's House maid can do *that* much for me in one minute. Jessie sees a great deal of cleaning needed, and will get at it better when the regular work of the House is not going on— THEN; sufficient for the day is the running up and down thereof![8] Besides, she will learn the ways of London Servants fast enough, without my hastening to initiate her therein!

In my dearth of company, I drove out to Denmark Hill yesterday to return a call old Mrs Ruskin made here in my absence. But I am decidedly unlucky at that House— Mrs Ruskin and son were changing the air at the Norwood Hotel![9] *He* writes to offer himself for Friday evening.

Such a fright Dr Carlyle's hand-writing on the address gave me![10]

Forster is better and off on his Inspecting.[11] You wont forget to go and see my Aunts! And *do* take a cab and go and see poor dear Betty! Stenhouse close by Greenend[.] Anybody can tell you which is the house

[no signature]

To Jessie Hiddlestone, Folkestone, 19 August 1865

Thanks, dear Jessie, for your note, which might have been *longer* without fatiguing my attention! And without exhausting your news I should say!

I continue to like my present quarters;[12] and no wonder; for I have *slept* more since I came here, than I have done in any given week thro'out the last three years!—have slept actually like a human-Being; without needing to have recourse to *Lucifers* [matches, for a candle], or *essence* of *beef*, or any other of those melancholy inventions of Sleeplessness! It is

8. Matthew 6: 34.
9. The Queen's Hotel in this south London suburb, adjacent to Denmark Hill, opened in 1854; it still operates, as part of the 'Best Western' chain.
10. Because Dr John might be sending bad health news.
11. John Forster served as Commissioner of Lunacy from 1861 to 1872, inspecting many asylums accordingly. Ann, Elizabeth and Grace Welsh, Jane's paternal aunts, lived in Morningside, Edinburgh. Betty is Betty Braid, resident in Stenhouse, south Edinburgh, not far from Morningside.
12. 4 Langhorne Gardens (now a hotel with a karaoke bar next door). The port of Folkestone developed and diversified as a resort in eastern Kent after the arrival of the railway in 1843. In its Edwardian heyday it was visited frequently by the royal family, but its palmy days have somewhat deserted it with the closure of its ferry service to France.

rather mortifying, however, that sleeping so well, I don't feel the least bit *stronger* for it! Twice that I have tried walking, about as far as twice the length of Cheyne Walk, I have had to get myself brought home ignominiously in a Donkey-Cart! And though I dine *twice* every day,—once at two o clock, under the name of *Luncheon*, and again at half after eight under the name of *Dinner*; I don't think I eat, putting it altogether[,] as much as would keep a couple of rabbits[,] nay—*one* rabbit, plump and sleek! I miss the oat-cakes; and I miss Mrs Warren's coffee, oh most dreadfully! And I need excessively to have my hair combed!— Tho' the *pain* is quite gone out of my arm, it is stiffer, I think, than ever! And then the Housemaid is so ugly!—I cant bear her to come within a yard of me! so I take an hour to dress *myself* every time, and look untidy after all.

Well, one of the two weeks I gave myself is past, and the other will soon be over too; and Heaven grant Mr Carlyle mayn't plump down on you in the meanwhile! He was to be back from his visits, on the other side of the Forth, next Tuesday I mean—back to his Brother's in Annandale—whence he would 'start homewards, he said in *one* day or *two*.' That sounds as if he might arrive at Cheyne Row about Thursday or Friday. I have written to beg him not to be in such desperate haste, exactly at the wrong moment! but to at least stop a day or two at Alderley Park (where WE should have stopt but for the *Baby*!) and so reach home in a calm state of mind, instead of driven distracted by the long journey all at one rush.

And then I held out the inducement that *I* should be there after Monday 28th to welcome him. But—I don't know—man is born to *contradiction*—as the sparks fly upwards![13] The very persuasion that he should absent himself a few more days may give him an unconscious but irresistible impulse towards home!— Any how Mrs Warren and you will not be found like the foolish Virgins, with lamps without oil![14] And besides, you may be sure of his giving you due warning. Have his bedroom all right—and the upstairs room *fit to be seen*, and no other preparations need be made till the hour and day of his coming has been announced to you by himself. I still *hope* he may not come till I myself am home first! but—if he should,—there is one thing that you must attend to, and which you would not think of without being told! *that cat*!!—I wish she were dead but *I* cant shorten her days! because—you see—my poor dear wee dog liked her! Well! there she is! and as long as she attends Mr C at his meals (she doesn't care a snuff of tobacco for him at any other times!) so long will Mr C continue to give her bits of meat,

13. Job 5: 7.
14. Matthew 25: 3.

and driblets of milk, to the ruination of the carpets and hearthrugs! I have over and again pointed out to him the stains she has made—but he won't believe them *her* doing!—and the Diningroom carpet was so old and ugly, that it wasn't worth rows with one's Husband about! Now however that nice new cloth must be protected against the cat-abuse. So what I wish is; that you would shut up the creature when Mr C has breakfast, or dinner, or tea. And if he remarks on her absence, say it was *my* express desire. He has no idea what a selfish, immoral, improper beast she is! nor what mischief she does to the carpets!

My bed had better be slept in occasionally.

Kind regards to Mrs Warren

Yours sincerely

Jane Carlyle

To Mary Carlyle Austin, Chelsea, 29 November 1865

Oh my Dear! I am so vexed that you should not have had your kind *Sending* acknowledged sooner.

It arrived when I was under a cloud—last Saturday, confined to bed in a perfect agony of sick headache! I had had nothing of *that* sort for many years, and it was really strange to me, the thought, how many such days I had passed formerly *without* being killed by them! But I am sure I couldnt live thro' many such at the present date! The Headache and sickness lasted only one day and night— But the effects of it have not yet passed. I am as weak and nervous as if I had just come thro' a course of mercury! And *that* is why I have let several posts pass without returning you our Thanks; but expressing them meanwhile in an approving consumption of the eggs and fowls— One was boiled on Monday (excellent!) the other is to be *roasted* today—according to *my* views about *variety* of food being requisite to the welfare of the human stomach[:] a consideration which Mr C makes light of but exemplifys in his own person, very convincingly the truth of—

I could very well account for that crisis the other day, several things had conspired to throw me on my back— First my black Mare who enjoys the most perfect health generally, got her foot hurt by a run-away cart—and has had to remain in the stable for more than a week, in a state of continual poultices! Not choosing to pay for another horse I agreed to go for exercise in an omnibus with Mr C—the first time I had entered an omnibus since the evening I had my fall—the beginning of all my woes [22 September 1863]!— I felt very nervous at the notion but I was to go to the end of the line and sit still while the horses were changed, and then come back again so as to avoid any walking or hanging about in the Streets! But Mr C, as usual, *dawdled* till we found ourselves too late, for going the whole way, and I had to get down at Charing-cross in a busy thoroughfare—and Mr C had to run after omnibuses to stop them—and I was like to cry with nervousness to find myself left alone in an open Street!—and couldn't *run* after him as he kept calling to me to do[;] *couldnt run* at all! and was besides paralysed at the sight of carriages so near me—so that I was terribly flurried, and felt quite ill when I had to go out to dinner with Mr C the same evening— Then I am sure the champagne they gave us was bad—that is; *poisonous*—and for two nights before I had had next to no sleep—owing to a terrible secret on my mind

One morning when I looked out of my dressing room window to see what sort of day it was; imagine the spectacle that met my eyes—a rubbishy hen-hutch—erected over night, in the garden *next* to ours—*next*! think of that! and *nine* large hens and one *very* large cock sauntering under our windows!!! I should have fainted where I stood, had I been in the habit of fainting[,] but *that* I never was. As Mr C said nothing, I could not guess whether he had made the discovery or not—The crowing which occurred several times during the night as well as abundantly in the morning certainly did not awake him—his mind being at present intent on 'Railway whistles'— But when he should have once opened his eyes to the thing and as the days should lengthen the crowing would increase—Ah—My Heaven what then?— [N]o wonder that I lay awake *thinking* 'what then!'— I have not time to give a detailed account of all that followed[.] Enough to say the poultry is all to evacuate the premises at Xmas and meanwhile the cock is shut up in a dark cellar from darkening till after our breakfast. And Mr C clasped me in his arms and called me his 'Guardian Angel' and all I have to pay for this restoration of peace and quietness, is giving a lesson three times a week in '*Syllables of two Letters*'—to a small Irish Boy!! rhyme that if you can![15]

Excuse this illwritten letter— I am not quite recovered from the crush of that poultry affair on my mind—altho the secret load is removed.

15. Thomas commented, typically, after Jane's death (*CL*): 'Some wretched people who had settled next door had brought poultry and other base disturbances; against which, for my sake, the noble soul heroically started up (not to be forbidden), and with all her old skill and energy gained victory, complete once more. For me—for me! and it was her last. The thought is cuttingly painful while I live.'

I will write soon when more up to writing— This is merely thanks and a kiss for the fowls and eggs— Oh if one never saw a fowl but like these—*dead*!

Love to them all—

Your ever affectionate / Jane W Carlyle

Jessie—the Thornhill Girl is going on quite satisfactorily since I ceased treating her too kindly—snubbing, and riding with a curb bridle is what SHE needs. All her former Mistresses warned me of that; but I wouldnt believe them the Girl *looked* so sweet and affectionate, the humbug! Mercifully Mr C sees no fault in her.

To Mary Russell, Chelsea, 26 January 1866

Dearest Mary

Let me instead of beginning with *apologies*, which you perhaps expect, begin with a piece of gossip which all Belgravia is ringing with! I heard it today when making calls, and might forget if I left it to the last page.

You have seen Dr Kitcheners cookery book I dare say?[16] He gave his well known name and a handsome fortune to a son who married a very lovely meek-looking Lady whom I know—that is to say I have dined twice in company with her. He was a terrible Blackguard the younger Kitchener—squandered his money, ill used his wife—even to beating her, till old Kitchener took her away from him, and settled her in a small house in Belgravia with her two little girls. There she lived on, after old Kitcheners death, entirely separated from her Scamp of a Husband. People pitied her and liked her; talked a little scandal about a Mr Chisholm ('*The Chisholm*'—the name he went by) making himself so much at home in her house, and acting as male Protector to the family; and were sure The Chisholm would marry Mrs Kitchener if her Husband would only die.— [B]ut The Chisholm *died* instead; and, having no near relations, left all his Fortune to Mrs Kitchener. The Heir at Law disputed the *will*, but could make nothing of that! Mrs Kitchener

16. William Brown Kitchiner (1775–1827), an appropriately named Regency 'celebrity chef', published *The Cook's Oracle; and Housekeeper's Manual: Receipts for Cookery and Directions for Carving* in 1817. It contains the first recipe for the potato crisp, and an astonishing confection called 'Wow-wow Sauce'. His (illegitimate) son William Brown Kitchiner (1804–1861) married Georgina Edgeworth (1808–1879) in 1828; her daughter (also Georgina) was born the following year. Jane the novelist *manqué* has some of the details wrong: see *CL*.

entered into possession of a good fortune and has remained a popular woman in Belgravia up to the present time; her eldest Daughter being now well on to thirty.

The other morning—I think they said; four days ago— The footman who was waiting at breakfast committed some stupidity which Mrs Kitchener reproved him for, and the man made her an insolent answer. Mrs K indignant said, she did not permit insolence from her servants[;] that he must change his tone or leave the House— He hadn't the least objection he said. 'Then said Mrs Kitchener you will give up the plate to the Housekeeper so soon as breakfast is over, and pack up your things and be off.'— 'Oh with pleasure returned the Man[,] when you have paid me my wages; but I will take my wife with me'!! 'What have *I* to do with your wife' asked the Lady?— Whereupon the fellow turned round towards the young Lady sitting at the Breakfast table (Miss Kitchener) and said 'Come along Georgie!—you hear?— Get ready your traps!' Mrs Kitchener could think nothing but that her footman had gone suddenly *mad*; and rushed out of the House, leaving the front door open, to a Street Sweeper who went messages; and implored him to run for the Police, that there was a mad man in the house! At which sight a mob began to collect about her door! The poor woman returned up stairs, and was met by the footman coming down followed by '*Georgie*,' with a bag in her hand!!! 'I am going Mama, said the young Lady, with my *Husband*, we were married at—church by Banns on Sunday gone a Fortnight.'[17] 'Nothing wrong said the Footman to the people outside only be so good as call me a cab'! Mrs Kitchener didnt see her Daughter drive off with the footman; for at the girls first words she had fallen down in a dead faint!

'Did you—ever?' To complete the disgrace the footman is two or three and twenty and the young Lady near thirty!

There! all these pages filled with a London Scandal.

It is time to give you a few details, of myself, trusting that I am more interesting to you, than ever so many scandals

When you last heard from me I was badly off for sleep, and generally out of sorts; tho still quite free of neuralgia. It seemed a case for a tonic, and I had *your* Dr's prescription made up, and persevered in taking it twice a day for a week. But the only effect I perceived from it was an ever increasing headache and sickness all the mornings—and a sort of sore throat like what I always got from trying cod liver oil! So at the end of a week I left it off *on trial*. I was immediately, almost, relieved from the

17. William Johnson and Georgina Edgeworth, married 18 January at Trinity Church, Marylebone, central London.

headache and sickness but slept no better, and felt miserably *low*. After leaving off for a week I tried the iron again, and the very second day of it the headache and sickness returned to me, so I considered it a made out case that the iron did not agree with me, and left it off altogether! I am sure *the Dr* would have advised me to do so, if he had been near me to *see*! Since the weather has been so temperate, I have felt better, and had more sleep. Except the two days when London was so snowed up that the Omnibuses struck work; I have never omitted my daily drive; and have even continued to go out occasionally to dinner!! Dr Quain told me I 'could do nothing more wholesome provided I drank plenty of Champagne.' Easy to do that! and really it is a fact that the night after I have been at an eight o'clock dinner with plenty of talk going on, I always sleep sounder than on other nights!

The Town is no longer 'empty.' All my most intimate friends are come back except Lady Ashburton, who alas WILL still remain on the Continent and give no certain promise of return— Her rheumatism is better; but there are family reasons for her avoiding England at present which she considers imperative, tho' her friends find them chimerical enough— Miss Davenport Bromley is back—The Alderley Stanleys—the Airlies—The Froudes &c &c—

We were much surprised by the Lothians coming to London some two or three weeks ago. They had not stirred from Newbattle Abbey for two years![18] The poor young Marquis came the whole journey in one day.— Some hope of Electricity had been put into his head, and they have been trying it on him. He said he 'did not think it had done him *any* HARM *as yet*; but *that* was the most he could say.' He is the saddest spectacle I have seen for long! His Body more than half *dead*, his face so worn with suffering; and the Soul looking out of him as bright as in his best days! I had not seen him since before my own illness, and I was shocked with the change—especially in his voice which from being most musical had become HARSH and husky. *She* poor soul bears up wonderfully! But is so white and sad, that I cannot look at her without dreading for her the fate of her Mother!

The House (ours) goes on peaceably enough on the whole. Not without crisises of ill temper of course!— But I have got Jessy pretty well in hand now. It is mortifying after all my romantic hopes of her, to find that *kindness* goes for nothing, indeed for worse than nothing with *her*, and that she is only amenable to good sharp snubbing. Well! she shall have it! At the same time I make a point of being *just* to her and being

18. I assume William Kerr, 8th Marquess of Lothian, and his wife, whose seat was at Newbattle Abbey in Midlothian, Scotland.

kind to her *as a* MISTRESS *to a* SERVANT! So she got the 'nice dress' at Xmas, along with Mrs Warren[;] at the same time I put no *affection* into any thing I do for her and let her see that I dont.

It was a lucky Xmas for *her*! Mr Ruskin always gives my Servants a sovereign a-piece at that season! 'The like never had happened to her before!' she was obliged to confess. She went to the Theatre one night with some Fergusons—and has acquaintances enough— So I hope she is happy—tho I don't like her!! Has the Dr seen young Corson who had to leave Swan & Edgar with a bad knee— He came here several times to see Jessy

Love to the Dr Yours ever J C [. . .]

To Thomas Carlyle, Chelsea, 2 April 1866

Dearest

By the time you get this, you will be out of your trouble, better or worse,—but *out of it*, please God! And if ever you let yourself be led or driven into such a horrid thing again, I will never forgive you! never!

What I have been suffering, vicariously, of late days, is not to be told! If you had been to be *hanged*, I don't see that I could have taken it more to heart! This morning, after about two hours of off-and-on sleep, I awoke—long before daylight—to sleep no more! While drinking a glass of wine and eating a biscuit at five in the morning; it came into my mind what is *He* doing, I wonder, at this moment? and then instead of picturing you sitting smoking, up the stranger chimney, or anything else that was likely to *be*; I found myself always dropping off into details of a regular *execution*! now they will be telling him it is time! now they will be pinioning his arms! and saying last words! Oh mercy! was I dreaming or waking? was I mad or sane?— Upon my word I hardly know *now*!— Only that I have been having next to no sleep all the week—and that at the best of times I have a too 'fertile Imagination,' like 'oor David'![19]

When the thing is *over* I shall be content—however it have gone, as to making a good 'appearance' or a bad one! That you have made your 'address' and are *alive*—*that* is what I long to hear, and please God *shall* hear in a few hours! My 'Imagination' has gone the length of representing you getting up to speak before an awful crowd of people; and what

19. 'A lying boy at Haddington, whom his mother excused in that way,' Thomas explains (*CL*).

with fuss and 'bad air' and confusion dropping down dead!— Why on Earth did you ever get into this galley!

JWC

To Thomas Carlyle, Chelsea, 3 April 1866

I made so sure of a letter this morning—from some of you! And 'nothing but a double letter *for* Miss [Margaret, 'Maggie'] Welsh!'

Perhaps I should, that is, *ought* to have contented myself with Tyndall's adorable Telegram, which reached me at Cheyne Row five minutes after six last evening! Considering the sensation it made!—

Mrs Warren and Maggie were helping to dress me for Forster's Birth-day when the Telegraph Boy gave his double knock— 'There it is!' I said. 'I am afraid cousin, it is only the Postman' said Maggie. Jessie rushed up with the Telegram. I tore it open and read '*from John Tyndall* (Oh God bless John Tyndall in this world and the next!) *to Mrs Carlyle*[':] '*A perfect triumph*'— I read it to myself and then read it aloud to the gaping chorus, and chorus all began to dance and clap their hands— '*Eh Mr Carlyle*! Eh Hear to *that*' cried Jessie. '*I* told you Mam! cried Mrs Warren; *I* told you how it would be!' 'Im so glad, Cousin! you'll be all right now Cousin!' twittered Maggie, executing a sort of leap-frog round me. And they went on clapping their hands, till there arose among them a sudden cry for—*Brandy*! 'Get her some Brandy'! '*Do* Mam swallow this spoonful of Brandy!—just a spoonful'! For you see the sudden solution of the nervous tension with which I had been holding in my anxieties for days nay weeks past, threw me into as pretty a little fit of hysterics as you ever saw.

I went to Forsters nevertheless with my Telegram in my hand and 'John Tyndall' in the core of my heart![20] And it was pleasant to see

20. John Forster ('Fuzz'), celebrating his fifty-fifth birthday. He left an intriguing account of Jane that evening: 'Tyndall had told her of the triumph just before dinner. She came to us flourishing the telegram in her hand, and the radiance of her enjoyment of it was upon her all night. Among other things she gave Dickens the subject for a novel, from what she had herself observed at the outside of a house in her street [No. 6]; of which the various incidents were drawn from the condition of its blinds and curtains, the costumes visible at its windows, the cabs at its door, its visitors admitted or rejected, its articles of furniture delivered or carried away; and the subtle serious humour of it all, the truth in trifling bits of character, and the gradual progress into a half romantic interest, had enchanted the skilled novelist. She was well into the second volume of her small romance before she left, being as far as her observation then had taken her; but in a few days exciting incidents were expected, the denouement could not be far off, and Dickens was to have it when they met again' (*CL*). Jane reported a similar plan to Mary Russell on Christmas Day 1865, but we have no evidence that she drafted anything.

with what hearty good will all there, Dickens, Wilkie Collins, as well as Fuzz, received the news. [A]nd we drank your health with great glee! Maggie came in the evening and Fuzz in his joy over you sent out a glass of Brandy to [Jane's driver] Silvester!! Poor Silvester by the by showed as much glad *emotion* as anybody on my telling him you had got well thro' it!

Did you remember Craik's paper[?] I am going to take Maggie to the Railway for Liverpool[.] I suppose I shall now calm down and get sleep again—by degrees[;] I am *smashed* for the present

J W C

❧

To Thomas Carlyle, Chelsea, 4 April 1866

Well! I do think you might have sent me a *Scotsman* this morning;[21] or ordered one to be sent! I was up and dressed at 7, and it seemed such an interminable time till a quarter after nine when the Postman came—bringing only a note about—Cheltenham from Geraldine [Jewsbury]!

The letter I had from Tyndall yesterday might have satisfied any ordinary man—or woman; you would have said. But I dont pretend to be an ordinary man—or woman[.] I am perfectly *extra*ordinary; especially in the power I possess of fretting and worrying myself into one fever after another, without any cause to speak of!

What do you suppose I am worrying about *now*, because of the Scotsman having *not* come? That there may be in it something about your having FALLEN ILL—*which you wished me not to see*! *This* I am capable of fancying at moments; tho' last evening I saw a man who had seen you 'smoking very quietly at Masson's,'[22] and had heard your speech, and, what was more to the purpose, (his semiarticulateness taken into account) brought me what *he* said was as good an account of it as any he could give,—*already in the Pallmall Gazette* written by a hearty admirer of long standing, evidently. It was so kind of Macmillan to come to me—*before he had slept.*[23] He had gone in the morning straight from the Railway to his Shop & Work— He seemed still under the *Emotion* of the

21. The great newspaper of Scotland, daily since 1855 but dating back to 1817.
22. David Masson (1822–1907), professor of English at University College London and thereafter at the University of Edinburgh; his later essays on the Carlyles are full of humanity and insight.
23. Alexander Macmillan (1818–1896), Ayrshire-born publisher, co-founder with his brother Daniel of the London publishing house: still one of the 'Big Five' UK publishers. The firm looked after Matthew Arnold, Lewis Carroll, Tennyson, Hardy, Kipling, Yeats and so on.

Thing[,] Tears starting to his black eyes every time he mentioned any *moving* part!!—

Now just look at that! If here isn't—at half after eleven when nobody looks for the Edinr post—your letter—*two* newspapers, and letters from my Aunt Anne Thomas Erskine, David Aitken besides.

I have only as yet read *your* letter. The rest will keep NOW— I had a nice letter from Henry Davidson yesterday—as good as a Newspaper *Critic.*

What pleases me most in this business—I mean the business of your *success*, is the hearty *personal affection towards you* that comes out on all hands. These men at Forsters, with there cheering, our own people; even old Silvester turning as white as a sheet, and his lips quivering when he tried to express his gladness over the telegraph, *all that* is positively delightful, and makes the success 'a good joy' to me— No appearance of envy or grudging in anybody, but one general, loving, heartfelt throwing up of caps, with young and old, male and female! If we could only *sleep* Dear, and what you call '*digest*'; wouldn't it be nice?

Now I must go— I promised to try and get Madame Venturi out with me for a little air. She has been at her Brothers quite near Forsters—since the Funeral— The history she herself gave me of the night of his Death was quite excruciating.[24]

He took these spasms which killed him, soon after they went to bed; and till five in the morning the two poor souls were struggling *on*, he positively forbidding her to give an alarm. Mrs Taylor had a child just recovering from scarlet fever, and sent from home for fear of infecting the others. When Emilie would have gone to the Taylors bedroom to tell them he said; 'Consider the poor *Mother*! If you rouse her suddenly, she will think there has come bad news of her Child! It might do her great harm.' '[A]nd I thought, Dear, there was no *danger*['] she said to me— [T]he Drs had so constantly said he had no ailment but ind[ig]estion'— *It was soon* after this that he 'threw up his arms as if he had been shot, and fixed his eyes with a strange wondering look, as if he saw something beautiful and surprising, and then fell to the floor *dead*!' I am so glad she likes *me* to come to her—for it shows she is not desperate—

Oh Dear I wish you had been coming straight back—for it would be so quiet for you here *just now*— There isnt a soul left in London but Lady William [Russell]—whom I havnt seen since the day you left. I am afraid she is unwell

24. Madame Venturi's second husband, Italian nationalist Carlo Venturi, had died suddenly of a stroke. The couple were staying with Annie and Herbert Taylor.

Good by—

We have the [*chimney*-]*sweeps* today in the Drawingroom and elsewhere.

Affly Jane W Carlyle

To Thomas Carlyle, Chelsea, 12 April 1866

Dearest

I sent you better than a letter yesterday—a charming *Punch*—which I hope you received in due course; but Geraldine undertook the posting of it, and as Ann said of her long ago, 'Miss [Jewsbury] can write Books but I'm sure it's the only thing she's fit for'!— Well! there only wanted, to complete your celebrity, that you should be in the chief place of Punch! And there you are, cape & wideawake, making a really creditable appearance.[25] I must repeat what I said before, that the best part of this '*success*' is the general feeling of *personal goodwill* that pervades all they say and write about you. Even *Punch* cuddles you and purrs over you as if you were his favourite son! From *Punch* to Terry the green grocer, is a good step; but let me tell you, he (Terry) asked Mrs Warren; *was* Mr Carlyle the person they wrote of as *Lord Rector*, and Mrs Warren having answered in her stage voice 'the *very* same'! Terry shouted out—'(quite *shouted* it Mam!)' [']I never was so glad of anything!—by George!—I *am* glad'!— Both Mrs Warren and Jessy rushed out and bought *Punches* to send to their families; and in the fervour of their mutual enthusiasm they have actually ceased hostilities—for *the present*. It seems to me that on every new compliment paid you, these women run and *fry something*; such savoury smells reach me up stairs!

Lady Lothian was here the day before yesterday, with a remarkably silly Mrs Leslie— I was to tell you that she (Lady L) was 'very impatient for your return' '*missed you dreadfully*'— I was to 'come some day before

25. A cartoon in the weekly of 14 April depicting 'Wisdom and "Wind-Bag"', in which Thomas is shown as Jane describes (holding a broad-brimmed 'wideawake' hat), while parliamentary reformer John Bright (1811–1889) is shown in the background, speechifying: 'The House of Commons is little better than a Sham and a Farce. Parliament is never hearty in any good work. It hated the Reform Bill, it hated the Repeal of the Corn Laws, it hates this Franchise Bill.' Only, *pace Punch*, one suspects that Thomas would have agreed with many of Bright's sentiments.

luncheon and then we could go—*somewhere*'— To Miss Evans is where we should go, still, if *you* would let us![26]

Dont forget about my oatmeal!— [Isabella] Edgar Yorstoun *died* (her family said) of having her oat cakes stopt when she went on a visit to Bath.

There is a large sheet from the Pall Mall Bank acknowledging the receipt of 70 pounds 'only'[.] I dont forward any nonsense letters come to you—this one inclosed has sex and youth to plead for it—so

Yours ever / JWC

[M]y kindest regards to [Thomas's sister] *Mary*—for whom I have made a cap, you may tell her—but, couldnt get it finished before you left

❧

To Thomas Carlyle, Chelsea, 21 April 1866

Dearest—it seems just a 'consuming of Time' to write today, when you are coming the day after tomorrow. But—'if there were nothing else in it'—(*your* phrase) such a piece of liberality, as letting one have letters on Sunday if called for, should be honoured, at least by availing oneself of it! All *long* stories however may be postponed till next week.

Indeed I have neither long stories nor short ones to tell this morning. Tomorrow, after the Teaparty, I may have more to say; provided I survive it! Tho', how I am to entertain, on 'my own base' eleven people, in a *hot* night, '*without refreshment*' (to speak of) is more than I '*see my way*' thro'! Even as to *cups*!—there is only *ten* cups of company-china, and *eleven* are coming; myself making 12! 'After all, said Jessie; you had *once eight* at tea! *three* mair won't kill us'!— I'm not so sure of *that*!— Let us hope the motive will sanctify the end, being 'the welfare of others'!—an unselfish desire to 'make two *Baiings* [beings] happy'! Principal Tulloch and Froude who have a great liking for one another! The Spottiswoods were added in the same philanthropic spirit. We met in a shop, and they begged permission to come again; so I thought it would be clever to get them over (handsomely,—with Froude and Mrs Oliphant) before *you*

26. Sadly, Thomas forbad Jane from socialising with George Eliot (Marian Evans) because she was living in a *de facto* relationship with critic George Henry Lewes, who was unable to annul his marriage to Agnes Jervis because he had countenanced her adultery by recognising her children.

came.[27] They couldn't '*ask for more*' for a long time! Miss Wynn offered herself, by accident, for that same night.

The Marchioness [of Lothian] was here yesterday *twice*; called at four when I hadn't returned, and called again at five. She brought with her yesterday a charming old Miss Talbot, with a palsied head but the most loveable Babyish old face! She seemed to take to me as I did to her; and Lady Lothian staid behind a minute, to ask if I would go with *her* some day, to see this Miss Talbot who had a Houseful of the finest Pictures.

You should have sent *the address* to Lord Lothian or Lady— I see several names on the List less worthy of such attention—

[. . .] I saw in an old furniture shop-window at Richmond a copy of the Frederich picture that was lent you.[28] *Not* bad—coarsely painted; but the likeness well preserved. Would you like to have it? I will, if so, make you a present of it—being to be had 'very equal'— I 'descended from' the carriage, and asked: 'what was *that*?' (meaning what price was it—)— The Broker told me impressively; '*that* Mam, is *Peter the Great*.' 'Indeed! and what is the price?'— '[S]even & sixpence'[.] I offered *five shillings* on the spot but he would only come down to six shillings. I will go back for it if you like, and can find a place for it on my wall—

Yours ever JWC

This must surely have been the last letter Jane wrote. Later that day, 21 April, she took her usual afternoon drive with her coachman, John Silvester. During it she died suddenly and it seems without pain, between the hours of three and four. Oddly—given the strained nature of their relations in life—her brother-in-law John Carlyle gave the

27. John Tulloch (1823–1886), academic theologian and principal of the University of St Andrews; James Anthony Froude (1818–1894), author, friend and Thomas's executor and biographer; William Spottiswoode (1825–1883), mathematician, publisher and future president of the Royal Society, and his wife Eliza. For Charlotte Williams-Wynn see 17 January 1848. Popular novelist Margaret Oliphant (1828–1897) had befriended Jane in the summer of 1860 as she sought materials for her biography of Edward Irving; they corresponded intermittently until the period just before Jane's death, when their relationship deepened, but few letters of substance remain.

28. A picture of Frederick the Great by German painter Heinrich Franke (1738–1792), whose portraits of the Emperor were widely reproduced, had been lent to Thomas by his friend William Vernon. The dealer would not be the first person to confuse *Peter* the Great of Russia with *Frederick* the Great of Prussia.

most circumstantial account of her decease. (He was a doctor, after all.) He wrote to his brother Alexander ('Alick') on 3 May.

My dear Brother,

On Saturday 21st April I was in Edinburgh, and Tom at Dumfries, when a piece of very sad news came to me from London, late in the evening by telegraph, which I had to forward to him at once. A second telegram came the same night at a still later hour, and it too had to be forwarded. The two joined together announced that Mrs Carlyle had died suddenly in the afternoon of that day while driving in her little carriage alone in Hyde Park. A small terrier [Tiny], left to her care by a friend (Mrs Chapman) who died lately (in March) of consumption, had been running alongside the carriage and had got itself either kicked or trampled on by the horses of another carriage and was left lying on the road. Jane got out, took it up, and spoke a few words to the lady of that other carriage who had got out to make an apology; then entered her own carriage again, and the driver went on as before noticing nothing particular about her and seeing that the dog had got very little if any injury. There was a string close to her by pulling which she could at once have stopped him. He first became uneasy at her not pulling it after he had gone on as far as usual; looked down through the front window, saw her hands lying quiet and open on her lap; went round the Park again, and on returning to the place (again) of which she used to pull the string, he stopt and saw her hands in exactly the same position—which of course gave him great alarm—and not being able to quit the horse he asked the nearest lady and gentleman to look into the carriage and see if aught had happened. They found her quite gone, reclining backwards with face looking placid in death and relieved of all sorrow. I joined Tom at Dumfries by the earliest train from Lockerbie, having come so far by the only Sunday train from Edinburgh; and we started together for London the same day (Monday), arriving here about half past ten at night. He had written to a friend on the Sunday from Dumfries, to make preparations for the funeral, and we found every thing in a state of forwardness. In the coffin her face still retained the expression of earnest placidity and relief from sorrow.

On wednesday went to Haddington with the coffin in next compartment of railway carriage before us, two friends from London accompanying us; on the Thursday the funeral took place from the house of Mr Dods, banker, an old friend and schoolfellow of hers. It was attended by many other old friends and acquaintances of the neighbourhood and passed off very quietly indeed, the weather being quite beautiful. She lies buried in the same grave as her Father, in the ruined choir of the old

Abbey church. She had written to Mr Dods about her burial more than twelve months ago; and she had told Tom before he went to Edinburgh, that she durst not go with him owing to some disease of the spine which sometimes took away her breath and stopped the action of the heart when aught agitated her suddenly; and the physician who attended her before, certified this spinal disease as the cause of death under the circumstances. She had talked of it to Tom as slight and so he had felt little or no alarm beforehand. He has felt the shock most severely of course, especially since we got back from Haddington on Friday, but he is quite calm and has had pretty good sleep for the last three nights. I intend staying here sometime with him. I will put three strokes on the newspaper address, if all goes well next week, as a signal. I could get no time to write earlier, or even to send off the newspaper last week.

We hear today from Dumfries, Gill, and Scotsbrig that all was well there. From the Queen downward there have been condolences, if any good were possible from them. Tom is as well as usual in body. Let us hope he may soon be able to adjust himself patiently to his great loss. I have not time to write more today. Please either send this on to Jenny without delay, or write her the substance of it, for I feel quite worn by writing.

Ever your affectionate / J A Carlyle

The kind of death which I have described, from that disease of the spine or brain, would be as sudden and as free from all pain as a simple fainting fit. The position in which the body was found reclining also shewed that there had been no struggle or suffering. She had written a letter to Tom, in excellent spirits, on the Saturday just before going out for her drive, and reached him at Dumfries on the Sunday. She had lunched with Mrs Forster too and been in high spirits only some 20 minutes before her death. Ever since her illness in 1864 she had been frail as possible, but had kept driving out daily and had never complained to any one; so that none of us felt alarmed about her. I did not hear of her spinal disease at all, or it might have alarmed me, as it did her physician whom I don't know personally and who had said nothing to Tom about it. She had suffered much from want of sleep all along, though she made no complaints. To herself such a gentle death would be a real benefit, though it has left our brother desolate and without his main stay in life. [. . .]

J A C [. . .]

Characters and Correspondents

Note: many entries in this section can be extended and supplemented by the excellent Carlyle Encyclopedia, edited by Mark Cumming (Madison, NJ, 2004). It should be consulted for many other issues, especially as regards TC's life and career.

Airlie, Henrietta Blanche (*née* Stanley), Countess of Airlie (1830–1921), whose husband succeeded to the earldom in 1849, putting her in charge of Airlie Castle, West Forfarshire, Scotland. An important friend of JWC's from 1850 on.

Aitken, Eliza; see Stodart.

Aitken, James; see Jean Carlyle Aitken.

Aitken, Jean; see Jean Carlyle Aitken.

Allingham, William (1824–1889), Irish-born poet, customs-officer and frequent visitor to London; introduced to TC by Leigh Hunt. His posthumously published *Diary* (1907) has important recollections of the Carlyles, but his relation with TC became substantial only after JWC's death.

Ashburton, Lady Harriet Baring (*née* Montagu; 1805–1857), hostess, socialite and *salonnière* with a large and slavish circle of male intellectual admirers, including Mill, Milnes, Tennyson and Thackeray: TC chief among them from 1839. JWC did not meet her until 1843, and by 1846 she had become understandably jealous of TC's devotion. Her mother, Lady Sandwich, remained a friend after Lady Harriet's death.

Ashburton, Lady Louisa Caroline Baring (*née* Stewart Mackenzie; 1827–1903), art collector and amateur painter (who studied with Ruskin); she made a deep and quasi-filial impression on JWC after her marriage to Baron Ashburton in 1858. Her daughter Mary became a surrogate granddaughter for JWC.

Ashburton, William Bingham Baring, 2nd Baron (1799–1864), banker and politician (MP 1826–1848), husband of both of the above. TC's gateway to high society in London in general and the Athenaeum Club in particular in 1853.

Bölte, Amely or Amalie (1811–1891), German writer, translator and governess, who arrived in England in 1839 and met the Carlyles in 1841. Despite her ardent feminism she maintained good relations with TC, and became close to JWC, who occasionally showed signs of exasperation. Returned to Germany in 1851.

Braid, Betty, Haddington servant of JWC's family, later resident in Edinburgh.

Brookfield, Rev. William Henry (1809–1874), clergyman and school-inspector, married Jane Octavia (*née* Elton; 1821–1896); friends of Harriet Ashburton, Thackeray and the Carlyles.

Browning, Robert (1812–1889), poet, in 1846 married Elizabeth (*née* Moulton Barrett; 1806–1861), poet and author of *Aurora Leigh*. TC and JWC both appreciated Elizabeth and her work, but JWC regarded Robert as a 'fluff of feathers'.

Buller family, Charles (senior; 1774–1848), Isabella (*née* Kirkpatrick; d. 1849), Charles (junior; 1806–1848), Arthur (1808–1869), Reginald (1813–1880). Employed TC as tutor to the eldest two sons (in Edinburgh, later in London) at Irving's recommendation in 1822–1824, upon the family's return from India, where Charles served as a judge. The arrangement ended but relations remained good, and JWC visited them in 1842. The family also adopted Theresa ('Tizzy') Revis: see JWC letter of 7 January 1851.

Carlyle, Alexander (1797–1876; 'Alick'), farmer, wife Janet Clow ('Jenny'); disliked by JWC on the grounds of his drinking and violence of temper at Craigenputtoch; emigrated to Canada in 1843.

Carlyle, James (senior; 1758–1832), stonemason, religious and irascible but vitally supportive of Thomas's early learning, and a key ingredient in his character: self-reliant, articulate, earnest and industrious. Originally at Ecclefechan; in 1826 the family moved to Scotsbrig.

Carlyle, James (junior; 1805–1890; 'Jamie' or 'Jemmy'), TC's youngest brother; married Isabella Calvert in 1834; most congenial of the siblings for JWC.

Carlyle, Janet (1813–1897; 'Jenny'), TC's sister; married Robert Hanning, 1836, who emigrated to Canada in disgrace, 1841, where she rejoined him ten years later.

Carlyle Aitken, Jean (1810–1888; 'Craw Jean'), TC's sister and JWC's frequent correspondent, despite a turbulent period under one roof in Craigenputtoch; married housepainter James Aitken, 1833.

Carlyle, John Aitken (1801–1879; 'Jack' or 'the Doctor'), TC's brother, only university-educated sibling, medical doctor and long-term translator of Dante, whose bumptious self-importance, combined with professional indecisiveness, eventually grated on JWC. Married wealthy widow Phoebe Fowler, 1852, who died in childbirth, 1854.

Carlyle, Margaret (*née* Aitken; 1771–1853), TC's mother, originally illiterate devout Calvinist, one-time servant, and matriarch of Ecclefechan;

in later life lived with James and Isabella at Scotsbrig. Had early hopes TC would enter the church.

Carlyle, Mary (1808–1888), TC's sister; married farmer James Austin, date unknown. JWC stayed with her in 1864 while recuperating from the Cheapside injury.

Carlyle, Mary Aitken (1848–1895), TC's niece, daughter of 'Craw Jean' Carlyle; married cousin Alexander Carlyle (TC's nephew, son of Alick), 1879. In 1868 moved into No. 5 with TC, and stayed with him till his death.

Cavaignac, Éléonore-Louis Godefroi (1801–1845), revolutionary French republican politician and journalist, in exile in London after 1835 after a period of imprisonment; returned to France in 1841. A saturnine but firm friend of the Carlyles between those dates: TC's favourite exile, one might say, where Mazzini was JWC's.

Chalmers, Dr Thomas (1780–1847), Scottish presbyterian minister and professor of theology at Edinburgh; mentor of Edward Irving and early acquaintance of JWC.

Chorley, John Rutter (1806–1867), book collector, editor and reviewer; advised on TC's 'soundproof' room at No. 5, 1854.

Craik, George Lillie (1798–1866), author and professor of English and history at Queen's College, Belfast; friend of the Carlyles from 1835 on. Daughter Mary (1827–1909) nursed JWC at St Leonards after the Cheapside accident of 1863.

Cushman, Charlotte (1816–1876), American lesbian actress and friend of Geraldine Jewsbury, via whom she met JWC and made a big, if short-lived, impression in the autumn of 1861.

Darwin, Erasmus Alvey (1804–1881), older brother of Charles and grandson of the more famous Erasmus, eighteenth-century poet and naturalist. Trained in medicine, he gave it up almost immediately to live a life of liberal thought, literary ease and eternal bachelorhood. An essential friend of both Harriet Martineau and JWC after 1835, whom he would transport around London in his carriage. (TC was a little more ambivalent, as was Erasmus regarding his conservatism.) Regrettably, her letters to him have disappeared.

Dickens, Charles (1812–1870), pre-eminent Victorian novelist and good friend of both JWC and TC on the London literary scene from the early 1840s. A profound admirer of TC, he dedicated *Hard Times* (1854) to him, and *A Tale of Two Cities* (1859) is substantially derived from *The French Revolution*. *A Christmas Carol* (1843) also shows signs of TC's moral views. The full extent of TC's influence is yet to be established.

Dilberoglue, Stavros (1821?–1878), Corfiote by birth, Manchester-based British representative of Greek trading concerns, admirer of TC, brother of Calliope, and connected to the Carlyles via fellow northerner Geraldine Jewsbury. He gave Nero the dog to JWC in 1849.

Dods, William, schoolfellow of JWC at Haddington.

Donaldson sisters of Sunny Bank, Haddington: Jean (1770–1860), JWC's godmother; Jess (1774–1860) and Catherine (1779–1852), friends of JWC's mother.

Eliot, George (Marian Evans; 1819–1880), second only to Dickens among the Victorian novelists, who sent her first two works of fiction to JWC in 1858 and 1859. They met only once (at the theatre in 1861), as TC forbad JWC from socialising with a woman living outside matrimony with a married man, George Henry Lewes. TC was perhaps more important in her development than we have yet established, in terms of her interest in German thought and her realism, and she repaid the compliment in an important article of 1855.

Emerson, Ralph Waldo (1803–1882), New England essayist and transcendentalist, who importantly sought out TC in Craigenputtoch in 1833 and supported him thereafter, particular as regards the Boston publication of TC's early books. He returned to London in 1847 to lecture, but the passage of time had opened up divisions both men tried to disguise from each other: his lofty idealism was something TC tolerated but JWC disparaged, finding him 'a considerable of a bore'.

Forster, John (1812–1876), editor, critic, biographer, historian and firm friend of Charles Dickens, whose biography he published in 1874. Advised TC on publishing, and a close and important male friend for JWC from 1839 on, who took a fellow sufferer's interest in Forster's poor health. Of working-class origins, he married a wealthy widow, Eliza Colburn, in 1861 and lived in some style in Kensington, west London.

Forster, William Edward (1818–1886), Quaker woollen manufacturer, philanthropist and Liberal politician with a strong interest in Ireland; Yorkshire friend of the Carlyles, with whom JWC stayed and travelled in 1847 and 1849, in the aftermath of Forster's exposure to TC's works around 1842. His passionate abolitionism eventually led to a cooling of relations with TC.

Gambardella, Spiridione (c. 1815–1886), Neapolitan-born painter who spent time in Boston, where he met Emerson, before coming to London in 1841 to paint TC. His portrait of JWC is a twee and sanitised affair. There is no portrait of TC, but one of JWC's Liverpool uncle, John Welsh, survives.

Garnier, Joseph (d. 1848), academic and editor in Germany, friend of the Carlyles from the mid-1830s, whom TC assisted into a clerkship at the Public Record Office, where he did not thrive. A 'big German refugee, dusty, smoky, scarred with duel-cuts', according to TC, who 'had picked up considerable knowledge in his wanderings', though with a 'tendency to go mad or half-mad,—as he did by and by', before disappearing in the German Democratic Legion of 1848.

Gaskell, Elizabeth (1810–1865), important Victorian novelist in both the working-class and middle-class modes; long-term resident of Manchester, whom JWC encountered on northern trips. Gaskell's biography of her friend, Charlotte Brontë (1857), brought out some of JWC's respect for social convention, and her suspicion of Gaskell's integrity. TC played a role in her fiction, too: especially in the social focus of *Mary Barton* (1848) and *North and South* (1855).

Gibson, William, friend of the Carlyles from 1835: 'a massive, easy, friendly, dull person, physically one of the best washed I ever saw' according to TC; 'American merchant, "who had made, and again lost, three fortunes"; originally a Nithsdale pedlar boy [. . .] "Silver Packman," he was often called here'; a trader with America, not an American as such.

Hiddlestone, Jessie (1835–1904), maid of the Carlyles, 1865–1866, as her mother had been maid to Grace Welsh. Only after Jane's death did she marry: a butler named Robert Broadfoot.

Howden, Agnes, Haddington friend of JWC, married to Thomas, a goldsmith; owners of Maitlandfield House.

Hunt, Leigh (1784–1859), poet, editor (above all of *The Examiner*) and essayist, who met the Carlyles on their first London foray and was a friendly neighbour in Chelsea in their early years; a remnant of the great Romantic generation, famously satirised as Mr Skimpole in Dickens' *Bleak House*. Mrs Hunt was Marianne.

Hunter, Susan; see Stirling.

Irving, Edward (1792–1834), Scottish clergyman and a kind of alter ego of TC, through whom he met JWC at Haddington (1821). Like TC of working-class background and educated at Annan and Edinburgh University, but he found brief fame as a powerful non-denominational preacher in early 1820s London. An inspiration and a warning, alike. JWC was powerfully attracted to him as a young woman (as he to her, but he was promised to another woman), and eventually admitted the fact to TC before their marriage. See TC, *Reminiscences*, and William Christie (ed.), *Letters of Francis Jeffrey to Thomas and Jane Welsh Carlyle* (Abingdon, 2008).

Jeffrey, Francis, Lord Jeffrey (1773–1850), Scottish advocate and literary intellectual, best known as editor of the innovatory and highly influential *Edinburgh Review* and ferocious reviewer in its columns. He edited the magazine throughout the Romantic era, and met Thomas in 1827, becoming a vital if perhaps superficial friend for the couple in the late 1820s and early 1830s, before they drifted apart in 1834—their views of the world ultimately being so different. The second part of his career was as a senior judge. See TC, *Reminiscences*.

Jewsbury, Geraldine (1812–1880), novelist and reviewer, who wrote to TC for literary advice in 1840 and became an important if occasionally stifling friend thereafter, with whom JWC had a serious tiff in 1858–1859. She destroyed JWC's letters to her. Her novels *Zoe* (1845) and *The Half Sisters* (1848) were both controversial, but JWC persisted in editing them and seeing them through to publication.

Larkin, Henry, Chelsea neighbour and cashier of the Chelsea Steamer Company, who contacted TC in 1850 and whom TC managed to involve, after 1856, as an assistant in the *Frederick* project, on indexes, maps and so forth. He it was who took JWC into No. 5 when she got home after her Cheapside fall of 1863.

Macready, William (1793–1873), the prince of Victorian actor-managers and frequent host and guest of the Carlyles after 1839, famed for his Shakespearean roles but also for promoting the dramatic efforts of Victorian writers and socialising alongside them. His wife Catherine was an important friend for JWC, who visited her on her deathbed at Sherborne in the West Country in August 1852.

MacTurk, Robert, ancient Haddington flame of JWC's, whom she rediscovered in Scotland in 1857 and nursed on his deathbed in 1860.

Martineau, Harriet (1802–1876), traveller, polymath, novelist and important female intellectual in sociological and economic fields, but also education and evolution. Succumbing to serious illness in the early 1840s, she believed she had been cured by mesmerism and published *Life in the Sickroom* (1844) and *Letters on Mesmerism* (1845), both of which JWC knew. A frequent visitor at Chelsea from 1836, and JWC in particular visited her in the north of England. She was of practical assistance in organising TC's first two series of lectures, but the friendship faded in time.

Mazzini, Giuseppe (1805–1872), the ideological genius among the quartet of Italians who made the Risorgimento (Cavour, Garibaldi and Victor Emmanuel II), who flitted between London and Italy constantly, much to the Carlyles' alarm as they (and JWC in particular) loved him dearly from the late 1830s on: which was not inconsistent with finding him unintentionally amusing, too. Alongside Erasmus Darwin, JWC's most important male friend.

Mill, John Stuart (1806–1873), one-time utilitarian and economist, perhaps the most influential anglophone philosopher of the nineteenth century. He and TC bonded on the Carlyles' arrival in London, and over the loan of materials for TC's *French Revolution*, the first part of which was incinerated by Mill's housemaid by mistake. As Mill was a powerful liberal and TC a powerful conservative their paths diverged—especially after Mill's *On Liberty* (1859)—but mutual respect remained. Of less importance to JWC.

Milnes, Richard Monckton, Lord Houghton (1809–1885), poet and Conservative politician, best remembered for his *Life and Letters of Keats* (1848); friend of the Carlyles from 1836. TC took pleasure in teasing him about the value of poetry. Mover and shaker rather than creative force, he supported Tennyson and Emerson, but (despite being an avid collector of pornography) also women authors such as Elizabeth Gaskell. A liberal whose views diverged from TC's, especially on matters like the Jews and the Catholics.

Montagu, Anna Dorothea (1773–1856), husband Basil, important and early London acquaintance of TC via Irving, dating from his first visit of 1824. She insisted on contacting JWC and played a role in their coming to marry, though his regard cooled after their move to Chelsea, partly because of her treatment of mutual friend John Badams. JWC re-encountered her in 1854. See TC, *Reminiscences*.

Neuberg, Joseph (1806–1867), German-born retired businessman, who met TC in 1848 and became his long-suffering (and unpaid) secretary and travelling companion on two German tours associated with the *Frederick* project.

Paulet, Elizabeth (b. 1806; 'Betsy'), married to Swiss businessman Étienne: society hostess, feminist and friend of Geraldine Jewsbury, whom JWC visited frequently at Seaforth House, near Bootle, Lancashire. Jewsbury's novel, *Zoe*, was originally intended to be a three-way venture, but Paulet and JWC fell away.

Pepoli, Conte Carlo (1796–1891), Italian nationalist politician, poet and journalist, who served as professor of Italian at University College London, 1838–1846. Married Elizabeth Fergus—sister of John, flax manufacturer of Kirkcaldy and friend of TC's—while in England, before returning to Bologna for good in 1859.

Plattnauer, Richard (1813–1895), radical refugee from Prussia and friend of Cavaignac, who introduced him to the Carlyles in the mid-1840s. Subject to periods of insanity through which JWC and TC loyally supported him; intermittently a tutor and resident of England and the Continent alike. Brother of Hedwig von Reichenbach.

Pringle, Janet (*née* Hunter; b. 1827), JWC's second cousin, resident of Thornhill, Dumfriesshire.

Rennie, George (1802–1860), sculptor, MP and ancient Haddington flame of JWC's, who re-entered her life somewhat stuffily in 1834, before disappearing to the Falkland Islands as its governor in 1847.

Ruskin, John (1819–1900), polymath, aesthete, prophet and activist; author of books (*Unto This Last*, *Sesame and Lilies*, *The Ethics of the Dust* and *Fors Clavigera*) much admired by TC, whom Ruskin came to call 'Papa'; but a firm friend of JWC, too.

Russell, Mary (*née* Dobbie; d. 1875), frequent correspondent of JWC, wife of Mrs Welsh's neighbour and doctor James Russell; they hosted JWC after her Cheapside injury at their home in Holm Hill, Thornhill, in 1864.

Simmonds, Isabella, daughter of the Carlyles' local medical practitioner, Dr Barnes; something of a surrogate daughter for JWC, and close to her around the time of the Cheapside accident of 1863.

Smith, Mary, poet and schoolmistress, resident in Carlisle, mentored by JWC in the mid-1850s. Her *Autobiography of Mary Smith, Schoolmistress and Nonconformist: A Fragment of a Life, with Letters from Jane Welsh Carlyle and Thomas Carlyle* (1892) shines with affection for JWC's kind frankness on literature as a career. She also published *Poems* (1860).

Southam, Charlotte (1842–1905), orphaned maid at No. 5, taken on in April 1858 aged only sixteen, who kept in touch thereafter, and for whom JWC, not surprisingly, had maternal feelings, despite dismissing her in June 1861.

Stanley, Katharine Russell, Viscountess Amberley (1842–1874; 'Kate'), sister of Lady Airlie, suffragist and feminist; married John Russell, Viscount Amberley, in 1864 and was the mother of British twentieth-century philosopher Bertrand Russell.

Sterling, Anthony (1805–1871), eldest son of Edward and brother of John, army officer active in the Crimean War and author of books relating to that conflict and his service; a friend of the Carlyles—and a one-time admirer of JWC—but less important than his brother. Married Charlotte Baird in 1829, who suffered from insanity and formed the belief that he and JWC were adulterously involved.

Sterling, Edward (1773–1847), Irish-born journalist and (essentially) editor at *The Times*, known as 'The Thunderer' for his fiery editorials. Vain, self-important and exasperating, accordingly, but also a steady friend, particularly of JWC. His long-suffering wife was Hester.

Sterling, John (1806–1844), Scots-born but Cambridge-educated poet and essayist, son of Edward and brother of Anthony, who abandoned religion for literature and was much loved by many, without fulfilling his promise before dying of tuberculosis. One novel: *Arthur Coningsby* (1833). The subject of one of TC's most attractive books, the *Life of John Sterling* (1851).

Stirling, Susan (*née* Hunter), old friend of JWC, with whom Leigh Hunt flirted ostentatiously on a visit to No. 5 in 1835.

Stodart, Eliza, long-standing Edinburgh friend of JWC: familiar enough for her to call Eliza 'cousin'; in 1829 married the Rev. David Aitken.

Stodart, John Riddle (1792–1871), ancient friend and suitor of JWC; brother of Eliza.

Tait, Robert Scott (1816–1897), artist and pioneer of photography (a technology the Carlyles valued highly), who left many images of the Carlyles including the unusual *Chelsea Interior*, still at the Cheyne Walk house, over which he laboured obsessively for months on site in 1857–1858.

Tennyson, Alfred, Lord (1809–1892), eminent Victorian poet, who first met the Carlyles in 1840 and enjoyed their (and Jane's) company intermittently thereafter, despite their inability to appreciate his (or anybody else's) verse; something of a tortured soul with depression and alcoholism running deep and broad among his male relatives. TC eventually found him passive; Tennyson found him dogmatic.

Thackeray, William Makepeace (1811–1863), novelist, satirist, editor and rival of Dickens, whose *Vanity Fair* (1848) remains an English classic, but whose other works have faded in currency. A vivid and vital member of the London literary circle, all the same, held in high esteem and affection by the Carlyles via mutual friends like John Sterling, the Bullers and Lady Harriet Ashburton. JWC held him and his daughters in particularly fond regard.

Twisleton, Ellen (*née* Dwight; 1828–1862), New England-born, and important confidante of JWC, who recorded the latter's perhaps embittered Craigenputtoch memories in November 1855.

Wedgwood, Hensleigh (1803–1891), philologist and lawyer, and cousin (and brother-in-law) of Charles Darwin. His pioneering *Dictionary of Etymology* was published in 1857; he also took an interest in spiritualism. His wife Frances, *née* Mackintosh (1800–1899; 'Fanny'), was a London acquaintance and near neighbour of JWC. Hensleigh was the cousin of Erasmus Darwin, who introduced the two couples in the mid-1830s.

Welsh, Ann (d. 1877), Elizabeth (d. 1877) and Grace (d. 1867): JWC's paternal aunts, living together in the comfortable suburb of Morningside, Edinburgh, when JWC visited them in the 1850s and 1860s.

Welsh, Grace (*née* Welsh; 1782–1842), JWC's mother; disagreed somewhat with her husband John's views on educating JWC (in a masculine style, in maths, Latin and so forth) and eventually had her sent to a girls' boarding school. Like JWC, of poor health, and their relationship was a somewhat stormy one—over TC as a future husband, in particular, given his social origins.

Welsh, Jeannie ('Babbie'), daughter of John and Mary, sister of Helen; married Andrew Chrystal in 1853, after which her lively and important correspondence with JWC came to an end.

Welsh, John (1775–1819), JWC's father, medical doctor born at Craigenputtoch. Married Grace—who was no relation, despite the shared surname—in 1800, and they moved together to Haddington. Died tragically of typhus when JWC was eighteen.

Welsh, John (d. 1853), JWC's 'only uncle of me'; brass and copper founder, resident at Maryland Street, Liverpool; wife is aunt Mary; daughters are Helen (1813–1853), Margaret (b. 1821; 'Maggie'), Jeannie and Mary.

Index

Jane Carlyle's letters to individuals are indexed in bold type; her themes and topics are listed throughout.